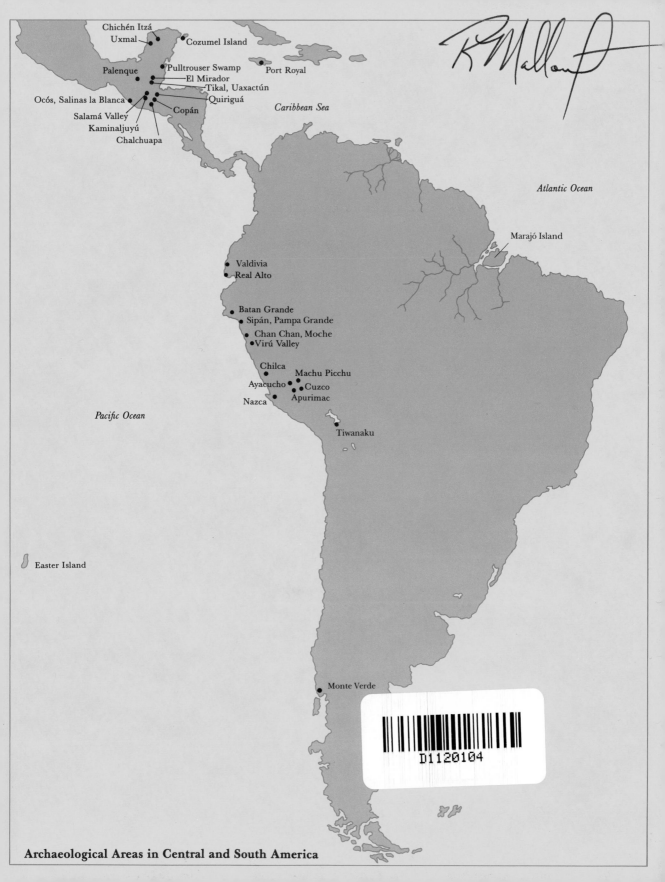

Chichén Itzá
Uxmal
Cozumel Island
Palenque
Pulltrouser Swamp
El Mirador
Tikal, Uaxactún
Ocós, Salinas la Blanca
Quiriguá
Salamá Valley
Copán
Kaminaljuyú
Chalchuapa

Port Royal

Caribbean Sea

Atlantic Ocean

Marajó Island

Valdivia
Real Alto

Batan Grande
Sipán, Pampa Grande
Chan Chan, Moche
Virú Valley

Chilca
Machu Picchu
Ayacucho
Cuzco
Nazca
Apurimac

Pacific Ocean

Tiwanaku

Easter Island

Monte Verde

Archaeological Areas in Central and South America

ARCHAEOLOGY

ARCHAEOLOGY
Discovering Our Past

SECOND EDITION

ROBERT J. SHARER
University of Pennsylvania

WENDY ASHMORE
University of Pennsylvania

MAYFIELD PUBLISHING COMPANY
Mountain View, California
London • Toronto

Library of Congress Cataloging-in-Publication Data

Sharer, Robert J.
     Archaeology : discovering our past / by Robert J. Sharer and Wendy
Ashmore. — 2nd ed.
          p.   cm.
     Includes bibliographical references and index.
     ISBN 1-55934-041-X
     1. Archaeology.   I. Ashmore, Wendy .   II. Title.
CC165.S44   1992
930.1—dc20   92-10838
                                                                  CIP

Manufactured in the United States of America
10 9 8 7 6 5 4 3

Mayfield Publishing Company
1240 Villa Street
Mountain View, California 94041

Sponsoring editor, Janet M. Beatty; production editor, Lynn Rabin Bauer; manu-script editor, Carole Crouse; art director, Jeanne Schreiber; text and cover designer, Donna Davis; associate designer, Jean Mailander; manufacturing manager, Martha Branch. The text was set in 10/12 Galliard by G & S Typesetters and printed on 45# Penntech Penn Plus by R. R. Donnelley and Sons.

Pages 109–112 adapted and reprinted by permission of the publisher from "A Visit to the Master" by Kent V. Flannery in *Guilá Naquitz* edited by Kent V. Flannery. Copyright © by Academic Press Inc.

Figure 4.8 used by permission of the publisher, Cornell University Press.

PREFACE

To many people, archaeology is especially fascinating. This book explores some of the reasons for that fascination: It explains what archaeologists do in their work, how they conduct research, and how they use the results to reconstruct the past.

In the following pages, we survey the techniques, methods, and theoretical frameworks of contemporary archaeology, with an emphasis on prehistoric archaeology, the discipline that focuses on the vast era of the human past before the dawn of history. In doing so, we have approached archaeology in a way that sets this book apart from others dealing with the same topic:

- In our presentation we view prehistoric archaeology as an integral part of the larger field of anthropology, conditioned by the historical development, concepts, and goals of its parent discipline.

- We treat the evolving perspectives of archaeological method and theory, together with their implications for understanding the prehistoric past, from a balanced scientific and humanistic perspective. The text is not a manifesto for any single doctrine or "school" within the field. Rather, it seeks to integrate those aspects of the more traditional and the recent innovative approaches that have contributed significantly to current archaeological understanding, including culture historical, cultural processual, and postprocessual approaches to studying the past.

- The text's organization reflects that of actual archaeological research. As in research, we begin on an abstract level, from the formulation of an idea or problem that stimulates research in the first place, and proceed to the more concrete steps of finding, manipulating, and describing the physical remains of past human activity. Finally, we go back to the abstract with the interpretation of the data in light of the original research questions and problems.

- In considering the research process, we keep a clear focus on the role of archaeology in the day-to-day world. Ours is not the "ivory tower" profession many think it is, and this point is underscored most forcefully in the opening and concluding chapters, which describe the major ethical, intellectual, and practical challenges to archaeology today and some of the ways these challenges are being met.

- As further evidence of archaeology's role in modern life, we present essays by our colleagues that relate incidents and issues from their personal perspectives. These essays, called "Archaeologists at Work," illustrate some of the points made in the text discussion from a fresh viewpoint, but also vividly demonstrate the varied lives and experiences that are part of a contemporary career in archaeology.

- Throughout the text we integrate generalized discussions of archaeological method and theory with actual case studies and examples from archaeological research around the world. We have elected to present a mix of detailed and relatively brief case studies and, when appropriate, we reintroduce the same example to illustrate later discussions. Extended consideration is given to recent field investigations at the Classic Maya site of Copán, Honduras, where each of us has been privileged to direct and collaborate in a multifaceted and truly exciting ongoing research effort.

- Throughout the book we stress two crucial themes. First, material remains providing a link with past societies are a finite and nonrenewable resource and should not be disturbed simply for weekend entertainment—let alone for monetary profit. Much knowledge can be gained from these remains, but only if they are handled with expert care. Second, the ways to study archaeological remains are varied, and an archaeologist's choice will depend on what he or she wants to know. Selecting one site over another, or one field method over another, is always a decision that follows from the specified research goals in each particular situation. The most useful skills an archaeologist can have are clear reasoning and incisive decision-making; these are far more important than an ability to wield a pick or a trowel.

We wish to emphasize that this book is not intended to be a blueprint for digging. Instead, we offer a review of what archaeology is today, how it developed over the years as a scientific and humanistic discipline, and how modern archaeology has allowed us to discover our human past from the material traces our ancestors left behind. In describing methods of data collection, analysis, and interpretation, we have tried to indicate criteria for choosing between one approach and another in specific situations. But there is much more to archaeology than digging, and the reader should not expect simply to take this (or any) book in one hand, a trowel in the other, and attempt to excavate or conduct any other kind of archaeological investigation. A textbook cannot substitute for active field participation and learning under the guidance of an experienced professional archaeologist.

AUDIENCE

The book is intended primarily for introductory college courses in archaeological method and theory. It is flexible enough to be useful also as a reference in introductory graduate-level method and theory courses. And because the organization follows the conduct of research, the text can easily be used in archaeological field schools to accompany the actual practice of field archaeology.

Depending on the course, this text can be complemented by books offering an outline of world prehistory, by manuals covering the more technical aspects of field methods, and/or by sets of selected readings amplifying discussion of the various topics covered here. We have, in part, geared our bibliography to include selections from standard readers to facilitate course organization, as well as to make it easier for students to locate supplementary materials. With its emphasis on archaeological reasoning and decision-making, this book can also be productively paired with any of several available workbooks, in which a series of exercises allows students to practice the kinds of reasoning they have learned from the text.

BIBLIOGRAPHY AND GLOSSARY

The bibliography is designed to introduce the newcomer to the archaeological literature; it thus provides a key to the huge library available on studies of the human past. Since no bibliography can hope to be comprehensive, we have tended to favor recent works and, whenever possible, publications that explicitly review relevant antecedent literature, while still including selected "classic" works. At the same time, we have tried to present varied positions in theoretical debates.

Bibliographic references are summarized topically at the end of each chapter in a "Guide to Further Reading." Full citation information for all references is given in the bibliography at the end of the book.

We have also included a glossary of key terms that includes references to the chapters where these concepts are discussed. Terms in the glossary are in boldface in the text.

ACKNOWLEDGMENTS

One never writes alone, and certainly we have been helped by many people in many ways during the writing of this book and its several predecessors. The first version, called *Fundamentals of Archaeology* (Benjamin/Cummings, 1979), originally grew out of the senior author's introductory archaeology method and theory course taught at the University of Pennsylvania. The students in this course were the first inspiration—as well as the first critics—and students in subsequent courses taught by both of us have continued to shape our ways of explaining how archaeologists discover the past.

When we moved to Mayfield to revise the original book, Janet M. Beatty enthusiastically assumed the role of sponsoring editor. Through two editions of this book, plus an abridged version, Jan has persistently pushed, praised, cajoled, and exhorted us onward. She has truly become our friend, as well as our editor. A number of other friends and colleagues read and criticized the manuscript at various stages; their advice may not always have been followed, but it was always considered and appreciated. Many others kindly allowed us to use photos and drawings from their research to help illustrate this text. And we thank Julia C. Miller, doctoral candidate at the University of Pennsylvania, for making all this possible by putting the previous edition on disk.

We acknowledge specifically the comments and suggestions for this edition received from several anonymous reviewers and from Sarah Campbell (Western Washington University), Paul Farnsworth (Louisiana State University), Kenneth L. Feder (Central Connecticut University), Gary M. Feinman (University of Wisconsin, Madison), Susan D. Gillespie (University of Illinois), Michael Love (Stanford University), Scott Madry (Rutgers University), Patty Jo Watson (Washington University), and Richard W. Yerkes (The Ohio State University).

We are also grateful to the colleagues who contributed the personal essays that enrich the narrative: Ronald L. Bishop (Smithsonian Institution), Robert J. Blumenschine (Rutgers University), Margaret W. Conkey (University of California, Berkeley), Lynne Goldstein (University of Wisconsin, Milwaukee), Steven A. LeBlanc (Southwest Museum, Los Angeles, and Mimbres Foundation), David W. Sedat (The University Museum, University of Pennsylvania), Payson D. Sheets (University of Colorado), and Patty Jo Watson (Washington University). Special thanks go to Kent V. Flannery (University of Michigan), who kindly allowed us to do severe bodily damage to his thoroughly enjoyable final chapter from *Guilá Naquitz* (Academic Press, 1986), that provides the essay after Chapter 3.

We extend deep appreciation to colleagues in the Instituto Hondureño de Antropología e Historia (IHAH) and the Proyecto Arqueológico Copán, who have supported our research at Copán and who, over the years, have generously shared with us information, guidance, and friendship. Their contributions are most readily apparent in Chapter 5, but collaboration with them has also had more general and sometimes quite profound effects on our thinking about the conduct of archaeological research. We would especially like to thank the several recent Directors of the IHAH, Dr. Adan Cueva, Lic. Ricardo Agurcia F., Lic. Victor Cruz R., and the current Director, Arq. José Maria Casco L., as well as respected colleagues who have directed various aspects of Copán research in the last two decades, Ricardo Agurcia F., E. Wyllys Andrews V, Claude F. Baudez, William and Barbara Fash, Carlos Rudy Larios V., Richard M. Leventhal, William T. Sanders, David W. Sedat, David L. Webster, and Gordon R. Willey.

There is one colleague whom the senior author came to know as a friend for far too short a time. Conversations with Glynn Isaac, just before his premature death in 1985, resulted in fundamental contributions to the discussions of the interpretation of the archaeological record found throughout this book. We include a photograph of Glynn in this book as an illustration for the discussion of reconstructing ancient behavior from the distribution of artifacts and ecofacts at Koobi Fora (Figure 12.2, p. 404)—one of the many endeavors in which he made substantial contributions to archaeology.

We would like to thank the professional staff at Mayfield Publishing Company for bringing the current edition to fruition. We are especially grateful to senior editor Jan Beatty, as well as to production editor Lynn Rabin Bauer, marketing manager Debby Horowitz, and associate designer Jean Mailander for their creativity, perseverance, patience, diplomacy, and good humor. Copy editor Carole R. Crouse gently corrected our grammar and offered helpful suggestions about how to say more clearly what we really meant.

We extend renewed thanks to our families for supporting us during all phases of this endeavor. And we thank each other, too, for intellectual stimulation, mutual respect and support, and a sturdy collegial friendship. As with earlier instances of writing and revising, we didn't always agree, but even the arguments were ultimately rewarding and often fun. We hope the result will stimulate others to think more—as we certainly continue to do—about the issues and choices raised in these pages.

The record of the human past is undeniably fascinating. But it is also very fragile. As in previous editions, we dedicate this book to those who may learn to be committed to studying and protecting our past heritage for the benefits of the future.

CONTENTS

CHAPTER FOUR   CONSTRUCTS: THE NATURE OF ARCHAEOLOGICAL DATA   113

CHAPTER FIVE   ARCHAEOLOGICAL RESEARCH   147

ARCHAEOLOGISTS AT WORK
Ronald L. Bishop: Pottery in the High Tech Lab   379

CHAPTER EIGHTEEN **CHALLENGES TO ARCHAEOLOGY 578**

INTRODUCTION

July 1987, Lambayeque Valley, Peru: Hopes were running high. Something extraordinary seemed about to happen. Along with the hopes, though, came realization that the odds still favored disappointment.

Archaeologist Walter Alva and his colleagues worked feverishly near the foot of Sipán's great earthen pyramid by day. By night, they posted armed guards to protect against determined tomb robbers. A rich burial from the ancient Moche culture (ca. A.D. 100–700) had been found by robbers in the same huge mound only the year before, and the gold and silver and other "art collectibles" had been ripped from the ground and quickly dispersed to the art market. One of the plunderers had been killed by police in attempting to recover the loot, and his neighbors wanted vengeance—and more gold. For the archaeologists, however, the prospective "treasure" of the Sipán excavations would not be the gold, but the unparalleled information to be gained from an unlooted tomb. Who was buried here? And when? And what could be learned about Moche society from the funerary customs?

The Moche were a powerful society, with sophisticated knowledge of irrigation agriculture, monumental building, and warfare more than a thousand years before the appearance of the more famous Andean civilization of the Inkas. The Moche were perhaps best known, however, for the beautifully painted and modeled pottery so coveted by modern collectors, and for the finely worked and similarly coveted copper, gold, and silver ornaments and armor produced by their highly skilled artisans. Now, however, what must have been lavish Moche tombs were "known" only from the gaping holes in the ground left by their gold-hungry discoverers, and by beautiful objects stocking the shelves of private collectors and museums.

From the time of the Spanish conquest in the 16th century, the looters had always won the race. Would the same be true this time? Had there perhaps been only the one tomb in this great mound? Or if there were more, would the archaeologists be able to keep the plunderers at bay until any new ones could be found, recorded, and safely removed for study?

Discovery of an area of looser mound fill hinted at an ancient pit, possibly another tomb, and tensions climbed. Imprints of long-rotted wooden beams showed where a chamber roof had been; below were more than a thousand pottery vessels, accompanied by the skeleton of a man, his body broken as he was killed in sacrifice. Clearly, by his treatment in

1

FIGURE I.1 Excavating the tomb of the "Lord of Sipán" required great care to recover the well-preserved but fragile remains. Here archaeologists have just removed the skeleton of this Moche lord, revealing lavish gold and feather ornaments on which he had lain. Whereas looters would have been concerned only with profit from selling the sumptuous offerings, archaeologists aim to recover the insights the tomb and its occupant, as well as the offerings, can give us about life and death in the Moche world. (Martha Cooper, © 1988 National Geographic Society.)

death, this man was not the subject of honor and awe that had prompted construction and furnishing of the chamber. Someone else must lie buried deeper within the mound.

Digging further, Alva encountered the skeleton of a young warrior, still clad in his copper helmet and shield. A more respectful burial, this, though the man had apparently lost his feet. But this physical mutilation and the relative simplicity of his burial were clues that the object of so much construction energy still had not been found.

Then came fragments of more wooden beams, elaborately lashed together with copper straps. The area covered by the beams measured seven feet long and four feet wide, and this huge timbered construction had slumped downward, indicating a chamber below. As Alva describes:

> For long seconds breath and words would not come; only a ripple of birdsong drifted into the excavation to break the enchanted silence. When we finally spoke, it was to babble: "A coffin! It's sealed. . . . Never opened!"

The tomb uncovered by Walter Alva that year was astounding in its complexity and preservation. The principal occupant, soon named the "Lord of Sipán," had been laid to rest in finery befitting a royal burial, from his copper sandals to his gold and turquoise bracelets, multiple gold head, ear, and nose ornaments, shell and copper chest ornaments, gold mask, and gold-decorated fabrics (Fig. I.1). He held gold and copper in-

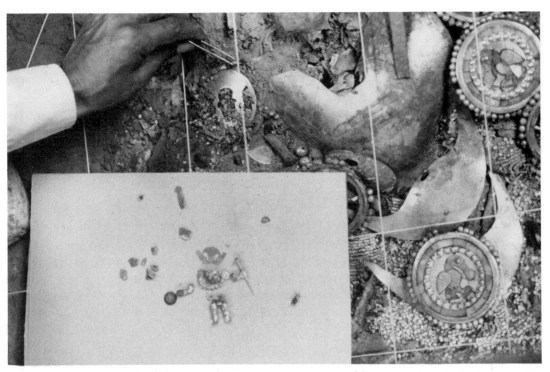

gots, a copper knife, and an elaborately embossed gold rattle, and had been laid out on a wooden frame and wrapped in three cloth shrouds before being closed in his coffin. Lying alongside him in the tomb were two men and two young women, plus a dog. Both the coffin and the surrounding chamber also contained elaborate offerings, from fragile feather fans to delicate thorny oyster shells, large gold and copper bells, and decorated pottery vessels.

Had all this been found by looters, the individual pieces of metal and pottery would have been separated and sold to multiple collectors of such antiquities, fetching prices ranging from $10,000 to $100,000 each! Broken or poorly preserved items, including both the feather fans and the turquoise-inlaid gold ear ornaments (Fig. I.2), would likely have been destroyed by frenzied digging or simply left behind, to disintegrate completely and be lost to human history.

Because the tomb was found by archaeologists, not only have smaller and more fragile items been saved, but the picture emerging from the tomb is immeasurably more complete than could be had from knowledge of any of its contents alone. Thanks to work by Alva and other Moche experts, the funerary trappings of the Lord of Sipán could be interpreted as clues to his ancient role in society. Regalia and belongings jointly identify the distinctive and powerful "chief" or "king" whom Christopher Donnan has recognized from scenes painted on Moche pottery vessels.

The vessel scenes depict these Moche leaders performing a variety of acts, especially ritual sacrifice of prisoners, and elements shown in the painted scenes were duplicated precisely in the tomb, from specific costume items to the hand-held gold rattle to the accompanying dog. The scenes therefore depicted ancient human actions, not mythical behavior by supernaturals.

The discovery made by Alva and his colleagues in Peru is dramatic because of the elaborate remains they found still intact, reflecting the wealth and power of the "Lord of Sipán." But the confrontation between archaeologist and looter occurs constantly everywhere in the world, including sites much closer to home. In the same year that the Lord of Sipán was discovered, another such confrontation erupted, with tragic results, on Slack Farm in rural Kentucky. The Slack Farm site, although not as exotic as Sipán, nevertheless fell victim to the same conflict between archaeology and those who would plunder the past for their own pleasure and profit.

For more than a hundred years, archaeologists had known that the remains of a large Native American town existed on Slack Farm, dating to about A.D. 1450–1650. This site belonged to the Mississippian culture, a way of life that dominated southeastern North America after about A.D. 900. Like other towns of this culture, the Slack Farm site was marked most prominently by earthen platforms, once occupied by the temples and chief's houses of these agricultural people. In size, the Slack Farm site was similar to other Mississippian towns, with a population estimated at 300–500. But what made it most remarkable was that, thanks to the care of the farm's owners, the Slack family, this site was the largest known of its kind that had escaped destruction by looters.

All that changed in 1987, when Mrs. Slack died, the farm changed hands, and its new owners pocketed a profit of $10,000 by leasing artifact-mining rights to a small group of pothunters. Within two months, this largely intact monument of Native American culture was transformed into a pockmarked wasteland, the edges of more than 450 looters' craters littered with bits of pottery and human bone (Fig. I.3). These plunder pits had destroyed at least 650 graves, their occupants' bones crushed or strewn aside, and the pottery and other mortuary offerings sold to collectors.

As at Sipán, once archaeologists learned of the destruction, they moved rapidly to salvage what information they could, but by that time the greater part of the site was destroyed, forever prevented from informing the present about ancient customs and people. Moreover, the wanton desecration of Native American graves was once again a callous insult to the living descendants of the ancient populace (Fig. I.4).

Neither of these sites will enlighten us on all aspects of an ancient society. But because peoples the world over have buried their dead with objects indicative of their roles in life, burials offer invaluable insights into the past. These objects were often prized possessions of or gifts to the deceased, and more often intact than items that ended up abandoned or

FIGURE I.3 This aerial view of Slack Farm illustrates dramatically the destruction wrought by looters: In just two months, ten men reduced this Native American site to a pitted wasteland, littered with pottery fragments and shattered human remains. (Kenny Barkley, Morganfield, Kentucky.)

FIGURE I.4 Archaeologists and volunteers from Kentucky and Indiana investigated the looters' holes and dirt piles at Slack Farm to document damage and to salvage information about this important habitation and mortuary site. (Courtesy of David Pollak, Kentucky Heritage Council, and Cheryl Ann Munson, Indiana University, Bloomington.)

Calvin and Hobbes

by Bill Watterson

FIGURE I.5 A well-known boy and his tiger share a wry view of the joys of archaeology. (Calvin and Hobbes copyright 1988 Watterson. Dist. by Universal Press Syndicate. Reprinted with permission. All rights reserved.)

broken in trash heaps. As we have already seen at both Sipán and Slack Farm, however, the same intact and information-rich objects are also tremendously appealing to collectors of "art" and antiquities. The result is that, from the United States to Peru, and in settings all over the world, archaeologists and others who want to understand the human past are in a constant struggle with those who would destroy it for personal gain. Whether the goal is finding a royal tomb or unearthing ancient arrowheads, the distinction and the struggle are the same: Why do people look for remains of the past at all, and once they find them, what do they do with these materials? The motivation for looters is obvious—to find valuable objects that can be sold for profit. The motivations for archaeologists may not be as obvious.

This book is about the questions that motivate archaeologists to find and study the past. Discoveries such as those made at Sipán, or at any other site that hasn't been devastated by looters, dramatize questions about who we are and why we behave as we do. What we are today, the way we act in various situations, our customs, our beliefs, and our entire civilization, are all the result of an incredibly long and complex tradition of human accomplishment that stretches thousands—even millions—of years into the past. At some point in our lives, each of us asks questions such as: What does it mean to be human? Where did we come from? Who *are* we? If we are to answer these questions and learn to understand ourselves, we must try to understand our past.

The desire for knowledge about ourselves motivates many people to pursue careers in fields such as anthropology, psychology, sociology, and other social sciences. These fields study different aspects of the fundamental questions raised above, but all are limited to examining our behavior and our society today, in the present. To fully understand ourselves, we need to know where we came from, our heritage from the past. The study of history does this, but its scope is limited to only the last few thousand years—the era of written documents. It also tends to downplay societies outside of our own Western civilization.

Only one field, **archaeology,** is designed to explore and reveal the full extent of the human past, from our most remote and obscure glimmerings to our greatest glories, in any and all areas of the globe. In pursuing the past, archaeology addresses questions such as: Where, when, and why did human life begin on earth? How and why did some early human societies develop increasingly complex cultures? Why did some others *not* become more complex? How and why do civilizations rise and fall?

Archaeology is the study of the human past through its material remains, and in this book we will outline how archaeologists go about discovering, studying, and making sense of those remains. Archaeology is exciting; it can also be tedious—"mind-numbing," in Calvin's immortal words (Fig. I.5). But it is always rewarding, not in money or fame, but in the satisfaction of contributing to understanding who we as humans are and how we've all gotten to where we are today.

CHAPTER ONE

VIEWING THE PAST

Consideration of the past removes us from the immediate concerns of the here and now . . . and plunges us directly into the larger common world which exists in the stream of time and hence bridges the mortality of generations.

William D. Lipe, "Value and Meaning in Cultural Resources," 1984

This book is about **archaeology** and how archaeologists carry out research to better understand the past. Archaeology holds a fascination for many people, for reasons that may be quite varied. For some of us, archaeology is appealing because it seeks answers to questions about ourselves. For others, the life of the **archaeologist** conjures up adventurous travel to exotic places and the prospect of making dramatic discoveries of "lost" civilizations. This romantic image of the archaeologist is perhaps best represented by recent movies about the character Indiana Jones. Fiction aside, certainly the general public's image of archaeology is shaped by real newspaper or television reports of spectacular finds. For instance, excavations like those we have described of Sipán tombs arouse tremendous public interest (Fig. I.1). Other recent archaeological discoveries, such as finding the 2000-year-old pottery army guarding the tomb of China's first emperor (Fig. 1.1), become front-page news. Even a discovery made more than half a century ago—Howard Carter's opening of the lost tomb of Pharaoh Tut-ankh-amun in Egypt—continues to excite the imagination.

But spectacular finds such as those at Sipán are very rare in archaeology, and few archaeologists find anything that even approaches the dramatic

FIGURE 1.1 Chinese archaeologists clear one of hundreds of pottery soldiers, part of the effigy army created to protect the tomb of Qin Shi Huang, the first Emperor of China, excavated from a collapsed underground vault near the village of Xiyang, Shaanxi Province, China. (Courtesy of Beijing Photo Studio.)

discovery made by Walter Alva. As we shall see, archaeologists are not motivated by the adventurous or dangerous exploits of an Indiana Jones, and they certainly do not recover evidence from the past for its monetary or aesthetic value. Instead, they are motivated by a hunger for the *information* their discoveries provide and for that information's contribution to understanding the human past. Yet popular fascination with archaeology is unabated, so perhaps there is a deeper reason for it.

⤏⤏

Dramatic archaeological discovery: Howard Carter and the tomb of Tut-ankh-amun

In November 1922, workers excavating in Egypt's Valley of the Kings for the British archaeologist Howard Carter and his patron, Lord Carnarvon, uncovered a rubble-clogged stone staircase leading down into the earth. When the rubble was cleared away, a plastered-over doorway was found at the foot of the stairs, bearing the hieroglyphs of a then little-known pharaoh, Tut-ankh-amun. The doorway was then broken through; it led to a rubble-filled corridor some 25 feet long. Clearing this debris brought the excavators to a second doorway. Despite his fears that it most likely had been pillaged by tomb robbers long before his arrival, Carter dared to hope that behind the second door he might find a tomb complete with the royal sarcophagus and the preserved remains of the pharaoh himself, along with the everyday objects of Tut-ankh-amun's life and the funerary paraphernalia used in the rituals surrounding his death. It was thus with considerable anticipation that, on November 26, 1922, Howard Carter removed several blocks from the plastered-over second doorway and, using the light from a lamp, peered into the dark chamber beyond.

> For the moment—an eternity it must have seemed to the others standing by—I was struck dumb . . . and when Lord Carnarvon . . . inquired anxiously, "Can you see anything?" it was all I could do to get out the words, "Yes, wonderful things. . . ." (Howard Carter's narrative of the opening of the tomb of Pharaoh Tut-ankh-amun)

When Howard Carter opened the door to the tomb of Pharaoh Tut-ankh-amun, he beheld a sight that left him speechless for several moments (Fig. 1.2). He was overcome by both the splendor of what he saw and the realization that his were the first eyes to gaze upon that scene for more than 3000 years. The "wonderful things" held him spellbound not only because of their beauty but also because they represented a moment suspended in time. Through those objects, Carter "saw" events surrounding the life and death of a king who had lived more than 3000 years earlier but events that were so vivid they might have happened the day before.

UNDERSTANDING OURSELVES THROUGH OUR PAST

It seems that at a deeper level the fascination of archaeology is its ability to examine the human past to answer questions about our own society and ourselves. Howard Carter's experience of awe was something that all archaeologists feel in their day-to-day confrontation with the past. Archae-

FIGURE 1.2 Howard Carter opening the doors of the second shrine, containing the remains of Tut-ankh-amun. (Griffith Institute, Ashmolean Museum, Oxford.)

ologists constantly face the paradox of individual human mortality and cultural immortality: Though each human life is finite, and though individual societies rise and fall, the cultural heritage of humankind is continuous and immortal.

Whenever archaeologists reveal the remains of an ancient house or study fragments of ancient pottery, they look into the past just as Carter did at the door of Tut-ankh-amun's tomb. Obviously, few of these views are as clear as Carter's, if only because they are based on much less completely preserved remains. Sometimes, deliberate destruction obscures the view even further. For instance, when the Spanish *conquistadores* led by Cortés entered the Valley of Mexico in 1519, they were also spellbound by what they saw (Fig. 1.3):

> and when we saw so many cities and villages built in the water and other great towns on dry land and that straight and level causeway going towards Mexico, we were amazed and said that it was like the enchantments they tell of in the legend of Amadis, on account of the great towers . . . and buildings rising from the water, and all built of masonry. And some of our soldiers even asked whether the things that we saw were not a dream. . . . I do not know how to describe it seeing things as we did that had never been heard of or seen before, not even dreamed about. (Diaz del Castillo [1632] 1956:190–191)

Yet that splendid scene was destroyed by those same Spaniards in a brutal war of conquest that saw the ancient cities of Mexico razed, thousands of people killed, and a whole way of life drastically altered. The *conquistadores* did more than wipe out a civilization; their destruction of buildings, tools,

Deliberate destruction of a civilization: Cortés and the Aztecs of Mexico

FIGURE 1.3 This view of 1981 excavations at the Templo Mayor, in the heart of Mexico City, reveals the series of temples the Aztecs built at the sacred center of their capital, Tenochtitlan. The temple's earliest archaeologically documented version, Stage II, is protected by the metal roof at right; the sets of stairs at the center are remains of renovations of the temple pyramid, built to encase its predecessors. The final stage, VII, was virtually obliterated by the Spanish *conquistadores*. (Courtesy Eduardo Matos Moctezuma and the Great Temple Project.)

records, and other products of Aztec culture also robbed future generations of much of the crucial evidence that would allow a fuller understanding of this civilization.

DESTRUCTION OF OUR HERITAGE

Looting of the past: The Deir el-Bahri mummy cache

Of course, the destruction of civilizations and their products is not confined to acts of war. Archaeological evidence is constantly being pillaged by **looters** who raid archaeological sites and sell their plunder. Looting is nothing new. There have always been individuals who view the remains of the past as a way to make money. Egyptian tomb robbers were plying their secret trade during the time of the pharaohs. The consequences of looting have even provided some unique archaeological discoveries, such as the finding in 1881 of a cache of more than 40 mummies in a single underground chamber at Deir el-Bahri in Egypt. The mummies had been brought to this spot in ancient times from their original tombs in the nearby Valley of the Kings to protect the dead rulers' remains from the depredations of tomb robbers. The plan was successful for more than 30 centuries, but the chamber was finally discovered—by none other than modern looters, heirs to an ancient and dishonorable tradition.

Today the plundering of archaeological sites is accelerating far faster than the pace of archaeological research. The simple truth is that much more money is available to purchase artifacts stolen from archaeological sites than to support archaeological research. As we shall explain in Chapter 4, thieves destroy immense quantities of irreplaceable knowledge even as they boast of recovering a handful of artistic objects. And the destructive toll increases when people alter the landscape for the public good, through works such as road building or agricultural development. We will return to these problems in Chapter 18. As a direct consequence of these destructive forces, however, the archaeologist is often in a fierce race against time to obtain and preserve as clear a view as possible of the past.

WHAT IS ARCHAEOLOGY?

Archaeology is the study of the human past through its material remains. As a field of inquiry, archaeology has grown during the past few hundred years from an amateur's pastime—or even a rich man's "sport"—to a scientifically based profession. In that time archaeology has emerged as the field that uses past remains to order and describe ancient events and to explain the human behavior behind those events. The material remains are referred to collectively as the **archaeological record.** To study the past, archaeologists have developed a series of *methods* by which they discover, recover, preserve, describe, and analyze the archaeological record (Fig. 1.4). To assess the meaning of this record, archaeologists are guided by a body of *theory*. Ultimately, this theory provides the means to interpret

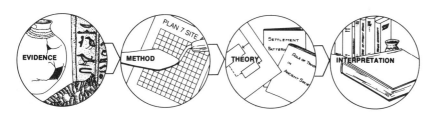

FIGURE 1.4 Archaeological reasoning relates evidence and interpretation by means of method and theory.

archaeological evidence and allows both description and explanation of the past. This book will explore both the methods and the theory used by archaeologists to understand the past.

Archaeology has four principal goals in studying the past (Fig. 1.5). The first is to reveal the **form** of the past: the description and classification of the physical evidence that is recovered. Analysis of form allows archaeologists to outline the distribution of remains of ancient societies in both time and space. The second goal is to discover **function:** by analyzing the form and interrelationships of recovered evidence, to determine the ancient behavior represented by the physical remains. The third is to understand **cultural processes:** by using the remains of ancient culture, to explain how and why they changed through time. Finally, the archaeologist attempts to derive *meaning* from the archaeological record.

The past was composed of countless individual lives that shaped events both petty and important. Although those individuals and their societies are dead and gone, their achievements and failures have lived on to shape our present world. The fascination of archaeology, ultimately, is that it bridges past and present. The past seen by archaeologists is nothing less than an imperfect reflection of our lives today.

ARCHAEOLOGY AND PSEUDOARCHAEOLOGY

To use the past to understand ourselves and our ancestors, we must look at a reflection that is as accurate as possible. As we shall see, the archaeological record is subject to alternative interpretations, but trained archaeologists are not the only ones providing accounts about our past. A multitude of other versions are readily available in books, magazines, movies, and television programs. These popularized descriptions of the past are often appealing, for they emphasize dramatic mysteries and baffling paradoxes supposedly found in the archaeological record. As we shall see, sometimes these accounts are even dangerous. But they are not archaeology; they are *pseudoarchaeology.*

Pseudoarchaeology refers to descriptions of the past that claim to be based on fact but actually are fictional accounts that distort our understanding of the past. Pseudoarchaeologists attack established interpretations with highly selective data, often accusing the proponents of accepted positions of narrow-mindedness and intellectual prejudice. In fact, it's the other way around: Pseudoarchaeologists are the ones who are narrow-minded and prejudiced. Pseudoarchaeology is something different from disagreement among scholars—falsified reconstructions of the past have had tragic consequences, as when used to support nationalistic or even racist political doctrines, such as those promoted by Nazi Germany.

Pseudoarchaeology has been with us for a long time. Included in the tradition are many of the accounts dealing with the "lost civilizations" of Atlantis and Mu, ancient mythical continents inhabited by precociously

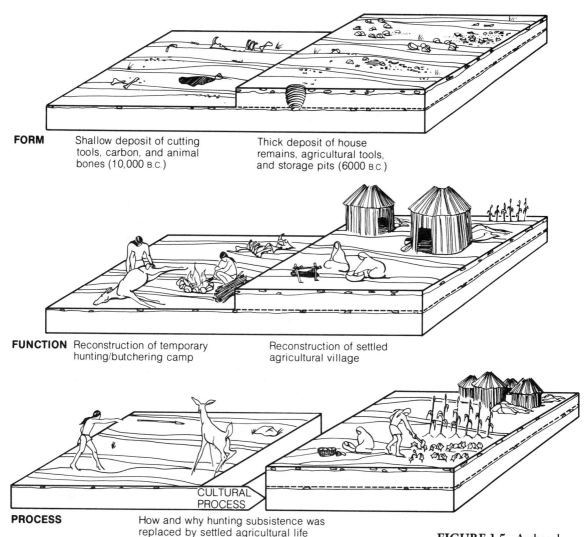

FORM   Shallow deposit of cutting tools, carbon, and animal bones (10,000 B.C.)   Thick deposit of house remains, agricultural tools, and storage pits (6000 B.C.)

FUNCTION   Reconstruction of temporary hunting/butchering camp   Reconstruction of settled agricultural village

CULTURAL PROCESS

PROCESS   How and why hunting subsistence was replaced by settled agricultural life

FIGURE 1.5 Archaeology is concerned with four primary goals. The first three are illustrated here: the description of form, analysis of function, and elucidation of process.

sophisticated peoples that supposedly disappeared beneath the waves of the Atlantic and Pacific oceans. Every so often reports of mysterious hieroglyphs or symbols from pre-Columbian contexts revive the theory that Old World cultures were the source of Native American civilizations. We will see in Chapter 2 that the debate over the identity of the "mound builders" of the ancient Americas grew quite heated in the 19th century, and peoples such as the Phoenicians, Assyrians, Romans, Chinese Buddhists, Norsemen, and Huns were suggested as the ones responsible for New World civilization. But archaeological research was then in its infancy, and to some extent the earliest proponents of those theories can be excused for a general lack of information. Today, however, pseudoarchaeology is characterized by ignorance or dismissal of accumulated evidence and of carefully reasoned archaeological interpretations, while the authors pick and choose those "facts" or bits of material evidence that seem to fit their case.

The efforts of the German prehistorian Gustav Kossinna (1858–1931) provide a glaring and ultimately tragic example of the manipulation of archaeological evidence to forge a racist reconstruction of the past. Kossinna was interested in showing the superiority of Germany to other nations. By exaggeration and falsification, he produced a version of **prehistory** claiming that everything of importance had begun in Germany before spreading to the surrounding "inferior" nations. It was this pseudoarchaeological view of the past that Adolf Hitler used in his book *Mein Kampf* to help justify the doctrine of German racial superiority. In this case, what began as pseudoarchaeological reconstruction ended up as part of the rationale for Nazi German military expansion, starting World War II in Europe and ultimately leading to the slaughter of millions of innocent people.

The terrible experience of Nazism provides a bitter lesson as to the power of racist ideology. But although blatantly racist pseudoarchaeological reconstructions have been rightfully discredited, more subtle fanciful versions of the past remain with us, many calculated to have a widespread, romantic appeal. In recent years, the most popular theory in this category has been that of Erich von Däniken, who sought to explain a series of archaeological and historical "mysteries" by invoking visits from ancient astronauts. According to one report, von Däniken's books have sold more than 25 million copies in 32 languages; they have also spawned television programs, movies, and numerous imitative books by other authors. Some responses from professional archaeologists and scientifically oriented laymen have appeared: Books and articles, college courses, and television programs have all dealt critically with von Däniken's propositions. But these and other pseudoarchaeological accounts continue to be more popular than scientific archaeology; and the public tends to regard the pseudoarchaeologist as more creative, imaginative, and open-minded, whereas the arguments of professional archaeologists appear stodgy and conservative. It seems that romantic speculations and the appeal of unsolved mysteries will always be more popular than the cold, hard facts.

Pseudoarchaeologists rationalize their theories by selectively citing only the "facts" that seem to support their position, often wrenching evidence from its total context. For example, von Däniken described the sculptured scene on the sarcophagus lid from the famous tomb at the Maya site of Palenque, Mexico, as "obviously" representing an ancient astronaut at the controls of his ancient rocket (Fig. 1.6). The author conveniently ignored all other evidence of Maya art and symbolism—the costume, the position of the figure, the representation of the ceiba tree, and the hieroglyphic inscription that ultimately identified the sculptured figure as the ruler buried in the sarcophagus. The pseudoarchaeologist takes the data out of their

Fanciful vs. scientific interpretation: The Palenque sarcophagus lid

larger context: Other material remains of the Classic Maya indicate nothing about ancient astronauts, but because this single example has a superficial resemblance to the launch position of an astronaut, it was advanced as positive evidence for the "space visitor" theory.

A related problem is the **ethnocentrism** of such interpretations, in which everything is interpreted from the perspective of the observer's culture, rather than that of the culture from which the material comes. Such items as the Palenque sarcophagus lid, the rock art of Africa and northern Australia, and the carved figures in the "Gateway of the Sun" at Tiwanaku in Bolivia have been interpreted as evidence of astronauts or gods from outer space. Even 19th-century ideas about New World civilizations being derived from transoceanic contacts, originating in Asia, Africa, or elsewhere, have been revitalized. But anyone who bothers to examine the full archaeological record for any of these times and places finds that the evidence indicates gradual development of local traditions: The supposed outside intrusions do not appear suddenly, they are not without parallels, and they are not followed by drastic changes in the archaeological record of the area. The record is there, but it does not speak for itself; it must be examined in its entirety, as responsible scholars examine it.

The problem of ethnocentrism (some would say racism) extends further. The basic questions underlying pseudoarchaeological theories are: How could ancient peoples possibly have built monuments such as the huge pyramids of Egypt? How could they have possessed the skills and the labor to erect these and other awesome monuments before the advent of modern technology, without the aid of some extraterrestrial power? These rhetorical questions do demand answers, but the pseudoarchaeologist phrases them so as to suggest that ancient peoples could not have accomplished these feats, despite firm archaeological evidence to the contrary. In fact, the accomplishments cited did not require superhuman skills or knowledge. Ancient Egyptians, for example, were quite able to move the huge and heavy stones of the pyramids—or entire obelisks—from the quarries by conventional water transport and by simple sledges and ramps; both methods are attested in written and pictorial Egyptian records. Certainly, we find the imposing accomplishments of the past awesome today. Perhaps, as William Rathje suggests, because the tasks involved are personally unfamiliar to us in our modern industrial culture, we find it difficult or impossible to accept that ancient preindustrial peoples could have accomplished such remarkable feats.

For example, the great sculptures of Easter Island have impressed everyone who has seen them (Fig. 1.7). Von Däniken asserted, among other things, that the stone was too hard to be carved with the tools locally available, that the time required to carve the statues—and there are hundreds of these huge monolithic sculptures—implied an impossibly large population on the barren volcanic isle, and that the sculptures were far too heavy to have been moved from their quarry site to the platforms where they were set up. He therefore concludes that Easter Island presents a clear case of extraterrestrial intervention.

FIGURE 1.6 Rubbing made from the sculptured sarcophagus lid found in the tomb beneath the Temple of the Inscriptions at Palenque, Mexico, representing the dead ruler surrounded by Maya supernatural symbols. (Rubbing, permission of Merle Greene.)

Experiments refute von Däniken: Easter Island monuments

FIGURE 1.7 View of the famous sculptured stone figures on Easter Island. Excavations and experiments indicate that these figures were quarried and transported by past inhabitants of the island, contrary to the speculations of pseudo-archaeologists. (Plate 12a from *The Art of Easter Island* by Thor Heyerdahl. Copyright © 1975 by Thor Heyerdahl. Used by permission of Doubleday & Company, Inc.)

Do von Däniken's claims hold up to critical examination? The stone statues are indeed steel-hard today, but experiments show that, when first quarried, the volcanic tuff is quite soft and can be cut with stone tools. After quarrying, this kind of stone becomes progressively harder by a common geological process called *case-hardening*. As for the time and labor involved, Thor Heyerdahl set out to find some answers. First he recruited modern Easter Islanders, gave them stone tools like those found in the ancient quarries, and asked them to carve a statue like the ancient ones. This simple experiment indicated that a mere twenty workmen could finish one statue within a year. And, since Easter Island is not nearly so barren as von Däniken would have us believe, during the 1200 years of known occupation it could have supported an ample population to provide the labor for the known sculptures. But what about the transport and placement of the idols? Von Däniken asserted there were no trees on the island to be used for rollers or sledges. This is untrue—trees are not plentiful, but some do exist on the island, and pollen studies indicate that in the past the island was forest-covered. Heyerdahl conducted another experiment in which 150 local people, using wooden sledges, succeeded in moving a 10-ton idol. Larger monuments would have required more people and more sledges. Evidence in archaeological settlements on the island supports the contention that enough people were present in prehistoric times to do the job. Finally, Heyerdahl's experiments demonstrated that, by using poles, ropes, and rocks, 12 men could raise a 25-ton statue from a horizontal to an upright position in just 18 days, by gradual leverage.

Archaeologists, of course, do not claim to have all the answers. As in all science, today's findings may be modified or even replaced by new interpretations based on new evidence. The famous lines marked on the Nazca plain in Peru are a case in point. Suggestions that the lines were used in astronomical observations have been contested, and there is no universally accepted explanation for the marks. But there is certainly no evidence to support their use as "ancient landing strips." And as for those examples that have elaborate shapes (constructed, according to von Däniken, to attract or please astronauts circling overhead), Peter White points out that modern features such as Christian churches also have symbolic (in this case, cross-shaped) forms that are best viewed from above. He goes on to remind us that

A disputed problem: The Nazca lines of Peru

> When men make designs that are best seen from the sky or take an interest in the stars it does not prove that there are astronauts. It proves that most people believe that gods are "up there" rather than down below us underground (though such beliefs are also known), or in the same world as we are but in some distant place. (White 1974:91)

What, then, is the challenge to professional archaeology? Why should archaeologists be concerned with the writings of pseudoscience? Aside from the obvious lesson learned from the use of pseudoarchaeology to support German Nazism, what is so harmful about these theories?

Prehistoric and preindustrial historic peoples were demonstrably capable of much more artistic, engineering, and other kinds of ingenuity than pseudoarchaeologists seem willing to allow them. Tales of extraterrestrial influences on cultural development make exciting science fiction, as anyone familiar with Arthur C. Clarke's classic film *2001: A Space Odyssey* or its sequel, *2010,* can well attest. But let these stories stay in the realm of fantasy where they belong, as good entertainment. Archaeology, the science seeking to understand the human past, has a responsibility to prevent pseudoarchaeologists from robbing humanity of the real achievements of past cultures. Such robbery is a subtle form of racism, for the underlying message of pseudoarchaeology is that people in the past required the assistance of outside "superiors" to accomplish what we see in the archaeological record.

ARCHAEOLOGY AND SCIENCE

Beyond robbing us of our true cultural heritage, pseudoarchaeology violates the rational and commonsense bases of all science. Archaeologists draw on these bases to develop as accurate and complete a picture of the past as possible. Thus archaeology, in contrast to pseudoarchaeology, is based on the same general approach taken by other scientists.

Considered in its broadest sense, **science** is concerned with gaining knowledge about the natural world and therefore seeks an understanding of all observable phenomena. Science is not concerned with phenomena that cannot be observed or examined; those remain the subject of theology, philosophy, the occult, and pseudoscience. Science proceeds by a disciplined search for knowledge, pursuing the description, ordering, and meaning of phenomena in a systematic manner. This search often involves controlled and repeatable laboratory experiments, such as those in chemistry or psychology. But it may also consist of detailed observation *without* experiment: Sciences such as **geology** deal with evidence that was formed long ago, or has accumulated over a long span of time, and that must generally be studied as it has come down to us, not through experimental manipulations. These are the so-called "historical" sciences; besides geology, they include evolutionary biology and archaeology.

In fact, however, the scientific quest for knowledge is almost as varied as the number of scientists making the quest. Some scientists strictly define their quest and rely on a uniform set of formal procedures, and reject all conclusions not derived from similar procedures. Later on (Chapter 3) we will consider one set of such formal procedures associated with archaeology, the hypothetico-deductive method. Other scientists, including many archaeologists, rely on less formally defined procedures, and we will discuss some of these in Chapter 3 as well. At this point, however, we should note that some scholars challenge the foundations of science and its claims to being objective and unbiased.

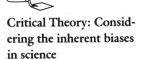

Critical Theory: Considering the inherent biases in science

One example is *Critical Theory*, named for its critique of how knowledge (including scientific knowledge) is gained. Drawing in part on Marxist theory, adherents of this school write of the biases inherent in the social, political, and ideological positions held by the individuals engaged in scientific inquiry, and how these biases affect the results of such inquiry. Incorporation of such a perspective can be seen in the writings of archaeologists such as Mark Leone or Russell Handsman. In the view of critical theorists, the fields of history and archaeology are a part of our own modern ideology, and thus the ways these disciplines interpret the past is biased by (and justifies) modern society's view of itself. Indeed, much of formal science itself is construed as part of an ideology of control because science declares there can be only a single view of the world and how it works.

Essential to this critique is the view that science itself has been traditionally controlled by a small, educated minority and that the rest of the world's population has had little or no input to scientific inquiry or access to its results. Thus critical theorists have called for incorporation of a broader constituency, including Nonwestern societies as well as other subgroups within Western society. Later on, in Chapters 3 and 18, we will consider such expansion more concretely, specifically with regard to native groups and women.

Whatever the specific form of its search, science follows an approach to acquiring knowledge that is continuously self-correcting, with continuous refinement of conclusions reached in earlier research. The widely accepted set of procedures that has been found to be trustworthy for gaining and testing our knowledge of the real world is called the **scientific method.**

The Scientific Method

Science discovers facts about the natural world by observing either objects or events. A scientist may draw conclusions by observing the real world and then test those conclusions by seeing if they hold true in other circumstances or cases. There are several ways of doing this. One starts from specific observation and proceeds to a generalization based on a series of such observations. Another goes in the opposite direction, deriving specific propositions from a generalization. For instance, if you purchased prerecorded cassette tapes and those from the Whizbang Company frequently went bad after only a few playings, you might generalize that Whizbang's products were unreliable in quality. If the same company started issuing videotapes, you might reason that the quality of these products might likewise be suspect. You could then *test* your conclusion about Whizbang's general manufacturing quality standards by buying and playing some of the new products.

To see how these reasoning processes work within archaeology, let us look at an example. Julian Steward, an anthropologist about whom we will have more to say in a later chapter, conducted extensive fieldwork in the Great Basin of the western United States in the 1920s and 1930s, studying the Native American peoples living in this region. From this work with living groups, he developed a generalization to describe the distribution of earlier, prehistoric Shoshone Indian activities and campsites, relating their locations to the seasonal cycle of food procurement.

Many years later, in the 1960s, David Hurst Thomas took Steward's description of shifting settlement in the Great Basin and derived a series of specific propositions from it. As Thomas phrased it, "if the late prehistoric Shoshoneans behaved in the fashion suggested by Steward, how would the artifacts have fallen on the ground?" If Steward's description of shifting settlement and seasonal exploitation of food resources in different locations were true, then Thomas could expect to find the tools associated with specific activities in predictable locations and densities. Hunting tools and butchering knives, for example, should be found more abundantly in the sagebrush zones, where hunting was argued to have been more important.

Thomas's research, in the Reese River Valley of central Nevada, supported more than 75 percent of the specific propositions, or *hypotheses,* derived from Steward's description. As a result, the original conclusions were refined, and new hypotheses were generated, which in turn allowed further improvement of our understanding of the Shoshone. This sequence of scientific hypothesis generation and testing could be continued indefinitely.

We have used the term **hypothesis.** What is a hypothesis, how is it generated, and how is it tested? A hypothesis is a tentative explanation, stated as a proposition that can be tested by observation. In the cassette tape example we used earlier, we derived the proposition that the Whizbang Company's products were unreliable in quality. We also derived the

The scientific method in archaeology: Research in the Great Basin (Reese River Ecological Project)

proposition that other Whizbang products might be bad. Other hypotheses are possible, for example, that the cassettes purchased all came from a single defective lot or, more broadly, that the entire Whizbang Company is unreliable. All of these alternative propositions are hypotheses because they can be tested by observation. To test a hypothesis, you evaluate how well it actually accounts for what you have observed—in this case, by buying other Whizbang products, asking friends about the quality of Whizbang products they've bought, writing the Better Business Bureau about Whizbang's reputation, and so forth.

Hypothesis testing: Reese River Ecological Project

Some hypotheses state a concrete relationship between two or more variables, based on certain assumptions or "givens." One type of hypothesis tested by the Reese River Project, for example, related the presence of archaeological sites (variable 1) to particular kinds of locations (variable 2). It said, in effect, that, if Steward's portrait of traditional Shoshone life were accurate, the specified kinds of locations would have been attractive places for occupation or use by the Shoshone's prehistoric ancestors. In the test, researchers found 65 sites, all but 2 of them in locales predicted by the hypothesis. They also found 11 locales where the hypothesis predicted that sites should be located but where no sites existed. Even so, the evidence strongly supported the relationship expressed by the hypothesis.

It is important to note that the scientific method does not attempt to prove one hypothesis correct. Rather, in its complete form, the testing operation seeks to test multiple contrasting hypotheses and eliminate those that are apparently incorrect, in order to isolate the one hypothesis (or set of related hypotheses) that best fits the observed phenomena. We have already seen how this works in the Reese River example, where the results of one round of testing allowed reformulation of more refined hypotheses.

Thus, there is no proof in science, only elimination or disproof of inadequate hypotheses. Science advances by disproof, promoting the most adequate propositions for the moment—in other words, what is most probable—knowing that new and better explanations will be advocated in the future with the availability of new data. Scientists, therefore, often disagree with each other, presenting alternative interpretations for consideration. This continuous self-correcting feature is the key to the scientific method.

Like other scientists, archaeologists apply the scientific method to a specified class of phenomena: the material remains of past human activity. Also, like other scientists, archaeologists attempt to isolate, classify, and explain the relationships among pieces of evidence, in this case, among the variables of form, function, time, and space or location. Archaeologists can observe the formal and spatial variables directly (for example, what are the size and shape of an item? where was it found?), but the functional and temporal variables must be inferred (what purpose did the item serve? how old is it?). Once these relationships are established, the archaeologist then infers past human behavior and reconstructs past human society from this evidence. In this sense, archaeology is a behavioral and a social science—its practitioners use the scientific method to understand past human social behavior.

Like many other scientific disciplines, archaeology today relies on computers in many ways. Because of the sheer volume of information that archaeologists often deal with, and the need to work with data that are quantified and can be statistically manipulated, computers have become virtually indispensable for archaeological research. But the use of computers or statistics should not be equated with "being scientific." It is the underlying philosophy governing the search for knowledge, and adherence to the scientific method, that establishes a discipline as a science. Computers and statistics are simply useful tools that enable scientists to conduct their research more efficiently and accurately.

As archaeology grows and matures as a scientific discipline, and as it relies increasingly on the scientific method to reach its goals, the less-than-rigorous research sometimes done in the past is giving way to the more painstaking procedures of science. We will discuss these matters again in Chapters 2 and 3, but we need to note here that archaeologists increasingly recognize that they must carefully state the assumptions under which they work and clearly formulate the questions they ask of their data. Interpretations of archaeological evidence can no longer be haphazard or intuitive. Instead, along with their data, archaeologists must present their assumptions and hypotheses and explain how these hypotheses were tested.

At the same time, it is important to recognize that although archaeologists, like other scientists, aspire to be completely objective in their search for knowledge, they can never escape their cultural milieu—the social, economic, political, and ideological settings in which they live and work. In this sense, the challenge expressed by such schools as Critical Theory should not be ignored by scientists, for although complete objectivity remains the goal, all scientific research is shaped to some degree by cultural factors. We should always be aware of potential biases and evaluate scientific results from a critical perspective.

The growth of scientific rigor in archaeology is reflected in the application of increasingly sophisticated bodies of *method* and *theory*. We briefly defined these terms (p. 13) as, respectively, the recovery procedures and the interpretive means used in dealing with the archaeological record. The remainder of this book explores the development and current status of archaeological method and theory. At this point, however, we would like to preview some of the distinctions made in archaeological theory.

Computers and statistics as archaeological tools

Theory: Constructs to Interpretation

In the first place, as archaeological theory has become more sophisticated, it has also become more explicitly defined and finely subdivided. We can discern at least three levels: constructs, "middle-range" theory, and general theory.

Constructs refer to the observable archaeological record and define the concepts archaeologists use for inferences about time, space, form, and function. Constructs are conceptual building blocks. They answer questions such as: What kinds of remains are left from the human past? How can we describe the conditions under which they are left behind and in which they are found? The basic constructs archaeologists use are defined in Chapter 4.

Middle-range theory makes correlations between ancient activities and their material traces. It does this by considering how the archaeological record was formed, as the collective result of human behavior and a myriad of other forces. Specifically, it connects the stones, bones, and potsherds we find to the ancient behaviors they represent, and it outlines the procedures for inferring the behaviors from the observed remains. At this level, for example, archaeologists seek clues to distinguish when animal bones represent the residue of people's meals, as opposed to leftovers from hyenas or other meat-eaters. They would also ask in what ways the form of an ancient building might identify the kinds of social groups that once used it, along with their activities. This is the level of theory that specifies how we make an observable record speak to us of the agents—human and otherwise—who produced it. The concepts dealing with formation of the archaeological record are also defined in Chapter 4.

General theory refers to the broader meaning and interpretation of the archaeological record, such as past cultural change and evolution and their explanations. The rise and fall of civilizations are common subjects (though certainly not the only ones) at this level of theory.

It is at the last two levels that the testing of hypotheses and models becomes the primary concern of archaeologists, as in the case of the Reese River Valley research described previously. After reviewing the growth of archaeology in Chapters 2 and 3, we will work our way through these levels of theory, from a primary concern with constructs in Chapters 4–9, to middle-range theory in Chapters 10–16, and arriving at general theory in Chapter 17. Practical application of theory—that is, archaeological method—will be treated at the same time. The theme throughout will be consideration of how archaeologists make scientifically valid inferences about the human past.

Although we will stress the scientific aspects of theory development, we will also argue strongly that a critical strength of archaeology stems from the diversity of its interests and its practitioners. This means that the value of the traditional historical and humanistic perspectives within archaeology should never be discarded. We have outlined how archaeology is a scientific discipline; let us turn now to consider its relation to the humanities, especially history.

ARCHAEOLOGY AND HISTORY

Archaeology is obviously related to the field of **history** in that both disciplines seek knowledge of the human past. The major difference between the two disciplines is the distinction in sources of information; this leads to differences in methodology, the techniques by which the past is studied.

History deals primarily with written accounts from the past. Archaeology, in contrast, deals primarily with the physical remains of the past.

These material remains are mute; their meaning and significance depend entirely on the inferences that trained archaeologists can make. In contrast, **historical records** contain messages that are direct and often deliberate communications from the past, although their meaning and significance are also subject to critical interpretation, to discover and get rid of exaggerations, lies, or other biases in written sources.

Another contrast between history and archaeology is that history tends to focus not only on literate societies (that is, those with people who can read and write) but also on their richest and most powerful members, their kings, queens, and high priests. Because of these people's leadership and prominence, records were more likely to have been kept about their lives and deeds. In many cases, literacy was confined to a privileged few, who wrote about themselves rather than the less privileged farmers, shoemakers, servants, or potters. Knowing how to write was seldom as widespread in the past as in our own society; many members of past societies (not to mention many whole societies) could not leave behind accounts of their lives, even if they had wanted to do so. Archaeology is less partial to rich or learned folk; everyone eats, makes things, discards trash, and dies, so everyone contributes to the archaeological record. Individual archaeologists may concentrate on one or another part or kind of society, but archaeology as a whole treats the whole range of humanity.

Historical documents, of course, are "physical remains of the past" and can be studied as such. Clay tablets marked in cuneiform writing, Egyptian hieroglyphic texts on papyrus, and inscriptions carved on Maya stone monuments are just as much documents as are the books published in 17th-century Europe. Obviously, therefore, many ancient historical texts are discovered through archaeological research. The distinction is that, given a particular document, historians are concerned primarily with its written message, whereas archaeologists deal with the document principally as a material object. This is not to say that archaeologists have no interest in what a historical text says. But whether or not a document can be read, archaeologists study it as an object made by humans; they study aspects such as its form, what it is made of, and where it was found, to gain information apart from its textual message. For example, archaeologists may identify an ancient library and infer its use or ownership from its size and location within an ancient settlement, even though its contents may be in an undeciphered script. But for historians, the information is in the message conveyed by the document.

Because of these contrasts, history and archaeology often complement each other, together providing a more complete record of the past than either can furnish alone. Whereas history often pertains to the movers and shakers, archaeology considers the remains of all levels of society. Conversely, although these remains may not represent the full range of past behavior, at least some of the archaeologically invisible activities may be described in historical documents.

For these reasons, archaeology and history have formed close alliances, drawing on the methods of both disciplines in the study of a particular era of the human past. For instance, the long-established field of **classical archaeology** combines the methods of archaeology with the use of historical sources to document the classical civilizations of Greece and Rome. Classical archaeology is also traditionally allied to the field of art history, which provides another route—the analysis of art styles and themes—to understanding the past. In recent years, scholars in history, art history, and archaeology, brought together by a common interest in a given subject and time period, have increasingly combined their expertise to add new insights to studies such as Medieval Europe, the Industrial Revolution, Maya civilization, and European colonization of the New World.

Most archaeologists, however, are concerned with aspects of the past that cannot be directly supplemented by historical studies. This is because written history is limited to a relatively recent era of human development, which began with the invention and use of writing systems. This "historical era" extends at most some 5000 years into the past, in southwestern Asia, the area with the earliest examples of writing. Within the two million years of human cultural development, the era of history represents less than 1 percent of the total (Fig. 1.8). Historical studies are even more limited outside southwest Asia, and they are not possible in areas where writing systems never developed, except where literate outsiders came in and wrote about what they saw.

HISTORICAL AND PREHISTORIC ARCHAEOLOGY

The contrasts (and growing partnerships) between history and archaeology further allow archaeologists to distinguish among kinds of research within their own field, on the basis of whether the subject society possessed a writing system. **Historical archaeology** refers to archaeological investigations carried out in conjunction with analyses of written records. **Prehistoric archaeology** focuses on societies and time periods that lack written historical traditions, seeking an understanding of the full sweep of human development on earth, from its earliest traces to its most remote variations. Although this is not a book about prehistoric archaeology alone, we leave the analysis of historical documents to historiographers. Because the methods and theoretical approaches discussed in this book are not dependent on historical supplements, they may be applied to any archaeological research, whether prehistoric or combined with documentary sources.

In making these distinctions, we should keep in mind that historical (documentary) and archaeological (material) data are complementary. As we shall make clear, both historical and archaeological data are fragmentary; neither, alone, can provide a complete reconstruction of the past.

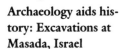

Archaeology aids history: Excavations at Masada, Israel

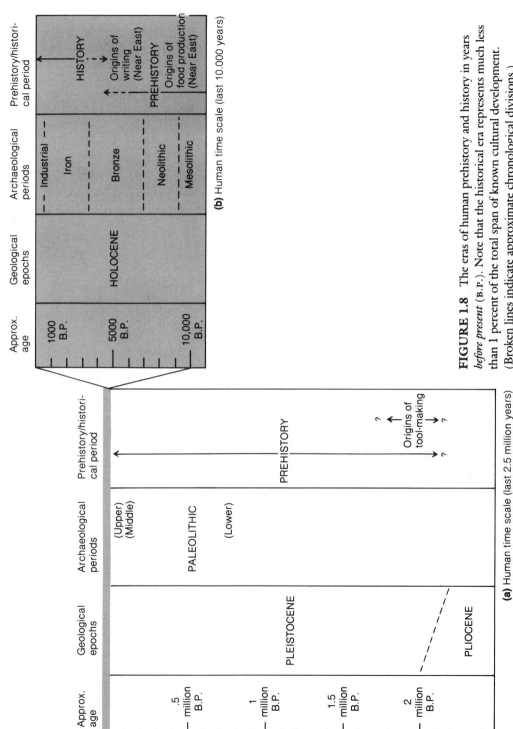

FIGURE 1.8 The eras of human prehistory and history in years *before present* (B.P.). Note that the historical era represents much less than 1 percent of the total span of known cultural development. (Broken lines indicate approximate chronological divisions.)

(a) Human time scale (last 2.5 million years)

(b) Human time scale (last 10,000 years)

FIGURE 1.9 Archaeologist at Martin's Hundred, Virginia, clears skeleton of a 17th-century woman who seems to have died of blood loss, in hiding after a devastating attack on the small community of Wolstenholme Towne. (By permission of the Colonial Williamsburg Foundation and Ivor Noël Hume.)

Archaeology rediscovers history: Martin's Hundred, Virginia

Thus, even when historical records are available, archaeological information can add to our understanding of that past era. A famous example in which history was illuminated by archaeology is the excavation of Masada, in Israel. The first-century historian Josephus Flavius described the construction and history of occupation of the fortress of Masada, where in A.D. 73 Jewish patriots chose suicide rather than surrender to besieging Roman troops. But it was archaeological excavation in 1963 through 1965 that revealed new information not described in the historical documents, such as the full length of occupation of the hilltop site, details of daily life there, and such information as the length of time—at least 40 years—that the Roman garrison remained after the end of the siege.

In the United States, a team of historical archaeologists directed by Ivor Noël Hume has painstakingly unearthed the fragile remnants of one of the earliest British colonial settlements of tidewater Virginia. Originally, the team had been seeking traces of buildings that were adjuncts to the main house of the 18th-century Carter's Grove plantation. They happened instead upon remains of house compounds, a fort, and a series of burials from the early 1600s. These remains were virtually all that was left of Wolstenholme Towne in a tract known as Martin's Hundred. The town was located close to Jamestown, the seat of colonial Virginia government. Martin's Hundred was established in 1619 by fewer than 200 English settlers, who faced disease and hunger as well as the unknowns of living in the New World. In 1622 the little community was attacked and burned, nearly 60 of its residents killed by the Indian attackers. Although Martin's Hundred was reoccupied, Wolstenholme Towne was subsequently lost to history.

Noël Hume's excavations in the 1970s rediscovered the settlement and documented the drama of the massacre. Ash and other traces of the fires were abundant, and several human skeletons attested to a quick, violent end (one bore evidence of scalping) and hasty burial. A woman, whose bones gave no indisputable indications of foul play, was found lying as if asleep, in a domestic refuse pit; perhaps this was a quickly chosen hiding place that failed to protect her from death, which probably occurred from loss of blood (Fig. 1.9).

As dramatic as these findings are, however, the deeper impact of the Martin's Hundred excavations lies in its documentation of daily life in early colonial Virginia. The products (including discards) of a resident potter speak of local provisioning, while the discovery of helmets and other pieces of armor constitute the earliest such pieces known for colonial America, and the traces of the wooden fort furnish a complete ground plan, the oldest one of this architectural form yet recovered. The original settlement was small, but its sometimes poignant traces have yielded important glimpses of life and death in—to use Noël Hume's words—"the teething years of American colonial history."

Other archaeological projects bridge the transition from prehistory to history—the period sometimes called **protohistory.** For instance, excavations at Winchester, England, directed by Martin Biddle over an 11-year

FIGURE 1.10 Excavations at Winchester, England, at the site of the principal cathedral of the Anglo-Saxon kingdom of Wessex, located to the left (north) of the present cathedral built after the Norman Conquest. (Courtesy of Martin Biddle, © Winchester Excavations Committee.)

period, were not oriented to a particular era of the past. Rather, the goal was to study the origins and development of Winchester as a town, from its prehistoric roots through its Roman, Saxon, and Norman periods, right up to the present. In this case, a research problem dealing with the local development of city life used archaeological data for the eras devoid of historical documents and combined historical and archaeological evidence for times when records were available (Fig. 1.10).

Some areas of the world that were once known to us from the more limited viewpoint of prehistoric archaeology are now beginning to develop a historical perspective. A case in point is Classic Maya civilization, which flourished between about A.D. 250 and A.D. 900 in what is now Mexico and Central America. The Maya developed a complex writing system that recorded political, religious, and astronomical events. But most of these records, sculptured on stone and wood, as well as written in folding books, could not be deciphered until recently. Now that decipherment of Maya writing has advanced significantly, historical information gleaned from these Maya texts, including records of political dynasties, marriages,

Bridging the transition between history and prehistory: Excavations at Winchester, England

Historical perspective emerges: Classic Maya civilization

warfare, and alliances, has added a whole new dimension to the archaeological research being conducted at Maya sites (Fig. 1.11). All this has happened because of the growing collaboration of scholars representing many disciplines, especially archaeology, history, art history, and linguistics.

In dealing with most areas of the human past, however, archaeology lacks any sort of historical record to supplement its studies. In such cases, prehistoric archaeology has drawn on the resources of several other fields, including cultural anthropology and geography. Traditionally, prehistoric archaeology has allied itself most closely with anthropology. Through the concept of culture, anthropology provides a framework upon which prehistoric archaeology can build both to describe and to explain the past.

ARCHAEOLOGY, ANTHROPOLOGY, AND CULTURE

FIGURE 1.11 Once considered prehistoric, ancient cultures such as the Maya emerge into history when their records are deciphered. The photograph shows a Maya calendric inscription in a tomb at Tikal, Guatemala. (The date is read as 9.1.1.10.10 4 Oc, equivalent to March 18, A.D. 457.) (Courtesy of the Tikal Project, The University Museum, University of Pennsylvania.)

In its broadest sense, **anthropology** is the comprehensive science of humankind—the study of human biological, social, and cultural form and variation in both time and space. In other words, anthropology seeks to study human beings both as biological organisms and as culture-bearing creatures. It also studies human society from two perspectives: a **diachronic** view that stresses development through time, and a **synchronic** view that emphasizes the state of one or more human societies at a particular point in time.

The field of anthropology is normally divided into a series of subdisciplines (Fig. 1.12). The subdiscipline that studies the human species as a biological organism is usually called **physical anthropology**. The diachronic aspect of physical anthropology investigates our biological evolution, while the synchronic perspective studies contemporary biological form and variation. The study of the human species as a cultural organism is usually referred to as **cultural anthropology**. The synchronic aspect of cultural anthropology includes two general approaches to the study of living cultures. The first, **ethnography**, refers to studies of individual cultures or cultural systems—studies of a single society or a segment of a complex society, such as a particular community. **Ethnology**, on the other hand, assumes a generalizing perspective, using comparisons among ethnographic data, in an attempt to understand the processes of culture. By comparing data from many societies, ethnology studies how and why contemporary cultural systems operate and change. In addition, some cultural anthropologists specialize in the study of human social institutions (social anthropology) or languages (anthropological linguistics). Archaeology is the diachronic aspect of cultural anthropology, the study of our cultural and social past.

The foregoing description of anthropology is a simplified view of a very complex field. The pursuits of anthropological research are as diverse as the varieties of human behavior and the complexities of culture.

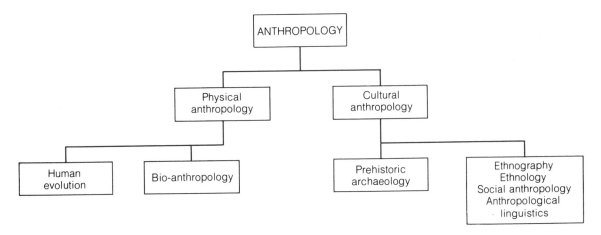

FIGURE 1.12 The field of anthropology may be divided into several subfields. In this view, archaeology represents the part of cultural anthropology that studies the social and cultural past.

Despite its internal diversity, anthropology is unified by one common factor, the concept of culture. The term **culture** has both a general and a specific connotation. In its general sense, culture refers to the customs learned by each generation from those that came before, and thus it describes the uniquely human addition to the biological and social characteristics we share with other life forms. It is culture in this general sense that we will be concerned with, and it is this concept that we will attempt to define below. But the term *culture* may also be used in a specific sense to refer to the particular and unique cultural system of an individual human society, such as "the culture" of the Maya, the British, or the Shoshone.

The concept of culture in the general sense is much too complex to define comprehensively in a few paragraphs, encompassing as it does the patterns of human behavior that span two million years of our evolution, as well as hundreds of unique and varied contemporary societies throughout the world. Yet one of the most often cited definitions, written more than 100 years ago by Edward Tylor (1871), remains useful today:

> That complex whole which includes knowledge, belief, art, morals, law, custom, and any other capabilities and habits acquired by man as a member of society.

Today many prehistoric archaeologists prefer to emphasize culture as the primary means by which human societies adapt to their environment, in contrast to the genetic (biological) adaptations of other life forms. According to this view, culture consists of the cumulative resources of human societies, perpetuated by language, that provide the primary means for nongenetic adaptation to the environment by regulating behavior on three levels: the technological (relationships with the environment), the social (organizational systems), and the ideational (belief systems).

We will return to these and other aspects of the concept of culture later in this book, when we discuss various views of culture that have developed along with the field of anthropology.

The concept of culture defined

Archaeology has benefited from the contributions of many other fields. In pursuing their goals, archaeologists often make use of the training and expertise of specialists in the other subfields of anthropology, as well as in art history, geography, history, biology, astronomy, physics, geology, and computer science. These fields contribute not only to the refinement of archaeological methods but in some cases also to the development of a body of archaeological theory by which the evidence of the past is interpreted.

ARCHAEOLOGY AS A PROFESSION

Because archaeology is both fascinating and important—it is the only bridge to our entire past heritage—many people are interested in the prospects for a career in archaeology. Archaeology is a diverse field, offering many career opportunities for all kinds of interests. Specialties within archaeology are sometimes based on different time periods, the broadest being the distinction between prehistoric and historic archaeology discussed earlier. More particular periods are also specialty areas, such as **medieval archaeology** in Europe, or **colonial archaeology** in the United States (both are subdivisions of historical archaeology). There are also specialties based on particular ancient cultures, such as classical and **biblical archaeology, Egyptology,** and Maya archaeology. And finally, some branches of archaeology are defined by specialized techniques, such as underwater archaeology or **ethnoarchaeology.**

Getting involved in archaeology

In most specialties, formal academic training is not a requirement for participating in archaeological research. Many people begin their experience in discovering the past by joining an archaeological dig or volunteering to help a museum preserve or study archaeological collections. Some individuals who are employed full-time in other jobs continue to follow their interest in archaeology as volunteers, working alongside professionals on weekends or during vacations. For those interested in pursuing archaeology as a profession, however, formal academic training is necessary.

Training in archaeology usually begins in the classroom, where methods and theory can be introduced by lectures and discussions. But archaeology cannot be learned solely in a traditional academic setting. Archaeological training must include time spent in the laboratory and in the field so that what is learned in college or university courses can be put into practice. In most cases, archaeological field schools are where students get their first taste of the practical application of research methods. After such training, students may return to an academic setting and take more advanced courses (in data analysis and theory, for example) leading to a college degree. Most prehistoric, and some historic, archaeological training in the United States is offered within anthropology programs, and the resulting undergraduate degrees and most graduate degrees are in anthropology, not archaeology.

Archaeological training and practice are generally uniform in that most archaeologists subscribe to the definition and goals outlined earlier in this chapter; yet, when it comes to the actual application of method and theory to meet these goals, a considerable diversity becomes apparent. Despite the increasing rigor in research procedures, there is still more variation than there should be in the standards by which archaeological sites are excavated and the results recorded. In some extreme cases, unfortunately, lack of proper standards leads to an irreparable loss of information about the past, rather than a gain in knowledge. For example, Kent Flannery describes the scene at a site in Mexico:

Destruction of archaeological evidence from substandard research

> Four stalks of river cane, stuck loosely in the ground, defined a quadrilateral (though not necessarily rectangular) area in which two *peones* [laborers] picked and shoveled to varying depths, heaving the dirt to one side. On the backdirt pile stood the archaeologist himself, armed with his most delicate tool—a three-pronged garden cultivator of the type used by elderly British ladies to weed rhododendrons. Combing through every shovelful of dirt, he carefully picked out each figurine head and placed it in a brown paper shopping bag nearby—the only other bit of equipment in evidence. This individual was armed with an excavation permit that had been granted because, in the honest words of one official, "he appeared to be no better or worse than any other archaeologist who had worked in the area." When questioned, our colleague descended from the backdirt pile and revealed that his underlying research goal was to define the nature of the "Olmec presence" in that particular drainage basin; his initial results, he said, predicted total success.
>
> As [we] rattled back along the highway in our jeep, each of us in his own way sat marveling at the elegance of a research strategy in which one could define the nature of a foreign presence in a distant drainage basin from just seven fragmentary figurine heads in the bottom of a supermarket sack. (Flannery 1976b:1–2)

This case might strike us as humorous until we realize that it is based on an actual incident and that, unfortunately, similar situations continue in the name of "archaeology" throughout the world. Partly in response to this problem, the **Society of Professional Archeologists (SOPA)** has attempted to define professional qualifications and standards for archaeologists, comparable to those set for lawyers by the American Bar Association or for doctors by the American Medical Association. These include the following criteria of training and experience:

Society of Professional Archeologists defines standards

1. Education and Training
   a. A professional archaeologist must have received a graduate degree in archaeology, anthropology, history, classics, or another pertinent discipline with a specialization in archaeology.
   b. A professional archaeologist must have supervised experience in basic archaeological field research consisting of at least 12 weeks of field training and 4 weeks of laboratory analysis or curating.
   c. A professional archaeologist must have designed and executed archaeological research, as evidenced by a Master of Arts or Master of Science thesis or an equivalent research report.

2. Experience—A professional archaeologist must have at least one year of experience in one or more of the following:
   a. Field and laboratory situations under supervision of a professional archaeologist, with a minimum of six months as a supervisor
   b. Analytic study of archaeological collections
   c. Theoretical, library, or archival research
   d. Administration of archaeological research
   e. Management of cultural resources
   f. Museum work
   g. Teaching
   h. Marine survey archaeology

In the United States there are seven national professional archaeological societies (see Table 1.1 for addresses of those with permanent national headquarters): the **Archaeological Institute of America (AIA),** the **Society for American Archaeology (SAA),** the Archeology Division of the **American Anthropological Association (AAA),** the **American Society of Conservation Archaeologists (ASCA),** the **Society for Historical Archaeology (SHA),** the **Society of Professional Archeologists (SOPA),** and the **Council on Underwater Archaeology (CUA).** Several of these have regular publication series. The AAA and AIA also publish annual listings of field schools and excavation opportunities. There are also numerous regional and state archaeological societies throughout the country. Further information about these and other archaeological organizations in your area can be found by contacting the office of your state archaeologist or the State Historic Preservation Office (SHPO) in your state capital.

CRM as fastest-growing area in American archaeology

Traditionally, most archaeologists have taken academic appointments in universities or museums, where they may teach archaeology as well as conduct fieldwork. Today, however, growing numbers of archaeologists are employed by private companies or government agencies, such as the National Park Service. Archaeologists in these positions are usually involved in **cultural resource management,** or **CRM,** concerned with the identification and evaluation of archaeological sites to protect them from disturbance or destruction and to investigate those that cannot be saved. CRM is the fastest-growing segment of the profession and now accounts for more than half of all professional archaeologists employed in the United States.

The growth of CRM is the direct result of an increasing concern over the accelerated destruction of archaeological sites, in this country and throughout the world. In the United States, as in many other countries, legislation has been enacted to protect our cultural heritage. This development may be seen as part of the larger awareness and concern in response to the destruction of our environment (natural as well as cultural resources). Like many natural resources, past cultural remains are a nonrenewable resource. Unlike natural resources, however, each archaeological site is a fragile and unique representative of our human heritage. Once an archaeological site has been destroyed, that portion of our past is lost forever.

Table 1.1 Professional Archaeological Organizations

Archaeological Institute of America
675 Commonwealth Avenue
Boston, MA 02215

Society for American Archaeology
808 17th Street, NW
Washington, DC 20006

American Anthropological Association
1703 New Hampshire Avenue, NW
Washington, DC 20009

Although some field archaeologists claim to have little or no interest in theoretical matters, they are, in fact, often confronting important theoretical issues and contributing to their resolution every day in their research. In addition to addressing theoretical concerns, CRM archaeologists frequently find themselves on the cutting edge of methodological and even legal issues, in deciding which sites have the greatest potential for increasing our knowledge of the past, by setting priorities for protection and recovery of archaeological remains.

SUMMARY

Some of the reasons for the popular fascination with archaeology may stem from the appeal of exotic adventure and dramatic discoveries. However, a deeper attraction is generated by the substance of archaeology itself—the study of the past—and by the realization that the reconstruction of the past mirrors the present. Our view of the past is distorted by pseudo-archaeology and may be destroyed by looting. Archaeology is the study of the human past from its material remains, and the general goals of the profession are: to consider the *form* of archaeological evidence and its distribution in time and space; to determine past *function* and thereby reconstruct ancient behavior; to delimit the *processes* of culture or determine how and why cultures change; and to understand cultural meaning.

Archaeology belongs to the general realm of science, for it, like any scientific discipline, involves a search for knowledge through a logical and consistent method, guided by a body of theory. It is related to several allied disciplines and concepts. In relation to history, archaeology can be divided into *historical* and *prehistoric archaeology*. In the United States, both historical and prehistoric archaeology are usually seen as part of the broader discipline of anthropology.

The training of professional archaeologists usually combines classroom, laboratory, and field experiences at both the undergraduate and the graduate level. Professional standards for the conduct of archaeological research have been defined, but considerable variation in their application still exists.

GUIDE TO FURTHER READING

Discovering the Past
Alva 1988a, 1988b, 1990; Arden 1989; Cottrell 1981; Fagan 1988; Mazar 1985; Swart and Till 1984; Topping 1978; Young 1989

Understanding Ourselves through Our Past
Carter [1922] 1972; Diaz del Castillo [1632] 1956; Fagan 1978, 1985; Layton 1989a, 1989b; Lipe 1984; McBryde 1985

Destruction of Our Heritage
Cleere 1984, 1989; Coggins 1972; Cook 1991; Fagan 1975; Greenfield 1989; Smith and Ehrenhard 1991

What Is Archaeology?
L. R. Binford 1968a; Butler 1987; Champion 1980; Clarke 1972a; Courbin 1988; Deetz 1967; Dunnell 1982; Fowler 1987; Gathercole and Lowenthal 1989; Green 1990; Leone 1972; Purdy 1990; Schiffer 1976, 1978, 1988; Sterud 1978; Trigger 1970, 1984; Wheeler 1954; Willey and Phillips 1958; Wiseman 1980

Archaeology and Pseudoarchaeology
Aveni 1990; Chippindale et al. 1990; Cole 1980; Feder 1990; Fell 1976; Flenley and King 1984; Heyerdahl 1961/1965; Isbell 1978; McKusick 1982, 1984; Numbers 1982; Rathje 1978; Sabloff 1982; Story 1976; Stover and Harrison 1979; Veit 1989; von Däniken 1969, 1970; Wauchope 1962; White 1974; Williams 1991

Archaeology and Science
Aldenderfer 1991; Bamforth and Spaulding 1982; Bettinger 1980; L. R. Binford 1968a, 1977, 1981b, 1983, 1987, 1989; Bintleff and Gaffney 1986; Clark and Stafford 1982; Clarke 1968, 1973; Conkey and Spector 1984; Cooper and Richards 1985; Flannery 1973; Gardin 1980; Gero and Conkey 1991; Gibbon 1989; S. J. Gould 1980, 1983, 1986; Hodder 1991a; Kelley and Hanen 1988; Lock and Wilcock 1987; Martlew 1984; Nelson and Kehoe 1990; Preucel 1991; Raab and Goodyear 1984; Renfrew, Rowlands, and Segraves 1982; Richards and Ryan 1985; Salmon 1982; Schiffer 1976, 1988, Shennan 1988; Spaulding 1968; Spector 1991; Stephen and Craig 1984; Steward 1955; Thomas 1973, 1983, 1986b; P. Watson 1973; R. Watson 1990, 1991; P. Watson, LeBlanc, and Redman 1971, 1984

Archaeology and History
Bamforth and Spaulding 1982; Beaudry 1989; Bintleff and Gaffney 1986; Deagan 1982; Deetz 1977, 1988a, 1988b; Falk 1991; Finley 1971; Grant 1990; Little 1991; Minchinton 1983; Noël Hume 1979; Platt 1976; Schuyler 1976, 1978; South 1977; Young 1988

Archaeology, Anthropology, and Culture
L. R. Binford 1962; Chang 1967; Charleton 1981; Gibbon 1984, 1989; Gumerman and Phillips 1978; Longacre 1970b; Taylor [1948] 1964, 1967; Tylor 1871; Willey and Phillips 1958

Archaeology as a Profession
Chapman 1985; Cleere 1984, 1989; Conkey and Spector 1984; Davis 1982; Flannery 1976b; Fowler 1982, 1987; Gathercole and Lowenthal 1989; Kramer and Stark 1988; Layton 1989a, 1989b; McBryde 1985; Mohrman 1985; Pearce 1990; Piggott 1959; Rowe 1961a; Society of Professional Archeologists 1978; Spector and Whelan 1989; Stone and MacKenzie 1989; Stuart 1976; Sullivan 1980; Turnbaugh, Vandebrock, and Jones 1983; Willey 1974

ARCHAEOLOGY AND SCIENCE

Patty Jo Watson

Patty Jo Watson grew up in rural parts of Iowa and Nebraska in the 1930s and 1940s and went to graduate school in anthropology/archaeology at the University of Chicago. She has carried out archaeological fieldwork in Iraq, Iran, Turkey, Arizona, New Mexico, Kentucky, and Tennessee and teaches at Washington University in St. Louis. She wrote this essay while a Fellow at the Center for Advanced Study in the Behavioral Sciences, Stanford, CA.

This topic sounds innocuous and rather dry, if not actually boring, but in fact it has generated very strong feeling among archaeologists over the past 20 years. That's because archaeology includes such a broad expanse of scholarship from the most intensely humanistic (e.g., Greek vase painting, Maya sculpture) to the most rigorously scientific (e.g., radiocarbon dating, obsidian and ceramic trace element analysis). Archaeology partakes liberally of both scientific and humanistic techniques and perspectives, but what is the *real* nature of this field? What should be the *ultimate* goals of archaeologists? To accumulate more and more facts about the past

simply for their intrinsic interest? Or to seek only those facts that are relevant to hypotheses, generalizations, and theories about the past? A tug-of-war between *particularizing* research (accumulating facts for their own intrinsic interest) and *generalizing* research (theory formulation, and seeking to establish generalizations incorporating or explaining many facts) is present in most scholarly fields, as it is in archaeology. But archaeology is unique because the traditional means of archaeological observation (excavation) destroys as it reveals. Once I have dug up a site or part of a site to answer *my* questions about it, no one else can make independent observations on that same body of evidence because I have destroyed it. This difficult situation is ameliorated somewhat by detailed record keeping, especially the latest forms of computerized techniques, but the basic paradox—observation as destruction—is still there. Hence, debates about differences in theoretical approaches to the archaeological record can be very intense.

Apart from these philosophical issues, and regardless of one's basic orientation (humanistic, his-

toricist, scientific, or other), all contemporary archaeologists rely routinely and heavily upon a wide range of scientific techniques as described in this textbook. These include site discovery procedures (e.g., satellite imagery, radar), dating methods, identification of raw materials, recovery and interpretation of biological remains (pollen, phytoliths and other plant remains, animal remains of various kinds, human bone), statistical sampling and analytical methods, and a great deal more. Any and all of these can be used in aid of generalizing or particularizing emphases, and every piece of research includes both. But the avowed goal of every scientist is to produce more and better generalizations that encompass (predict and explain) more and more particulars. Scholars—archaeological or other—whose ultimate concern is only for the specifics and not for potential generalizations to which those particulars are relevant are not working scientifically. Although specific details and masses of individual facts are essential to all facets of archaeology whether practiced in the field, laboratory, or study, I believe with many other archaeologists that the most effective way to practice archaeology is as a social science. We want not only to know *what* kinds of human cultures there were in the past, *when* they flourished, and when they overlapped in time, but also to delineate the patterns and processes explaining *how* and *why* those cultures appeared, changed, and disappeared.

To illustrate some of these points about particularizing and generalizing foci in research, here are some examples from work I've directed in west central Kentucky over the past few decades. This long-term research project began in 1963 in Salts Cave, one of several caves making up the Flint Ridge Cave System in Mammoth Cave National Park. The Flint Ridge System joins the Mammoth Cave System under an intervening valley, and the combined passage complex constitutes the longest cave known anywhere in the world (well in excess of 300 miles, with more being mapped every year). Several miles of Salts Cave and Mammoth Cave were known to prehistoric inhabitants of this portion of eastern North America. We have spent hundreds of hours following (and documenting with notes, maps, and photos) the traces of prehistoric cavers in big passages, narrow canyonways, small crouchways, and crawlways. The research group has spent many hundred more hours analyz-

ing, describing, and interpreting the remains.

In the initial stages of the research, I was all wrapped up in what were to me intrinsically fascinating details of this unusual archaeological situation: At what times in the past did prehistoric people enter the cave? How far into the cave did they go and what did they do there? What did they use for light and what were their caving techniques like?

As we recorded, discussed, and argued about the prehistoric remains in Salts Cave and Mammoth Cave, we began to get answers to these questions. Our observations and radiocarbon dates indicated that the Indians went into the cave between 4000 and 2000 years ago, that they were mining cave minerals and crystals very skillfully and very persistently (possibly for trade as well as for their own use), and sometimes they were just exploring quite remote and somewhat dangerous cave passages. They lighted their way with cane and dried weed stalk torches, that our experiments showed to be very effective sources of illumination.

While we were seeking answers to these and other specific questions about this one place and this one piece of archaeology, we realized that some of these details and some of the prehistoric remains in Salts Cave and Mammoth Cave are directly relevant to—and in fact have helped restructure our un-

derstanding of—a very important general process: the origins of plant cultivation in eastern North America.

The ancient but perfectly preserved and highly abundant botanical remains in these dry caves (including scores of ancient human fecal deposits) date to an early stage in the creation of an indigenous horticultural complex that helped sustain many thousands of Eastern Woodlands people for millennia before maize ever reached this region from Mexico. The minute particulars of Salts Cave–Mammoth Cave archaeology are thus applicable to broad issues of far-reaching significance: How and why do foraging groups anywhere change from gathering or collecting wild species to relying significantly or even exclusively on domesticated ones? How and why are cultivated species exported or diffused from one region or population to another?

Thanks to the great abundance and the high quality of evidence preserved in the dry passages of Salts Cave and Mammoth Cave, these sites have contributed significantly to answering both particular and general research questions. The particular information we have gathered demonstrates that these prehistoric Indians were world class cavers who performed subterranean feats not equalled for

(continued)

(continued)

two millennia. The general information we obtained demonstrates that these same Indians were early farmers and food producers as well as skillful exploiters of wild forest resources, and helps us understand how and why they invented an agricultural lifeway.

Delineating and understanding broad cultural patterns and processes like the origins and consequences of food production can help us think about and predict where we might be going in the future, and even indicate how to influence future trajectories. That is perhaps the ultimate reason why practicing archaeology as a social science is so important.

CHAPTER TWO

THE ORIGINS OF ARCHAEOLOGY

The Growth of Scientific Disciplines

Collectors and Classifiers

Professional Disciplines

Antiquarians and the Origins of Archaeology

Early Archaeological Collectors and Classifiers

Early Archaeological Issues

The Transition to Professional Archaeology

The Problem of Interpretation

The Influence of Anthropological Ideas

The Emergence of Modern Archaeology

Historical Interpretations

Anthropological Interpretations

Summary

Guide to Further Reading

The city was desolate. No remnant of this race hangs round the ruins. . . . It lay before us like a shattered bark in the midst of the ocean, her masts gone, her name effaced, her crew perished, and none to tell whence she came . . . perhaps, never to be known at all.

Stephens and Catherwood at the ruins of Copán, Honduras, in 1839–1840

THE GROWTH OF SCIENTIFIC DISCIPLINES

The growth of science is one of the hallmarks of modern civilization. Its development can be traced back several millennia to roots in the ancient civilizations of the Old World, including those of southwest Asia, China, and the classical Mediterranean world. Science and the scientific method have taken their present forms in the 500-year period since the Renaissance. Regardless of origins, each branch of science has had its own pace and trajectory of development; different branches have seemed to take the lead in importance during different periods. Thus, one can argue that the development of modern science began with the astronomical discoveries made by Nicolaus Copernicus and Galileo Galilei in the 16th century. Similarly, the middle and late 19th century might be characterized as the age of evolutionary biology, because of the influential work of men such as Alfred Wallace, Charles Darwin, and Gregor Mendel. In contrast, the first half of the 20th century was dominated by advances in nuclear physics. However, no branch of science has grown in isolation; each has benefited from contemporary developments in other fields. For example, Darwin's theory of biological evolution depended not only on his own observations of biological variety but also—among other things—on the concurrent development of important discoveries in **geology.**

In this growth process, **archaeology** is a relative infant. But it has followed and is following a course of development similar to other scientific disciplines. To better understand the present status of archaeology, we need to see how the underlying ideas and theories that guide the field have developed. Obviously, the history of science is far too complex to describe fully here. To illustrate the process, we will consider one of several themes that have permeated this complicated development, namely, the emergence of specific professional disciplines from their amateur beginnings.

Collectors and Classifiers

Most scientific fields, including archaeology, begin their development with amateur **collectors.** Indeed, many fields continue to have a vigorous amateur constituency. These individuals, often part-time hobbyists, pursue their various interests because they value the objects they collect or study, often as things of beauty or as curiosities. For instance, the modern science of biology has firm roots in 17th- and 18th-century European collections of local plant and animal species, made by the English country parsons and other gentlemen of leisure who flourished at the time.

Amassing a collection leads naturally to attempts to bring order to the assembled material, resulting in the first efforts at **classification.** Early classifications usually group together objects that are similar in their most obvious traits, especially **form.** Long before the biological collectors of the 17th and 18th centuries, Aristotle constructed the oldest recorded biological classification. It divided life forms into classes called *species,* according to observable and describable physical and behavioral characteristics. As he observed in *History of Animals* (Book I, Chapter 1), "Animals differ from one another in their modes of subsistence, in their actions, in their habits, and in their parts." The most exhaustive biological classification system, the 18th-century Linnaean system still used today, was simply a refinement of this approach.

Attempts to classify often lead to the first questions concerning the meaning or significance of the phenomena being studied. Why do the observed classes exist? Why should these differences and regularities among them exist? How can they be explained? Such questions were answered in many cases with pure speculation but at times with conclusions based, at least in part, on systematic observation. More often than not, the first answers to such questions have since been discarded. For example, in the development of biology, questions about the origins of certain forms of life were answered by such "explanations" as the theory of spontaneous generation. This thesis held that mice were spawned from piles of dirty linen and flies from dead flesh. To quote Aristotle again: "So with Animals, some spring from parent animals according to their kind, whilst others grow spontaneously . . . some come from putrefying earth or vegetable matter, as is the case with a number of insects" (*History of Animals,* Book V, Chapter 1). The ultimate "explanation" for the Aristotelian–Linnaean classification of life, "the Great Chain of Being," was theologically based—a static scheme of unchanging life forms created by God (Fig. 2.1).

Professional Disciplines

In time, concern with **function** and **explanation** replaced concern with form. With this step, in many branches of science, the first professionals can be discerned. Amateurs never disappear completely and often continue to make important discoveries that lead to scientific advances. But, in every scientific discipline, true professionalism has meant the rise of full-time specialists interested in "understanding" rather than "collecting."

As attention shifted to questions of function and explanation, it became obvious that descriptive classifications based solely on lists of isolated traits could not provide sophisticated answers about the origins and significance of observable phenomena. In biology, for example, the interrelationship of organs within individual life forms began to be studied, to reveal how the organs worked together to maintain the total living animal or plant.

Classification by form: Aristotle's *History of Animals*

Speculation from classification: Aristotle and the Great Chain of Being

FIGURE 2.1 An early attempt at classification and explanation is represented by the Great Chain of Being, a theologically based scheme for ordering natural and supernatural life forms.

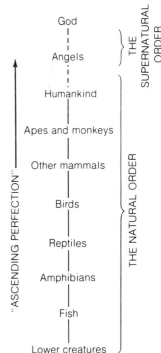

The next step toward understanding a set of phenomena is the attempt to comprehend the processes of its development—to explain the causes of change. Again using biology as an example, this step in the development of science is illustrated by the breakthrough made by Darwin and Wallace, the synthesis that produced the theory of evolution by natural selection.

ANTIQUARIANS AND THE ORIGINS OF ARCHAEOLOGY

These trends of scientific development—with emphasis gradually shifting from collecting to classifying and then to explaining—are visible in the emergence of archaeology as a professional discipline. Archaeology did not spring forth fully developed but emerged gradually from diverse origins. Like other disciplines, it has roots in the work of amateur collectors and speculators, often called **antiquarians,** who in this case were the collectors of remains from the past. In looking back at those early efforts, we can see that the search for knowledge was often combined with treasure hunting. With today's perspective that makes a clear distinction between scientific motives and those of financial or personal gain, it is somewhat ironic that the origins of professional archaeology were so intertwined with looting. But archaeology did not begin to develop as a formal discipline until it went beyond collection and acquired the means to interpret the materials being assembled.

In this section we will trace the growth of archaeology from its antiquarian roots to its emergence as a professional discipline. This development begins with the first attempts to classify the remains from the past and proceeds from purely speculative explanations of the past (often with only token reference to the actual remains) to efforts to use the archaeological evidence to infer what happened in the past. The means of archaeological interpretation, taken largely from history and anthropology, have been refined ultimately by the scientific method.

It should be noted that refinements in methods of recovery (especially excavation) accompanied and aided the growth of interpretive schemes. But, because of space limitations, we cannot trace both developments in detail here. Since the chief goals of a science are explanation and understanding, we will focus on the development of archaeological interpretations as the means for explaining and understanding the past.

Early Archaeological Collectors and Classifiers

Innumerable individuals have encountered the remains of the past, often accidentally or, in the case of **looters,** as the result of treasure seeking. As more and more discoveries were made, however, some individuals began to realize that the objects recovered from the earth had more than monetary value—they were, in fact, clues to the understanding of past lives and of entire societies that had long since disappeared.

Interest in the past can be found among the earliest historical accounts. For example, Thutmose IV, pharaoh of Egypt in the 15th century B.C., ordered the excavation of the Great Sphinx at Giza, then already centuries old and nearly buried by sand. He left a record of his work inscribed on a stone tablet between the paws of the sphinx. Nearly a millennium later, in the mid-6th century B.C., Nabonidus, the last king of Babylon, conducted excavations to probe the ancient civilizations that had given rise to his own, which was by then already 2500 years old. It is reported that Nabonidus even exhibited the artifacts from his excavations. Although these two individuals were obviously not professional **archaeologists,** their work exhibited several crucial components of archaeological research—excavation to reveal ancient remains, records of the work, and preservation of the finds.

The Greeks, too, were interested in their own past. The Greek historian Herodotus wrote and speculated at length about the past of non-Greek peoples, especially the antiquity of Egyptian civilization. Roman interest in the past was not always so constructive. The Romans systematically looted many sites of the Mediterranean for sculpture and other works of ancient art, but they seemed to have had little concern for using their finds to understand the past.

During the Dark Ages, the centuries following the collapse of the Roman Empire in A.D. 476, little attention was given to antiquities, classical or otherwise. However, one account that comes down to us from the succeeding Middle Ages holds a special interest, because it represents one of the earliest examples of the use of excavation to discover a specific relic of the past for very practical purposes. (Alternatively, we might view it as one of the first attempts at archaeological forgery for financial gain.) It appears that in the 12th century the monks of Glastonbury Abbey in England were interested in discovering evidence for the existence of the already legendary King Arthur. At the very least, such a discovery would provide the monks with considerable financial benefit from pilgrimages to an Arthurian shrine. In a practical sense, such proceeds would be useful for rebuilding the abbey, which had burned in 1183. According to the 12th-century account, excavations in 1191 in an ancient cemetery south of the abbey produced a lead cross with the following inscription (translated from the Latin): "Here lies buried the famous King Arthur in the Isle of Avalon." Beneath the cross, the excavators found a large oak log; inside the hollowed log were the remains of a human skeleton. The skeleton was reported to be that of a large male, and the conclusion seemed obvious: The excavators had found the remains of King Arthur. The story does not end there, however. Archaeological excavations in 1962 in the area south of the abbey revealed the remains of a large pit that had been opened and refilled sometime in the late 12th century. It is thus possible that the medieval monks did indeed excavate and find an early burial at the abbey; but there is, of course, no proof that they found Arthur. Unfortunately, neither the original inscribed cross nor the reputed remains of Arthur, subsequently reburied in Glastonbury Abbey, have survived the ravages of time (Fig. 2.2).

Early excavations: Nabonidus, king of Babylon

Excavations at Glastonbury: King Arthur discovered?

FIGURE 2.2 Within the ruins of medieval Glastonbury Abbey, situated on the legendary Isle of Avalon in southwest England, a plaque (visible in the middle of the church) marks the site of a 12th-century tomb, built for the reburial of the purported bones of King Arthur, discovered in an ancient cemetery on the Abbey grounds.

Antiquarians and Looters It wasn't until the Renaissance (from the 14th to the 17th century), an era of reawakened European interest in the arts, literature, and learning in general, that interest in the past began to flourish. One of the leading advocates in the 15th century was Ciriaco. Although he didn't conduct excavations, he traveled throughout the ancient Mediterranean world to study the monuments of past civilizations. Excavation and direct recovery of antiquities came into vogue as Roman ruins were probed in search of antiquities. In 1594, excavations at a villa garden near Naples led to one of the most important discoveries of the period, that of the lost Roman city of Pompeii (Fig. 2.3). Excavations there continue to the present day. Activities such as these began a general frenzy of looting in Italy and other countries of Europe. The 16th, 17th, and 18th centuries were highlighted by expeditions, conducted by "gentlemen of leisure" from countries such as England, France, and Germany, to sites all over the classical world, to recover sculpture and other remains from the past.

The term *antiquarian* began to be applied to those inquiring individuals who recovered ancient remains more to preserve the past than to realize economic gain. This is not to say that all antiquarians had the highest motives. On the contrary, the distinction between those who were trying to learn about the past and those who wished only to profit by the discovery and sale of long-lost treasures was sometimes impossible to make. And even the highest of motives did not guarantee that an overzealous digger would not destroy much precious evidence.

This was the heyday of the antiquarian, but archaeology as we know it has at least some of its roots in this period. Despite the damage, some useful contributions to archaeology resulted. Knowledge of the past was gained, monuments were saved, and specific excavation techniques began to be developed; all these were contributions to the modern discipline of archaeology.

As the looting and destruction of antiquities continued in Europe and other areas of the world, some individuals began to stand out not only as collectors but also as people seeking to learn about the past through attempts to classify and interpret the remains. One of the earliest of these was an English gentleman named William Camden; in 1587, he produced *Britannia,* the first comprehensive directory of British antiquities. Camden's work is significant in that he compiled a descriptive list of all archaeological sites and artifacts then known in England. Through his work, interest in British prehistory had its start. Two other British antiquarians of the 17th and 18th centuries, John Aubrey and William Stukeley, are important for their speculative attempts to use material remains to interpret the prehistoric past of England. Both men took an interest in the great stone enclosures of Avebury and Stonehenge (Fig. 2.4); they fostered the still persistent interpretation that these were druid temples.

Elsewhere in Europe, people were similarly probing their prehistoric past. In 16th- and 17th-century Scandinavia, for example, royally commissioned antiquarians such as Ole Worm of Denmark and Johan Bure of Sweden were recording ancient runic inscriptions, excavating burial sites, and compiling inventories of national antiquities. At the same time, they were encouraged to connect their findings with the semilegendary accounts of national history (Fig. 2.5).

William Dugdale, a 17th-century prehistorian from Warwickshire, gathered and studied extensive collections of the stone hand-axes common throughout the English countryside. His interpretation of their origin and

Early classifier of archaeological remains: William Camden in England

FIGURE 2.3 A street in the Roman city of Pompeii, Italy, after excavation and partial reconstruction. (Courtesy of Elizabeth K. Ralph.)

FIGURE 2.4 The ancient function of Stonehenge, located on the Salisbury Plain of England, remains a subject of popular speculation—regardless of the archaeological evidence.

FIGURE 2.5 Runic inscriptions were used as early as the 16th and 17th centuries to aid archaeological investigation in Scandinavia. (By permission of the British Library.)

Early interpreter of archaeological remains: William Dugdale

use was revolutionary for his time: "These are weapons used by the Britons before the art of making arms of brass or iron was known." The prevailing view at that time held either that such artifacts were manufactured by elves or other mythical beings or that they were products of thunder, fallen from the sky. Dugdale's account thus represents one of the first reported interpretations that credited prehistoric people with making these stone tools.

Speculative interpretation of the prehistoric past in Europe gradually gave way to more solidly based interpretations, as evidence accumulated that demonstrated the association of human bones and tools with the bones of animals known to be extinct. However, another two centuries would pass before the implications of these discoveries for human prehistory would be generally accepted. The initial reaction to these discoveries was to ignore or reject them, since they conflicted with the prevailing view, based on the version of creation given in the Old Testament, that human existence was confined to the 6000 years since the earth's creation.

Early Archaeological Issues

The early development of archaeology was intertwined with one central question: How long had the human species existed on earth? On the one hand, the theological position held to a literal interpretation of the Old Testament about the length of human prehistory. On the other hand, a growing number of scholars accepted an increasing body of evidence implying that human prehistory extended much farther into the past than biblical accounts indicated. Before archaeology could develop further, the issue of the length of human prehistory had to be settled.

The Discovery of Old World Prehistory   The controversy was centered in the Old World, where accumulating archaeological discoveries pointed to the great antiquity of the human species. In London, in the year 1690, a man named Conyers discovered a series of stone axes that were apparently as old as the extinct elephant bones with which they were found. But critics dismissed this dramatic find with the speculation that Conyers had discovered the remains of an ancient Briton's attempt to defend his homeland against Roman elephants during the historical conquest by Emperor Claudius! More than a century later, in 1797, John Frere described the discovery of chipped flint in association with bones of extinct animals from Hoxne, a gravel pit also in England. These finds, from a depth of 12 feet below the modern surface, were sealed in place by three higher, and therefore later, deposits. Frere described the remains as belonging "to a very remote period indeed; even beyond that of the present world." In this case the discovery was simply ignored. Between 1824 and 1829, another excavator, Father MacEnery, discovered more stone tools associated with extinct animal bones, sealed by a stalagmite deposit in Kent's Cavern, Devon. One of the leading English geologists of the day, William Buckland, dismissed the Kent's Cavern finds as a mixture of ancient animal bones with relatively recent weapons; the latter were again assigned to the historical Britons.

Elsewhere in Europe, material evidence for human antiquity met similar reactions. In France in the 1830s, a customs inspector named Jacques Boucher de Perthes discovered an assemblage of crude hand-axes and extinct animal bones in the Somme River gravel beds. Convinced of the significance of his finds, he tried without much success to persuade his scientific contemporaries that the stone tools indeed represented antediluvian (before the biblical flood) human existence. In 1856, some fossilized human bones were retrieved from the Neander Valley in Germany. These bones are now seen to be important fossils of Neanderthal man, but

Stone tools associated with extinct animals: John Frere, Father MacEnery, and Boucher de Perthes

at the time, their "primitive" and possibly ancient anatomical attributes were explained by Rudolph Virchow, the leading pathologist of the day, as coming from a pathological modern individual.

The tide of scientific opinion finally turned, however; the year 1859 marked several important events in the change. In that year, two prestigious English scholars, Sir John Prestwich and Sir John Evans, announced to their fellow scientists that, as a result of their studies of Boucher de Perthes's finds, they concurred that the Somme River artifacts were indeed ancient. This influential assessment coincided with the vindication of MacEnery's earlier discoveries by the work of William Pengelly, who had conducted excavations in both Kent's Cavern and Windmill Hill Cave. And 1859 was the year of publication of Darwin's *On the Origin of Species*. In sum, in the mid-19th century, the theory of evolution and the archaeological evidence combined to challenge successfully the theological opposition to prehistoric human development in the Old World.

The Discovery of New World Prehistory   As early as the 16th century, Europeans encountered and destroyed sophisticated urban civilizations in both Mexico and Peru. However, remains of earlier cultures—mounds, temples, sculptures, and burials—were often said to be the work of Old World peoples. Because American Indians were believed incapable of such impressive accomplishments, speculation identified the lost cities of America with immigrant groups of ancient Egyptians, Hebrews, Babylonians, Phoenicians, Hindus, Chinese, and even the mythical inhabitants of Atlantis and Mu. Even such a sober scientist as Benjamin Franklin attributed the construction of the mounds of the Mississippi Valley to the early Spanish explorer Hernando de Soto.

First recorded excavation in America: Thomas Jefferson in Virginia

Accumulating archaeological data eventually established rightful credit for the ancient New World monuments. One of the first contributors of such data was Thomas Jefferson. Soon after the American Revolution, Jefferson conducted the first recorded archaeological excavation in America: The subject was a 12-foot-high mound in the Rivanna River valley, Virginia. Jefferson wrote: "I proceeded then to make a perpendicular cut through the body of the barrow, that I might examine its internal structure." Jefferson found the mound to be stratified, with several differentiated levels of earth containing human burials. He noted that the burials lower in the mound were less well preserved than those near the surface; this led him to interpret the mound as a place of burial that was used and reused over a long period of time. Beyond this, he credited the work of building the mound to American Indians. Jefferson's achievement is remarkable; besides being a pioneer in systematic excavation and accurate recording of results, he was one of the first individuals to use *stratigraphy* (see Chapter 7) to interpret his discoveries, by observing the sequence of earthen layers (or *strata*) as reflecting the passage of time.

Neither Jefferson's attribution of burial mound construction to American Indians nor his admonitions for careful fieldwork were accepted by all. The battle lines had been drawn in the New World: During the first half

FIGURE 2.6 Publication of drawings by Frederick Catherwood sparked public interest in ancient New World civilizations in the mid-19th century. (From an original print, courtesy of the Museum Library, The University Museum, University of Pennsylvania.)

of the 19th century, a great dispute raged between those who saw the American Indians as builders of the archaeological wonders of the Americas and those who thought one or another of the Old World civilizations was responsible. Speculation flourished in both camps. Eventually, as more excavations were conducted, evidence accumulated to give strong support to the thesis of indigenous origin. Although we cannot mention all the evidence that led to this conclusion, a few of the more important discoveries will illustrate its development.

In 1841 and 1843, John Lloyd Stephens and Frederick Catherwood published their illustrated accounts of the discovery of spectacular ruins of the lost Maya civilization in the jungles of Central America. The books became best-sellers, revealing the wonders of the ancient Maya civilization to the populace of England and America (Fig. 2.6). This publicity helped spur the often romantic and frenzied search for lost civilizations, not only in the New World but also in Africa, Asia, and elsewhere. But Stephens's own appraisal of the origin of the Maya civilization stands in marked contrast to the unfounded speculations popular at the time: "We are not warranted in going back to any ancient nation of the Old World for the builders of these cities. . . . There are strong reasons to believe them the creations of the same races who inhabited the country at the time of the Spanish Conquest, or of some not-very-distant progenitors."

Other writers had reached the same conclusion by different routes. In 1839, for example, studies of skeletal evidence led Dr. Samuel Morton of

Popular appeal of archaeological discovery: Stephens and Catherwood in Central America

Philadelphia to declare that contemporary American Indians were members of the same population as the builders of the ancient mounds. Albert Gallatin, founder of the American Ethnological Society, noted in 1836 the similarities of form between the platform mounds of the Mississippi Valley and the pyramids of Mexico; on the basis of that likeness, he postulated a gradual diffusion of cultural influences from Mexico to the United States. And he saw no reason to attribute construction of these monuments to other than native New World peoples.

Early mound classification: Squier and Davis in the Mississippi Valley

Still the debate went on. In 1848, when E. G. Squier and E. H. Davis published the results of their research into the mounds of the Mississippi and Ohio valleys, they provided valuable descriptive data, including one of the first classifications of the mounds into different functional categories. But in trying to identify the builders of the mounds, they lapsed into pure speculation, refusing to believe that the American Indians—or their ancestors—could be responsible. In contrast, Samuel F. Haven's sober appraisal of American Indian prehistory makes his study, *Archaeology of the United States,* published in 1856, a landmark in the development of archaeology. Haven used the available archaeological evidence to dismiss many fantastic theories about the origins of the American Indian: He concluded that the prehistoric monuments in the United States were built by the ancestors of known tribal groups. Although the controversy continued for another quarter century, careful empirical work such as Haven's, rather than speculations like those of Squier and Davis, finally carried the day.

Indigenous origin of mounds: Samuel Haven's *Archaeology of the United States*

The works of Haven and of Squier and Davis represent the culmination of antiquarian research in the New World. By midcentury, similar studies in Europe were already leading to the emergence of archaeology as a professional discipline. Archaeology was gaining recognition as a separate field of endeavor and a legitimate scholarly activity in its own right.

Prehistorians and Looters Unfortunately, as the discipline of archaeology began to emerge in the 19th century, its long-time companion, looting, also gathered momentum. The principal motive for these destructive activities remained financial or personal gain, but other forces were also responsible for an increase in looting. In particular, as European and American colonial powers expanded into previously unexplored areas of Asia, Africa, and Latin America, proprietary claims were staked over ruins in these areas, and archaeological sites were often mined like mineral deposits, to stock the shelves of museums and private collectors alike. For instance, from 1802 to 1821, Claudius Rich, a British consular agent in Baghdad, collected and removed thousands of antiquities and sent them home to England. An extraordinary Italian, Giovanni Belzoni, working for the English government, systematically looted Egyptian tombs; he even used battering rams to enter the ancient burial chambers.

As destructive as many of these activities were by today's standards, many important discoveries were still made. Discoveries of ancient civilizations—even those made by plunderers—were sometimes used to supplement documentary history. This work was made easier by the decipherment of Egyptian **hieroglyphs** in 1822 by Jean Jacques Champollion and of Mesopotamian cuneiform writing by Henry Rawlinson soon thereafter.

THE TRANSITION TO PROFESSIONAL ARCHAEOLOGY

By the late 19th century, the impact of the accumulating evidence of the human past was impressive. And the increase in finds was accompanied by a gradual refinement of recovery and classification methods that made the record even stronger. But what did all this new information mean? How could it be interpreted? Collection and classification certainly continued in various forms, but as explanation and interpretation took center stage in importance, archaeology emerged as a professional pursuit, to study the human past through its material remains.

The Problem of Interpretation

The problem of elucidating the past from physical remains was immense. Archaeologists usually have only scattered remnants of past cultures to work with. One way to visualize the problem is to imagine what could survive from our own civilization for archaeologists to ponder some 5000 or 10,000 years from now. What could they reconstruct about our way of life on the basis of scattered soft-drink bottles, porcelain commodes, plastic containers, spark plugs, parking structures, fast-food restaurants, and other durable products of our civilization? In approaching the problem of interpreting the past, the archaeologist needs a framework to help put the puzzle together. As an analogy, imagine an incredibly complex three-dimensional jigsaw puzzle. If we knew nothing about its size, form, or subject matter, the puzzle would be impossible to reconstruct. But if we proposed a scheme that accounted for the puzzle's size, form, and subject, we could use this scheme to attempt to put it together. Thus, by proposing a hypothetical size, form, and subject matter for the puzzle, we might be able to reconstruct it. If one scheme failed to work, we could propose another in its stead, until we succeeded.

By the beginning of the 19th century, the rapidly accumulating body of archaeological materials, together with the inadequacy of the traditional theological interpretation of the past, made dedicated antiquarians realize that they needed some scheme to aid them in understanding and interpreting all the data about the past.

The solution to this problem came with the gradual definition of a new discipline—anthropology. The development of anthropology is beyond our scope here, but we can highlight the themes that are most important to both anthropology and archaeology.

The Influence of Anthropological Ideas

Anthropology developed during the 19th century as a fusion of several diverse philosophical trends. These include the idea of biological evolution, the doctrine of social progress, and the idea of cultural evolution.

The Idea of Biological Evolution
The idea that the forms of biological life are the result of gradual, long-term alterations is an old one. But by the 1800s, this evolutionary view had long been out of favor with theologians because it ran counter to the description given in the Book of Genesis. The theological view was that the history of the earth was relatively short and that all species of life were of fixed and unchanging form. But the theological position was gradually weakened by accumulating evidence that the earth was far older than the approximately 6000 years allowed by orthodox religious accounts. Eventually, the growing discrepancy between the religious interpretation and the geological and paleontological evidence led to the emergence of two schools of thought for interpreting this evidence.

The first school is generally known as *catastrophism*. Catastrophists held that during the history of the planet a series of geological disasters took place that destroyed all life forms of their time. Each disaster was followed by a new creation. This view was often seen as a reconciliation of the geological and paleontological evidence with the theological position, since the creation recorded in Genesis could be interpreted as the creation after the most recent catastrophe, and the older forms of life revealed through fossils could represent earlier creations.

Competing with this interpretation was another view of the geological evidence, the theory of *uniformitarianism*. This theory saw the structure of the earth's crust as the result of a gradual, continuous interaction between processes of erosion and of deposition. The word *uniformitarianism* derives from the idea that a single, uniform set of processes can account for both past and present geological forms. This position, supported by the stratigraphic evidence revealed by 18th-century geologists, implied that the earth was much older than the biblical accounts would allow. Thus the uniformitarian point of view was often in conflict with the theological interpretation.

The uniformitarian theory—along with the fossil evidence that life on the planet was also much older than 6000 years and that it too had changed gradually over time—contributed directly to the formulation of the concept of biological evolution. The grand synthesis of many ideas into a theory of biological evolution was put into print by Charles Darwin in 1859 in *On the Origin of Species*. As we have said, Darwin did not "invent" the idea of biological evolution. But his version of it incorporated the perspective of the long geological history of the earth and proposed a mechanism—**natural selection**—through which the changes took place. That is, over this vast time span, the gradual process of natural selection, in which better adapted forms produced more offspring and multiplied, while less "fit" forms died out, operated to produce the incredible diversity of life forms on earth. And, although Darwin's views were meant to be applied to biology, they also provided unintended encouragement for theories of cultural evolution of that period.

The Ideas of Progress and Positivism Like biological evolution, the idea that the forms of human society change and evolve is a relatively ancient view. By the 18th century, many European philosophers were arguing that change—and **progress**—was a part of the natural human social order. In the 19th century, a complementary theme was also current: that all natural and social phenomena could be understood by determining their causes. This philosophical position, called **positivism,** made natural selection seem as plausible a mechanism for social evolution as for biological evolution. Just as Darwin used the diversity of modern species as evidence for biological evolution, so the positivists used the diversity of human societies encountered by Europeans in the 19th century as evidence for social evolution.

The Idea of Cultural Evolution By the 19th century, European colonial expansion had brought Western society into contact with a tremendous variety of human societies with diverse physical characteristics. Some of these human variations appeared to be so different from Europeans that one of the questions in the 16th century was whether these newly discovered peoples were human beings. The issue was settled by the Papal Bull of 1537, which declared that the inhabitants of the New World were indeed human! However, the question of the technological and cultural diversity of these alien peoples remained. In this context, anthropology developed in the 19th century as a discipline that attempted to gather and analyze information about Nonwestern societies, largely to create a universal theory of human cultural and social differences. That theory is often known today as the theory of **cultural evolution.**

During this period, some scholars were studying and writing about human origins, using the archaeological evidence then available. Others were interested in human **culture**—how it developed and how the diversity in human customs originated. These investigators combined current intellectual ideas with firsthand evidence from their own fieldwork and with previously recorded descriptions of so-called primitive peoples, such as missionary accounts. We now refer to many of these researchers as "early anthropologists." Whatever we label them, these 19th-century scholars were, for the most part, generalists: people who attempted to use any and all of the somewhat limited data available to them to answer very broad questions. Their goal was to provide a history where none existed—to write a universal history of human culture.

Unilinear Evolutionary Anthropology Typical of these 19th-century scholars was Herbert Spencer, a cultural evolutionary thinker as well as an apologist for colonialism; he coined the phrase "survival of the fittest." Spencer believed that the present human social order was imperfect but that it was constantly adapting (progressing) to become more perfect. Spencer's explanation for the success of some cultures was simple: Successful evolution was due to an innate superiority. In fact, a good number of scholars at this time were concerned with the idea of cultural evolution. Many, including pioneers such as Sven Nilsson, who proposed a four-stage evolutionary scheme in 1838, had relatively little impact on archaeology. On the other hand, two early anthropologists, Lewis Henry Morgan and Edward Tylor, became very influential in the development of archaeology.

L. H. Morgan's unilinear evolutionary scheme

Lewis Henry Morgan, the 19th-century American anthropologist whose studies of the Iroquois are classics to this day, saw cultural evolution somewhat differently from the way Spencer did. Morgan advanced the concept of the *psychic unity of mankind*. By this concept, Morgan meant that the mental ability of all humans was essentially the same, since we all react to similar conditions in similar ways. Using this line of reasoning, Morgan concluded that all cultures move or evolve in a parallel fashion through formally defined stages, which he labeled "savagery," "barbarism," and, ultimately, "civilization." But some cultures move faster or progress further than others; Morgan considered those that are furthest advanced to be superior.

The foremost English anthropologist in the 19th century, Edward Tylor, attempted to catalog all aspects of human culture, including their variations as well as their similarities. Tylor felt that European superiority in the 19th century could be explained by environmental factors, such as an advantageous geographical position.

The universal theory of cultural evolution, as developed by these scholars and others, was based on comparisons among societies. Data from any source—ethnographic, archaeological, or whatever—were acceptable in assessing a society's "evolutionary status." Above all, cultures were compared to determine their relative positions on a single scale of development or success. This assumption that all human cultures develop along a single or *unilinear* path, perhaps best expressed by Morgan's evolutionary stages, stands out as the greatest weakness in 19th-century cultural evolutionary theory.

The errors of the unilinear evolutionists are readily apparent now, with the benefit of more than 100 years of hindsight. In the 19th century, however, little thought was given to the possible effects of vast differences in time and space. Since all cultural evolution was thought to proceed along the same course, ancient societies were assumed to be directly comparable to contemporary societies. A definite bias is evident in the use of technological criteria for defining stages and for assigning a developmental status to a given culture. And many errors were committed in interpreting or evaluating the data used; sources were often not evaluated critically. Above all, these 19th-century evolutionists were **ethnocentric**—their assessment of the developmental stages of other societies was heavily biased by their assumption that 19th-century Western culture represented the current pinnacle of evolutionary achievement.

Today, the ideas that human behavior does change and that societies and cultures do evolve remain important in modern anthropological theory; we shall return to the theme of evolution later. But by the turn of the 20th century, it was evident that the weaknesses of the case made for **unilinear cultural evolution** outweighed its strong points, and the attempt to write a universal history of human culture was cast aside or altered to remove its inherent weaknesses.

Franz Boas and Empirical Anthropology   The next stage in the emergence of modern anthropology and archaeology took place in America through the efforts of Franz Boas and his students during the early part of the 20th century. In opposition to the unilinear evolutionists, these scholars emphasized further data collection, seeking to improve the quality and quantity of information available about the world's cultures. This better data base, they argued, would be the foundation for rigorous development and testing of sound theory and explanation. Theirs was an understandable reaction to the still highly speculative approach current among the unilinear evolutionists.

Indeed, Boas felt that scholars could reconstruct the cultural history of even a single given society only after rigorous collection of all kinds of data—archaeological and linguistic as well as ethnographic. Thus, as part of his approach Boas emphasized the importance of archaeology for the gathering of prehistoric data. In fact, he sponsored the first stratigraphic excavations in the Valley of Mexico, conducted by Manuel Gamio in 1911.

Empirical emphasis in anthropology: Franz Boas and the use of archaeology

THE EMERGENCE OF MODERN ARCHAEOLOGY

Modern professional archaeology emerged during this period of debate in the 19th century. As we have said, one of the essential points that distinguishes archaeologists from their antiquarian predecessors is the use of interpretive schemes to understand the evidence of prehistory. Archaeologists and other scientists now generally refer to interpretive schemes as **models.**

A model is essentially a form of hypothesis; it is constructed and tested according to the scientific method (see Chapter 1). Although various kinds have been devised, all models are schemes based upon a set of assumptions (or givens) that are compared with the available data and used to bring order to those data. As data are placed in order according to the model, two things can happen. Either the data "fit" or they do not. If the data agree with the model, then the two together form a basis for an adequate interpretation—subject, of course, to further testing. If the data do not fit the model, then the model might be revised or replaced and the new one tested. However, this method always contains potential sources of error:

FIGURE 2.7 Model testing in archaeology is an important means of refining our understanding of the past.

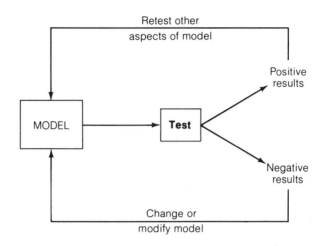

The data may be biased, for example, or our assumptions may be incorrect. As a result, even when a "fit" occurs, we cannot be sure we have found *the* solution, we have found only the best available under the circumstances. Thus, in keeping with the scientific method, we can reject a model, but we can never completely prove its applicability (Fig. 2.7).

The models used to interpret archaeological data are of two types: descriptive and explanatory. As the names imply, *descriptive models* merely describe observable characteristics—the form and structure of phenomena—whereas *explanatory models* seek to determine the causes of those forms or structures. In archaeology, both kinds of models can be subdivided into **synchronic** and **diachronic** aspects. *Synchronic models* are static; they describe or explain phenomena at one point in time. *Diachronic models* are dynamic, describing or explaining phenomena through time. An example of a synchronic descriptive model would be the classical biological classification scheme of Linnaeus or "the Great Chain of Being" (Fig. 2.1, p. 43). Diachronic descriptive models are exemplified by most chronological historical schemes, such as those commonly used in European history: classical period, Dark Ages, medieval period, Renaissance, and so forth. Sir Isaac Newton's explanation of the rotation of the moon about the earth is a synchronic explanatory model. Biological evolution by means of natural selection provides a diachronic explanatory model for the sequence of life on earth.

The earliest archaeological interpretations were based on historical models: Typically, they were diachronic and descriptive. The application of such historical models was especially prevalent in areas with documented historical traditions, such as Europe and southwest Asia. But early scholars also applied historically based schemes to prehistoric evidence. Later, models borrowed from anthropology, including evolutionary schemes that anthropology had in turn derived partly from biology, were used to interpret prehistoric data from both the Old and the New Worlds.

The early models used to interpret archaeological data were not always formally defined, nor were the assumptions underlying the schemes made explicit. In fact, rather than rejecting a model when the data did not fit, investigators often forced facts to conform to their expectations. Explicit definitions of interpretive schemes and of the assumptions behind them, as well as the procedures for testing those schemes, had to await the further development of archaeology as a scientific discipline. We can trace the beginnings of this trend even before the 19th century.

Historical Interpretations

The first historical scheme widely used in archaeological interpretation was the well-known *three-age technological sequence,* which held that prehistoric society developed progressively through ages of stone, bronze, and iron technology. The idea behind this theory can be traced to historical writings from several ancient civilizations, including those of Greece, Rome, and China.

Among the first to propose a **three-age sequence** for European prehistory were two early 19th-century Danish scholars, Christian Thomsen and Jens Worsaae. Thomsen, one of the true pioneers of modern archaeology, organized the collections in the Danish National Museum of Antiquities according to this scheme, not only as a convenience but also because it seemed to reflect chronological stages of human progress. The energetic Jens Worsaae, assisted by funds from the king of Denmark, conducted excavations in burial mounds to demonstrate the validity of the three-age sequence. These excavations verified that stone tools were located in an earlier position underlying those of bronze, which in turn underlay the later tools of iron. Worsaae also stressed the importance of careful excavation technique and of preserving all available evidence. For Worsaae, the goal of excavation was far more than simply to collect artifacts for museum display—it was to learn about the development of human culture.

Three-age sequence in Europe: Thomsen and Worsaae in Denmark

The three-age scheme was refined by further excavations, and, as time went on, the sequence grew more detailed. In 1865, for example, Sir John Lubbock distinguished between an earlier chipped-stone technology ("old stone" or paleolithic) and a later ground-stone technology ("new stone" or neolithic). In 1890, the Swedish archaeologist Oscar Montelius integrated most of Europe into a single chronology through comparison of artifact styles. In 1871, Heinrich Schliemann used a quasi-historical source—Homer's *Iliad*—in his efforts to discover Troy, thereby initiating investigation of the predecessors to classical Greek civilization.

Thus, by the end of the 19th century, European archaeology was based on a well-developed historical chronological framework. To this day, many European archaeologists regard their discipline as allied more closely with history than with any other field.

Anthropological Interpretations

In the 19th century, archaeological method was refined to near-modern precision by the work of the Englishman Augustus Lane-Fox, more commonly known as General Pitt-Rivers. At the dawn of the 20th century, American archaeologists were borrowing the excavation methods developed largely in the Old World, but they were taking a rather different path from their Old World counterparts in their attempts to interpret the past. The difference was due largely to contrasting circumstances.

For one thing, the New World, unlike many areas of the Old World, generally lacked a native tradition of written history. In addition, cultural development in the Americas did not have the time depth found in the Old World: The earliest migration in the New World appeared to be relatively recent, taking place during the last glacial epoch. This meant that the historical (or historically based) schemes used in the Old World could not be meaningfully applied in the New. In fact, New World archaeologists shared closest interests with New World ethnologists and linguists, for all of them were concerned with understanding Native American societies, past or present. As a result, for New World archaeologists, anthropology ultimately became the main source of interpretive models—in essence, it replaced history. Indeed, many anthropologists of this period did archaeological as well as ethnographic and linguistic fieldwork.

Use of ethnographic data in archaeology: Cyrus Thomas, F. H. Cushing, and others

The most obvious approach to interpreting ancient New World remains was to accept the earlier conclusions of Gallatin, Morton, Haven, and their contemporaries that continuity existed from the past to present-day Native American societies. If that was true, then the archaeologist could use ethnographic (anthropological) studies of living groups to interpret the past. This was done by comparing contemporary artifacts with those recovered archaeologically—working from the present back through time as far as possible. This method, often called the **direct historical approach** (something of a mislabel), was pioneered by the investigations of the Bureau of American Ethnology established in 1879. Under the auspices of the bureau, Cyrus Thomas, like his associates from several other institutions (the Peabody Museum of Harvard University, the American Museum of Natural History, the New York State Museum, and others), used this approach to study the history of the prehistoric mound builders of the American Midwest. It was Thomas's 1894 report that finally removed lingering doubts and established that native New World peoples had built the splendid monuments in America.

In the southwestern states, F. H. Cushing, taking pottery as his key, used this same method in 1890 to trace the connections between the contemporary Pueblo peoples and their ancient forebears. Much later, ethnographic studies of tribal groups on the Great Plains, such as the Cheyenne, were combined with archaeological research to trace the prehistoric origins of the tribes back to the Great Lakes region. We will discuss the direct historical approach in more detail in Chapters 3 and 13.

Although successful in certain cases, the direct historical approach has serious limitations. To use it, researchers move backward from artifacts and sites identified with a historically known group to similar but earlier archaeological materials. The method works only so long as a given cluster of artifacts remains coherent—recognizably distinct from those of other prehistoric societies. Because these conditions are not fulfilled in all cases, other means of interpreting the past were soon found to be necessary. Archaeologists needed a far more inclusive and flexible framework to guide their interpretations. This was provided by anthropology and its concept of culture. However, anthropology has developed several different cultural models or concepts that apply somewhat differently to archaeological interpretation. Each of these models conditions archaeological research to some degree by influencing the questions being asked, the kinds of data sought, and the types of analyses performed. In the next chapter, we shall briefly review the development of these cultural models and their use as the basis of archaeological interpretation.

SUMMARY

This chapter has traced the origins and growth of the discipline of archaeology. Like other branches of science, archaeology has its roots in the work of amateur collectors. As collections of antiquities grew, attempts were made to bring order to them by classification. Some individuals tried to understand the meaning of their collections—what they were and what they could tell us about the prehistoric human past—but early "explanations" were largely speculative. All too often, evidence from the past was misconstrued to fit inflexible theories. Growing dissatisfaction with this approach was illustrated by the study of human antiquity in both the Old and the New Worlds. Ultimately, empirically based works of such scholars as Boucher de Perthes and Haven broke the hold of speculative theories.

The emergence of archaeology as a professional, scientific discipline was marked by the rise of full-time specialists committed to understanding the meaning behind the physical remains of the past. This commitment to meaning implied the adoption of one or more interpretive frameworks or models that could be tested against the evidence. Models developed in the Old World, such as the three-age system, were derived primarily from history. In the New World, where the aboriginal cultures lacked a historical tradition, archaeology became allied with the new field of anthropology and adopted a variety of cultural frameworks to interpret the past.

GUIDE TO FURTHER READING

The Growth of Scientific Disciplines
Eiseley 1958; Gould 1982, 1986; Kuhn 1970; Lovejoy [1936] 1960; Mayr 1972; Toulmin and Goodfield 1965

Antiquarians and the Origins of Archaeology

General Histories of Archaeology: Christenson 1989; Daniel 1962, 1967, 1976a, 1981a, 1981b; Daniel and Chippindale 1989; Fagan 1978; Grayson 1983; Heizer 1962; Trigger 1989; Trigger and Glover 1981, 1982

Old World—Issues and Personalities: Alcock 1971; Daniel 1943, 1971b, 1976b; Fagan 1975; Klindt-Jensen 1975; Lloyd 1955; Lynch and Lynch 1968; Piggott 1985; Poole and Poole 1966; Wheeler 1955; Wood 1985

Old World—Classic Studies: Camden [1789] 1977; Frere 1800; Lubbock 1865

New World—Issues and Personalities: Brunhouse 1973; Fitting 1973; Gorenstein 1977; Griffin 1959; Meltzer 1983; Rowe 1954; Rowlett 1982; Schuyler 1971; Thompson 1963; Wauchope 1965; Willey and Sabloff 1980

New World—Classic Studies: Cushing 1890; Gallatin 1836; Haven 1856; Koch and Peden 1944; Squier and Davis 1848; Stephens [1841] 1969, [1843] 1963; Thomas 1894

The Transition to Professional Archaeology

General Studies: Brew 1968; Daniel 1981a, 1981b; Grayson 1983; Harris 1968; Kardiner and Preble 1961; Keesing 1974; Rowe 1965; Trigger 1989; Trigger and Glover 1981, 1982; Willey and Sabloff 1980

Classic Works: Boas 1948; Darwin 1859; Lyell 1830–1833; Morgan 1877; Spencer 1876; Tylor 1871

CHAPTER THREE

CONTEMPORARY APPROACHES

We must continually work back and forth between the contexts of explaining the archaeological record and explaining the past; between the contexts of proposition formulation . . . and proposition testing. . . .

    Lewis R. Binford, "Some Comments on Historical versus Processual Archaeology," 1968

The ongoing business of archaeology is a progression toward improved knowledge and understanding. Sometimes this progression will advance through pattern recognition, at other times it will advance through the use of low-level inductive procedures, the hypothetico-deductive method, heuristic use of covering laws, classification, or just an ability to count: no one technique can be expected to work in all situations.

    Jane H. Kelley and Marsha P. Hanen, Archaeology and the Methodology of Science, *1988*

Many interpretations of prehistory reflect a kind of archaeological "econothink" which has seen more effort put into following the changing tactics of technological adaptation in the environment than into trying to understand what it may have been that prehistoric peoples found worthwhile to live for.

    Robert L. Hall, "An Anthropocentric Perspective for Eastern United States Prehistory," 1977

For most of the 20th century, two theoretical schools have dominated archaeology. The earlier one, *culture history,* paralleled the work of Boas described at the end of the last chapter. In the 1960s, a second approach, *cultural process* or *processualism,* sought to revolutionize the pursuit of the discipline under the banner of the "New Archaeology." A third, more loosely defined set of theoretical orientations has emerged since the 1980s, all grouped under the heading of *postprocessual* archaeology.

The emphasis in culture history is outlining the *what, when,* and *where* of the past, whereas study of cultural process seeks to explain the *how* and, in broad, comparative terms, the *why* of what happened in the past. Postprocessual archaeologists also aim at the *why* of past developments, but from the perspective of the ancient people involved—to gain an insider's understanding rather than an outsider's explanation.

Sometimes the three approaches have been viewed as contradictory or mutually incompatible. Indeed, some members of each "school" have claimed theirs was the only acceptable kind of archaeology. As we shall see in this chapter, however, the three are better seen as mutually complementary. They are also to some degree interdependent: It is unlikely that processualism could have developed without the solid accomplishments of culture historians, and in a similar way, postprocessual archaeology emerged in the wake of culture historical and processual developments.

Each of the three approaches asks different questions, and doing so requires somewhat different constructs and methods. But taken together, these approaches address all four of the fundamental goals of archaeology outlined in Chapter 1—the form, function, process, and meaning of the past. We will discuss two important aspects of contrast (and attendant complementarity!): the definitions of culture assumed by each school and the methods of inquiry used by each.

CULTURE HISTORY

The **culture historical approach** is usually associated with a normative model of culture and with a rather informally defined research methodology. Within these frameworks, the central goal of culture history is outlining the sequence and geographical distribution of past events. As we will see later, in Chapter 17, the culmination of the culture historical approach is therefore a chronicle of events and general trends of cultural change and continuity in the prehistoric past.

Origins of the Culture Historical Approach

In the culture historical orientation, both the research methodology and the specific model of culture are firmly rooted in the American school of anthropology founded by Franz Boas and his students at the beginning of the 20th century. Boasian anthropology, often called "historical empiricism" or "historical particularism," was in part a reaction against the accumulated abuses of 19th-century unilinear cultural evolutionary theory (see Chapter 2). A critical flaw in the approach, however, was the lack of testing of the model to allow for its possible refutation. Reacting to this approach, Boas and his followers adopted a research methodology by which descriptive data were to be gathered first; models of change and continuity and specific problems for interpretation were not to be formulated until the data base was sufficient for such purposes.

Prehistoric archaeology in the United States, emerging at the same time as the Boasian school of anthropology, inherited much of the methodology of its parent discipline. Although philosophically a product of the theoretical conditions prevailing within American anthropology at the turn of the century, culture historical archaeology was also conditioned by the unique circumstances under which prehistoric archaeologists worked in the New World. Particularly important was the lack of historical records for periods before the 16th-century European conquest, a situation that contrasts markedly with the long historical tradition available in much of the Old World. There simply was no established framework into which to fit pre-Columbian archaeological data. Since archaeologists of the early 20th century were unwilling to accept the model used in the Old World, they set out to collect the "hard data" from which they could reconstruct the events of American prehistory. These archaeologists applied their newly won data to the prevailing concept of culture of the time.

The Normative Model of Culture

Not surprisingly, the first model of culture to be applied to archaeology derived from the Boasian tradition of American anthropology. It is usually called the *normative* concept. As a model for interpretation, the **normative concept of culture** is descriptive rather than explanatory. Although it is based on a synchronic analysis of culture, it is adaptable to a diachronic perspective, viewing culture through time. Its advantage for a culture historical approach is its emphasis on culture as idealized, so that variant forms and styles (e.g., of pottery decoration) can be seen as straightforward clues to cultural boundaries in time and space.

All human behavior is patterned, and the form of the patterns is largely determined by **culture.** The normative concept of culture holds that within a given society, behavior patterns are the result of adherence to a set of rules, or *norms,* for behavior. The rules are passed from one generation to the next—some within the family (parent to child), others within schools (teacher to student) or occupations (master to apprentice). Some behavior, of course, is idiosyncratic—unique to the individual—and is not passed on, but most behavior is regulated by norms.

In any given cultural system, however, a range of behaviors is tolerated; what the norms really specify are the ranges and their limits. Each such range represents only a portion of the potential behaviors in a given behavioral realm. For instance, one realm of behavior is location of the residence of newly married couples. The potential choices for such residence are many: A couple could reside with the bride's parents, the groom's parents, or an uncle's family, or they could establish a new and separate residence. In fact, however, all cultures restrict the choice. Individuals learn which residential behavior is considered correct within their culture. Deviance from the norm may be corrected by a variety of methods, such as gossip or threats of violence. The mere existence of these measures will lead most individuals to follow the acceptable norm; by doing so, they gain a measure of security and well-being.

By observing actual human behavior in as many contexts as possible, anthropologists attempt to abstract the "rules" that describe and even predict forms of behavior. This is comparable to the grammar (a set of abstracted rules) that describes and predicts the regularities within a language. In the example just cited, residence behavior is often abstracted in **residence rules** that describe and predict where married couples will live under given circumstances. Of course, there are always discrepancies between the "ideal" of behavior and the observed behavior, but the norms should always predict the majority of actual, observed behaviors.

The archaeologist often makes use of the normative view of culture to reconstruct or describe the nature and sequence of past behavior. The remains of past cultures recovered by the archaeologist may be assumed to represent past behavioral norms. For instance, pottery, because of its durability, is often considered a useful indicator of past cultural behavior. According to the normative concept of culture, pottery can be viewed as a

Residence rules viewed as normative behavior

Reconstruction of past behavior: Pottery as reflection of cultural norms

reflection of norms governing technological behavior. Although the methods for making and decorating pottery are potentially numerous, each culture uses only a few of these techniques. The behavior of potters, then, is controlled in much the same way as the behavior of married couples selecting a new residence. The potter is bound by the manufacturing techniques learned from the older generation; departures from those standards may be discouraged by both social and economic sanctions. The archaeologist can infer the ancient "rules" governing pottery making by studying the pattern of similarities and variations in the surviving pottery, just as the anthropologist discovers the "rule of residence" by studying actual behavior.

Thus, the normative view sees culture as the set of rules that regulate, maintain, and perpetuate appropriate behavior within society. Because such behavior is patterned and to a degree predictable, archaeologists can infer past cultural norms from surviving products of a culture. The patterns and variations apparent in this evidence enable archaeologists to reconstruct variations and changes in behavioral norms in both space and time.

The Emergence of Culture Historical Research

Under the influence of such scholars as Franz Boas and Alfred V. Kidder, the normative model of culture dominated anthropological archaeology during the first half of the 20th century. The bulk of prehistoric archaeological interpretation, especially in the New World, has been based on the normative concept either implicitly or explicitly. Until quite recently, the general procedures followed by most prehistoric archaeologists have reflected not only the normative cultural concept but also a general research strategy based on Boasian anthropology. Refinements in excavation and classification methods and the construction of site and regional chronologies were the most common concerns of normative archaeologists in the first half of the 20th century. These emphases have been an efficient and appropriate means of gaining an integrated data base for the prehistoric past from most areas of the world. Culture historical archaeology has been quite successful in providing a descriptive outline of the prehistory for vast expanses of time and space. However, it tended to address only one of the four fundamental concerns of archaeology. Only the first goal, that of outlining the distribution in time and space of the material forms from the past, was being pursued. The remaining goals—reconstruction of past behavior, delineation of culture process, and interpretation of meaning—were not usually addressed by use of a normative cultural framework. Different views of culture were needed to focus on these concerns.

The culture historical approach was forged by many individual scholars, using data collected in hundreds of separate archaeological investigations; as a result, it is impossible even to mention most of these in our brief review. We will concentrate on the career of one American archaeologist who, more than any other individual, pioneered and refined the tenets of

FIGURE 3.1 In this 1916 photograph, taken at Pecos Pueblo, A. V. Kidder is flanked by Harvard mentor, Alfred E. Tozzer (left), and Kidder's assistant, Carl E. Guthe. (Alfred Kidder Guthe.)

Survey in the American Southwest: Hewett's field school

Foundations of Southwest prehistory: Kidder at Pecos, New Mexico

culture historical interpretation in prehistoric archaeology: Alfred V. Kidder (1885–1963)(Fig. 3.1).

Kidder's archaeological career began in 1907, while he was an undergraduate student at Harvard University. That summer, he and two other Harvard students joined Edgar L. Hewett's expedition to the southwestern United States. Kidder's actual initiation into the realities of archaeological fieldwork came as Hewett led his students to the top of a mesa in the Four Corners area of the Southwest. The view encompassed several hundred square miles—to Kidder it seemed "about half the world." Gazing out over this vast area, Hewett pointed out several principal landmarks and simply said, "I want you boys to make an archaeological survey of this country. I'll be back in six weeks. You'd better get some horses."

Kidder and his two companions went on to complete their first summer's fieldwork according to Hewett's rather terse instructions. After graduating from Harvard, Kidder visited several excavations in the Mediterranean area and was exposed to stratigraphic procedures for the first time. His education in state-of-the-art rigor in data collection continued in his graduate school years at Harvard, and he returned to the Southwest to apply the principles he had learned.

In 1915, Kidder began investigations at Pecos, New Mexico, to document the sequence of prehistoric cultures in the Southwest, which was at that time almost completely unknown. Kidder chose Pecos (Fig. 3.2) for this work for a very good reason: It was a historic contact site, still occupied at the time of the first Spanish colonization in the 16th century, and it had thereafter become a Spanish mission center. Kidder hoped to discover and excavate stratified deposits through which, by applying the **direct historical approach** (discussed in Chapters 2 and 13), he could link the known historic Spanish period with successively earlier remains, to reveal the full sequence of prehistoric occupation. The results of the Pecos excavation—which lasted until 1929—more than fulfilled this expectation. The data from stratified midden deposits at Pecos provided the basis

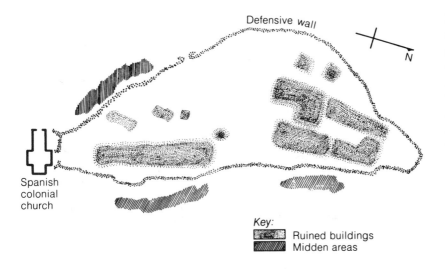

Defensive wall

N

Spanish
colonial
church

Key:
▓▓▓ Ruined buildings
▨▨▨ Midden areas

for the first long-term chronology of human occupation in this part of the New World. This sequence, in turn, provided the foundation for the first area synthesis in the Southwest. At Kidder's invitation, archaeologists from all over the Southwest met in 1927 at a conference at Pecos to pool their findings and reconstruct the temporal and spatial distributions and interconnections of their data. The resulting temporal and spatial synthesis still provides the basic framework for all Southwest archaeologists (Fig. 3.3); although subsequent research has refined the synthesis, the basic structure remains.

After 1929, Kidder was appointed Director of the Division of Historical Research for the Carnegie Institution of Washington; in this position he was able to sponsor and oversee a multitude of anthropological and archaeological research projects during the next three decades. The focus of this research was in the Maya area of Mesoamerica. Kidder viewed the Maya as a unique, pristine laboratory for anthropological study. The study he planned was based on a multidisciplinary investigation, in which archaeologists were joined by ethnographers, ethnohistorians, linguists, and a variety of other specialists to gather data spanning the prehistoric and historical past, along with the ethnographic present. Contemporary Maya communities preserved many traditional (or non-European) aspects of culture; immediate ethnographic documentation was therefore needed to record this culture before it disappeared. Archives held rich resources of ethnohistorical information about the Maya from the time of the Spanish Conquest to the present day. Both ethnographic and ethnohistoric sources could provide comparisons for the reconstruction of ancient Maya civilization.

But the direct study of past Maya civilization was Kidder's primary interest, for in 1929 the temporal and spatial dimensions of ancient Maya life were largely unknown. In Kidder's view, the first priority was there-

Foundations of Maya prehistory: Kidder with the Carnegie Institution

Space: Regions of the Southwest

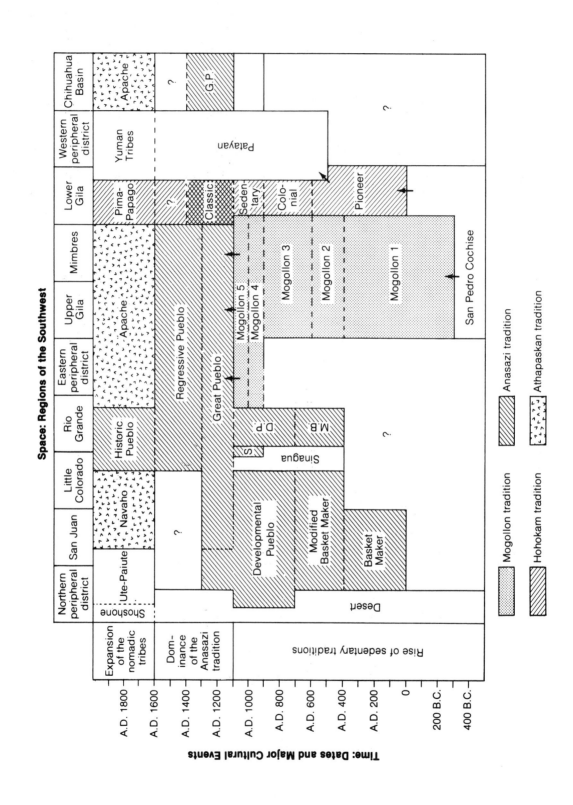

Time: Dates and Major Cultural Events

Legend:
- Mogollon tradition
- Hohokam tradition
- Anasazi tradition
- Athapaskan tradition

fore to gather archaeological data to establish the basic sequence and distribution of prehistoric Maya culture; these considerations were prerequisites for any attempt to answer such questions as: What were the origins, development, and demise of Maya civilization? Accordingly, Kidder and the Carnegie Institution sponsored the first large-scale archaeological investigations in the Maya area, selecting a series of sites in each of the principal environmental regions that promised to cover the estimated time span of Maya occupation.

Projects at Uaxactún, in the Petén rain forest of Guatemala, and at Chichén Itzá, in arid Yucatán, were two of the major pioneering undertakings. In the Guatemalan highlands, the focus was the site of Kaminaljuyú—in Mayan, the "hills of the dead." Work began at Kaminaljuyú in 1935, directed by Kidder himself. Its results were surprising. Although evidence was discovered of an occupation contemporary with the great lowland centers of the **Classic** period (ca. A.D. 250–900), much of the material culture from the Kaminaljuyú Classic period included obvious non-Maya attributes. In fact, some pottery and architectural styles found there were virtually identical to those from Central Mexico. This was the first indication that the Maya highlands, during the early portion of the Classic period at least, were intimately related to the political and economic power of the Central Mexican city of Teotihuacan. An even more significant surprise emerged from the Kaminaljuyú excavations. Kidder and his colleague Edwin M. Shook discovered an earlier, **Preclassic** civilization that appeared to have reached its peak several hundred years before the development of civilization in the Maya lowlands. Building on this research, Kidder hypothesized that Classic Maya civilization may have had substantial roots in the southern region of the highlands and Pacific coast of Guatemala—a hypothesis fully supported by subsequent archaeological investigations.

Kidder's archaeological research played a crucial role in the development of the culture historical approach. His work was instrumental in establishing rigorous standards for archaeological research. His emphasis on refinement of data-gathering techniques, such as careful and detailed recording of excavations and the use of stratigraphic excavation, continues to influence contemporary archaeologists. Kidder's overall research strategy—exemplified in his use of the direct historical approach at Pecos and in the building of site sequences into area syntheses in both the Southwest and the Maya area—shaped the culture historical approach. But, as Kidder himself realized, this research method never realized its ultimate goal—an understanding of the processes of culture, the explanation of how and why civilizations such as that of the Maya rose and fell.

As we shall see, a culture historical approach can be used to outline the temporal, the spatial, and even the functional dimensions of prehistory, but it is less suited to documenting cultural process or the specific causes of cultural development and change. Before considering these larger issues, however, we shall describe exactly how the culture historical approach

FIGURE 3.3 (opposite page)   Kidder's excavations at Pecos helped define the chronological and spatial distributions of prehistoric societies in the southwestern United States. The culture historical approach leads to the development of such *time–space grids* to summarize ancient events and cultural relationships. (From *An Introduction to the Study of Southwestern Archaeology,* by A. V. Kidder. Copyright © 1924 by Yale University Press. Revised edition. Copyright © 1962 by Yale University. All rights reserved.)

Kaminaljuyú excavations: Kidder and Shook

provides temporal, spatial, and functional frameworks for chronicling the past.

The Culture Historical Method

Following the research method associated with the culture historical approach, investigators begin with specific data from individual sites and combine these to increase the scale and scope of coverage. Data collection is used to formulate cultural sequences. These sequences are often tested by subsequent work. We will briefly describe a standard culture historical methodology by recounting the steps normally followed in conducting archaeological research in a previously uninvestigated area.

Once the zone of archaeological research has been selected, a reconnaissance program identifies archaeological sites, and surface survey provides the initial round of data collections (these procedures will be considered in Chapters 5 and 6). From these collections, the archaeologist selects the traits that seem most sensitive to temporal change and that will therefore best allow the preliminary collections to be arranged in a tentative chronological sequence. The traits used may be characteristics of features, such as architectural form or style; more commonly, however, they are attributes of pottery or of stone tools. Once the surface survey data are classified and analyzed, the archaeologist sets up a tentative chronological sequence, using the direct historical method or other techniques.

After the preliminary chronological scheme has been worked out, excavations are undertaken to test the sequence and to provide data for its refinement. Other goals may also be pursued in excavation, but the emphasis in the culture historical approach usually is placed on discovery and investigation of deposits that enable the archaeologist to document further or to rework the tentative time scheme. When the excavated data have been classified and analyzed in comparison with the initial collections, the changes observed in the sequence of artifacts are used to define broad chronological subdivisions. Thus, separate sequences are defined for pottery, chipped stone, houses, and so on.

Correlating sequences across data categories, the archaeologist next defines chronological **periods** or **phases** for the site as a whole. These are blocks of time, but since it is unlikely that all data categories will change simultaneously or at the same rate, phase boundaries are arbitrary. For example, pottery styles may change fairly rapidly, while house form may stay the same over a long time span. In many cases, the artifact sequences that are most sensitive to change are emphasized and adopted as the principal criteria for defining site phases; this is one reason why pottery typologies are commonly the backbone of archaeological sequences.

The next step is to expand beyond the individual site to encompass ever wider geographical areas. This enlargement of scope is accomplished by repeating the research procedures outlined above at sites adjacent to those already investigated. Newly acquired data can be compared with the sequences already defined, thus facilitating the task of chronological ordering at sites investigated later. Of course, not all the artifacts and features found will duplicate previous finds; new types, sequences, and phases may be defined as new sites are studied. In this way, not only is the cultural chronology refined, but the archaeologist can also begin to plot the spatial distributions of artifact and feature types. As more and more sites are investigated, the prehistoric sequences within ever larger geographical regions become established, like that worked out by Kidder and his collaborators at the 1927 Pecos conference. These are often termed **time–space grids** (see Fig. 3.3).

As a rule, the working unit of culture historical synthesis is the **culture area,** a conceptual unit originally based on ethnographically defined cultural similarities within a geographical area (Fig. 3.4). Archaeologists working within a given culture area facilitate the process of temporal and spatial synthesis by using common terminology and classificatory concepts to make information from different sites comparable. The first culture historical synthesis of an entire culture area in the New World was Kidder's, for the Southwest. Since that time, other prehistoric culture area syntheses have been worked out, both in the New World and in the Old. Compilations of time–space grids for many regions of the Old World were published in 1990 and for the New World in 1978.

Some archaeologists have been able to continue basing their area syntheses on evolutionary stages derived from the 19th-century unilinear theorists. Thus, chronological stages labeled Paleolithic and Neolithic, for example, still form a usable framework for prehistoric reconstructions in Europe, for this was the area for which the sequence was originally developed. Definitions of the divisions have been refined, of course, resulting in many detailed local chronological subdivisions for each stage (Fig. 3.5); but in much of the Old World, including Europe, the basic approach has continued to focus on testing and refinement of that original model. In the New World, on the other hand, the outline of prehistory specifically avoided using the 19th-century evolutionary model. As a consequence, the Paleolithic–Neolithic scheme has never been successfully applied to New World prehistory, although these terms are occasionally used to note general similarities to Old World finds.

Somewhat ironically, as the culture historical approach yielded ever broader and more general syntheses in the New World, archaeologists became increasingly aware that some kind of overriding scheme very much like the Old World evolutionary model would be necessary. Such a framework was worked out in the mid-20th century; a temporal–spatial synthesis for the entire New World. The terminology is distinct from that used in the Old World evolutionary model, and the resulting scheme is explicitly *not* founded on evolutionary theory. Yet the New World synthesis implicitly suggests a course of cultural development from simple to complex, certainly not identical to, but clearly parallel to, the course of Old World prehistory.

This New World model, developed in the late 1950s by Gordon R. Willey and Philip Phillips, is based on the complementary concepts of

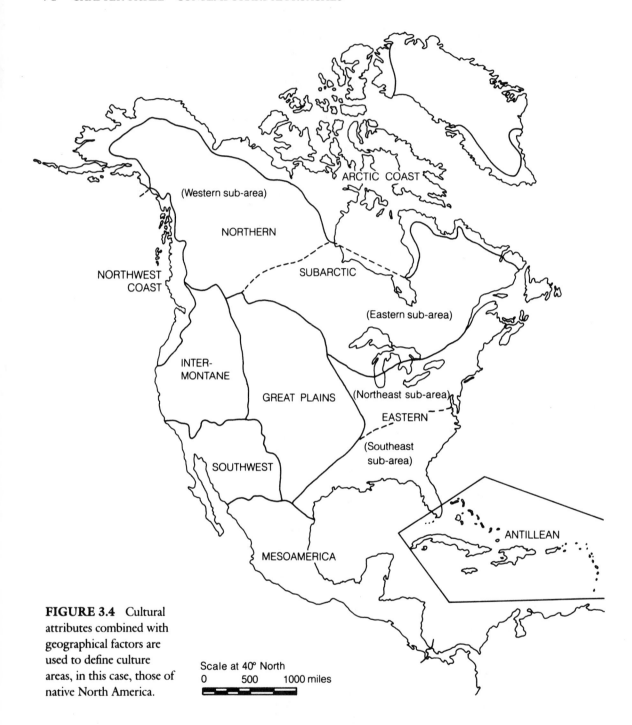

FIGURE 3.4 Cultural attributes combined with geographical factors are used to define culture areas, in this case, those of native North America.

Scale at 40° North

0   500   1000 miles

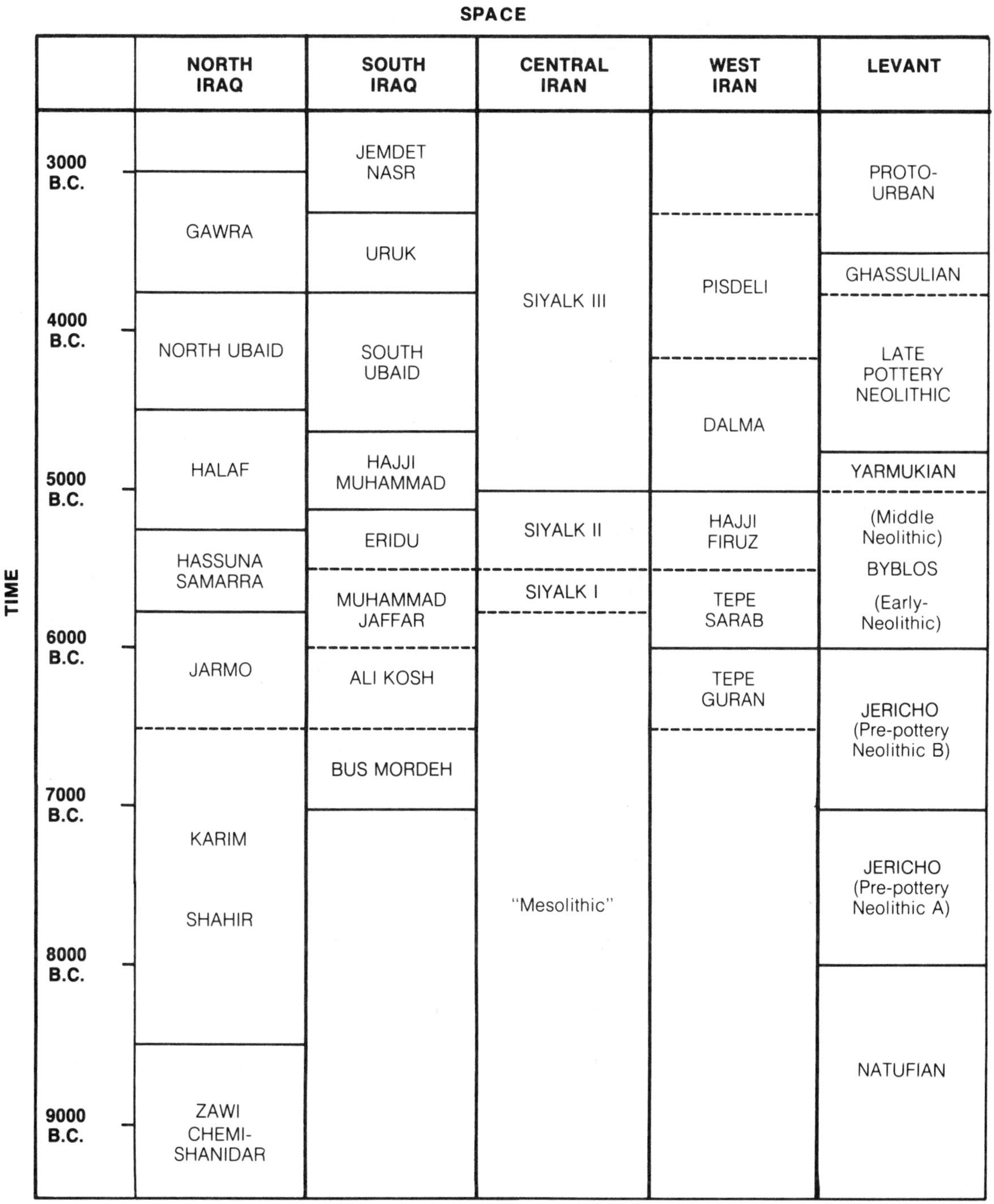

SPACE

TIME	NORTH IRAQ	SOUTH IRAQ	CENTRAL IRAN	WEST IRAN	LEVANT
3000 B.C.		JEMDET NASR			PROTO-URBAN
	GAWRA	URUK	SIYALK III	PISDELI	
					GHASSULIAN
4000 B.C.	NORTH UBAID	SOUTH UBAID			LATE POTTERY NEOLITHIC
				DALMA	
	HALAF	HAJJI MUHAMMAD			YARMUKIAN
5000 B.C.		ERIDU	SIYALK II	HAJJI FIRUZ	(Middle Neolithic)
	HASSUNA SAMARRA	MUHAMMAD JAFFAR	SIYALK I	TEPE SARAB	BYBLOS (Early-Neolithic)
6000 B.C.	JARMO	ALI KOSH		TEPE GURAN	JERICHO (Pre-pottery Neolithic B)
		BUS MORDEH			
7000 B.C.	KARIM		"Mesolithic"		JERICHO (Pre-pottery Neolithic A)
	SHAHIR				
8000 B.C.					NATUFIAN
9000 B.C.	ZAWI CHEMI-SHANIDAR				

FIGURE 3.5 One version of the chronological and spatial distributions of the major cultural periods of prehistoric societies in the ancient Near East. (After Mellaart 1965.)

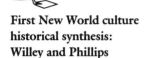

First New World culture historical synthesis: Willey and Phillips

tradition and horizon. **Tradition** refers to cultural continuity through time, and **horizon** deals with ties and uniformity across space in a relatively restricted span of time (Fig. 3.6). Applying these concepts to data from all areas of the Americas, Willey and Phillips defined a series of five developmental stages, or, as they have been more commonly applied, chronological periods. The exact temporal boundaries for each "stage" differ from area to area, but overall, Willey and Phillips's scheme represents a culture historical synthesis for the entire New World. Variants of this scheme are still cited as broad frames of reference, although—especially for the Classic and the **Postclassic**—sequences tend to be tied to particular culture areas within the Americas.

CULTURAL PROCESS

The **cultural processual approach** is the second major way of conducting archaeology. **Cultural process** refers to an explanation both of how the components of a culture work at one point in time and of how cultures change through time. Although the culture historical and cultural processual approaches are both concerned with the dynamics of culture, the former emphasizes *identification* of synchronic ties and of cultural change through description of a sequence of events, whereas the latter is concerned with discovering the *causes* of interactions and change. That is, the cultural processual approach seeks not only to identify and describe similarities and differences across time and space but also to delineate the cause–effect relationships that explain the observed distributions. For example, change can be explained by identifying an alteration in one variable, such as family structure, which leads to adjustments and changes in other variables, such as pottery production.

How does the cultural processual approach attempt to identify the causes of change and thereby explain the processes involved in prehistoric cultural dynamics? The study of cultural process uses a methodology in which, at the outset of research, multiple hypotheses specify the working model of change (or interaction) and the kinds of data that will support or refute each hypothesis. Competing hypotheses are then tested against the archaeological data to eliminate those that are not supported by the evidence. Hypotheses that are supported in the first test are retested and refined by further research to isolate the factors involved in a given situation of prehistoric cultural change.

Of course, the cultural processual approach is rooted, either directly or indirectly, in the culture historical approach. A direct link may be apparent when the tested hypotheses have been derived from culture historical models. In a direct way, however, *all* cultural processual interpretation is built on a culture historical foundation, since the latter approach has provided the temporal and spatial frameworks of prehistory. These frameworks furnish the analytical controls without which cultural process

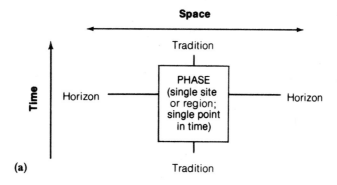

(a)

DEVELOPMENTAL STAGES	ATTRIBUTES		
	Technological	*Social*	*Ideological*
Postclassic	Metallurgy	Complex urbanism, militarism	Secularization of society
Classic	Craft specialization, beginnings of metallurgy	Large ceremonial centers, beginnings of urbanism	Developed theocracies
Formative	Pottery, weaving, developed food production	Permanent villages and towns; first ceremonial centers	Beginnings of priest class (theocracy)
Archaic	Diversified tools, ground stone utensils, beginnings of food production	Beginnings of permanent villages	?
Lithic (or Paleo-Indian)	Chipped stone tools	Nonsettled hunters and gatherers	?

(b)

FIGURE 3.6 New World cultural history was comprehensively outlined by Willey and Phillips, by (a) integrating the dimensions of time and space through the concepts of tradition and horizon (a *phase* represents the form or content of a particular tradition on a particular horizon) and (b) summarizing the course of cultural development through five generalized stages. (After Willey and Phillips 1958; part (a) copyright 1958 by The University of Chicago Press.)

cannot be discerned. The cultural processual approach represents an essential component in the scientific method as applied to archaeology; that is, after initial inquiry, new questions or hypotheses are formulated that may be tested by new data.

Origins of the Cultural Processual Approach

The cultural processual approach can best be understood in the context of its origin and development within prehistoric archaeology and within anthropology generally. It follows several complementary culture models and research strategies. Both models and strategies reflect the two themes inherent in the very meaning of process mentioned earlier—an understanding of how cultures work synchronically and diachronically. We will trace the development of each theme before considering their synthesis in modern processual research.

The Emergence of a Synchronic Perspective

The core of the synchronic theme in processualism came from the rise in the 1930s of the idea of functionalism in anthropology. This concept provides the background for studying culture as a system of interrelated parts. From a functional view, each aspect of culture—whether residence rules, pottery production, religious organization, or anything else—is a useful and well-integrated part of the whole and cannot be understood except as part of the overall system.

The Functional Model of Culture Although the normative view of culture is usually associated with American (Boasian) anthropology, the **functional concept** developed primarily within French and British social anthropology, under the name of *functionalism*. Although the development of the traditional functional school involves the important roles of such scholars as Emile Durkheim and A. R. Radcliffe-Brown, we shall briefly outline one of the most refined versions of this concept—that presented by Bronislaw Malinowski (Fig. 3.7).

Functional relationships within culture: Bronislaw Malinowski's view

Culture, for Malinowski, consists of "inherited artifacts, goods, technical processes, ideas, habits, and values." In literal definition, this idea is not too different from other definitions of culture. But Malinowski goes further, asserting that each cultural whole consists of a set of inseparably interrelated aspects, each serving the dual function of maintaining the whole and of fulfilling the society's (and the individual's) basic needs for survival. More specifically, Malinowski begins with a list of universal biological needs—metabolism, reproduction, health, and so on. Culture, then, is fundamentally the human response to fulfill these basic needs, permitting both the individual and the society *physically* to survive. At the same time, for humans as *social* beings to survive, a secondary set of "derived" needs must be met, such as the need for social control (through

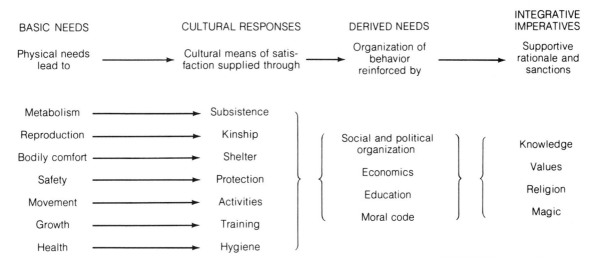

BASIC NEEDS	CULTURAL RESPONSES	DERIVED NEEDS	INTEGRATIVE IMPERATIVES
Physical needs lead to	Cultural means of satis-faction supplied through	Organization of behavior reinforced by	Supportive rationale and sanctions

Metabolism ⟶ Subsistence

Reproduction ⟶ Kinship

Bodily comfort ⟶ Shelter

Safety ⟶ Protection

Movement ⟶ Activities

Growth ⟶ Training

Health ⟶ Hygiene

Social and political organization

Economics

Education

Moral code

Knowledge

Values

Religion

Magic

FIGURE 3.7 A functional view of culture as presented by Bronislaw Malinowski.

law) and for education. A third level of needs, which Malinowski calls "integrative," involves the symbols—values, art, religion, and so on—by which the above solutions could be codified and communicated. The forms of a given culture can be understood as the totality of that culture's particular solutions to the hierarchy of needs. These solutions are interrelated, so that the proper functioning of each aspect (the family, economic activities, magic, and so on) is dependent on and contributes to the functioning of all other aspects. This network of relationships constitutes the structure of the society or culture.

In this way, according to the functionalist view, cultural systems provide for the various needs of the members of society both individually and collectively. Each component of the cultural system has a *function* (its contribution to the maintenance of the system) and is related to the remainder of the system through a *structure* (network of relationships).

We can illustrate this view of culture by returning to the example discussed previously. Instead of viewing residence choices of newly married couples within a normative range of behavior, the functional approach examines the relationship of this trait to other aspects of the society (structure) and its consequences within the total cultural system (function). Thus, a particular pattern of residence (such as living with the bride's family) may be linked directly to other traits (such as marriage patterns, power and authority figures, inheritance, and parent–child relationships). Furthermore, this residence pattern may contribute to the continuity of economic and political responsibilities held by women (since daughters continue to reside with their mothers after marriage), thus maintaining social stability and minimizing disruption between female generations. Residence patterning does not affect the survival of the society directly (as do most technological aspects of culture), but it has an indirect role in

Residence rules viewed via functional relationships

maintaining the social system by facilitating the orderly transferral of responsibility and authority between generations, reducing tension and conflict, and providing the circumstances for effective cooperation and interaction in the residence group.

The functional approach provides a synchronic view of culture; it tends to picture society as a constantly adjusting, yet stable, internally regulated system. With a functional approach, each archaeological trait can be seen, not in isolation, but as part of a network of interrelated traits, each with functions contributing to the maintenance of a larger system.

Although functionalism as such never gained widespread application in prehistoric archaeology, its counterpart has been the incorporation within archaeology of **general systems theory,** a theory for describing and interpreting the "behavior" of all kinds of systems, including living organisms, digital computers, and cultures. As we shall see, cultural ecological models also view culture as a constantly adjusting, stabilizing system. The principal difference is that cultural ecology regards cultural systems as being externally regulated by means of their adaptation to their environment.

Functionalism in archaeology: Lewis Binford's scheme

A later refinement of the functional approach for archaeology was made by Lewis Binford, who classified archaeological materials into three categories according to function. **Technofacts** are those artifacts that function directly to maintain the survival of society by providing food, shelter, and defense. **Sociofacts** function to maintain social order and integration. **Ideofacts** function to furnish psychological security, well-being, and explanations for the unknown.

This is not to say that each artifact must be assigned to only a single category or that each artifact has only a single function. On the contrary, each artifact will have at least one function, but many will have more than one. For instance, one of the most common archaeological materials, pottery, can obviously be assigned to the category of technofact. Most pottery vessels function directly for the acquisition, transport, storage, or preparation of food or water. Thus, many characteristics of pottery (the kind of clay used, the way it is made, its shape and size, and so on) are directly related to or dependent upon its function as a part of the food acquisition system. However, the same vessel may also have attributes that relate to social functions and may thus be a sociofact. For example, the vessel's decoration may signify social status or affiliation with specialized groups such as a family or lineage. These characteristics of a pottery vessel function as symbols of membership and social solidarity. Other attributes, such as special shapes and decorative traits, may have ideological functions, making the vessel an ideofact as well.

Multiple functions of artifacts: The Yir Yoront of Australia

A striking ethnographic example of the multiplicity of functions served by some artifacts is provided in a description by Lauriston Sharp of the Yir Yoront Aborigines of Australia. A group of missionaries contacted the Yir Yoront and, full of the best intentions, started distributing abundant steel axes to replace the less efficient, less numerous stone axes. What the missionaries did not realize was that their action affected more than the technological realm: The stone axes also served as sociofacts and ideofacts for the Yir Yoront. As sociofacts they symbolized the social order, for the owners were all senior men; women and junior men had to defer to the authority of these men every time they needed to borrow an axe. Trade in stone axes was also an important reason for annual gatherings of multiple Yir Yoront bands. As ideofacts, the stone axes were sacred possessions with clear symbolic status in the traditional cosmology. The unrestricted introduction of steel axes disrupted the social order, both by threatening the established patterns of dependence and subordination and by decreasing interest in and need for annual gatherings. It also undermined the traditional belief system by forcing the Yir Yoront to question a cosmology that could not easily account for the steel tools. Even the technological realm had not been clearly "improved": Sharp suspects that whatever time was saved may have been used for extra sleep! In his words, "the steel axe . . . is not only replacing the stone axe physically, but is hacking at the supports of the entire cultural system." Although the missionaries had hoped to "protect" the Yir Yoront from the intrusion of Western society, their misunderstanding of the many roles of the stone axe had effects rather opposite to their goals.

Using an approach of this kind, a study of the patterns of the various characteristics of artifacts and of their interrelationships as technofacts, sociofacts, and ideofacts may lead to conclusions not only about ancient **technology** (kinds of food used, methods of acquisition, transportation, and preparation, and so on) but also about the social organization and the belief system. Furthermore, changes in the various kinds of attributes may come about independently. That is, changes in the attributes that reflect use as sociofacts or ideofacts probably result from processes different from those that affect technofacts. Therefore, changes in social institutions, status relationships, or even belief systems might result in changes in certain attributes of pottery without affecting other attributes, which derive from the function of the vessels as technofacts.

The foregoing theoretical contributions have become integrated in the current widespread concept of culture as a **system**—a complex entity composed of interrelated parts, in which the relationships among components are as important as the components themselves. Such a concept is static but potentially dynamic. The crucial concept that provided the dynamic quality to the functional-systemic view of culture was **cultural ecology.** Thus, we can view the development of cultural ecology in anthropology and archaeology as the critical transition between the synchronic and diachronic themes within the cultural processual approach.

The Emergence of Cultural Ecology

An American anthropologist, Julian H. Steward (1902–1972), is considered the father of cultural ecology (Fig. 3.8). As we have seen in Chapter 1, Steward conducted ethnographic studies in the Great Basin of the American West. From this and other ethnographic data concerning the

FIGURE 3.8 Julian Steward in 1919. (Courtesy of Thomas J. Riley and the Department of Anthropology, University of Illinois.)

Cultural ecology: Steward's model

adaptations of specific societies to specific environments, he refined a concept of cultural ecology that focused on the individual society's total adaptation to and transformation of its **environment** (see below). The primary agency of adaptation, as responses to environment, is seen in what Steward called the *culture core*—basically, the technology defined as that aspect of culture that interacts directly with its surroundings. This perspective attributes the observable regularities in the panorama of human societies to the finite number of environmental conditions under which they exist and the limited number of cultural responses or adaptations possible within each kind of environment. That is, people in similar environments tend to solve their problems by adapting in similar ways. Certain environments provide more potential or flexibility for successful human exploitation than do others, but the cultural response is neither predetermined nor dictated by a particular environment: A range of adaptive choices is open to any given society.

The Ecological Model of Culture   The ecological model is based on the adaptive aspects of culture. It views culture, and especially technology, as the primary means by which human societies adapt (with varying degrees of efficiency) to their environment. Culture change—and, ultimately, **cultural evolution**—stems from changes within this adaptive relationship between culture and environment. For instance, if the environment changes, the technology will make an adaptive adjustment, leading in turn to further changes in the total cultural system, as components of both the organizational and the ideational aspects adjust to the technological change.

This model is analogous to biological evolution, which views each species as adapting to a particular set of conditions that defines its environment. The analogy generally holds when we turn to the relationship of human societies with their environment, but some significant differences must also be considered. The environment that animal species adapt to consists of two components: the **physical environment** (geography, climate, and so on) and the **biological environment** (other species of plant and animal life). Human societies adapt to these components of the environment, but they must also adapt to a third component—the **cultural environment** (neighboring groups or societies). More important, in strictly biological evolution the mechanism responsible for transmission of physical or behavioral traits within a species is genetic inheritance, from parent to offspring. Therefore, the ability of a species to respond or adapt biologically to environmental change is, in the short run, relatively limited and inflexible. As a result, the pace of adaptive change—**evolution**—is limited by the length of a generation. This means that biological evolution can be perceived only over a span of multiple generations.

Human societies, however, have an additional mechanism for variation that is not genetically controlled: culture. To a large degree, human behavior is determined by culture (see the discussion of the normative model of culture on p. 66). And because culture is transmitted socially—that is, we learn it—changes need not wait for a new generation before they spread.

As a result, cultural evolution is often detectable over short periods of time. This does not mean that all cultures are constantly undergoing rapid and dramatic changes. The point is simply that culture has the *potential* for speedy and flexible response if a change in the environment occurs.

It must be stressed that cultural ecology does not imply that the environment *determines* the nature of culture. On the contrary, through the course of cultural evolution even the physical and biological components of the environment have become increasingly determined by human culture. We need only look at our own environment to see the changes our culture has made—altering the landscape and the very composition of the water we drink, the food we eat, and the air we breathe.

Every human society exploits and changes its environment in some way. And each society's technology basically determines which portions of the total environment will be utilized. For example, the Great Plains region of the United States has supported a succession of different cultures, each exploiting a different aspect of its resources. The earliest hunters and gatherers on the plains were limited in their mobility; they exploited a wide variety of subsistence alternatives (hunting small game, occasionally hunting large game, gathering wild plant foods, and so on) in small, localized groups. A dramatic change in the biological environment—the arrival of herds of horses introduced by the Spanish—presented a new subsistence choice. Some groups adapted to the changed environment by creating a new technology focused on the horse; they gained an increased mobility that enabled them to specialize in the hunting of large game animals (bison). But, because of their specializations, these same groups proved vulnerable to outside invaders who had a different technology. That technology included the repeating rifle, which was used to decimate the herds of bison and destroy the subsistence base of the mobile plains societies. The same technology included the plow, which allowed the invading settlers to harness a previously unexploited portion of the environment for extensive agriculture. Of course, in the 20th century a still newer technology has led to the exploitation of yet another portion of this same environment—the vast deposits of fossil fuel located beneath the surface of the plains.

The environment has not determined each of these successive ways of life it has supported; it has merely provided the opportunities for human technological exploitation. Each technology exploits a different niche in the environment, thereby redefining the effective environment. And, since each technology is different, the organizational and ideological aspects of each culture, which follow the technological adaptation, will obviously be unique.

Although the choices each environment offers to human exploitation are not preordained, some environments offer more alternatives—and more lucrative alternatives—than others. In another parallel with biological evolution, societies that are less specialized in their environmental adaptations tend to be less vulnerable to changes in their environment than more specialized societies. Just as the 19th-century Plains Indians were

Cultural ecology: Successive adaptations in the Great Plains

vulnerable because of their heavy dependence on bison, so the 20th-century urban, industrialized Americans are vulnerable because of their dependence on fossil fuels. When environmental conditions change, societies either change their cultural adaptations or face extinction.

But we must remember that not all culture change results from environmental change. And environmental change can stem from specific shifts in the physical, biological, or cultural realms. The arrival of the horse altered the biological environment of the plains. But the changes stemming from use of plow agriculture resulted from a technological innovation, not from a shift in the environment. This technological change altered the effective environment of the Great Plains. The link between culture and environment goes two ways: a change in either one will cause a change in the other.

Archaeologists who use the ecological model of culture seek to identify as many components as possible of the ancient interactive system. It is usually possible to distinguish among the physical, biological, and cultural aspects of ancient environments and to identify segments of the technology adapted to each; for instance, classes of technofacts such as digging sticks and baskets relate to exploitation of plant life. It may be possible to identify at least some of the sociofacts or ideofacts associated with each of these technofacts. For example, digging sticks and baskets may be found associated with individual houses but in an area separate from artifacts that represent hunting activities. This situation enables the archaeologist to reconstruct at least a portion of an ancient cultural system. The division just described might be interpreted as reflecting an ancient division of labor and suggesting what parts of the environment were exploited by each side.

If the system can be reconstructed, and if a change in one of its components can be identified, then the consequences of that change for other components can be traced. For instance, the introduction of metal tips for digging sticks may lead to increased horticultural production, a decrease in reliance upon food gathering, and perhaps a more concentrated grouping of houses. This innovation might also involve shifts in the organizational system, beginning with changes for the people using the digging sticks, and then perhaps modifications of residence rules and kinship. Eventually, changes in the belief system could follow, such as increased importance of agricultural deities. By viewing the archaeological record from this perspective, the archaeologist begins to move to a diachronic perspective from a well-established synchronic baseline. Thus, cultural ecology provides a way to discover the cause and consequences of change instead of merely describing the changes in form (new artifacts, new housing patterns, and so on) and shifts in proportions of various artifacts. In other words, rather than merely describing what has changed, the archaeologist begins to unravel the process of change.

In this way, cultural ecology is a bridge between synchronic and diachronic aspects of the processual approach. Julian Steward, in fact, is properly considered one of the founders of the theory of multilinear evolution.

Cultural ecology shows us that cultural systems, as in biology, evolve not as part of a single uniform sequence. Rather, cultural evolution is a many-channeled process, governed by each society's ecological adaptation. Specific societies adjust and change according to their own cultural and environmental circumstances.

The Emergence of a Diachronic Perspective

The diachronic theme in processual archaeology can be traced to the rise of cultural anthropology in the late 19th century, for, as we mentioned in Chapter 2, anthropology at that time was characterized by emphasis on the idea of cultural evolution. But the 19th-century concept of cultural evolution, usually labeled *unilinear*, treated all human societies, past and present, as part of a single evolutionary line. The position of a society along this line was measured by its progress toward a "higher" society, as measured principally by development of an increasingly complex technology. As we have seen earlier, in the United States, most anthropologists rejected the idea of unilinear evolution early in the 20th century. European anthropologists and archaeologists, however, along with a few hardy American scholars, endeavored throughout the 20th century to modify and redefine the theory of cultural evolution in light of the accumulated criticism and conflicting data that had made the old, oversimplified, unilinear concept untenable.

An exception to this trend may be seen in countries such as the People's Republic of China. In line with political ideological considerations, archaeology in some countries has continued to use unilinear cultural evolution as an interpretive base, since the founders of modern Communism, Karl Marx and Friedrich Engels, accepted many of the tenets of 19th-century unilinear theory, especially as set forth in the works of Lewis Henry Morgan.

In the West, however, a new concept of cultural evolution eventually emerged, **multilinear cultural evolution.** This concept also has strong roots in Marx and Engels, as modified by the neo-Marxist school seeking to apply the 19th-century Marxist ideas to a more contemporary setting of today's world. Thus, instead of holding to the original 19th-century concepts of cultural evolution accepted by Marx and Engels, the multilinear concept has provided a viable theory of cultural dynamics that has been much more successful in accounting for long-term cultural change.

There are two principal anthropological underpinnings to multilinear cultural evolution, the cultural ecological and cultural materialist models of culture. We have already examined the first of these; it is now time to look at the second.

The Cultural Materialist Model of Culture   Within cultural anthropology, cultural materialism has been a strong force behind the application of objective scientific methods to the study of human societies. According to this model, the realm of study is defined as observable human behavior,

in contrast to human thought, which cannot be directly observed but only inferred indirectly from behavior. Like the functionalism of Malinowski, cultural materialism holds that there are biological and psychological needs common to all humans, such as hunger, sex, protection, and so on. But unlike their role in functionalism, for cultural materialists these shared needs provide a common cross-cultural means for measuring input, output, costs, benefits, and other measures of a given society's adaptation and efficiency. Human needs are satisfied most directly by the core components of culture, the technological, economic, and demographic factors that cultural materialists call the *infrastructure* (we prefer the term *technology* for these factors). The infrastructure, especially as observed in technology, is the focus of change as it responds to changing human needs and environmental conditions, and acts to optimize benefit versus cost for the society. It also transmits change to the rest of the system, the social, political, and ideological subsystems.

While cultural materialism derives its main inspiration from the tenets of neo-Marxist theory, two historical figures stand out as critical to its application in archaeology. One, V. Gordon Childe (Fig. 3.9), was himself an archaeologist. The other was an important cultural anthropologist, Leslie White.

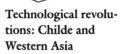

Technological revolutions: Childe and Western Asia

One of the most influential scholars of the early 20th century was V. Gordon Childe (1892–1957). Childe was born in Australia and educated in England; he devoted most of his archaeological career to understanding cultural development, especially that in the "cradle of civilization," Western Asia. His formulation of cultural evolution kept technology as the prime causal factor, holding that human societies evolved through the invention of new technological means for more efficient use of the environment. To Childe, some of these technological innovations were truly revolutionary, rapidly and radically transforming entire cultures. The first of these profound advances, the agricultural revolution, transformed wandering hunting and gathering societies into communities of settled farmers. The second was the urban revolution that gave rise to the earliest civilizations. The concept that revolutionary technological change was the **prime mover** in cultural evolution was not in itself a departure from the evolutionary ideas of the 19th century. However, after viewing the sum of the available archaeological evidence, Childe concluded that the specific courses followed by different societies were distinct. Although there were parallels between cases, no single developmental trajectory could describe cultural evolution in detail.

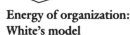

Energy of organization: White's model

Leslie White (1900–1975) was a major figure in American anthropology, defending a modified version of general cultural evolution at a time when this was clearly not in vogue. While recognizing the problems in the 19th-century version of unilinear cultural evolution, White argued that broad, general stages could be defined to describe the overall trajectory of known cultural evolution. White's definition of culture as "man's extrasomatic (nonbiological) adaptation" has been widely adopted by archaeologists studying cultural process, as has his return to technological forms as

FIGURE 3.9 V. Gordon Childe stands beside a 4500-year-old stone dwelling at Skara Brae, in Scotland's Orkney Islands, where he had directed excavations in the late 1920s. (Copyright: Royal Commission on the Ancient and Historical Monuments of Scotland.)

the primary data sources for understanding cultural adaptation. The developmental model worked out by White and his students focuses on increases in efficiency in harnessing energy and organizing human labor as the key to evolutionary change in human society. Critical changes occurred when, for example, people harnessed animals to pull plows or serve as beasts of burden, allowing individual humans to conduct a greater range of tasks, with greater output volume, and to complete the work in less time. Another transition took place when inanimate power sources, from water (as in mills) to electricity, oil, or the sun, were put under human control and use.

Multilinear Cultural Evolution The theory of multilinear cultural evolution has taken a number of specific forms, but as in Childe's and White's theories, most multilinear views portray technology as the primary factor in change, determining to varying degrees the nature and relative rapidity of cultural evolution. Different versions of the theory also vary in the degree to which they consider the roles of the other two aspects of culture, the social-organizational and the ideational factors that may be involved in culture change, although all usually attempt to demonstrate the links between these last two components and technology.

When viewed over the long term, each individual culture manifests change resulting from the accumulation of its specific behavioral adaptive responses. This is the process of adaptation and change already referred to as cultural evolution. Unlike 19th-century unilinear evolutionary theorists, however, the proponents of current cultural evolutionary theory do not rely on speculation or implied causes for evolution. Instead, the contemporary concept of cultural evolution is based on objective data, gathered and tested (for the most part) by the scientific method. Most important, the modern evolutionary concept is *multilinear:* As Julian Steward originally emphasized, this view portrays each society as pursuing an individual evolutionary career rather than changing in a predestined, unilinear course. Although the origins of cultural evolution, as applied by archaeologists, lie in the writings of 19th-century social evolutionists such as Lewis Henry Morgan, the model has been refined for its modern applications. For example, documentation from individual anthropological studies has replaced the pure speculation that marred the 19th-century theory.

The multilinear evolutionary model: Stability vs. growth in cultural development

Multilinear evolutionary theory, as used by some archaeologists, is based on cultural ecology and cultural materialism insofar as it assumes that each human society adapts to its environment primarily through its technology and secondarily through its organizational and ideational subsystems. But the evolutionary model goes beyond considering the particular instances of adaptation and change stressed by the ecological model; it emphasizes the degree of success or efficiency each system manifests in its development, consistent with the tenets of cultural materialism. According to the theory, the efficiency of cultural development can be measured by two consequences over time: social *survival* and *growth.* A particular society may be well adapted to its environment so that it achieves a stable balance or *equilibrium.* In this case, adaptation involves refinements in the existing technology, as well as in the organizational and ideational aspects of culture, but no profound change in the overall culture. In such cases, survival is the measure of adaptation efficiency. Societies such as that of the Inuit (Eskimo) have reached this kind of stability, which results in survival without growth. Human societies in many other environments have achieved similarly stable adaptations. This fact suggests that there are some optimum organizational and ideational systems for given technologies within certain environments.

In other cases, human societies become involved in growth cycles. Changes originating either from the environment or from within the society trigger changes in the technological system (and, in some cases, in the organizational and ideational systems as well). If these technological changes result in increases in food production, and if the organizational and ideational changes allow for increases in population size, a process of growth may begin. Continued growth will eventually place new strains upon the technology (amount of food produced), the organization (control of people), and the ideology (belief system). This pressure may trigger further changes in the society—technological innovations to increase food production further or new forms of social and political organization to mobilize the population. At some point, every society reaches its limit of growth; every specific environment and particular technology has an upper limit on the number of people it can support.

Obviously, some environments have greater potential and some technologies are more efficient in this growth process than others. Fertile temperate zones populated by peoples who practice plow agriculture can produce more food and thereby support larger populations than desert zones occupied by hunters and gatherers. In the same way, certain organizational systems are more efficient than others at mobilizing and harnessing human resources that may be essential to an expanding society. Specialized labor under centralized control is generally more efficient than nonspecialized individual enterprise. Finally, ideational systems may also differ in the degree of efficiency they produce. In a growth situation, a belief system that provides sanctions for centralized organization and gives its adherents security and confidence will have an advantage over a system without clear-cut sanctions or one that instills fear and insecurity in the population.

Why do some societies appear to seek a stable equilibrium with their environments, while others maintain growth cycles? Under certain circumstances, adaptive changes appear to trigger "chain reaction" growth. In such cases, emphasis is placed on technological innovation leading to continual increases in food supplies and population. This growth spiral is evident in the archaeological record of the development of the world's complex civilizations in both the Old and the New Worlds.

To illustrate a sophisticated recent version of multilinear evolutionary theory, we will look briefly at *The Evolution of Human Societies,* by Allen W. Johnson and Timothy Earle. In this book, Johnson and Earle argue that the driving force behind cultural evolution is population growth within a given economic system. Such growth ultimately leads, through mechanisms like overexploitation of local natural resources, to a decline in the security and standard of living for at least some families in the population. To avoid shortages of food and other necessities, those at risk allow one or a few individuals to act on their behalf, to accomplish group economic security by means individual families could not pursue alone. These new leaders or elite regulate production and distribution, control competition over resources (such as farmland), direct communal technological developments (such as construction of an irrigation system), and engage in trade for locally scarce or absent resources (such as metals, high-quality chipping stone, or other raw materials). These key changes lead to further shifts, in the social, economic, and political systems (leaders become wealthier and more powerful, for example), as well as further population growth—which, of course, leads to a new round of changes. Johnson and Earle illustrate these spiraling changes in abundant ethnographic, historical, and archaeological case studies drawn from all over the world. Although this is certainly feasible as a hypothesis, many archaeologists wonder whether archaeological evidence is ever precise or complete enough to document the timing and scale of population growth per se, let alone to demonstrate whether population increase is the cause or the consequence of other changes being investigated.

Although at first glance Johnson and Earle's approach appears unilinear, it is fundamentally multilinear, for the authors emphasize the diversity in how specific cultures reflect the basic evolutionary spiral. In other words, there are recognizable broad regularities in cultural evolution, but there is no single or preset series of specific changes a given culture will experience. Johnson and Earle's theory is also a materialist view, in that it stresses the primary role of population growth, subsistence, and other economic systems, in the broadly parallel evolution of cultures.

Nonmaterialist emphasis: Adams compares Mesopotamia and Mesoamerica

The theme of separate but parallel cultural evolutionary paths has also been developed by archaeologists who don't base their ideas in cultural materialism. An example of this is the work of Robert M. Adams. Adams outlined specific sequences of changes and cultural developments that culminated in the emergence of complex, urban civilizations in the particular cases of Mesopotamia and Mesoamerica. In contrast to Childe, Adams argued against any single prime mover, asserting that changes in the realms of social and political organization generally took precedence in the evolution of civilization: Development of the social hierarchy and of managerial efficiency fostered changes in technological, subsistence, and ideological systems. All of these factors reinforced each other, leading to complex cultures of cities and civilization. Adams postulated a specific set of interrelated changes in social organization whose emergence could be tested by well-designed archaeological investigation.

Similar nonmaterialist approaches to cultural evolution have been explored by archaeologists such as Geoffrey Conrad and Arthur Demarest (see Chapter 16) with respect to Inka and Aztec civilizations, and Richard Blanton, Kent Flannery, and Joyce Marcus, with respect to ancient Zapotec civilization in Oaxaca, Mexico. Whereas a cultural materialist approach would identify a component such as subsistence efficiency as the crucial variable in determining the capability of a society to grow in size and complexity, the multilinear approach emphasizes the specific subsystem unique to each situation to attempt to reconstruct the process of evolution.

The range of cultures and societies that result from this multilinear evolutionary process can be classified, and the cultural classification most used today combines criteria of technological and organizational complexity to define broad evolutionary stages. This classification is discussed in detail in Chapter 17; here we wish only to make clear that this revived cultural evolutionary model does *not* imply that the societies with the most complex organization and sophisticated technological adaptation represent the inevitable end product of cultural evolution. On the contrary, although multilinear evolution *may* lead to increasing complexity, this is only one general pattern of cultural change. Other evolutionary routes may lead to stability—or no change—and still others may result in decreasing complexity and even extinction.

The Emergence of Cultural Processual Research

The methodology of the cultural processual approach has had a somewhat separate developmental career. The overall rationale of the original unilinear evolutionary theory involved a rather loose research strategy. But one of the greatest accomplishments of cultural processual archaeology has been the use of a rigorous, scientific methodology in archaeological research. The application of such a formal methodology had its roots in the first critiques of the approaches associated with culture history.

In 1938, Julian Steward and Frank M. Setzler took culture historical archaeologists to task for placing such a heavy emphasis on description of the temporal and spatial distributions of prehistoric data. Steward and Setzler asserted that preoccupation with temporal and spatial description had become an end in itself: Once all the time–space distributions had been worked out, archaeologists would be left with nothing to do. Instead, they argued, archaeologists should be asking fundamental anthropological questions about the process of cultural change and then using archaeological data to answer such questions.

Soon thereafter, a young graduate student named Walter W. Taylor wrote a critique of the prevailing practice of the culture historical approach. This work, *A Study of Archeology,* was published in 1948; it represents the most thorough evaluation of the contributions and shortcomings of the descriptive emphasis then current in culture historical archaeology. Taylor's fundamental criticism was not directed at the goals of the culture historical approach—that is, understanding form, function, and process—for these remain valid objectives for all archaeologists. Rather, Taylor pointed out the failure of archaeologists to meet their stated goals—failure to integrate data into a picture more functionally and socially meaningful than, for example, noting artifactual similarities and differences between sites. And he found a complete lack of worthwhile effort directed at understanding how and why cultures change. As a solution, Taylor called for what he termed a **conjunctive approach,** to reveal the interrelationships of archaeological data by considering them in their original social context rather than simply as interesting but isolated material finds. By looking at functional sets of archaeological data, investigators could reconstruct the ancient activities they represented and ultimately begin to understand the processes of cultural change.

In 1962, Lewis R. Binford made the first explicit, unmistakable call for an entirely new archaeological research strategy based on a formalized methodology, with **hypothesis testing** as its central emphasis. The impact of Binford's critique of the prevailing practice of culture historical archaeology, which had changed little since Taylor's original appeal some 15 years earlier, has been profound. Whereas Taylor had been largely ignored, the work of Binford and his students has been the most important factor in the general acceptance of an explicit hypothesis-testing research method and of the cultural processual approach in general. Robert Dunnell has made the important point that culture historical archaeology did, in fact, involve hypothesis testing. The hypotheses remained implicit, however, and were essentially restricted to questions about the accuracy of time–space grids. Other topics were addressed only through speculation. With this in mind, let us now examine the cultural processual approach more closely.

Steward and Setzler's critique of archaeology

Walter Taylor's critique of archaeology

Lewis Binford's critique of archaeology

The Cultural Processual Method

The basic data-gathering procedures used in the cultural processual approach are the same as those used for the culture historical approach, but the orientation of the research is critically different: The strategy and research questions are formally defined, and the latter explicitly include questions of the sort Taylor, Steward, Setzler, and other critics had urged archaeologists to ask. In practice, this means that research begins with the formulation of propositions to be tested about ancient adaptation and change, and the definition of relevant data—the kinds of data that provide appropriate tests for the propositions (Fig. 3.10). As we have noted, in many cases, previous culture historical reconstructions and speculations are the source for propositions to be tested.

The Hypothetico-Deductive Method The label *hypothetico-deductive* refers to a specific, formal scientific method based on the philosophy that there is a real world composed of observable phenomena that behave in an orderly manner. By observation, formulation of hypotheses, and testing of those hypotheses, one can explain how the world works.

The testing of hypotheses in archaeology, as in any scientific discipline, follows an explicit, fully documented procedure. In many sciences, from physics to psychology, hypotheses are tested by a repeatable *experiment*. For example, one could hypothesize that the weight of the earth's atmosphere—atmospheric pressure—supports the column of mercury in a barometer. Any change in atmospheric pressure should change the height of the column supported. One such change is produced by variation in weather conditions; another, if the hypothesis is true, should result from variation in altitude. That is, much more atmosphere is located above a barometer at sea level than at, say, 5000 feet. If a barometer is moved from sea level to 5000 feet above sea level, the reduction in pressure should lead to an increase in the column's height. An experiment to test this hypothesis would involve moving one barometer to a new altitude while a second remained at the first altitude as a check against change in weather conditions. This experiment is controlled, in that it rules out interference by other factors (in this case, weather). It is also repeatable: It can be performed any number of times.

This example helps highlight a fundamental distinction raised in Chapter 1 between the *physical* and the *historical* sciences (including evolutionary biology, geology, and archaeology). In the words of Stephen Jay Gould, "historical sciences are different, not lesser. Their methods are comparative, not always experimental; they explain, but do not usually try to predict; they recognize the irreducible quirkiness that history entails" (1985:18).

As a historical science, archaeology cannot rely on controlled, repeatable experiments to test hypotheses. The archaeological record already exists, and, except through computer simulation and specific limited replications (discussed in Chapter 13), archaeologists cannot manipulate vari-

The distinction between physical and historical sciences: Gould

FIGURE 3.10 An archaeologist records ancient architectural remains at Broken K Pueblo as part of James Hill's research project, an important early application of the cultural processual method. (Courtesy of James N. Hill.)

ables or create special situations to test hypotheses. They can, however, provide rigorous tests by explicitly and clearly stating the conditions and expectations of their hypotheses and by adhering to certain principles governing nonexperimental research.

The testing procedure for archaeological hypotheses actually begins in the research formulation stage (see Chapter 5), with the formulation of multiple hypotheses that make mutually exclusive predictions about the data. The use of **multiple working hypotheses** means that as many explanatory alternatives as possible are considered. This minimizes the opportunity for explanatory bias on the part of the investigator and maximizes the chance of finding the best available explanation.

For example, in studying the island of Cozumel, off the coast of the Yucatán peninsula, Jeremy Sabloff and William Rathje postulated on documentary grounds that the island had served as an ancient Maya port-of-trade, where exchange was conducted on a large scale (Fig. 3.11). To investigate the exchange system specifically, they outlined the kinds of facilities they expected, such as warehouses, and even postulated the artifact style variability they would expect to find, assuming different sets of ancient political conditions. If the port had been controlled by a single political authority, for example, the goods should show a preponderance of one style; if the place had been a free port, with free exchange protected by mutual agreement of trading parties, the styles found in goods exchanged should show more diversity and closer to equal numerical representation. These predictions (called *test implications*) are based on logical expectations, and exemplify the crux of the hypothetico-deductive method

Multiple working hypotheses: Cozumel Island, Mexico

FIGURE 3.11 Working on the Caribbean coast of Mexico's Yucatán peninsula, archaeologists Sabloff and Rathje sought to test the hypothesis that the Island of Cozumel had been an ancient Maya port-of-trade. Here two project members excavate a small coastal shrine. (Courtesy of the Cozumel Archaeological Project.)

in cultural processual archaeology. That is, archaeologists frame explicit hypotheses about social, economic, and political aspects of ancient society, and then specify the data whose discovery will distinguish which hypotheses best fit the actual record of the past.

When the hypotheses are set forth and the relevant data assembled, the archaeologist checks the observed data against what was expected. The latter process usually begins with the test of *compatibility:* Do the data agree or conflict with the expectations of a given hypothesis? In many cases, the compatibility test eliminates all but one hypothesis, which is advanced as the best available explanation. In other instances, however, several hypotheses may survive this test, and other criteria must be used to decide among them.

If two hypotheses account equally well for the observed data, other **hypothesis-testing criteria** can be applied to distinguish between them. The principle of *parsimony,* or Occam's razor, gives preference to the most economical, least complex explanation. A hypothesis that requires a complicated combination of circumstances is less likely to be accurate than one requiring only a few conditions. (Note that this principle can be used *only* to choose between explanations that otherwise account for the data equally well.) The criterion of *completeness* is also important: The greater the amount of detailed observed data a given hypothesis accounts for, the stronger the evidence in favor of that explanation. Finally, the criterion of *symmetry* directs selection of the most internally unified, well-articulated hypothesis.

As we have seen, these criteria are applied with the goal of invalidating all but one hypothesis. The surviving hypothesis may then be advanced, not as proved, but as the best possible explanation given the present state of knowledge. Scientists assume that contemporary explanations will eventually be modified or completely replaced, as new implications of them are tested by other data. It is also possible that the data base currently available is not complete enough to allow the elimination of all but one hypothesis; two or more may survive all tests. In such cases, both survivors are retained, in the expectation that subsequent research may provide new data that will isolate the best explanation.

POSTPROCESSUAL ARCHAEOLOGY

Postprocessualism is the third and most recent of the developments we discuss. As its name suggests, this approach (really a set of loosely related approaches) has been shaped largely as a reaction against both culture history and cultural process, and primarily the latter. Just as some cultural processualists argued that culture history was invalid, so some postprocessualists contend that all earlier approaches to archaeology are invalid, because of the biases of their practitioners (see Archaeology and Science in Chapter 1). We take the position that just as processualism has proven to complement rather than replace culture history, so postprocessualism will also add balance rather than replace its antecedents. In many ways, we find the term *postprocessualism* unfortunate, since it emphasizes negative reaction over positive contribution; because it has gained widespread acceptance, however, we will use it here.

FIGURE 3.12 Ian Hodder teaching at Cambridge. (Courtesy of Ian Hodder.)

Ian Hodder's critique of archaeology

In what ways is postprocessualism a reaction to its predecessors? Ian Hodder (Fig. 3.12), for example, one of postprocessualism's chief advocates, was originally trained in processual archaeology. He became dissatisfied, however, with what he perceived as the shortcomings of that school, especially its inability to deal with the roles symbols play in people's lives. Whereas processual archaeologists treat culture as adaptation and portray culture change as response to shifts in one or another aspect of the environment, Hodder and some of his colleagues began to argue for a more humanistic approach that would recognize the primacy of worldview in guiding people's lives. These archaeologists contend that forms and changes in behavior—and in its material expression, through pottery styles, burial practices, house form, or whatever—can be understood only in the context of the particular set of cultural values, attitudes, and other beliefs that give the world meaning. (Indeed, Hodder uses the term *contextual archaeology* as a label for the variant of postprocessualism he finds most intellectually promising.) In the view of postprocessualists, then, behavior is to be understood as meaningfully constituted and that meaning as expressed through symbols. Rather than being secondary or derivative aspects of culture, symbols and their meaning are portrayed as primary and determinative. Since the early 1980s, Hodder and a growing number of colleagues have worked to develop archaeology's capacity to reveal the way in which ancient lives were meaningfully constituted.

More broadly, we see four ways in which postprocessualism complements both culture history and cultural process. First, believing that all previous cultural models (normative, ecological, and evolutionary) present people as passive, postprocessual archaeologists have called for a more active or dynamic model of culture. As already noted, previously existing models emphasized nonhuman factors, such as fixed "rules" of behavior or the environment or prime movers, as determining how societies operate and change. Instead, postprocessualists focus on human factors, on our unique ability to think and to create and modify idea systems, as the source of how societies operate and change. Second, postprocessual archaeologists perceive culture historians and processualists as dealing with time in large undivided blocks, often many centuries long. Here, too, the response has been to take a more dynamic view, to treat time in much smaller segments, more like the continuous flow in which people actually live their lives. As viewed by postprocessualists, culture is constantly being adjusted and reinterpreted with the flow of time. Third, whereas both culture history and cultural process are concerned with collective behavior at the level of entire past societies, postprocessualists attempt to get at the smallest-scale behaviors, the components of past societies such as those of the individual, family, or ethnic groups. (In some ways, this importance of individual decisions hearkens back to Stephen Jay Gould's comment on the "quirkiness" of history.) And fourth, whereas culture history and cultural process deal with interpretation of the archaeological record from an outsider's point of view, postprocessualists aim to achieve an insider's perspective, to infer ancient meaning, or how the people who created the material remains saw their world.

For these reasons, many argue that postprocessual archaeology is not a substitute for earlier approaches and, in fact, depends in part on prior existence of both culture historical and cultural processual reconstructions. In the first place, like cultural processual studies, postprocessual archaeology must have a culture historical foundation to provide the temporal and spatial frameworks for the past. Postprocessualists also draw on processualists' reconstructions of large-scale systems and long-term change, whether accepting them as frameworks or seeing them as interpretations to be challenged. Hodder has depicted modern archaeology as standing on two "legs," one of which is the processual approach, the other being the postprocessual (or the variant he calls "contextual") approach. The problem, as Hodder sees it, is that the processual leg has dominated the postprocessual leg, so that archaeology can achieve a balanced posture only if the postprocessual leg achieves equal strength.

Origins of Postprocessual Archaeology

Although many of its proponents view postprocessualism as a British and European response to an Americanist processual episode in the history of archaeology, the origins of postprocessual archaeology are intertwined with broader trends within social sciences and humanities in many parts of the world, including North America. The trends can be seen in part as reflecting a cycle of changing emphasis in understanding human culture, a cycle alternating between knowledge gained by formal "objective science" and that from "subjective insight" (see Chapter 1). Whereas processual archaeology clearly belongs to the formal, objective science category, postprocessual archaeology often incorporates subjective insights. For many processual archaeologists, the goal of objective science is **explanation**—the definition of functional relationships and points of change within past cultural systems. For many postprocessual archaeologists, the goal of subjective insight is understanding—determining the meaning of past events within their own cultural contexts.

Among the trends involved in the origins of postprocessual approaches, we can identify three that seem paramount. Although each has a complex history in its own right, we will mention only those characteristics that seem crucial to the emergence of postprocessual archaeology.

The first of these is the rise of *structural* and *symbolic* schools in anthropology. The former, a school once closely associated with the French scholar Claude Lévi-Strauss, holds that cultures are systems of symbols in highly structured relations. In these systems, different entities can substitute symbolically and stand for their structural equivalents. For example, Robert McGhee has outlined a structured series of symbolic equivalences in Thule culture, a prehistoric culture ancestral to the Inuit (Eskimo) in Canada. McGhee noted that Thule arrowheads were consistently made of antler, whereas other weapons had been made from ivory. There seemed to be no technological reason why such a pronounced distinction should exist. McGhee therefore decided to look further at the distribution of raw materials, implements into which they were made, and the activities for which those implements were used. What he found was a set of structured relationships linking ivory (derived from sea mammals), sea animals (hunted with harpoons), and women (for whose possessions ivory was consistently used), on the one hand, and on the other, linking antler (derived from a land mammal), land animals (hunted with arrows), and men. Each of these and other items in the linked series had a clear counterpart in the other set—women with men, sea animals with those of the land, ivory with antler—and all these oppositions accorded with recorded Inuit worldview and belief structure. In fact, this example illustrates *structural archaeology,* a specific and early form of postprocessual archaeology, whose proponents stress synchronic reconstructions of past symbolic relations. Symbolic anthropology, as well as its counterpart expressions in archaeology, partially embraces structural approaches. They go beyond structural relationships, however, to elucidate in more varied ways the actual meanings and behavioral implications assigned to interrelated symbols in specific cultures.

A second and related development important to postprocessual archaeology is the rise of Critical Theory and parallel critiques of science, outlined in Chapter 1. Key to this argument is that no science is objective and

Structured meaning in the Canadian arctic: McGhee's analysis of Thule artifacts

that events and meanings can be understood in multiple ways. Such a view is obviously congruent with postprocessualists' recognition of the myriad interpretations of the universe offered in the worldviews of different cultures.

A third trend we would cite is an outgrowth of systems analyses in archaeology, as most closely associated with multilinear evolutionary models (see above and Chapter 17). In applying systems models to archaeological data, archaeologists such as Kent Flannery and Joyce Marcus have emphasized the importance of ideological components in specific past cultural systems. By using data from the prehistory of the valley of Oaxaca, Mexico, in combination with ethnohistoric information about the religious beliefs of the native Zapotec peoples of Oaxaca, Flannery and Marcus have shown how incorporating religious and other ideological factors contributes to a far more complete understanding of ancient Oaxacan societies, especially in maintaining and modifying such systems through time.

In all three areas just listed, the role of meaning is central. In archaeology, postprocessualism has brought the issue of determining meaning to the forefront (the fourth goal of archaeology, considered in Chapter 1). This issue, which has been debated within the parent discipline of anthropology for several decades, centers on the distinction between **etic** and **emic** points of view in describing cultural systems.

The term *etic* comes from *phonetic*—a linguistic term referring to the total inventory of sounds available for use in human language. In anthropology, then, "etic" refers to the perspective of the observer, the anthropologist who describes the culture being studied in reference to cultures worldwide. The contrasting perspective is *emic,* from *phonemic*—a linguistic term referring to the specific inventory of sounds used by a particular human language (for example, a phonemic contrast between English and Spanish is that English speakers distinguish between the sounds we write as *b* and *v,* whereas Spanish speakers do not). In anthropology, "emic" refers to the perspective of the culture being studied, an internal, culture-specific point of view.

In both culture historical and cultural processual approaches, the interpretation of the archaeological record is considered on an etic basis—it is determined by the observer (the archaeologist) from his or her point of view, and the inside view is generally regarded as impossible to discover. As we have said, however, postprocessualists assert the opposite, arguing that an emic view is more than just possible, it's necessary. These archaeologists argue that because each culture interprets the world differently, an "objective" and etic view is impossible! (We will take up this point again in Chapter 13.)

The need to consider emic meaning was only one of the perceived "flaws" of processualism that gave rise to postprocessual archaeology. Others include downplaying or ignoring ideology and the role of the individual in past cultural systems; processualism's close ties to science to the exclusion of links to history and the humanities; and the emphasis on process itself, rather than individual decisions and actions. Some of the most pointed assertions and criticisms made by postprocessualists appear to owe at least part of their fervor to a need to stake out a new position with clear-cut distinctions from that of processualism—just as the "new archaeologists" did a generation before in their reaction to culture history. We believe that although the disparities between the cultural processual and postprocessual approaches are real, they need not define mutually exclusive archaeologies; each can contribute to a richer understanding of the past.

The Cognitive Model of Culture

As we have seen, the models for culture used by culture historians and processualists emphasize, respectively, ideal norms and adaptive systems. In both cases, whether portrayed as following norms or as prospering or failing because of a system's adaptive capacity, the people practicing a culture are treated collectively and as passive participants rather than active agents. According to postprocessual archaeologists, however, this attitude misses the defining attributes of culture and humanity. For these archaeologists, the key distinction is that, unlike other living creatures, humans interpret the world around them. Postprocessualists therefore use a **cognitive model of culture,** one in which culture is the set of meanings (categories and relationships) people construct for making sense of their lives. By saying culture is constructed, postprocessualists portray people as active agents, individually reworking learned norms and traditions, reconstructing the systems of cultural meanings to fit the contexts of their own lives. In contrast to other cultural models we have discussed, the cognitive model places individual human beings as the central focus for understanding how cultures operate and change. Because culture is seen as perpetually changing, even on a short-term basis, this model of culture is diachronic, its adherents trying to address spans of time "between the moment and the long-term," which they feel earlier archaeologists have ignored.

The cognitive model incorporates notions of culture as a set of durable grammars. In many ways, such "grammars" correspond to the "systems" and "norms" used in other models of culture; this suggests there *are* aspects in common among the different models. But beyond these labels, the similarities quickly fade. In the first place, with the cognitive model, the norms do not determine human behavior. Rather, they define options available to individual members of a culture, and each person draws on and adapts those that suit his or her needs. In this way, culture is constantly in flux, and its specific forms are redefined in each situation. Second, the norm options explicitly relate to meaning. Available norms within a given culture are seen as variant expressions of deep-seated and highly structured patterns unique to that culture. Material culture is to be "read" as if it were a text, expressing those patterns.

To return to our example of how different culture models guide our view of artifacts such as pottery, culture historians see decoration on ceramics as idealized sets of styles that allow isolation of cultures in time and space. Processualists see the same decoration from a functional and evolutionary perspective, having served the ancient society as means of defining social groups and boundaries, and having changed through time in response to shifts in those boundaries. Postprocessualists, on the other hand, look at the content of the decoration and the context in which it occurs, as well as how it relates in form to other expressions within the specific culture. They attempt to decipher the message being conveyed by the choice of particular pottery styles *and* by the choice of pottery vessels as the medium for their expression.

The Emergence of Postprocessual Research

Postprocessual archaeologists seek access to meaning beyond the technological, the environmental, or even the social dimensions on which archaeologists have traditionally relied. Some of these dimensions may be more difficult to reconstruct than others, and those targeted by postprocessualists are undoubtedly the most elusive of all. As we have stressed, however, these different levels of meaning should not be seen as mutually exclusive. It should be obvious that it is important to reconstruct, and ultimately understand, as many aspects of past human behavior as possible.

Levels of meaning in Native American societies: Hall's analysis of the *calumet*

These multiple levels of meaning can be approached by examining specific artifacts and features known from the archaeological record. For example, artifacts used by native North American societies have immediate and recognizable technological functions, but have social and ideological meanings as well. Although completed before the emergence of postprocessualism, Robert Hall's analysis of these different levels of meanings, and their changes through time, shows how valuable this kind of research can be to flesh out a more complete reconstruction of past human behavior. Whereas the etic view of an implement such as the *atlatl*, or spear-thrower, portrays this as a weapon, the emic view adds important social and ideological meanings.

In North America the atlatl was ultimately replaced by a more efficient weapon, the bow and arrow, by about A.D. 500. But, as Hall points out, instead of disappearing, the ancient atlatl survived in various forms well into historical times, transformed over time into the *calumet,* or "peace pipe," to become an important social and religious symbol (Fig. 3.13). Its social function involved use as an emblem for specific groups, such as clans. Its religious meaning involved its use in rituals of peace or friendship celebrated between adversaries. In this way, a former weapon evolved into a symbol for peace used in meetings between potential enemies, much like our handshake derives from a gesture to demonstrate that no weapon is being held in the hand.

It is not surprising that historical archaeology has produced some of the best-known attempts at interpreting both ancient symbols and the cultural meaning they represent, because documents give us access into emic mean-

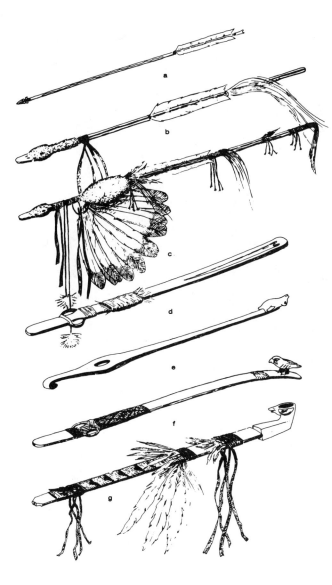

FIGURE 3.13 Historic (b–d, g) and prehistoric (e, f) materials illustrate similarities in form between spear-throwers (d, e) and *calumet* and other Native American pipes (b, c, g), as well as their co-occurrence sometimes in the same item (f). The arrow (a) is shown for scale. (After Hall, reproduced by permission of Robert L. Hall and the Society for American Archaeology from *American Antiquity* 42:4, 1977.)

ings otherwise difficult to reconstruct. In separate studies that presaged postprocessualism, folklorist Henry Glassie and archaeologist James Deetz have traced changes in form and decoration of 18th- and 19th-century Anglo-American houses, cooking and serving pots, gravestones, and other items of everyday life. What they see in these changes are trends away from communal sharing and personal involvement, toward a more individualistic and interpersonally anonymous way of life. Where people had eaten stews from a common pot, they came to use individual plates and bowls. Where houses had been asymmetrical in layout, and built to encourage entry into the living quarters (Fig. 3.14), they came to be more symmetrical and to incorporate an entry hall or foyer as a buffer, delaying or even

Levels of meaning in North American historical archaeological data: Deetz and Glassie

FIGURE 3.14 (top) The Lesser Dabney House, an 18th-century Virginia dwelling. (bottom) Plan of the same house, showing direct access into living areas from outside, without the entry hall found in most American homes today. (After Glassie 1975.)

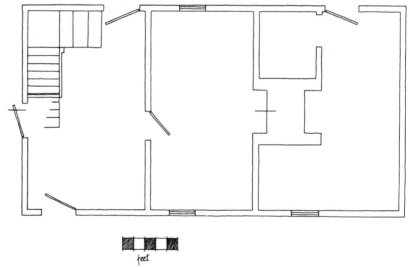

feet

preventing entry of visitors (or intruders) into the family's living space (as in most modern American houses). Where gravestones had been highly individualized, made from various colors of stone and carved to portray angels' and other faces, they became standardized, in white stone decorated with impersonal themes, such as willows or urns. Deetz and Glassie relate these trends to other cultural shifts taking place at the same time, such as the fragmenting of family togetherness through factory or similar employment, and they argue that the material remains are symbols that together eloquently describe profound changes in how the world and life were viewed.

The Postprocessual Method

We have pointed out a central tenet in postprocessual archaeology—the need to gain meaning from the archaeological record, using material culture to reconstruct an emic view of an ancient symbol system. Ethnographers may interact with living people in their attempt to gain an emic view from the study of other cultures, but discerning an emic perspective for an extinct prehistoric society is obviously much more difficult. Under some circumstances, historical or ethnohistoric documentation may provide clues, as with the calumet and early American houses. For prehistoric situations, structuralist principles based on observed regularities or patterns in artifacts may suggest potential meanings for aspects of the archaeological record, as we saw in McGhee's analysis of Thule culture.

The prevailing form for generating and testing propositions used by postprocessualists differs little in its initial stages from methods used by other archaeologists. That is, the archaeological record is examined for regularities and patterns, and these patterns are interpreted by propositions that can be tested by subsequent research. Consistency between patterning and the propositions offered to account for the patterns seems to be the hypothesis evaluation criterion cited most often by postprocessual archaeologists like Hodder.

But for many archaeologists schooled in hypothetico-deductive procedures, the fundamental question is how one can derive and test a proposition describing an ancient symbolic system that once existed in the minds of long-dead people. The reply from many postprocessualists is not to deny the difficulty of using formal scientific method to this end; indeed, some do use many of the same criteria to test propositions. Other postprocessualists conclude, however, that traditional science is simply inappropriate for the task, since it is an inherently etic perspective bound to a Western cultural tradition. Instead, in cases where archaeological data are linked to specific and known ethnic groups, an emic perspective of specific cultural values, gained from ethnographic or ethnohistorical accounts, may be used as the basis for understanding similar patterns in situations in the past. But in cases without such documented links to the past, as with much of prehistoric archaeology, an alternative procedure has been advanced by Ian Hodder to reconstruct the ancient meaning of material remains, based on the method of "reenactment of the past" proposed by the British historical philosopher R. G. Collingwood.

The reenactment method attempts to reconstruct behavior and events by placing the observer, the archaeologist in this case, in the role of an individual in the past. To do so, of course, the observer must learn as much as possible about conditions, motives, techniques, and any other available information that might have a bearing upon the situation under study.

The goal is to use these facts to determine the most consistent proposition describing the situation. Although the reenactment method does not call for the generation of multiple hypotheses, it would seem possible to evaluate a proposition derived from this method by the recognition of consistent patterns, as mentioned above. Because it is inherently speculative, however, we doubt that the reenactment method will ever become widely accepted by prehistoric archaeologists.

Because of its emphasis on the individual and the emic perspective, postprocessual archaeology has been described as particularistic, incompatible with reconstruction and interpretation beyond the confines of a particular cultural tradition. Hodder and his colleagues categorically deny this equation, asserting that postprocessual archaeology can and does contribute to general theory. At this point, it seems most likely that such contributions will concentrate on enhanced appreciation of how people have used symbols to define worlds different from our own.

THE INTERPLAY OF CULTURE HISTORY, CULTURAL PROCESS, AND POSTPROCESSUAL ARCHAEOLOGY

Archaeologists today use all three approaches in their research, but as we have recognized, some have questioned whether these are alternative or mutually exclusive ways of interpreting the past. This is a fundamental concern, since each approach has been defined as a **paradigm**—an overall strategy with its unique research methods, theory, and goals. According to this viewpoint, prehistoric archaeology consists of three research traditions, each of which has evolved under different circumstances, defining its own problems for investigation and the set of data it considers relevant to such problems.

Competition between two or more paradigms is not unique to archaeology. Instead, it is inevitable in scientific study. According to the view of one philosopher of science, Thomas Kuhn, the development of any scientific discipline through time is marked by periods of fairly tranquil acceptance of a single paradigm, interrupted by periods of conflict between the old paradigm and a newly emerged one that seeks to "revolutionize" the concepts and orientation of the discipline. This developmental view appears to explain rather neatly the turmoil of the 1960s in archaeology—the conflict between the traditional culture historical advocates and the followers of the then-emerging cultural processual approach, associated with the rise of the "new archaeology." In fact, some archaeologists, such as Mark Leone, explicitly interpreted this conflict as a case of Kuhn's thesis. A new cycle of paradigm conflict emerged a generation later in the 1980s and continues today, with the former revolutionaries, the advocates of the "new archaeology," now cast in the role of defending what had become the traditional tenets of archaeology against the "new revolutionaries" advocating postprocessual archaeology. Exactly 20 years separates the flowering of the two movements, seen in Binford's 1962 key article, "Archaeology as Anthropology," and Hodder's 1982 counterpart, "Theoretical Archaeology: A Reactionary View." One wonders what archaeologists will be saying 20 years hence.

According to Kuhn's view of the development of science, however, a new paradigm does not necessarily provide the discipline with a better understanding of its subject matter than the previous one. Thus, in Kuhn's view, science should "relinquish the notion, explicit or implicit, that changes of paradigm carry scientists . . . closer and closer to the truth."

Kuhn bases the latter point on the realization that the conflict between paradigms is not resolved solely by the cold logic of rational science but by psychological and emotional factors as well. In other words, one paradigm replaces another only when scientists, as individuals, reject the old scheme and accept the new concepts. Interestingly, Kuhn speaks of this intellectual transfer process as a "conversion experience." In the case of prehistoric archaeology, Paul Martin, a former exponent of the culture history approach, wrote a now-famous article describing his acceptance of the "new archaeology" in terms comparable to a religious conversion. As we have seen, one of the most prominent of the postprocessualists, Ian Hodder, was originally an advocate of processual archaeology. But, of course, not all the defenders of the old concepts convert to the new. Thus, according to Kuhn, full acceptance of the revolutionary view relies on the emergence of a new generation of scientists trained in the new paradigm.

Kuhn's thesis holds that scientific disciplines develop by successive replacements of paradigms but that these changes are strongly influenced by nonrational factors. The result is often the acceptance of a paradigm that is more psychologically satisfying but no better equipped than its predecessor to understand the real world. This tends to contradict the view held by many of the "new archaeologists" and postprocessualists, that their paradigms are superior to earlier ones for understanding the past. According to this position, archaeologists still pursuing earlier interpretive paths are at best outmoded, if not actually making invalid inquiries.

Science does progress through conflict between competing paradigms. Kuhn's thesis has been valuable in revealing the role of this aspect of scientific development, as well as the importance of other than strictly scientific factors in this process. Science also progresses in a cumulative sense, for rather than new paradigms always replacing old ones, they can also complement each other to produce a more complete picture. Although postprocessualists have challenged the exclusive appropriateness of the hypothetico-deductive method as a means for attaining archaeological understanding, this does not remove the scientific method generally as the foundation for archaeological research.

To the degree that each of the three approaches outlined provides reasonable and testable propositions about the past, it should be among the avenues of inquiry available in archaeology. Each asks different questions, and provides a different perspective on the past. Thus, rather than being mutually exclusive, these approaches can work together to form a coherent overall paradigm for archaeology with the aim of producing a more comprehensive view of the past.

SUMMARY

Since the beginning of the alliance between archaeology and anthropology at the end of the 19th century, archaeology has gained interpretive power and sophistication as it developed and applied successively more useful models of culture, in concert with anthropology. Culture historical interpretation is built on the temporal and spatial synthesis of archaeological data. It emphasizes a chronicling of events, a demonstration of shifting cultural connections between sites, and an outline of relative change and stability of cultural forms within sites. Descriptions are usually broad, general ones, founded in a normative concept of culture, focused both synchronically and diachronically on the form of cultural attributes. Data gathering and hypothesis testing follow the scientific method, but the hypotheses involved center on the accuracy of existing time–space grids as models for ordering data.

The second major approach to archaeological interpretation emphasizes identification and explanation of cultural process—how cultures operate at any one point in time and why they change (or remain stable) through time, based on several complementary cultural models. The functional model stresses synchronic study of the purpose of behavioral components within the overall structure of a culture. With the reemergence of evolutionary models of culture, emphasis is on change and the delineation of cultural process. Processual models view human culture as a means of adaptation, maintaining an equilibrium with the physical, biological, and cultural environment. An ecological approach to culture emphasizes specific interactions within particular systems of culture and environment. Multilinear cultural evolution attempts to establish general cross-cultural trends of human prehistory, often arguing that the technological realm of culture has played the leading role in cultural evolution.

Delineation of cultural process is based on a hypothesis-testing research strategy, working with a series of competing propositions about a broad range of questions. These are tested against archaeological data to eliminate inadequate explanations. At a practical level, archaeologists use hypotheses in attempting to reveal the cultural processual factors that operate in each specific case being investigated. Regardless of the specific strategy employed, the testing of multiple and mutually exclusive hypotheses about a range of topics lies at the very core of the cultural processual approach.

A third approach, represented by postprocessualism, focuses on understanding the past by using a more active or dynamic model of culture, a more human time scale, and individual, family, or ethnic group behavior. In contrast to other cultural models, which are passive, the cognitive model places human beings as the central focus by portraying culture as the set of meanings people construct for making sense of their lives. These meanings, or "systems" of "norms," define available options, each person adapting those that suit individual situational needs. Culture is constantly in flux, and its specific forms are redefined in each situation. Within a given culture these options are seen as variant expressions of deep-seated and highly structured patterns, allowing material culture to be "read" as if it were a text, provided the analyst assumes an emic perspective.

Postprocessual archaeology derives from trends within social science seeking to understand human culture by "subjective insight" rather than to explain it through "objective science." And where culture historical and cultural processual approaches use an etic interpretation of the archaeological record—that is, from the archaeologist's point of view—postprocessualists attempt an emic interpretation, from the point of view of the ancient people who produced that record. Although historical or ethnohistoric documentation may help discern an emic perspective, it is far more difficult to do this for an extinct prehistoric society. The challenges to postprocessualism are clearly great, but they also point out the potential for multiple interpretations of the archaeological record, and may allow greater understanding of the use of symbolic meaning in ancient societies.

Finally, although over the past few decades archaeologists have debated the relative merits of the culture historical, cultural processual, and, more recently, postprocessual approaches, it seems clear that all contribute importantly to the development of the most complete and accurate understanding of the past.

GUIDE TO FURTHER READING

Culture History
Dunnell 1986a; Ehrich 1990; Fitting 1973; Flannery 1967; Ford 1969; Gibbon 1989; Kelley and Hanen 1988; Kidder [1924] 1962; Kidder and Guernsey 1919; Kidder, Jennings, and Shook 1946; Kroeber 1939; McKern 1939; Rouse 1953; Shook and Kidder 1952; Taylor [1948] 1964 and 1967; Taylor and Meighan 1978; Trigger 1968a; Watson 1973; Willey 1966, 1971; Willey and Phillips 1958; Willey and Sabloff 1980; Woodbury 1973

Cultural Process and Processualism
Adams 1966; L. R. Binford 1962, 1968a; Chamberlain 1897; Childe 1954; Cordell and Plog 1979; Deetz 1988a; Flannery 1986; Gibbon 1989; Gould 1985; Johnson and Earle 1987; Kelley and Hanen 1988; Kosso 1991; Meltzer 1979; Plog 1974; Sabloff and Rathje 1973; Sahlins and Service 1960; Steward 1955; Steward and Setzler 1938; Taylor [1948] 1964, 1967, 1972; P. J. Watson 1986; R. A. Watson 1991; Watson, LeBlanc, and Redman 1971, 1984; White 1949; Willey and Sabloff 1980

Postprocessual Archaeology
Bapty and Yates 1990; Bourdieu 1977; Collingwood 1946; Earle and Preucel 1987; Geertz 1983; Gero and Conkey 1991; Gibbon 1989; Hall 1977, 1989; Harré and Secord 1972; Hodder 1982a, 1982b, 1985, 1987, 1989, 1990,

1991; Lévi-Strauss 1963; McGhee 1977; Miller and Tilley 1984; Paddayya 1990; Pinsky and Wylie 1990; Preucel 1991; Shanks and Tilley 1987; Tilley 1990; Trigger 1989; P. J. Watson 1986; Wolf 1982

The Interplay of Culture History, Processualism, and Postprocessual Archaeology

L. R. Binford 1968a; Christenson 1989; Dunnell 1986a; Flannery 1967, 1973, 1986; Gibbon 1989; Hodder 1985, 1990, 1991; Kelley and Hanen 1988; Kuhn 1970; Lamberg-Karlovsky 1988; Leone 1972; Martin 1971; Meltzer 1979; Paddayya 1990; Preucel 1991; Trigger 1984, 1989; P. J. Watson 1986; R. A. Watson 1991; Young 1989

PLATE 1: Extensive stratigraphic excavations at the site of Koster, Illinois, have revealed fourteen superimposed occupation levels spanning the period from 7500 B.C. to A.D. 1200, providing a wealth of information about the development of food production among the peoples of North America. (Photography by D. Baston, courtesy of the Center for American Archeology, Kampsville, IL.)

PLATE 2: The Pueblo people of the American Southwest constructed huge, apartment-like residential compounds, such as Chetro Ketl in Chaco Canyon, New Mexico. This thriving center was abandoned in the twelfth century A.D., probably because drought and human-induced environmental degradation made the landscape unproductive for farming. (Courtesy Linda M. Nicholas.)

PLATE 3: Buildings in the Mexican city of Teotihuacán were decorated with wall murals. This mural from the residential compound of Tepantitla shows a deity iconographers call the Great Goddess, from whose hands spring fountains of water, a precious substance in Teotihuacán's semiarid valley. The scene illustrates elements of an ideological system otherwise unavailable for archaeological study. (Courtesy Mary Ellen Miller.)

PLATE 4: Town markets have been important economic institutions in many cultures for thousands of years. Traditional markets that can be observed today, such as this one in highland Guatemala, help archaeologists reconstruct ancient economic behavior. (Marion Patterson/Photo Researchers.)

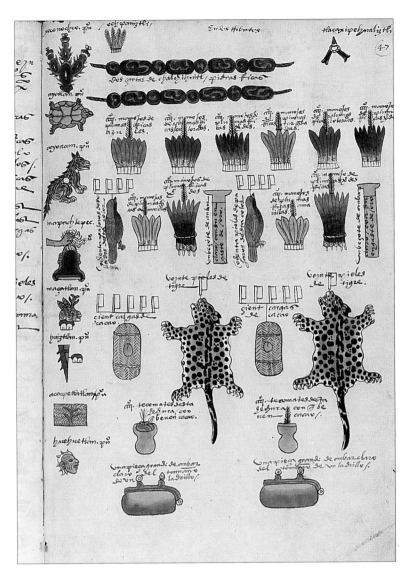

PLATE 5: Aztec kings of Mexico recorded the tribute they exacted from conquered peoples in books called codices. This page from the Codex Mendoza shows the name symbols of tributary towns and the kinds and amounts of tribute they owed. Such documentary evidence supplements data available from the archaeological record. (Bodleian Library, Oxford University.)

PLATE 6: This wall mural from the Classic Maya site of Bonampak, Mexico, depicts the ritual designation of a royal heir. Such representative art is enormously helpful in understanding ancient cultures. (Mural from reproduction of Room 1, Structure 1, Bonampak Chiapas, Mexico, for the Florida Museum of Natural History, Gainesville, Fla. Reproduction painted by Felipe Davalos and Kees Grootenboer, assisted by Janis Gore. Photo by Stan Blomeley.)

PLATE 7: This artist's conception of a sacrificial ritual at the Classic Maya center of Copán, Honduras, is based on the archaeological discovery of jaguar skeletons buried beneath this stone altar depicting a dynasty of sixteen successive kings. (H. Tom Hall, © 1989 National Geographic Society.)

PLATE 8: The superbly preserved Inka administrative center of Machu Picchu, high in the Peruvian Andes, was discovered by Hiram Bingham in 1911 during his attempt to find the final capital of the Inka empire. (Robert Frerck/Woodfin Camp & Associates.)

PLATE 9: The Rift Valley system of East Africa has revealed evidence of human activity that extends back several million years. The geological strata of Olduvai Gorge, Tanzania, shown here, provide the evidence that has allowed dating of the associated fossil remains of our early ancestors. (K. Cannon-Bonventre/Anthro-Photo.)

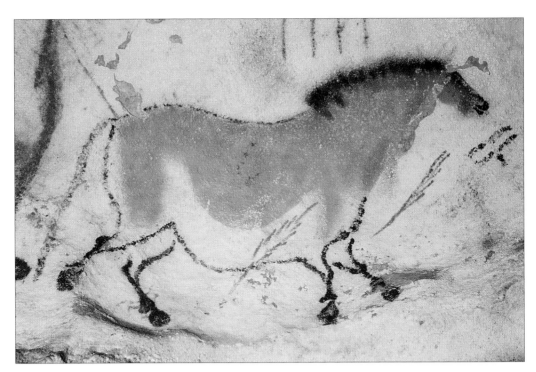

PLATE 10: The earliest clear examples of human symbolic behavior, dating to more than 15,000 years ago, are recorded in the elaborate cave art of Europe. Images of animals, such as this one from Lascaux in France, are not only aesthetically sophisticated but probably had complex and important meanings which may never be fully understood by modern scholars. (© Jean Vertut, Issy-les-Moulineaux, France.)

PLATE 11: Pharaohs of Old Kingdom Egypt (2600–2200 B.C.) built enormous pyramid complexes at Giza, near modern Cairo, to glorify themselves and provide for the survival of their souls. These elaborate complexes preserve much tangible information concerning ancient Egyptian belief and ritual. (PHOTRI, Inc.)

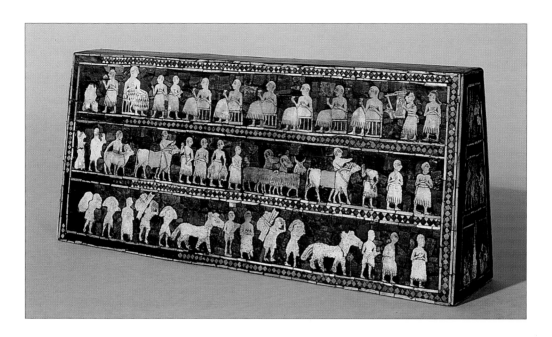

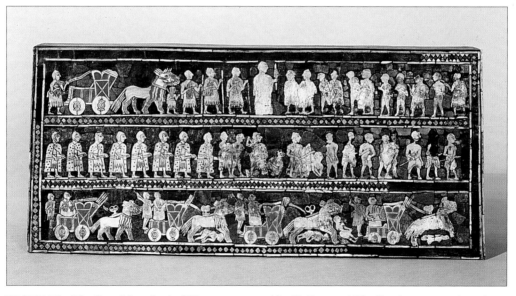

PLATE 12: The Royal Standard of Ur was recovered by Sir Leonard Woolley from a complex of royal graves at Ur, an ancient city in southern Mesopotamia. Presumably a symbol of political authority, it records scenes of peace and prosperity on one side (top) and war and discord on the other (bottom). (Courtesy of the Trustees of the British Museum.)

PLATE 13: One of the best-preserved early cities in the world is Mohenjo-Daro, in the Indus Valley of modern Pakistan. Abandoned in about 1500 B.C., its houses and public buildings, built of fired brick, have survived remarkably intact and provide insights into the social and economic organization within the ancient city. (© Dilip Mehta 1984. All rights reserved./Woodfin Camp and Associates.)

PLATE 14: The vast wealth and power of the first emperor to unify all China (221 B.C.) is reflected by his enormous mortuary complex just outside the modern city of Xian. Near the mountain-like tomb itself, huge pits hold life-sized ceramic replicas of soldiers, horses, and chariots representing the army he led during his life. (Wally McNamee/Woodfin Camp & Associates.)

COPING WITH EXPLANATION IN ARCHAEOLOGY: ADVICE FROM THE MASTER

Kent V. Flannery

This account is from the final chapter of Flannery's report of research conducted at the Guilá Naquitz cave, Oaxaca, Mexico. Entitled "A Visit to The Master," it considers explanation and causality in archaeology by means of an imaginary encounter with an amazingly sophisticated archaeological sage.

The issues of causality and explanation are heated topics in archaeology, ones that have carried some archaeologists to the threshold of philosophy. A whole series of logical positivists—many of them named Karl—have raised nagging questions about the way we conduct our profession. . . .

Quite frankly, I do not feel comfortable at the threshold of philosophy, and when it came time to write this chapter I felt I should seek the aid of an expert. Someone who had spent a lifetime considering the organization, methods, and principles of knowledge, and the mysteries of a universe where cause and effect seem often to confound human logic. . . .

A visit to The Master, such as I made in 1983, begins with a long, hot climb up Antelope Mountain. One is met . . . by an acolyte in a saffron robe who examines your credentials and guides your trip up the winding trail. . . . You are ascending to a calmer and less materialistic world, one where the theoretical issues of archaeology become sharper and clearer, unencumbered by fads and grant proposals and publishing or perishing. . . .

The Master seemed unexpectedly petite, with piercing black eyes set in a face like tanned leather. . . . The Master sat hunched over a wooden bowl into which he periodically dipped his fingers, each time forming a small ball of rice which he transferred casually to his mouth. I say "casually" because not every grain of rice made it to its destination, and this may have been the one flaw in an otherwise imposing presence. Visitors to The Master were supposed to be gripped by the candlelight reflections in his penetrating eyes, but

this was hard to achieve if your attention was riveted on the stray grains of rice in his beard.

"Tell me the reason for your visit," he suggested, in a voice that put me at ease without being condescending or overly familiar.

As best I could, I explained that I was an archaeologist working on the origins of agriculture in Mexico. After reviewing a number of current theories on the topic, I had designed a multivariate model based on the best data available to me from Tehuacán. One of my colleagues had converted it to a mathematical model that could be run on a computer, and with that we had been able to simulate the pattern of subsistence activities seen in a whole new batch of data collected more recently in Oaxaca. The results allowed us to reject some current opinions on the origins of agriculture, defend others, and contribute some new opinions of our own.

"But you are still not satisfied," he said knowingly.

(continued)

(continued)

"No," I said. "In today's archaeology, people want you to come up with clear-cut *causes* for prehistoric phenomena. They want those causes to be explained in terms of universal covering laws of human behavior. I think I can suggest *how* the transition from foraging to agriculture in Oaxaca was accomplished, but if you asked me, 'Why did agriculture begin?' I'm not sure what I'd give you as a cause. And if you asked me, 'What law did you come up with?' I'm not sure what I'd say."

An understanding smile, marred only by an errant grain of rice, illuminated The Master's face. "Tell me something," he said. "Of all the other sciences, which one do you feel most resembles archaeology: mathematics, physics, chemistry, or biology?"

"In my opinion, biology," I replied. "Specifically, within biology, I feel that archaeology most resembles paleontology. We both attempt to reconstruct evolutionary sequences on the basis of an incomplete fossil record."

"In that case," said The Master, "why don't we look at what a distinguished senior biologist has to say about covering laws?"

By the flickering light of the candles, his hand moved along a wooden shelf behind his seat, and for the first time I saw that it was stacked with books of every shape and size. He stopped at a thick brown volume; his fingertips moved gently over the gold printing on the spine, and withdrawing the book he opened it on the carpet before me.

"Ernst Mayr is one of the architects of the modern evolutionary synthesis," said The Master. "This is his new book, *The Growth of Biological Thought* (Mayr 1982). I have opened it to his second chapter, 'The Place of Biology in the Sciences and its Conceptual Structure,' so that we can read it together." . . .

Perhaps the most striking characterization of biology by Mayr . . . was that it proceeds virtually without laws such as those in physics. . . . Virtually every law proposed for biology has too many exceptions to be a covering law; "they are explanatory as far as past events are concerned, but not predictive, except in a statistical (probabilistic) sense" (p. 37). That is why generalizations in biology are almost invariably of a probabilistic nature, and predictions about evolution are impossible. "No one would have predicted at the beginning of the Cretaceous that the flourishing group of dinosaurs would become extinct by the end of this era" (p. 58). . . .

"Then how can biologists prove anything?" I asked The Master.

"By ridding themselves of the notion that proof in biology is the same thing as proof in a predictive science such as physics," he replied. . . .

"According to Mayr," [I replied, picking up his line of thought] "in biology, and particularly in evolutionary biology, explanations take the form of what he calls 'historical narratives' (p. 58). Narrative explanations use concepts but are constructed without mentioning any general laws (p. 71). For some sciences, such as paleontology, historical narratives play an important role, and Mayr actually uses the phrase 'historical narrative theory.' He goes on to say that historical narratives 'have explanatory value because earlier events in a historical sequence usually make a causal contribution to later events' (p. 72)." . . .

The Master's fingers strayed momentarily to his beard, and I was relieved to see at least a couple of rice grains disappear into the cave floor. "All right," he said. "Why don't you start by giving me a historical narrative explanation for the origins of agriculture in Oaxaca? When you have finished, we'll talk a little about causality."

"That could take all night," I said, somewhat apologetically.

"Quite literally," said The Master with a knowing smile, "I have all the time in the world." . . .

Choosing my words carefully, I tried to explain to The Master that it might be no accident that *Cucurbita pepo* [squash] was one of Oaxaca's first domesticates. It belonged to the same family as the bottle gourd and would probably have been recognized as just as simple to cultivate. It was a weedy annual whose seeds could be roasted, stored, and carried and eaten on trips. Unknown to its early cultivators was the fact that its seeds could provide them with the extra dose of protein their diet needed, but this unsuspected nutritional benefit could have conferred a selective advantage on early squash cultivators. *Susí* nuts could have done the same, but the *susí* is a perennial shrub and therefore not nearly as amenable to casual cultivation as a weedy annual.

Why would Naquitz phase [8900–6700 B.C.] foragers begin to cultivate squash? Surely not because their population was so high that they had exhausted all sources of wild food. No, I explained, I preferred to see early agriculture as a logical extension of the preagricultural pattern. Our simulated foragers had shown a concern with reducing [the food] search area; cultivation did that by concentrating lots of squash in a small area. It also made the location of the densest squash stands totally predictable from year to year; and it increased a storable seed crop, which extended the harvest season. . . .

Selecting for greater numbers of seeds per fruit, we suspect that preceramic cultivators unwittingly selected for a fruit with edible flesh, positively reinforcing the advantages of cultivation and eventually producing a phenotype that could not survive without human intervention. As agriculture increased the efficiency of their search for calories and protein, they increased the number of agricultural tasks in virtually all their

strategies and eventually moved agriculture out of the piedmont and onto the alluvium where its greatest strides would be made. Thus a very small initial change in behavior, amounting to no more than an extension of the preagricultural strategy, was amplified into a major change by time and positive feedback. . . .

"And in the end," said The Master, "you came to prefer a probabilistic ecosystem model to a mechanistic-deterministic theory?"

"For several reasons," I replied. "For one thing, such a model leaves open the options for several different responses to systemic change. For example, if a group's strategy of reducing search area leads to a protein deficit, there are several alternative changes that might be selected for. They could move in the direction the Naquitz phase people moved, domesticating a high-protein plant while further reducing search area. Or they could move in the direction of more intensive hunting or fishing; this may have happened in parts of the world where agriculture *didn't* arise between 10,000 and 5000 B.C. If we make agriculture the *only* possible outcome of our model, we fail to account for those areas where it *didn't* appear independently." . . .

The Master signaled to the acolyte to bring him another bowl of rice. "And are there still further reasons for your choice of model?" he wondered.

"Yes," I replied. "In addition to

information, it even allows me to include such features as world view or ideology: for example, the Zapotec notions that mesquite 'as thick as your arm' is an indicator of good corn land, or that land is not worth clearing unless the corn yield will be around 250 kilos per hectare. These notions may have some underlying basis in ecology or economics, but essentially they are arbitrary cultural beliefs. Yet we need to take them into account because they help determine when land is cleared or taken out of fallow. If you lower your arbitrary threshold to 50 kilos per hectare, or raise it to 1000 kilos, it significantly affects the rate at which maize gets moved to alluvium." . . .

" . . . I sense," said The Master, "that you regard culture as so flexible that it confounds most mechanistic-deterministic models."

"Exactly," I said. "If the biological world is made up of complex feedback loops and recurrence relationships, as biologists like . . . Mayr evidently believe—and if even paleontologists depend on historical narrative explanations—can we really expect to reduce cultural behavior to a set of laws like those of physics?"

Patiently, The Master formed a new ball of rice between his fingertips. I swear, I didn't know where he was putting it all, but I decided not to worry about it.

"Did anything strike you as familiar about your historical narrative explanation?" he asked.

(continued)

(continued)

"It struck me that it was not unlike the kind of summary and conclusions that many archaeologists have offered in the past," I admitted. "Does that mean that it's been all right to do that all along?"

"Would that surprise you?" he asked.

"It would certainly be reassuring to a lot of archaeologists over 35," I told him.

The Master struggled to suppress a laugh. He suppressed it partly because it would have spoiled his dignified image and partly because it would have caused him to spit a lot of rice back into his bowl. . . .

We stood together at the mouth of the cave, enjoying . . . the view of dawn spreading over the valley below.

"I don't know how to thank you," I said at last. "I had no idea how I was going to deal with causality. Now I think I can write my last chapter."

The Master smiled. "Do not thank me too hastily," he said. "I really only tried to direct you away from the laws of physics and toward the concepts of biology. To fully understand the origins of agriculture, you will have to eschew science completely and ascend to a higher spiritual level where there is no essential difference between plants and man. You are not yet ready for that level. . . .

"You see," said The Master, "now that we have finished talking I can admit to you that I was present at the origins of agriculture. It was in an earlier life, of course, and in another land and another cave. And it did not happen just the way you think. At that time I did not expect that it would become as important as it has. I was too young then to understand."

"Could you give me just a hint?" I asked.

"No," said The Master. "That would take away the whole reason for your search. In some fields, such as archaeology and paleontology, the search is half the fun."

CHAPTER FOUR

CONSTRUCTS: THE NATURE OF ARCHAEOLOGICAL DATA

Too often we dig up mere things unrepentantly forgetful that our proper aim is to dig up people.

Sir Mortimer Wheeler, Archaeology from the Earth, *1954*

Data relevant to most, if not all, the components of past sociocultural systems are preserved in the archaeological record. . . . Our task, then, is to devise a means for extracting this information.

Lewis R. Binford, An Archaeological Perspective, *1972*

In this chapter, we consider the kinds of information archaeologists work with and the ways this material is acquired. Most people are familiar with the commonest kinds of archaeological evidence; they have probably read about archaeologists "piecing together the past" by studying ancient pottery, "arrowheads," or other tools found by excavation. However, tools represent only one of several kinds of evidence that archaeologists study, and excavation is only one of several means of collecting information about the past. The many and varied kinds of information, together with the ways they are recovered, are all crucial to archaeologists' efforts at understanding what happened in the past. In this chapter we examine the characteristics of the evidence archaeologists seek. But first we consider the basic forms of archaeological data.

THE FORMS OF ARCHAEOLOGICAL DATA

We have defined the archaeological record as all the material remains of past human activity, from the smallest stone-chipping debris to the most massive architectural construction. Parts of this record become archaeological *data* when the archaeologist recognizes their significance as evidence from the past and collects and records them. The collection and recording of remains of the past constitute the acquisition of archaeological data. Later, in Chapters 6 and 7, we will discuss the various methods by which archaeologists acquire data. Here we are concerned with defining and describing the three basic classes of archaeological data (artifacts, features, and ecofacts) along with the two composite classes (sites and regions).

Artifacts

Artifacts are portable objects whose form has been modified wholly or partially by human activity (Fig. 4.1). Objects such as a stone hammer or a fired clay vessel are artifacts, because they are either natural objects modified for or by human use (such as the stone hammer), or new objects

FIGURE 4.1 Artifacts are portable objects whose form is modified or wholly created by human activity, whereas ecofacts are nonartifactual remains that nonetheless have cultural relevance. Here a project point (an artifact) lies embedded among the bones (ecofacts) of an extinct form of bison at Folsom, New Mexico. (All rights reserved. Photo Archives, Denver Museum of Natural History.)

formed completely by human action (such as a vessel made of clay). The shape and other characteristics of artifacts are not altered by removal from the surroundings in which they are discovered: A stone axe and a pottery vessel both retain their appearance after the archaeologist takes them from the ground. This portability distinguishes artifacts from features in a fundamental way.

Features

Features are nonportable artifacts; that is, they are artifacts that cannot be recovered from the settings in which they are found (Fig. 4.2). Position and arrangement are key aspects of features; for this reason they cannot be removed after their discovery without either altering or destroying their original form. They may, however, be reconstructed after removal, as in a museum display. Some common examples of archaeological features are hearths, burials, storage pits, and roads. It is often useful to distinguish between simple features such as these and composite features such as the remains of buildings. The latter (whether houses, storage buildings, temples, palaces, or whatever) are usually revealed archaeologically by the patterned arrangements of floors, postholes, walls, and doorways, as well as by associated simple features such as hearths, refuse pits, and the like.

FIGURE 4.2 Features are artifacts that cannot be recovered intact, here represented by a partially excavated cremation burial pit.

Ecofacts

Ecofacts are nonartifactual material remains that nonetheless have cultural relevance (see Fig. 4.1). That is, although not directly created or modified by human activity, ecofacts do provide significant information about past human behavior. Examples of ecofacts include remnants of both wild and domesticated animal and plant species (bones, pollen granules, and so forth). Such material contributes to our understanding of past human behavior by indicating the environmental conditions and the kinds of food and other resources used.

Sites

Sites are spatial clusters of artifacts, features, and/or ecofacts (Fig. 4.3). Some sites consist solely of one form of data—a surface scatter of artifacts, for example. Others consist of any combination of the three forms of archaeological data. But, no matter what their specific form and content, all sites identify where humans have occupied the landscape.

The boundaries of archaeological sites are sometimes well defined, especially if features such as walls or moats are present. Usually, however, a decline in density or frequency of the material remains is all that marks the limits of a site. In some cases, the archaeologist may be unable to detect clear boundaries and may have to assign arbitrary limits for convenience of research; examples include extensive sites in dense rain forest cover and sites partially buried by flood deposits or volcanic ash. However boundaries are defined, the archaeological site is usually a basic working unit of archaeological investigation.

Sites can be described and categorized in a variety of ways, depending on the characteristics the investigator wants to note. For instance, location—sites in open valley positions, cave sites, coastal sites, mountaintop sites, and so forth—may reflect past environmental conditions, concern for defense, or relative values placed on natural resources located in different areas. Sites may be distinguished by the functions they may have served in the past. For example, there are habitation sites, trading centers, hunting (or kill) sites, quarry sites, ceremonial centers, and burial areas. Sites may also be described in terms of their age or cultural affiliation. For example, a southwest Asian site may be described as belonging to the Bronze Age, or a Mexican site may be termed "Aztec."

Since all sites are places where people occupied the landscape, the nature and depth of cultural deposits at a site can reveal the time span of activities—whether overall occupation was brief or extended. People leave behind artifacts and other traces of their presence, and at some sites occupation (and deposition of artifacts) may have been continuous. Other sites may have had multiple occupations interspersed with periods of abandonment, which are marked by naturally deposited (nonartifactual or "sterile") layers, such as windblown sand. Depth of accumulation is not a perfect indicator of length of occupation; at one spot a great deal of ma-

FIGURE 4.3 Sites are spatial clusterings of archaeological remains. Stonehenge is an example of a site with well-defined boundaries. (English Heritage Photo Library.)

terial can be deposited very rapidly, whereas elsewhere a relatively thin deposit of trash might represent many, even thinner layers laid down intermittently over hundreds or thousands of years.

It is still true, however, that "surface" sites—those with no appreciable depth of deposition—are usually the result of short-term, erratic, or temporary human activity such as hunting and gathering camps. Examples include some of the seasonal camps studied by David Hurst Thomas in the Great Basin of the United States (see Chapter 1), where ancient stone tools and bone fragments still litter the ground. Most archaeological sites, however, have both surface and depth components. Surface manifestations may be apparent at such sites, but a considerable accumulation may also be hidden beneath the surface. These sites, more typical of permanent stations of past activity, may range in size from small shell heaps, common on coast and shore lines, to large, complex, urban centers such as Teotihuacan in Mexico or Uruk in Iraq.

Other sites may exist completely beneath the surface of the ground. In these cases, the surface gives no indications of the presence of a site—all evidence of previous human activity has been buried by forces of deposition such as windblown sand or volcanic ash or water-laid alluvium (Fig. 4.4). Detection of buried sites presents special problems to the archaeologist; these will be discussed in Chapter 6.

Some "buried" sites lie not under ground but under water. The most

Depositional characteristics: Surface, subsurface, and underwater sites

FIGURE 4.4 Completely buried sites pose special problems of detection. Here, an ancient Maya stone house platform at Quiriguá, Guatemala, had been covered by ancient flood silts (background) making it invisible to surface detection.

Regional archaeology: Willey, MacNeish, Binford, and Struever

common underwater sites are sunken ships. However, sites that were once on dry land may also become submerged because of changes in water level (sometimes resulting from human activity such as dam building) or land subsidence. A famous example of the latter is Port Royal, Jamaica, a coastal city that sank beneath the sea within minutes after an earthquake in 1692. In some cases, human activity may intentionally submerge artifactual material; for example, refuse may have been dumped into lakes or oceans or ritual offerings thrown into sacred bodies of water, such as the famous sacred *cenote* at Chichén Itzá in Mexico. The Gallo-Roman sanctuary of Sequana, at the source of the Seine River, has yielded 190 carved wooden figures; whether they were originally left as trash or as ritual offerings, these fragile figures owe their unusually long survival to 2000 years of submersion.

We will return to the issue of the definition of archaeological sites later in this chapter, in discussing the ways archaeological data are structured. But next we consider the ways archaeological data may be distributed beyond the level of individual sites.

Regions

Regions are the largest and most flexible spatial clusters of archaeological data. Definition of a region allows archaeologists to investigate a wider range of ancient activities—beyond those restricted to a single site. Indeed, turning attention to areas separating obvious sites frequently yields subtle but important traces of human presence that might otherwise be missed. Occasional artifact finds, for example, might be considered too widely scattered to define sites; taken together, however, in a regional context, they contribute to better understanding of people's overall use of the landscape.

The region is basically a geographical concept: a definable area bounded by topographic features such as mountains and bodies of water. But the definition of an archaeological region may also consider ecological and cultural factors. For instance, a region may be defined as the sustaining area that contains a series of interrelated human communities sharing a single cultural-ecological system (Fig. 4.5).

Obviously, the nature and scope of an archaeological region vary according to the complexity of the prehistoric society and the subsistence system it used. Part of the archaeologist's task is to identify the factors that define a region under study, as well as to show how these factors changed through time. In other words, the archaeologist usually works with a convenient natural region defined beforehand by geographical boundaries and then seeks to determine that region's ancient ecological and cultural boundaries as well.

By emphasizing the region as the basic spatial unit for archaeological research, several scholars have defined a new approach to prehistory. Lewis Binford is often cited as the first North American archaeologist to call explicitly for a regional approach; he was followed shortly by Stuart

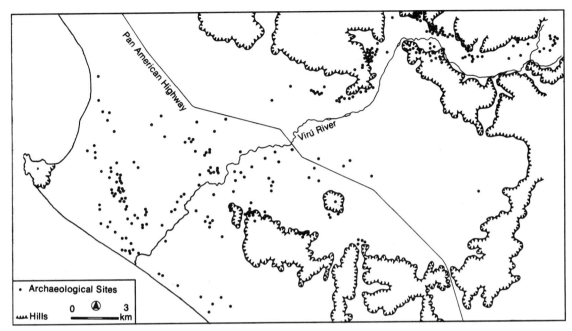

FIGURE 4.5 An archaeological region is often defined by topographic features; in this case, hilly areas and seacoast define the limits of the Virú Valley, Peru. (After Willey, 1953.)

Struever. At that time—in the mid-1960s—other archaeologists, such as Richard MacNeish in his investigation of the Tehuacán Valley in Mexico (see Chapter 6), had already shown tangible evidence of the value of this approach. And Gordon Willey had pioneered regionally oriented research in his famous study of the Virú Valley in Peru in the 1940s (see Fig. 4.5). Although other early projects with a regional focus can be named, however, only recently have archaeologists begun to adopt a regional orientation to any marked degree. In some places, notably the American Southwest, the new orientation has been a leading factor behind important changes in interpretation.

Why was the regional approach attractive and productive? Traditionally, archaeologists have tended to consider the site as their investigative unit. Conclusions about larger areas were based on comparisons *between* sites. In other words, the prehistory of geographical spaces between sites was "filled in" from what was known about a few specific points, the sites. But, as noted earlier, a regional approach frees archaeological investigations from restriction to a single site or even to all the identified sites within a region. Intersite areas or seemingly vacant terrain may also be examined to provide useful archaeological data that may be hidden from view or otherwise ignored. In the Southwest, for example, a regional approach has recently helped archaeologists to recognize previously unsuspected complexities in prehistoric culture. The most dramatic reevaluation involved the Chacoan culture of the 10th to 12th centuries A.D. As summarized by Linda Cordell and others, hundreds of communities, large and small, were newly discovered in thousands of square miles of northwestern New Mexico and adjacent areas. In addition, archaeologists found that, despite great distances, all communities were linked together effectively by trade in various goods such as turquoise (and quite probably food); the links were sometimes indicated materially by an extensive system of Chacoan roads.

Overall, the regional approach stresses a research strategy aimed at sampling an entire region; the data gathered enable the archaeologist to reconstruct aspects of prehistoric society that may not be well represented by a single site. Of most obvious importance here is the reconstruction of ancient subsistence and social organizational systems. Of course, beyond gathering better data bearing on these specific concerns, regional archaeology remains oriented to meeting the overall objectives of all prehistoric archaeology (see Chapter 1).

How does the regional approach meet its objectives? Obviously, translating any fragmentary remains left by past peoples into a reconstruction of ancient society is a difficult task. Some of the ways archaeologists do this will be discussed in Chapters 14–16. Here we shall consider how past human behavior is transformed into archaeological evidence and how the characteristics and distribution of these remains become the basis for archaeological interpretation.

THE DETERMINANTS OF ARCHAEOLOGICAL DATA

Now that we have defined the various forms of archaeological data, we can describe the processes responsible for creating evidence of past human behavior and how the archaeologist detects those processes to reconstruct that behavior.

Behavioral and Transformational Processes

Archaeological data are the result of two factors: behavioral processes and transformational processes. This is the domain of middle-range theory (Chapter 1), or the frameworks that link the archaeological record with the behavior that produced it. We will describe the general dimensions of both processes here, and discuss middle-range theory again in Chapter 13.

All archaeological sites, from the smallest temporary overnight hunting camp to the largest, longest-occupied urban center, represent the products of human activity. Of course, not all human activity or behavior produces tangible remains. Entire unwritten languages, philosophical concepts, and belief systems that existed in the past may be completely lost, having left little or no direct evidence. Most kinds of human behavior, however, do modify the natural environment to some degree; every society affects its surroundings in some way. Forests are felled, animals hunted, plants gathered, rivers diverted, and minerals extracted, all to satisfy the needs of human societies. The material products of this behavior—the tools, food, roads, buildings, and so forth—are the artifacts, ecofacts, and features that the archaeologist recovers. And the activities that affect the environment to produce tangible remains (later recovered as archaeological data) are what we call ancient **behavioral processes.**

In recovering these data, the archaeologist attempts to determine what specific kinds of ancient behavior they reflect. All archaeological data potentially represent a cycle of four (ideally consecutive) stages of behavior: **acquisition, manufacture, use,** and **deposition** (Fig. 4.6). Each of the stages in the behavioral cycle may be complex. Acquisition refers to the gathering of raw materials, either directly or through intervening agents (such as by purchase or barter). Manufacture refers to the modification of raw materials by a variety of means, often comprising a series of definable steps, discernible either from waste products or from traces on the artifact itself. Use may result in further modification of artifacts, sometimes leaving similar clues that allow archaeologists to reconstruct artifact functions. Deposition, which may occur at *any point* in the behavioral cycle, defines the entry of material residues of human behavior into the archaeological record.

Artifacts such as tools are made, used for one or more specific purposes, and then discarded when broken or worn, at which point they enter the archaeological record. Features such as houses are constructed and then occupied; when they are no longer habitable or needed, they enter the archaeological record by being abandoned, torn down, or burned. Ecofacts such as animals used for food pass through similar stages: The animal may be hunted (acquisition), butchered and cooked (manufacture), and eaten (use), and both the digested and the undigested waste products discarded (deposition). The combinations of these activities at a site delineate the same four stages in the life span of the site as a whole: selection of the locale, setting up areas or structures to house activities (shelter, work, ritual, and so forth), use of these areas for the various activities, and, ultimately, destruction or abandonment of the site.

The remains of human behavior may pass through *all* these stages, or they may enter the archaeological record by deposition at any point in the cycle. On the other hand, remains may pass through more than one such cycle. Some items are modified for new uses or recycled, involving new manufacturing and use activity.

Thus the archaeologist can use all forms of archaeological data, individually and together, to reconstruct the acquisition, manufacture, use, and deposition stages of ancient behavior. Clues to all four kinds of ancient behavior may be found in characteristics of the data themselves and in the circumstances of their deposition (Fig. 4.7). In Chapters 10–16 we will discuss how the archaeologist reconstructs past behavior from data analysis; and later in this chapter we will see how the archaeologist can determine aspects of ancient behavior from the circumstances under which material remains are found.

ACQUISITION

MANUFACTURE

USE

DEPOSITION

FIGURE 4.6 Archaeological data represent at least one behavioral cycle of acquisition, manufacture, use, and deposition.

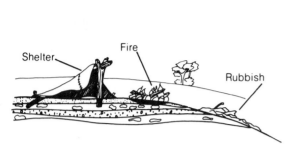

2000 years ago: Hunting camp (acquisition, manufacture, use, and deposition behavior)

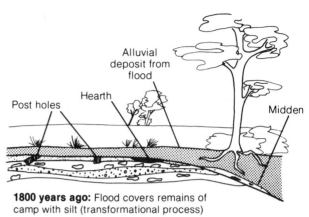

1800 years ago: Flood covers remains of camp with silt (transformational process)

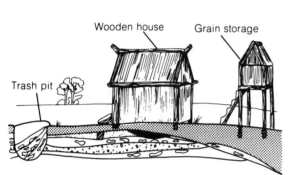

1500 years ago: Farming village built on silt (new cycle of acquisition, manufacture, use, and deposition behavior)

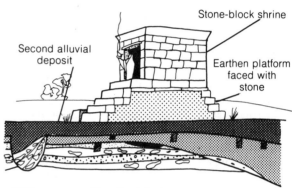

1000 years ago: New flood destroys farming village (transformational process); stone shrine built on new ground surface (new cycles of acquisition, manufacture, use, and deposition behavior)

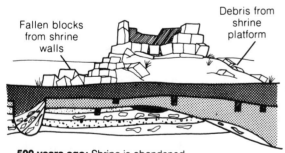

500 years ago: Shrine is abandoned and begins to disintegrate, forming mound (depositional and natural transformational processes)

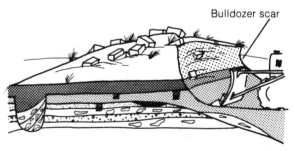

Today: Mound is mined for fill to be used in highway construction (cultural transformational process)

FIGURE 4.7 The characteristics of archaeological data and their deposition reflect both behavioral and transformational processes.

These behavioral processes represent the first stage in the formation of archaeological data. After material remains have entered the archaeological record through deposition, a second stage begins, consisting of **transformational processes.** These processes include all conditions and events that affect archaeological data from deposition to the time the archaeologist recognizes and acquires them. These include transformations by natural agents (*natural transforms*), such as organic decay of materials or their burial by a volcanic eruption, and by human activity (*cultural transforms*), such as recycling of artifacts, their uprooting through plowing, retention of artifacts as heirlooms (*curation*), or demolition of buildings. The transformations that affect the archaeological record are continuous, dynamic, and unique to each situation.

The tangible products of ancient human behavior are never completely indestructible, but some survive better than others. As a result, the data recovered by the archaeologist always present a picture of the past that is biased by the effects of transformational processes (see Fig. 4.7). To gauge this bias, it is crucial to determine the nature of the processes that have been at work in each archaeological situation. Both natural and human events act either to accelerate or to retard destruction. Natural agents of transformation include climatic factors, which are usually the basic influence acting on the preservation of archaeological evidence. Temperature and humidity are generally the most critical: Extremely dry, wet, or cold conditions act to preserve fragile organic materials, such as textiles and wooden tools, as well as bulkier perishable items such as human corpses (Fig. 4.8). Organic remains have been preserved under these circumstances along the dry coast of Peru, in the wet bogs of Scandinavia, and in the frozen steppes of Siberia.

Natural destructive processes (such as oxidation and decay) and catastrophic events (such as earthquakes and volcanic eruptions) also have profound effects on the remains of the past. Underwater remains may be broken up and scattered by tidal action, currents, or waves. Catastrophes such as volcanic eruptions may either preserve or destroy archaeological sites; often the same event may have a multitude of effects. For example, sometime around 1500 B.C. both an earthquake and a volcanic eruption struck the island of Thera, in the Aegean Sea near Greece. Part of the island blew up; another part collapsed inward and was filled by the inrushing seawater. Still other areas were immediately buried under a blanket of ash. The local population abandoned the island, but the remains of its settlements were sealed beneath the ash. Recent excavations have disclosed well-preserved buildings, some intact to the third story—a rarity in more exposed sites—as well as beautiful wall paintings (Fig. 4.9). Such fragile artifacts as baskets have also been found, thoroughly disintegrated but recoverable through specialized techniques.

One of the most decisive factors in the transformational process is subsequent human activity. Reoccupation of an archaeological site by a later people may destroy all traces of previous occupation. Earlier buildings are often leveled to make way for new construction or to provide construction

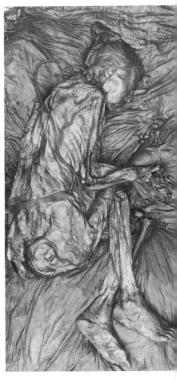

FIGURE 4.8 Tollund man, a corpse preserved for some 2000 years in a Danish bog. (Reprinted from P. V. Glob: *The Bog People: Iron-Age Man Preserved.* Copyright © P. V. Glob 1965.)

Transformational processes: Thera

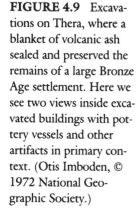

FIGURE 4.9 Excavations on Thera, where a blanket of volcanic ash sealed and preserved the remains of a large Bronze Age settlement. Here we see two views inside excavated buildings with pottery vessels and other artifacts in primary context. (Otis Imboden, © 1972 National Geographic Society.)

materials. In other cases, however, later activity may preserve older sites by building over and thus sealing the earlier remains (Fig. 4.10). Of course, large-scale human events such as war, conquest, and mass migration usually have destructive consequences for archaeological preservation. Finally, economic conditions that support a flourishing market in antiquities have a profound negative effect by encouraging the looting and consequent destruction of archaeological sites.

Thus the archaeologist must carefully evaluate the preservation status of data gathered, to determine what conditions and events have acted to transform the materials originally deposited by past human behavior. The most fundamental distinction to be made is between natural and human agents of transformation. Obviously, the transformational processes that have modified the data are specific to each site, so each archaeological situation must be evaluated individually.

As we have seen, the form of archaeological data is the result of sequential behavioral and transformational processes. To derive as much information as possible from the available data, the archaeologist must understand both sets of processes. As we have noted, the propositions governing the links between the revealed archaeological data and the past are usually labeled *middle-range theory* (see Chapter 1). These propositions allow the archaeologist to infer ancient human behavior by understanding how material remains enter the archaeological record and how that record

FIGURE 4.10 Structure E-VII sub at the Maya site of Uaxactún, Guatemala, preserved by a later overlying construction completely removed in 1928: (l) view before reclearing and restoration in 1974; (r) restoration completed, 1974. (Courtesy of Edwin M. Shook.)

is subsequently transformed. These inferences may be supported by modern observations of the processes at work or by experiments designed to replicate links between human behavior and material residues, or the ways these remains are transformed under varying conditions. We will consider these subjects in Chapter 13; at this point, we need to examine how the archaeologist begins to reconstruct behavioral and transformational processes from the circumstances under which data are recovered, including their matrix, provenience, association, and context.

Matrix, Provenience, Association, and Context

All archaeological material, from the smallest arrowhead to the grandest temple complex, occurs within or relative to a matrix. **Matrix** refers to the physical medium that surrounds, holds, and supports the archaeological material (Fig. 4.11). Most frequently this medium consists of earthen substances, such as humus, sand, silt, gravel, and pumice. The nature of a matrix is usually an important clue to understanding the artifacts, features, or ecofacts it contains. For instance, artifacts recovered from an alluvial matrix (deposited by running water) may themselves have been deposited by natural action of a river. A matrix may also be the product of human activity such as the deposition of immense amounts of soil to construct an earthen platform. In this case, the soil is not only a matrix for any artifacts contained within it but also a constructed feature.

Provenience simply refers to a three-dimensional location—the horizontal and vertical position on or within the matrix—at which the archaeologist finds data. Horizontal provenience is usually determined and

FIGURE 4.11 In this photograph, a human burial has been excavated from most of its matrix, but the relationship of the remains to the matrix is still readily apparent. (Courtesy of the Ban Chiang Project, Thai Fine Arts Department/The University Museum.)

recorded relative to a geographical grid system using known reference points. Vertical provenience is usually determined and recorded as elevation above or below sea level. The determination and recording of provenience for all kinds of archaeological data are necessary for the data to be useful. Provenience information allows the archaeologist to record (and later to reconstruct) the material's association and context.

Association refers to two or more archaeological items (artifacts, ecofacts, or features) occurring together, usually within the same matrix (Fig. 4.12). Once physical proximity is established, the archaeologist must still determine the behavioral significance of the association, evaluating whether it is the product of behavioral or transformational processes (e.g., a modern bottle cap redeposited by a gopher next to a 10,000-year-old human bone).

Context is the interpretation of the significance of an artifact's deposition in terms of its matrix, provenience, and association—that is, where it is and how it got there.

Importance of provenience, association, and context: The archaeologist vs. the looter

One point of sharp contrast between the archaeologist and the looter is that when the looter finds "buried treasures"—let us say, two beautifully painted pottery bowls within a tomb chamber—he or she does not bother to record either provenience or association. Being interested only in the money to be gained from selling the vessels, such a person does not care that archaeologists might know the age of one of the kinds of vessels but not of the other. If archaeologists knew the provenience, association, and matrix of these two vessels—that is, if they knew that the two were discovered in association on the floor of an ancient tomb—they would prob-

FIGURE 4.12 A group of pottery vessels found in association as a result of intentional ritual deposition (primary context). This indicates that they were used together as part of an ancient ceremony (ca. first century A.D., El Portón, Guatemala).

Reconstruction of early human occupation of the Western Hemisphere: Folsom, New Mexico

ably infer that the two were deposited at the same time and had remained undisturbed until their discovery. The unknown vessel could then be assigned the same date as the known one. When the information goes unrecorded, however, these insights are forever lost. Although the vessels themselves are recovered and preserved, their significance as sources of information about past human behavior is destroyed.

Another example of the importance of context arises in discoveries of stone projectile points in clear association with the bones of extinct prey animals. These finds have been important keys to the reconstruction of early human occupation of the Western Hemisphere. In the mid-1920s, finds at Folsom, New Mexico, revealed such points in undisturbed context, associated with bones of a species of bison that had been extinct for 10,000 years or more (see Fig. 4.1). Similar finds at other sites, such as Lindenmeier, Colorado, established firmly that bison hunters lived and stalked their prey in North America at least 10,000 years ago. The dates were supplied by paleontological study, but archaeological association and contextual interpretation were critical in establishing the cultural significance of the finds.

The point is that any kind of excavation, by archaeologists or anyone else, destroys matrix, association, and context. The only way to preserve the information these factors convey is in drawings, photographs, and written records. Such records will be discussed in Chapter 7; here we wish only to underscore the importance of keeping accurate records of archaeological work. Without them, even the most painstakingly controlled excavation is no more justifiable or useful than a looter's pit.

Evaluating Context

The archaeologist uses the products of past behavior—archaeological data—to reconstruct both the behavior and the cultural systems by which they were produced. As the first step in linking the data to a past cultural system, the archaeologist must assess the effects on the data of the processes we have discussed in this chapter: the kinds of ancient behavior—acquisition, manufacture, use, and deposition—that originally produced the evidence (the behavioral processes), and the natural or human events that have affected these data from the time of their deposition to the moment of archaeological recovery (the transformational processes).

Understanding these sets of formative processes begins with evaluating the context of archaeological data. *Context* refers to the characteristics of archaeological data that result both from their original behavioral associations and from their postdeposition transformational history (Fig. 4.13). Context is evaluated at the data acquisition stage (see Chapter 5) by careful observation and recording of the matrix, provenience, and association of all data.

Archaeological contexts are of two basic kinds: primary (undisturbed) and secondary (disturbed). Each of these may be divided into two categories to produce four kinds of context. We shall first define each of the four kinds and then examine brief examples to clarify the relationships among these context categories (see Table 4.1). The following discussion illustrates both the differences among the types of archaeological context and the significance of determining context.

Primary context refers to conditions in which both provenience and matrix have been undisturbed since deposition of the artifacts or other materials by people who made and used them. There are two varieties, **use-related** and **transposed primary context,** which we will define in the following paragraphs. Both may have involved deliberate ancient activity or may have been the result of casual or even accidental behavior.

As we have already indicated, any artifact may be used over an extensive period of time; furthermore, it may be modified to be reused for a different kind of activity throughout its use span. Thus a single pottery vessel

Table 4.1 Kinds of Archaeological Context

Primary (Undisturbed) Context	Secondary (Disturbed) Context
Use-related: Resulting from abandonment of materials during acquisition, manufacture, or use activities.	*Use-related:* Resulting from disturbance by human activity after original deposition of material.
Transposed: Resulting from depositional activities, such as midden formation.	*Natural:* Resulting from natural disturbances such as erosion and animal and plant activity.

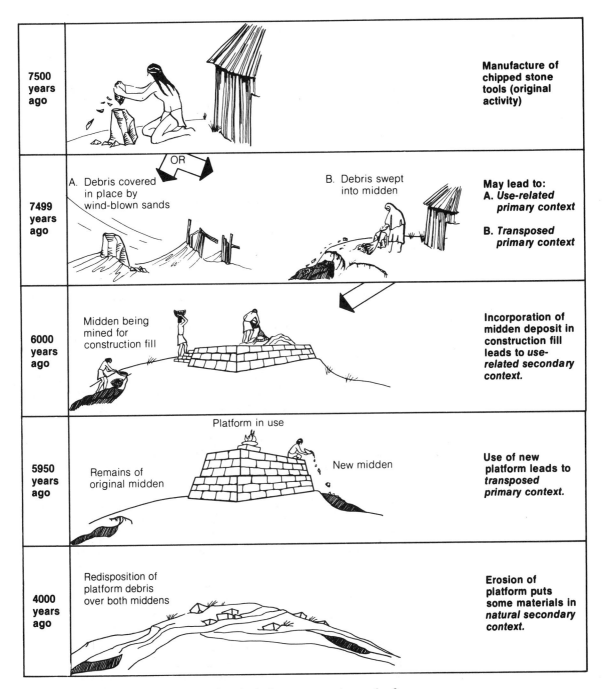

FIGURE 4.13 Different kinds of archaeological contexts are the result of varying combinations of behavioral and transformational processes.

may be manufactured to be used for water transport, food storage, and meal preparation, as well as to serve, when inverted, as a mold for other pottery—and if it remained within an undisturbed matrix together with its associated artifacts, ecofacts, and features, then its archaeological context upon discovery would be *primary* (undisturbed) and *use-related* (representing an ancient human behavior pattern). Knowing the provenience, association, matrix, and context, in this case reflected in the find of an inverted vessel surrounded by other vessels in various stages of manufacture along with clay-shaping tools and so forth, the archaeologist would be able to reconstruct not only a kind of manufacturing behavior (pottery making) but also many of the specific details of the process of pottery making. Determination that a context is primary and use-related allows the direct reconstruction of ancient behavior.

The survival of use-related primary contexts depends on transformational processes that act to preserve rather than to destroy. Truly undisturbed archaeological contexts, however, are very rare; most primary context situations have been altered to some degree by natural transformational processes. Casual or accidental use-related primary context results from the discard of unwanted artifacts or ecofacts at their point of acquisition, manufacture, or use. For example, broken tools and bones may be discarded at the place of their use. Specific kinds of behavior can often be reconstructed by careful excavation and recording of such "scatters" of artifacts or ecofacts. Provided there is evidence of contemporaneity, accumulation of this kind of debris may define "living floors"; the next time you move, just look at your old floor (especially in the corners!) when you're getting ready to leave for your new house or apartment.

Other kinds of use-related primary context involve deliberate acts of deposition. One of the most familiar of these deliberate forms is called a *cache,* referring either to the deposition of offerings in important or sacred locations or to the stockpiling of food or other resources for later use. Caching of offerings is analogous to the laying of cornerstones in new buildings in our own society. One of the best examples of use-related deposition is provided by burials and tombs. In many areas of the world, elaborate funerary customs developed in the past; the resultant tombs, when undisturbed, provide opportunities to reconstruct ancient ritual activity and belief systems. A good illustration of this is the Royal Tombs of Ur, excavated by Sir Leonard Woolley in the late 1920s (Fig. 4.14).

The Royal Tombs of Ur: Use-related primary context

King A-bar-gi and Queen Shub-ad were buried in adjacent tombs, accompanied by more than 80 other people. The actual chamber in which A-bar-gi lay had been plundered in ancient times—perhaps, as Woolley argues, when the next chamber over was prepared somewhat later for the queen. But the original entry pits and ramps of both tombs were undisturbed; excavation gradually disclosed an astounding retinue, including soldiers with gold- and silver-headed spears, female attendants wearing headdresses of lapis, carnelian, and gold, a decorated chariot accompanied by asses and their grooms, and an array of spectacularly beautiful artifacts such as gaming boards and harps. Recovery was slow and painstaking,

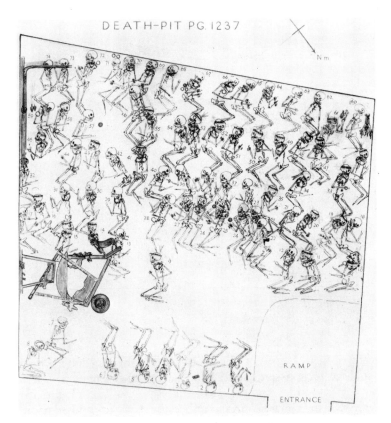

DEATH-PIT P.G. 1237

FIGURE 4.14 This plan shows positions of bodies in the "Great Death-Pit" adjacent to the royal tombs at Ur. (From Woolley 1934; by permission of The University Museum, University of Pennsylvania.)

because of the quantity and, in many cases, the fragility of the remains. As a result of the careful recording of the provenience and associations, a nearly complete funerary scene could later be reconstructed.

Other examples of use-related primary context have been preserved by natural events. The deposition of soil by wind and water has buried countless sites under deep layers of earth; a famous example of a suddenly buried site is the Roman city of Pompeii, which was covered by volcanic ash from the eruption of Mount Vesuvius in A.D. 79 (Fig. 2.3, p. 47).

Overall, while use-related primary contexts represent a wider range of ancient activities, archaeological remains in primary contexts are more commonly found in *transposed* situations. This means that before the remains were deposited, they were moved (or transposed), either intentionally or unintentionally, from where they had been made or used. Unintentional deposition may result from loss of artifacts away from the point of manufacture or use. Intentional deposition may result from the discard of items after they are damaged, broken, or no longer useful. In some cases, this intentional discard activity produces a **midden,** or specialized area for rubbish disposal removed from other human activity areas. Middens contain artifacts and ecofacts that are usually undisturbed from

Archaeological middens: Transposed primary context

SE

SW

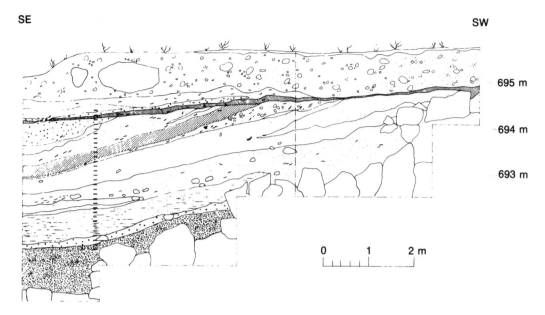

695 m

694 m

693 m

0   1   2 m

FIGURE 4.15 Cross-section drawing of a stratified midden representing nearly 2000 years of accumulation at Chalchuapa, El Salvador. One of the characteristics of transposed primary context, such as this midden, is that the artifacts from a given layer are contemporaneous but cannot be assumed to represent the same set of ancient activities.

Recognition of use-related secondary context: The tomb of Tut-ankh-amun

the moment of their deposition. Furthermore, if used over long periods of time, middens may become stratified, or layered (see Chapter 7), with each layer corresponding to a period of rubbish deposition (Fig. 4.15). Middens are thus in primary context, but because of the transposed nature of their deposition, the only past behavior directly reflected by this context is the general practice of rubbish accumulation and disposal. For this reason, the use or function of an artifact cannot be inferred directly from associations in transposed primary context. Of course, in either kind of primary context, association can be used to establish chronological contemporaneity: In the absence of later disturbance, items associated by provenience and within the same matrix are contemporary.

Secondary context refers to a condition in which provenience, associations, and matrix have been wholly or partially altered by processes of transformation. It is subdivided into use-related and natural variants. **Use-related secondary context** results from subsequent disturbance by human activity. Once identified, such disturbances can often aid the archaeologist in understanding how artifacts came to be associated. On the other hand, if the disturbed context is not recognized as such, chaotic and erroneous interpretation can result. For example, the contents of a heavily disturbed tomb might include not only some portion of the original furnishings but also material such as tools and containers that were brought in and left behind by looters. During the excavation of the tomb of the Egyptian pharaoh Tut-ankh-amun, ancient looting was recognized by evidence of two openings and reclosings of the entry; the final sealings of the disturbed areas were marked by different motifs from those on the un-

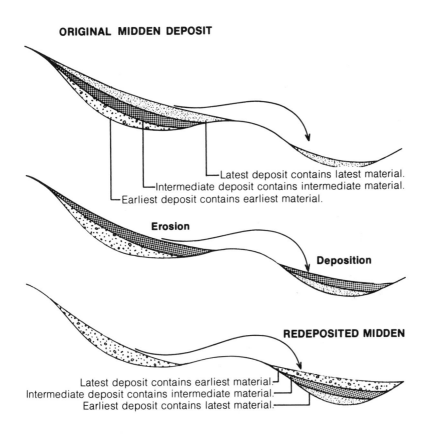

ORIGINAL MIDDEN DEPOSIT

Latest deposit contains latest material.
Intermediate deposit contains intermediate material.
Earliest deposit contains earliest material.

Erosion

Deposition

REDEPOSITED MIDDEN

Latest deposit contains earliest material.
Intermediate deposit contains intermediate material.
Earliest deposit contains latest material.

FIGURE 4.16 Schematic depiction of inverted layering. Uppermost (latest) material in the original deposit erodes first, and is redeposited as the lowermost layer downstream, resulting in natural secondary context.

disturbed portions. If the disturbance had not been recognized, the associations and arrangements of recovered artifacts might have been wrongly interpreted as representing burial ritual behavior.

Natural secondary context results from disturbance by nonhuman agents, including burrowing animals, tree roots, earthquakes, and erosion (Fig. 4.16). For example, at Ban Chiang, a site in northern Thailand, a series of ancient burials are juxtaposed in a very complex fashion, with later pits intruding into or overlapping earlier ones. But the job of segregating originally distinct units was made even more difficult by the numerous animal burrows, including those of worms, crisscrossing the units, so that the task of tracing pit lines and other surfaces was exacting and intricate work.

Archaeologists, then, not only must record carefully the associations, provenience, and matrix they are working with but also must use this information with great care to determine the context of their data. Unless they do so, the significance of the data will be lessened or even destroyed.

Recognition of natural secondary context: Ban Chiang, Thailand

THE STRUCTURE OF ARCHAEOLOGICAL DATA

We shall now examine the structure of the basic forms of archaeological data—that is, the ways artifacts, ecofacts, and features tend to be distributed with respect to one another. This structure, conditioned by the behavioral and transformational processes discussed above, provides the basis for reconstructing prehistoric behavior and culture. Our discussion assumes that the materials are found in primary context; for most practical purposes, this is further limited to use-related primary context.

The structure of archaeological data allows the archaeologist to infer certain kinds of ancient activity. This structure, together with the kinds of inferred activities (behavior), is summarized in Figure 4.17. Inference of prehistoric behavior relies on two basic factors: spatial clustering and comparison of functional characteristics. Individual artifacts, ecofacts, and features that are recovered in association with one another define **data clusters,** often referred to as **activity areas.** Clusters that show some consistent functional characteristics are used to define the kinds of ancient activity. The latter step involves an inference of function from the individual units. Repeated clustering of data with similar characteristics tends to reinforce such functional inferences. For example, the discovery of cutting tools (artifacts) in association with disarticulated and broken animal bones (ecofacts) allows the archaeologist to infer ancient butchering activity.

Of course, archaeologists do often encounter isolated remains. Although such finds reflect the past activities of individuals or groups, the lack of spatial clustering or functional patterning largely prevents the archaeologist from making inferences about prehistoric behavior. For convenience, we can refer to material of this kind as **isolated data.**

Setting aside these exceptions, at the most basic level of structuring the archaeologist may encounter data clusters that relate to a single function. For example, the discovery of several projectile points together with animal remains suggests ancient hunting activity. Similarly, clusters of stone-chipping debris, broken stone tools, and antler "punches," or clusters of raw clay, polishing stones, molds, and burned areas both indicate ancient manufacturing activity (for making chipped-stone tools and pottery, respectively). Clusters indicative of single activities may be termed **simple data clusters.** Simple data clusters may consist of any combination of artifacts, ecofacts, and features. Since buildings and other composite features are usually associated with multiple activities, however, they are less likely to be associated with simple data clusters.

At the next level (see Fig. 4.17), data clusters may be more varied internally, while still showing consistent functional patterns. These clusters may be interpreted as indicating two or more distinct activities that are often spatially segregated; the clusters can be referred to as **differentiated data clusters.** They frequently reflect activities divided along differences in age and sex. Since all known human societies manifest at least some be-

Data Structure   Inferred Behavior

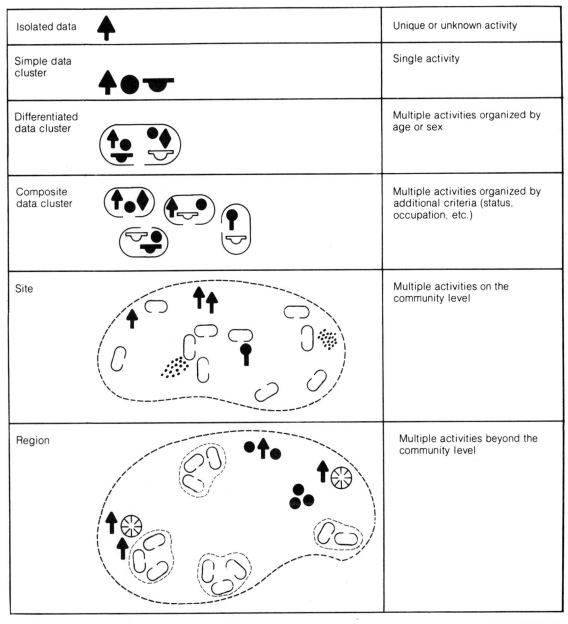

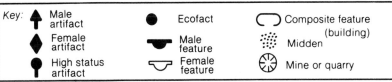

FIGURE 4.17 The hierarchical structuring of archaeological data found in use-related primary context.

havioral distinctions between males and females and between adults and children, some reflection of these distinctions can be expected in the archaeological record. For example, a composite feature such as house remains (consisting of foundation, floors, walls, and so on) may contain a hearth associated with cooking utensils and food residues in one area, along with hunting tools and weapons in another area. This kind of patterned diversity may reflect, respectively, female and male activity areas within a household. Child-size utensils and toys similarly reflect nonadult activities. These differentiated data clusters often mark residences housing nuclear families or larger kin groups.

Beyond the level of the differentiated data cluster, the archaeologist may find clusters that indicate multiple activities based on other social distinctions besides age and sex. Such behavioral distinctions include those involving occupational specialization, wealth or status distinctions, and class or caste differences. For example, a cluster of several composite features representing residences may contain the patterning of artifacts, ecofacts, and features reflective of the male/female activity distinction discussed above. In addition to this patterning, one of the residences may be associated with such noteworthy artifacts as unusually decorated pottery and imported jewelry; these may be indicative of higher status or greater wealth. Other buildings may differ in their size, shape, or decoration and be associated with distinct clusters of artifacts, ecofacts, or features. Depending on such criteria, these clusters may reflect civic activities, ceremonies, markets, and so forth. Clusters that embody distinctions beyond age and sex may be termed **composite data clusters.**

By viewing archaeological data according to a hierarchical structure based on cluster, pattern, and inferred functions, we may also define more precisely two concepts discussed earlier: site and region. Although the archaeological site remains a convenient unit for investigation, it can be defined as a contiguous concentration of the kinds of data clusters we have just discussed. Thus a site may be composed of one or more of any single kind of data cluster, or any combination of such data clusters. The archaeological region, the preferred means of establishing the limits to archaeological research, may be defined as a coherent geographical area containing two or more related sites.

The structure of archaeological data: David Clarke's reanalysis of Iron Age Glastonbury

To illustrate in more detail the various levels of structure in archaeological data, we will describe David L. Clarke's reanalysis of the remains of an Iron Age settlement at Glastonbury, England. During its occupation in the last two centuries B.C., this site grew to comprise what its original excavators in 1911 termed an "amorphous agglomeration" of clay floors, hearths, and wooden structures, all enclosed by a stockade wall. Clarke's detailed reexamination of the recorded evidence a half century after its recovery allowed identification of examples of all the kinds of data clustering we have defined here (Fig. 4.18).

On the edges of the ancient settlement, Clarke found *isolated data,* some of which (such as irregular clay patches) might represent severely eroded early buildings, but none of which was clearly linked to a particular ac-

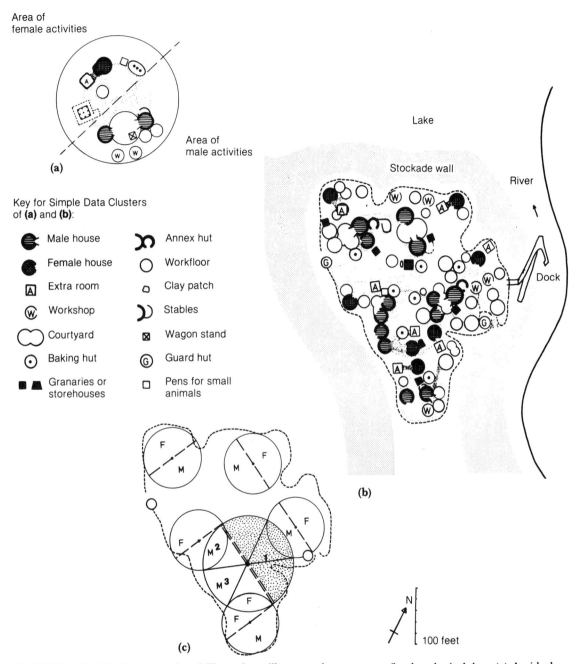

FIGURE 4.18   The Iron Age site of Glastonbury illustrates the structure of archaeological data. (a) An idealized house compound consists of one *differentiated data cluster*. Within this are multiple *simple data clusters* inferred as representing either male or female activities. (b) The site of Glastonbury at the peak of its growth, showing the location of individual houses and other features. (c) A schematic plan identifies the individual house compounds, each with its male-associated (M) and female-associated (F) areas. The large, partly shaded circle at the lower right defines a *composite data cluster*, which includes both the wealthiest (1) and the poorest house units (2 and 3) in the ancient community. (After Clarke 1972b.)

tivity. Many kinds of individual activities were discerned in other areas of the site, however, and these *simple data clusters* of artifacts, ecofacts, and features marked the locations where pursuits such as wool spinning, leather working, iron smelting, carpentry, weaving, milking, and animal husbandry took place. *Differentiated data clusters* defined a series of residential compounds, each having separate houses for males and females. Each of these gender-defined dwellings was associated with distinct work and storage features, so that carpentry, metal working, and small corral areas were found in male subdivisions, while baking, spinning, and granary areas were found in female subdivisions. Distinctions among these compounds indicated wealth and status differences, and the central compounds constituted a *composite data cluster* in which both the richest and the poorest residents of the settlement could be identified. The wealthiest, associated with a locally unique array of luxury and imported artifacts, such as jewelry and fine pottery, occupied the area closest to the dock (Compound 1) and provided the pivot around which the small community grew. Their adjacent neighbors to the southwest (Compounds 2 and 3) also had sizable compounds but, in contrast to Compound 1, lacked both wealth and status goods and facilities for the production of metal and other commodities. These inferences demonstrate that careful analysis of well-recorded archaeological data from primary contexts, even if recovered many years before, can yield a wealth of information about ancient human behavior.

At Glastonbury the *site* was a large composite data cluster composed of the six residential compounds plus paths and intervening open spaces that connected them, an encircling palisade with guardhouses at the entrances, and a small pier linking the east entry to the adjacent river. On a more inclusive scale, Clarke defined a series of three, progressively larger *regions* beyond the site proper. The smallest of these regions was a territory of 10-mile radius around the site, defined as the area within which Glastonbury residents would have spent most of their time and energies. This region embraced diverse economic resources such as pastureland, sources of potting clay or chipping stone, and fishing areas, as well as the "social resources" marked by neighboring settlements. The larger regions, up to 20 and 30 miles from Glastonbury, comprised areas with which its ancient residents were less constantly involved but that contained social, political, and economic sites and resources important to their lives.

The use of the data cluster concept provides only one way to organize archaeological data, and can produce valuable new insights, as Clarke's application to the Glastonbury material demonstrates. But more recently, John and Bryony Coles have reexamined the original data, in light of new finds, and critiqued some of Clarke's conclusions. Iron Age Glastonbury, then, illustrates vividly how the interpretation of the past is never final. In this one case, the original excavators' findings were reinterpreted by Clarke, and then again by Coles and Coles. We expect that Bulleid's and Gray's original data will continue to offer new information, in response to new questions phrased by future archaeologists.

APPROACHES TO ARCHAEOLOGICAL DATA ACQUISITION

Now that we have defined the forms of archaeological data, discussed their determinants, and examined the way this evidence is structured, we will consider the basic approaches to data recovery. The archaeologist gathers evidence of past human behavior as a first step toward understanding that ancient behavior and toward meeting both the specific objectives of the research and the general goals of archaeology (see Chapter 1). Realization of these objectives requires discovery of as much as possible about the characteristics of the data. Ideally, the archaeologist seeks to recover the full range of variation in the archaeological data relevant to his or her research questions. What was the range of activities carried on at a site? What was the range of places chosen for location and settlement? What was the range of forms and styles of pottery? To the extent that such variation existed but is not known, the research findings are incomplete, and conclusions based on them may be misleading or wrong. This means that the archaeologist must do everything possible to avoid acquiring an unrepresentative set of data—evidence that reflects only a part of the variation in the archaeological record. In a sense, archaeological data are always unrepresentative: Not all behavior produces tangible evidence, and, even for behavior that does, not all the remains will survive. So the ideal goal is seldom realized. But to some extent the unevenness in the availability of data can be compensated for by understanding the processes that affected the production and preservation of the evidence. At this point we need to consider how the archaeologist chooses data acquisition strategies to maximize the usefulness of the evidence that is available.

Data Universe and Sample Units

The first step in data acquisition is defining the boundaries of the area being investigated, to place a practical limit on the amount of evidence to be collected. A bounded area of investigation may be referred to as a **data universe.** An archaeological data universe is bounded both in geographical space and in time. Thus an investigator may define a data universe to correspond to a single site, or even to a portion of a site. In the regional approach the investigation extends over a much larger universe, such as an entire valley or mountain range containing many individual sites. The archaeologist may also draw temporal boundaries. One investigator may seek data corresponding to a relatively short period of a century or so; another archaeologist might be interested in a much longer span, such as the several thousand years of the most recent interglacial period.

Once defined, the archaeological data universe is subdivided into **sample units.** A sample unit is the unit of investigation; it may be defined by either arbitrary or nonarbitrary criteria. **Nonarbitrary units** correspond either to natural areas, such as environmental zones, or to cultural entities, such as rooms, houses, or sites (Fig. 4.19). **Arbitrary units** are spatial

FIGURE 4.19 A universe with nonarbitrary units, in this case, rooms in a prehistoric Southwestern pueblo; the shaded rooms were the ones excavated. (By permission from *Broken K Pueblo, Prehistoric Social Organization in the American Southwest,* by James N. Hill, University of Arizona Anthropological Paper #18, Tucson: University of Arizona Press, copyright 1970.)

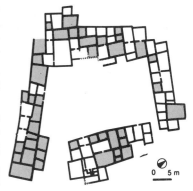

0   5 m

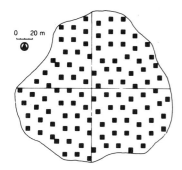

FIGURE 4.20 A universe with arbitrary units at Girik-i-Haciyan, Turkey; the black areas were the units investigated. (After Redman and Watson, reproduced by permission of The Society for American Archaeology, adapted from *American Antiquity* 35:281–282, 1970.)

divisions with no inherent natural or cultural relevance (Fig. 4.20). Examples of the latter include sample units defined by a grid system (equal-size squares, called **quadrats**), by geographical coordinates (points where coordinates cross, called **spots**), or by axes (linear corridors of equal width, called **transects**). In general, larger numbers of small arbitrary sample units are preferable to fewer units of larger size.

Sample units should not be confused with data: For example, if an archaeologist is looking for sites (as data), the sample units will be geographical areas where sites might be located. On the other hand, if sites are the sample units, the data to be gathered will be the artifacts, ecofacts, and features within the site.

The choice between arbitrary and nonarbitrary sample units is made by the investigator; it reflects the specific objectives of the study (see Chapter 5). But, in any case, all sample units are (or are assumed to be) comparable. That is, nonarbitrarily defined units are assumed to yield similar or complementary information about ancient behavior. For example, if sites are the sample units, one "cemetery" site will give information similar to that from another cemetery site and complementary to information from "habitation" sites and other sample units within the data population. Arbitrarily defined units, on the other hand, are comparable because they are always regular in size or shape or both.

The combined set of all sample units is the **population.** Note that if the universe is a region and the sample units are defined as known sites, for instance, the population will not include unknown sites, even though these areas are part of the universe. Nevertheless, conclusions drawn about the population are often inferred to be true of the universe as well.

The archaeological **data pool** is the total of the evidence available to the archaeologist within a given area of study (the data universe), conditioned by both behavioral and transformational processes. Remember that the data pool is the total potential data, while the population is the sum of the sample units. The amount of material actually recovered from a given archaeological data pool depends on the acquisition methods used and whether the goal is to collect all or only a portion of the available data.

Total Data Acquisition

Total data acquisition involves investigation of all the units in the population. Of course, the archaeologist never succeeds in gathering every shred of evidence from a given data universe. As we shall describe in later chapters, new techniques of recovery and analysis are constantly being developed that broaden the definition of data. A change in the definition of a research problem also alters the definition of what observed materials and relationships are data. It is nonetheless important to distinguish between investigations that attempt to collect all available archaeological evidence (by investigation of all sample units) and those that set out to collect only a portion of the available data. Something approaching total data acquisition, in this sense, is often attempted by salvage situations, when a site or a region is threatened with imminent destruction by construction of a new road or dam.

Sample Data Acquisition

In most cases, however, only a portion or **sample** of the data can be collected from a given archaeological data pool. With such **sample data acquisition,** the limits to the sample recovered are often partly dictated by economic realities—the archaeologist seldom has the funds to study all potential units. Nor is research time unlimited: Factors such as seasonal weather conditions and scheduling commitments often limit the time available to gather data. Access to archaeological data may be restricted: Portions of a single site or some parts of a region may be closed to the investigator because governmental agencies or private property owners have not granted access permission. In other cases, access may be hampered by natural barriers or by lack of roads or trails. Even in the absence of these limiting factors, in many cases, especially when excavation is involved, it would still be desirable to collect only a part of the available archaeological evidence. Except in such cases as a site or an area under threat of immediate destruction, most archaeologists recommend that a portion of every archaeological site or region be left untouched to allow future scientists, using more sophisticated techniques and methods than those in use today, a chance to work with intact sources of archaeological data. In this way future investigations can check and refine the results obtained using present techniques.

Probabilistic and Nonprobabilistic Sampling

Since most archaeological situations demand that only part of the available data be collected, we need to consider the methods used to determine which units will actually be investigated. Two approaches are available for selection of data samples: probabilistic and nonprobabilistic sampling methods.

Nonprobabilistic sampling uses informal criteria or personal judgment in the selection of data samples. Such sampling techniques have been used since the early days of archaeology and usually involve gathering data from the most obvious or most easily investigated available archaeological remains. This is not to say that such uncontrolled sampling methods are wrong; no archaeologist should ignore prominent or obvious remains. And no one can deny the ability of skilled investigators to locate archaeological evidence, whether on the basis of experience, intuition, or some "sixth sense." It is also true, however, that nonprobabilistic sampling has often been accompanied by disregard for defining the units being sampled, the population, or the data universe. Without this information, no one else can judge how well the sample (a building within a site, for instance, or a site within a region) represents the universe as a whole—or even what universe it is supposed to represent.

Nonprobabilistic sampling can lead to significant and sometimes spectacular discoveries, and it is often useful when the area of study has never been investigated before. It is also the appropriate choice when something specific is sought, such as an ancient ritual offering, whose contents may then indicate the age of the particular construction in which it was buried. In this case, data are being acquired for a specialized purpose, and the unit is not chosen as an example of all units of its kind. But, if a sample is supposed to substitute for total data acquisition and is therefore intended to represent a cross-section of some larger population, nonprobabilistic sampling techniques are not the best ones to use.

Probabilistic sampling techniques come from the field of statistics and allow the archaeologist to specify mathematically how a sample relates to a larger population. The individual techniques are all based on probability theory, and although these statistical sampling procedures can never ensure that a sample is fully representative of the whole population, they do maximize the probability that it is.

Once the universe, sample unit, and population have been defined, the archaeologist proceeds with probabilistic sampling by labeling all the units and making them into a list. This list is the **sampling frame,** from which a number of units will be chosen. The total number of units chosen, called the **sample size,** may also be expressed as a percentage of the population size; it is then called the **sampling fraction.** Although archaeologists are still evaluating what sampling fractions are most appropriate for particular research situations, there will never be a single figure that is right for all circumstances. In practice, sample size is usually greatly influenced—if not altogether dictated—by limits of time and funds.

Of course, the closer one gets to a sample size of 100 percent (total data acquisition), the more closely the characteristics of the sample can be expected to reflect those of the population. But the absolute size of the sample and the population are also very important. In a population of 10, for example, 20 percent is 2 units and each unit represents 10 percent of the population. In a population of 1000, however, a 20 percent sample contains 200 units, and each unit accounts for only 0.1 percent of the total. As the sample and population sizes increase, the probable importance of any one unit thus decreases; at the same time, the risk of missing an example of important variation by excluding any one unit declines. That is one reason why samples based on very large populations—such as national opinion polls—can often use relatively small sampling fractions. In the United States, a sample of less than 1 percent of the total population would still include over two million people. Archaeological populations and samples are seldom so large: Regional populations of site units typically total in the tens and hundreds, but pottery sherd populations typically may have ten thousand to more than a million individual sherd units.

There are three basic probabilistic sampling schemes—simple random, systematic, and stratified.

Sample size: Advantages of large numbers

Simple Random Sampling   **Simple random sampling** is the most basic method of probabilistic sampling. Random sampling does not mean haphazard, hit-or-miss sampling; rather, it means that each unit in the sampling frame has a statistically equal chance for selection. It removes the element of choice—and therefore any opportunity for selection bias—from the archaeologist's hands.

Once the sample units have been defined, totaled, and listed in a frame, they are labeled with a series of consecutive numbers. After the sample size has been determined, the required number of units is selected in a random manner from the frame—such as by matching the unit's numbers to a table of random numbers from a statistics book. The archaeologist then proceeds to investigate the units so chosen. If any of the selected units cannot be investigated—for instance, because a landowner refuses entry to a site, or an artifact to be analyzed is lost—the sample is no longer random and cannot be subjected later to statistical analyses that assume random sample selection. One "solution" to this problem is to settle questions of access before drawing the sample, to exclude units that cannot be examined anyway; in that case, the sample will be random, but the definition of the population will have been changed to include only accessible units.

In general, simple random sampling has a limited use in archaeology, since it treats all sample units as equivalent and ignores any known dimensions of variation—such as location of some sites on hilltops and others on the valley floor. An archaeologist who already has knowledge about variation within a population should take that information into account in designing a sampling strategy.

Systematic Sampling In a **systematic sample,** the first unit is selected with a random number table or some other randomizing technique. All others are selected at predetermined, equal intervals from the first (every 4th unit, or every 27th unit, or whatever). This method eliminates one potential problem encountered in simple random sampling: The latter could easily yield a sample with units concentrated in one or a few areas of the population—sites in only the north and west parts of a region, for example; systematic sampling ensures spatial (or other kinds of) separation among the units, so that all portions of the population are represented.

On the other hand, if any aspects of the data happen to have the same kind of distribution as the systematic intervals used for sample selection, this kind of sampling runs into problems. For instance, suppose rooms within a structure are used as sampling units; if, unknown to the archaeologist, every third room had a fireplace, systematic sampling with an interval of three starting with a fireplace room would hit only those rooms—or, with a different starting point, would hit none of them (see Fig. 4.21).

Stratified Sampling In many archaeological situations, it is obvious from the onset of investigation that the data units are not uniform. When the nature of this variation is believed (or known) to be important to the research questions, **stratified sampling** may be used, to ensure that sample

FIGURE 4.21 Hearths (not visible without excavation) occur in every third room; a systematic sample with an interval of three would encounter either all or none of these features.

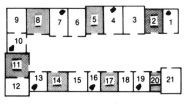

□ Systematic sample of rooms excavated
● Hearth

units are drawn to represent each kind of observed variation within the population.

In this method, sample units are divided into two or more groups (called **sampling strata**), which correspond to each kind of observed variation within the population. For example, in looking for sites within a valley, sampling strata might correspond to ecological zones. Once the strata are defined, simple random or systematic samples may be chosen from each. The key advantages of stratified random sampling are that the known kinds of variation in the population can be recognized and assured of representation in the sample, while the individual units actually chosen to represent them are still selected randomly.

Choice of a Sampling Strategy   Other, more complex sampling techniques have been devised, but these are the basic ones. The criteria for choosing among them in a given situation can be quite complex. A thorough background in statistics is necessary to make the best choice—but so is a thorough consideration of the particular archaeological circumstances. Archaeologists who are not well trained in statistics should at least know how to consult a statistician to get help. And it is crucial to consult the statistician *before* the sampling (unit selection *or* data collection) begins. This is because many statistical techniques of data analysis can be used only if the sample data were selected by probabilistic sampling; if difficulties in sampling occur, a statistician will not be able to cure them afterward.

There are two final general rules on choice of sampling techniques. First, the more the archaeologist knows beforehand about the population to be sampled, the more sophisticated the sampling procedures may be. Political pollsters, who are among the best-known users of sampling techniques, are able to make the predictions they do because of the quality and detail of the census data they use to stratify their population. In archaeology, we know much less about the populations we seek to study, which limits the utility of probabilistic sampling in many situations.

Second, sampling techniques (and sample size) should be appropriate to the scale of the archaeologist's research and the quality of the data. There is no point in working out a complicated sampling design when the sample is so small that, for example, each stratum will be represented by only one or two numbers. Nor will complicated sampling designs be very useful with "poor" data pools, such as sites that have been nearly obliterated or artifacts whose original form is undefinable. This kind of methodological overkill wastes time, energy, and funds.

The application of probabilistic sampling is of great benefit to archaeological data acquisition. However, no single method can anticipate all the normal complexities of archaeological data. Archaeologists cannot allow their methods to restrict their research rigidly; the means by which they acquire data must remain flexible. If, for instance, an archaeologist encounters a new and unique site within the defined universe after drawing a stratified random sample of different-size sites, the fact that the new site is outside the chosen sample does not mean that it should be ignored. Instead the investigator collects data from the new site and uses that information to shed light on the variation in the overall sample. Because it was not chosen by probabilistic sampling techniques, the new site cannot be included in statistical analyses that assume such selection procedures, but to avoid all consideration of relevant data because of this is to lose potentially vital insights.

Thus, in many cases, probabilistic and nonprobabilistic sampling methods are both used, to yield the most representative overall sample possible. These approaches to sampling are used in archaeology not only for site location and field data acquisition—including the surface surveys and excavations to be discussed in the next few chapters—but also in later analysis of the data. This is true for any category of data, from the analysis of artifacts such as ceramics or stone tools to the analysis of entire sites and of settlement patterns. Whenever possible, from the onset of the investigation to its conclusion, the archaeologist chooses sampling methods that maximize the chance that the samples are actually representative of the populations from which they were drawn.

SUMMARY

Archaeological data have several forms: artifacts, features, and ecofacts. In addition to these, archaeologists also examine distributions of data within sites and regions. Further information about the past is gleaned from determining the matrix, provenience, and association of the data and evaluating their context. The understanding of archaeological context (more specifically, discrimination among various kinds of contexts) is the crucial link that allows the investigator to evaluate the significance of data—that is, to reconstruct the kinds of behavior that the data represent.

Archaeologists can never recover data representing all kinds of past behavior. Some behavior leaves no tangible evidence. The evidence of other kinds of ancient behavior may be transformed through time by a variety of processes, both human and natural in origin. These processes act selectively either to preserve or to destroy archaeological evidence. Thus the data available to the archaeologist constitute a sample determined first by ancient activity (behavioral processes) and then by human and natural forces acting after the evidence is deposited (transformational processes). Assuming they have data in primary (undisturbed) context, archaeologists can infer various kinds of ancient behavior directly, by the ways the data are spatially clustered and functionally patterned. We have defined five levels in this data structure (beyond that of isolated data): the simple data cluster, the differentiated data cluster, the composite data cluster, the site, and the region.

The resulting archaeological data form the base that the investigator attempts to recover, either totally (by collection of all available evidence) or by sampling methods. Whatever methods are used, the archaeologist seeks data that represent, insofar as possible, the full range of human behavior.

It is generally practical and desirable to collect only a sample of the data pool. The methods used to acquire data samples may be either probabilistic or nonprobabilistic, but only probabilistic samples allow reliable projections concerning the nature of the overall data base. In the past, archaeologists often collected samples in a manner that was biased toward discovering the most prominent and spectacular remains. Today, however, specific research goals and field conditions call for a flexible mix of sampling schemes to enable the archaeologist to learn as much as possible about the past.

GUIDE TO FURTHER READING

The Forms of Archaeological Data
> Bass 1966; L. R. Binford 1964; Coggins and Shane 1984; Coles 1984; Cordell 1984b; Courty, Goldberg, and Macphail 1989; Deetz 1967; Fish and Kowalewski 1990; Flannery 1976b; Hamilton and Woodward 1984; Hayes, Brugge, and Judge 1981; Johnson 1977; Lightfoot 1986; MacNeish 1964a; Parsons 1974; Spaulding 1960; Struever 1971; Willey 1953

The Determinants of Archaeological Data
> Ascher 1968; L. R. Binford 1981b, 1982; Butzer 1982; David 1971; Deal 1985; Fehon and Scholtz 1978; Frink 1984; Gero and Conkey 1991; Gifford 1981; Glob 1969; Hayden and Cannon 1983; Heider 1967; Kosso 1991; Lange and Rydberg 1972; Moseley 1983; Patrik 1985; Schiffer 1972, 1976, 1985, 1987; Stein 1983, 1987; Villa 1982; Villa and Courtin 1983; White and Kardulias 1985; Wood and Johnson 1978; Woolley 1934

The Structure of Archaeological Data
> Ascher 1968; L. R. Binford 1981a; Clarke 1972b; Coles and Coles 1986; Flannery 1976b; Schiffer 1985; Spaulding 1960

Approaches to Archaeological Data Acquisition
> Bellhouse 1980; L. R. Binford 1964; Carr 1985; Clark 1982; Clark and Stafford 1982; Cowgill 1968, 1977, 1986; Doran and Hodson 1975; Hill 1966, 1967; Hole 1980; Kintigh 1988; Mueller 1974, 1975; Orton 1980; Ragir 1975; Redman 1973, 1974; Rowlett 1970; Struever 1971; Thomas 1978, 1986b

CHAPTER FIVE

ARCHAEOLOGICAL RESEARCH

The research design must be directed by a well-trained anthropologist capable of making interpretations and decisions in terms of the widest possible factual and theoretical knowledge of general anthropology.

Lewis R. Binford, "A Consideration of Archaeological Research Design," 1964

The excavator without an intelligent policy may be described as an archaeological food-gatherer, master of a skill, perhaps, but not creative in the wider terms of constructive science.

Sir Mortimer Wheeler, Archaeology from the Earth, *1954*

Today's archaeologist is primarily a scientific researcher. Most archaeologists in all nations either work for research institutions (including museums, governmental agencies, and CRM consulting firms) or have academic appointments in universities. Although archaeologists employed by governmental agencies may devote virtually all their professional energies to field research, some museums and most universities require the archaeologist to teach as well. In any case, good archaeological research requires teaching skills: The professional archaeologist must train and supervise the individuals working on a project, whether they are students, volunteers, or day laborers.

This chapter will examine the nature of archaeological research from various points of view. We will begin by considering the complexity of modern archaeology and the archaeologist's consequent need for the aid of specialists from a variety of other disciplines. Next we will discuss archaeological projects and the design of archaeological research. We then use a detailed case study to illustrate how modern archaeological research is conducted.

THE SCOPE OF RESEARCH

Scientific archaeology demands a broad range of expertise. Today's archaeologist must be a theoretical scientist, a methodologist, a technician, and an administrator. Although the archaeologist must be able to perform all these functions, in reality it is nearly impossible for one individual to do everything; usually, the archaeologist must bring together specialists from a wide variety of disciplines. Doing so requires a multidisciplinary approach—coordinating the efforts of many scientists, each of whom focuses on a particular aspect of the research. Thus one extremely important skill the archaeologist must have is recognizing when the proper specialist should be consulted. Only by depending on others can the archaeologist ensure that the data collected are best used.

As a theoretical scientist, an archaeologist should be able to define appropriate research problems based on a thorough knowledge of current problems and relevant research. These problems are usually broad areas, such as the origin and development of food production (when? where? under what conditions?). A research problem delineates the general and specific goals to be met and the hypotheses to be tested. The archaeologist then must be able to evaluate, synthesize, and interpret the results of research.

As a methodologist, an archaeologist plans the approaches (methods) to be used to meet the theoretical goals. This task includes choosing tactics of data collection and analysis. The analysis of data in modern archaeology almost invariably requires consultation with specialists from allied disciplines. If the archaeologist is a well-trained anthropologist, she or he may be able to assume the role of an ethnographer to document contemporary culture, or a physical anthropologist to analyze skeletal remains. Most archaeologists will consult with geologists or geomorphologists, ecologists, botanists, zoologists, geographers, paleontologists, and other specialists at one time or another. In addition, statisticians, computer programmers, and other individuals may help in processing and analyzing data.

As a technician, an archaeologist collects archaeological data by various means. The archaeologist may have to assume, or employ others to assume, the roles of explorer, surveyor or cartographer, photo interpreter, architect, and geologist, as well as excavator. Recording and processing data may require drafting, photography, and conservation skills, among others.

The final function of the archaeologist is that of administrator. To carry on archaeological research effectively, an archaeologist must be an executive who keeps all phases of the project on schedule. The archaeologist must have—or furnish through specialists—the other skills necessary for administering an archaeological project. Such specialists may include an agent or troubleshooter for arranging permits and the like, an accountant, a secretary, and—when the research reaches the publication stage—an editor.

The effectiveness of a research organization depends on the archaeologist's application of overall management skills to integrate the four functions just discussed. In some cases, the archaeologist may find most of the required support specialists housed under one roof, as they are in large museums and research institutions in many parts of the world. In the United States, the Smithsonian Institution provides one of the most complete support facilities for archaeology. Many university museums, through their laboratories and other facilities, provide more than adequate support for their research archaeologists. However, no single institution can furnish all the specialists and facilities that today's archaeologist requires. Thus, at some point, all archaeologists seek outside assistance to complete their research successfully.

RESEARCH PROJECTS

The size and duration of archaeological research projects depend on the scale of the problems being investigated and the kind of investigation, if any, that has been done in the area previously. Research concerned with complex civilizations, such as explorations of large urban sites in southwest Asia and Mexico, usually calls for a large staff and a huge labor force (Fig. 5.1). Such projects employ teams of on-site specialists and may occur over many years or even decades. In other situations, a few months of a single individual's work may suffice to gather data. Like most activities, archaeological research is limited by the availability of time and money. In some cases, when nationalistic and economic priorities favor archaeological study, governments may spend millions of dollars on such work. But many archaeologists have considerable difficulty securing enough research funds—and enough time away from their other duties—to undertake their own research projects. A far greater problem, however, threatens the very existence of archaeological research: the increasing pace of destruction wrought by our rapidly expanding world. The destruction of archaeological remains has reached such proportions that we may well ask, "Does the past have a future?" We will consider the problem of the destruction of archaeological sites in the final chapter of this book.

RESEARCH DESIGN

Traditionally, most archaeological research has been "site-oriented": The primary or sole objective was to excavate a particular site and, often, to collect spectacular material. Research was conducted by choosing a prominent site, forming an expedition, excavating the site, and transporting the recovered artifacts to a museum storeroom or other facility. In many cases, the full results of such investigations were never published.

With the emergence of archaeology as a scientific discipline, more systematic approaches to research have become the rule. Among the first explicit calls for systematic **research design** in archaeology were the mid-20th-century critiques of Walter Taylor and Lewis Binford. Binford's appeal for scientific research design in archaeology emphasized regional "problem-oriented" research projects.

Site-oriented research has gradually given way to investigations that are regional in scope, as archaeologists have sought a broader and more complete frame of reference for their interpretations of the past. Regional problem-oriented research seeks to solve specific problems or test one or more hypotheses by using controlled and representative samples of data from a particular region. Because of its complexity, research of this kind demands a thorough, systematic plan to coordinate all its facets successfully. Problem-oriented research begins with the definition of the research problem and the geographical or cultural region to be investigated.

FIGURE 5.1 The modern large-scale archaeological excavation at Quiriguá, Guatemala, involved over 100 people and continued over a six-year period. (Quiriguá Project, The University Museum, University of Pennsylvania.)

Systematic research design involves a formal process that guides the conduct of the investigation, both to ensure the validity of research results and to maximize efficiency in use of time, money, and effort. The design is systematic and formal because it divides the research process into a series of steps or stages, each with specific functions (Fig. 5.2). Each functionally distinct stage forms a part of an overall sequence of investigation that extends from origin (formulation stage) to conclusion (publication stage). We will discuss these stages in sequence below. Note, however, that the clear-cut sequence we outline is idealized. In most cases, aspects of two or more stages take place simultaneously, and some stages may be delayed or postponed until later in the research sequence.

Furthermore, since each archaeological sequence is unique, this research design must be flexible enough to adapt to a wide variety of individual needs. Thus the following design, while outlining broadly the stages of archaeological research, does not attempt to specify the actual ways in which research is conducted at any stage in the process. Nor does it assume a particular cultural model, which usually influences the specific research plan, as we mentioned in Chapter 3. Later chapters discuss the various alternative procedures used to discover, gather, process, analyze, and interpret archaeological data.

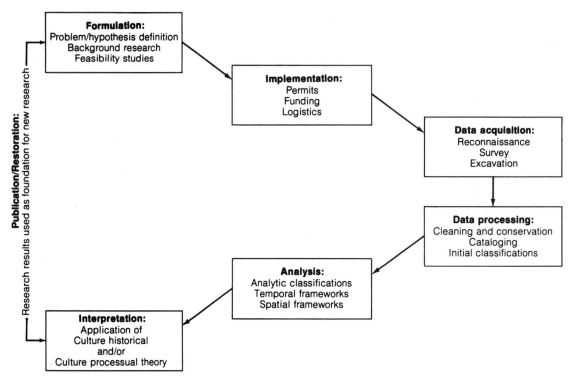

FIGURE 5.2 Diagram of stages of archaeological research.

Formulation of Research

Long before fieldwork begins, an archaeologist must formulate a plan for the research. **Formulation** involves defining the research problem, doing background investigations, and making feasibility studies.

A decision regarding the geographical area or problem of interest both limits and guides further investigation. Once that choice is made, the archaeologist conducts background research, locating and studying previous work. Previous archaeological research in the same region or even within the same site is obviously crucial, but investigations that covered adjacent regions or concerned similar problems are important as well. Useful background information includes geographical, geological, climatological, ecological, and anthropological studies, if available. Some information may be readily available in published form in any good research library. In many cases, however, such data are not published and must be pursued in archives, laboratories, and storerooms. Consultations and interviews with individual experts may be necessary and advisable.

Because archaeological research customarily requires fieldwork, a feasibility study including a trip to the region or sites to be investigated is usually advisable. Its objective is evaluation of the archaeological situation and of local conditions such as accessibility and availability of labor force. If the area under study has never been investigated archaeologically, or if previous work has been inadequate, archaeological reconnaissance (see below) is usually needed to identify and locate archaeological remains.

Thorough background investigations facilitate the actual archaeological research by refining the problem under investigation and defining specific research goals. The goals of most archaeological research include testing of one or more specific hypotheses. Some hypotheses may derive from previously proposed models; others may arise during the formulation of the research problem. As the research progresses, of course, new hypotheses will be generated and tested. It is important to remember, however, that the initial formulation of a research problem is what leads the archaeologist to look for particular kinds of data. One theory about the change from food gathering to food production, for example, might predict that the transition took place in a mountain valley setting; another theory might predict a seaside locale. In either case, the archaeologist would need to define not only where to look but also what kinds of data to look for: the specific artifacts, ecofacts, and features believed to be evidence for and against the changes being documented. Data collection will certainly include more than just these materials, but the formulation stage of research must include definition of the kinds of data necessary to test adequately and fairly the hypotheses set forth.

Implementation of Research

Implementation involves all arrangements necessary to the success of the proposed fieldwork. These arrangements may be complex, especially if the research is to be carried out in a foreign country. The first step, in any case, is to secure the necessary permissions for conducting field research, usually from special government agencies charged with overseeing archaeological activities. Sometimes archaeologists are invited or hired to investigate a particular site or area, as in CRM research (see Chapter 1). More often, it is the archaeologist who initiates research and who therefore must seek official permission. Since archaeological research often requires access to wide areas of land and involves a measure of disturbance of this property through excavation, the owners of the land on which the work is to take place must also grant permission before investigations can proceed. Since the laws governing access to and investigations of archaeological sites vary from country to country, the archaeologist must be aware of the relevant laws and customs within the country where the project is to take place. Crossing international boundaries also requires special arrangements for the import and export of research equipment, research funds, and other materials. Import and export permits must therefore be secured from the appropriate government agencies.

Once permissions have been secured, the archaeologist must raise funds to finance the research. In some cases, funds may be available from the inception of the research, but more often the archaeologist must submit a research proposal to either private or governmental institutions that fund archaeological investigations. In the United States, one of the most active governmental funding agencies has been the National Science Foundation. The National Park Service and other agencies also underwrite a great deal of work within sites located on government lands. And a variety of private foundations are active in supporting archaeological work in the United States and abroad.

When the research is funded, the archaeologist can turn to logistic arrangements. Research equipment and supplies must be acquired. Field facilities must be rented or built for safekeeping this equipment and for processing and storing artifacts and research records. Most projects require a supervisory staff, which must be recruited, transported, and housed. Although short-term projects often house the staff in temporary quarters such as tents, long-term projects may use permanent facilities that may be rented for, donated to, or even built by the project. Major items of equipment, such as vehicles, should be insured; staff members should carry health and accident coverage (most projects require that all members obtain their own insurance). Many projects rely on trained local labor forces for moving the massive amounts of earth involved in large-scale excavation. In such cases, the workers must be hired, trained, supervised, and in some cases housed. Other projects use volunteer nonprofessional or student labor for excavation, but these work forces still must be recruited, transported, supervised, and cared for.

Acquisition of Data

Archaeological **data acquisition** involves two basic procedures: examination of surface characteristics and excavation. Probabilistic sampling techniques can be used with either to maximize the likelihood that the data collected are representative of the total data pool. We will discuss these procedures only briefly here, since they will be treated in depth in Chapters 6 and 7.

Archaeological **reconnaissance** is the means for locating and identifying archaeological sites. Sites may be found by direct observation (by foot, mule, or jeep) or by remote sensors such as aerial or satellite photography, radar, or other instrumentation (see Chapter 6). Once sites are located, **surface survey** records as much as possible about archaeological sites without excavation (Chapter 6). Recording often includes photography (aerial or ground-level), mapping, and sampling by subsurface probes such as remote sensors and mechanical devices. Most commonly, samples of artifacts are collected from the ground surface of sites. **Excavation** is undertaken to reveal the subsurface configuration of archaeological sites. The archaeologist uses a variety of techniques both to retrieve and to record excavation data; these will be treated in Chapter 7.

Data Processing

Once archaeological evidence has been collected, it must be processed in the field. Portable data—artifacts and ecofacts—are usually processed in a field laboratory or museum, undergoing several steps (cleaning, numbering, and cataloging) to ensure that they are preserved and stored so that they are easily retrievable. Artifacts are often recorded in the lab, using a card or log registration system, drawings, and photography. Because features cannot be moved, they are always recorded in the field through notes, photography, scaled drawings, and similar methods. These recorded data are normally not further processed in the laboratory but must be stored for easy retrieval and later use. Sorting involves division of the data into categories, both as the initial step in classification and as an aid to later manipulation during analysis. Both raw and recorded data are usually sorted and stored in the field laboratory. **Data processing** is described in detail in Chapter 8.

Analysis of Data

Data **analysis** provides information useful for archaeological interpretation. Analyses are of various kinds, including typological classifications based on form or style, determination of age, and various technical studies, such as identification of what the artifact is made of and how it was made. Some analyses, such as classification, can be done in the field laboratory. However, the more technical analyses are usually undertaken at permanent laboratory facilities. When the quantity of data precludes analysis of the entire collection, the archaeologist may study a controlled sample of the total collection. We begin to consider the analysis of archaeological data in Chapter 9.

Interpretation of Data

The use of scientific procedures in interpreting data differentiates professional archaeologists from their antiquarian predecessors. **Interpretation** involves the synthesis of all results of data collection, processing, and analysis in an attempt to answer the original research questions. In most cases, historical and anthropological models provide the most consistent reconstructions and explanations of the past. Chapters 13–17 discuss data interpretation.

Publication of Results

Once all stages of research are completed, the professional archaeologist must publish both the data and the results of the data analysis and interpretation as soon as feasible. **Publication** makes the research accessible so that its results can be used and retested by fellow archaeologists, other scholars, or any interested individual. In this way the research furthers the broadest objectives of archaeology and of science in general. Too often archaeologists have failed to match the scale of their data acquisition effort with the scale of their publication effort; but data acquisition is justified only if the information is later made public (see Chapter 18).

A CASE STUDY IN RESEARCH DESIGN: MODERN ARCHAEOLOGICAL RESEARCH AT COPAN, HONDURAS

To illustrate the research design just outlined, we will devote the rest of this chapter to a case study of actual research, focusing on archaeological investigation at the Classic Maya site of Copán, Honduras. Copán was chosen for the case study for several reasons. First, archaeological research there has been almost continuous since 1975, the senior author of this text was involved in the formulation of the original research plan for the site, and both authors have directed aspects of some of the most recent investigations. Second, this research has been carried out as a series of at least seven distinct but related projects, addressing different questions from different theoretical perspectives at a variety of scales (see Table 5.1). Some have emphasized figuring population size and sketching the internal workings of society at large; others have centered on the activities of Copán's rulers and their royal entourage. Each set of questions has required its own specific research design, its own definition of what data are appropriate to examine, and its own interdisciplinary cast of scholars.

Because of all this, recent research at Copán highlights exactly how archaeological investigation is guided by the questions being asked, and how each round of research builds on what has been learned before. It is the integration of richly varied data *and* equally varied thinking about the data that makes the results so exciting and rewarding. And third, the same rich variety in questions and investigations illustrates the principal theoretical orientations described in Chapter 3—culture historical, cultural processual, and postprocessual archaeological approaches—and shows how the contributions of each broaden the findings of the others.

In what follows, we outline the research design and some of the accomplishments (as of 1991) of recent archaeological investigation at Copán. Individually and together, these offer a useful illustration of the steps required to plan, prepare, organize, and conduct archaeological research,

Table 5.1 Copán Archaeological Projects since 1975

Name	Dates	Directors
Valley Project	1976–1977	Gordon Willey
PAC I	1977–1980	Claude Baudez
PAC II	1980–1985	William Sanders
Mosaics Project	1985–present	William Fash, Barbara Fash
PAAC	1985–present	William Fash, Ricardo Agurcia, E. Wyllys Andrews V, Rudy Lários, Robert Sharer (Codirectors)
Rural Sites Project	1985–1988	David Webster
North Group Project	1988–1989	Wendy Ashmore

using an interdisciplinary perspective to accomplish scientific objectives, while dealing with the political, economic, and social realities of the contemporary world.

Background: Ancient Maya Civilization

Classic Maya civilization flourished between approximately A.D. 250 and 900 in the tropical lowlands of southern Mexico and northern Central America (Fig. 5.3). In settings ranging from the dense rain forest of Guatemala to the scrub growth of the Yucatán plain, the Maya built beautiful and imposing cities, created masterpieces of sculpture, perfected elaborate astronomical calculations, and developed a system of writing that has only recently been deciphered (see Fig. 1.11, p. 30). Because of their accomplishments, the ancient Maya have fascinated archaeologists and the public at large for well over a century. The last few decades, however, have produced an explosion of research whose results have led to important new interpretations of Classic Maya society.

For a long time, the Maya were portrayed as simple farmers, living in scattered groups and tending small, family-held cornfields. These farmers supported a small group of priestly rulers whose principal job was to ensure the success of each year's harvest. Toward that end, the priests occasionally used great architectural centers to celebrate public rituals, but mostly they kept quietly to themselves, conducting private ceremonies, recording accurate counts of the days and years, and tracking the movements of the stars.

Today, however, combined evidence from archaeology and epigraphy (the decipherment of inscriptions) has changed this view, indicating instead a complex society of farmers, craft workers, merchants, and kings, all in far greater numbers than previously thought. Rulership was hereditary, and individual rulers not only governed their local populace but also

FIGURE 5.3 Map of the Maya area. Copán is located in the southeastern portion of this area.

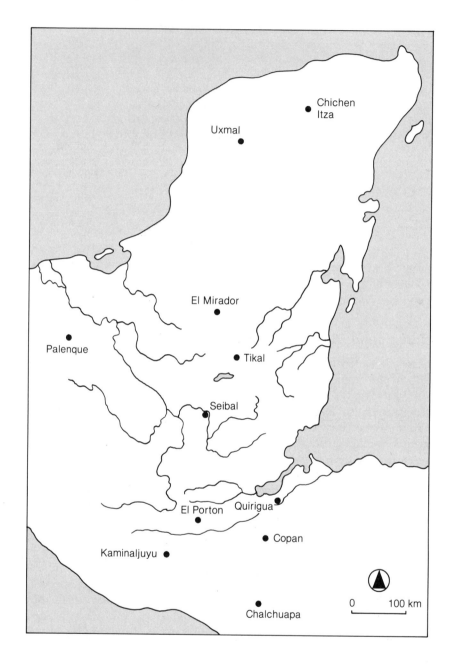

forged alliances with powerful neighbors, while waging war against others—a far cry from the quiet priests of earlier interpretations. These active rulers were also the likely sponsors of the extensive hillside terracing, swamp modifications, and other efforts that increased agricultural productivity for the large communities. Despite this seeming abundance, however, archaeological data confirm the not-surprising fact that the upper classes had better diets (as well as more elaborate houses and richer burials) than did their poorer subjects.

Archaeology has gone on to reveal that imposing architecture and other hallmarks of Maya civilization began in the Preclassic period, well before the earliest known lowland inscriptions used to define the onset of the "Classic" period (ca. A.D. 250). Moreover, we can now see clearly that the form of Classic-period society had roots both in the lowlands themselves (at El Mirador, for example) and in the highlands farther to the south, at places such as Kaminaljuyú. Finally, archaeologists continue to grapple with the question of why Maya civilization declined around A.D. 900. Continued research has shown that many dramatic changes did occur in powerful centers such as Tikal, Seibal, and Copán, and that the causes were probably a combination of factors: Local populations caused resources to be spread too thin, non-Maya outsiders disrupted supply networks, and increased warfare led to the destruction of some Maya cities. There is also growing evidence that some Maya centers managed to survive and prosper, and even in areas that saw drastic changes, a good number of farmers and other commoners stayed on their land, more or less as before. Furthermore, lowland civilization as a whole clearly kept on after 900 as more northerly capitals such as Uxmal and Chichén Itzá thrived.

Many aspects of ancient Maya life are now well documented, but questions inevitably remain. Some of these are broad issues (the causes of the origin and decline of lowland civilization, for example); others are more specific (the political and economic relations between centers in a particular period, for example). In this exciting time of changing interpretation, the research at Copán described below was formed and carried out to address some of these unresolved concerns.

Formulation

The ruins of Copán occupy a small but fertile river valley perched in the mountains of western Honduras, in the southeastern corner of the Maya area. Curiosity about the history of the place goes back to the Spanish explorers of the 16th century. In the mid-19th century, explorers Stephens and Catherwood (see Chapter 2) were awestruck by the elegance of the sculpture and the grandeur of the ruined buildings. Despite nearly a century of intermittent archaeological investigation, by the 1970s, it was clear that despite the fame and fascination of the place, we really knew very little about when and why it was founded, how it grew, who lived there, and what had happened to the civilization that flourished at Copán.

Modern archaeological research at Copán began with the establishment of the Copán Valley Project (1976–1977), sponsored by the Peabody Museum of Harvard University and directed by Gordon R. Willey. The specific goals of this and subsequent projects will be indicated in a moment. The Valley Project was followed by the first phase (1977–1980) of the Proyecto Arqueológico Copán (hereafter PAC I), sponsored by the government of Honduras and directed by French archaeologist Claude Baudez. The second phase of this government-sponsored project, PAC II, continued with a new research orientation (1980–1985), led by William Sanders. Since 1985, a series of more specific projects have carried on in various ways, including the Copán Mosaics Project, directed by William and Barbara Fash; the Proyecto Arqueológico Acrópolis de Copán (Copán Acropolis Archaeological Project) (PAAC), codirected by William Fash and four other archaeologists; the Copán Valley Rural Sites Project (1985–1988), directed by David Webster; and the Copán North Group Project (1988–1989), directed by Wendy Ashmore.

Formulation of all these projects grew out of the development of the original investigation, the Valley Project. This, in turn, grew from the interest and concern of people in Honduras to study Copán and preserve the site for the future. In 1974, Gordon R. Willey was invited by the Instituto Hondureño de Antropología e Historia (IHAH) to review the need for, feasibility of, and promise for renewing archaeological investigations at Copán. Together with William Coe and Robert Sharer (who were then working at the neighboring site of Quiriguá, across the Guatemalan border from Copán), Willey outlined the highest priorities for research, preservation, and development at the site. This required Willey, Coe, and Sharer's joint assessment of what had been done in the past (background study), as well as of what should and could be done in the near future (problem formulation and feasibility study).

Background study not only noted the travelers' accounts mentioned above but also traced the investigative history of the site. The record begins with Juan Galindo's 1834 excavation of a chambered tomb in the huge architectural complex called the Acropolis (Fig. 5.4). More formal investigations commenced at the end of the 19th century and continued intermittently through the onset of World War II. Almost all of this work focused on the area with the greatest concentration of architecture and sculpture, usually called the Main Group. The most enduring accomplishments of these efforts were documenting sculpture and buildings, some of which were subsequently damaged or destroyed by erosion, and outlining an initial culture historical sequence.

Interest in the architecture led to concern for its preservation. The most important result of this concern was the Carnegie Institution of Washington's diversion of the Copán river, which had long been undermining the east edge of the Acropolis. Between 1890 and the river's diversion by the CIW in the 1930s, at least three major buildings toppled from the Acropolis summit and were lost (Fig. 5.5), leaving only scant traces in the huge erosional cut called the *corte*.

Culture history was outlined first by the CIW's Sylvanus Morley, in 1920, drawn from Copán's abundant Maya hieroglyphic dates and from study of the sculpture on which they occurred. In 1952, another CIW researcher, John Longyear, published a somewhat different view, based

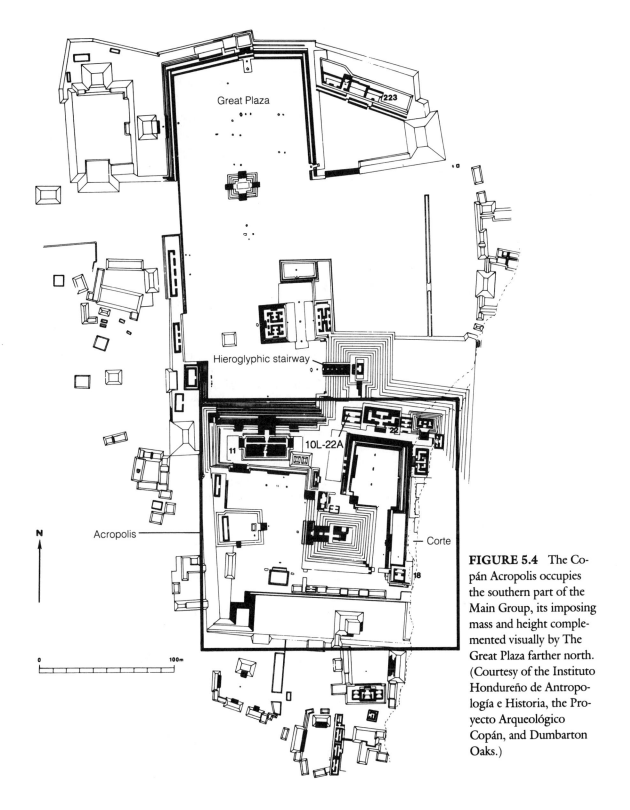

FIGURE 5.4 The Copán Acropolis occupies the southern part of the Main Group, its imposing mass and height complemented visually by The Great Plaza farther north. (Courtesy of the Instituto Hondureño de Antropología e Historia, the Proyecto Arqueológico Copán, and Dumbarton Oaks.)

FIGURE 5.5 Until its rerouting in the 1930s, the Copán river undermined construction along the east side of the Acropolis, causing several buildings to collapse and revealing a complex cross-section of architectural remains. (After Morley 1920.)

principally on pottery analysis, with incorporation of Morley's hieroglyphic study. Because pottery was made before and after the Classic period, when hieroglyphic texts were used, Longyear's outline covered a longer time span than did Morley's. But the two authors agreed on a number of important interpretive points, including the intrusion of Maya leaders and elite culture to Copán sometime in the Early Classic (ca. A.D. 250–600).

Longyear's views on Copán remained the most current ones available in 1975. In short, Copán was known to have been an important Maya center, thought to have been occupied from sometime around 1000 B.C., through intrusion of elite Maya culture early in the Classic period, to a developmental peak in the eighth century A.D., with a sudden and mortal collapse soon thereafter. In its heyday, Copán must have been powerful and prosperous, boasting sculptors and architects who created some of the most beautiful monuments of the ancient Americas (Fig. 5.6). And research elsewhere was showing that evidently the ancient Maya held Copán in similarly high regard, for its "emblem glyph," a shorthand reference to the place itself or its ruling family, was named in important texts of rulers at other centers, even at the opposite end of the Classic Maya world.

But these results posed more questions than answers, especially since ideas both about the ancient Maya and about archaeological interpretation had changed during the intervening years, as outlined earlier. For example, what were the reasons for and precise timing of Copán's founding, growth, and demise? What were Copán's foreign relations, in trade and diplomatic spheres? And although Longyear's summary of occupational history was well grounded in the evidence available to him, archaeologists wanted to test those conclusions with new data.

The 1975 research proposal outlined two foci for investigation: the Main Group and the surrounding valley. Despite previous emphasis on the Main Group, a great deal of very basic information about this civic and ceremonial core of the site remained unknown. When did this complex begin and how did it develop through time? What were the functions of the buildings found there? A coordinated program of excavations, conservation of the buildings, and study of the inscriptions was designed to answer such questions and preserve the site for the future. There was even less to go on regarding ancient settlement in the surrounding valley, and the sparse evidence available to Longyear from outside the Main Group had not been systematically gathered. The 1975 proposal therefore contained a series of questions that settlement research in the Copán valley was designed to answer. How was ancient settlement patterned and organized across the landscape? What were the size and the social composition of the ancient population? What were their economic, political, and religious organizations?

The need to answer questions such as those led to *problem formulation*. For one thing, the traditional conclusions outlined above—such as that involving an Early Classic Maya "intrusion" at Copán—were recast as hypotheses for testing. Other problems, however, more clearly broke new investigative ground. One of the most pressing research needs was clearly a systematic study of how many people had lived at or near Copán and how their homes and activities had been situated across the settled landscape. Archaeological thinking about the Classic Maya in the mid-1970s suggested that a relatively dense population should have resided in the vicinity of the Main Group, and previous investigations hinted that there were hundreds of small mounds (the likely remains of ancient houses) in the area. But no one really knew how many there were, their age, or whether they were in fact remains of houses! Initiation of a "settlement pattern" study (see Chapter 15) was therefore a central goal of Willey's Valley Project, a study extended and complemented by later programs of PAC I, PAC II, and the Rural Sites Project.

Other problems were also outlined, to be taken up by subsequent projects (some of which are discussed below.) For example, since the late 19th century, investigators had commented on the abundance of stone sculpture lying scattered throughout the Main Group (and elsewhere), the fallen remains of collapsed building façades. The 1975 proposal called for the inventory and study of these potentially informative remains, a task that is being successfully addressed by the Copán Mosaics Project. Another priority spelled out in 1975 was the "problem" of the huge Acropolis corte. Although recognized as early as the 1890s as an extraordinary opportunity for study of architectural stratigraphy and growth, only with work of the PAAC has long-term systematic study of the full history of Acropolis construction taken place, beginning in 1989.

It would be unrealistic, however, to expect that all future research concerns and questions could be anticipated in 1975—or, for that matter, at any single point in time. Some Copán programs had separate formulation

FIGURE 5.6 Copán sculpture is deservedly famous for its beautiful rendering of human, animal, and mythical beings, as well as of hieroglyphic texts. This monument, Stela A, is one of many portraits of 18 Rabbit, the 13th ruler in Copán's dynasty. Alfred E. Maudslay, who pioneered archaeological research at Copán in the late 19th century, is seated to the right of 18 Rabbit. (Courtesy of the Instituto Hondureño de Antropología e Historia and the Proyecto Arqueológico Acrópolis de Copán.)

histories, because the questions they addressed grew out of discoveries and interpretations that did not exist in 1975. In the case of the North Group Project, analysis of architectural patterns at many Maya sites had suggested by the early 1980s that building arrangements conveyed clues about Maya directional symbolism. For example, north was specifically hypothesized to be the home of powerful royal ancestors. Such hypotheses about Maya symbolic meaning could be tested at Copán in the late 1980s, largely because of the archaeological information gathered there in the preceding decade.

The third component of the formulation stage, *feasibility study*, took place in several steps. After completing backgound studies, in February 1975 Willey was joined at Copán by Coe, Sharer, and a (then) graduate student, Richard Leventhal, to gather information that would be used to prepare the research proposal. Over a period of several days, all portions of the Main Group and several outlying sites in the valley were inspected, after which an outline of the proposal was prepared. In April, Willey returned to Copán and, together with several IHAH officials, conducted a pilot reconnaissance of the Copán valley to assess the number, size, and state of preservation of settlement remains. This resulted in a trial classification of remains, which was included in the research proposal. The feasibility study also included assessments of practical needs for conducting research, including the availability of housing, lab space, vehicles, and labor.

The final research proposal made specific recommendations for the organization of the research staff and contained a budget for the project's first five years (1976–1981), totaling about 1.5 million (1975) dollars. The proposal included provisions for building a permanent research laboratory and storage facility near the site, a publication program to disseminate the results of the investigations, and improvements to the local archaeological museum. The proposal also recommended that ways be found to improve local roads, hotel facilities, and the airfield, all to make the site more accessible to the general public.

Implementation

All these recommendations have been implemented, but the scale of research at Copán has greatly exceeded the original 1975 plan. Instead of a 5-year project, more than 15 years of investigations have taken place, and are still continuing. And the 5-year budget estimate of 1.5 million dollars has been exceeded several times over. For each of the projects that have been realized over the past 15 years, contracts were negotiated with IHAH as permits for the research, and funds were raised from various sources, in Honduras, the United States, and Europe.

The original Valley Project was designed to be short-term, to provide an initial nonprobabilistic sample of settlement remains (see Reconnaissance, below); implementation procedures were appropriate to the scale

FIGURE 5.7 These laboratory and storage facilities at Copán were originally built during PAC I and have been expanded in later years to accommodate growth in research programs and to house the abundant artifacts recovered by that research. (Courtesy of the Instituto Hondureño de Antropología e Historia and the Proyecto Arqueológico Acrópolis de Copán.)

of the project. Once the research contract was approved, funding was procured from the National Science Foundation (NSF). A vehicle and supplies were purchased, and housing was rented in the town of Copán Ruinas to serve as both residential and lab space for the small project staff. Permission for access to private property had to be negotiated with each landowner involved. Local people were hired to help in survey, excavation, and lab processing, and the project was ready for its two six-month field seasons in 1976 and 1977.

Implementation for PAC I was somewhat more complicated. Because this project was officially sponsored by the Honduran government, it was they who selected a director, Claude Baudez, to pursue research already broadly outlined in the 1975 proposal. Moreover, unlike the Valley Project, PAC I was charged with beginning the permanent site protection and touristic development priorities spelled out in the 1975 proposal. The latter included constructing and furnishing a research lab facility to serve as a permanent research center, with library, research archive, drafting and photographic facilities, artifact and equipment storage areas, and administrative offices (Fig. 5.7). PAC I was also much larger than the Valley Project in diversity of research programs, size of staff, and duration of investigation. In all, some 57 staff members carried out ecological and ethnographic studies, as well as epigraphic, art-historical, and more strictly archaeological inquiry, working virtually year-round from July 1977 through 1980. Since 1975, researchers from nearly a dozen nations have worked at Copán. In addition to all this, there were still the usual logistical arrangements. Funding for all the foregoing was clear, however, and came directly from the government of Honduras through the Secretary of State for Culture and Tourism (SECTUR) and the Banco Centroamericano de Integración Económica (BCIE).

The subsequent PAC II was larger in scale than PAC I, and its specific research programs and objectives differed. The director, William Sanders, was likewise selected by IHAH, and he assembled a professional staff ultimately totaling some 87 individuals. The research center had already been completed, and funding came from the Honduran government and NSF, together with support from Sanders's home institution, The Pennsylvania State University. The Rural Sites Project, described below, was an excavation program that grew directly from PAC II, and was conceived and executed by Sanders's codirector, David Webster. Logistical implementation for both PAC II and the Rural Sites Project was similar to both the preceding projects.

The Mosaics and Acropolis projects addressed two of the most pressing remaining needs specified in the 1975 proposal—namely, the sculpture cataloging and study (Mosaics Project) and a clearer outline of the growth of the massive architectural complex of the Acropolis (PAAC). To pursue both, William Fash (who had worked at Copán since 1977) negotiated contracts with IHAH, raised funds from multiple sources (National Endowment for the Humanities, National Geographic Society, National Science Foundation, U.S. Agency for International Development, and support from his home institution, Northern Illinois University), and assembled a still-growing staff of professionals and students from art history and epigraphy, as well as archaeology and architectural restoration. The goals and excavations of the Acropolis work have become enormous, so Fash has invited archaeological colleagues to become codirectors of the PAAC and assume specific aspects of the task. This has also added new institutional support to the Copán research from the University of Pennsylvania and Tulane University. Logistic arrangements have been similar to preceding projects, and although Fash's team still used the lab and study center originally built by PAC I, the success of the Mosaics Project's sculpture recovery and cataloging, along with the Acropolis excavations, required the construction of substantial new storage areas. Since the onset of these two projects, field research (and/or architectural restoration) has continued nearly year-round.

In contrast, the North Group project was a short-term and very focused program, with an appropriately smaller staff and relatively few equipment needs. Contract and land-access negotiations were comparable to other projects, however, and space was made available by IHAH in the lab and study center. Research funds were obtained from the National Geographic Society and Rutgers University for two field seasons totaling about four months.

Acquisition of Data

Different kinds of data acquisition were appropriate for each of the projects described above. In this way, cumulative recent research at Copán amply illustrates the relation between what archaeologists want to know (problem orientation) and what they do to find out (method).

Reconnaissance and Surface Survey   Obviously, the existence of Copán's Main Group was known long before any of these recent projects was conceived. Reconnaissance was nonetheless vital, beginning with the original Valley Program, which reconnoitered widely outside the Main Group in search of ancient occupation traces. The reconnaissance universe and the sampling program were defined formally according to natural constrictions that divide the Copán river valley into six "pockets," or widened valley bottom lands with good farming soil. The Copán pocket, where the Main Group is located, is the largest of these, measuring about 25 km² in extent. The Valley Project defined the Copán pocket as its universe. Coverage was designed ultimately to be complete (100 percent), though the Valley Project staff knew their time limits meant that the reconnaissance would have to be completed by succeeding projects, then already in the formulation and implementation stages. Thus research concentrated on the 1.25 km² area immediately east of the Main Group, along with areas along the foothills north of the Main Group and south of the river. Search tactics concentrated on visible remains of ruined architecture (mounds). In all, approximately 13 km² were examined, and 378 sites, of one or more mounds each, were located.

In PAC I, the complete-coverage reconnaissance continued, but Baudez added probabilistic sampling of locations lacking visible mounds, and an initial foray into areas beyond the Copán pocket. The primary sampling universe was the Copán pocket and adjacent hills. The sample units and population were redefined by a valley grid system, with grid-square quadrat units measuring 52 meters on a side within the valley and 500 by 500 m in the more difficult hillslope terrain. The sampling fraction was 4 percent on the low terrace north of the river and 1 percent elsewhere. Besides ground reconnaissance, tactics included test-pitting to seek buried traces not visible at ground level.

Beyond the valley and foothills, ground reconnaissance also followed natural corridors connecting the Copán pocket with other zones. These corridors, the valleys of Copán river tributaries, were nonarbitrarily defined sample units, and the population was the total set of such tributary valleys. Sampling was nonprobabilistic, with special emphasis given to corridors leading to other known site areas, especially the nearest neighboring Maya center of Quiriguá, 50 km to the north in Guatemala. In this program, 97 sites were found in 300 km² of coverage area.

Reconnaissance was a key aspect of PAC II, and again the stimulus was to complement previous coverage. Although the Copán pocket was essentially completely reconnoitered by the close of PAC I, little remained known of settlement in the adjacent pockets of the valley, especially outside the tributary corridors. Moreover, study of settlement distribution (see discussion of surface survey, below) suggested the geographic "edges" of the ancient community had not yet been encountered. During PAC II, David Webster recognized the need to seek occupation traces beyond the Copán pocket, in a systematic fashion. This resulted in the discovery of 1066 new structures.

Taken together, Copán's reconnaissance coverage (of all but the corridors) was 62 km². Within this sizable expanse, 1425 sites were recorded, containing a total of 4509 individual structures.

In all the reconnaissance programs described above, mapping and surface collection proceeded simultaneously. All mounds were mapped using surveyor's instruments (see Chapter 6) by the Valley Project, PAC I, and PAC II. The maps of the Copán pocket were published in 1983 by PAC I, at scales of 1:2000 and 1:6250 (Fig. 5.8). From the range of site size and complexity of arrangement evident in mapping during the Valley Project, Willey and Leventhal proposed a five-part typology of sites (see Table 5.2), a refinement of the hierarchy outlined by Willey during the feasibility stage. Single, isolated mounds and irregular pairs of mounds were recognized as sites but were not labeled within the typology.

Along with mapping, surface collections of artifacts were made at each site, from which to make a first estimate of occupation history and site function. Coverage was 100 percent; collections were attempted from every site discovered. Sampling within sites was nonprobabilistic and focused on ceramic and stone artifacts. Often, however, few or no artifacts were visible on the surface, because of localized site-formation processes (see Chapters 4 and 6). This prompted development of an alternative artifact collection program using test pits (see Excavation, below).

The Valley Project site typology, along with Valley Project and PAC data from surface collections, has proven very productive for suggesting

Table 5.2 Copán Valley Site Typology

	Defining Criteria			
Type	Plazas	Mounds	Mound Ht	Materials
I	1	2–5	0.3–1.5 m	Cobbles
II	1–2	6–9	2.5–3 m	Some cut stone
III	1–2	6–9	<4.75 m	Frequent cut stone
IV	3+	9+	<10 m	Stone vaults; sculpture
V	[Copán Main Group]			

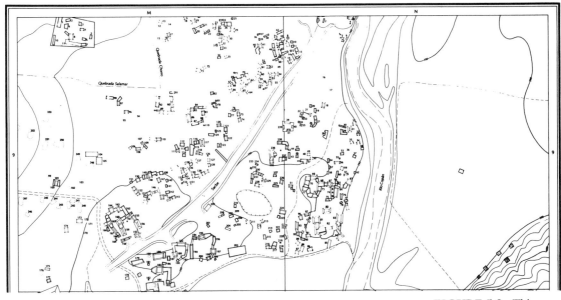

hypotheses about social structure in the ancient community at Copán. For instance, almost all mound sites outside the Main Group were identified provisionally as residential compounds, on the basis of their architectural form and artifact associations (e.g., food preparation gear, such as corn-grinding stones). Sites of Type IV were posited as being the households of wealthier and more powerful families, with those of Types I through III correspondingly lower in socioeconomic standing.

Moreover, the clustering of sites across the landscape defined three distinct occupation zones within the Copán pocket (Fig. 5.9). The first, the Main Group, had long been recognized as visually (and socially) the dominant complex, containing the largest buildings, as well as most of the sculpture and hieroglyphic texts. It has two principal architectural components, the Acropolis (the center of royal residential, administrative, and ritual activities) and the Great Plaza (the public assembly area containing most of the dynastic monuments and the Great Ballcourt). Newly recognized since the late 1970s, however, are two further zones that subdivide the valley pocket. The first is roughly 0.6 km² of densely concentrated settlement containing 1071 structures immediately surrounding the Main Group. This zone, labeled here the Residential Core, was posited as having contained the household compounds for the bulk of Copán's population. The remainder of Copán's ancient inhabitants lived in more dispersed compounds in the Copán pocket, in what we call the Valley Settlement

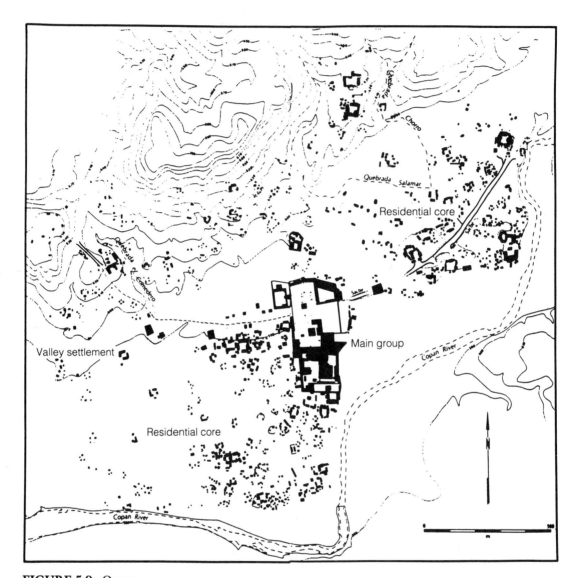

FIGURE 5.9 Occupation zones at Copán include the Main Group, Residential Core, and Valley Settlement Zone. (Courtesy of the Instituto Hondureño de Antropología e Historia and the Proyecto Arqueológico Copán.)

Zone (736 sites, containing 2372 structures). Most of the residents of this zone are hypothesized as having been farming families, producers of the food that sustained the entire ancient community. Together, the typology and this three-part zonation provide a working model of settlement (and indirectly, social) organization, and with it, a set of specific propositions for testing by excavation.

Two kinds of remote sensing were used in Copán reconnaissance and survey, both by PAC I. Specifically, aerial photographs were used for valley reconnaissance, and resistivity testing (Chapter 6) was employed to locate and map construction features buried under later plaza surfaces in the area north of the Acropolis. Indications of approximately two dozen buried features were recorded and later confirmed by excavation.

Excavation Excavations at Copán have taken many forms, with specific kinds chosen because of their appropriateness to address particular project research goals.

Test pits were used by the Valley Project, PAC I, and the North Group Project to gain artifact and other samples from sites so they could be provisionally dated and their functions (residential, ritual, etc.) inferred. In the Valley Project and PAC I, these tests were usually placed in the middle of the central open space, or plaza, of the mound groupings, to further reveal the number of times the plaza surface had been smoothed or paved, as clues to occupation history. PAC I archaeologists also excavated test pits in areas without known sites, to look for buried traces of occupation (see above). Whereas PAC I excavations were aimed at all occupation periods, PAC II settlement excavations focused on the Late Classic era, when valley occupation reached its peak. A later program of test-pitting was conducted by AnnCorinne Freter as an offshoot of PAC II and the Rural Sites Project. In this program, sites (the sampling units) for testing were randomly chosen from sampling strata defined by each of the site types (I–IV). Excavations were placed both in plazas and off the back (nonplaza) sides of mounds, to recover midden debris, especially obsidian (see Analysis of the Copán Data, below).

More extensive excavations were incorporated within several projects. In the Valley Project, for example, trenches bisected mounds of several (nonprobabilistically selected) sites in the Residential Core Zone, to examine cross-sections revealing the construction and occupation history of individual buildings and compounds. Usually, however, these trenches were combined with clearing excavations to reveal greater detail of architectural form of the buildings. Comparable strategies were followed in the Main Group in PAC I (e.g., Str. 10L–4) and II (e.g., Str. 10L–223).

Combined clearing and penetration had its greatest expression in PAC II, when another nonprobabilistically chosen sample of sites within the Residential Core Zone was examined. The central goal was to test social structural inferences (outlined earlier) derived from the site typology and settlement zonation. Were these residences? If so, of whom? Did differences in mound size reflect ancient socioeconomic contrasts? What activities were pursued within the compounds? And over what span of time? Plaza surfaces as well as mounds were cleared, to recover both midden debris and collapsed building components, including sculpture from fallen façades. This clearing recovered a wealth of detailed information attesting to the distribution of specific activities both in and outside of buildings, activities ranging from food preparation to shell and stone artifact manufacture to storage of ritual ballgame gear. Trenching by PAC II archaeologists was largely confined to plaza areas, however, because an additional goal of the project was restoration of excavated buildings. Restoring the buildings required not only painstakingly accurate recording of collapsed elements, but also leaving the core of the mound (including earlier buried versions of the building) largely intact. Hence, little architectural penetration was done because of its highly destructive nature. Trenches in the plazas, however, proved very productive, and in one notable case William Fash discovered a very early (ca. 1050–900 B.C.) cemetery whose jade-bedecked occupants suggested a previously unknown degree of social complexity on this early time level.

Similar combinations of clearing and penetration were adopted by the Rural Sites Project. Entire mound compounds were cleared, to gain information on rural architectural forms and activity-identifying artifacts. Small penetrating excavations tested for buried features, but since the sites involved were so small in both horizontal and vertical dimensions, these test pits were less informative (and therefore less emphasized) than were the clearing operations. Because of the smallness of the sites as well as their relative distance from both ancient and modern settlement, the rural excavations were refilled but no restoration was undertaken.

Combined test-pit penetration and clearing was used on a more focused scale by the North Group Project. Following from the project's goals of investigating Maya symbolism, excavation sought primarily to locate materials with most obvious symbolic content, including burials, other ritual deposits, and sculpture fallen from the faces of stone buildings. Excavation placement was nonprobabilistic, based on accumulated knowledge about likely locations for the deposits of most interest.

One of the most dramatically productive recent excavation programs at Copán has involved tunneling in the Acropolis. Tunneling is always risky in principle, because of the danger of collapse. Tunnels into the Acropolis, however, have benefited from the remarkable stability of Copán constructions. CIW archaeologists opened some tunnels, but the PAAC has created a much more extensive system, revealing thus far more than 70 buildings and platforms sealed within later construction masses. One of these yielded the earliest hieroglyphically inscribed stone monument now known from Copán, Stela 63, deliberately buried by the Maya in Classic times (Fig. 5.10) and important to epigraphers as the earliest known reference to the first named king of Copán, called Yax K'uk Mo'. Although Yax K'uk Mo' was cited in many later inscriptions, a lack of texts dating to his lifetime suggested to some that he was no more than a legendary or mythical king. Stela 63 was carved after his death, but was commissioned by one of his immediate successors, himself a very real king, and helps confirm the reality of Yax K'uk Mo'.

As part of the PAAC, the Early Copán Acropolis Project (ECAP) has used tunnels to take on the challenge of the corte. Some 300 meters long and, in places, 45 meters high, the vertical surface of the corte reveals the floors, buildings, and other constructions cut through by the Copán river

FIGURE 5.10 Stela 63, with the earliest known reference to Yax K'uk Mo', the founder of Copán's dynasty, was discovered as seen here, wedged in a niche inside a temple buried beneath the Hieroglyphic Stairway (see Figure 5.4). (Courtesy of the Instituto Hondureño de Antropología e Historia and the Proyecto Arqueológico Acrópolis de Copán.)

before its diversion by the CIW earlier this century. Starting at these river-exposed sections, ECAP has opened over 1 km of interconnecting tunnels, at different levels, to reveal highly detailed sequences of construction, partial destruction, and rebuilding spanning the fifth through early ninth centuries A.D. The ECAP tunnels, and all others in the Acropolis, are nonprobabilistically placed, deliberately following particular promising architectural traces. The tunnel systems have been augmented by test pits in the East Court, as well as a large clearing operation there. The latter exposed an important and well-preserved building that had lain just under the final court surface but was first recognized in a tunnel from the corte. Recording the masses of architecture exposed in these tunnels has presented special problems, but these have been solved by using a computer-assisted mapping (CAD) program to process the survey data generated by a laser transit (Fig. 5.11).

Altogether the tunnel finds have provided a framework for understanding the growth of the overall Acropolis and have, in some of the earliest levels, documented impressive buildings that must pertain to Yax K'uk Mo' and his contemporaries. Like Stela 63, these provide irreplaceable (and irrefutable) demonstration of the power and authority of these early kings. The size and frequency of monumental constructions also provide a barometer of the waxing and waning of Copán's fortunes that can even be correlated to the reigns of individual kings.

FIGURE 5.11 The complex recording needs of the Early Copán Acropolis Project are met by a laser transit and a computer-assisted mapping program that produce maps of the many deeply buried buildings, such as those seen here, discovered by a series of tunnel excavations beneath the Acropolis. (Courtesy of the Instituto Hondureño de Antropología e Historia and the Proyecto Arqueológico Acrópolis de Copán/Early Copán Acropolis Project.)

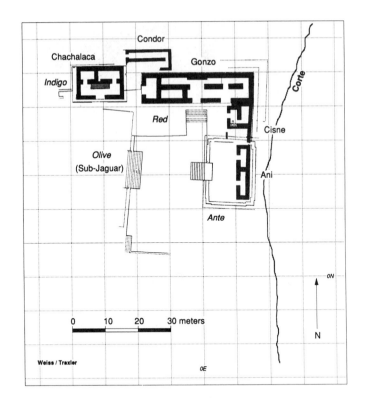

Other Data Acquisition Programs Archaeologists in almost any project rely on consultation and contributions from specialists in other fields, and those of the various Copán projects have been no exceptions. To list only a few of the more prominent examples, ecological studies were done in conjunction with both PAC I and PAC II. The former, by B. L. Turner and William Johnson, comprised a survey of natural resources in the Copán pocket, especially as these related to agricultural productivity. In PAC II, David Rue gathered samples of pollen from ancient deposits of varying specific age, and has outlined land-use histories as told from changing vegetation patterns—including inferences of accelerating deforestation and environmental degradation within and beyond the pocket during the Classic period, followed by recovery of the natural forest after abandonment of the valley by human populations.

Another set of specialists increasingly crucial to any Maya archaeological project are art historians and epigraphers who provide expert analysis of sculptural, pictorial, and textual records. Advances in hieroglyphic decipherment have transformed the "prehistoric" ancient Maya into a historical society, and research combining historical (textual) and archaeological (material culture) study provides insights from both data sources. Each source has its own limitations, as described in Chapter 1, but when they can be examined jointly or "conjunctively," they provide complementary insights that allow mutual correction and filling in the blanks left by the limitations of one approach alone. Such interplay was illustrated above with respect to the evidence for the actual (as opposed to mythical) existence of Copán's earliest kings, as provided in late texts, the early text of Stela 63, and the imposing early buildings revealed in the ECAP tunnels.

The excavation of Str. 9N–82 during PAC II provides a vivid example of how the combination of archaeology and epigraphy produces results more complete than either could furnish alone. In the words of one of the excavators, David Webster:

> If we had only the results of our surveys and excavations but no texts of any kind, we probably would be able to generate and confirm the same basic model of the place of the House of the [Scribes] in the larger Maya sociopolitical system at Copán. We would lack, however, the precision and independent confirmation of chronology derived from the inscriptions, as well as detailed insights into the way elite individuals related to the royal establishment and to each other. And we would certainly have a much poorer concept of how such elites manipulated ritual and ideology to legitimize and reinforce their positions and vie for authority and power. (1989:106)

At Copán, epigraphic and art historical specialists such as Berthold Riese have been integrally involved in ongoing research since PAC I, and Linda Schele, David Stuart, and Nicolai Grube (among others) have been invaluable collaborators in study of data from the PAAC (and ECAP) and Mosaics Project. Together these specialists have outlined the dynastic history of Copán, identified specific buildings, and linked their construction with individual rulers, as we shall see later on. In general, this historical information adds a dimension to our understanding of Copán simply unavailable from archaeological data—insights on what the ancient Copanec rulers and their scribes were actually saying about themselves and their world.

Processing the Copán Data

All data recovered in archaeological research are processed in some way, and the Copán archaeological lab built by PAC I provides facilities for washing, labeling, and storing artifacts, drafting scaled drawings, photographic darkroom work, flotation, and other processing. All original field records—notes, data forms, drawings, photographic negatives—are kept in the archives of the Copán lab, where current and future researchers may consult them. Any archaeological lab should be able to accommodate special project needs; an example in the case of Copán is the large sandbox developed by William and Barbara Fash, to allow trial reassembly of sculpture mosaics before reconstruction—whether reconstruction takes place on a building façade or simply by photography or drawing (Fig. 5.12).

FIGURE 5.12 Mosaic sculptures fallen from façades of Copán buildings are (left) reassembled on a trial basis in huge sandboxes before (right) being replaced on the buildings themselves. (Courtesy of the Instituto Hondureño de Antropología e Historia and the Proyecto Arqueológico Acrópolis de Copán/Copán Mosaics Project.)

Analysis of the Copán Data

The first data analysis undertaken is classification of artifacts and features. At Copán, artifact collections are broken down into categories defined by industry—that is, by raw material and manufacturing technique. Categories thus defined at Copán include pottery, chipped stone, ground stone, figurines, and so on. Further, more formalized classification and study take place within each category, such as René Viel's PAC I typological study of Copán pottery, refining and expanding the still-sound work done earlier by Longyear. In PAC II, Mary Spink analyzed *metates* (corn-grinding stones) to examine how specific form and raw material of these basic, durable artifacts might relate to social and economic standing of the owners. John Mallory of PAC II has studied intensively an unusually specialized obsidian tool-manufacturing household.

More technical artifact analyses have also been done, sometimes requiring export of artifact samples to U.S.-based labs. For example, Ronald Bishop led a team of analysts using neutron activation techniques to examine the chemical composition of pottery clays, thereby identifying the sources of raw materials and location of manufacture for particular kinds of pottery. This kind of analysis allows inference of exchange patterns, both locally and over long distances. Other materials are subject to technical analyses for purposes of dating archaeological deposits. One exciting development at Copán has been the program of obsidian hydration dating (see Chapter 9) conducted by AnnCorinne Freter for PAC II and the Rural Sites Project. Her test-pitting program was mentioned earlier; the obsidian recovered from those excavations has yielded material more than a thousand age assessments, and these give important new insights about the timing of the final collapse of Copán society (see below).

Analysis of features is also central to the Copán research, whether the subjects be constructed or cumulative features. Both Charles Cheek (for PAC I) and Elliot Abrams (for PAC II), for example, have studied energy investment in construction projects, to get a clearer idea of how many people, how much time, and how much care were involved in construction of both monumental architecture (e.g., in the Acropolis) and households of various sizes and elaborateness (e.g., in the Residential Core Zone). Although the evidence tends to suggest somewhat less energy was required than might at first be thought, still there are marked differences across time and space in how intensively and skillfully energy was harnessed for construction—in other words, some household heads (and some kings) commanded more work effort than did (or could?) others. Other studies exploit the wealth of information on spatial distributions of artifacts, ecofacts, and features uncovered in PAC II's extensive clearing excavations in the Residential Core. Analysts including Julia Hendon, Melissa Diamanti, and Randolph Widmer have made detailed inferences about the distribution of ancient activities represented by these archaeological remains, and give us an unusually vivid view of the workings of some ancient households. James Hatch is examining the mortuary customs represented by the more than 500 human burials discovered by PAC II, and physical anthropologists Rebecca Storey and Stephen Whittington are analyzing the human remains themselves for clues to ancient health, diet, and causes of death.

The examples listed here are but a small set of the multifaceted analyses conducted on recently gathered Copán data, by archaeologists and other specialists. They do, however, give an idea of the strong base available for interpretation of what has been found at Copán in recent years.

Interpretation of the Copán Data

What interpretations have the last two decades of work made possible? What have we learned that changes or expands on Longyear's views of half a century ago? How do the new views relate to the perspectives we have discussed as culture history, cultural process, and postprocessual archaeology?

Like Longyear, we now view the span of occupation at Copán as beginning in the Preclassic, peaking in the eighth century of the Classic, and ending in the Postclassic. But we have now a much clearer view of the exact timing of events and developments within the overall span. Thanks to chronometric dating techniques (see Chapter 9), we can place the earliest occupants at before 1000 B.C. Fash's cemetery excavation, containing local leaders buried with exotic jade necklaces and other symbols of wealth and prestige, indicates some form of social stratification at this time. But the data available from this time span is still too sparse to know any detail about life in the Copán valley during the Early and Middle Preclassic.

Drawing on settlement data collected by the Valley Project and PAC I, we know that after 400 B.C. or so, local occupation declined, for reasons that are still poorly understood. By A.D. 400, however, combined data from archaeology (especially from PAC I and PAAC), art history, and epigraphy (especially from the Mosaics Project) show that Copán was a growing, thriving, and socially complex agricultural community, beginning to exhibit hallmarks of Classic Maya civilization, such as monumental sculpture and hieroglyphic inscriptions. By A.D. 456, at least, Copán had its first historically recognized king, Yax K'uk Mo'. As we have seen, Yax K'uk Mo's literal and physical existence is attested directly in both text (Stela 63) and monumental construction (early buildings found by ECAP), and he is described in later texts as having been the founder of the Copán royal dynasty.

Was he a foreigner, "importing" elite Maya culture from far north, consistent with the original suggestions of Morley and Longyear? The epigraphic record is still fairly silent on Yax K'uk Mo's personal origins, but the archaeological record has given us further clues, not available at the time of the CIW work, about the roots of Early Classic population and culture more generally. These clues stem from studies of settlement patterns and artifact styles as these changed through time. Thanks to settlement study by the Valley Project and PAC I, we can see a rather abrupt upswing in size and density of occupation in the early centuries A.D. The population increase is so great it seems most likely due to migration of people into the Copán valley, and not simply "natural" increase of the populace already resident there. Did they come from the north? The answer is not simple, but artifact styles suggest the immigrants came from both north and south, where various Early Classic Copán styles have recognizable precedents. According to Arthur Demarest, the bulk of the new Copanecos most likely arrived from the area that is now western El Salvador. Others may have arrived from the north and west, where Classic Maya society had already a well developed elite culture, including hieroglyphic writing and royal portrait sculpture. Some of these traits could have been borrowed, though, with immigration of no more than artisans to execute these new material expressions of power.

After this relatively sudden florescence in the fifth century, there began a nearly linear sequence of growth, culminating with the prosperity, dense population, and strong, centralized political authority of seventh- and eighth-century Copanec society. This mirrors Longyear's interpretation. Unlike Longyear, however, we have epigraphic decipherments to tell us who the rulers of this society were, their names, and when they reigned.

What is more, we also know from archaeological study what they built and how much power they had, both within and beyond the confines of the Copán pocket. It is here that PAAC and ECAP tunneling has been particularly informative in revealing the shrines and palaces built by these kings for themselves and their courts.

In A.D. 738, however, Copán's fortunes took a disastrous turn. Epigraphy tells us the 13th king of Copán, whom we call 18 Rabbit, was captured and beheaded by his rival (and previous subordinate), the contemporary ruler of Quiriguá. Archaeology has been even more informative with respect to the results of that confrontation at both Maya cities. At Quiriguá, construction and prosperity increased dramatically after its victory over Copán, almost certainly because of a newly won independence resulting in freedom from channeling tribute to Copán and controlling its own lucrative trade routes. At Copán, in contrast, there was a 20-year period of depressed construction and dynastic activity. Even when Copán recovered its power and prestige, the constructions of 18 Rabbit's successors were poorer in quality, almost hasty in their execution. In an elegant convergence of archaeological and epigraphic analyses, William and Barbara Fash have identified a critical clue to what happened. It consists of Str. 10L–22A, a relatively small building at the north end of the Acropolis (see Fig. 5.4). Stratigraphically it is later than neighboring Str. 10L–22, the "palace" of 18 Rabbit, and clearing 10L–22A for restoration (within the Mosaics Project) recovered the sculptured decoration of the exterior. The latter consisted of designs like woven mats—to the Maya, a symbol of authority, for rulers sat on such mats—plus a set of glyphs designating places (Fig. 5.13). According to the Fashes' interpretation, 10L–22A is a *popol na*, or "house of the mat," a council house like those known in Maya society at the time of the Spanish conquest but never before identified from the Classic period. On this and other evidence it appears that Copán rulers after 18 Rabbit no longer held absolute power, instead being obliged to share sovereignty with powerful nonroyal landowners who lived in elaborate residences just outside the Main Group. Moreover, excavation showed that the situation continued through the dynasty's end in A.D. 822, for later rulers added interior features to the building.

As a further symbolic response to Copán's defeat, the 15th king, Smoke Shell, had the magnificent Hieroglyphic Stairway built (see Fig. 5.4). The stairway, each step of which carries a glyphic text, is the longest inscription in the Maya world, and has been justifiably famous since its excavation in the 1890s by the Peabody Museum. Only the lowest ten steps were still in place when found, however, the rest having fallen in a jumbled heap. The irony of this is that the content of the inscription—deciphered by Mosaics Project epigraphers—is a propagandistic account of the glory of the ruling dynasty, built to reestablish Copán's ancient power and prestige. Yet, as the Fashes point out, it was so poorly built that it was one of the least stable and worst-ruined structures ever encountered at Copán. It was the

FIGURE 5.13 Structure 10L−22A has been identified as a "house of the mat," where Copán's later rulers shared governing authority with powerful local landowners. (Courtesy of the Instituto Hondureño de Antropología e Historia and the Proyecto Arqueológico Acrópolis de Copán/ Copán Mosaics Project.)

final version of a series of better-made buildings occupying the same ritually important spot, an early one of which had housed Stela 63 (see Excavation, above)—a perfect location for a declaration of dynastic continuity and clout.

While the message of the Hieroglyphic Stairway was one touting past greatness, particularly of the expansionistic 12th king, Smoke Imix, it was ultimately the untimely and unexpected death of the 13th ruler, 18 Rabbit, that inspired a need to create such a monument. Elsewhere in Copán, other buildings were created to celebrate dynastic continuity. Among these was Str. 8L−74, where North Group Project excavations recovered sculpture and ritual deposits with links to sacrifice, ceremony, and the person of 18 Rabbit. Ashmore interprets these as supporting assertions about identification of the northern direction with royal ancestors and their immortality, and also as further testimony for the lingering need of late eighth-century Copanec society to resolve the disaster of Copán's defeat and 18 Rabbit's death.

It is for this final period of dynastic rule, particularly during the reign of the last known ruler, Yax Pac, that we have the fullest picture of life at Copán across all social and economic levels. Filling in such a picture had been the prime goal of PAC II data acquisition strategies outlined above, and the results of that work have well repaid the efforts made. Population reached a peak at this time, Webster and Freter estimating between 9300 and 11,500 residents in the 25 km² of the Copán pocket. Families of varied social standing were packed densely into the Residential Core, and this packing, according to physical anthropologist Storey, resulted in a high rate of infectious disease, even among the well-to-do. A few families seem to have held exalted positions within the Copán nobility, the best known of these being the family head who lived at Str. 9N–82, the interior and exterior sculpture of which identifies him as having been a royal scribe of Yax Pac. The scribe was surrounded by family, servants, and others, in a highly complex household spread over more than a dozen adjoining patio compounds. There is evidence the scribe had multiple wives, and at least one group living in the complex followed customs identifying them as foreigners to Copán.

The houses of the Residential Core occupied the best farmland, but there was not enough space left between or around the houses to grow the quantities of food needed to support Copán's large population. Data from the Valley Project, PAC I and II, and the Rural Sites Project suggest the bulk of the farmland and farmers were located in the Valley Settlement Zone, increasingly distant from the civic center of Copán through time, and pushed increasingly to farming poorer land. David Rue's pollen studies combine with earlier ecological and archaeological analyses to suggest the eighth-century Copanecos had cut down too many trees, both for use of the wood and to clear land for planting; the natural environment was being overtaxed. At the same time, the political clout of the royal dynasty remained diluted, as rulers were forced to share authority with nonroyal nobles.

In A.D. 822, the weakened dynasty disappeared with the end of the historical record. The final royal sculpture was dedicated in that year, but it was never completed. The timing of this political collapse fits roughly with Longyear's views, but recent research has shown that the social decline of Copán was not as abrupt as Longyear had thought. Freter's probabilistic sample of test-pitting sites for obsidian hydration dating (see Excavation and Analysis, above) suggests that both the valley's farmers and the nobility (including the family of the scribe in Str. 9N–82) carried on, at ever decreasing levels of prosperity, for another two to three centuries. And although the dynasty was gone, it was not forgotten. In the North Group, an elaborate tomb with distinctive imported pottery was constructed, probably about A.D. 842. Occupants of the tomb were perhaps sacrificial victims, for the position and contents of the tomb appear to mark a further monument to the immortality of 18 Rabbit and his now-vanished dynasty.

The foregoing account illustrates how the multiple data sets, research strategies, and disciplinary orientations of recent Copán projects have provided crosscutting and mutually complementary insights. Texts describe the actions of rulers and nobles; archaeology informs us about the way of life of the whole population. Settlement reconnaissance and surface survey give the big picture of where people were living and at what time periods; excavation tells us what they were doing there. The examples of complements could be greatly expanded, but the point is made: All data, adequately gathered and interpreted, contribute to the whole, and no one view, no single investigation, will answer all questions.

What about the complementarity of culture history, cultural process, and postprocessual archaeology, outlined in Chapter 3? How does recent research at Copán illustrate these trends and approaches?

Culture history yields the chronological framework for the developmental sequence. Dating the occupation span, relating it to cultural periods such as the Preclassic and the Classic, and recognition of mechanisms for change—such as migration—are all aspects of culture history. At Copán, the chronological framework and general sequence of occupation were worked out before 1975. The recent research has added considerable detail to provide a far more complete culture history for Copán.

Cultural process, on the other hand, looks at the processes by which aspects of culture and society are interrelated, to explain (rather than just describe) the dynamics of stability and change. The interpretive interrelation of differently documented phenomena such as great population growth, environmental overexploitation, the capture and execution of a particular named king, construction of a *popol na* and the Hieroglyphic Stairway—all these and other elements are examined together as clues to events and developments that together can be explained as stimuli or responses to changing conditions in Late Classic Copán. It's not simply the *list* of events and trends but, rather, the use of each to help account for the occurrence of the others. For example, the construction of the *popol na* is less important in itself, as a building, than is the implication its establishment carries for changes in the system of government at Copán, from rule by a single divine sovereign to joint governance by a king and his most powerful nobles. Any such accounting is provisional, a hypothesis subject to future modification in the light of new data or newly proposed explanatory links. But together they are examples of cultural process.

As for postprocessual archaeological approaches, these are evident in the identification of active agents—named kings and scribes, as well as textually unnamed individuals—and interpretation of specific symbolic meanings in Copán's occupational record. Most broadly, there is the increasing incorporation of art historical and epigraphic study in such projects. More specifically, the *popol na* and Hieroglyphic Stairway analyses, as well as the work of the North Group project (described in Chapter 16), illustrate the additional insights to be gained from such approaches.

Archaeology at Copán continues even as this book goes to press and will likely be pursued, in many forms, for decades to come. New data will be discovered, new models and interpretations will be proposed. The summary here is no more than an interim statement, but one that illustrates how interpretation reflects research design and how different kinds of investigation are individually suited to different kinds of questions.

Publication of the Copán Data

One of the most important stages in research design involves sharing the results of research with professional colleagues and a broader public. This sharing most obviously takes the form of publication, in books and articles of various kinds. It also includes presentations in the mass media, in films and TV programs, along with restoration of architecture and artifacts for public view, at a site or in a museum. All kinds of sharing are illustrated by recent Copán projects.

Publication of research results has generally been the responsibility of individual projects, although reports from a given project certainly draw on insights gained through other projects. The Valley Project has given rise to several articles, for both popular and professional audiences, with its final technical reports to be issued in a series of monograph volumes published by the Peabody Museum of Harvard. PAC I and II have likewise yielded numerous articles on specific aspects of research, published in Spanish and English. A three-volume monograph set published in Honduras, in Spanish, in 1983, provides details of PAC I programs. PAC II has begun publication of a multivolume monograph series, again in Spanish, the first volumes of which appeared in 1986 and 1990. A special monograph, in English, detailing investigations at the scribe's palace, Str. 9N–82, was edited by David Webster and published in the United States in 1989. The other projects are more recent, several of them ongoing, and have just begun publication of results, in article form. The Mosaics Project has a special publication series, called *Copán Notes*, in which project epigraphers (using computer desktop publishing and copier reproduction) make new decipherments and related interpretations immediately available to colleagues.

In all these publications, the archaeologists remain aware of multiple responsibilities, multiple reading audiences that must be addressed. One consideration is that research in a place where English is not the native language should be published in the language of the home country as well as the investigators' native tongue. Accordingly, Copán publications occur at least as often in Spanish as in English or other languages. Efforts are also made to balance technical, formal reporting with more popular articles and broadcasts to reach the general public. Articles in *Archaeology* magazine, as well as several series for television (including those produced by the National Geographic Society and by The Pennsylvania State University), and a book written for a nonprofessional audience—all these are either completed or in production at this time, and more are sure to follow.

In addition, much thought and energy has been devoted to development of information for visitors to Copán. Most obvious, tremendous effort has been invested in restoration (directed by Rudy Lários), both in the Main Group (by PAC I, II, PAAC, and the Mosaics Project) and in a part of the Residential Core called Las Sepulturas (by PAC II). A visitors' center, adjacent to the Main Group, contains a scale model of the Acropolis and Great Plaza areas, as well as several exhibits on the history and continuing process of investigation at Copán. New guidebooks, in Spanish and English, were prepared in the mid-1980s, and a well-arranged and very informative museum in the nearby modern town displays and explains recent finds. Plans for the future include a new museum to display the vast array of beautiful sculpture found at Copán.

SUMMARY

An archaeologist must command a broad range of expertise to conduct scientific research successfully. He or she must have knowledge of field method, theory, administration, and a range of technical skills. But no single individual can perform all the tasks demanded by the complexities of today's archaeological investigations, so in almost all cases the archaeologist calls on a variety of specialists to assist in the research process. Although the scale of archaeological research projects varies from that conducted by a single person in a few weeks or months to that performed by large research teams over several years or decades, in each case the research process follows the same generalized stages (illustrated in this chapter by a synopsis of a series of research projects at Copán).

Research design begins with *formulation* of a problem to be investigated, supported by background and feasibility studies. This is followed by *implementation,* which usually involves solving a series of practical problems such as fund raising, securing of permits, and making logistical arrangements. The next stage is *data acquisition,* including reconnaissance (locating unknown sites), survey (gathering data from the surface), and excavation (gathering data by digging beneath the surface). *Data processing* follows, to ensure that material remains are cleaned, conserved, described, and classified, and that all data records are completed and accessible. Such processing facilitates *analysis,* in which data are broken down by a variety of techniques to extract as much information about the past as possible. *Interpretation* involves the synthesis of this information, and the application of theoretical models, to reconstruct the past. Finally, *publication* of the results of archaeological research makes this knowledge accessible to others and usable to formulate new research.

Except for the first two stages, formulation and implementation (not considered further in any detail), these components of archaeological research design will provide the basic organization of the remainder of this book. Data acquisition will be described in greater detail in Chapters 6 (reconnaissance and surface survey) and 7 (excavation). Data processing is considered in Chapter 8. Data analysis is treated in Chapters 9–12. Interpretation is the subject of Chapters 13–17. Finally, in Chapter 18, we discuss some of the important challenges to, and responses by, archaeology in today's world, including the obligation to publish research results.

GUIDE TO FURTHER READING

The Scope of Research

Brown and Struever 1973; Butzer 1982; Fish and Kowalewski 1990; Gladfelter 1981; Gumerman and Phillips 1978; MacNeish 1967; Olin 1982; Rapp 1975; Rapp and Gifford 1985; Struever and Carlson 1977; Wiseman 1980

Research Projects

Agurcia Fasquelle 1986; Alexander 1970; Bleed 1983; MacNeish 1967; Schiffer 1976; Shook and Coe 1961; A. L. Smith 1973; Weiss 1983; Wheeler 1954; Willey 1974

Research Design

L. R. Binford 1962, 1964; Brown and Struever 1973; Carr 1985; Clarke 1978; Cronyn 1990; Daniels 1972; Gero and Conkey 1991; Goodyear, Raab, and Klinger 1978; Grinsell, Rahtz, and Williams 1974; Gumerman 1984; Joukowsky 1980; Olin 1982; Powell et al. 1983; Redman 1973, 1982; Staski 1982; Struever 1968; Taylor [1948] 1964 and 1967; Thomas 1969; Tuggle, Townsend, and Riley 1972

A Case Study in Research Design: The Copán Project

Lowland Maya Civilization: Adams 1977; Ashmore 1981; Chase and Rice 1985; Culbert 1973, 1991; Hammond 1982; Morley, Brainerd, and Sharer 1983; Sabloff 1990; Sabloff and Andrews 1986; Schele and Freidel 1990; Schele and Miller 1986; Willey 1982

Copán: Ashmore 1991; Baudez 1983; Boone and Willey 1988; Fash 1988, 1991; Fash and Fash 1990; Fash and Sharer 1991; Longyear 1952; Morley 1920; Sanders 1986, 1990; Urban and Schortman 1986; Webster 1989; Webster and Abrams 1983; Webster and Freter 1990a, 1990b; Webster and Gonlin 1988; Willey, Coe, and Sharer 1976; Willey and Leventhal 1979; Willey, Leventhal, and Fash 1978

CHAPTER SIX

ARCHAEOLOGICAL RECONNAISSANCE AND SURFACE SURVEY

One's ears are filled with chatter about assorted magnetometers and how they are used to pick up the traces of buried objects and no one has to guess at all. They unearth the city, or find the buried skull . . . then everyone concerned is famous overnight.

Loren C. Eiseley, The Night Country, *1971*

Of the three of us, Vay [Sylvanus G. Morley] was the only one who knew what an archaeological survey was all about. It should, he said, be a stocktaking of all the remains in an area and their description in the form of notes, plans, and photographs in as full detail as possible without excavation.

From A. V. Kidder's journal written during E. G. Hewett's Colorado Plateau expedition, 1907

Most people think archaeologists spend the bulk of their time digging. In fact, however, excavation usually follows **data acquisition** by various other less intensive and less destructive means, methods used to gain an initial familiarity with the local archaeological record. These other means are **reconnaissance** and **surface survey,** by which sites are discovered and their surface characteristics recorded. Data acquired by these nonexcavation methods can tell us a great deal about the past, and often—whether by design or by necessity—excavation is not undertaken at all.

In this chapter, we will describe the objectives and methods of reconnaissance and surface survey, and how their applicability depends on the questions being asked in a particular research situation. At the close of the chapter, we will consider the pros and cons of relying on surface data without excavation.

OBJECTIVES OF RECONNAISSANCE AND SURFACE SURVEY

Transformational processes affect the sites of past human activity in a variety of ways. Some sites, such as Stonehenge, remain obvious to any observer. Others may be nearly destroyed or completely buried under tons of earth; in such cases, identification and study may be extremely difficult. The systematic attempt to identify archaeological sites is called *archaeological reconnaissance.* By identification, we mean both discovery and location (determination of geographical position) of sites. *Surface survey* involves mapping the surface characteristics of sites discovered by reconnaissance, and collecting samples of artifacts and ecofacts for inferring each site's age and function.

Obviously, it may be more efficient in many instances to combine identification and data gathering. This is especially true if the same sample

FIGURE 6.1 Definition of the Tehuacán Region was based on both cultural and ecological criteria. (After MacNeish et al. 1972.)

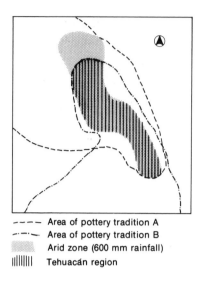

- - - - Area of pottery tradition A
-·-·-· Area of pottery tradition B
▓ Arid zone (600 mm rainfall)
‖‖‖‖‖ Tehuacán region

units can be used for site identification and for the acquisition of surface data. But in other situations these objectives may have to be pursued separately. For instance, a project may undertake total coverage of its data universe to identify and locate sites but have the resources to cover only a sample of the universe for gathering surface data. Because reconnaissance is an initial step in the research process, it is sometimes more profitable to limit efforts at this point to discovery and location. The information thus gained—through repeatable and nondestructive procedures—can be used to formulate or refine hypotheses to be tested through surface survey or excavation. This is especially true when the reconnaissance is taking place in geographical areas with no prior archaeological information or as part of a feasibility study for a larger overall project.

Archaeological reconnaissance yields data concerning the range in form (size and internal arrangement) of sites as well as their total number and spatial distribution within a region. The distribution data may reveal patterns in the placement of sites, relative both to each other and to variables of the natural environment, such as topography, biotic and mineral resources, and water. Sometimes these findings may be used to define the region for later, more intensive study: For the Tehuacán Project (discussed further below), one phase of research helped to define the study region by indicating the correlation between limits of the arid Tehuacán Valley and distribution limits of two pottery styles (Fig. 6.1).

Uses such as these for archaeological reconnaissance also emphasize the need for ecological studies of the region, either before archaeological reconnaissance (as part of background research) or in conjunction with the site identification process. Defining ecological zones within a study area can guide the archaeologist in searching for sites if site distribution can be correlated with the distribution of different environmental variables. The archaeologist may thereby gain an initial understanding of possible ecological relationships between past peoples and their environment.

Archaeological reconnaissance can begin during background investigation using documents, records, maps, previous reports, local informants, and other sources to learn as much as possible about the area before going into the field. Reconnaissance at this stage is often part of a feasibility study to determine the practicability of pursuing the planned research. Preliminary reconnaissance can also indicate the best areas (or the only possible areas) in which to test a given hypothesis. For example, by the late 1950s New World archaeologists had documented much of the sequence of human occupation from the earliest settlers of the New World to the time of European conquest. However, very little information had been obtained about one particular era of crucial importance: the transition from societies subsisting by hunting and gathering to sedentary, agriculture-based societies. As a result, a team of archaeologists and paleobotanists led by Richard MacNeish planned a research project specifically to locate and investigate archaeological sites spanning this critical period.

Previous research—much of it done by MacNeish—indicated that the most important agricultural species, corn (*Zea mays*), had been domesticated before 3000 B.C., probably somewhere between the Valley of Mexico and the Mexican state of Chiapas. Within this general area, the research location selected would have to combine two environmental characteristics: First, it would have to be in the highlands where the wild ancestor of corn would have been likely to grow; second, it would have to contain dry caves in which ancient and continuous stratified deposits with well-preserved organic remains could have accumulated. Preliminary reconnaissance in the areas meeting the first requirement allowed MacNeish to eliminate those that did not also meet the second. Government permit in hand, he scouted out a series of rock shelters or caves on his own, but the most promising sites were those shown to him by local inhabitants in the Tehuacán Valley, located in the state of Puebla. In this case, the feasibility study was capped by a week of exciting and fruitful test excavations in one rock shelter, Ajuereado cave. This led to the formation of the Tehuacán Archaeological–Botanical Project (1961–1964), which has become a standard for systematic and productive archaeological research.

Reconnaissance may be conducted in many ways, but the actual techniques and procedures used often depend on the kinds of archaeological sites being sought. The methods used to locate surface sites differ greatly from those intended to discover deeply buried sites. Likewise, a small, poorly preserved seasonal hunting camp requires a different means of detection from that used to find a large, well-preserved urban center. In most cases, limitations of time and money prevent the archaeologist from covering every square meter of the research area in attempting to identify sites. Accordingly, carefully selected sampling procedures should be used, to maximize the chance that the number and location of sites in the areas

Reconnaissance defines area of Tehuacán Project

actually searched are representative of the universe under study. In some cases, a systematic sample may be taken by dividing the reconnaissance universe into squares (quadrats) and covering as many squares as time and money will allow. In other cases, knowledge about the area may enable the archaeologist to use a stratified random sampling procedure. For instance, previous accounts might indicate that archaeological sites are found in only two ecological zones—along coasts and on hilltops. The research area could then be stratified into these zones and sample areas within each zone selected and searched. In such a case, it would be advisable to test the posited distribution by also reconnoitering sample areas of the other ecological zones to verify that, in fact, no sites are located in these areas.

Finally, it is worth noting that some environments are simply more conducive to reconnaissance than others. Dry climates and sparse vegetation offer nearly ideal conditions for both visual detection of archaeological sites and ease of movement across reconnoitered terrain (Fig. 6.2). Such environments have greatly aided archaeologists in discovering sites in southwest Asia, coastal Peru, highland Mexico, the southwestern United States, and similar areas.

Whereas reconnaissance is used to discover sites, surface survey is used to extract data from the surface of the sites. The way surface survey is conducted in a given situation depends on the nature of the site or area and the kind of data being gathered. To begin with, in surface surveys archaeologists attempt to detect and record surface features at their location. Many substantial archaeological features, such as the remains of ancient buildings, walls, roads, and canals, exist on the present ground surface, where they can be detected by direct observation. Features so preserved are recorded in surface survey by mapping. Buried archaeological features, however, may not be directly detectable from the surface. In some cases, buried remains can be located and mapped by one or more of the remote sensing methods, such as aerial photography, described later in the chapter.

Surface surveys also include detection and recording of artifacts and ecofacts. When these kinds of archaeological remains are found on the surface, their provenience is recorded, and they are often taken to a field laboratory for processing and later analysis. Like features, artifacts and ecofacts are sometimes buried beneath the surface; unlike features, they cannot usually be detected by remote sensors. In some cases, probes, using shovels, augers, or corers, can be used to determine whether artifacts or ecofacts are present below ground. But such probes yield only limited samples of small items. As a rule, recovery of buried artifacts and ecofacts in useful quantities for detailed study must await archaeological excavation.

Whether or not it is combined with reconnaissance, surface survey is, in most research situations, an essential complement to subsequent excavation. It is also possible to conduct archaeological research by gathering

FIGURE 6.2 Present environmental conditions have a great influence on reconnaissance: (left) tropical rain forest greatly reduces visibility whereas (right) arid landscapes are often conducive to detection of surface sites. (Courtesy of the Tikal and Gordion Projects, The University Museum, University of Pennsylvania.)

Agriculture in the desert: Landscape modification in Arizona

data solely by surface survey methods. These methods may be the only alternative when research time and money are limited, especially when relatively small-scale projects investigate large regions or complex sites, or when difficulties in securing the necessary permissions preclude excavation as a means of acquiring data. In other cases, remains are so low in frequency or density that excavation is not warranted. Whatever the reasons, productive archaeological research can be conducted by relying on surface survey for data gathering. As an example, let us consider a survey project conducted recently in the southwestern United States, near Tucson, Arizona.

As part of a large-scale program of reconnaissance and surface survey, Suzanne and Paul Fish and their colleagues encountered extensive series of small piles of unmodified stones. Not very impressive individually, these cobble features were usually less than 1.5 m in diameter and under a meter in height, and although scattered reports of such piles had been made before, no one had appreciated their great numbers or spatial extent. The Fishes' project, however, documented 112 rock-pile fields, ranging in size from less than a hectare (2.5 acres) to more than 50 ha (125 acres), encompassing some 42,000 individual piles (Fig. 6.3). Fields also contained fire-cracked rock and roasting pits, and the complexes were associated with artifacts whose style dated to the Classic period of Hohokam culture (ca. A.D. 1100–1450). Experiments showed the rock piles most likely served to slow evaporation of soil moisture in the dry Arizona climate and were probably used specifically for cultivation of agave, later roasted in the adjacent pits. Taken together, the field complexes attest to impressive and previously unrecognized Hohokam achievements in making this part of an unforgiving landscape productive for agriculture. Since the Tucson

FIGURE 6.3 This map shows the distribution of rock piles and other prehistoric cultivation features in an extensive Hohokam agricultural field near Tucson, Arizona. (After Fish, Fish, and Madsen 1990.)

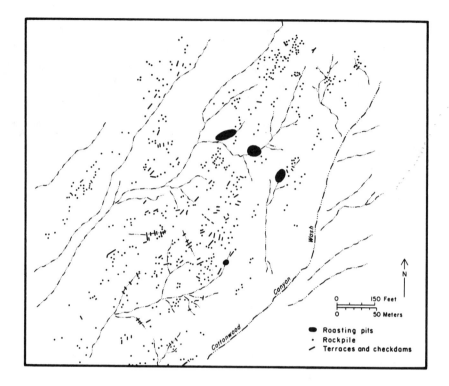

Roasting pits
Rockpile
Terraces and checkdams

work, the Fishes and their colleagues have identified similar previously ignored features in other parts of Arizona. The results of these investigations obviously point to the need for archaeologists to be alert to unanticipated or subtle traces of human landscape modification. They also illustrate the great interpretive potential of reconnaissance and survey programs, even without excavation.

LITERATURE, LUCK, AND LEGENDS

Of course, not all sites are located through reconnaissance. To begin with, some archaeological sites are never lost to history: In areas with long literate traditions, such as the Mediterranean basin, the locations and identities of many archaeological sites are well documented. Obviously, the locations of Athens, imperial Rome, and many other sites in the ancient world have never been forgotten. Most sites, however—even many documented by history—have not fared so well. Many once-recorded sites have been lost, razed by later conquerors or ravaged by natural processes of collapse and decay. Ancient Carthage, for example, was systematically destroyed by its Roman conquerors in 146 B.C.; it has only recently been rediscovered near Tunis. Similarly, the Greek colony of Sybaris, still re-

FIGURE 6.4 A contemporary view of Heinrich Schliemann's excavations at Troy. (From Schliemann 1881.)

membered for its luxurious and dissolute ("sybaritic") way of life, was lost for centuries.

Sometimes histories and even legends provide the clues that lead to the relocation of lost cities. Literary references were valuable in the case of Sybaris. But the most famous quest of this sort was Heinrich Schliemann's successful search for the legendary city of Troy (Fig. 6.4). As a child, Schliemann became fascinated with the story of Troy and decided that someday he would find that lost city. By age 30 he had become a successful international merchant and had amassed the fortune he needed to pursue his archaeological goals. He had learned more than half a dozen languages and had quickened his appetite for Troy by reading Homer's tales of the Trojan War in the original Greek. Study of textual descriptions of the location of the ancient city convinced him that it was to be found at Hissarlik in western Turkey. Accordingly, in 1870, he began excavations that ultimately demonstrated the physical existence of Priam's legendary city. Later it was found that the buried remains Schliemann had called Troy were really an earlier settlement, and that he had cut right through the Trojan layers in his determined digging! Nonetheless, Schliemann is credited with the discovery of Troy, and his successful persistence there, and later in Greece at Mycenae and Tiryns, gave great impetus to the search for the origins of Greek civilization.

Mapmakers observe and incidentally record many archaeological sites. In areas of the world covered by accurate maps, the archaeologist may be able to rely on distributional information provided by cartographers. In England, for instance, the excellent coverage provided by the Ordnance Survey Maps, made mostly from **ground survey,** includes identification of many archaeological sites. Similar coverage exists for the United States (U.S. Geological Survey maps) and many other countries. Even though

The discovery of Troy: Heinrich Schliemann

FIGURE 6.5 This oblique aerial photograph of Olduvai Gorge, Tanzania, amply illustrates the erosional forces that exposed evidence of human physical and cultural development. (Emory Kristof, © 1975 National Geographic Society.)

The Templo Mayor of the Aztecs: Excavations beneath Mexico City's streets

preexisting maps may be used to locate archaeological remains, these sources must always be field-checked to test their accuracy.

Perhaps more archaeological sites come to light by accident than by any other means. The forces of nature—wind and water erosion, natural catastrophes, and so forth—have uncovered many long-buried sites. The exposed faces of Tanzania's Olduvai Gorge (Fig. 6.5), from which Louis and Mary Leakey and others have retrieved so much evidence on early humans, are the product of millennia of river bed-cutting action. And the famous Neolithic lake dwellings of Switzerland were discovered when extremely low water levels during the dry winter of 1853–1854 exposed the preserved remains of the wooden pilings that once supported houses.

Chance discoveries of ancient sites occur all the time. For example, it was French schoolboys who, in 1940, first happened on the Paleolithic paintings of Lascaux cave: The boys' dog fell through an opening into the cave, and when they went after their pet, they discovered the cavern walls covered with ancient paintings. As the world's population increases and the pace of new construction accelerates, more and more ancient remains are uncovered. Unfortunately, many are destroyed before the archaeologist has a chance to observe and record them. In the heart of modern Mexico City a momentous discovery was made in 1978 by electrical workers excavating near the national cathedral (Fig. 6.6).

The workers found a large stone sculpture and wisely stopped work to notify archaeologists from Mexico's Institute of Anthropology and History. Once on the scene, the archaeologists realized the stone sculpture had to be associated with the main temple complex of Tenochtitlán, the Aztec capital now covered by Mexico City (Chapter 1). The centerpiece of that complex, the Templo Mayor, was architecturally and symbolically

FIGURE 6.6 This aerial view of Mexico City illustrates the reconstructed form and the location of the Aztec Templo Mayor, with the modern cathedral and plaza beyond, to the southwest. (Photograph by David Hiser with overlay by Ned Seidler, © 1980 National Geographic Society.)

the most important building in Tenochtitlán. Because of its importance, the Spanish conquerors had destroyed what they could, and buried the rest beneath their newly rising colonial capital of Mexico City.

The sculpture's discovery immediately spawned a major excavation, directed by Eduardo Matos Moctezuma, that exposed the remains of the great temple itself and the remains of rituals conducted there before the arrival of the Spanish in 1519. First constructed in the 14th century, six major rebuildings over the next two centuries had encased each older temple in the larger version that replaced it. Human sacrifices and other offerings were made at each rebuilding, and on many occasions in between. The remains of more than 80 such offerings were discovered during the excavation. These included deposits containing materials brought from the far-flung regions of the growing Aztec realm. Archaeology thereby documented what later historical accounts had always asserted, that the Templo Mayor had a central role in the integration of the Aztec state. All in all, the excavation of the Templo Mayor is a landmark in the archaeology of Mexico, and it all began with the alertness and care of the electrical workers who made the original discovery.

Similar incidents occur constantly throughout the world. In many countries, laws require building contractors to stop work immediately when they encounter archaeological materials. In most cases, work cannot resume until archaeologists, whose work is funded either by government agencies or by the contractors themselves, excavate and remove the material. More and more frequently, archaeologists work hand in hand with builders to minimize both the destruction of the past and delays in construction.

Many sources, then, provide the archaeologist with information concerning the location of archaeological sites. But identification of sites by these means must always be verified by archaeological investigation. Too often researchers have assumed the location of archaeological sites without rigorous checking. For instance, the ancient Toltec capital of Tollán was identified with the famous ruins of Teotihuacan near Mexico City. But subsequent ethnohistorical and archaeological work at a much smaller site near Tula, Hidalgo, about 50 miles north of Mexico City, has indicated that this city was Tollán and that the earlier assumptions were wrong.

METHODS OF RECONNAISSANCE AND SURFACE SURVEY

Two basic methods are used to conduct archaeological reconnaissance and survey: direct observation and remote sensing. Each requires specialized techniques, and each is effective in identifying and studying sites under specific conditions.

Direct Observation

The oldest and most common method of searching a study area is by visual inspection at ground level. Direct observation has been used for archaeological reconnaissance since the days of antiquarian interest, when exploration by such men as William Camden in 16th-century England or

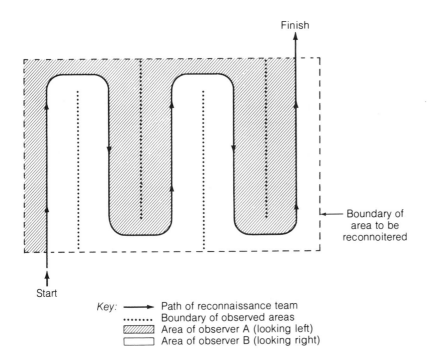

Finish

Boundary of
area to be
reconnoitered

Start

Key: ──▶ Path of reconnaissance team
.... Boundary of observed areas
▨▨ Area of observer A (looking left)
☐ Area of observer B (looking right)

FIGURE 6.7 A schematic illustration of one efficient technique of conducting ground reconnaissance. (After Mueller, reproduced by permission of The Society for American Archaeology, adapted from *American Antiquity* 39 [2, part 2, Memoir 28]:10, 1974.)

Stephens and Catherwood in 19th-century Central America led to the discovery of countless sites. Today, well-defined sample areas such as transects or quadrats are covered systematically by moving back and forth or across in sweeps (Fig. 6.7). Most **ground reconnaissance** is still conducted by walking—the slowest method, but also the most thorough. Often the efficiency of reconnaissance on foot may be increased by using teams of archaeologists to sweep through designated areas. Many archaeologists increase the speed of ground reconnaissance by using horses, mules, or motorized transport (four-wheel-drive vehicles are frequently necessary). Combinations of these methods are very commonly used. For example, Robert Adams relied on several methods in the Warka (ancient Uruk) area of southern Iraq, where some 2800 km² were covered in 4½ months.

Ground reconnaissance can be greatly aided by the cooperation and assistance of local inhabitants, who may serve as guides and indicate the location of sites. Of course, the site sample gained from local informants will not be a random one, but in some cases it is the most feasible one. For example, in the dense rain forest of Guatemala, an inexperienced traveler can easily become lost and, during the dry season, literally die of thirst (among other things). Explorers and archaeologists, from the 19th century to the present day, have wisely and profitably employed local *chicleros*—men who gather the resin from the *chicozapote* tree and sell it to be processed into chewing gum—to lead them through the rain forest—to ruins as well as water holes.

Identifying Sites How does the archaeologist recognize sites on the ground? Many, of course, are identified by their prominence. Some sites in southwest Asia are called **tell** or **tepe**—both of which mean "hill"—because they stand out as large mounds against a relatively flat plain. In other cases, only a slight difference in elevation or a seemingly unnatural rise or fall in the landscape may indicate a buried ancient wall or other feature. Semisubterranean Inuit (Eskimo) dwellings, for example, appear as slight depressions after their roofs have collapsed. At some sites, construction features such as building walls, earthen platforms, or paved roadways are sufficiently well preserved to be easily recognizable. Many sites are identified by concentrations of surface artifacts such as potsherds and stone tools. Shahr-i Sokhta in eastern Iran was recognized as a site from its densely littered surface. Because of its richness, this artifactual layer was long thought to be the sole remnant of a thoroughly wind-eroded hilltop settlement; as it turned out, the "hill" was the buried—and beautifully preserved—site!

Some sites leave no direct surface indications. This is a problem often encountered in areas, such as many parts of the eastern United States, with thick vegetation, urban buildup, or other extensive masking of the ancient landscape. Recent exposures of underlying material, including road cuts, eroded stream banks, or newly plowed fields, provide access to subsurface possibilities. Although buried sites are often missed by ground reconnaissance, they may leave clues to their location. Low-growing vegetation, such as grass or grain, is often sensitive to subsurface conditions. Many plants grow higher and more luxuriantly where remains of ancient human activity, such as canals, middens, or burials, have improved soil moisture and fertility. For example, at the Salmon Ruin of New Mexico, a large underground chamber was clearly distinguishable in 1973, without excavation, as a circular patch of green amid the drier, browner surrounding vegetation. In contrast, solid construction features such as walls or roads immediately below the surface will often impede vegetation growth. For example, at certain times of day, differential absorption of salt made the tops of the buried mud-brick walls at Shahr-i Sokhta stand out as whiter than the rest of the surface of the mound (Fig. 6.8). Patterned differences in the distribution of plant species may also indicate archaeological sites. In the dense jungle of lowland Central America, early explorers were aided in locating Maya sites by looking for concentrations of a large tree known as the *ramón* (breadnut tree). These trees bear an edible fruit, and the stands seen today may actually be descended from trees cultivated a thousand years ago by the pre-Hispanic Maya.

In most cases, however, these and other differences in soil and vegetation conditions are invisible to the ground observer. Solutions to that invisibility are offered by *remote sensing,* discussed below.

Surface debris identifies site at Shahr-i Sokhta, Iran

Vegetation contrast identifies feature at Salmon Ruin of New Mexico

Ramón trees as indicators of lowland Maya sites

Plotting Sites   Discovery is only half the task of reconnaissance. The other half is recording the location of the sites encountered. The central objective of recording is to relate the new finds to their spatial setting, to place the previously unknown within the realm of the known. Usually, but not always, this involves plotting on preexisting maps or aerial photographs. Sometimes base maps may be specially drawn for reconnaissance purposes; but, since most reconnaissance uses preexisting maps, we shall confine discussion here to that circumstance.

Good maps are essential for reconnaissance; they may be supplemented in some cases by aerial photos. Maps are used first to plot the boundaries for sample units and later to plot the location of new archaeological sites discovered. Plotting of sample unit boundaries enables the archaeologist to indicate which areas have been covered and which have not so that sampling adequacy can be assessed and possible distributions in nonreconnoitered areas can be posited. Plotting of new sites is necessary for distributional studies within the sampled area—and, of course, for returning to the sites later. Techniques for making and using maps will be discussed later in this chapter.

Location is most commonly recorded by plotting on maps or aerial photos. Aerial photos with vertical coverage and maps made from them are frequently available for the area of interest. Sometimes archaeological sites are already indicated on the maps or visible on the photos. This lessens the archaeologist's work somewhat, but it is not a substitute for checking the "ground truth" of the marked features. The date of the base map or photo can be important here: Since that date, new roads may have been built or old ones overgrown, sites may have been obliterated, and cultivated crops may have changed. Since ground pattern clues, reference points, and even the archaeological data may have altered since publication of a map or a photo, it is wise to be aware of the recent—as well as the long-term—history of the study area.

When an archaeological site is encountered, its position is plotted by noting its distance and direction from one or (preferably) more reference points. Bearings to reference points are usually determined from a compass, and distance from a single reference point can be taped, paced, estimated, or determined by a range finder. If at least two reference points are used, such as hilltops, and if they are far enough from the site and from each other, triangulation will give the site's location exactly. To determine location by triangulation, the bearings of the compass readings to the reference points are plotted on the map; they will intersect at the point of observation—that is, at the location of the site. The accuracy of these procedures, of course, depends on the accuracy of the base map, the compass, and the compass readings as well as the separation and distance of the reference points. **Global positioning system (GPS)** receivers now provide an easier and more accurate, if still somewhat expensive, method of plotting sites. The GPS receiver calculates the user's location by triangulation from a constellation of satellites in orbit 11,000 miles above the

FIGURE 6.8   Traces of a building visible on the surface of Shahr-i Sokhta. (Courtesy of Centro Studie Scavi Archeologici in Asia of IsMEO, Rome.)

**Plotting site location:
The Virú Valley, Peru**

earth. Hand-held receivers are the size of a small portable radio, weigh only a few pounds, and yield locational data accurate to within 30 meters; more sophisticated systems are accurate to within centimeters. Use of GPS systems has particular promise in heavily forested or other areas where visual triangulation is difficult.

In the Virú Valley Project in Peru (see Fig. 4.5, p. 119), a pioneer effort to locate and map all sites within a single valley, air photo sheets were mounted on the lowered windshield of the project's jeep. This procedure not only provided a stable plotting surface but also reduced the risk of getting lost: The jeep could be aligned with the "north" of the photos, and photo reference points could then be sought by looking in line with their position on the car hood. The match between base map and "ground truth" was so vivid in this case that one of the workmen claimed he could watch the jeep move across the photo as reconnaissance progressed!

At the end of each day's or week's work, the field plots should be transferred to a base map, usually located at the project's field headquarters. The base map provides a complete record of the reconnaissance as well as insurance against loss of the field plots. It often represents a larger area—either a large, uncut original map or a mosaic of smaller original sheets—on which overall progress can be gauged and emergent distributional patterns examined.

As part of the reconnaissance record, verbal data often add useful details to a location map. For example, notes on road conditions, or on local friendliness or hostility, can be handy when investigators return to a site found earlier. Verbal information can even substitute for plotting on a map or a photo, if the latter are unavailable. In such an instance, the description should relate the discovered remains to multiple known, permanent features that are easy to locate. Rivers, towns, roads, and—where available—surveyors' benchmarks are all examples of reference points. The archaeologist should bear in mind, however, that landscapes change; sites have been "lost" when their verbal reference points were destroyed.

Increasing numbers of archaeologists are using **Geographic Information Systems (GIS)** technology to store and use locational data. Kenneth L. Kvamme (1989:139) has described GIS as "database management systems with a spatial component; in other words, GIS are designed for the manipulation, analysis, storage, capture, retrieval, and display of data that can be referenced to geographic locations." In GIS, locational information from maps, aerial photographs, remote sensing (see below), and other sources is converted to digitized format and entered in a computer. Information on soils, water systems, and other aspects of the natural environment is usually included along with archaeological (and other) data. The resulting data sets are usually extensive and complex, but the memory and analytic capacities of the computer allow storage and study of these data in ways literally impossible to achieve by traditional, noncomputerized means. We will explore some of the accomplishments and potentials of GIS in this chapter, as well as in Chapters 14 and 15.

Along with recording its location, the archaeologist must give each site a label. Numbers are easiest. They may run in a single consecutive series or be subdivided and coded to indicate location; for example, each grid square or map sheet might have an independent series. The system commonly used in the United States combines a number designation for the state, a letter code for the county, and a number for the site. Thus, site 28MO35 refers to the 35th site recorded in Monmouth County, New Jersey. Names can be descriptive and easy to remember, but they also tend to be more cumbersome than numbers for data analysis. The whole point of labeling is to tie the locational data to other information—physical descriptions of the remains, surface collections taken, drawings, maps, and photographs made, later excavations conducted, and so forth. With the identification and plotting of sites accomplished, the archaeologist moves from reconnaissance to the surface survey of individual sites.

Surface survey encompasses techniques of direct observation used to gather archaeological data present on the ground surface at specific sites. These are used to detect and record whatever surface artifacts, ecofacts, and features may be present. Archaeologists use one set of survey techniques to record surface features and another for surface artifacts and ecofacts. The first set consists of **mapping** techniques; the second involves **surface collections.** Insofar as the spatial arrangement of artifacts and ecofacts in primary context can be considered a feature (being nonportable; see Chapter 4), it too is subject to mapping; surface features, however, are by definition not subject to collection.

Mapping Sites   A map is a scaled symbolic representation of a segment of the earth's surface as viewed from above; it is a two-dimensional rendering of a three-dimensional reality. Archaeologists use two basic kinds of maps: planimetric maps and topographic maps (Fig. 6.9). Archaeological **planimetric maps** depict archaeological features (buildings, walls, tombs, or whatever) without indicating relief or other three-dimensional data. **Topographic maps,** in contrast, show not only archaeological remains but also the three-dimensional aspects of land forms, using conventional symbols such as contour lines. In addition to depicting relief, topographic maps usually contain symbols for natural features such as rivers, springs, and lakes, and for modern cultural features such as roads and buildings. It is important to note that planimetric maps usually include more interpretation of archaeological remains than do topographic maps.

Both kinds of maps must contain a scale, expressed either as a numerical ratio (such as 1:200, where 1 cm on the map represents 200 cm [or 2 m] on the ground) or in graphic form (such as a bar scale like the one in Fig. 6.9). The map scale is critical, since it determines the amount and detail of the data that can be presented on a map. Although most topographic maps give scales in both the metric and the English systems, nearly all archaeological work is now done in the metric system. The English system

FIGURE 6.9 Comparison of information conveyed by (top) topographic and (bottom) planimetric archaeological maps of the same site, Cahokia, Illinois. (After Fowler 1989, courtesy of Melvin Fowler and the Illinois Historic Preservation Agency.)

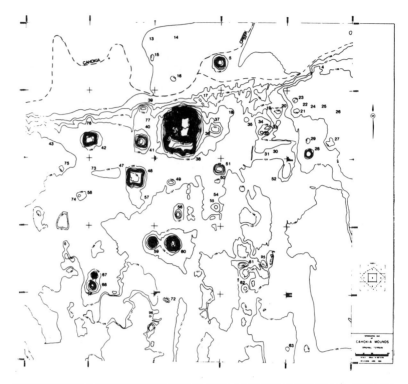

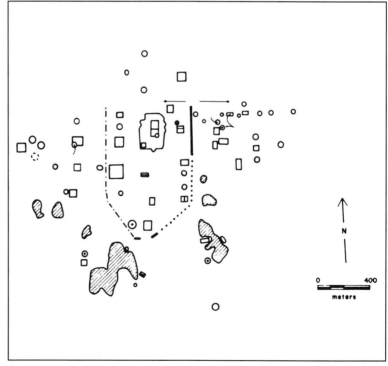

remains particularly useful for work at sites such as those of British colonial North America, where the original inhabitants measured in yards, feet, and inches. In most situations, however, archaeologists use the metric system, for purposes of standardization and comparison of recordings.

Maps also indicate orientation information—often an arrow pointing north—and usually include the survey date and magnetic declination (difference between magnetic north and true north; see Chapter 9). Decisions about proper scale or choice of map type depend on the kind of information and amount of detail that are required, along with the amount of time and funds available. These considerations will become more apparent as we discuss different kinds of maps.

Regional maps **Regional maps** are designed to depict archaeological sites within their local environmental setting (region) and are most useful as tools in reconnaissance, as noted earlier. They are especially important in presenting the relationship of the site to aspects of the natural landscape, such as rivers or hills. The optimum scale for the map depends, of course, on the numbers and sizes of sites being depicted, but regional maps are generally small in scale (1:10,000 to 1:50,000). Because of their function, they do not attempt to depict individual archaeological sites or features in any detail. Sites are usually indicated just by triangles, circles, or other simple symbols. It is normally beyond the means of most archaeologists to prepare regional maps "from scratch" because they cover such extensive areas. However, existing topographic maps can usually be adapted for this purpose (Fig. 4.5, p. 119, is an example of a regional map), and growing numbers of archaeologists are incorporating such maps into computerized GIS data bases.

Site maps **Site maps** depict archaeological sites in detail. They normally serve as the basic record of all surface archaeological features, as well as of relevant details of the natural landscape, as these aspects appear at the beginning of investigation. Site maps also indicate the **site grid** system used to designate and record archaeological features and other data. Limits to areas investigated, such as sample areas for surface collections or areas excavated, are often marked on site maps. Scales vary according to individual cases, but they range from about 1:1000 to 1:5000. Site maps may be purely topographic, with both natural and archaeological features indicated by the same conventional symbols, such as contour lines (see Fig. 6.9a). In some site maps only the natural relief is shown by contour lines, while archaeological features are depicted in distinct symbols (Fig. 6.13, p. 206, is an example).

Site plans **Site plans** are used to show details of site components, usually archaeological features such as buildings, tombs, and walls. They are almost always planimetric, emphasizing only the relevant feature and its

FIGURE 6.10 Plan of a masonry structure. Solid lines indicate walls and platforms revealed in excavations or visible on the surface; broken lines represent extensions from known architecture to complete the structure. Excavation limits are also shown. (Drawing by Diane Z. Chase; Quiriguá Project, The University Museum, University of Pennsylvania.)

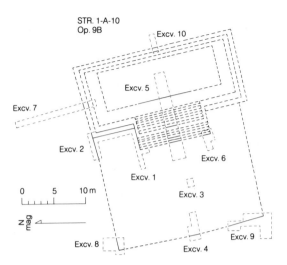

constituent parts (Fig. 6.10). Because they show great detail, these are relatively large-scale maps, generally 1:250 or larger. In many cases, site plans are used to present the results of excavation, by first presenting a plan of the feature before excavation, then depicting the same feature after excavation. This is especially useful in cases of superimposed construction; often a complex sequence of constructional activity can be clearly recorded only by a series of plans, each corresponding to a single stage in construction. Site plans will be discussed again in Chapter 7 when we consider the recording of excavation data.

Preparing archaeological maps   For regional maps the archaeologist can often use available topographic maps at suitable scales as base maps. A regional map can be prepared simply by adding the relevant archaeological data, such as the location of sites. Increasingly this is the core of (or can be added to) a GIS data base. But the archaeologist may not find preexisting maps of suitable quality and adequate scale to serve as site maps. And, because scientific standards change and objectives differ, even archaeologists who reinvestigate a site that has already been mapped may find previous maps inadequate for their needs. Good quality, large-scale maps may sometimes be available for an archaeological site located within or adjacent to a modern town or city that is itself well mapped. These maps usually contain accurate topographic data, such as contour information, and can be converted to site maps by simply plotting the location of archaeological features on them.

   If such a large-scale map is not available, the preparation of a site map is the first field priority in any archaeological investigation, for the map will serve as the basic spatial control in all records of provenience. In addition to both archaeological and topographic features, the site map must

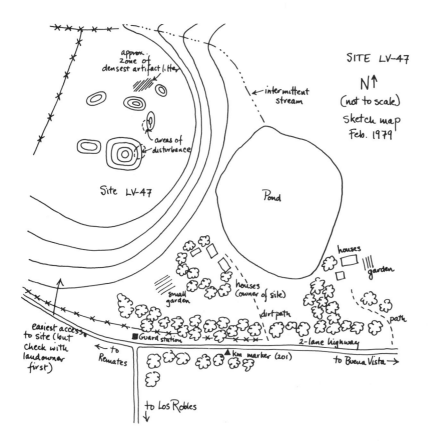

FIGURE 6.11 Sketch map, made without instruments, recording both surface features and other useful information.

indicate the location of source areas of surface collections and the limits to all excavations. In many cases, the site map will control the selection of probabilistic samples, with units based on either archaeological criteria (such as features) or arbitrary criteria (grid systems).

There are four basic kinds of archaeological maps. For those interested in mapmaking procedures, several excellent field manuals describe these techniques (see Guide to Further Reading at the end of this chapter). The simplest maps, and the quickest ones to make, are sketch maps (Fig. 6.11). **Sketch maps** are impressionistic renderings made without instruments. They are often made during feasibility studies or archaeological reconnaissance efforts, to record graphically the general characteristics of a site. In this role sketch maps can be valuable supplements to written descriptions and photographs. However, sketch maps do not have a uniform scale, do not accurately depict the topography, and cannot reliably delineate the forms or relationships of archaeological features; for these reasons they represent a preliminary record and should always be replaced by more accurate mapping as research progresses.

Compass maps are more accurate representations, since they are made

FIGURE 6.12 Compass map, accurately recording planimetric information without depicting topographic relief. (After Sedat and Sharer 1972.)

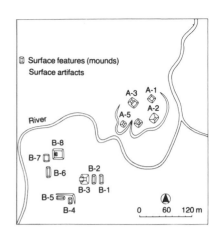

FIGURE 6.13 Grid square 5C from the Tikal, Guatemala, site map, a planimetric and topographic map originally published at 1:2000. This grid square is located within the overall map in the diagram below. (From Carr and Hazard 1961, Tikal Report no. 11, The University Museum, University of Pennsylvania.)

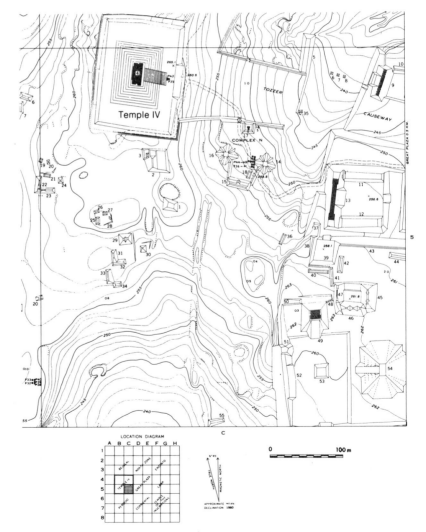

using the most basic instrument usually available to the archaeologist, a good quality magnetic compass. Several good pocket-transit compasses are available for all-round use, including mapmaking.

The use of compass and tape is the fastest method of making a reasonably accurate planimetric map (Fig. 6.12). However, this method is not as efficient or as accurate for measuring differences in elevation, so it is usually not preferred for making topographic maps. Although instruments such as pocket-transit compasses are indispensable to the archaeologist, they should be used for mapmaking only when more accurate instruments are not available. In some cases, compass-and-tape methods have been used to extend the coverage provided by more accurate instrument mapping. At the huge site of Tikal, Guatemala, the central area, 9 km², was mapped by surveying instruments over a period of four field seasons (Fig. 6.13). Another 7 km² surrounding the central area, a set of 28 squares each 500 m on a side, was mapped by compass and tape during the fourth season.

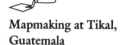

Mapmaking at Tikal, Guatemala

Aerial photographic maps are planimetric representations made by tracing ground features directly from an aerial photograph. Of course, the usefulness of such a map depends on the scale of the photograph. Many aerial photographs are at too small a scale to be useful for site maps, but they may be of great help as base maps in reconnaissance efforts and surveys that cover wide areas. Other factors besides scale affect the quality of this kind of map. Every camera lens produces distortions, which increase toward the edges of the photograph; thus features traced from the edges of an aerial photograph will always be less accurately rendered than those traced from the photograph's center. In addition, in some situations (such as heavy vegetation) archaeological features are not detectable on aerial photographs. On the other hand, as we shall see later in this chapter, under the right conditions aerial photographs can reveal buried features, as in crop marks (Fig. 6.18, p. 212), and detect topographic information.

Instrument maps are often the preferred method for archaeological mapping. They are made using one or both of two basic kinds of surveyors' instruments: the **transit** (or *theodolite*) and the **alidade.** Generally speaking, the transit or theodolite (Fig. 6.14) is the more accurate instrument for taking bearings and measuring angles; for this reason it is often preferred for making planimetric maps and site plans. Measurements are recorded in a surveyor's notebook and plotted later, out of the field. This makes a transit easier to transport than an alidade, since the latter must be accompanied by a **plane table** (Fig. 6.15). The plane table is a special drawing surface that can be accurately leveled. Although the plane table and alidade are certainly bulkier to carry around, their use produces a map on the spot and ultimately saves time. The alidade is therefore more efficient for measuring and plotting both elevations and distances and is preferred by many for making topographic maps, especially site maps.

In recent years the development of electronically automated laser instruments with digital distance and elevation readouts has made mapping an easier and less time-consuming task. Because the laser equipment is still

FIGURE 6.14   Field recording of planimetric and topographic information by surveyors' transit.

FIGURE 6.15 Field recording of planimetric and topographic information by plane table and alidade. The person in the background holds a specially marked pole at the point for which the data are being measured.

quite expensive, however, many archaeologists continue to use optical surveyors' instruments.

Another timesaving innovation has been computer-generated maps and field drawings. Survey data can be fed into a computer programmed to plot the finished map. This method can be used either with the traditionally formatted data from a surveyor's notebook or, in the case of laser instruments, with data recorded on computer-compatible tape or disks.

Surface Collection   At one time or another, almost every archaeologist has used artifactual data from surface proveniences to provide at least a preliminary evaluation of a site under study. In most areas of the world, many archaeological sites are recognized by surface scatters of durable artifacts such as stone tools and pottery sherds. The recovery of artifacts such as these often provides an immediate clue to the age and even the function of the sites.

Surface remains may be collected from archaeological sites in a variety of ways. Some archaeologists prefer to select their collection by choosing only the diagnostic artifacts from the surface. *Diagnostic,* in this case, refers to those artifacts that are significant to the particular research problem under investigation. To determine the probable occupation period of a site littered with surface pottery, for example, the archaeologist may collect only decorated sherds, because they may be the best chronological indicators. Alternatively, an archaeologist interested in ancient function might collect only sherds from the rims of vessels, because they may be the best functional indicators. The remaining sherds and all other artifacts would be left behind as "undiagnostic." Other archaeologists prefer to collect all available surface remains, allowing later laboratory analysis to evaluate which artifacts are significant. Of course, the collection of every kind of surface artifact is especially important in areas about which there is little previous archaeological knowledge. In most cases, collection of all kinds of surface artifacts is probably best: Sometimes the most uninteresting lump proves significant once it has been examined in the laboratory.

Artifacts and ecofacts may be collected with or without first plotting (mapping) their surface location. The decision to map surface provenience usually depends on two factors—the context and the amount or extent of the remains. If the surface artifacts or ecofacts appear to be in secondary context, badly disturbed by human or natural events, plotting individual locations may not be necessary or useful. However, if the surface material appears to be in primary context, it is usually advisable to plot the provenience of each artifact accurately. Whether this is feasible may depend on how many artifacts are present and how large an area they cover. It may be possible to map accurately the location of each of several dozen chipped-stone tools and animal bones lying on the surface of a site that covers only several hundred square meters. In such a case, the provenience of each artifact is recorded by plotting its location on a site map or plan and then numbering each item as it is collected, keying the same number to the artifact symbol on the map or plan. To study association patterns at the exposed sites of China Lake Valley, California, archaeologists plotted individual artifacts and ecofacts for a number of squares, each about 300 m on a side (Fig. 6.16).

When the archaeologist is confronted with several hundred thousand pottery sherds scattered across an ancient village site covering several thousand square meters, however, plotting the location of each artifact may not be possible. In such a situation, the surface area of the site is usually divided into small provenience units called **lots**. These units can be defined either arbitrarily (for instance, by grid squares) or nonarbitrarily (for example, using archaeological features to subdivide a site—in other words, artifacts are collected and provenience-keyed to their association with structures, rooms, and so forth). In either case, each artifact's provenience is recorded as part of a lot, but not by its precise individual location. Thus the provenience of any single artifact—say a sherd—will indicate that it was found on the surface of a particular grid square or structure, along with dozens of other artifacts from the same lot.

Individual plotting of artifacts and ecofacts at China Lake, California

Remote Sensing

Remote sensing involves a number of techniques in which the observer is not in direct contact with the archaeological remains. These techniques may be used in both reconnaissance and surface survey, but for different purposes—to identify previously unknown archaeological sites, or to detect and record components of individual sites. Remote sensing techniques

FIGURE 6.16 Detailed plot of surface finds at China Lake, California. (After Davis 1975, reproduced by permission of The Society for American Archaeology, adapted from *American Antiquity* 40:51, 1975.)

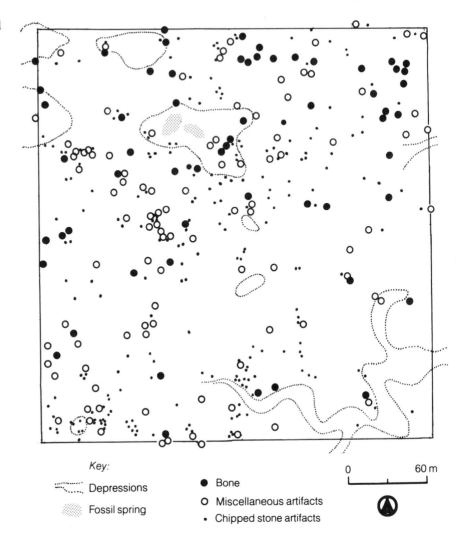

Key:

⋯⋯ Depressions

▨ Fossil spring

● Bone

○ Miscellaneous artifacts

· Chipped stone artifacts

0   60 m

can be divided into two principal categories: those done from the air and those done from ground level (subsurface detection).

Aerial Methods The development of aerial methods for archaeology is an outgrowth of military necessity. Somewhat ironically, the techniques designed to improve the destructive capabilities of modern warfare have also been of great benefit to archaeologists in their efforts to record and preserve past human achievements. The same techniques of aerial observation that gather information for the world's armies, by permitting observers to see large-scale spatial distributions and patterns, aid archaeologists in identifying ancient sites.

FIGURE 6.17 Vertical aerial photograph, shot by remote control, from a balloon moored over the site of Sarepta, Lebanon. (Photo by Julian Whittlesey.)

Direct observation from the air is usually inefficient without some method of simultaneously recording what is observed. **Aerial photography** is the most common means of recording.

Aerial photography   The most common approach to aerial photography is use of a small airplane. Helicopters and balloons have also been used (Fig. 6.17), as have kites and drones equipped with remote-controlled cameras.

Aerial photos are of two types: vertical coverage, in which the ground is photographed from directly above, with the camera pointed straight down; and oblique coverage, in which the ground is photographed at an angle, for example as viewed from an airplane window. Vertical aerial photography is generally the most versatile. Because the scale is constant throughout the photo, patterns in ground features can be seen with minimal distortion. In addition, because plan measurements can be drawn directly from the photo, these are the kinds of photographs most useful as aids in mapping. With oblique shots, the scale varies throughout the photograph, and because of distortion, the location of reference points on the ground may be difficult to determine. On the other hand, oblique views reveal more area per photo, and, since the perspective is from the side, slight changes in elevation—including some archaeological features—are often easier to see.

Aerial photography is useful to archaeologists in a number of ways. First, it provides data for preliminary analysis of the local environment and its resources. Second, it yields information on site location. Although aerial photography can reveal sites from their surface characteristics or

FIGURE 6.18 A pair of vertical aerial photographs of the same area at different times. Detection of buried archaeological features has been greatly enhanced with the maturation of the barley growing in the field: (top) taken June 4, 1970; (bottom) taken June 19, 1970. (Courtesy of the Museum Applied Science Center for Archaeology, The University Museum, University of Pennsylvania.)

prominence, one of its most useful applications is in detecting buried sites. The same phenomena of differential vegetation growth that are useful to ground reconnaissance are often vividly revealed in aerial photography (Fig. 6.18). The best circumstance for such detection is a uniform, low-growing plant cover, such as that found in grassy plains, savannahs, or croplands. Areas of luxuriant growth are usually darker than poor growth areas. As we noted, some ancient activity may produce areas that promote growth; other archaeological features retard the growth of overlying vegetation.

Aerial methods are not always helpful in locating archaeological sites. For one thing, in low-altitude work—the kind most archaeologists do—the coverage area must be relatively free of dense vegetation. Thus, with some exceptions, the technique is seldom useful in heavily forested regions. Another difficulty is that differences in elevation that are obvious to the ground observer may be imperceptible in aerial photography. Elevation differences can best be seen in photographs through shadows; for this reason, aerial photos are often most useful if taken under brightly sunlit conditions when shadows are longest, either early in the morning or late in the afternoon. Differences in elevations can also be detected by the use of stereo photography. The principle of stereo photography is the same as that of stereoscopic vision; it is occasionally used commercially, for example, in 3-D movies. Aerial stereo cameras are programmed to take vertical photographs with overlapping coverage (usually 60 percent of each frame overlaps the area covered by the previous photo). By placing any two adjacent frames under an instrument called a *stereoscope,* an observer can see the area of overlap in three dimensions. Stereo photography can reveal slopes and heights even when the sun's shadows do not indicate their relief. Cartographers use stereo coverage and sophisticated equipment to make contour maps.

Because vertical aerial photos are so useful for mapmaking, extensive coverage already exists for many areas. Depending on the range in altitude of the aircraft and the type of camera used, coverage may be available at one or more scales. As a general rule, scales from 1:4000 to 1:10,000 are the most useful for locating ancient archaeological sites. But some smaller scales (up to 1:50,000) may be useful for such purposes as plotting the regional distribution of sites relative to environmental resources. The larger-scale photos can sometimes be used as a basis for mapping individual sites. Most existing vertical photos are available from government agencies or from private cartographic companies. They are usually easy to obtain and relatively inexpensive.

Black-and-white panchromatic film is generally used, because it is more economical than color. Black-and-white photography also has better resolution—it can be enlarged more effectively to show detail—and it is better for recording contrasts in the brightness and texture of ground features. Other film types, however, such as **infrared,** are useful for specific goals such as increasing the contrast among some types of trees. In addition, special filters can sometimes enhance detection capabilities. Just as oblique and vertical images serve complementary purposes, so multiple coverage using more than one type of film (or filter or camera) allows the advantages of the various types to complement, rather than substitute for, one another. But, because flight time is expensive, it is worthwhile to combine coverages to maximize the number of photographs taken in a given flight.

Like data from all remote sensing techniques, aerially gathered data require knowledge of the corresponding **ground truth** for reliable interpretation. In other words, the archaeologist must determine, by some degree of surface investigation, what the various contrasting patterns and features on a photograph represent on the ground. Features such as rivers and towns may be self-evident. But even familiar things such as modern golf courses can sometimes go unrecognized by an individual who is not acquainted with the area or experienced in reading aerial photographs. After doing some ground checking, the researcher may be able to pick out the distribution of specific crops or the like. Local inhabitants can be of great help in this work. In general, successful interpretation of aerial photography depends on firsthand investigation of a sample of covered areas on the ground.

Aerial thermography Aerial observational data can also be recorded by a variety of nonphotographic—and usually much more expensive—devices. Infrared or heat radiation can be detected and recorded by thermal sensors (**thermography**). The resulting image indicates the differential retention/radiation of heat. **Aerial thermography** has been used to locate such archaeological features as buried ditches and prehistoric fields. Note that infrared photographic film detects reflected radiation from the sun, whereas thermography (infrared thermal sensing) detects heat emitted from the object being examined.

SLAR Radar images, such as **side-looking airborne radar** (**SLAR**), which provides an oblique image of the ground surface, have also been used for archaeological purposes. Radar is effective in penetrating cloud cover, and to a certain extent it will "see through" dense vegetation (as in a rain forest) to record abrupt changes in topography or large archaeological features (Fig. 6.19). As always, the archaeologist needs to check directly any apparent discoveries picked up by remote sensing; for example, although SLAR images suggested the presence of large-scale ancient agricultural fields in many parts of the Guatemalan lowlands, ground-level inspection showed a good number of these to represent natural changes in the landscape.

Satellite imagery Several nonmilitary satellites provide data useful for archaeological purposes. For example, the Earth Resources Technology Satellites—now called **Landsat**—have multispectral scanners that record the intensity of reflected light and infrared radiation. The minimum units

FIGURE 6.19 A SLAR image taken through extensive cloud cover from 35,000 feet over the rain forest of northern Guatemala. The darker zones in the center to lower right corner are probably areas of standing water; the regular outline of this area is of interest, since it may represent agricultural modifications made by the ancient Maya (the visible straight lines are from 3 to 5 km long). (SLAR image courtesy of NASA–Jet Propulsion Laboratory.)

recorded are called **pixels** (a word coined from "picture elements"). Early pixels were 80 m on a side, a size Scott Madry and Carole Crumley likened to that of a major-league baseball field. More recently, resolution has been reduced to 20 or even 10 m, and now even traces as small as 3 m across can sometimes be detected.

Data for these pixels are converted electronically to photographic images that can be built up, in a mosaic, to form a very accurate map. The resolution of the images, however, is still often low; study units must normally exceed 10 acres for this method to be useful. Early images were frequently projected at a scale of 1:1,000,000, so that even massive features such as the great pyramids of Egypt are barely visible (Fig. 6.20). Although higher-resolution imagery is now available, studies involving regional or interregional distributions are still the most frequent applications of satellite data. For example, by identifying unexplored pixel areas similar to pixel areas containing documented sites, Jay Custer and his colleagues have used Landsat data to predict the location of unknown sites in central coastal Delaware.

Use of satellite imagery, and remote sensing at the regional scale more generally, has a valuable and flexible new tool in computerized Geographic Information Systems (GIS), described earlier in this chapter. After digitizing information from a base map (often simply a government topographic map), analysts incorporate details from multiple other sources, such as satellite imagery, historical maps, or ground survey. The result is a richly textured computer data base on landforms, vegetation, water systems, cultural features, and so on, for a specified region. On the computer screen or summarized in numerical form, the analyst can view selected aspects of the landscape at will, highlighting individual or sets of elements, such as terrain of particular slope angle, geological composition, or whatever. At the same time, the digitized data can be subjected to statistical analyses, to examine the composition of the landscape, co-occurrence of cultural and natural features, and the like. As we shall see in Chapters 14 and 15, GIS offers great archaeological potentials in relating traces of ancient occupation to environmental features. For one thing, GIS contributes to increasingly detailed analyses of resources available to ancient occupants. And although examination of GIS data (like satellite imagery) doesn't in itself reveal new sites, it allows archaeologists to accurately locate areas in which—based on previous research—new sites are likely to occur. Searches of such signature areas can then test site distribution hypotheses. GIS therefore serves as both an ever-expandable data base and an interactive tool for refining models of settlement distribution. As Jay K. Johnson and his colleagues have demonstrated in Mississippi, for example, GIS has particular promise in regions like the eastern United States, where direct observation and analysis of the landscape are often hampered by dense ground cover.

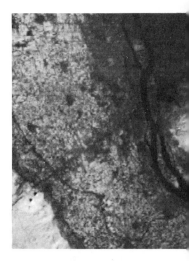

FIGURE 6.20 Landsat image of a portion of the Nile Valley in Egypt, with the Great Pyramids visible on the desert margin at lower left. (Produced by John Quann, Goddard Space Flight Center, from Landsat photo E–1165–08002, Band 7.)

Subsurface Detection   Not all buried sites are detectable by either direct observation on the ground or aerial methods. Furthermore, sites that are identified on the surface by either of these means may have unknown subsurface components. It is often necessary, therefore, to use methods of **subsurface detection** in both reconnaissance and survey. Various methods have been developed, ranging from the rather simple and commonplace to the exotic and expensive. Most of the procedures we will discuss have been adapted or modified from geology, where they were originally developed for petroleum and mineral prospecting. Usually these techniques provide limited coverage and are time-consuming and expensive. For these reasons they are used primarily for defining subsurface characteristics within archaeological sites (survey), but they may sometimes be used to locate entire sites (reconnaissance).

Bowsing   The simplest and most straightforward approach is often called **bowsing;** it involves thumping the earth's surface with a heavy bat or mallet. Using this technique—analogous to tapping walls to find studs for hanging pictures—a practiced ear can successfully detect some subsurface features, such as buried walls and chambers, by differences in the sound

FIGURE 6.21 Conventional photograph of the interior of a recently discovered Etruscan tomb; such tombs are often discovered by subsurface probes. (Courtesy of Ellen Kohler and Fondazione Lerici.)

Lerici periscope: Etruscan tombs in Italy

produced. Several sophisticated electronic elaborations of this idea have been tested. All are based on differential reflection or transmission of seismic waves by buried features—the same principle used in submarine sonar detection. Unfortunately, few of these experiments have enjoyed success.

Subsurface probes Another simple technique, designed to be used in earth matrices, is **augering** or **coring.** An auger is a large drill run by human or machine power. It is valuable in ascertaining the depth of deposits such as topsoil or middens. *Corers* are hollow tubes that are driven into the ground. When removed, they yield a narrow column or core of the subsurface material. Depending on the depth of the site or deposit involved, cores can provide a quick and relatively inexpensive cross-section of subsurface layers or construction.

A specialized subsurface probe called a **Lerici periscope** uses either a camera or a periscope equipped with a light source; it has been used to examine the contents of subterranean chambers (Fig. 6.21). The best-known application of this technique was in examination of underground Etruscan tombs previously identified by aerial photography. The probes were placed through a small opening drilled in the top of the tomb to see if the contents were undisturbed (in primary context) or had been looted. Since only undisturbed tombs were worth excavation, the technique saved the archaeologists time and money.

Shovel testing An alternative method commonly used in North America is **shovel testing.** Where remains are near the visible ground surface, but obscured by soil, vegetation, or both, quick, shallow probes with a shovel, or sometimes a posthole digger, can turn up artifacts or other traces of occupation. Because the volume of each probe is small, however, many need to be dug to get an idea of subsurface distribution. This means that although equipment costs are low, labor expense can be high. Moreover, there has been considerable debate concerning the effectiveness of these tests for discovering sites. Both the size of the tests (generally as squares 25 cm to 1 m on a side) and the spacing between them (anywhere from 5 m to 100 m apart) affect the likelihood of encountering archaeological remains—as do, of course, the size, internal density, spacing, and other characteristics of the sites themselves.

Some archaeologists, such as Michael Shott, conclude that shovel-test surveys have been unreliable guides to the distribution of archaeological remains. Many others, however, including Francis McManamon, Jack Nance, Bruce Ball, and Kent Lightfoot, argue that thoughtfully designed shovel-test programs can be quite productive and accurate. For this reason, and because they are relatively easy to implement, shovel-test samples will likely continue as central to archaeological reconnaissance and survey in the eastern United States and other areas with dense ground cover.

Magnetometry The **magnetometer** is an instrument that discerns minor variations in the magnetism present in many materials. Unlike the compass, which measures the direction of the earth's magnetic field, magnetometers measure the intensity of that magnetic field. These instruments have been successfully applied to archaeological reconnaissance and surface survey because some remains create anomalies in the earth's magnetic field. For example, iron tools and ceramic kilns are especially easily found. Buried features such as walls made of volcanic stone, ditches filled with humus, and even burned surfaces may be detected by the magnetometer (Fig. 6.22). Its primary use, then, is to locate features within a site. Magnetic readings are usually taken by the instrument at regular intervals, often 1 m, and the numbers are recorded on graph paper (Fig. 6.23); some machines, however, give continuous magnetic readings. The readings are then converted into a magnetic contour map by connecting areas of equal magnetism. Areas of high magnetism stand out on the map as "peaks"; areas of low magnetism form "valleys."

Areas with steep gradients of magnetic intensity may indicate archaeological features. Sometimes the shape of a magnetic anomaly suggests what lies buried (such as a wall), but the source of the anomaly is not always a cultural feature. To distinguish "signals" from "noise," the anomalies must be tested by excavation. The function of the magnetometer is to tell the archaeologist where to dig.

The magnetometer was first applied archaeologically in England in 1958, to search for sites in the path of a new highway. An improved version, the cesium magnetometer, was used several years later as part of the

FIGURE 6.22 Magnetometers are important aids in subsurface detection; (top) the person in the foreground carries the detector while the two in the background (bottom) read and record the magnetic values. (© Nicholas Hartmann, MASCA, The University Museum, University of Pennsylvania.)

Magnetometer locates Sybaris in Italy

FIGURE 6.23 Field plot of magnetic values with contours superimposed, revealing a pronounced linear anomaly (top to bottom in the figure) later found to correspond to a buried wall. (Courtesy of the Museum Applied Science Center for Archaeology, The University Museum, University of Pennsylvania.)

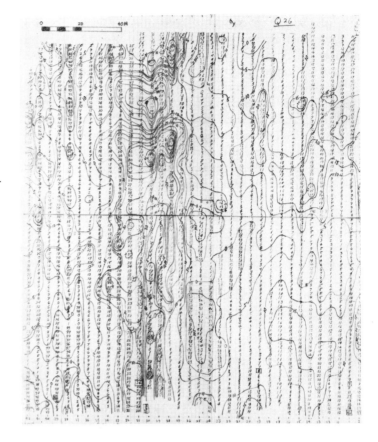

search for the Greek colonial city of Sybaris mentioned earlier in this chapter. Sybaris had a history and a reputation, but no tangible remains had been located. It had been founded in 710 B.C. and had become notorious for the self-indulgent way of life of its inhabitants; in 520 B.C., it was destroyed by its neighbors from the city of Croton. It was known to be located somewhere on the plain of the River Crati in the instep of Italy's boot; beyond this, all attempts at locating the ancient city had been unsuccessful. Then, in the 1960s, a multiseason, joint Italian–American expedition succeeded in locating Sybaris (Fig. 6.24). The investigators used a variety of approaches, including coring and resistivity techniques (see below), but the center of attention was the magnetometer. Several versions were tried; a cesium magnetometer was found to combine enough sensitivity with enough portability to trace the outlines of part of the buried remains, and this was the key both to final location of the elusive site and then to mapping its internal features.

Resistivity, conductivity, and radar Other techniques exist and new methods are constantly being developed. Resistivity surveys measure localized differences in how freely an electrical current passes between probes placed in the ground (Fig. 6.25). Moisture gives most soils a low resistance, and electricity passes easily through them. Its passage is impeded, however, by buried walls or similar solid features. By mapping differences in resistance, possible subsurface features can be located; their identity and characteristics may be tested by later excavation. Conductivity surveys are like resistivity studies in principle, but measurements are made above ground, and no probes are involved. Consequently, conductivity studies are easier to perform, but the equipment can be nearly ten times as expensive as **resistivity detectors** and is more subject to interference from power lines and the like.

Ground-penetrating radar units have been developed for archaeological applications. They detect potential buried features from differing "echoes" of electromagnetic pulses (Fig. 6.26). The result is a vertical cross-section showing the relative depth of changes in the echo patterns, each of which could mark the top or the bottom of a feature. A series of these can be used to create a map of the distribution of suspected subsurface remains, but again the remote sensing data must be tested by excavation. Radar sensing is more expensive and often more time-consuming than other methods, but if soil and other conditions are right, it can yield much more detail about what lies below the ground level—showing, for example, the approximate depth of both the ceiling and the floor of a buried chamber, as well as its horizontal extent.

When employed together, the various techniques described above can usefully provide complementary views of subsurface remains. Prehistoric

FIGURE 6.24 Excavations at Sybaris, following reconnaissance by magnetometer, expose Roman construction superimposed on the remains of the earlier Greek colony. (Courtesy of the Museum Applied Science Center for Archaeology, The University Museum, University of Pennsylvania.)

FIGURE 6.25 Subsurface detection by resistivity at a historical site in Pennsylvania. (Courtesy of the Museum Applied Science Center for Archaeology, The University Museum, University of Pennsylvania.)

FIGURE 6.26 Ground-penetrating pulse radar being used at Valley Forge, Pennsylvania, to locate subsurface remains of the Revolutionary War encampment: (left) the portable radar transmitter yields the cross-section of subsurface strata seen at right. (© Nicholas Hartmann, MASCA, University of Pennsylvania.)

Combining remote sensing techniques: Marajó Island at the mouth of the Amazon

sites in the South American lowlands are traditionally thought to preserve little, beyond pottery, of archaeological significance. Based on her work in Venezuela, Anna Roosevelt knew much more potential existed in at least some of these sites. She wanted to explore the potentials in similar settings, but knew that excavation to reveal the range of details she sought would be time-consuming, expensive, and destructive. Instead, she decided to apply a battery of remote sensing techniques, and in 1985, she and her colleagues conducted magnetometry, conductivity, resistivity, and radar surveys at a 6-acre (2.5-hectare) site on Marajó Island, at the mouth of the Amazon river in Brazil.

Each technique used identified a somewhat different kind of anomaly. For example, the black areas on Figure 6.27 were identified by magnetometry as possible fired-clay hearths, within a meter of ground surface; resistivity and conductivity data were consistent with such an interpretation, and also identified artificial earthworks, shown in cross-hatching in the figure. The combined survey results allowed Roosevelt to outline a detailed working interpretation of the surbsurface structure of the site, including site limits as well as the location of hearths, middens, residences, and a wall-and-moat defense system. Those interpretations were then tested and confirmed in limited but strategically placed excavations. From ceramics encountered, the site could be dated to the Marajoara period, A.D. 400–1300. But the overall interpretive yield from the project was much richer—a highly detailed description of a large, late-prehistoric village site. Not only did the project net more information than is usually recovered from such Amazonian sites, but also the subsurface details were outlined in a relatively short time with relatively little destruction from excavation.

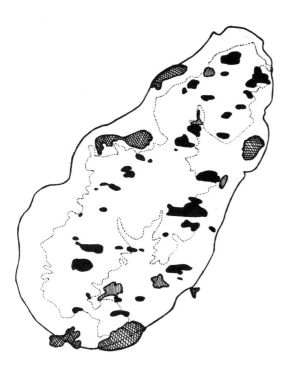

FIGURE 6.27   Magnetometry, resistivity, and conductivity surveys at this prehistoric site on Marajó Island, Brazil, suggested where various kinds of archaeological features likely lay buried. For example, black areas on the map were identified as possible fired-clay hearths; this identification and others could then be tested by excavation. (Courtesy of Anna Roosevelt.)

APPROACHES TO RECONNAISSANCE AND SURFACE SURVEY

Total Coverage

Because reconnaissance, unlike survey and excavation, seldom entails disturbing the landscape or removing archaeological evidence, total reconnaissance coverage does not often raise the issue of leaving a portion of data intact for future investigators. In fact, it is usually preferable to cover an entire study area whenever possible, especially when prior knowledge of the area is limited. As was illustrated in the Tucson Hohokam research discussed earlier in the chapter, large-scale spatial patterns are best revealed with total coverage, and rare or inconspicuous data will less likely be missed. The practicality of complete coverage depends in part on the methods to be used; for example, **aerial reconnaissance** can often cover large areas quickly for the detection of sites. In other cases, total or near-total coverage has been achieved by combining ground-based and air-based techniques, especially by use of GIS. For instance, once the archaeologist has done enough general local ground reconnaissance to be able to read local air photos accurately, sample areas that are not accessible on the ground may be covered by searching the photographs for evidence of sites. Ground checking is always advisable, even if it is not always possible.

Similarly, when surface features are being identified and recorded by mapping, total coverage of a given data universe is preferred. The only reason to use a sampling strategy in mapping would be excessive size or inaccessibility of the study universe, or potential erosion damage to archaeological remains by removal of vegetation. If, on the other hand, the surface survey includes actual collection of surface remains (artifacts and ecofacts), the need to leave some data intact for future investigations favors a sampling strategy. In archaeological salvage situations, where complete destruction is inevitable anyway, total coverage remains the preferable approach to surface collecting.

If the survey universe is defined to correspond to a single site, then total coverage implies surface survey of every square meter of that site. If, on the other hand, the universe is defined to correspond to an archaeological region containing more than one site, then total coverage implies surface survey of every site in that universe.

As an example of total survey coverage, let us consider the investigation of Hatchery West, one of a set of sites on a terrace overlooking the Kaskaskia River just east of Carlyle, Illinois. A grid of 6 m squares was laid out by Lewis Binford and his associates over the whole Hatchery West site, covering almost 15,000 m². Once all the observed artifacts and ecofacts were collected and recorded, contour maps were prepared showing the distribution density of five artifact/ecofact categories—ceramics, cracked cobbles, chipped-stone debris, chipped-stone artifacts, and ground-stone artifacts (see Fig. 6.28). Each category showed different distribution limits and different areas of concentration, but the 14 identified concentration areas could be grouped into eight types by their content. Using only this surface-derived information, the researchers formulated a number of preliminary postulates. For one thing, the site was posited to include several distinct occupations, separable both temporally and functionally. Like Roosevelt later at Marajó, excavators at Hatchery West used survey information to place key excavation units to test their hypotheses. They also made the critical observation that a representative picture of this variability in time and activities could not have been gained by surface collections from one area alone or by attending to only one of the artifact categories.

At Hatchery West the archaeologists had the opportunity to make complete survey coverage; when total coverage is not possible, however, the Hatchery West example should serve as a reminder that uncontrolled samples may offer less than adequate clues to the makeup of a site.

Total survey coverage: Lewis Binford at Hatchery West, Illinois

Sample Coverage

Total reconnaissance or surface survey of a given universe may not be feasible for any of several reasons. The method chosen may preclude total coverage. For instance, use of ground-based remote sensors is time-consuming and expensive and thus can cover only very restricted areas, as

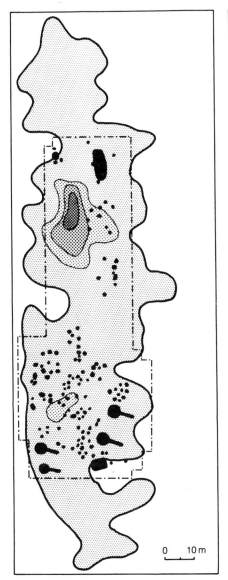

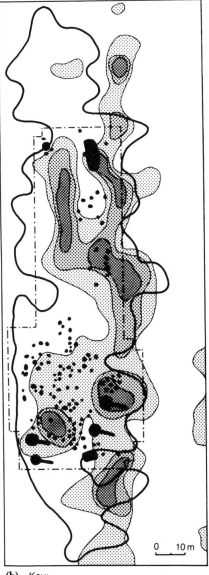

FIGURE 6.28 Surface densities of (a) pottery and (b) chipped stone at Hatchery West, Illinois. (After Binford et al., 1970, reproduced by permission of The Society for American Archaeology, adapted from *American Antiquity*, "Archaeology at Hatchery West" [Memoir of the Society for American Archaeology] 24: Figs. 5 and 10, 1970.)

(a) *Key:*

- 1–5 sherds/36 m^2
- 6–10 sherds/36 m^2
- 11–15 sherds/36 m^2
- 16–20 sherds/36 m^2
- Features
- Excavation limits

(b) *Key:*

- 10–15 chert artifacts/36 m^2
- 16–20 chert artifacts/36 m^2
- 21–25 chert artifacts/36 m^2
- Features
- Excavation limits
- Limits of surface sherds

at the Marajó Island site described above. Or the data universe may be too vast to undertake total coverage in a reasonable length of time. The highland valleys of central Mexico have been subjected to intensive and extensive reconnaissance work by scores of researchers over decades of time, yet there are still gaps. Also, in many areas of the world unsuitable environmental or political conditions may preclude complete reconnaissance. Finally, for surface survey, issues of preservation may dictate less than total coverage. In circumstances such as these, sample coverage is the only alternative. Both probabilistic and nonprobabilistic methods have been applied to select the samples.

Surface surveys using sample coverage also include two kinds of investigations, again depending on the nature of the data universe. When the universe corresponds to a single site, sample coverage implies a surface survey of only a portion of that site. If the universe corresponds to a region containing two or more sites, then sample coverage implies surface survey of only a portion of the sites in the universe, survey of only a portion of each selected site, or both.

In many cases, when archaeologists are working with multiple-site universes, they may prefer to combine sample coverage with total coverage. This means either conducting a surface survey of portions of every site in the universe (total coverage of sites combined with sample coverage of individual sites) or conducting a surface survey of the entire extent of a portion of sites in the universe (sample coverage of sites combined with total coverage at each individual site).

Nonprobabilistic Sampling The first question the archaeologist faces is whether to select the data samples by probabilistic or nonprobabilistic means. Reconnaissance and surface surveys using nonprobabilistic samples have dominated archaeological research until recently. Thus, for example, surface collections have usually been gathered from the most prominent or accessible archaeological sites, or from portions of such sites. This kind of **nonprobabilistic sampling** has certain advantages: It is often the fastest and easiest means of conducting surface surveys. Speed and ease, in turn, usually result in less expenditure of research funds. However, nonprobabilistic sampling has serious disadvantages, the chief being the inability of the archaeologist to judge the reliability of the data.

As an example of the reconnaissance difficulties imposed by environmental conditions, we shall consider the case of the ancient Maya of Mesoamerica. For years, the tropical environment that harbored one of the New World's most brilliant civilizations has hampered dozens of reconnaissance attempts to discover pre-Columbian Maya sites. Until recently, the vast, almost impenetrable lowland rain forest of northern Guatemala had made travel for any purpose—let alone archaeological reconnaissance—nearly impossible. As a result, nonprobabilistic sampling has forcibly governed most reconnaissance undertaken in this region. Ground reconnaissance has been largely restricted to the system of narrow trails

Nonprobabilistic sampling in the Maya lowlands

kept open by *chicleros*. During the past decade, access to the region has been improved by the opening of a network of unpaved roads and a few landing strips. Nevertheless, ground reconnaissance has remained difficult, because the thick jungle growth restricts visibility to a few feet on either side of the trail or road. Numerous tales are told of travelers and explorers who have passed directly through the ruins of large Maya centers, unaware of their existence. Even trained archaeologists have failed to observe large structures hidden in the dense vegetation.

These difficulties made the Maya lowlands the focus of some of the pioneer attempts at aerial reconnaissance. In 1929, Dr. A. V. Kidder (see Chapter 3) of the Carnegie Institution of Washington flew with Charles Lindbergh over the central and eastern parts of the Yucatán peninsula; in the process, he discovered more than half a dozen new sites. The following year, Percy Madeira led an aerial expedition over a somewhat wider area, recording several new sites as well as a number of unmapped lakes. On the other hand, one well-known and precisely located large site—Yaxchilán—could not be detected, even from as close as 150 feet! To this day, however, large Maya sites continue to be discovered by airline and private pilots flying over the area. Air reconnaissance has also been useful more recently in searching for differential tree-growth patterns that may indicate such extensive features as causeways (roads) and canals. Recent discoveries of remains of intensive agriculture (raised fields and terracing), which have altered previous conceptions of the tropical environmental adaptations of the Maya, have been largely due to aerial photography and airborne radar.

As a result of several centuries of sporadic exploration and perhaps a century of serious archaeological reconnaissance, hundreds of Maya sites have been identified and located. However, as one might expect with basically nonprobabilistic sampling, most of these are large sites located within traveled areas, and they were discovered because of their prominence and accessibility. There is little doubt that more Maya sites remain undiscovered in the areas that are most inaccessible. The case of El Mirador illustrates the problem: One of the largest of all Maya sites, it is located in an almost unexplored region near the Mexican border. El Mirador was first reported by the Madeira air reconnaissance expedition of 1930 (Fig. 6.29), but because of the site's inaccessibility, few archaeologists and explorers visited it in succeeding years, and even the ones who tried could not always find it. With its location reliably established, however, archaeologists in the late 1970s and early 1980s completed several seasons of successful research at the site.

On the other hand, it is probable that the vast majority of the smaller Maya sites—representing the villages and farmsteads of the ancient population that once sustained the larger elite centers—have not been documented. We know of their existence primarily because in a few cases fairly large areas of the jungle have been deliberately cleared to locate such sites. For instance, during the archaeological research at Tikal, the largest

Finding an inaccessible giant: El Mirador, Guatemala

FIGURE 6.29 Although El Mirador (arrows) is an imposing site, two of its largest platforms (over 200 ft high) barely disturb the rain forest canopy, illustrating the difficulty of finding sites in such a forested environment. (© University of Pennsylvania Museum—Fairchild Aerial Surveys Photo.)

Probabilistic sampling in the Maya lowlands

known Maya site, a series of four transects, roughly cardinally oriented and about 500 m wide, were searched for a distance of up to 12 km from the site core to document the distribution of Maya occupation. Numerous sites were found as a result, representing individual houses, house clusters, hamlets, and even small specialized centers that perhaps served as markets or religious areas. Although this reconnaissance still represents a non-probabilistic sample—the areas sampled were not selected by probabilistic procedures—it does indicate the amount and variety of archaeological remains that previous attempts at reconnaissance have missed.

Probabilistic Sampling   We may conclude from the above example that if future reconnaissance in the Maya lowlands were based on attempts to secure controlled samples, the results would yield a more representative picture of Maya sites, exposing the full range from the largest to the smallest. Work by Don and Prudence Rice, involving randomly placed transects of equal length radiating from several northern Guatemalan lakes, was a pioneering program in probabilistic reconnaissance and survey sampling. The results of such studies allow the investigators to project not only the total number of sites in the study area but also such things as the proportion of smaller (satellite) sites to larger centers. Thus, for example, a 20 percent controlled sample within a given universe (perhaps a single drainage basin) that identified 10 sites (9 satellites and 1 larger center) would allow the archaeologists to project a total data pool of 50 sites (45 satellites and 5 larger centers) within their study area. Of course, statistical manipulations such as these are based upon probability theory and are accurate only as estimates within certain tolerance limits or ranges of error.

With surface surveys, **probabilistic sampling** schemes produce data that stand a better chance of being representative of the total data pool. For this reason, such controlled sampling methods are preferable, despite greater expense in time and funds. This is especially true for research that involves surface collection of artifacts and ecofacts. Most of the specific sampling designs discussed in Chapter 4, such as stratified random sampling, can be of great benefit to the archaeologist. After the data universe is defined, either arbitrary or nonarbitrary sample units are selected to control the acquisition of surface data. Three forms of arbitrarily defined sample units—*quadrats, transects,* and *spots*—have been used successfully by archaeologists to secure representative collections of surface artifacts.

To conduct a surface collection using **quadrats,** the data universe must be gridded to define the sample units on the ground. This is usually done by placing stakes at grid line intersections. The examination and collection of surface material then proceeds within each of the quadrats selected by the sampling design being used. This strategy was used at Copán by PAC I (see Chapter 5). Similar means may be used to define linear survey areas (**transects**) and to collect surface data from a designated sample of this kind of sample unit.

Spot sample units are usually defined by the intersection of grid lines or coordinates, but they may be defined by nonarbitrary criteria such as surface features. Each spot (usually located on the ground by a stake) becomes the center point of a uniform circular sample unit. This circular area is defined by its radius, such as 10 m. Definition of spot sample units is also the most useful procedure for controlling mechanical subsurface probes such as augers and corers.

Nonarbitrary sample units may also be used to control surface collections. This means is best suited to situations characterized by well-defined archaeological features, such as individual structures or rooms within structures, or by natural divisions, such as ecozones. At the great pre-Columbian city of Teotihuacan, discussed in some detail at the end of the chapter, architectural units were quite productively used as sample units for surface collection.

Even with probabilistic sampling schemes, the archaeologist should remain flexible enough to include new areas of unexpected finds if the need arises. At Çayönü, Turkey, for example, when the randomly selected quadrats left some large areas untested, other units from the latter areas were added to the sample for spatial balance (Fig. 6.30). Evidence from such additional units cannot be included in later statistical analyses that presume random sample selection, but it may still yield valuable information.

In Chapter 4 we noted that archaeologists are still testing the relative efficacy of various schemes of probabilistic sampling. Several tests of sampling effectiveness in reconnaissance have been done by James Mueller, Stephen Plog, Kenneth Kvamme, and others, simulating the effects of different sampling designs applied to areas that have been previously completely searched. These studies indicate that stratified and/or systematic designs consistently produce more accurate samples, reinforcing the point made in Chapter 4 that sampling strategies profit from increased knowledge about the data universe and pool under study. Beyond this, however,

Combined probabilistic and nonprobabilistic survey: Çayönü, Turkey

FIGURE 6.30 Map of sampled areas at Çayönü, Turkey: Stippled quadrats represent the original probabilistic sample, and open quadrats are non-probabilistically selected sample areas added for more uniform spatial coverage of the site. (After Redman and Watson 1970, reproduced by permission of The Society for American Archaeology, adapted from *American Antiquity* 35:281–282, 1970.)

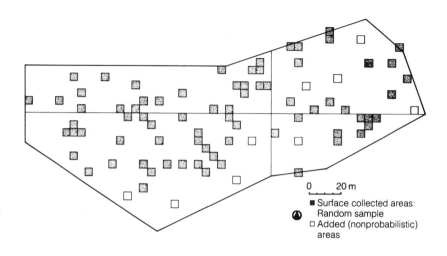

no simple or single solution exists for all situations, and the archaeologist must choose a sampling approach based on the goals and working conditions pertaining to each study.

RELIABILITY OF SURFACE COLLECTIONS

How reliable are surface-collected data for archaeological interpretation? In this section we will consider the degree to which surface artifacts and ecofacts are representative of subsurface remains. This question is of fundamental importance because of the prominence of surface collections in data acquisition. Surface collection is a quick and relatively nondestructive means of gathering information over large areas, and in some cases such collection has been relied on as the primary data source for chronological, functional, and processual interpretations. As we shall see below, in the case of Teotihuacan, test excavations supported the assumed reliability; but is such assumption valid in all cases? We shall examine the merits of this assumption by looking at several cases in which surface collections were followed by excavations to test the reliability of the survey findings. In so doing, we will also see how archaeologists use various approaches to surface survey.

Surface collection reliability: Hatchery West, Illinois

Case Studies

Our first test of the reliability of surface collections comes from the investigations at Hatchery West, described earlier in this chapter. This prehistoric site in Illinois was surface-collected over its entire extent of nearly

15,000 m² using 6 m grid squares as provenience units. Contour maps were prepared showing the relative surface density and distribution of the various kinds of artifacts. After excavations at the site were completed, the results of the surface work were compared with results from excavation. The excavations first demonstrated that Hatchery West was a shallow site: The depth of archaeological materials averaged only about 45 cm beneath the ground surface. The excavations also revealed the remains of prehistoric houses; interestingly, these features were generally in site areas with the lowest surface densities of pottery sherds. The areas of highest surface sherd densities were found upon excavation to correspond to middens. Evidence of earlier occupation was found to correlate with areas with the highest surface concentrations of cracked rock. In general, then, the Hatchery West findings indicated that the distribution and density of surface artifacts were directly (if sometimes negatively) related to the presence of subsurface features, involving at least two kinds of use-related primary contexts (houses and occupation areas) and one kind of transposed primary context (middens).

For our second test of surface collection reliability, let us look at some results of an extensive nonprobabilistic sample of surface materials from the site of Chalchuapa, El Salvador. The surface samples at Chalchuapa were nonprobabilistic because surface collections could be made only in limited portions of the site zone. The remainder was inaccessible because of modern cultivation (coffee trees were the biggest obstacle) and, in a few cases, property owners who refused to open their land to the survey. In addition, the modern town of Chalchuapa covers the western portion of the site, making it inaccessible. Most of the remaining area, some 2.5 km², was examined by ground survey, including surface collection. Areas showing high concentrations of surface artifacts were subsequently excavated on a priority basis. Three areas with unusually high concentrations of surface artifacts, especially pottery sherds, were predicted to represent middens. All three areas were excavated, and all three were revealed to be stratified middens (Fig. 6.31). However, none of the surface collections indicated the full time-depth of the middens as revealed by excavation; only the uppermost levels of the middens were represented in the surface collections.

Also at Chalchuapa, the excavations of eroded adobe platforms (mounds) were always preceded by surface collections. The surface materials here, though frequently badly weathered, generally *did* reflect the range of artifacts recovered from the subsequent excavations, even though some of the latter materials came from 3 to 4 m below the mound surface. However, excavations also revealed that the artifactual material associated with these adobe platforms was almost exclusively from use-related secondary contexts. The artifacts were in a matrix of construction fill that had been mined from previous structures, middens, and so forth, resulting in a mixture of cultural debris from a variety of time periods. The artifacts collected from the surface of the mounds had reached the surface through

FIGURE 6.31 Excavation of a stratified midden at Chalchuapa, El Salvador; materials from the lower levels seen here were not represented on the surface.

Surface collection reliability: Chalchuapa, El Salvador

Surface collection reliability: Joint Site, Arizona

processes of transformation, specifically the erosion of the earthen construction fill and its artifactual contents, caused by rainwater and modern agricultural activity.

At the Joint Site in east-central Arizona, a 6400 m² area was divided into 1 m squares, which were grouped into larger squares 20 m on a side (Fig. 6.32). Within each of the larger units, smaller units (4 m squares or 2 m strips) were selected randomly to a total of 36 percent coverage of the area (a stratified random sample). Then archaeologists chose locations for test excavations to examine the surface–subsurface relationship: A stratified random sample of units was drawn, with the strata defined by different densities of surface materials. The result was a *lack* of correspondence: Surface densities, whether high or low, were not reliable predictors of buried deposits. Going beyond this observation, however, the researchers showed how surface distributions could have been combined with an understanding of transformational processes such as wind and rain erosion patterns to yield more accurate predictions. As an obvious example, surface materials on a slope may be windblown or washed downhill from their original location. Chapter 4 discussed the fundamental importance of considering the effects of postdepositional transformations; the Joint Site example points up as well that surface debris does not necessarily indicate what lies underground.

Site Formation and the Surface–Subsurface Relationship

These examples, along with other studies not summarized here, show that the relationship between surface artifacts and ecofacts on the one hand and subsurface archaeological evidence on the other is both complex and highly variable. In some cases, there may be a good correspondence, but in others, there may be little or no direct relationship. Obviously, the relationship between surface and subsurface configurations depends on the processes of site formation—both the nature of the site and the transformational processes that have either preserved or altered the surface evidence of occupation.

As an example of the former variable, consider a site that is deeply stratified, with ancient remains extending to a great depth beneath the surface. Under normal circumstances, only the uppermost levels of the site will be represented on the surface. This effect was noticeable in the middens at Chalchuapa, where artifacts from only the uppermost levels were represented in surface collections. Later excavation revealed pottery and other artifacts in the lower levels of the middens more than 1000 years older than the materials from the surface collections. The degree of correspondence between surface remains and subsurface evidence exposed by excavation at Hatchery West appears to have resulted primarily from the fact that the occupation levels were close to the surface and not very thick.

The other main factor responsible for the distribution of surface materials is the combined forces of transformation. These transformational pro-

FIGURE 6.32 Schematic representation of sampling strata based on density of surface collections at the Joint Site, Arizona; shaded areas contain architectural remains and were sampled separately. (After Schiffer 1976.)

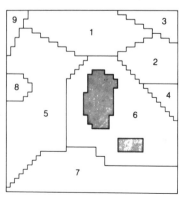

cesses were discussed in detail in Chapter 4, but it may be useful to review them here to indicate specifically how they affect the surface–subsurface relationship.

Natural agents of transformation include wind and water; we saw earlier how river-laid soil had completely buried the site of Sybaris. The study at the Joint Site showed that wind and water are also erosive, displacing surface remains from their original positions. Kent Flannery reports a similar case from the Valley of Oaxaca, Mexico. There, at an unnamed preceramic site, the results of a total-coverage surface collection were plotted on a distribution map, revealing that projectile points tended to be distributed in a ring around the edges of the site. It soon became apparent, however, that since the site was elevated in the center, this curious pattern resulted from water erosion.

Plants and animals also affect surface remains. Tree roots may dislodge buried artifacts, sometimes pulling them to the surface when the tree falls. Animal burrows can either unearth buried artifacts or allow surface materials to move into subsurface positions. Grazing animals may cause some lateral displacement of surface remains; heavy animals such as cattle may even pulverize cultural debris such as sherds.

Human agents of transformation are also important to the nature of surface–subsurface relationships. At Chalchuapa, erosion had exposed artifacts from disturbed and uniformly mixed construction fill (use-related secondary context) of earthen mounds; in this case, surface samples usually reflected excavated materials regardless of their depth. In another area of Chalchuapa, surface collections produced a baffling variety of artifacts and ecofacts, including prehistoric pottery from several time periods, human bones, bits of rusted iron, several lead bullets, and at least one brass button. The significance of these finds was revealed with the discovery of a historical account that described a decisive victory by defending Salvadoran forces over an invading Guatemalan army at the Battle of Chalchuapa in 1885. The historical account related that the major action was fought among a group of "low hills" northwest of the town. The only low hills northwest of the town of Chalchuapa are the several dozen mounds that represent the remains of pre-Columbian platforms. At least part of the battle, then, was fought in this part of the archaeological site. Further examination of the area from which the puzzling surface materials originated indicated that the collections were from what appeared to be the remains of defensive earthworks from this battle. The 19th-century soldiers who dug trenches and built earthworks probably brought pre-Columbian artifacts to the surface; the bullets and the button were evidence of the battle itself; and the human bones may testify to the usual results of warfare. However, examination of the area, including several subsequent test excavations, indicated that the area had also been badly disturbed by recent coffee cultivation and by looters' pits. The result of all this activity, from the battle in 1885 to the time of the archaeological investigations, was a badly disturbed array of both prehistoric and historic artifacts lying mixed and scattered on the present ground surface.

Transformations of surface remains: Valley of Oaxaca, Mexico

Transformation of surface remains: Chalchuapa, El Salvador

Other earth-moving activities frequently figure in the surface–subsurface relationship. Discards from looting excavations provide an example; the effect of plowing is a more common one. When confronted by surface disturbance from plowing, the archaeologist must try to estimate the degree of displacement. Sometimes, when site areas are known to have been plowed previously but have since become recompacted, archaeologists have resorted to replowing before collection. This loosens the already disturbed materials, in effect reestablishing a surface component. Such an approach was used, for example, at the Hatchery West site.

SITE DEFINITION BY RECONNAISSANCE AND SURFACE SURVEY

Well-executed reconnaissance and surface survey using one or more of the methods described in this chapter permit the archaeologist to define the study universe, whether it consists of a single site or a region containing many sites. This definition should also describe the *form, density,* and *structure* of archaeological remains within the study universe. The range in the forms of various classes of features may be assessed by both mapping and remote sensing. The range in the forms of artifacts and ecofacts may be assessed by surface collecting. Surface survey information may then be used to determine the relative density of each kind of data, together with their interrelationships (structure). Thus by plotting the spatial distribution of one artifact class, say grinding stones, the investigator may find areas in which these artifacts cluster. Furthermore, it may be possible to relate these relative densities to the distribution of other classes of artifacts, as well as of ecofacts and features. Surface survey data of this kind are often transformed into maps to show the distribution and density of artifacts, ecofacts, and features within a site. By evaluating such results, the archaeologist may be able to formulate working hypotheses to account for the surface data distributions and patterns. For example, in the China Lake Valley of California, artifact/ecofact distributions were used to infer that two different stone tool types represented different parts of one tool kit rather than different populations. A more complex example is provided by the Teotihuacan Mapping Project of the University of Rochester.

Famous among tourists as well as archaeologists, Teotihuacan is a complex, pre-Columbian, urban site located in a semiarid side valley of the Valley of Mexico, northeast of modern Mexico City. The population of Teotihuacan reached its peak in the period A.D. 1–700, when 150,000 or more people lived there. In part because of the overall size of the ancient city, even as late as the mid-20th century, no comprehensive, detailed map of the site had ever been made. Yet such a map should be a prerequisite for studies of the city's growth and decline and of the distribution of the presumably numerous activities carried on there. Fortunately, Teotihuacan lends itself well to surface inquiry, for archaeological materials tend to be

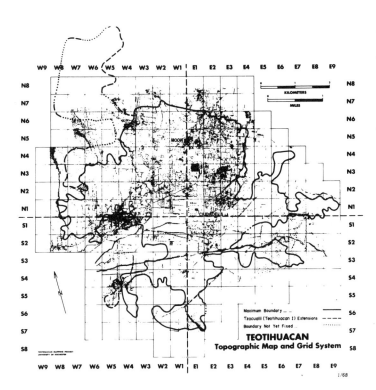

FIGURE 6.33 Overall archaeological map of Teotihuacan, Mexico, originally published at 1 : 10,000. (From *Urbanization at Teotihuacan, Mexico*, vol. 1, *The Teotihuacan Map*, copyright © 1973 by René Millon, all rights reserved.)

at or near surface level, and, in contrast to the *tells* and *tepes* of southwest Asia, the discrete buildings and courts that make up the city remain individually perceptible. With all these factors in mind, René Millon and his associates designed a program that coordinated reconnaissance, mapping, and surface collections to record the pre-Columbian metropolis. The investigation covered an area of about 53 km² using aerial photographs and maps (Fig. 6.33) as guides. This operation defined the limits of the aboriginal city; the 20 km² within these limits then became the principal focus of intensive mapping and surface collections. More than 5000 structural units and activity areas were recorded. Some excavations were conducted to test survey-derived interpretations, but the primary direction of research was toward reconnaissance and surface survey. The resulting published maps (Fig. 6.34) and accompanying verbal descriptions contain a wealth of archaeological data that will be mined by archaeologists for decades to come. For example, George Cowgill has plotted surface potsherd density for different time periods to study growth and decline of population (Fig. 6.35). In surface-oriented research, these insights are an "end product" of the investigation. In most cases, however, such survey results are preliminary findings; they assist the archaeologist in choosing where to excavate to explore promising areas and test specific hypotheses.

FIGURE 6.34 Detailed pair of archaeological maps (originally published at 1:2000) representing one grid square of the map in Figure 6.33. Map (a) records topographic and archaeological information; map (b) provides the archaeological interpretation of that information. (From *Urbanization at Teotihuacan, Mexico,* vol. 1, *The Teotihuacan Map,* copyright © 1973 by René Millon, all rights reserved.)

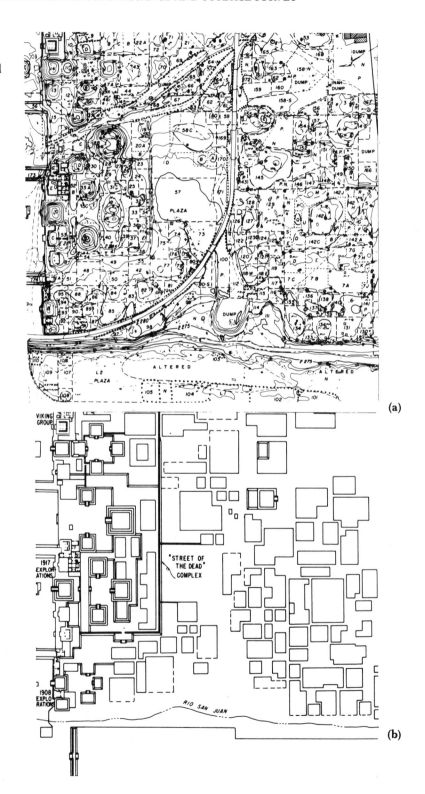

(a)

(b)

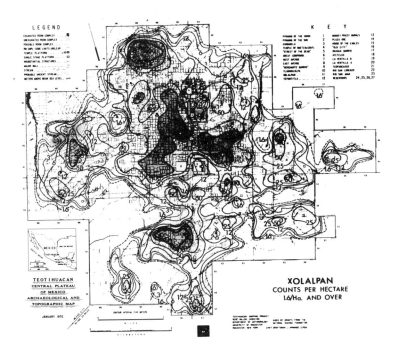

FIGURE 6.35 Surface densities of recovered pottery at Teotihuacan, Mexico, ca. A.D. 450–650. (After Cowgill 1974.)

Thus reconnaissance and surface survey remain most commonly preludes to excavation, gathering data that guide subsequent archaeological research.

SUMMARY

This chapter has discussed the basic objectives and methods archaeologists use in conducting reconnaissance and surface survey. Both are designed to yield representative data from archaeological sites without resorting to excavation. In some cases, data acquired in this way are the primary or sole basis on which the archaeologist formulates reconstructions of the past. More often, however, the acquisition of data through reconnaissance and surface survey is a prelude to the next stage of research, excavation. Surface data thus aid in selecting areas to excavate, as well as in providing specific problems or hypotheses for the archaeologist to test by excavation.

Archaeologists have developed several methods and techniques for discovering and locating archaeological sites. Each approach has its advantages and disadvantages. Ground reconnaissance is the oldest and most thorough way to identify sites that have surface manifestations, but it is often slow and in most cases cannot detect buried sites. Aerial reconnaissance provides rapid coverage of wide areas; in addition, it is perhaps the best way of detecting buried sites, provided some surface indications exist.

However, aerial reconnaissance may not detect all sites, and it may fail to distinguish smaller ones. Subsurface detection is perhaps the slowest and most cumbersome means of site identification; its coverage area is the most limited. Nonetheless, it may be the only choice in situations where sites are deeply buried. No single technique can guarantee success, but by learning as much as possible about the search area before reconnaissance, the archaeologist can design a program that combines methods to provide the highest probability of success. If total coverage of the reconnaissance universe is impractical, the archaeologist should choose sampling techniques that will maximize the extent to which data from the actual reconnaissance may be generalized. No matter what discovery or sampling techniques are used, the spatial location of the archaeological remains must be recorded. Other information may be recorded at the same time, but discovery and geographical location are the essential aspects of reconnaissance.

Most surface surveys consist of ground surveys. Ground surveys acquire data by mapping the surface characteristics of sites, including features such as surviving remains of buildings, walls, roads, and canals, as well as relevant topographic and environmental information. Ground surveys usually rely heavily on the collection of surface artifacts and ecofacts. Surface surveys also use remote sensors (either aerial or ground-based) to map the form and extent of obscure or buried features. Remote sensors and mechanical devices may be used to determine whether artifacts or ecofacts are present beneath the surface. Together, ground surveys and remote sensors are used to produce site maps and maps showing the distribution and density of surface artifacts and ecofacts. Increasingly, computer data bases (and especially Geographic Information Systems) are used to store and manipulate this mapped information.

Surface surveys may aim for total or only sample coverage of the study universe, whether that universe is defined as a single site or as an area containing two or more sites. Many surface surveys use either probabilistic or nonprobabilistic samples of the study universe. Probabilistic sampling designs are preferable under most circumstances. However, all sampling should be flexible enough to include unexpected discoveries that may add to the investigator's knowledge of the full range of data present within the study universe.

The reliability of data collected by reconnaissance or surface survey is a concern to archaeologists. As some studies dealing with this question show, it may be dangerous simply to assume that surface data are a direct reflection of the evidence beneath the ground. Instead, the archaeologist should couple the surface evidence with inferences about the probable transformations that have acted upon it, in selecting promising areas for excavation. Not only are subsequent excavations guided spatially by the results of surface survey, but they may also be used to test specific functional questions and hypotheses generated by the distribution and density patterns of surface data. At the same time, the inferences about transformational processes should be tested by excavation.

GUIDE TO FURTHER READING

Literature, Luck, and Legends

Matos Moctezuma 1988, 1989; Müller-Beck 1961; Schliemann [1881] 1968; Wood 1985

Objectives and Methods of Reconnaissance and Surface Survey

Adams 1965; Adams, Brown, and Culbert 1981; Adams and Nissen 1972; Aitken, Webster, and Rees 1958; Allen, Green, and Zubrow 1990; Ammerman 1981; Aronoff 1989; Aston and Rowley 1974; Atkinson 1953; Barker 1977; Benner and Brodkey 1984; Breiner and Coe 1972; Carr 1982; Carr and Hazard 1961; Cowgill 1974; Cowgill, Altschul, and Sload 1984; Custer et al. 1986; Davis 1975; Dillon 1989; Dinsmoor 1977; Ebert 1984; Edgerton 1976; Elachi 1982; El-Baz et al. 1989; Estes, Jensen, and Tinney 1977; Fish and Kowalewski 1990; Fish, Fish, and Madsen 1990; Frink 1984; Fry 1972; Gibbons 1991; Gumerman and Lyons 1971; Harp 1975; Johnson et al. 1988; Joukowsky 1980; Kelley, Dale, and Haigh 1984; Kennedy 1989; Kennedy and Riley 1990; Kenyon and Bevan 1977; T. F. King 1978a; Krakker, Shott, and Welch 1983; Kvamme 1989; Lynch 1980; McCauley et al. 1982; McManamon 1984; MacNeish 1964b, 1974; Mason 1984; Millon 1973, 1974, 1981; Mueller 1974; Myers and Myers 1985; Napton 1975; Palmer 1977; Parrington 1983; Pugh 1975; Pulak and Fey 1985; Roosevelt 1989, 1991; Schliemann [1881] 1968; Schorr 1974; Scollar et al. 1990; Sever and Wiseman 1985; Shapiro 1984; Shott 1985; Steponaitis and Brain 1976; Vogt 1974; Weymouth 1986; Willey 1953; Wood 1985

Approaches to Reconnaissance and Surface Survey

Alexander 1983; Allen, Green, and Zubrow 1990; Altman et al. 1982; Binford et al. 1970; Byrd 1980; Chartkoff 1978; Cowgill, Altschul, and Sload 1984; Dunnell and Dancey 1983; Fish and Kowalewski 1990; Flannery 1976d; Foley 1981; Fry 1972; Gibbons 1991; Kvamme 1989; Lightfoot 1989; Lovis 1976; Madeira 1931; Mueller 1974, 1975, 1978; Nance 1981, 1983; Nance and Bell 1989; Plog 1976, 1978a; Plog, Plog, and Wait 1978; Puleston 1974; Read 1986; Redman 1982, 1987; Redman and Watson 1970; Rice 1976; Schiffer, Sullivan, and Klinger 1978; Shott 1989a; Thomas 1975, 1978; Wobst 1983

Reliability of Surface Collections

Ammerman 1985; Ammerman and Feldman 1978; Baker 1978; Binford et al. 1970; Cherry 1983, 1984; Dunnell and Dancey 1983; Flannery 1976d; Frink 1984; Hanson and Schiffer 1975; Hirth 1978; Hope-Simpson 1984; Kintigh 1988; Koch 1989; Lewarch and O'Brien 1981; Redman and Watson 1970; Rick 1976; Roper 1976; Schiffer 1987; Sharer 1978; Tolstoy 1958; Tolstoy and Fish 1975; Wood and Johnson 1978

Site Definition by Surface Survey

Cowgill 1974; Davis 1975

CHAPTER SEVEN

EXCAVATION

There must always be an element of chance and of opportunism in an excavation, however carefully planned. But scientific digging is not on that account a gamble. . . .

Sir Mortimer Wheeler, Archaeology from the Earth, *1954*

Excavation is the principal means by which the archaeologist gathers data about the past. Excavation is used both to discover and to retrieve data from beneath the ground surface. As we have seen, surface survey is often an essential prelude to excavation. Collections of artifacts and ecofacts from the surface often provide clues to what lies beneath the ground, guiding the archaeologist in planning excavations. Remote sensors such as magnetometers or radar equipment may detect the existence of buried archaeological features. But the only way to verify what lies below the surface is through excavation.

Data retrieved through excavation are especially important for the archaeologist, since subsurface material remains are usually the best preserved and the least disturbed. Surface artifacts and ecofacts are seldom in primary context and are usually poorly preserved. Surface features such as ancient walls or roads, although in primary context, are often less well preserved than similar features buried—and therefore protected—below the surface. Most important, excavation often reveals associations of artifacts, ecofacts, and features in primary contexts. As we have seen, this kind of information is the most useful for inferring ancient function and behavior.

The two basic goals of excavation are, first, to reveal the three-dimensional patterning or *physical structure* among the artifacts, ecofacts, and features uncovered, and, second, to assess the functional and temporal significance of that patterning. The finding of stone tools, pottery vessels, and animal bones associated with each other and with house remains tells us far more than recovering any of these items in isolation. Determination of this three-dimensional patterning depends on establishing provenience and associations of the individual artifacts, ecofacts, and features, with respect both to each other and to their surrounding matrix. At the same time, evaluation of provenience and association allows the assessment of context. As Chapter 4 pointed out, it is attention to these relationships—to the links among the elements of archaeological data, as established by records of provenience, association, and context—that differentiates the archaeologist from the antiquarian and the looter. Only by knowing which of these elements were found together (provenience and association) and by inferring how they got there (association and context) can the archaeologist reconstruct ancient behavior. Once uncovered, these relationships must be thoroughly documented, so proper records of an excavation are just as crucial to its interpretation as proper methods of excavation. Of course, behavioral reconstruction also depends on analysis of what the individual artifacts, ecofacts, and features were used for; this analysis, in turn, is based partly on their provenience and association and partly on the form and other attributes of each artifact, ecofact, and feature. Such analysis of individual elements will be discussed in Chapters 8–12.

If we consider the three-dimensional structure of an archaeological deposit, what do the three dimensions represent? We must make a fundamental distinction between the single vertical dimension (depth) and the two horizontal ones (length and width). The combined horizontal dimensions represent, in an idealized situation, the associated remains of a *single point in time.* The case of Pompeii, where a whole community was buried and preserved as if in suspended animation, provides an extreme illustration. The point is that artifacts and features on the same horizontal surface ideally represent use or discard that is approximately contemporaneous (Fig. 7.1). Over time, new surfaces are created, usually by leveling and covering the old; repetition of this process creates a vertical dimension (Fig. 7.2). Thus the vertical dimension in an archaeological deposit represents accumulation through time. This distinction and its implications are crucial in excavation. Before turning to excavation methods, then, we shall discuss the structure of archaeological deposits in more detail.

STRATIFICATION AND STRATIGRAPHY

Archaeological **stratification** refers to the observed layering of matrices and features. These layers, or **strata,** may be sloping or roughly horizontal; they may be thick or thin. In some cases, they are well defined by contrasts in color, texture, composition, or other characteristics, but in others, their boundaries may be difficult or impossible to discern; one apparent stratum may simply grade into another. Whatever the specific characteristics, the layering of stratified deposits reflects the geological **law of superposition:** The sequence of observable strata, from bottom to top, reflects the order of deposition, from earliest to latest. Lower layers were deposited before upper layers. The individual strata of an archaeological deposit may represent formal occupation surfaces, as in the example of Pompeii, or they may be the result of other acts of deposition, such as accumulated layers of trash in a midden. Strata may also be deposited naturally, for instance, when floods cover an area with a layer of alluvium, or volcanoes deposit layers of ash (see Fig. 7.1).

Note, however, that the law of superposition refers to the *sequence of deposition,* not to the *age* of the materials in the strata. Although in most cases, the depositional sequence of materials found in stratified matrices does reflect relative age, this depends on the context of such remains. Special caution must be used if stratified remains are in secondary context. For

FIGURE 7.1 Recovery of evidence representing a single moment in time at Cerén in El Salvador. Excavations have here exposed the remains of an adobe house, buried by a local volcanic eruption that collapsed and carbonized the roof beams and thatch. Later eruptions are represented by the upper deposits of ash. (Courtesy of Payson D. Sheets.)

FIGURE 7.2 This view of a modern village in Iran shows that occupation at a single point in time does not always mean occupation of a single, level, ground surface. The different elevations of the houses shown here are the product of accumulation of occupation debris, not hilly topography. (Courtesy of Ilene M. Nicholas.)

example, pits or burrows, dug either by humans or by animals, may insert later materials into lower levels (see Chapter 4). In other cases, stratified matrices may be formed of redeposited material, for instance, when water erosion removes soil from a location upstream and redeposits it downstream. If this soil contains cultural material, chronologically late artifacts could be removed and redeposited first, followed by redeposition of chronologically earlier artifacts (see Fig. 4.16, p. 133). Thus the redeposited matrix contains later artifacts in its lower strata and earlier artifacts in its upper strata. Similar effects can occur as a result of human activity. Note, however, that even in cases of "reversed stratification" the law of superposition holds: The lower layers were redeposited first, followed by the upper layers.

Stratigraphy is the archaeological evaluation of the temporal and depositional meaning of the observed strata. In stratigraphic analysis, the archaeologist combines use of the law of superposition with a consideration of context. Since intact features are invariably in primary context, problems of temporal determination usually arise with portable data—artifacts and ecofacts. In essence, the archaeologist must judge whether the artifacts and ecofacts associated with stratified deposits are the undisturbed result of human activity (primary context) or whether they have been transported and redeposited by either human agents or natural events (secondary context). If the archaeologist can demonstrate primary context with reasonable assurance—that is, if there is no evidence of redeposition disturbance—then the temporal sequence of the archaeological materials within the deposit may be assumed to follow that of the strata. In this way, stratigraphic sequence is established.

Let us consider some examples of stratigraphy. In the Lindenmeier Valley of northern Colorado, bison hunters some 11,000 years ago camped in the area now called the Lindenmeier site. The hunting groups left evidence of their presence in the form of stone tools, tool-making debris, hearths, and the bones of prey animals. Although each individual group probably spent only a brief time camped at Lindenmeier, repeated use of the campsite over time led to a gradual accumulation of occupation debris. We do not know exactly how long the site was used, but during that period the level of the ground surface was being raised by natural processes: Small depressions would flood with water from a nearby stream, after which plants would grow in the wet areas and eventually die and decay. The humic soil from the decayed plants would fill the old depressions, and the stream overflow would begin the process in another low area. The new, raised surfaces created by such filling-in were used as camping stations, and older debris would be buried and sealed in place when a given locale was flooded. In this way, the combined effects of geological buildup and repeated reoccupation produced a stratified deposit in which the matrix accumulation resulted from natural causes but included (and preserved) evidence of human occupation. At Lindenmeier the law of superposition is relatively unaffected by disturbing factors: The basic stratigraphy is simply vertical accumulation upward through time, and the relative age of artifactual remains correlates well with stratigraphic position.

In many sites, however, intrusions of various kinds disrupt stratigraphy. Earthworms, along with other burrowing species, can present the archaeologist with serious transformations of the original stratigraphy. In Kentucky, for instance, Julie K. Stein documented extensive and complex

Stratigraphy: Lindenmeier, Colorado

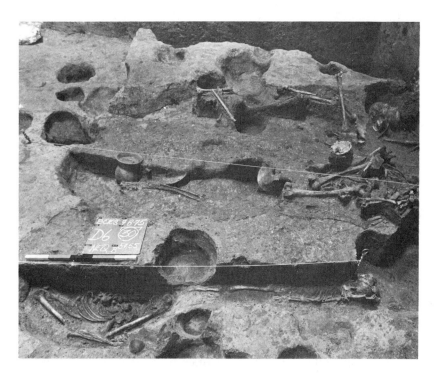

FIGURE 7.3 Excavators at Ban Chiang, in northeastern Thailand, were confronted with a complex stratigraphy of multiple intrusive pits. The light surface at left and in the background is an occupation surface through which the later pits, some of them human graves, were excavated, and sometimes the pits intruded on each other. Note that the lower leg of the skeleton in the right foreground has been cut by the pit of the later grave in the left foreground. (Courtesy of the Ban Chiang Project, Thai Fine Arts Department/ University Museum.)

earthworm disturbance of stratigraphy at the Carlston Annis mound, a shell midden originally formed between 4000 and 5000 years ago. Human activity also creates disturbances. For example, in a cemetery used over long periods, later burials may intrude into earlier ones (Fig. 7.3). Sometimes the walls of earlier burial pits are broken by later pits so many times that their outlines are difficult to trace. Later pits may also be dug deeper than earlier ones; thus, when dealing with pits, the archaeologist must tie the top of each one into the overall stratigraphy. In other words, one establishes what level the pit was dug down from. At Ban Chiang and other village sites in northeastern Thailand, the intrusive pit problem is further aggravated by—of all things—the repeated burrowing of insects, riddling pit walls and other stratification levels with holes that may be as large as tennis balls.

As stratigraphic assessments are made, archaeologists need to be able to convey them clearly to others, whether in words or in diagrams. In the early 1970s, Edward C. Harris outlined a new technique for doing just that. The schematic forms shown in Figure 7.4 are used to depict stratigraphic relations, including superposition, stratigraphic equivalence, and lack of demonstrable direct relation between elements. Combining all stratigraphic assessments for a single excavation yields a Harris Matrix as

FIGURE 7.4 A Harris Matrix depicts stratigraphic relationships as taking one of three forms: (a) no direct connection between the elements; (b) one is superimposed on the other; or (c) apparently distinct units are interpreted as previously parts of a single whole. (After Harris 1989.)

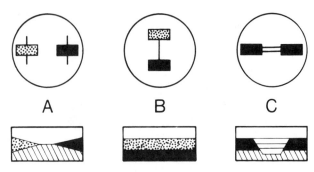

A   B   C

a stratigraphic summary for the excavation. Figure 7.5 illustrates a cross-section through an imaginary mound, along with the Harris Matrix outlining the mound's stratigraphic sequence.

Not only have many archaeologists found this a convenient means of integrating large and often complex bodies of stratigraphic information, but Harris has also used the technique to highlight interpretive distinctions he believes archaeologists too often overlook. For example, along with the more obvious "solid" stratigraphic elements, such as earthen strata, walls, or hearths, we must also pay attention to the surfaces bounding and linking other elements. Sometimes the surfaces, or interfaces, are separable and important stratigraphic entities in their own right. In Figure 7.5, for example, element 12 is the interface between 11 and 13; stratigraphically, 12 marks the surface of a pit. Its excavation (12) was an event quite distinct from processes accounting for adjacent deposits, obviously both later than deposition of the matrix (13) into which the pit intruded, and earlier—possibly by a considerable amount of time—than when the pit was filled (11).

Whether using a Harris Matrix or not, archaeologists must correlate stratigraphic sequences from separate excavation units to form a master sequence for the entire site. In some cases, this process may be facilitated by physically linking excavation units—removing barriers between adjacent test pits and trenches—to create a continuous cross-section of the stratified deposit. The problem is more difficult in large or complex sites in which linking of excavation units is impossible or impractical. In such cases, the characteristics of each individual layer—its thickness, color, composition, apparent extent, and position with respect to other strata—must be carefully defined to avoid mismatching similar features in the sequence. Photography can be an important aid in this process; ultraviolet film, for example, may pick up subtle differences that are not otherwise visible. Or direct comparisons may be made by taking physical samples of each stratum and either visually comparing them or, if necessary, submitting them to soil laboratories for analysis. Comparing strata from each excavation may enable the archaeologist to create a full composite stratigraphic sequence for the entire site.

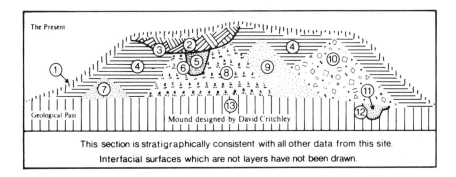

The Present

Geological Past

Mound designed by David Critchley

This section is stratigraphically consistent with all other data from this site.
Interfacial surfaces which are not layers have not been drawn.

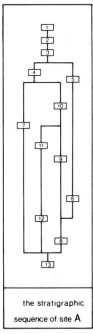

the stratigraphic
sequence of site **A**

FIGURE 7.5 Stratigraphic components of a mound are depicted (left) in a relatively realistic cross-section view and (right) in a Harris Matrix summarizing abstractly the stratigraphic relationships among the components. (After Harris 1989.)

The functional dimension of stratigraphy involves distinguishing which layers in the stratified deposit are culturally deposited features and which are naturally laid soils. For some deposits, evidence of past human activity is obvious: burials, house foundations, refuse deposits, and so on. More subtle clues to human occupation include the presence of unusually high concentrations of organic remains, which may give occupation layers a dark, "greasy" appearance. Tests have been developed to detect organic residues, such as determining the presence and amounts of phosphorus in soils.

Once the archaeologist has distinguished cultural strata from natural strata, a further functional distinction may be made between architectural and nonarchitectural features. Nonarchitectural features include middens, burials, tamped-earth floors, hearths, and quarries. Architectural features include walls, prepared or plastered floors, platforms, staircases, and roadways. Of course, nonarchitectural features such as hearths and burials are often associated with architectural units. The analysis of features will be discussed further in Chapter 12.

Stratigraphic evaluation, then, incorporates both temporal and functional aspects. Combining the law of superposition with assessments of context, the archaeologist interprets the depositional history of the physical matrix. Functional interpretation begins with a distinction between those parts of the sequence that are natural strata and those that are cultural features. On the basis of these evaluations, the archaeologist establishes first a stratigraphic sequence for each excavation and then, by comparing stratigraphy between excavations, an overall (composite) stratigraphic sequence for the entire site. This stratigraphic sequence forms the underlying framework for all further interpretation.

Stratigraphy thus emphasizes sequence and accumulation over time; it is primarily related to the vertical dimension of archaeological deposits. Distribution in the two lateral dimensions—that is, the spread of features and artifacts through a given horizontal layer—associates these data with one another in a single point or span of time. Because horizontally associated materials within a stratum are ideally the remains of behavior from a single unit of time, these lateral distributions fill in the functional picture and provide data to reconstruct the range of activities carried on simultaneously. Taken together, stratigraphy and association—the vertical and the horizontal—constitute the three-dimensional physical structure that excavation attempts to reveal. We now turn to the means used to reveal these three dimensions.

APPROACHES TO EXCAVATION

Surface survey information, such as maps of distributions of features or collections of surface artifacts, is indispensable in choosing the location of excavations. These data may define the approximate limits of sites and even suggest the probable location, nature, and function of subsurface activity areas. For instance, distribution patterns of surface artifacts often suggest hypotheses concerning the nature and function of buried activity areas that can be tested only by excavation. A concentration of surface pottery debris may indicate the location of a midden, or surface scatters of grinding stones might signal the presence of buried house remains. The formulation of such working hypotheses is useful in guiding subsequent excavations, for excavation provides the means to *test* the hypotheses—in these examples, to document the presence or absence of a midden or of house remains. The time and thought involved in an organized and detailed surface survey is a worthwhile investment: The more that is known about surface remains, the better the archaeologist can estimate the variability that excavation may encounter. This estimate may be inexact, of course, for surface configurations do not always reflect subsurface ones. But the potential guiding capacity of surface data should be exploited— and, indeed, if the surface–subsurface configurations do not match, disconformities (such as the 19th-century buttons and bullets at pre-Columbian Chalchuapa; see Chapter 6) should be explained.

As we have seen (Chapter 6), not all material traces of human activity are concentrated in sites. To deal with human modifications of the natural environment, another specialized branch of archaeology has emerged, often termed **landscape archaeology.** One example would be the study of Hohokam agricultural features in Arizona, discussed in Chapter 6. Another example is provided by the investigation of 18th-century gardens in Annapolis, Maryland, directed by Mark Leone. This work illustrates two premises of landscape archaeology: Spaces between buildings and other features are as important as the features themselves, and the definition of such spaces reflects social and ideological meanings important to their creators. With the investigation of three Annapolis gardens, using both historical documents and archaeological excavation, Leone and other landscape archaeologists point out how gardens were planned as physical and social barriers to access to the adjacent imposing houses of the wealthy gentry. Beyond this role, such 18th-century gardens were carefully planned to create optical illusions of larger spaces that enhanced the owner's claims of power and status.

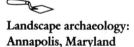

Landscape archaeology: Annapolis, Maryland

Total Coverage

Once the surface variability of a site or an area has been analyzed, the archaeologist must decide how much of the site to examine further by excavation. Total excavation, either of all sites in a region or of the whole of a single site, is extremely rare. Most archaeological projects have neither the time nor the funds for such an undertaking. More important, archaeologists should leave a portion of a site undisturbed for potential future investigations. In salvage situations, however, where the remains will be destroyed by nonarchaeological means anyway, total coverage may be chosen. At Hatchery West, for example, after removing the disturbed plow layer from the entire area of the site, Binford and his associates excavated every feature they encountered—a total of 8 structures, 109 pits, and 7 human burials.

Total coverage: Hatchery West, Illinois

Sample Coverage

In most situations, total coverage is not appropriate. The sites, features, or areas to be excavated may be selected by either probabilistic or nonprobabilistic sampling procedures; often the two means are combined. When the sampling units—whether grid squares, structures, sites, or other forms—appear similar in surface characteristics, **probabilistic sampling** maximizes the extent to which data from the sample can be generalized to the overall population. But generalization is not always the archaeologist's goal: If a number of apparently unique units call for investigation, or if a particular kind of information is required and the archaeologist can predict, from past experience, where to find it, then a **nonprobabilistic sampling** scheme is preferable.

To illustrate the use of a nonprobabilistic sample in excavation, let us consider work in the Salamá Valley of highland Guatemala in 1972. Preliminary reconnaissance indicated that a site called El Portón was the largest and apparently the focal site of the valley. The principal structure at the site, and the largest in the valley, was an earthen "pyramid" some 15 m high. Within the overall research goals of this archaeological project, a prime concern was establishment of the date and the probable function of this unique and presumably important structure. But the project had neither the time nor the funds necessary to undertake extensive excavations, and the excavators did not want to devote all efforts to this single structure. From past experience, however, they knew that the ancient builders often placed dedicatory offerings or **caches** along the center or axial line of the structure, in front of or beneath the staircase leading to the summit. Caches such as these often contained pottery vessels that could be dated to a time span as short as 100 to 200 years. Furthermore, since caches were usually associated with ceremonial structures ("temples") and not with other kinds of buildings, the mere presence of such a deposit would be an indication of ancient function.

Nonprobabilistic sampling: Test excavations in the Salamá Valley, Guatemala

FIGURE 7.6 Dedicatory deposit at El Portón, Guatemala, found beneath the base of a buried staircase (remains of which are visible above). (Verapaz Project, The University Museum, University of Pennsylvania.)

Location of the front of the structure—the side containing the staircase—was made difficult by the badly eroded state of the pyramid's surface. But the east face was considered the best candidate, both because it faced the center of the site and because it showed a slight bulge that might have been the remnants of the staircase. The midline of the east face was calculated and located on the ground. A small test excavation was then made along this line, some 10 m in front of the pyramid, at the point where the slope angle of the mound surface led the archaeologists to expect that the buried base of the staircase should be. After several days of excavation, they discovered the bottom step and balustrade of a plastered adobe staircase about 2 m below the present ground surface. Carefully digging under the bottom stair and the ancient plaza surface in front of the staircase, the archaeologists found the predicted cache (Fig. 7.6), containing some 60 pottery vessels, 2 elaborate jaguar-effigy incense burners, obsidian knife blades, and remnants of burned materials. The pottery vessels were characteristic of the end of the Preclassic era of Maya prehistory, corresponding to about 200 B.C.–A.D. 1 in our calendar. This information enabled the archaeologists to make a reasonable chronological and functional evaluation of this large structure by means of a small and simple excavation, costing only two weeks' time and a few hundred dollars in project funds.

On the other hand, when the archaeologist encounters an area with relatively uniform surface characteristics, probabilistic sampling is most useful in selecting excavation locations. As an example, we will describe some of the excavations at the Joint Site in Arizona (Chapter 6 discussed surface survey at this site). For the selection of the excavation sample, sampling units were defined by a grid of 2 m squares (a total of 1506 squares), excluding areas of visible architecture. Because one of the proj-

Table 7.1 Stratified Random Sample of Test Pits (Joint Site, Arizona)

Sampling Stratum	Stratum Size (Number of 2 m Squares)	Sample Size (Excavated)
1	216	4
2	113	2
3	56	1
4	36	1
5	369	7
6	378	8
7	278	6
8	30	1
9	30	1
Total sample size		31

SOURCE: After Schiffer 1976, Table 7.2.

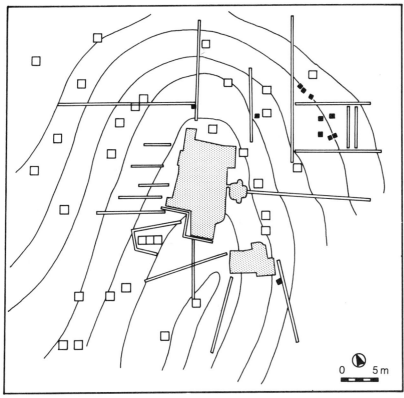

FIGURE 7.7 Map of nonarchitectural excavations at the Joint Site, Arizona, showing original test pits selected by probabilistic sampling of the strata defined in Figure 6.32 (p. 230), along with later nonprobabilistically located excavations. (After Schiffer 1976.)

Key:

 Areas with architecture

☐ Test pits, location probabilistically selected

⬭ Test trenches

◼ Supplementary test pits

ect's goals was to test the relation of surface remains to those recovered by excavation, the population of grid squares was divided into nine sampling strata, each with a different density of surface artifacts (see Fig. 6.32, p. 230). Then a 2 percent stratified random sample was drawn: Using a table of random numbers, 2 percent of the units in each stratum were chosen for excavation (Table 7.1 and Fig. 7.7). (For strata containing fewer than 50 sample units, the "2 percent samples" were rounded off to a single whole unit.) In this case, as in the survey at Çayönü, Turkey (discussed in Chapter 6), supplementary excavations not located probabilistically were added to fill in spatial gaps; data from these additional units could not be used in statistical analyses based on random samples, but they provided checks on how well the sample units represented the area. This sampling strategy maximized the efficiency and statistical reliability of an investigation over a large area with a limited amount of actual excavation.

Probabilistic sampling: Test excavations at the Joint Site, Arizona

EXCAVATION METHODOLOGY

An archaeological excavation is usually a complicated, painstaking process. The aim of an excavation program is the acquisition of as much three-dimensional information relevant to its research objectives as possible, given the available resources. The success of any particular program depends on a variety of factors, the most important of which is the overall organization or strategy of the excavations. This strategy guides the archaeologist in choosing the locations, extent, timing, and kinds of excavation to meet the research goals with maximum efficiency.

Many of the factors involved in organizational and strategic decisions are unique to each research situation, such as the kinds of problems being investigated, the nature of the site or sites, and the availability of resources, but the range of choices is limited. At this point, decisions concerning the conduct of reconnaissance and survey will already have been made. The archaeologist chooses an excavation sampling scheme to fit the objectives and scale of the excavation program. To make the best decisions for a given project, the researcher should be thoroughly familiar with all the alternatives and the ends they are best suited to accomplish.

We shall now consider four aspects of excavation methods: first, the kinds of archaeological excavations and the relationship of each kind to a general **data acquisition** strategy; second, the various techniques used to carry out excavations; third, the ways to control provenience of excavated data; and finally, the recording of excavated data.

Kinds of Excavations

The two basic kinds of excavations mirror the vertical and horizontal aspects of archaeological site formation. **Penetrating excavations** are primarily deep probes of subsurface deposits: Their main thrust is vertical; their principal objective is to reveal, in cross-section, the depth, sequence, and composition of archaeological remains. They cut through sequential or adjacent deposits. **Clearing excavations,** in contrast, aim primarily at horizontal investigation of deposits: Their main thrust is outward or across, and their principal objective is to reveal, in plain view, both the horizontal extent and the arrangement of an archaeological deposit. Clearing excavations emphasize tracing continuities of single surfaces or deposits. Although they are often used in combination, each kind of excavation has specific advantages and disadvantages.

Penetrating Excavations The most basic kind of penetrating excavation is the **test pit.** Test pits are extensive only in the vertical dimension; that is, they can probe the full depth of a deposit but not its horizontal extent. Their horizontal area is only big enough to accommodate one or two excavators (about 1–2 m square). Even more restricted test pits may be excavated using shovels, posthole diggers, or augers. Because they are so small and reach such limited depths, however, these probes are often restricted to survey testing (see Chapter 6).

The objectives of test pits are to sample subsurface artifacts and ecofacts and to gain a limited cross-sectional view of the site's depositional history. For this reason, test pits are often the first excavations placed within a site. Some archaeologists prefer to place their initial test excavation outside the main areas of known or suspected archaeological interest. This kind of test pit, often called a **sounding pit (sondage),** is used to preview what lies beneath the ground or to probe the full vertical extent of cultural deposits. In the latter case, excavations are usually made down to the natural soils beneath the lowest cultural layers, so that the cross-section shown on the walls of the pit represents a complete stratigraphic record. Sounding pits are usually considered entirely exploratory and are not intended to acquire large samples of artifacts or other kinds of data.

Test pits may also be excavated within specific surface features such as mounds, to evaluate composition and, if possible, temporal position and function. The excavation at El Portón discussed earlier in this chapter is an example of this kind of test pit. The archaeologist may then evaluate the results of test-pit excavations to determine whether more extensive excavations are justified. In other words, test pits are often a prelude to more elaborate vertical and horizontal excavations.

The archaeologist may use sets of test pits to gain information about the large-scale distribution of data in, and the overall composition of, an archaeological site. Such extensive coverage may be achieved by defining a grid over the site, each square of which then defines a test pit. This kind of test-pit program is well suited to a probabilistic sampling design (Fig. 7.8); Schiffer's test pits at the Joint Site have already been described as an example. In other cases, preselected intervals, such as alternate squares of a grid, may be used to acquire extensive site coverage.

The chief limitation of test pits is their lack of a horizontal dimension. Their deliberate emphasis on depth yields much evidence on sequence or accumulation over time but very little information on the materials associated with any one time. A compromise solution to this problem is the **trench,** a narrow linear excavation used to expose both the full vertical extent of a deposit and its horizontal extent in one direction. Trenches, then, are essentially excavations in two dimensions (the vertical dimension and one horizontal dimension). They resemble extended test pits, often 1 to 2 m wide but as long as necessary to cut through the feature or area being probed. Thus trenches explore both vertical accumulation and horizontal association. A trench often begins as a single test pit within a conspicuous feature; it becomes a trench by extension of one axis of the pit to provide a fuller cross-section of the feature. Alternatively, a line of individual test pits may provide a nearly continuous cross-section. Like test pits, trenches cut through deposits and often serve as a prelude to more extensive lateral excavations.

Trenching excavations can be used in many ways. One of their most

FIGURE 7.8 A systematic line of test pits at Quiriguá, Guatemala, located at regular 15 m intervals and aligned with the site grid, used to define the limits of a Late Classic period (A.D. 600–800) paved plaza. (Quiriguá Project, The University Museum, University of Pennsylvania.)

familiar uses is in probing individual surface features such as mounds (Fig. 7.9). Burial mounds, ruined earthen platforms, and the like are usually examined either by a single trench or by two perpendicular cross-cutting trenches. Similarly, when a whole site consists of a single mound—as in the *tells* and *tepes* of southwest Asia or the town and village sites of Thailand—trenches may reveal the overall stratigraphy of the site. Trenches for these purposes may be aligned with the axes of the mound being excavated or with cardinal directions. The archaeologist may follow trench penetration with lateral clearing excavations designed to expose discovered features—floors, burials, hearths, and so on—in horizontal association. Of course, deeply buried features are often difficult to expose fully. When the deposits being cut are very deep, the excavation may take the form of a step trench (Fig. 7.10) so that greater depths may be reached with less risk of the trench wall collapsing for lack of support.

Occasionally, the location of the trench operations may be guided by probabilistic sampling methods. In most cases, however, the means are nonprobabilistic: The archaeologist uses trenches to cut into areas of some particular interest for some specified reason. For example, a trench may be

FIGURE 7.9 View of an earthen structure at Las Tunas, Guatemala, revealed by a trench; a second, smaller trench has now penetrated this structure and its supporting platform. (Verapaz Project, The University Museum, University of Pennsylvania.)

FIGURE 7.10 A step trench used to probe a large (23 m high) mound at Chalchuapa, El Salvador. (Chalchuapa Project, The University Museum, University of Pennsylvania.)

cut on the axis of a structure to reveal the stratigraphic relationships between successive renovations of the building and floors or pavements that might lie adjacent to it. Or a trench into the end of a single mound could be used to determine whether the site boundary at surface level was the same as that below the surface.

One final kind of excavation may be mentioned in this section—the **tunnel.** Archaeological tunnels resemble test pits that have been rotated to a horizontal plane (Fig. 7.11). Like test pits, tunnels are essentially one-dimensional excavations, but that dimension is a horizontal one. Unless supplemented by test pits or trenches, tunnels do not reveal the vertical dimension of a feature or deposit. They may still yield information on temporal sequence if, for example, a series of tunnels is cut into successively renovated constructions, as at Copán, Honduras (Chapter 5).

Tunnels are best suited for testing within features or site areas that are too deeply buried to be reached by other means of excavation. Then they are a useful and efficient means of exploring, because they reach deeply buried areas without destroying overlying features, and generally expend less time and money. These advantages have been amply demonstrated at Copán, where tunnels from the exposed river cut of the Acropolis have proven to be an efficient and minimally destructive means for gaining extensive information about the scale and patterning of deeply buried architecture (see Fig. 5.11, p. 174). It should be remembered, however, that tunnels are potentially dangerous enterprises that should be undertaken only after the matrix has been evaluated for stability, and they must be equipped with lights, adequate ventilation, and emergency exits.

FIGURE 7.11 A tunnel used to probe the center of a large earthen mound at Chalchuapa, El Salvador. (Chalchuapa Project, The University Museum, University of Pennsylvania.)

FIGURE 7.12 A labeled photograph of House 14 at Divostin, Yugoslavia. This was the largest dwelling (18 m long) found and cleared at that Neolithic site. Three hearths (a, b, c) and nearly 100 pottery vessels were found on the fired mud-and-chaff floor. (Courtesy of Alan McPherron.)

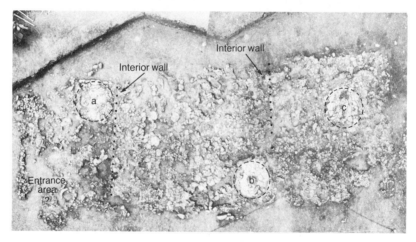

Clearing Excavations The primary objective of clearing excavations is to expose the horizontal dimensions of subsurface archaeological data. Clearing excavations are not usually initiated until penetrating operations (usually test pits or trenches or both) have revealed the basic stratigraphic relationships of the site and its components. With this information in hand, the archaeologist can expose as much as possible of the three-dimensional patterns and relationships of features, artifacts, and other data within the site (Fig. 7.12).

Area excavations are used to expose the horizontal extent of data, with the vertical stratigraphic record preserved in *balks,* unexcavated divisions between excavations. Area excavations usually consist of squares, often 5 or 10 m on a side, which resemble large test pits, but because of their broad exposure, their information yield is much different. Vertical penetration takes place more slowly because a much larger horizontal area is

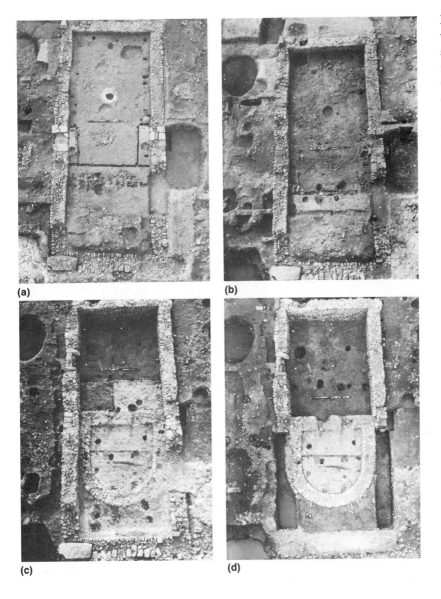

(a)   (b)   (c)   (d)

FIGURE 7.13 Nearly vertical views of successive stages, (a) through (d), in the excavation of the Church of St. Mary, Winchester, England. Foundations visible in (a) date from ca. A.D. 1150; those exposed in (d) represent an earlier building dated at ca. A.D. 1000. (Courtesy of Martin Biddle, © Winchester Excavations Committee.)

being investigated at one time. The archaeologist usually places a small control pit within the excavation to preview the stratigraphy beneath. Clearing to a given stratigraphic level is then done across the square by peeling away the *overburden* (overlying matrix) to reveal the full horizontal distribution of remains within the square at that stratigraphic level, including remains of architecture as well as other features and artifacts. Once recorded, all the features and artifacts at this level are removed, and the next lower level is exposed. When completed, the archaeologist will have revealed a series of successive remains (Fig. 7.13). Of course, the larger the

FIGURE 7.14 The ground-plan of the seventeenth-century fort at Martin's Hundred, Virginia, was revealed clearly by stripping excavations. (By permission of the Colonial Williamsburg Foundation and Ivor Noël Hume.)

site, the more multiple squares will be needed to produce such a sequential record. The balks, or matrix left standing between adjacent squares, provide a record of the stratigraphic position of each layer after it has been removed. Area excavation techniques have been the primary excavation approach at such varied sites as Hasanlu in Iran (Fig. 17.4, p. 551), Ban Chiang in Thailand (Fig. 7.3), and the Abri Pataud rock shelter in France (Fig. 7.21).

Stripping excavations (or open area excavations) are used to clear large expanses of overburden to reveal uninterrupted spatial distributions of data, such as the foundations of large buildings, remnants of entire settlements, and other extensive remains (Fig. 7.14). Stripping excavations do not leave balks to preserve stratigraphic relationships, but this information should always be recorded as excavation proceeds. Mechanical equipment is sometimes used to strip vast amounts of earth or stone overburden from a buried site. But this can be done only after the depth of the overburden is first established by penetrating excavations. The same basic strategy—first penetrating vertically to discover the nature and depth of the subsurface strata, then clearing laterally to expose their horizontal extent—can also be applied to archaeological situations that do not involve formal occupation surfaces. For instance, middens are usually probed by test pits or trenches to determine the nature and depth of the deposit; then a lateral excavation may be initiated at the face of the vertical cut to follow the surface of the uppermost stratified layer and to discover its limits. By this method, each layer in turn can be "peeled back" to expose the extent of the next. In such transposed primary contexts, especially if the deposit is extensive, the main objective of clearing excavation is often to acquire a larger sample of artifactual and ecofactual data from each layer rather than to define its exact horizontal extent. The vertical excavations may be used to isolate a block or column of the midden. The column is then peeled back one layer at a time, and the artifacts and ecofacts are collected from each level.

Variants and Combinations Clearly, most excavation projects will involve both penetration and clearing operations. Each type has its advantages (Fig. 7.15); as always, choices among the alternative techniques depend on the nature of the deposits and the goals and resources of the project.

In the Tehuacán Valley, Mexico, during a project described in Chapter 6, excavation of each site began with a trench through the apparently deepest part of the deposit. Along with evaluation of the stratigraphy of each trench, Richard MacNeish and his colleagues assessed the time span represented by the deposit and the range of materials being recovered from it. They were especially interested in the recovery of organic remains, over a long time span, that would bear on the question of the development of domesticated plants. On the basis of these excavations, the archaeologists selected 11 of the 39 tested sites, most of which were caves, for more extensive excavation. These excavations proceeded by peeling horizontal strata, moving away from the trench wall, in alternate small "squares" (or descending columns) 1 m wide. Eventually the intervening 1 m balk columns were removed, and horizontal clearing continued via these small discrete vertical segments away from the trench face. In this way, each stratum was traced, little by little, yielding information on horizontal arrangements (and thus on possible use-related association) as well as larger numbers of remains.

Excavation methods at Tehuacán, Mexico

A different combination, stressing clearing, was used in the Abri Pataud site of the Dordogne region of France (see Fig. 7.21). The rock shelter was occupied between about 34,000 and 20,000 years ago, and the 14 strata of habitation surfaces and debris accumulated during this time formed a deposit some 9.25 m deep. The excavations, directed by Hallam L. Movius, Jr., were organized by a 2 m grid system. Instead of a central trench as at Tehuacán, a set of 1 m test trenches bordering a central area 4 m wide served as control pits for previewing stratigraphy. With these test trenches as stratigraphic guides, individual layers were cleared across the larger gridded area, exposing broad living areas including hearths and associated evidence of human occupation.

Excavation methods at the Abri Pataud, France

A striking contrast to the Abri Pataud in site and research goals is provided at Tikal, Guatemala. The North Acropolis of this Maya site covers an area of about 1 hectare or 2½ acres. Its uppermost plaza level, 10 m above limestone bedrock, represents the accumulation of more than a millennium of construction, beginning about 600 B.C. The primary goal of investigations here, directed by William R. Coe, was to understand the

Excavation methods at Tikal, Guatemala

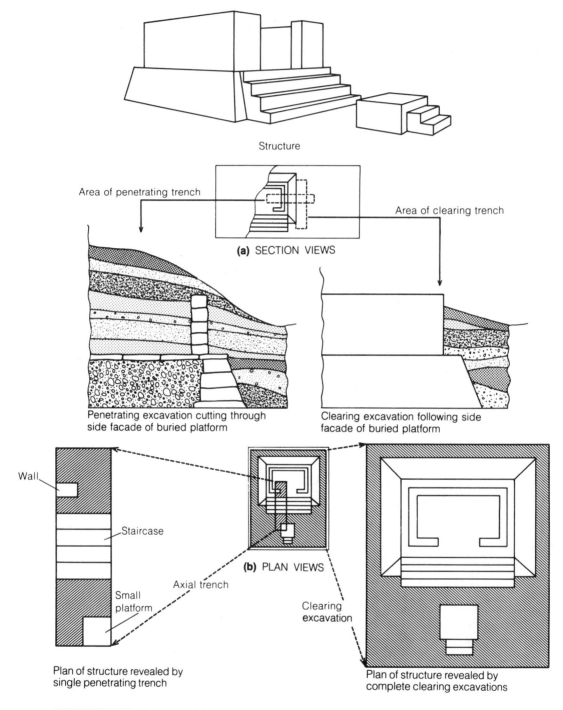

Structure

Area of penetrating trench

Area of clearing trench

(a) SECTION VIEWS

Penetrating excavation cutting through
side facade of buried platform

Clearing excavation following side
facade of buried platform

Wall

Staircase

(b) PLAN VIEWS

Axial trench

Small
platform

Clearing
excavation

Plan of structure revealed by
single penetrating trench

Plan of structure revealed by
complete clearing excavations

FIGURE 7.15   Contrast of the kinds of information provided by penetrating
and clearing excavations of the same hypothetical feature.

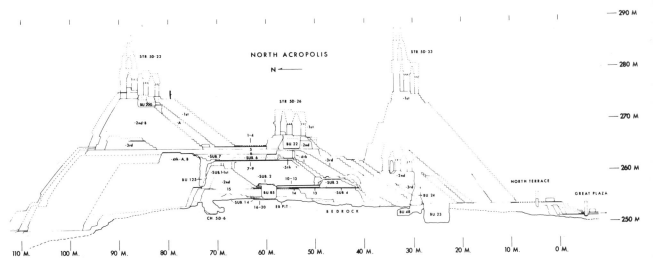

FIGURE 7.16 Simplified cross-section of some 1000 years of superimposed construction at the North Acropolis of Tikal, Guatemala. (Courtesy of the Tikal Project, The University Museum, University of Pennsylvania.)

constructional development of the architectural complex; as a result, penetrating excavations were emphasized. A huge trench was cut through the overall feature; myriad small, secondary clearing excavations and radiating tunnels linked component features—buildings, tombs, and so on—located outside the main trench to the master construction sequence (Fig. 7.16).

Clearly, many strategies are possible for excavating an archaeological site. More than one archaeologist has compared the excavation task to solving a three-dimensional jigsaw puzzle. Of course, excavation does not attempt to put the pieces together; rather, it takes them apart. The archaeologist "reassembles" them later, on paper and by notes and drawings. To reassemble the pieces, the investigator must not only use care in taking them apart (excavating) but also observe and record precisely how they originally fit together. In the following sections we will consider the techniques for conducting and recording excavations—techniques that, when properly executed, enable the archaeologist to reconstruct and interpret the original three-dimensional site.

Excavation Tools and Techniques

The kind of equipment used to move earth varies with particular excavation situations. The actual tools and techniques used reflect the relative requirements for precision and attention to detail as opposed to speed and capacity for earth removal. The alternatives range from the largest mechanical earthmovers, such as front-end loaders and backhoes, to the finest hand-held brushes and dental picks.

If great quantities of sterile overburden or badly disturbed debris cover a site or a feature, removal of this material with heavy-duty equipment

FIGURE 7.17 Casts of victims of the Vesuvius eruption of A.D. 79, recovered at Pompeii when careful excavation revealed voids in the ash, which the investigators then filled with plaster. (Courtesy of The University Museum, University of Pennsylvania.)

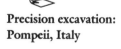

Precision excavation: Pompeii, Italy

may be helpful. At some sites, such as deeply buried Sybaris, mechanical earthmovers are the only feasible way to reach the necessary depths (see Fig. 6.24, p. 219). In other cases, one or more test pits may be placed to gauge the depth of the overburden, to guide its removal by mechanical means.

In many excavation situations, pick-and-shovel crews provide the appropriate combination of precision and speed, especially for removal of overburden and penetration of material in secondary context, such as construction fill. When intact features are encountered or artifacts are found in apparent primary context, archaeologists resort to finer tools to remove surrounding matrix.

The sharpened mason's pointing trowel is one of the most valuable tools for fine work, because its shape is well suited for such tasks as clearing and following plastered floors or masonry walls. With careful trowel scraping, tamped-earth floors can be distinguished from overlying soils by changes in texture and hardness. The edges of "negative" features such as post molds, pits, and drainage ditches can also be detected and traced by troweling, through changes in color and texture. At the famous site of Pompeii, excavation revealed voids in the volcanic matrix that when filled with plaster, produced the original forms of now decomposed human and animal victims of the eruption of Mount Vesuvius (Fig. 7.17).

When very small or fragile materials are encountered, the finest excavation instruments are used to free them from their matrix. Small brushes of assorted sizes, dental picks, and air blowers are very useful in clearing remains such as plaster or stucco sculpture, bones, burials, and other organic items (Fig. 7.18). When such finds are poorly preserved (for

FIGURE 7.18 Excavation of a burial mound at Los Mangales, Baja Verapaz, Guatemala, showing initial exposure of (left) the principal stone-lined tomb chamber and (right) an earlier burial (the outline of the burial pit can be seen above the label). (Verapaz Project, The University Museum, University of Pennsylvania.)

example, crumbling bones), they must be treated in the field for strengthening and protection before removal to a laboratory for further conservation.

The full inventory of archaeological equipment is quite extensive. It includes not only excavation tools but also survey and drafting instruments (some of which were discussed in Chapter 6), cameras, and notebooks. Table 7.2 lists the items in a standard archaeological "dig kit" used by members of many research projects.

Using appropriate excavation tools, the archaeologist proceeds to isolate archaeological materials and clear away their encasing matrix. The manner in which matrix is removed is extremely important. One approach is to remove the matrix in **arbitrary levels;** the other is to work in units corresponding to visible strata or **natural levels.** Most archaeologists strongly favor the stratigraphic method, excavating each visible layer as a discrete unit before proceeding to the next. We have already mentioned the basic method for this procedure: use of a preliminary sounding pit to give the archaeologist a general indication of the sequence of strata to be encountered in other excavations, of the relative thickness and composition of each stratum, and of any special precautions to take with, or attention to give to, particular strata.

Table 7.2   Inventory of Individual Excavator's "Dig Kit"

1 2¼ × 2¼ format camera and film	1 plumb bob
1 mason's trowel	1 plastic metric ruler
1 pocket compass	Ballpoint pens
1 small palette knife	Assorted drawing pencils
1 Swiss army knife	(with erasers and sharpener)
1 wooden 2 m folding rule	String tags (provenience labels)
(English and metric units)	1 marking pen (waterproof ink)
1 steel 3 m tape	Assorted cloth artifact bags
1 steel 15 m tape	Assorted plastic ecofact bags
Nylon line	Notebook and extra notepaper
2 line levels	Graph paper (8½ × 11 inches)
Assorted dental picks	1 clipboard
Assorted small paintbrushes	1 canvas "dig kit" bag

In some cases, however, the matrix may be devoid of visible strata. Then, rather than excavating the entire deposit as a single unit, the archaeologist may subdivide it into uniform blocks of arbitrary thickness—usually 5, 10, or 20 cm—and remove one level at a time. Such a procedure is preferable to excavation in larger units for two reasons. First, by dislodging smaller volumes at any one time, the archaeologist maximizes control of the provenience of artifacts and ecofacts encountered. Second, even in matrices lacking visible stratification, temporal distinctions in deposition may exist. By removing material in relatively small units, the archaeologist may preserve at least an approximation of the original stratigraphic relationships. For the same reason, many archaeologists recommend subdividing observed strata—especially when these are relatively thick—into several arbitrary levels, both to facilitate excavation and to maintain any depositional distinctions that may later be suggested, in laboratory analysis, for artifacts recovered from the same gross stratum.

Once features, artifacts, or ecofacts are located and isolated within their matrix, their provenience must be determined and recorded. Provenience control allows the archaeologist to determine data associations—the three-dimensional relationships among features, artifacts, and ecofacts. Since these variables are crucial ingredients in the evaluation of context, determination of provenience is a basic task for all forms of archaeological data and in every excavation situation.

Provenience Control: Units and Labels

Archaeologists have developed a variety of methods to ensure accurate control over vertical and horizontal provenience during excavation. Horizontal location is determined with reference to the site map or grid. All

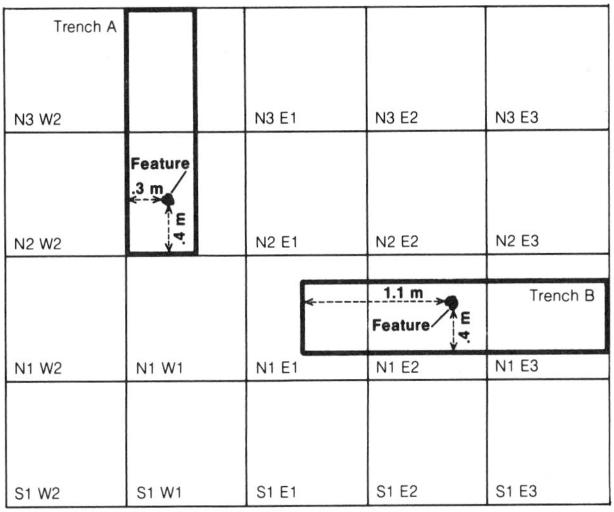

Trench A					
N3 W2			N3 E1	N3 E2	N3 E3
	Feature .3 m E		N2 E1	N2 E2	N2 E3
N2 W2					
N1 W2	N1 W1	N1 E1	N1 E2	N1 E3	Trench B
S1 W2	S1 W1	S1 E1	S1 E2	S1 E3	

Trench B detail: 1.1 m, Feature, E, Trench B

FIGURE 7.19 A site grid may be used to designate the horizontal provenience of excavated features. In Trench A, measurements are made north and east of the N2 W1 stake, to record provenience as "(N2)40cm/(W1)30cm." In Trench B, horizontal provenience is measured from the excavation limits, as "110 cm east of west wall, 40 cm north of south wall." The latter is convertible to a site grid designation as long as the location of the trench walls in relation to the grid is known.

excavation operations must be accurately plotted. Within each operation, then, the location of artifacts and features can be related to the overall site either by direct reference to specific grid coordinates or by location within the limits of the excavation (Fig. 7.19). These determinations may be made by instruments such as the surveyors' transit, by measuring angle and distance from a known reference point such as a grid intersection stake. Or location can be measured directly by means of a steel measuring tape; however, this must be done precisely, maintaining right angles with respect to reference points.

Vertical location is determined with respect to a known elevation; this may be done with surveyors' instruments or by direct measurement. A level or transit may be used to obtain a measurement, or the investigator may measure with a line level, steel tape, and plumb bob (Fig. 7.20).

In an innovative adaptation to a rock-shelter setting, Hallam Movius used an elevated grid as a provenience control system for the Abri Pataud site in France. He set up a frame of pipes to form a grid of 2 m squares over the excavation area. Plumb bobs suspended from the frame defined the grid on the surface of the excavation, thus providing horizontal referents; measurements down from the pipes defined vertical provenience (Fig. 7.21). A similar pipe grid has been used to control horizontal provenience in underwater sites (Fig. 7.22). In open sites—mounds or mound groups—provenience controls are usually set at a horizontal rather than a vertical distance from the excavations. But the principle of establishing a permanent, accessible set of horizontal and vertical reference points is the same.

Provenience control for artifacts and ecofacts is often complicated by

Provenience control: Abri Pataud, France

FIGURE 7.20 Two ways of determining vertical provenience: In (a) an instrument of known elevation is used in conjunction with a stadia rod; in (b), an elevation is measured along a plumb line intersecting a level string of known elevation.

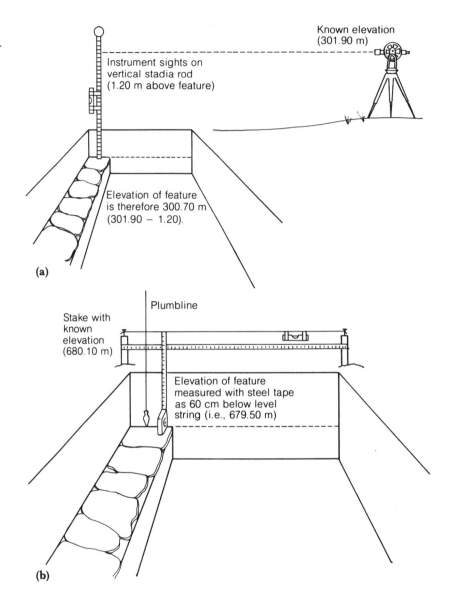

Known elevation (301.90 m)

Instrument sights on vertical stadia rod (1.20 m above feature)

Elevation of feature is therefore 300.70 m (301.90 − 1.20).

(a)

Plumbline

Stake with known elevation (680.10 m)

Elevation of feature measured with steel tape as 60 cm below level string (i.e., 679.50 m)

(b)

their small size and abundance. When artifacts are relatively few in number, or when they are being encountered in primary context, each item discovered must be individually and precisely plotted. The same means for determining provenience positions that have already been discussed can be used for artifacts; means for graphic recording, such as photographs and drawings, will be considered below. After they are recorded, artifacts are removed from their matrix and placed in a bag or other container to be

FIGURE 7.21 During excavation of a Paleolithic rock shelter at Abri Pataud, France, provenience control was maintained by a pipe grid suspended over the site. (By permission of the Peabody Museum, Harvard University, and Hallam L. Movius, Jr.)

FIGURE 7.22 A pipe grid was used to control provenience during the underwater excavation of the Roman shipwreck at Yassi Ada, off the coast of Turkey. (© National Geographic Society.)

taken to the field laboratory for processing. From this point on, they must always carry a label relating them to their provenience.

A number that refers to a finds registry or object catalog provides one kind of label. For example, provenience and other data for object #347

FIGURE 7.23 Screening at Copán, Honduras. This technique provides a means of recovering small artifacts and ecofacts that might otherwise be missed during excavation. (Courtesy of the Peabody Museum of Harvard University and Gordon R. Willey.)

may be found by looking through a numerically ordered log. But in some cases, such as potsherds found in a midden deposit, artifacts may be too numerous to be individually registered. In such circumstances, archaeologists usually use a collective unit called a **provenience lot.**

A lot is a minimum provenience unit within an excavation. Lots may be used to control data in **secondary contexts,** such as surface artifacts from a specific area or concentration. Within an excavation, each level recognized to have internal uniformity may be defined to correspond to a lot. For instance, if the archaeologist is excavating a test pit by arbitrary 20 cm levels, each level may be defined as a lot as long as the matrix within it appears homogeneous. If a change occurs in the observable characteristics of the matrix, such as the appearance of a new texture or color, the excavator closes the previous lot and defines a new one to incorporate material recovered from this distinct stratum. Of course, if an excavation is proceeding by natural levels, each observed stratum would be defined as a distinct lot. Any other kind of discrete deposit encountered, such as a burial pit, would be segregated and defined as a distinct lot. A lot is, therefore, a general kind of unit; the size, form, location, and composition of each actual lot must be defined specifically. Exact horizontal and vertical limits of lots may be determined by either tape or instrument, using the provenience techniques already discussed for operations and features.

Use of a lot label provides a general provenience designation for items too small or plentiful to be plotted individually. This in turn encourages controlled recovery of more of these items through bulk processing of matrix units. The most common means of recovering artifacts and ecofacts under bulk conditions is by **screening.** Matrix may be shoveled directly into a screening box (Fig. 7.23) adjacent to the excavation or transported by wheelbarrow, basket, or bucket to a central screening area. Material to be separated can be passed through one or more screens (of diminishing mesh size) either by gravity (dry screening) or by washing with water (wet screening). In all cases, of course, it is crucial to maintain the separation of material from distinct lots. Once the matrix has passed through the screen, the recovered artifacts and ecofacts are removed from the screen surface and bagged. At this point, the lot label is attached to the bag, which is then securely closed to prevent losses and mixups.

Flotation or water separation is another method of bulk processing that has been of special benefit for recovery of organic materials. When matrix is submerged in water, lighter organic materials such as seeds and bone will sink more slowly than soil, stones, and burned clay; the lighter material can then be skimmed off, dried, and bagged (Fig. 7.24). (Plastic bags, sealed and labeled by lot, are the preferred field containers for most organic remains.) Chemicals such as sodium silicate or zinc chloride may be added to water used for flotation (sometimes in a second stage of flotation) to increase its specific gravity and hence its ability to segregate bone from plant remains. Flotation techniques have proven so valuable for recovery of organic remains that in arid environments such as the southwestern United States, archaeologists have developed adaptations to "float" as much matrix as possible although they have very little water.

FIGURE 7.24 Flotation is used to recover organic remains from matrix, here being collected in a fine-mesh screen. (Arizona State Museum, University of Arizona, Susan Luebbermann, photographer.)

Because each excavation situation is unique, each poses somewhat different problems for data recovery; the archaeologist must be ready to improvise to recover as much information as possible. For instance, archaeologists excavating within construction fill of earth mounds of the Salamá Valley, Guatemala, noted that dry screening of the earth matrix failed to segregate very fine fragments of jade that appeared to be redeposited workshop debris. So that at least a sample of this material could be recovered efficiently for identification, several lots of matrix were sluiced through a second wet screening system, using running water from a nearby irrigation canal. As a result, the archaeologists recovered a full range of jade particles, from small chips and flakes to sand-size grain, that indicated ancient jade-working activities in the vicinity.

All artifacts and ecofacts, once removed from their matrix, are transported in labeled containers to the laboratory. There the provenience label or catalog label is applied directly to each object; this and other aspects of laboratory processing will be discussed in detail in Chapter 8.

Recording Data

Apart from artifacts and other samples physically removed and preserved by research operations, all data retrieved by the archaeologist are in the form of photographs or verbal or graphic descriptions. Furthermore, because any portion of a site that is excavated is thereby destroyed, the only record of the original matrix, proveniences, associations, and contexts of data is the investigator's set of field notes, drawings, and photographs. The manner by which archaeological research is recorded is therefore of prime importance.

There are many specific ways to record data; we will discuss some of the most useful means later in this section. No matter which specific recording methods are used, however, all data records should have certain common characteristics. First, they must be permanent: Acid-free paper should be used to record data to ensure a long life span. Inks should not be water soluble or subject to rapid fading. Whenever possible, copies should be made of all records as protection against loss. Computerized records not only act as a backup for hard copies but also allow much more rapid retrieval, manipulation, cross-referencing, and indexing, as well as linkage to data generated later in laboratory processing and analysis (see Chapter 8). Laptop microcomputers allow archaeologists to generate a variety of data records in the field.

Field Notes   **Field notes** are usually the fundamental record of any archaeological research project. They normally consist of a running chronicle of the progress of research, most commonly divided into daily entries. When completed, a record of this kind provides a thorough history of the investigations. Since no one can anticipate what kind of information will be useful at a later date, it is better to record as much potentially relevant information as possible in the field notes than to regret later that some useful fact or insight was omitted.

The core of field notes is the day-to-day description of the progress of excavation or surface operations. Each excavator should keep an individual notebook to describe his or her research responsibilities. Some archaeologists prefer to create a standard form for field notes; others write in regular notebooks with no set format. Word-processing programs allow field notes to be backed-up on microcomputers, often in the field.

The minimum required information usually includes daily observations of the weather and other working conditions, methods of data acquisition, and short- and long-range objectives. A daily record in the progress of a particular excavation might include the number of people actually at work; descriptions of matrix and stratigraphy; provenience and association information about each artifact or ecofact encountered (or definitions of each provenience lot, if that system is being used); descriptions of features; and preliminary assessments of context. In addition, the researcher should use the field notes to orient or focus thoughts on larger issues raised by the investigations—defining working hypotheses, proposing tests for hypotheses, stating priorities of research, and so on.

Standardized Forms   Whether or not an archaeologist uses **standardized forms** for field notes, such forms are usually included in the overall field recording system. Precisely because they are standardized, these forms assure that comparable information is gathered about all examples of a particular kind of data, regardless of who completes the form. Forms are especially useful, therefore, in large-scale research programs involving

SGS ARCHAEOLOGICAL PROJECT

Human Burial Form

Context: □ Primary*   Site:

            □ Simple burial   Operation/Lot(s):

            □ Prepared chamber   Excavator:

        □ Secondary   Date(s):

            Give circumstances: Cross-references:

                                                          Notebooks:

            _____   Drawings:

            _____   Photos:

            _____

*Dimensions of grave or chamber: DESCRIPTION OF SKELETAL REMAINS:

Length: _____ cm   Completeness or Number
                                                        (left)   (right)
Width: _____ cm
                                                Skull   _____
Orientation: Vertebrae   _____
                                                Sternum   _____
Position of principal skeleton: Sacrum   _____
                                                Innominates _____
    □ Supine   Scapula   _____ _____
                                                Ribs   _____ _____
    □ Prone   Humerus   _____ _____
                                                Radius   _____ _____
    □ On side (□ left/ □ right)   Ulna   _____ _____
                                                Carpus   _____ _____
    □ Flexed   Metacarpals _____ _____
                                                Phalanges   _____ _____
    □ Extended   Femur   _____ _____
                                                Tibia   _____ _____
Orientation: Patella   _____ _____
                                                Tarsus   _____ _____
Main axis of body   Metatarsals _____ _____
                                                Phalanges   _____ _____
With head to: Clavicle   _____ _____

Face to:
                                                Note any obvious pathologies:_____
Estimated age:

    □ Fetus   □ Child   _____

    □ Young adult   _____

    □ Mature adult   _____

Sex: □ Male   Preservatives used, if any: _____

       □ Female

       □ Indeterminate   _____

Cross-reference to other skeletons
   if this is a multiple burial:

Associated artifacts/samples	Field no.	Provenience	Cross-references

THIS FORM MUST BE ACCOMPANIED BY SCALED 1:10 PLAN AND SECTION DRAWINGS.

large numbers of investigators. For example, use of a standardized burial form (Fig. 7.25) leads to acquisition of the same categories of data for all burials.

FIGURE 7.25 An example of a standardized form for recording burial data.

FIGURE 7.26 This excavator is using a line level, on a taut string, and a tape measure to draw a scaled section of the test pit at Quiriguá, Guatemala. (Quiriguá Project, The University Museum, University of Pennsylvania.)

Standardized forms can also provide a link between field recording and computerized storage of recorded data. There are a variety of computer programs that allow the archaeologist to use microcomputers to design forms and enter data. In fact, it is commonplace for field records to be completely computerized, either in the field or after return to the home institution.

It is important, however, that forms retain enough flexibility to assure that the data are not being distorted, or that other information is not being ignored simply because the form makes no specific provision for it. Open-ended sections for miscellaneous comments and observations may help to prevent such difficulties.

Scaled Drawings **Scaled drawings** are always essential data records, but they are much more detailed and elaborate for excavations than for most surface operations. Plan and cross-section views are normally required to record, respectively, the horizontal and vertical aspects of observed strata, features, and artifact/ecofact distributions encountered during excavations. Some archaeologists prefer to keep graph paper in the field notebook for doing scaled drawings; surveyors' notebooks often provide alternating pages of plain and gridded paper to facilitate making both notes and drawings. Computer-assisted surveying instruments allow field measurements to be electronically recorded and processed. Computer-assisted drawing (CAD) programs have become extremely useful tools for generating archaeological drawings, especially records of complex architectural features.

Section drawings document the stratigraphic sequence of matrices, features, and associated artifacts/ecofacts encountered in an excavation (Figs. 7.26 and 7.27). As a normal rule, the walls of all types of excavations should be recorded by such drawings as well as by photography. If, however, all walls of a given excavation show the same stratification, then recording one north–south wall and one east–west wall is usually sufficient. Before recording is done, excavation walls must be plumbed to be vertical and cleaned and scraped smooth with a trowel or similar tool. This ensures the most accurate and detailed scale recording possible, by reducing distortions caused by sloping or uneven surfaces. Under some circumstances, brushing or spraying the walls with water may help to define the strata boundaries and features more clearly. Some archaeologists use a trowel to cut shallowly along the upper and lower limits of each stratum, making them easier to see and record. If this is done, however, photographs should be taken first, to have an "unbiased" record of the excavation.

Scaled **plan drawings** are used to record the horizontal relationships of features and associated artifacts or other materials (Figs. 7.28 and 7.29). The scale of plans may vary according to the size of the area being depicted, although most researchers adopt a set of standard scales for specific categories of plans. For instance, detailed plans of features such as burials

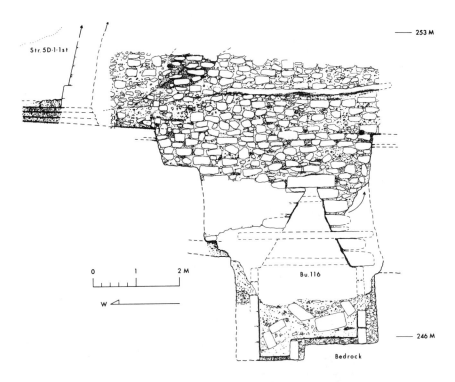

FIGURE 7.27 An example of a detail from a larger section, portraying excavated matrix and construction at Tikal, Guatemala, in a realistic manner (broken lines represent projections in unexcavated or destroyed areas). (Drawing by William R. Coe. Courtesy of the Tikal Project, The University Museum, University of Pennsylvania.)

may be rendered at 1:10, plans of larger features such as buildings may be 1:50, and composite plans depicting groups of structures may be done at 1:100. If an excavation encounters superimposed features—such as sequent living floors, each with associated artifacts and debris—a separate plan will be required to document each floor. The archaeologist should avoid crowding a single plan with superimposed data from different excavation levels.

Gridded site areas may also be recorded by scaled vertical photographs taken from overhead platforms or scaffolding or from balloons (see Fig. 7.28); scaled plan drawings can be traced directly from the photographs. Most plans of underwater sites, such as ancient shipwrecks, are recorded in this manner.

Other kinds of drawings supplement plans and sections when the need arises. **Profile drawings** are like silhouettes: They portray the outline of a feature without showing its internal composition (Fig. 7.30). Profile data are therefore included within section drawings, but not the other way around. Profiles are useful to show the exposed form of an unpenetrated feature or an unpenetrated part of a feature. **Elevation drawings** are straight-on views of exposed feature surfaces, such as the façade of a building (Fig. 7.31). A **perspective drawing** is often a reconstructed interpretation of field data, showing what the feature is believed to have looked

FIGURE 7.28 Preparing a balloon and radio-controlled camera for early morning flight to record excavations at Sarepta, Lebanon. (Courtesy of the Museum Applied Science Center for Archaeology, The University Museum, University of Pennsylvania.)

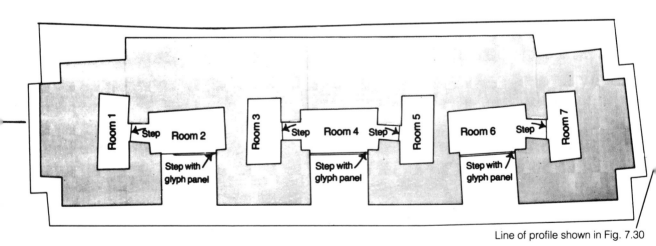

Line of profile shown in Fig. 7.30

FIGURE 7.29 Plan drawing of Structure 1B–1 and its platform at Quiriguá, Guatemala (walls are symbolized by the shaded area). (Based on a drawing by Kevin D. Gray.)

Outside wall | Room 1 | Room 2 | Wall | Room 3 | Room 4 | Room 5 | Wall | Room 6 | Room 7 | Outside wall

FIGURE 7.30 Longitudinal profile of Quiriguá Structure 1B–1 along the line indicated in Figure 7.29.

like when in use, rendered in a three-dimensional view (Fig. 7.32). **Isometric drawings** also portray features in three dimensions, but maintain constant scale in all three; because the depth dimension doesn't appear to diminish, these depictions look less realistic to the eye, but they are valuable as technical illustrations. Some of these drawings can now be computer-generated, saving considerable time and effort.

Photographs **Photography** is an indispensable aid in recording all facets of archaeological data acquisition. Archaeological sites and site areas should be thoroughly photographed before, during, and after the research process. Preexcavation photos are important, to document the appearance of sites and features before excavation disturbs them. Once excavation is under way, a continuous series of photographs should be taken of each excavation unit as a chronicle parallel to that in the field notes (see Fig. 7.13). Important features—burials, building foundations, and the like—should also be photographed from a variety of perspectives.

Each photograph must contain an easy-to-read scale (usually a boldly painted metric ruler); it may also include information concerning the orientation and identification of the excavation or feature being recorded. The latter information may be written on a slate or letterboard and placed so that it will appear in one corner of the photograph. Alternatively, to avoid cluttering the photograph, this information may be entered in a separate photographic record notebook.

Most archaeological photography is done in black and white. Given the quantity of film necessary to record most research programs, color film

FIGURE 7.31 Front elevation drawing of Quiriguá Structure 1B–1. Solid lines indicate platform and walls standing in 1977; broken lines show restoration based on work in 1912, when the building was more complete.

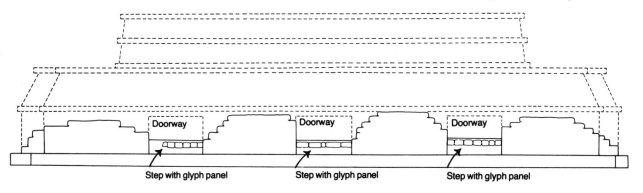

Doorway   Doorway   Doorway

Step with glyph panel   Step with glyph panel   Step with glyph panel

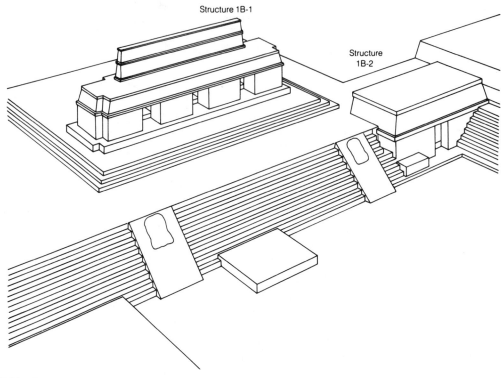

Structure 1B-1

Structure 1B-2

FIGURE 7.32 Perspective reconstruction of Structure 1B–1 and adjacent construction in the Quiriguá Acropolis. (After Morley 1937–1938.)

would be prohibitively expensive. Color film may be used in special instances, such as recording stratified deposits in which soil color changes or differences are significant. Ultraviolet or infrared film may similarly be useful for particular "detection" needs.

With the advent of relatively inexpensive hand-held video recorders, archaeologists are expanding use of this medium as well. Video has the advantages of motion, continuity, and immediacy. The photographer can record multiple perspectives of a scene in a fluid sequence, covering a larger and more continuous area than a single photograph. Single frames can later be isolated from the tape, as needed, and even incorporated in computer data banks. And because a video can be played back immediately, material removed by excavation can be reexamined, as if still "in place," before leaving the field.

SUMMARY

The objectives of excavation are to investigate the three-dimensional structure of buried archaeological remains and to understand the temporal and functional significance of this structure. In combination, the three dimensions of an archaeological deposit represent the processes of site formation: Occupation at any one time was distributed horizontally in space (having length and width); through time, new occupation surfaces and accumulations of occupation debris buried older remains, giving the site a vertical (depth) dimension. The archaeologist therefore investigates stratigraphy—the interpreted sequence of deposition—and examines the remains within individual stratigraphic layers for evidence of activities carried on during single periods in the sequence.

A program of excavation begins with an assessment of the surface variability within the site or area under investigation, as determined by surface survey. The archaeologist then must decide how much of the total to examine further by excavation. Part of this decision is a choice first between total and sample coverage and then, if sample coverage is selected, between probabilistic and nonprobabilistic sampling schemes.

There are basically two kinds of excavations: Penetrating excavations cut through deposits to reveal the depth, sequence, and composition of archaeological sites; clearing excavations are aimed at revealing the horizontal extent and arrangement of remains within a single stratigraphic layer. Most excavation projects use some combination of the two approaches to investigate fully the complementary vertical and horizontal dimensions of site structure.

Excavation begins with the selection of appropriate tools. A full inventory of excavation equipment ranges from front-end loaders and backhoes to shovels, trowels, and even dental picks and air blowers. Specific choices are based on the relative requirements of a particular excavation for precision and attention to detail, on the one hand, and speed and quantity of earth removal, on the other.

In actually removing archaeological matrix, the archaeologist must decide whether to extract units that correspond to observed stratigraphic layers or blocks, or to define the excavation units arbitrarily. It is preferable to follow observed stratigraphy whenever possible, removing archaeological matrix and materials by the same units in which they were deposited, although in reverse order. Exceptions are cases in which different stratigraphic layers cannot be distinguished, or in which observed strata are very thick and subdivision provides for more controlled removal.

Provenience control is crucial: To reconstruct later how the site was formed, the archaeologist must be able to reestablish the precise locations where all the discovered materials were found. All data from excavations or surface collections are given distinctive labels and plotted with reference to horizontal location and vertical elevation. Features and stratigraphic deposits can then be located either by direct reference to the map and elevation system or indirectly by reference to the operation in which they were discovered. Portable remains—artifacts and ecofacts—may be individually plotted, but because of their usual great quantity they are often more conveniently and efficiently handled in bulk provenience units called *lots.* All artifacts and ecofacts are then labeled with their lot provenience before they leave the excavation area; particular artifacts and ecofacts may be further identified or more precisely plotted when their unusual nature or their location within a significant context so requires.

Because excavation destroys a site, detailed records are essential to all later reconstruction and analysis. The four kinds of recorded data from field operations are field notes, standardized forms, scaled drawings, and photographs. Each type contributes indispensably to the record of an archaeological excavation; for maximum utility, the four should be cross-referenced so that all records pertaining to a given excavation or a given feature can be readily located. Computerization of these records is being adopted by a growing number of archaeologists.

With this set of cross-referenced records, data recording in the field is complete. At this point, the work emphasis shifts to the field laboratory. Data processing in the field laboratory is the subject of Chapter 8.

GUIDE TO FURTHER READING

Stratification and Stratigraphy
  Adams 1975; Casteel 1970; Courty, Goldberg, and Macphail 1989; Davies 1987; Drucker 1972; Harris 1975, 1989; Hawley 1937; Lloyd 1963; Movius 1977; Stein 1983, 1987; Villa and Courtin 1983; Wilmsen 1974

Approaches to Excavation
  L. R. Binford 1964, 1981a; Flannery 1976c; Hanson and Schiffer 1975; Harris 1989; Hill 1967; Kenyon 1961; Moeller 1982; Mueller 1975; Redman 1974; Redman and Watson 1970; Schiffer 1985; Wheeler 1954; Winter 1976

Excavation Methodology
  Adkins and Adkins 1989; Alexander 1970; Barker 1977, 1988; Bass 1966; Bass and Throckmorton 1961; Bement 1985; Bird 1968; Bird and Ford 1956; Bodner and Rowlett 1980; Butzer 1982; Coe 1967; Coles 1984; Davies 1987; Dillon 1985, 1989; Dorrel 1989; Harp 1975; Harris 1989; Hester, Heizer, and Graham 1975; Hole, Flannery, and Neely 1969; Hope-Taylor 1966, 1967; Joukowsky 1980; Karata 1989; LeBlanc 1976; Lennstrom and Hastorf 1992; Levin 1986; Limp 1974; Lloyd 1976; McIntosh 1977; MacNeish et al. 1972; Movius 1974, 1977; Piggott 1965; Reed, Bennett, and Porter 1968; Sterud and Pratt 1975; Struever 1968; Wagner 1982; Wheeler 1954

A DAY IN THE LIFE OF A FIELD ARCHAEOLOGIST

David W. Sedat

Sedat is a Research Associate at the University Museum, University of Pennsylvania. Both a Guatemalan and U.S. citizen, he has directed excavations over the past 23 years at sites in El Salvador, Guatemala, and Honduras. As Field Director of the Verapaz Project, he experienced the unexpected incident described here.

Because archaeological research often produces the unexpected, the field worker may be called on to cope with surprises and demonstrate skills not usually thought of as part of scientific investigation. This became all too apparent to me one day in 1972 while I was directing archaeological excavations at the site of El Portón, Baja Verapaz, in the highlands of Guatemala. I was still a graduate student at the time, having just completed my master's degree in anthropology the previous spring. Although I had several seasons of archaeological fieldwork under my belt, as Field Director of the Verapaz Project I was, for the first time, in charge of an entire research program—which included supervising both the excavation of sev-eral large structures at El Portón and the field laboratory in the nearby town of San Jerónimo.

I recall the day—clear and warm, like almost every day in the beautiful highlands. It was mid-morning, I had just finished assigning several excavation workers new tasks, and I was about 8 feet down in a deep trench, beginning to record some newly found adobe floors of one of the smaller temple mounds. I was so engrossed in my work that I didn't hear two helicopters approach until, with a sudden and awesome roar, they made a pass right over my trench and landed in the tomato field about 50 yards away.

With some alarm I leaped out of the trench and was instantly engulfed in a choking cloud of dust. Disoriented, I could barely make out two army green Huey choppers already disgorging a horde of uniformed men. In the panic-stricken confusion of the moment, my mind raced—was our government permission to excavate really in order (where were all those papers?), or had our excavations been mistaken as an antigovern-ment guerilla installation? My work crew of twenty obviously shared my apprehension; some of them appeared ready to bolt for the hills, while several others had already thrown themselves on the ground either out of fear or to protect themselves from the still rotating chopper blades (or were they trying to surrender?).

I had no time to reflect on this scene, for out of the nearest chopper bounded a familiar figure in a crisp khaki uniform and a military cap encrusted with gold. He was obviously an important officer and surely, I thought, I have seen this man before—perhaps in a newspaper photo. As he came striding toward me, he exclaimed in Spanish, "Who is the archaeologist in charge here?" I had no choice but to admit that I was the guilty one, so as I stumbled over the furrows, I extended my hand and replied, "I'm directing this work, and I'm at your service." As we shook hands, I suddenly realized with a shock that this was General Carlos Arana Osario, president of Guatemala, and I could hear several of

(continued)

(*continued*)

my workers collectively gasp, "¡Es el presidente!"

As President Arana and I shook hands, the members of his entourage gathered around us, and I could see several television cameras trained on us. (I later learned they were from an Italian TV network filming a documentary about the president.) As I introduced myself, my feelings of panic were rapidly replaced by self-consciousness; here I was, dressed in muddy boots, faded and dusty blue jeans, with a red bandana around my head, in the midst of a crowd of neatly dressed government officials and military officers, making small talk with the president of Guatemala! General Arana must have been expecting a more impressive-looking figure, for he turned to an aide and asked if this tattered and dusty figure was really the archaeologist they had come to see. By a stroke of luck, the aide was an old childhood friend, and after I exchanged long-overdue greetings with him, he cheerfully verified that I was, indeed, the archaeologist in charge.

President Arana then declared, in his characteristic style, "We are here for only a short while before going on to visit Tikal, so tell us what this is all about as quickly as you can!" In the space of two or three minutes, I found myself shifting gears from recording ar-

chitectural details in a trench to engaging in a running discourse (in both Spanish and English) on the history of the site as revealed by our excavations and the importance of the site in the overall development of Pre-Columbian civilization. As I led the presidential party through the trenches, we were joined by a quickly growing crowd of local people from the nearby town. Although I worried over possible cave-ins or other disasters in the excavations, the only apparent casualties were the neatly pressed uniforms of my visitors, which picked up a considerable sample of the local matrix in the hot and humid confines of the trenches!

After we toured the site, General Arana wanted to see the artifacts recovered by the project, housed in our field laboratory. Naturally, with piles of potsherds in the process of being numbered, broken pottery vessels in various stages of repair, and more spectacular objects, such as jade artifacts, stored on open shelves, I was somewhat uncomfortable with the picture of our now greatly expanded group crowding into the small rooms of the laboratory. And I wondered how my wife, who was busily cataloging artifacts at the lab, would cope with this unexpected onslaught. But I could not refuse the president's request. So, after strolling into town, picking

up still more curious people along the way, and issuing polite admonitions of "please don't touch," I led the swelling horde into the laboratory and toward the last surprise test of the day.

Although my wife was somewhat startled by the sudden arrival of the president and an entourage of about a hundred people, everyone seemed pleased by the chance to tour our laboratory. After I explained how we had developed a ceramic sequence from the various piles of broken pottery littering the lab, one of the presidential aides and some government officials took me aside and suggested, in low voices, that it would be a wonderful gesture if I would give the president a memento of his visit to El Portón and San Jerónimo. What, I reluctantly asked, would they suggest as an appropriate gift? They replied quickly that President Arana much admired the large and elaborate jaguar effigy incense burners that we had excavated a few months before [see Fig. 7.6, p. 248]. Delicately, I tried to explain how important these artifacts were to science, and how our contract with the government forbade such action, but to little avail. After all, they argued, President Arana *was* the government!

At that point I noticed that the president and a few of his group had moved to the veranda, where they were obviously admiring our very plump turkey that we were fattening up for Thanksgiving, then only a few weeks away. Excusing myself, I joined them in time to hear President Arana extolling the virtues of his wife's recipe for roast turkey. Hearing this, I was struck with a sudden inspiration. "Señor Presidente," I said, "I would like your wife to have that turkey as a memento of your visit that has so honored us today. Who knows, maybe someday you can invite my wife and me

to enjoy her recipe!" With a great roar of laughter from the group, President Arana graciously accepted the present.

Several days later my wife and I were invited to a series of presidential functions in Guatemala City, and after that we were asked to accompany the president and his entourage on a tour of the country's archaeological sites. President Arana was obviously deeply interested in the heritage of his country's past, and throughout

his term of office he remained personally supportive of archaeological research in Guatemala. But when I think back to that day when he and his party suddenly descended from the sky over El Portón, I am always thankful that, in the end, it was our Thanksgiving turkey that was presented as a memento of that surprise visit, and not one of the 2,000-year-old jaguar incense burners!

CHAPTER EIGHT

FIELD PROCESSING
AND CLASSIFICATION

Classification, like statistics, is not an end in itself but a technique . . . to attain specific objectives, and so it must be varied with the objective.

Irving Rouse, "The Classification of Artifacts in Archaeology," 1960

Next time, be sure, you will have more success, when you have learned how to reduce and classify all by its use.

Johann Wolfgang von Goethe, Faust

Once acquired, all forms of archaeological data are processed in some way—cleaned, labeled, sorted, and so on—before analysis. In addition, some forms of data may be classified or broken into groups in preparation for further study. Preparation and organization are thus the basic goals of the initial stages of analysis. Portable microcomputers, small enough to be used in the field, are already revolutionizing this process.

Processing and classification have to be done while fieldwork is still going on, usually in a field laboratory. This allows the archaeologist to evaluate the data as they are recovered and to formulate and modify working hypotheses that can then be tested through new or continuing acquisition strategies. For example, if the archaeologist recognizes that evidence being recovered suggests occupation during a little-known period, excavation efforts in that locale (site, mound, trench, or whatever) can be expanded by adding new excavations or enlarging old ones. If, however, processing and classification of data are postponed until active fieldwork has ended, the archaeologist loses the chance to use such evaluations to guide continuing data acquisition.

DATA PROCESSING

Of all the types of archaeological data, artifacts usually undergo the most complex and thorough **processing.** They are nearly always classified in some way in the field, before being subjected to more detailed analysis. Ecofacts are generally handled more simply in the field laboratory, and features, because they are not portable, are not "processed" at all beyond field recording. (Of course, the constituent elements of some features—such as the bones and mortuary goods in a burial—*are* processed, but they are treated as artifacts and ecofacts, not as "parts of features.") Field data records also pass through the laboratory system, and when computerized, allow for a more flexible and rapid system for the addition of information as the analysis process proceeds. However, since artifacts receive the most attention in the field laboratory, we will deal primarily with artifactual data in this chapter, but the processing of other data forms will be discussed when appropriate.

We begin by considering the field laboratory itself. Once we have described the physical and organizational setting, we will outline the flow of artifacts through the stages of laboratory handling. The remainder of the chapter is concerned with the final step in field processing, which is also the first step in analysis—classification.

The Field Laboratory

Most archaeological projects have a specialized facility or field laboratory in which to carry out processing, initial classification, and storage of archaeological data. The size and complexity of the field laboratory depend on the kind and amount of data being collected. Tents or other portable structures are sometimes used, especially for short-term seasonal projects. Most archaeologists, however, prefer to house the field laboratory in a permanent building to provide security for the collected data. Whatever its form, the field laboratory should be close enough to the site under investigation to facilitate day-to-day transport of artifacts, ecofacts, records, and equipment. If the project includes many sites within a broad area, a central location for the field laboratory has obvious advantages. Figure 8.1 shows a schematic plan of the field laboratory used by a recent large-scale research program in Guatemala, the Quiriguá Project.

Portable data—artifacts and ecofacts—should be brought to the field laboratory for processing at the close of each workday. Field records—notebooks, standardized forms, and drawings—are usually stored in the laboratory when not in use in the field. Laboratory storage of all kinds of data and equipment must be systematic and orderly so that any item can be quickly retrieved. Distinct, clearly labeled areas for each category of data make retrieval much easier (Fig. 8.1).

The field laboratory is staffed according to the needs of the project. If research is being conducted by a single person, the same individual may undertake both data collection and laboratory processing. At the other end of the continuum, large-scale projects often require a specialized staff of laboratory workers, supervised by a full-time laboratory director. Regardless of the project's size, the laboratory must have sufficient staff to process archaeological data as soon as possible after they are collected. This promptness is important to guard against errors, such as loss of labels on artifacts or lot bags, and to allow quick evaluation of the data as a guide for ongoing research.

Processing Procedures

Artifacts are usually processed in five stages: cleaning, conservation or repair, labeling, inventory, and cataloging (Fig. 8.2). Each newly arrived bag of artifacts must be accompanied by a tag to identify its provenience. To guard against loss of provenience information, many archaeologists rec-

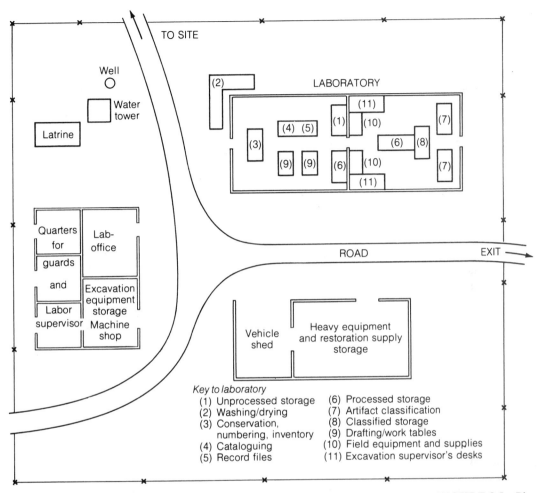

TO SITE

Well

Water tower

Latrine

LABORATORY

(2)

(11)

(4) (5)   (1)   (10)   (7)

(3)

(6) (8)

(9) (9)   (6)   (10)   (7)

(11)

Quarters for guards and Labor supervisor

Lab-office

Excavation equipment storage Machine shop

ROAD   EXIT →

Vehicle shed

Heavy equipment and restoration supply storage

Key to laboratory
(1) Unprocessed storage
(2) Washing/drying
(3) Conservation, numbering, inventory
(4) Cataloguing
(5) Record files

(6) Processed storage
(7) Artifact classification
(8) Classified storage
(9) Drafting/work tables
(10) Field equipment and supplies
(11) Excavation supervisor's desks

FIGURE 8.1 Plan of a laboratory compound designed to house a large and self-sufficient archaeological project (Quiriguá, Guatemala).

ommend that each bag of artifacts be accompanied by two provenience tags: one inside the bag and the other outside. As the artifacts are processed and analyzed, an appropriate **standardized form** (hard copy or computerized format) should be used to record additional information as it is generated.

Cleaning Processing begins with cleaning. Most pottery and stone artifacts must be washed in water to remove any earth that remains on them. It should be stressed that washing of even such durable pieces is a delicate process, to be entrusted only to trained individuals, since improper treatment can damage or even destroy the artifact. As a general rule, washing can be done with soft brushes, as long as they do not erode or scratch the surface of the artifact (Fig. 8.3). Artifacts that require special treatment

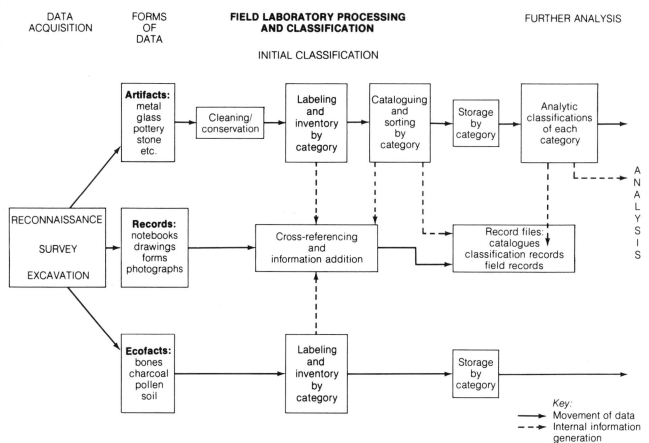

FIGURE 8.2 Flow chart to illustrate the data processing and analysis stages normally undertaken in a field laboratory.

must be segregated by the archaeologist before washing. For instance, pottery vessels that contain remains of ancient food or other substances must be handled specially: They may be washed and the wash water saved for analysis, or they may be left unwashed and reserved for later treatment to identify their contents.

Conservation Conservation involves repair, consolidation, and other means of preserving material remains. It may entail strengthening weak substances, for example, by gradually applying a solution of plastic to crumbling bone. As the liquid in the solution evaporates, the plastic is left, holding the bone together. Repair of artifacts includes such common activities as gluing together smashed pots or broken projectile points. When positive protective measures are unnecessary or impossible in the field, treatment may involve no more than careful protective packing, such as that for fragile textile or basketry materials.

Conservation requirements vary from one project to another, and the

FIGURE 8.3 Washing artifacts in the field. Note the compartmentalized drying tray and attached provenience labels.

sophistication of conservation techniques available to archaeology continues to grow rapidly. If recovery of fragile remains is expected in a field project, it is best to call in a professional conservator who can then apply the best available measures. An extreme example is given by Ozette, a site in northwestern Washington excavated by Richard Daugherty. There, a wealth of fragile organic materials, including cedar house planks, wooden bowls, baskets, and dried foods, were preserved by waterlogged (anaerobic) surroundings; it was necessary to work out a number of on-the-spot treatment schemes to cope with the abundance of perishable remains. Similarly, Vindolanda, in England, has yielded such incredible finds as leather shoes, woolen textiles, thin wooden documents, insects, tanners' combs (complete with cattle hair), and uncorroded metal, all from a 1900-year-old Roman garrison settlement near Hadrian's Wall. Most sites do not promise such riches—or such headaches—but it is wise to be prepared. If the field laboratory staff will not include a professional conservator, the archaeologist is well advised to consult such a person before fieldwork begins.

Conservation situations: Ozette, Washington; Vindolanda, England

Labeling When artifacts are removed from their bag for washing or conservation, they become separated from the containers that carry their provenience identification. Great care must therefore be taken to ensure that provenience information is not lost during these stages: Until each item is individually labeled, it can be identified only by its proximity to the field tag for its provenience unit (lot). For this reason, artifacts are washed in groups corresponding to separate lots and then removed to distinct areas for drying. Portable drying trays, such as screens with wooden frames, are usually used (see Fig. 8.3). The provenience tag can be pinned to each tray to identify its contents, or a piece of chalkboard can be affixed to the end of the tray and the lot label changed with each use.

The best way to avoid loss of provenience information is to place a permanent label on each artifact as soon as possible after cleaning. Permanent ink, such as black India ink, is most often used; white ink may be necessary for dark artifacts. The label should be placed in an inconspicuous spot, and not on any surface that may be important in later analysis, such as the cutting edges of tools or decorated surfaces of pottery.

Inventory Once an artifact bears a permanent provenience label, it need no longer remain grouped or bagged with its original lot. At this point it is usually convenient to classify artifacts initially into gross categories that provide the basis for inventory and detailed description. These categories (Table 8.1) are defined both by substance—the raw material used to make the artifact—and by general technique of manufacture. The combined criteria of substance and technology yield convenient categories called **industries,** such as a chipped-stone industry or a ground-stone industry.

Inventory consists simply of counting and recording the quantity of artifacts within each industry. These counts are usually recorded on a standardized form or in a computerized format. If a lot system is being used, for instance, the numerical totals of each industrial category within each lot are entered on the card or form for that lot. Record forms of other "special" provenience units, such as burials, receive the same treatment. This quantitative information can be valuable in interpretive assessments of the data. For example, the relative amounts of specific artifact categories found in secondary contexts such as construction fill may be constant and may contrast strikingly with the amounts of artifacts found in primary contexts.

Table 8.1 Representative Artifact Industries

Lithic Industries	Ceramic Industries	Metal Industries	Organic Industries
Chipped stone	Pottery	Copper	Bone
Ground stone	Figurines	Bronze	Ivory
	Musical instruments	Iron	Horn
	Beads	Gold	Wood
		Silver	Shell
		Tin	Hide
			Basketry
			Textiles

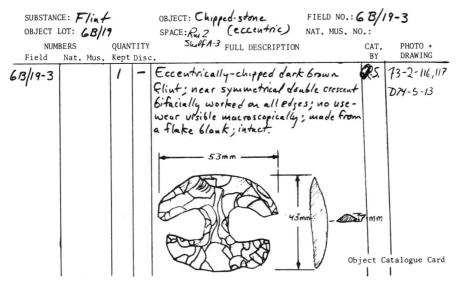

SUBSTANCE: *Flint* OBJECT: *Chipped-stone* FIELD NO.: *6 B/19-3*
OBJECT LOT: *6B/19* SPACE: *Rm 2* *(eccentric)* NAT. MUS. NO.:

NUMBERS		QUANTITY		*Shelf A-3* FULL DESCRIPTION	CAT. BY	PHOTO + DRAWING
Field	Nat. Mus.	Kept	Disc.			
6B/19-3		1	—	*Eccentrically-chipped dark brown Flint; near symmetrical double crescent bifacially worked on all edges; no use-wear visible macroscopically; made from a flake blank; intact.*	R.S.	73-2-116,117 D74-5-13

53mm

43mm 7mm

Object Catalogue Card

FIGURE 8.4 Cataloging: an example of a completed artifact catalog card.

Cataloging After inventory has taken place, many artifacts are described and recorded in detail. This individualized description constitutes cataloging. Standardized forms are used for cataloging; the format may be a notebook, a bound registry log, or a card system (Fig. 8.4). The catalog format is usually designed for computerized recording of artifacts using microcomputers in the laboratory. Catalog information usually includes a record of substance, color, and form (description of overall shape and measurements of length, width, and thickness) as well as provenience information and the catalog number. The description of the artifact's form is often supplemented by a **scaled drawing.** In all cases, the cataloged artifact should be photographed and the appropriate negative number cited on the catalog form. Once an artifact has been described, a catalog number is usually added to the provenience label, both in the catalog and on the artifact, to identify the individual item.

Cataloging is a time-consuming process. For this reason, many archaeological programs that produce large quantities of artifacts cannot afford to catalog each individual item recovered. In such cases, the most plentiful artifact categories—such as pottery fragments—are usually not cataloged. Exceptions may be made—in particular, it may be advisable to catalog all whole vessels and any fragments derived from use-related primary contexts (occupation floors, burials, and so forth). But, most often, bulk items are simply given bulk provenience labels and then counted.

Cataloging completes the basic sequence of artifact processing. At this point, processed artifacts either are placed in storage or undergo the preliminary step in analysis, classification.

CLASSIFICATION

In all branches of science—and in everyday life—classification provides a base for further understanding and study. Much of the work of early archaeologists was devoted to the description and classification of objects from the past. Although classification is no longer the archaeologist's sole or principal concern, it remains a fundamental analytical step toward interpretation of the past.

Classification is the process of ordering or arranging objects into groups on the basis of shared characteristics. These characteristics are termed **attributes.** Groups determined by directly observable attributes constitute **primary classification.** Examples include classifications of decoration on the basis of inferred characteristics, or of attributes measurable only by tests more complicated than simple visual inspection, such as microscopic inspection or chemical analysis. Ordering based on inferred or analytic attributes constitutes **secondary classification.** An example is the sorting of obsidian (volcanic glass) tools according to the chemically identifiable source of the raw material. Secondary classifications are less often carried out in the field, since they usually require specialized laboratory facilities and technicians—either archaeologists with special training or outside consultants. Computer applications have aided artifact classifications, like other archaeological procedures, especially when a large number of attributes must be considered.

Objectives of Classification

All classifications serve a variety of purposes. Their first and most fundamental purpose is to create order from apparent chaos by dividing a mass of undifferentiated data into groups (classes). Classification thus allows the scientist to organize vast arrays of data into manageable units. As a very basic example, "artifacts" are distinguished from "ecofacts" and "features" in terms of their collection and processing requirements. Artifacts are often further subdivided into gross categories or industries, such as lithics, ceramics, or metalwork. These classes may then be subjected to detailed primary and secondary classification, breaking them down into kinds of stone artifacts, kinds of ceramics, and kinds of metalwork.

Second, classification allows the researcher to summarize the characteristics of many individual objects by listing only their shared attributes. Most archaeological classifications result in definition of **types.** Types represent clusters of attributes that occur together repeatedly in the same artifacts. For example, the potsherds and whole vessels in a given pottery type will share attributes such as color and hardness of the fired clay; but other attributes, such as evidence of ancient vessel repair or of ritual vessel breakage, may not be defining traits of the type class. Thus, reference to types enables the archaeologist to describe large numbers of artifacts more economically, ignoring for the moment the attributes that differentiate among members of a single type.

Third, classifications define variability within a given set of data. Such variability may be explained, eventually, by a broad range of factors, including temporal and spatial separation, or, more specifically, by behavioral differences reflecting functional, social, economic, or similar distinctions. For example, definition of several types of projectile points might reveal the existence of specialized equipment once used for hunting different kinds of animals. Recognition of different styles of decorating pottery might reveal distinctions in social status within an ancient society. In any case, the recognition and explanation of variability in the archaeological record is one of the cornerstones of all archaeological research.

Finally, by ordering and describing classes and types, the scientist suggests a series of relationships among classes. The nature and degree of these relationships should generate hypotheses that stimulate further questions and research. For instance, the most obvious question that may emerge from a classification concerns the meaning of the classification: How did the order originate, and what is its significance? As we saw in Chapter 2, in biology, the descriptive classification of plant and animal species and the questions it generated gradually led to the theory of biological evolution as an attempt to account for the origin of the described order and to ascribe meaning to the hierarchical relationships among the classes. In classifications of artifacts, the described order and relationships among categories or types represent aspects of the artifacts' raw materials, techniques of manufacture, use (function), and decorative style.

Emic versus Etic Classification

From a broader philosophical viewpoint, questions about the meaning of classification plunge scientists into debate about whether classifications reflect the *discovery* of a "natural" order inherent in the data or an *imposition* by the scientist of an "artificial" order. For archaeology (and anthropology) this corresponds to the **emic–etic** distinction discussed in Chapter 3. This debate has a long and colorful tradition in archaeology. We shall briefly review the basic positions involved, since they lie at the root of all assumptions about the significance of archaeological classifications. The debate focuses on whether classifications and types represent an ancient cultural order (the emic position) or whether they are categories imposed by the archaeologist (the etic position).

Archaeologists recognize that members of all cultural systems, past and present, organize and categorize the world they observe and live in. For example, animals may be categorized by whether they walk or fly, whether they are edible, or whether they are good beasts of burden. People may be ordered by age, sex, occupation, status, wealth, and so on. Pottery vessels may be classified according to whether they are suited for storage, valuable, homemade, and so on. And human activities can be differentiated into such categories as food preparation, tool manufacturing, and disposal of the dead. Thus all societies maintain a kind of cultural classification or "cognitive structure," and different activities—including those forms that produce material evidence recovered by archaeologists—should reflect the cognitive structure of the people who perform them. The debate, then, concerns whether (or to what degree) archaeologists can rediscover aspects of such an ancient emic cultural order by (re)classifying the material remains of past behavior.

Archaeologists such as Krieger, Spaulding, Deetz, and Gifford maintain that this *can* be done. They argue that by carefully considering the distribution of specific characteristics within any given category of artifact, the archaeologist can pick out clusters of attributes that co-occur regularly. Traditionally, most observations of co-occurrence have been made impressionistically, but today these "impressions" are increasingly being replaced by statistical tests of co-occurrence. Since the clustered attributes occur together more than chance would predict, the proponents reason, the clustering must represent selection and grouping by the ancient makers and users of the artifacts. Therefore the "types" form an emic classification that represents the ancient cognitive structure.

The opposite position is taken by scholars such as Brew, Rouse, and Ford, who hold that cognitive structure or emic classification is too complex to be captured in a single typology. They argue for etic classifications because artifacts have so many attributes that, depending on which attributes the investigator considers, a number of crosscutting classifications could result, each an arbitrary breakdown of the total array (Fig. 8.5). And types grade into each other, so that some artifacts could as justifiably be put in one type as in another (Fig. 8.6). The proponents of this point of view do not suggest that classifications be abandoned; they do insist, however, that they be recognized as arbitrary impositions by archaeologists. These archaeologists suggest creating *more* etic classifications, using differing attributes to define the classes; they suggest choosing the different attributes with a view toward studying different kinds of variation, such as use, manufacture, or decorative treatment. Rouse has argued also for the study of distributions of isolated attributes themselves.

Historical documentation may provide archaeologists with evidence for the ways in which objects are categorized by specific cultures. Inventories, manufacturers' specifications, and even inscriptions on the artifacts themselves are sources of potential clues for the reconstruction of emic classifications. At many colonial North American sites, for example, fragments of the metal portions of muskets and pistols may be classified as to the types known to have been used by various military units. More likely to survive intact, gun flints can be classified by their size and shape into categories reflecting place of manufacture and even specific weapon types. In a different time and place, recent decipherments of texts inscribed on some

Emic classifications from historical documentation: Colonial American artifacts and Maya pottery

FIGURE 8.5 One difficulty in classifying archaeological materials is illustrated by this hypothetical example. The complex variation in house forms makes it difficult to define a single classification based on all observable attributes. (Reproduced by permission of the American Anthropological Association from *American Anthropologist* 56:1, February 1954. Not for further reproduction.)

pottery vessels reveal the names used by the Classic Maya to refer to the shape and even the uses of some vessels ("chocolate pot"), thus providing emic classifications for both form and function.

But in contrast to such historical situations, we can see that in most prehistoric contexts, the question of whether archaeological classifications correspond to ancient cognitive structures may be too complex for a simple answer. A given set of statistically demonstrated attribute clusters of types may well represent ancient emic decisions and groupings, but selection of different attributes for attention may produce different, crosscutting etic types that are equally useful for the analyst. In fact, the selection of attributes used to define types depends directly on the archaeologist's research design: The particular attributes the investigator chooses to look at depend on the research questions he or she is interested in exploring. For example, a researcher studying food storage patterns would look at the shapes and sizes of storage vessels rather than the designs used to decorate them.

The point is that classification is a convenient ordering tool, organizing

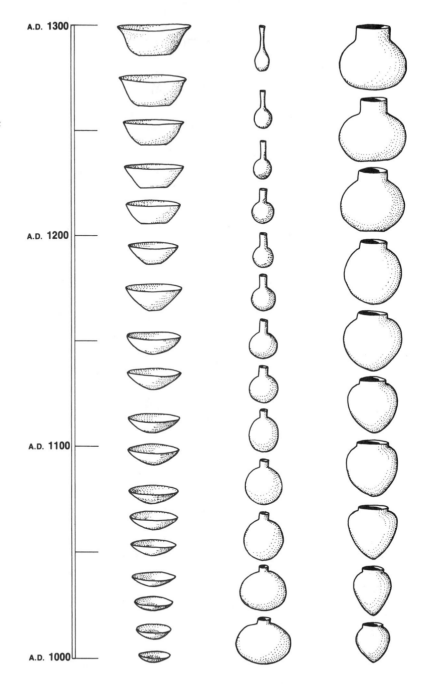

FIGURE 8.6 Another problem in classifying archaeological materials is illustrated in this example of gradual changes in three pottery forms through time, which make it difficult to divide each column into distinct types. (After Ford, Pan American Union, General Secretariat, Organization of American States, 1962.)

artifacts or other archaeological data into manageable groups. The significance of the types in terms of ancient human behavior is a question that must be answered for each classification.

Kinds of Classification

As we stated above, archaeological classifications are based on attributes. Three basic categories of attributes apply to archaeological data: stylistic, form, and technological attributes. **Stylistic attributes** usually involve the most obvious descriptive characteristics of an artifact—its color, texture, decoration, secondary alterations, and other similar characteristics. **Form attributes** include the three-dimensional shape of the artifact as a whole as well as the forms of various parts of it. Form attributes include measurable dimensions such as length, width, and thickness ("metric attributes"). **Technological attributes** include characteristics of the raw materials used to manufacture artifacts ("constituent attributes") and any characteristics that reflect the way the artifact was manufactured ("manufacturing attributes").

To be meaningful, an attribute must potentially have two or more alternative states. Some attributes may be expressed qualitatively: a grinding stone either has leg supports or does not (presence/absence), and it takes one of a number of forms (basin, trough, and so on). Other attributes may be expressed quantitatively, such as the angle of the working edge of a chipped-stone tool. Attributes in all three categories may be expressed either qualitatively or quantitatively. For example, the surface attributes of a pottery vessel can be qualitatively described as "red, well-smoothed, and moderately hard" or quantitatively described according to a standardized color scale, such as the Munsell system ("5YR 4/6"), and a hardness scale, such as the Mohs system ("5.1"). Further examples of pottery attributes are listed in Figure 8.7.

To classify any given category of artifacts, the archaeologist identifies the attributes to be considered and defines their variable states. The classification itself can proceed either by manipulating and physically grouping the artifacts according to their attributes (hand-sorting) or by coding attributes and recording them by computer to establish attribute clusters statistically. For example, in most pottery classifications, the potsherds are hand-sorted into groups by similarity of appearance—color, smoothness, thickness of vessel wall, decorative techniques and motifs, and so on. The other approach may be exemplified by the work of James Sackett, who studied a collection of a traditional category of European Upper Paleolithic tool called an Aurignacian end-scraper (Fig. 8.8) to define the attribute clusters represented. Sackett isolated a small set of attributes and their potential alternative states (Fig. 8.9). By statistical analysis, he was able to divide the collection of end-scrapers into three attribute-cluster categories, probably indicating differences in use:

Definition of attribute clusters: James Sackett and Aurignacian end-scrapers

1. Those that were retouched (chipped along the edges to increase or decrease sharpness) and any two of the following: rounded front contour; narrow piece width; convergent (triangular) body contour.

2. Those attribute combinations not included in Classes 1 and 3.

3. Those that were not retouched and any two of the following: medium shallow front contour; wide piece width; parallel-sided body contour.

FIGURE 8.7 Classification of pottery: examples of kinds of attributes used to define stylistic, form, and technological types.

STYLISTIC ATTRIBUTES

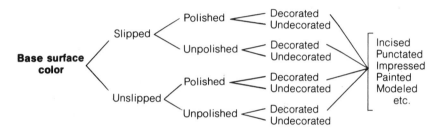

FORM ATTRIBUTES

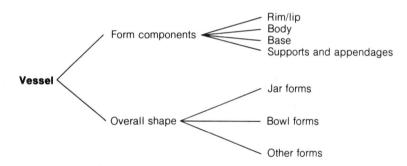

TECHNOLOGICAL ATTRIBUTES

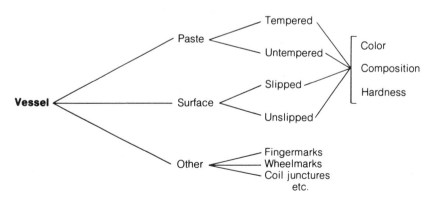

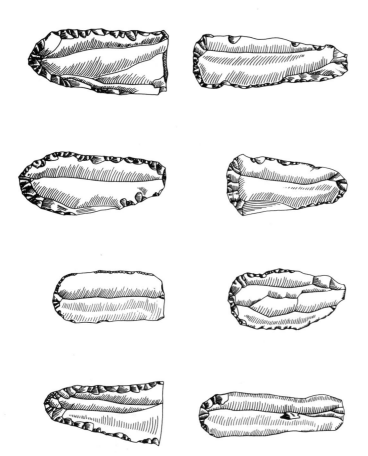

FIGURE 8.8 Examples of Aurignacian end-scrapers showing variation of form within this artifact category. (Reproduced by permission of the American Anthropological Association from *American Anthropologist* 68:2, Part 2, April 1966. Not for further reproduction.)

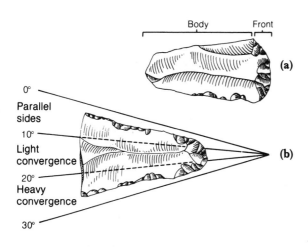

FIGURE 8.9 The systematic definition of attributes for Aurignacian end-scrapers may be based on (a) the extent and location of retouch and (b) the angle between the longer sides. (Reproduced by permission of the American Anthropological Association from *American Anthropologist* 68:2; Part 2, April 1966. Not for further reproduction.)

Another related distinction can be made in classificatory procedures—namely, whether the investigator considers all attributes to be equally important or whether some are more important than others in defining types. Obviously, the mere selection of an attribute for consideration in a classification implies that it is more important than those not selected. But, within the set chosen as the basis for classification, the archaeologist may choose whether to weight the various attributes equally.

The **taxonomic** approach involves a series of decisions that break the larger collection of artifacts into ever smaller groupings; the divisions at each decision point are based on the alternative states of one or several attributes. Different "types" result from considering the same attributes in different order. The taxonomic approach has been used in pottery typologies, and it can be illustrated graphically for a North American pottery typology (Fig. 8.10).

In contrast, **paradigmatic** classifications weight all attributes equally. The order in which attributes are considered makes no difference to the definition of types, for each type is defined by particular states of all the attributes (Fig. 8.11). Sackett's study of Aurignacian end-scrapers illustrates this approach; indeed, most statistically derived typologies have tended to be of this kind.

The term **mode** has been used in several different ways by archaeologists. We follow only one such definition by using modes to refer to those attributes that have special significance, as in defining types and distinguishing among them. Although some modes are recognized as important because they cluster to form types, others occur across types as markers of a particular time period or a restricted area. For example, the use of iridescent paint on pottery in southern Mesoamerica is a stylistic mode found on a very early time level—about 1500–1200 B.C.—regardless of the other attributes or the "type" of the vessel or sherd on which it is found. There are also, of course, technological modes, such as wheel-made pottery, and form modes, such as restricted mouths on vessels. Modal analysis allows the archaeologist to study particular aspects of technology, form, and surface treatment apart from the way the modes were combined within the artifacts. For example, one may study the distribution in time and space of resist painting as a decorative technique, or of effigy feet as pottery supports, separately from the study of the pottery types on which they occur.

As we have noted, the kinds of attributes selected will determine the kind of archaeological typology or modal analysis that results. Depending on the nature of the artifacts and the objectives of the study, the archaeologist may choose to define technological types, form types, or stylistic types. **Technological types** may be based on one or both of the major groups of technological attributes defined earlier—constituent attributes and manufacturing attributes. For example, in southwest Asian metal artifacts, different copper alloys may be distinguished by their constituents, such as brass (copper and zinc) or bronze (copper and arsenic or copper

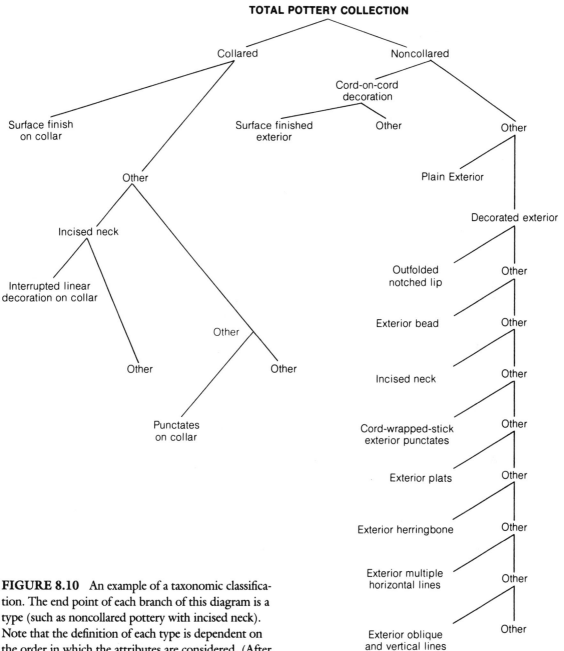

FIGURE 8.10 An example of a taxonomic classification. The end point of each branch of this diagram is a type (such as noncollared pottery with incised neck). Note that the definition of each type is dependent on the order in which the attributes are considered. (After Whallon, reproduced by permission of the Society for American Archaeology, adapted from *American Antiquity* 37:17, 1972.)

FIGURE 8.11 An example of paradigmatic classification. Each box represents a type in the classification (such as unslipped sand-tempered bowls). Note that the definition of each type is *independent* of the order in which the attributes are considered.

		TEMPER ATTRIBUTES			
		Shell-tempered		Sand-tempered	
DECORATIVE ATTRIBUTES	Unslipped	Bowls	Jars	Bowls	Jars
	Slipped without decoration	Bowls	Jars	Bowls	Jars
	Slipped with decoration	Bowls	Jars	Bowls	Jars

and tin). And drilled beads may be classified according to whether their holes were drilled from one direction only or from both sides, with the two drill holes connecting in the middle.

Form types are based on component shape attributes, metric attributes, or both. Component shape attributes, such as body shape, are especially important in classifying fragmentary artifacts, such as pottery sherds; metric attributes such as vessel height are usually more useful in working with largely intact specimens. An example of form types is the common classification of hand-held grinding stones by their cross-sectional shape (round, subrectangular, and so forth).

Stylistic types are generally based on color, surface finish, and decorative attributes. Pottery classification systems usually emphasize surface attributes, such as the presence or absence of painted decoration and, if decoration is present, the number and choice of paint colors used.

Unfortunately, the archaeological literature is crowded with references to a multitude of confusing labels for typologies. For instance, "natural" or "cultural" types and "arbitrary" types refer to the emic–etic controversy mentioned earlier in this chapter; actually, these terms are evaluations of typologies, not descriptive labels. In the past, archaeologists also used categories called "functional" types that were based on the uncritical assumption that form can be used directly to infer ancient function. As a result, the archaeological literature contains a series of labels such as "scrapers," "batons," and "gravers." Some of these labels may be accurate; more often than not, however, the functional labels were applied without any contextual evidence to support them. To avoid further misunderstandings, most archaeologists today avoid applying functional labels to classifications, except where solid evidence supports their use.

Given the great variety of potential ways of classifying artifacts, how does the archaeologist make a choice? The answer lies both in the objectives of the classification to be undertaken and in the nature of the data. The archaeologist selects a classification that is suitable to the artifacts under study and that will meet the particular objectives of the investigation.

Uses of Archaeological Classifications

Archaeologists often use types to reconstruct ancient human behavior; they do this by correlating hierarchical classifications with various levels of behavior. The most widely cited example of such behavioral reconstruction is that outlined by James Deetz (Fig. 8.12). According to this scheme, the *individual* creators of artifact *types* (archaeologically defined by consistent patterning of *attributes)* adhere to culturally defined standards. Patterned *sets* of artifacts used by occupational *groups* (archaeologically classified by criteria of form and function), such as the various tools used by hunters or farmers, are called **subassemblages.** Patterned sets of subassemblages, representing the sum of social activities, define the **assemblage** of the ancient *community*. At the highest level, patterned sets of assemblages are used by archaeologists to define **archaeological cultures,** corresponding to ancient *societies*.

It should be made clear that, unlike the structure of archaeological data discussed in Chapter 4 (see Fig. 4.17, p. 135), reconstructions of the kind just described are built on artifact classifications alone, and not on the context and associations of the data. But only if we assume that the scheme in Figure 8.12 is an emic classification can it be used as a *behavioral* reconstruction, that is, by assuming that it reflects ancient cognitive structure. We have already raised questions concerning the universal correctness of this assumption. We will consider it further (in the relations between artifact style, artifact form, and behavior) in Chapters 13–16, where we also outline alternative sources for the reconstruction of behavior.

The point here is simply that the classification of archaeological data is undertaken to meet a variety of objectives. And recognition of subassemblages, assemblages, and archaeological cultures reminds us that this classification can be carried out at a number of scales. It also points to the fact that only by operating at the levels of assemblages and archaeological cultures can we really begin to understand the workings of an ancient society. Individual potsherds and stone chips are each small clues to the whole. But the archaeologist must consider the fullest recoverable range of artifact types and industries used by a society, together with the ecofacts and features from that society—*all preferably combined with information on association and context*. Only then can the rich texture of ancient life be revealed.

In the following chapters, we will begin to discuss how artifacts, ecofacts, and features are analyzed to reveal ancient life. Chapters 10–12 consider each of these categories and its interpretive potentials, and Chapters 13–16 indicate how different kinds of data are combined to document the human past.

SUMMARY

In this chapter we have discussed what happens to archaeological data, primarily artifacts, when they are brought from the field.

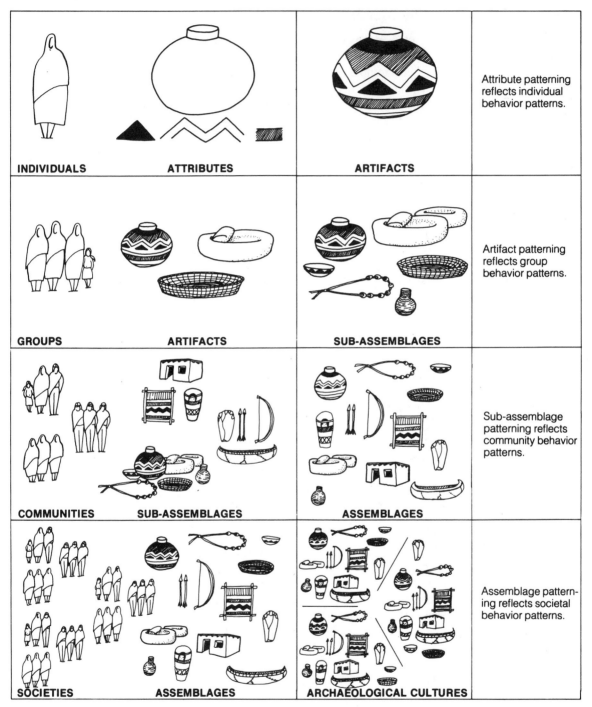

FIGURE 8.12   Behavioral reconstruction based on hierarchical classification, independent of archaeological context (compare with Fig. 4.17, p. 135). (After *Invitation to Archaeology,* by James Deetz. Copyright © 1967 by James Deetz. Used by permission of Doubleday, a division of Bantam Doubleday Dell Publishing Group, Inc.)

In the field laboratory, specimens are cleaned, conserved or repaired (when necessary), and labeled. Bulk items are then inventoried (tallied) by industry for each provenience unit; some items receive detailed individual descriptions through cataloging. The field laboratory also provides space for storage of archaeological data, both processed and unprocessed, as well as storage of data records and some excavation equipment. Once archaeological materials have passed through the stages of laboratory processing, they are available for analysis.

Analysis begins with classification. The objective of classification is to organize the mass of undifferentiated data into manageable units. Such organization also suggests relationships among sets of data—the type classes of the remains. Whether or not these categories would have been meaningful to the makers and users of the artifacts, they are useful tools for the archaeologist, providing a starting point for analysis and interpretation of the collected data.

Classification is based on attributes or descriptive characteristics of the artifacts. The classes may consist of single attributes (modes) or clusters of attributes (types). There are three basic kinds of attributes: stylistic, form, and technological attributes. Selection of different kinds of attributes results in correspondingly different classifications (stylistic, form, and technological types). Classifications may be the basis for analyses of each kind of archaeological data, according to a variety of specific objectives, discussed in Chapters 10–12.

GUIDE TO FURTHER READING

Data Processing
Addington 1985; Adkins and Adkins 1989; Chenhall 1975; Coles 1984; Cronyn 1990; Dillon 1985, 1989; Dorrel 1989; Dowman 1970; Hope-Taylor 1966, 1967; Joukowsky 1980; Kenworthy et al. 1985; LeBlanc 1976; Marquardt, Montet-White, and Scholtz 1982; Organ 1968; Richards and Ryan 1985; Sease 1987; UNESCO 1968

Classification
W. Adams 1988; Aldenderfer 1983; Beck and Jones 1989; Brew 1946; Clarke 1968; Deetz 1967; Doran and Hodson 1975; Dunnell 1971, 1986b; Ford 1954; Gifford 1960; Hill and Evans 1972; Hodson 1970; Klejn 1982; Krieger 1944, 1960; Rouse 1939, 1960; Sackett 1966; Schiffer 1976; Spaulding 1953, 1977; Whallon 1972; Whallon and Brown 1982

TEMPORAL FRAMEWORKS

It is possible to refine the sense of time until an old shoe in the bunch grass or a pile of nineteenth-century beer bottles in an abandoned mining town tolls in one's head like a hall clock. This is the price one pays for learning to read time from surfaces other than an illuminated dial.

Loren C. Eiseley, The Night Country, *1971*

The structure of archaeological data has three dimensions: time, space, and behavior. For example, to trace the development of specialized production and the rise of craft workers and artisans in a particular area, the archaeologist must be able not only to identify the material remains that represent craft production but also to indicate when such materials first appeared in the area and where and how quickly their occurrence spread. Or, to reconstruct ancient political and economic systems, an archaeologist must be able to specify which sites were occupied at the same time, before discussing the relations between their inhabitants.

In this chapter we shall review the ways archaeologists control the temporal dimension—that is, ways to establish which remains are from the same period and which are from different periods. In succeeding chapters we shall examine inferred behavior systems at single points in time and the ways these systems change through time.

Archaeologists have been preoccupied, during most of the discipline's history, with establishing dates and sequences for their materials. Consequently, a sizable variety of methods have been developed for analyzing the age of archaeological materials. This traditional emphasis, combined with recent advances in such fields as chemistry and nuclear physics, has produced a wide—and still growing—assortment of methods for temporal **analysis.** In fact, probably the single most important implication of the wealth of new dating techniques is that they have freed archaeologists from their traditional concern with dating. The "radiocarbon revolution" of the 1950s has been followed by development of a series of other dating techniques, all of which allow the archaeologist to focus research on behavior-oriented studies rather than chronological ones. The archaeologist must still understand the basis for the dating techniques used; the difference is that today a range of relatively reliable techniques can more easily relate one researcher's data temporally to that of other scholars.

Before we discuss specific techniques, however, we must consider a few basic definitions. Age determination may be direct or indirect. **Direct age determination** involves analysis of the artifact, ecofact, or feature itself to arrive at a chronological evaluation. **Indirect age determination** involves analysis of material associated with the data under study to derive a chronological evaluation. For example, an obsidian blade found in a cache might be dated directly by obsidian hydration analysis (discussed later); other materials in the cache and the cache feature itself can then be dated indirectly by assigning them the same age as the obsidian with which they were associated. Of course, the reliability of age determination by indirect means depends completely on the security of the contextual association—in this case, evidence that the obsidian and other materials were deposited at the same time.

Another distinction to be considered is that between **relative** and **absolute** (or **chronometric) age determinations** (Table 9.1). Relative determinations are made by methods that evaluate the age of one piece of data compared with another—for example, artifact A is older than artifact B. Absolute determinations are made by methods that place the age of the material on an absolute time scale, usually a calendrical system (artifact A was manufactured in 123 B.C.), or years before the present (B.P.), and therefore assign an age in years.

A common mistake is to assume that absolute methods refer to precision in age determination. In fact, absolute methods are seldom precise, because it is usually not possible to fix the age of a given artifact to an exact calendrical position. Instead, most absolute methods assign an age expressed as a time span or range, such as A.D. 150–250; they often include a statement of the degree of statistical certainty that the "true" age of the piece falls within that range (expressed, for example, as A.D. 200 ± 50, referring to the midpoint and spread of the range).

Exceptions to this are artifacts or features inscribed with calendrical dates, even if these refer to a calendrical system different from the one we use today. For instance, most coins minted during the Roman Empire carry at least one reference to a specific year in the reign of a particular emperor. And most stelae carved by the Maya of the Classic Period are inscribed with one or more dates in the Maya calendrical system. If the ancient calendars involved can be correlated with our own, the notations on these artifacts can be assigned to a precise position in time—in the case of the Maya system, even to the month and the day. Such materials can thus be dated both directly and absolutely; they can then be used to provide indirect absolute dates for associated remains.

Determining the age of deposits containing datable objects raises the distinction between the concepts of **terminus post quem** and **terminus ante quem.** Terminus post quem (or TPQ) refers to the date *after* which an artifact or a feature must have been deposited. The finding of a Roman cache containing a variety of coins with dates that span A.D. 35–65 means that the date of the deposit must be after the latest dated coin (i.e., A.D. 65), but exactly how many years after that date may be unknown (since it is possible that only "old" coins were placed in the cache). Terminus ante quem (TAQ) refers to the date *before* which an artifact or feature must have been deposited. In the same example, if the Roman cache had been covered by volcanic ash from the A.D. 79 eruption of Vesuvius (see Fig. 7.17, p. 260), then we could conclude that the cache must have been before that year, but exactly how many years before would remain unknown. In this instance, then, by combining TAQ and TPQ determi-

Absolute dating by notations on Roman coins and Maya stelae

Table 9.1   Major Archaeological Age Determination Techniques

Relative Methods	Absolute (or Chrono-metric) Methods
Stratigraphy	Varves
Seriation	Obsidian hydration
Sequence comparison ("cross-dating")	Dendrochronology
Geochronology	Radiocarbon
Bone age	Potassium–argon
	Uranium series
	Fission track
	Archaeomagnetic
	Calendrical

nations, we would conclude that the date of the cache must have been between A.D. 65 and A.D. 79, or a span of only 14 years.

Absolute dates answer one of the two questions about the temporal dimension: How old is it? But relative dates—those that indicate whether A is older than B—usually have broader and more comprehensive significance, for they lead to definition of chronological sequences. By determining the age of a multitude of data sets relative to each other, and arranging these in chronological order, the archaeologist defines a sequential framework that can be used to organize all subsequent data. Finding out the individual absolute ages of the data sets is only one of many ways of determining their relative ages. Establishing chronological sequences has been one of the prime objectives of prehistoric archaeology, since those sequences provide a basic framework for reconstructing the order in which ancient events took place. In many areas of the world these basic sequences are well defined, and newly discovered data can simply be placed in the existing scheme. In other areas, however, the basic chronological sequences have yet to be defined or tested; there the process of establishing the sequence of prehistoric data is still of prime concern.

In this chapter we will briefly discuss the most important methods used by archaeologists and other specialists to determine age and chronological sequence. To present these methods in a meaningful manner, we have categorized them according to their basis of age determination: archaeological methods, geological methods, floral and faunal methods, radiometric methods, magnetic methods, and calendrical methods.

ARCHAEOLOGICAL AGE DETERMINATION

Patterns of human behavior change continually; as the behavior changes, so do its material products, including the various kinds of data recovered by archaeologists. We have all observed how changes through time in design and style alter familiar products such as clothing and automobiles in our own society. Furthermore, most of us can identify the trends of change in these and other artifacts, so that we can place any particular example in its proper position in the time sequence. For instance, when shown several automobiles of varying ages, many people in our society can arrange them at least roughly in order of their age (Fig. 9.1); similar sequential changes are noticeable in clothing, furniture, jewelry, and so on.

The artifacts and features studied by archaeologists are no different, and the archaeologist, by observing and studying various attributes, can usually determine trends of change through time. Changes in manufacturing methods, function, style, and decoration all result in shifts of corresponding attributes. By determining which attributes are most sensitive to changes through time—that is, which traits change most rapidly—the archaeologist can use these characteristics to form a **classification** that will best record changes through time. This classification may be either a typology or a modal study (see Chapter 8). In most cases, stylistic attributes—especially those of surface decoration—change most rapidly and most freely; they thus tend to be the best indicators of time change. This is because stylistic attributes are least affected by functional or technological requirements. For example, a water storage vessel may be of any color and bear any (or no) decorative design, but it must be deep enough to hold water, and it should, if possible, have a restricted mouth to lessen spilling. Similarly, artifacts made from such plastic or malleable materials as clay or metal are usually good sources for deriving temporal sequences, because they are amenable to surface-treatment manipulation. It is not surprising, then, that in most areas of the world, pottery—the infamous potsherd—is the archaeologist's principal gauge of temporal change.

Stratigraphy

In discussing stratification as a geological concept in Chapter 7, we pointed out that **stratigraphy** refers to the archaeological interpretation of the significance of stratification. We have also seen how archaeological stratigraphy may result from both behavioral and natural transformational processes (for example, a midden may be composed of alternating strata of materials in primary context and redeposited **alluvium**). As long as the context—and, therefore, the temporal order—of a stratified deposit is clear, the archaeologist can use stratigraphy to determine the proper sequence of artifact classes from the deposit.

Accordingly, an archaeologist who is fortunate enough to be dealing with artifacts excavated from a long-term, undisturbed stratified midden

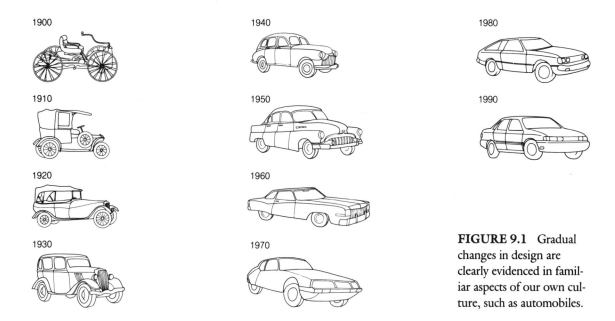

1900 1910 1920 1930 1940 1950 1960 1970 1980 1990

FIGURE 9.1 Gradual changes in design are clearly evidenced in familiar aspects of our own culture, such as automobiles.

deposit will be able to determine the temporal sequence of the types or modes from the order of deposition. Once a given category of artifacts, such as pottery, has been classified, the classes can be placed in a time sequence by plotting their distribution according to their provenience within the stratified deposit (Fig. 9.2). In this situation, the temporal ordering of artifact classes is clearly based on the accurate recording of provenience and determination of context.

Seriation

Seriation is a technique that seeks to order artifacts "in a series" in which adjacent members are more similar to each other than to members further away in the series. Seriation has two basic applications: stylistic seriation and frequency seriation.

Stylistic Seriation   **Stylistic seriation** orders artifacts and attributes according to similarity in style (Fig. 9.3). Here the variation observed may be ascribable to either temporal change or areal differences. It is therefore up to the archaeologist to interpret which dimension is represented in each situation. Generally, the more limited the source area of the artifacts—such as a small valley or a single site, as opposed to a region such as southern France—the more reliably the seriation relates to time changes. Such temporal seriation depends on observable trends—such as decreasing size—

FIGURE 9.2   In this diagram, pottery types have been arranged chronologically by their stratigraphic order in a midden (excavated at Chalchuapa, El Salvador). Charting the gradual increases and decreases in the occurrence of each type through time creates the lenslike pattern called *battleship-shaped curves.* (After Sharer 1978, vol. III, p. 106.)

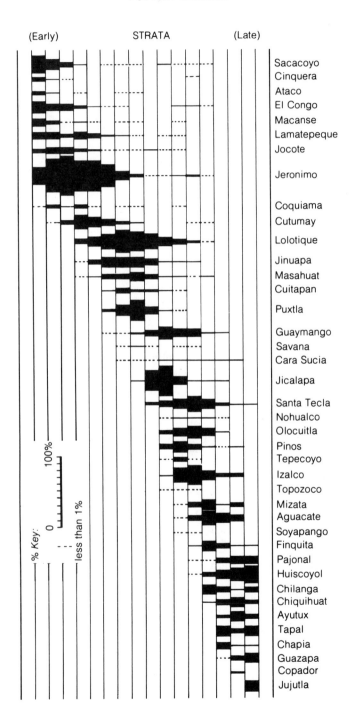

POTTERY CLASSES

(Early)   STRATA   (Late)

Sacacoyo
Cinquera
Ataco
El Congo
Macanse
Lamatepeque
Jocote
Jeronimo
Coquiama
Cutumay
Lolotique
Jinuapa
Masahuat
Cuitapan
Puxtla
Guaymango
Savana
Cara Sucia
Jicalapa
Santa Tecla
Nohualco
Olocuitla
Pinos
Tepecoyo
Izalco
Topozoco
Mizata
Aguacate
Soyapango
Finquita
Pajonal
Huiscoyol
Chilanga
Chiquihuat
Ayutux
Tapal
Chapia
Guazapa
Copador
Jujutla

% Key:
100%
0
less than 1%

in the gradual change of attributes or artifacts; it also involves the assumption that such trends do not change direction capriciously. Our ability to place familiar artifacts from our own culture—such as cars or clothes—into approximate chronological order is based on our knowledge of this kind of gradual change, and it is comparable to what the archaeologist attempts to accomplish by seriation.

One of the first studies to use stylistic seriation successfully was the Diospolis Parva sequence done by Sir Flinders Petrie at the close of the 19th century. Petrie was faced with a series of predynastic Egyptian tombs that were not linked stratigraphically, but each had yielded sets of funerary pottery. To organize the pottery and its source tombs chronologically, he developed what he called a **sequence dating** technique. He ordered the pottery by its shape (see Fig. 9.3) and assigned a series of sequence date numbers to the seriated pots. The "dates," of course, did not relate to a calendar of years but indicated instead the relative age of the materials within the series. Nonetheless, the sequence dating technique allowed Petrie to organize the pottery chronologically and, by association, to order the tombs as well.

Petrie's study also provides evidence that the archaeologist cannot assume that the trend of change is always from the simple to complex or that it implies "progress" as our own culture defines that term. In the Diospolis Parva sequence, the vessel handles began as functional attributes and ended as decorative lines "mimicking" the handles. Thus, for a sequence to be valid, the archaeologist must ensure that it is free from presumptions of "progress," increasing complexity, or other ethnocentric biases. This example also points out a constant problem—how to determine which end of the sequence is earliest and which is latest in age. In fact, this question is usually answered by linking seriation with other (usually absolute) dating methods.

Stylistic seriation: Sir Flinders Petrie and the Diospolis Parva sequence

Frequency Seriation **Frequency seriation** is a method that is more strictly oriented to chronological ordering. It involves determining a sequence of sites or deposits by studying the relative frequencies of certain artifact types they contain. These seriation studies are based on the assumption that the frequency of each artifact type or mode follows a predictable career, from the time of its origin to an expanding popularity and finally decline to total disuse. Of course, the length of time and the degree of popularity (frequency) vary with each type or mode, but when presented diagramatically, most examples form one or more lenslike patterns known as **battleship-shaped curves** (see Fig. 9.2). The validity of this pattern has been verified by plotting the frequencies of artifact types from long-term stratified deposits and by testing historically documented examples. The best-known historical test is that by James Deetz and Edwin N. Dethlefsen, involving dated tombstones from the 18th and early 19th centuries in New England. This study demonstrated that the popularity of various decorative motifs on the headstones did indeed show battleship-shaped distribution curves over time. (Fig. 9.4).

Frequency seriation: Deetz and Dethlefsen and New England tombstones

ARBITRARY   SEQUENCE
DATES

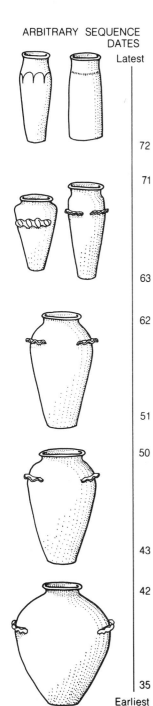

Latest

72

71

63

62

51

50

43

42

35

Earliest

FIGURE 9.3   One of the earliest applications of stylistic seriation was Petrie's chronological ordering of tombs at Diospolis Parva, Egypt, based on changes in associated pottery vessels. (After Petrie 1901.)

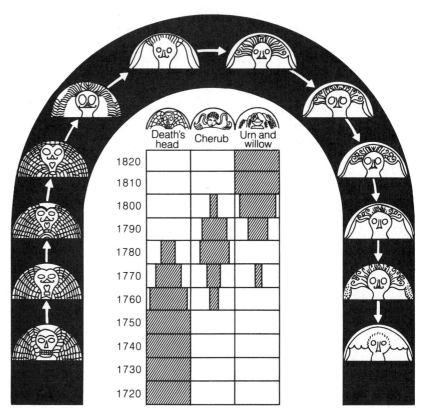

	Death's head	Cherub	Urn and willow
1820			
1810			
1800			
1790			
1780			
1770			
1760			
1750			
1740			
1730			
1720			

FIGURE 9.4   A study of dated New England tombstones shows that the changes in popularity of particular styles is aptly described by battleship-shaped curves, and it supports assumptions used in both stylistic seriation and frequency seriation. The outer ring shows the gradual change in one motif, the death's head. (After *Invitation to Archaeology* by James Deetz. Copyright © 1967 by James Deetz. Used by permission of Doubleday, a division of Bantam Doubleday Dell Publishing Group, Inc.)

To seriate an artifact collection—let us say a set of surface sherd collections from a number of different sites in a valley—the archaeologist can construct a battleship-shaped curve diagram using a technique described by James Ford. On a sheet of graph paper, the researcher designates

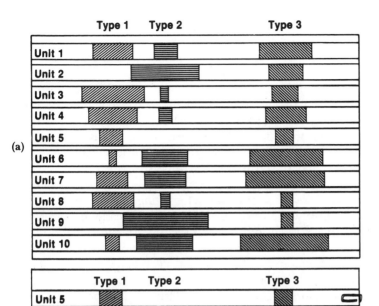

FIGURE 9.5 The archaeologist can seriate an artifact collection by taking strips of paper that graphically record type frequencies for each provenience unit (a) and by finding the arrangement of the strips that yields a set of battleship-shaped curves (b). (After Ford, Pan American Union, General Secretariat, Organization of American States, 1962.)

vertical lines or positions to represent the types in the collections, and horizontal rows or positions to represent individual collections from the various sites, each containing one or several of the range of types (Fig. 9.5). Each horizontal row is marked with a bar for each type represented; the horizontal extent of the bar indicates the percentage of that collection accounted for by that type. When all collections have been tallied for all types, the paper is cut into horizontal strips. The strips—each standing for a different collection or, in this case, a different site—are then physically ordered and reordered by hand until the order is found that best approximates battleship patterns. Of course, the archaeologist must also have some idea of which end of the resulting seriation is "up"—that is, which is the earlier end and which the later. In most cases, comparisons with established sequences will provide this information. Computer programs have been developed to facilitate the search for the best arrangement to reflect chronology. Indeed, several computer-based seriation techniques

Frequency seriation method: James Ford

have been worked out; see the Guide to Further Reading. Overall, seriation must be cross-checked against stratigraphy and absolute dates whenever possible and requires additional information to indicate which end is "early" and which is "late."

Seriation in historical times: Colonial pipes

Under some conditions, a seriation can be converted from a relative to an absolute means of dating. Clay smoking pipes in colonial sites of North America have provided evidence of sequential change in a number of attributes, including stem thickness, stem length, and aspects of the pipe bowl. Historical records allowed archaeologists to match the series of such changes to firm and reasonably limited time spans. Because these and other pipe attributes changed fairly quickly, the pipe fragments could thus potentially furnish a very sensitive index for dating colonial archaeological deposits. But there was a catch: Because they were easily breakable, the pipes were frequently replaced; this left them well represented in the archaeological record, but the parts that survived most often—fragments from any part of a pipe stem—seldom included the pertinent attributes. In 1954, however, J. C. Harrington proposed that focusing on the diameter of the pipe stem *hole* could solve the dilemma: Not only did this diameter decrease at a fairly constant rate between the early 1600s and the late 1700s, thus making the sequence an easy one to fit pipes into, but also the critical measurement could be made on any portion of a stem of any length.

In 1961, Lewis Binford derived from Harrington's work a formula for estimating the mean (statistical average) age of a sample of pipe stems made before 1780, a calculation that would, in turn, approximate the median age (midpoint of the time span) of a particular deposit or site. But then work at Martin's Hundred—a locality described in Chapter 1—yielded a dramatic reminder of the limits of the technique. A trash pit in one of the more interesting, but then undated, areas yielded abundant artifacts including more than 200 pipe stems. Binford's formula suggested a median date of around 1619 for the pipe stems, and therefore for the pit deposit as a whole. But, on reaching the lowest, and therefore earliest, levels of the pit, archaeologist Noël Hume found a potsherd with a clearly marked date of 1631! This evidence provides a terminus post quem (TPQ) date a minimum of 12 years later than that suggested by Binford's formula.

Although a discrepancy of 12 years sounds small, it presents a problem when judged against the kind of dating precision often possible in historical archaeology. Yet it does not mean that Binford's formula should be discarded: It did yield an approximate age for the collection of pipe stems. Other factors, however, affected the broader utility of the date in the Martin's Hundred case. First, the formula has been found to be most reliable for materials made between 1680 and 1760, so the earliness of this set of pipes may have skewed the age estimate somewhat. More important, though, is the relation between the objects being dated directly (the pipe stems) and those dated indirectly (pit contents as a whole, dated by association with the pipe fragments). The 1631 TPQ date provided by the sherd indicates clearly that deposition of trash into the pit had not begun until a decade or more after the pipes had been manufactured. The lesson is that there are limits to this—as to any—dating technique, and archaeologists must always keep these in mind.

Sequence Comparison

If seriation is not feasible, the archaeologist has another recourse for constructing a temporal sequence. If other well-documented artifact sequences exist in the geographical area being investigated, the artifact classes in question may be compared with those already defined from nearby sites and placed into a temporal order corresponding to those already established. This comparative method, however, makes the assumption that some past cultural connections, such as trade, did exist and that the resemblances are therefore not accidental. Furthermore, even if connections can be documented, two similar types or modes may not be exactly contemporaneous. The work of Deetz and Dethlefsen, for example, showed that even among colonial communities as close together as Plymouth, Concord, and Cambridge, Massachusetts, the temporal limits to the occurrence of tombstone motifs were rather variable (see Fig. 9.4). Because of these difficulties, the comparative method is usually the weakest means for inferring a local chronological sequence; it should be used only when other means are impossible.

Sequence comparison is very useful, however, for building broad areal chronologies. By matching sequences already established for individual sites or regions, archaeologists produce the time–space grids important to culture historical interpretation, as discussed in Chapter 3. These time–space grids allow identification of trends and regularities in cultural change and stability across broad expanses of space and time. Summaries of comparative chronologies are available in volumes edited by Robert Ehrich (Old World) and R. E. Taylor and Clement Meighan (New World).

GEOLOGICAL AND GEOCHEMICAL AGE DETERMINATION

The age of archaeological materials can sometimes be assessed by their association with geological deposits or formations. Often these assessments are relative, for instance, in cases based on the rule of superposition, which states that materials in lower strata were deposited earlier than those higher up. But sometimes geologists have determined the age of geological formations using radiometric or other techniques; these allow the archaeologist to assign an approximate date to artifacts found with such deposits. Geological dating of archaeological materials is thus often indirect, requiring valid association in primary contexts.

Geochronology

The effects of long-term geological processes such as glacial advance and retreat or fluctuations in land and sea levels can sometimes be useful in dating archaeological remains. If the chronology of the geological events is known, then the associated archaeological materials can be fitted into that scheme. For instance, changes in sea level related to the cyclical advance and retreat of glaciers during the **Pleistocene** (Ice Age) had marked effects on the action of rivers on their beds. In general, as sea levels fall (or land levels rise), rivers increase their down-cutting action; on the other hand, a rise in sea level encourages deposition or terrace building. Sequences of erosion and deposition have been worked out for a number of river valleys, especially in Europe, and in some cases archaeological materials or fossil human remains can be dated by their association with geological features of known position within a sequence. The "Heidelberg jaw," for example, a complete *Homo erectus* mandible (lower jaw) found by German gravel-pit workers in 1907, has been dated by its location in the "Mauer sands," a known feature of the sequence of Rhine river terraces. The Mauer sands, in turn, were fixed in time—during the interglacial period about 500,000 years ago—by both faunal and radiometric dating techniques.

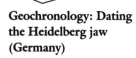

Geochronology: Dating the Heidelberg jaw (Germany)

The dating of archaeological remains by association with a particular geological deposit or formation, as in the Heidelberg case, is most commonly done with extremely old sites. For example, archaeologists and physical anthropologists interested in the remains of early hominids are working closely with geologists and others in reconstructing the environment and prehistory of the past several million years in the Rift Valley of East Africa. The latter group of scholars are basically the "producers" of the chronology for this work, and the archaeologists and physical anthropologists are the "consumers." As the subject of study moves closer to the present, archaeologists turn increasingly to other means of dating. In fact, Frederick Zeuner notes that for later periods, especially after 3000 B.C. or so, the producer/consumer roles may sometimes be reversed: Geological features may be assigned dates for their association with "known" archaeological materials!

Geochronology: Sequence of beaches at Cape Krusenstern, Alaska

Even in attempting to date relatively recent remains, however, the archaeologist will find an understanding of geological processes very useful. For example, the successive formation of post-Pleistocene shorelines at Cape Krusenstern, Alaska, provided J. Louis Giddings with a means of chronologically ordering sites. As the beach expanded seaward through time, people continued to locate their camps near its high-water limit or crest. In this progression, the younger beaches—and, through association with them, the more recent sites—are those located closer to the current beachfront. Today, more than 100 old beachlines are discernible at Cape Krusenstern, representing some 5000 years of accumulation (Fig. 9.6). Through this beach sequence—which some have called **horizontal stra-**

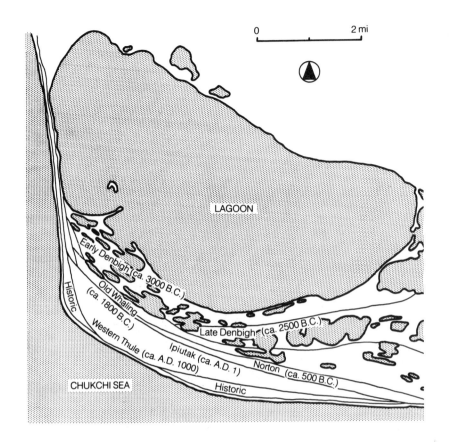

0   2 mi

LAGOON

Early Denbigh (ca. 3000 B.C.)

Old Whaling (ca. 1800 B.C.)

Historic

Western Thule (ca. A.D. 1000)

Late Denbigh (ca. 2500 B.C.)

Ipiutak (ca. A.D. 1)

Norton (ca. 500 B.C.)

CHUKCHI SEA

Historic

FIGURE 9.6 This map of Cape Krusenstern, Alaska, emphasizes some of the series of ancient beach ridges that have been related to particular periods of occupation during the last 5000 years. (Redrawn from *Ancient Men of the Sea* by J. Louis Giddings. © estate of J. Louis Giddings, New York: Alfred A. Knopf, Inc., 1967.)

tigraphy—Giddings arranged the sites in temporal order. By applying other dating techniques, he then converted the relative dating to an absolute scheme.

Varve Accumulation

In the case of the Cape Krusenstern beaches, accumulation of new land surfaces has proceeded at varying rates through time. It is sometimes possible, however, to find geological processes that follow a calculable rate. Such is the case with **varves,** the paired layers of outwash deposited in glacial lakes by retreating ice sheets. The first to recognize that this phenomenon could be used for assessing age was a Swedish researcher, Baron Gerard de Geer, in the late 1870s. He noted a regular alternation between coarser silts, deposited by glacial meltwater in the summer, and finer clays, deposits of suspended particles that settled during the winter months when the lakes were covered with ice. The recurring pattern of coarse and fine sediments could be read as a yearly record of glacial discharge

Varve dating: Ertebölle sites in Finland

FIGURE 9.7 Varves are sediment layers deposited by melting glaciers. When the ice retreated to position A, the sediments contained in the melted waters settled to form the lowermost varves. In successive years, more sediments were deposited, each varve extending horizontally to the point where that winter halted the glacier's thaw and representing in thickness the amount of glacial discharge. When varves from several glacial lakes have been recorded, they can be correlated, to create a master sequence for an area. (After Zeuner 1958.)

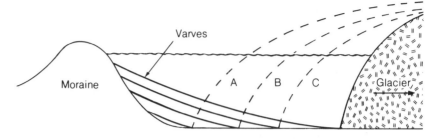

(Fig. 9.7), and, by moving back in time from a recent layer of known age, researchers could establish an absolutely dated sequence of varves. The thickness of the varve pairs varies from year to year, depending on the amount of glacial melting; this gives the sequence recognizable landmarks and allows sequences from different bodies of water to be linked. Through

FIGURE 9.8 Map of an area of southern Finland where varve analysis has indirectly provided a date for many of the Ertebölle sites by dating the shoreline with which they are associated. Note that the Ertebölle sites are on or near ancient shorelines rather than present-day shores. (After Zeuner 1958.)

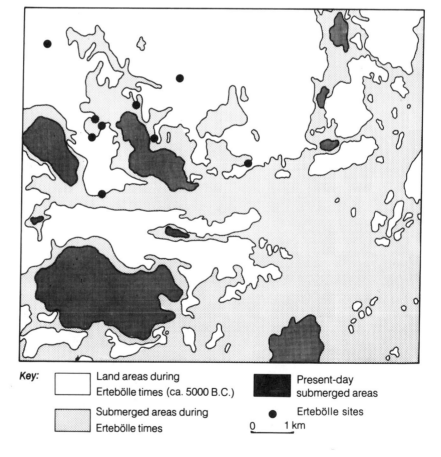

Key:
- ☐ Land areas during Ertebölle times (ca. 5000 B.C.)
- ░ Submerged areas during Ertebölle times
- ■ Present-day submerged areas
- ● Ertebölle sites
- 0   1 km

such links, the varve record in Scandinavia has been extended back some 12,000 years and has been used to chart changes in sea level in the Baltic region. By providing dates for some ancient shorelines, the varve sequence has also indirectly yielded dates for sites associated with those shorelines. For example, sites of the Ertebölle culture in Finland are found only at or above a shoreline dating to about 5000 B.C. (Fig. 9.8). After that time the waterline dropped, but Ertebölle sites are not found on this newly exposed land. Varve sequences have also been established for other parts of the world, including North America, South America, and East Africa; however, these are much shorter than the Scandinavian sequence.

Obsidian Hydration

It has long been observed that the surfaces of many geological materials undergo chemical alteration through time. These weathering reactions create a visibly distinct surface layer or *patina*. Among stones that are subject to such changes are flint and obsidian, common raw materials for prehistoric stone tools. Because the amount or degree of patination has been assumed to be a function of time, some archaeologists have used the observed patina as a rough guide to the relative age of stone artifacts. However, we now know that patina formation is a complex process that seems to follow no consistent rate of accretion. In fact, even as a clue to relative age, the amount of visible patina is not a reliable indicator.

Another kind of change also affects the surface of obsidian, however, and this one *can* be related to a time scale. In 1960, Irving Friedman and Robert L. Smith announced a new age determination technique based on the cumulative *hydration*, or absorption of water, by obsidian. Over time, the water forms a hydration layer at the surface of the obsidian (Fig. 9.9). This layer is measured in microns (μ) ($1\mu = 0.001$ mm) and is detectable microscopically. Since the hydration layer penetrates deeper into the surface through time, the thickness of this layer can be used to determine the amount of time that the surface has been exposed. In other words, the age of manufacture or use—either of which could fracture the obsidian, exposing a new surface for hydration—can be calculated if the rate of hydration (expressed as μ^2 per unit of time) is known. Once this rate is established, the thickness of the hydration layer from a given obsidian sample can be compared with a chronological conversion table to determine the sample's age.

Unfortunately, since the method was originally applied, problems have emerged that have somewhat diminished its early promise, especially as an absolute technique. First, we now know that the hydration rate varies with the composition of the obsidian. Since each obsidian deposit was formed under slightly different conditions, it has slightly different characteristics.

Interior of obsidian specimen   Hydration zone

FIGURE 9.9 In this magnified view, the 3μ-wide hydration zone appears as a wide band at the edge of the obsidian. (From Michels 1973; by permission of the author and Seminar Press.)

Therefore, this method of age determination can be applied to a given sample only if the source of the sample can be identified and if its particular hydration rate is known. Also calculation of hydration rates is difficult: They must be worked out by measuring the hydration of a series of known-age samples, such as obsidian artifacts whose age has been determined indirectly by association with radiocarbon-dated materials. This means not only that we lack a single, globally applicable hydration rate but also that archaeologists cannot assume, as they did initially, that all obsidian from a single site can be dated using a single rate. Many sites contain obsidian brought in from several different obsidian sources, and these will absorb water at different rates.

A more complicated problem has emerged with the realization that the hydration rate also changes through time, in response to variations in the temperature conditions to which the obsidian has been subjected. Unless these rate fluctuations are known, accurate age determination by obsidian hydration is difficult at best. For some areas, correction factors have been worked out on the basis of a long sequence of known-age samples. But since such sequences of known-age samples are difficult to accumulate, most areas of the world do not yet have a reliable means to assess hydration rates accurately.

In Chapter 5 we discussed the use of obsidian dates at Copán, Honduras, where the results indicate that domestic occupation continued long after the demise of the traditional political system. This and other examples indicate that **obsidian hydration** holds great promise as an accurate, simple, and inexpensive means to determine the age of obsidian artifacts directly. Even if its potential as an absolute technique has yet to be fully realized, it can often be used as a relative method within a single site or region. However, its potential can be realized only when the variations resulting from composition and environmental conditions are fully controlled.

FAUNAL AND FLORAL AGE DETERMINATION

Archaeological dating methods involving floral and faunal material fall into two categories. One entails application of analytic techniques designed to indicate when an *individual organism* died or how long it has been in the ground. We will discuss several of these techniques, such as dendrochronology and fluorine dating.

Faunal Association

The other general category involves dating simply by identification of the *species* present. Many animals have (or had) a rather restricted existence in time and space; they are called **index species.** Faunal remains of various species, from insects to elephants, have been used as markers for particular time periods. For example, the sequence of elephant species in Europe has been used to divide the Pleistocene into three periods:

1. *Elephas primigenius:* Upper Pleistocene (ca. 200,000 to 20,000 B.C.)
2. *Elephas antiquus:* Middle Pleistocene (ca. 700,000 to 200,000 B.C.)
3. *Elephas meridionalis:* Lower Pleistocene (ca. 2,000,000 to 700,000 B.C.)

In the New World, too, such **faunal associations** are sometimes important. One notable case was the 1926 discovery near Folsom, New Mexico, of stone projectile points in association with the bones of an extinct bison (see Fig. 4.1, p. 115). Human presence in the New World was, at the time, widely believed to be restricted to the last 3000 to 4000 years. But since the type of bison found in the Folsom site had died out by 8000 B.C., its association with these artifacts was clear evidence that people had been in the New World for at least 10,000 years.

Dating by faunal associations: Folsom, New Mexico

Presence of particular floral species is more often an indication of past local climatic conditions than, directly speaking, of dates. Particular plant species are often sensitive indicators of temperature and humidity conditions, as well as whether an area was covered by forest or grassland. Stratified palynological (pollen) data have been used to reconstruct climate and general environmental sequences in a number of places, especially in Europe; in those areas, pollen recovered from an archaeological site can indicate the site's position in the climate sequence, thereby indirectly placing it in time.

The dating inferences in the preceding examples rely on the occurrence of particular faunal *species* in an archaeological deposit. Let us now consider several dating techniques that involve direct technical analyses of the *individual* faunal or floral specimens encountered in an archaeological context.

Dendrochronology

The best-known method of directly determining absolute age for floral materials is **dendrochronology,** an approach based on counting the annual growth rings observable in the cross-section of cut trees. This means of determining the age of a tree has been known for centuries; it was even used fairly commonly in the 19th century to date archaeological features. In 1848, for instance, Squier and Davis reasoned that the minimum age of mounds in the Mississippi Valley could be ascertained by learning the age of the oldest trees growing on the ruins. Assuming that trees would not be allowed to grow on mounds before abandonment of the site, one could say that if the oldest tree growing on a site were 300 years old, the site itself had to be at least that old.

Early dendrochronology technique: Squier and Davis (Mississippi Valley mounds)

The modern method of dendrochronology involves a refinement of such tree-ring counts. The basic refinement is the cross-linkage of ring-growth patterns among trees to extend a sequence of growth cycles into

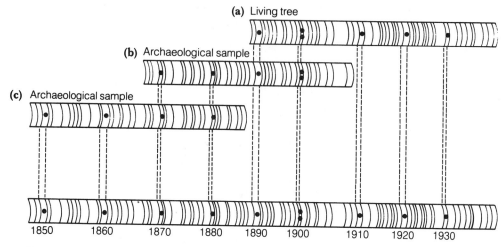

Reconstructed master sequence

FIGURE 9.10 Like a varve sequence, a master dendrochronological sequence is built by linking successively older specimens, often beginning with living trees (a) that overlap with archaeological samples (b, c) based on matching patterns of thick and thin rings. Provided the sequence is long enough, specimens of unknown age can be dated by comparison with the master sequence. The rings are marked with dots at 10-year intervals for ease of reading. (After Bannister 1970.)

the past, far beyond the lifetime of a single tree (Fig. 9.10). The compilation of a long-term sequence of tree-ring growth patterns is analogous to the development of the varve sequence; it was first established by an astronomer, A. E. Douglass, working in the southwestern United States in the first decades of the 20th century. Douglass's original research was aimed at relating past climatic cycles—as reflected in cycles of wider and narrower tree-ring growth—to sunspot cycles. Although variations in tree-ring growth do provide valuable clues to past climatic cycles, the additional usefulness of this method in establishing an absolute chronological sequence was soon realized. By counting back from a known starting point, the tree-ring segment could be projected back for thousands of years; a given tree segment could be dated by matching to a part of the known sequence. In the case of the bristlecone pine in southeastern California, the record spans more than 8000 years. As we shall see, the bristlecone pine has been archaeologically important in the refinement of radiocarbon dating; it is not, however, generally found in archaeological sites. Other species, such as the Ponderosa pine, do not provide as long a total record as the bristlecone pine but are more often found in archaeological contexts and so are more often useful for dendrochronological dating of these deposits.

This method has been of prime importance for establishing a chronological sequence in the southwestern United States. Although it is potentially useful anywhere in the world where trees were used by prehistoric peoples, dendrochronology has in fact been applied in only a few parts of the world: the southwestern United States, Alaska, northern Mexico, Germany, Norway, Great Britain, and Switzerland. The method has found only limited use because it depends on the presence of four conditions that cannot everywhere be met. First, the proper kind of tree must be present: The species must produce well-defined annual rings and be sensitive to minute variations in climatic cycles. Many species of trees produce roughly uniform rings regardless of small changes in climate. Regional variations in climate also prevent comparison of tree-ring sequences from one area to another. Second, the ring-growth variation must depend primarily on one environmental factor, such as temperature or soil humidity. Third, the prehistoric population must have made extensive use of wood, especially in construction. Finally, cultural and environmental conditions must allow for good archaeological preservation of tree segments.

Dendrochronology determines the age of a tree by placing its last or outermost growth ring within a local sequence. This date represents the time when the tree was cut; if the outermost ring is missing from the tree sample, the cutting date cannot be certainly assessed. But even if a tree can be assigned a cutting date, that may or may not be related to the time when the tree was used. The validity of an archaeological date based on dendrochronology also depends on correct assessment of the archaeological context and association of the wood. Wood specimens that form parts of construction features—and that are therefore in primary context—are more reliable. Even so, Bryant Bannister has listed four types of errors in interpreting tree-ring dates, three of them involving wood used as a construction element.

1. The wood may be reused and therefore older in date than the construction in which it was used.

2. Use of the construction feature—house or whatever—may have extended well beyond its construction date, so that the wood is older than this use date.

3. Old, weakened beams may have been replaced by newer, stronger ones, so that the wood is younger than the original construction.

4. Wooden artifacts or ecofacts found within a construction feature—such as furniture or charcoal in a house—may be younger or older than the building date for the feature.

To help offset these problems, the archaeologist should try to recover multiple samples for dendrochronological analysis. The dates from the various specimens can then be used to check each other: Good agreement among several samples relating to the same feature creates a strong presumption that the date is correct.

Dendrochronology offers the archaeologist the rare opportunity of specifying a date that is accurate to the year, sometimes even to the season. If used correctly and with appropriate caution, it is indeed a precise and valuable dating tool.

Bone Age Determination

Several techniques are available for determining the age of bone specimens. These techniques can be used to date bone ecofacts, including human skeletal material, as well as bone artifacts. Some of the techniques yield relative dates, but absolute determinations can be made by radiocarbon dating of bone collagen.

The relative age determinations enable the archaeologist to determine whether bones found in the same matrix were indeed deposited together. The fundamental premise involved is that a given bone will lose organic components, principally nitrogen, and gain inorganic components, such as fluorine and uranium, at the same rate as other bones buried at the same time in the same deposit. Nitrogen is a component in bone collagen that begins to be depleted when the organism dies; fluorine and uranium, on the other hand, are absorbed by the bone from groundwater through a process of chemical substitution. Within a single deposit, then, a bone with more nitrogen, less fluorine, and less uranium will be younger than a bone with less nitrogen, more fluorine, and more uranium. Since the rates of nitrogen depletion and fluorine accretion vary on the basis of such local environmental conditions as temperature and humidity, the rates are not the same for separate deposits. Thus the method cannot be used to establish absolute dates. Two bones from different sites but with the same relative amounts of nitrogen and fluorine *cannot* be assumed to be of the same age, since the depletion and accumulation rates will not have been the same. Nitrogen and fluorine measurements are, however, useful for distinguishing whether any of the bones in a single deposit are younger (intrusive) or older (redeposited) than the rest.

The classic demonstrations of the usefulness of these relative dating techniques concerned evaluations of some human skeletal remains of disputed antiquity. The first was the Galley Hill skeleton, reported in 1888; it was said to have come from the Swanscombe gravels of the Thames River, from an undisturbed context that had also produced Lower Paleolithic tools and fossil bones of extinct mammals. The importance of the Galley Hill skeleton was that it seemed to indicate that anatomically modern humans already existed very early in the Pleistocene, thereby contradicting the evolutionary evidence of the rest of the human fossil record. Fluorine measurements made in 1948 by Kenneth Oakley finally settled the 60-year-old controversy by demonstrating that the Galley Hill bones contained far too little fluorine to be contemporary with the fossil animal bones (Table 9.2). The same tests indicated, however, that the Swanscombe skull, an anatomically "earlier" hominid from the same gravel deposit, did have fluorine and nitrogen contents appropriately equivalent to those of the extinct mammals, thus confirming its position in the evolutionary record.

The great Piltdown hoax was unmasked by the same methods. The Piltdown finds, unearthed between 1911 and 1915, revealed an apelike

Bone age determination: Galley Hill and Swanscombe, England

Table 9.2   Fluorine and Nitrogen Content of the Galley Hill Skeleton, the Swanscombe Skull, and Other Bones

Remains	Percentage of Fluorine	Percentage of Nitrogen
Neolithic skull, Coldrum, Kent	0.3	1.9
Galley Hill skeleton	0.5	1.6
Swanscombe skull	1.7	Traces
Bones of fossil mammals from Swanscombe gravels	1.5	Traces

SOURCE: After Oakley 1970, Table A, p. 38.

jawbone apparently paired with a modern-looking human cranium. Over-all, the two were anatomically mismatched, but the geological evidence, combined with the uniformly discolored appearance of age in all the bones and some hominid characteristics in the otherwise apelike jaw, soon convinced all but a few disbelievers that "Piltdown man" represented a significant new discovery, altering conceptions about the course of human evolution. The skeptics, however, finally prevailed. In 1950, Oakley tested the bones for fluorine content and later for nitrogen; he found that the jaw was markedly younger than the cranium (Table 9.3). Uranium tests reinforced these findings. On further examination, the "hominid" aspects of the jaw were shown to be due to deliberate alteration of a modern chimpanzee jaw. The whole forgery was publicly unraveled in 1953 by Oakley, J. S. Weiner, and Sir Wilfred E. LeGros Clark.

Piltdown hoax exposed by bone age determinations

Table 9.3   Fluorine, Nitrogen, and Uranium Content of Piltdown and Related Bones

Remains	Percentage of Fluorine	Percentage of Nitrogen	Uranium Parts per Million
Fresh bone	0.03	4.0	0
Piltdown fossil elephant molar	2.7	—	610
Piltdown cranium	0.1	1.4	1
Piltdown jaw	0.03	3.9	0

SOURCE: After Oakley 1970, Table B, p. 41.

Table 9.4 Half-Lives and Utility Ranges of Radioactive Isotopes

Isotopes	Half-Life (in years)	Limits of Usefulness for Archaeological Dating
$^{14}C \rightarrow {}^{14}N$ (Radiocarbon) (Cambridge half-life)	5730 ± 40	Normally 100,000 years and younger
^{230}Th & ^{231}Pa (Uranium series)	—	Normally 50,000–500,000
$^{40}K \rightarrow {}^{40}Ar$ (Potassium–Argon)	$1,300,000,000 \pm 40,000,000$ $(.04 \times 10^9)$	100,000 years and older
$^{235}U \rightarrow {}^{207}Pb$ (Uranium-235–Lead)	ca. 700,000,000	Too slow to be of archaeological value
$^{238}U \rightarrow {}^{206}Pb$ (Uranium-238–Lead)	ca. 4,500,000,000	Too slow to be of archaeological value
$^{232}Th \rightarrow {}^{208}Pb$ (Thorium–Lead)	ca. 14,000,000,000	Too slow to be of archaeological value
$^{87}Rb \rightarrow {}^{87}Sr$ (Rubidium–Strontium)	ca. 50,000,000,000	Too slow to be of archaeological value

RADIOMETRIC AGE DETERMINATION

A variety of age determination techniques exploit the principle of radio-active decay—transformation of unstable radioactive isotopes into stable elements. These methods are all usually termed **radiometric** techniques. Although they can sometimes be used to date archaeological materials directly, they more frequently provide indirect age determinations. The radiometric technique most commonly used by archaeologists is **radiocarbon age determination;** the following discussion will emphasize this particular technique. Most other radiometric techniques are applicable to extremely long time spans (Table 9.4), usually beyond the time range of human existence. They are used mainly by geologists to determine the age of geological formations.

The physical properties of radioactive decay can be used for dating purposes only if three facts are known: (1) the original amount of the radioactive isotope present at the onset of decay; (2) the amount now present; and (3) the rate of radioactive decay. In most cases, the first factor cannot be directly determined, but it can be computed as the sum of the radioactive material now present plus the amount of the "daughter" isotope—the stable residue of the decay process. The amount of the radioactive isotope now present is "counted" directly, using different methods according to the isotope being measured. The decay of any unstable isotope is a random

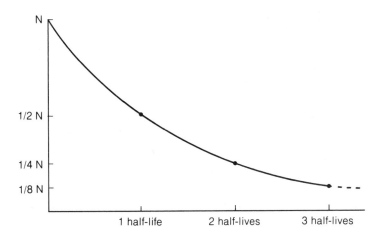

FIGURE 9.11 The decay rate of a radioactive isotope is expressed by its half-life, or the period after which half of the radioactive isotopes will have decayed into more stable forms. After two half-lives, only one-quarter of the original amount of radioactive isotopes will remain, and by the end of the third half-life, only one-eighth ($\frac{1}{2} \times \frac{1}{2} \times \frac{1}{2}$) will remain radioactive.

process, so (except for directly counted radiocarbon) there is really no strictly determinable rate; it is possible, however, to calculate the statistical probability that a certain proportion of the isotope will disintegrate within a given time (Fig. 9.11). This disintegration rate is usually expressed as the **half-life** of the isotope—the period required for one-half of the unstable atoms to disintegrate and form the stable daughter isotope. It is important to remember that the half-life of any radioactive isotope does not represent an absolute rate but, rather, a statistical average with a range of error that can be specified.

Radiocarbon Age Determination

One of the effects of the bombardment of the earth's atmosphere by cosmic rays (n) is the production of ^{14}C, the radioactive isotope of carbon from nonradioactive nitrogen (^{14}N):

$$^{14}N + n \longrightarrow {}^{14}C + {}^{1}H$$

This heavy, radioactive isotope of carbon (radiocarbon) is, however, unstable. It decays by releasing a beta particle to return to the stable ^{14}N form:

$$^{14}C \longrightarrow \beta^- + {}^{14}N$$

The extremely small quantities of ^{14}C distribute evenly through the atmosphere, and they combine with oxygen in the same way as normal carbon to form carbon dioxide. Through photosynthesis, carbon dioxide enters the chemistry of plants, which are in turn eaten by animals; thus all living things constantly take in both ordinary carbon—^{12}C—and ^{14}C throughout their lifetimes. The proportion of ^{14}C to ^{12}C in an organism remains constant until its death. At that point, however, no further ^{14}C is taken in, and the radioactive carbon present at that time undergoes its normal decrease through the process of radioactive decay. Thus measurement of the amount of ^{14}C still present (and emitting radiation) in plant and animal remains enables us to determine the time elapsed since death. In other words, by calculating the difference between the amount originally present and that now present, and comparing that difference with the known rate of decay, we can compute the time passed in years. The radiocarbon decay rate is expressed in a half-life of about 5730 ± 40 years, and the amount of ^{14}C present in a fresh, contemporary organic specimen emits beta particles at a rate of about 15 particles per minute per gram of carbon (15 cpm/g). By comparison, a sample with an emission count of about 7.5 cpm/g would be about 5730 years old, since that is the amount of time necessary for one-half of the original radioactive material to disintegrate. After about 22,920 years, or four half-lives, the emission rate will be less than 1 cpm/g.

Any archaeological specimen of organic origin is potentially appropriate for direct radiocarbon dating. Charcoal from burned materials, such as that found in ancient hearths or fire pits, is most commonly used, but unburned organic material such as bone collagen, wood, seeds, shells, and leather—sometimes even the carbon in worked iron—can also be dated. Most of the unburned materials require larger sample amounts because they contain a smaller proportion of carbon (Table 9.5).

Laboratories vary in the size of samples they can handle; the estimates for the conventional method are listed in Table 9.5. Any sample to be used for radiocarbon age determination should be kept free from contamination by modern carbon, which would cause an erroneous age measurement. To avoid contamination, excavators should refrain from excessive handling of the material to be dated, preferably touching it only with glass

Table 9.5 Recommended Minimum Amounts of Sample for Conventional Radiocarbon Dating

Sample Material	Minimum Amount (in grams)
Charcoal or wood	25
Ivory	50
Peat	50–200
Organic/earth mixtures	100
Shell	100
Bone	Up to 300

FIGURE 9.12 Determining age by conventional radiocarbon analysis requires (left) facilities to purify and convert the sample into carbon dioxide (CO_2) and (right) a counter to measure its current radioactivity. (© Nicholas Hartmann, MASCA, The University Museum, University of Pennsylvania.)

or metal tools, such as a trowel. Samples should be sealed immediately in clean protective containers. Of course, obvious impurities such as earth, roots, and twigs should be removed; the technicians at the radiocarbon laboratory will remove other impurities before measuring the ^{14}C. The final step in preparing the sample for shipment to the laboratory is labeling with descriptive information, including when, where, and how the material was recovered as well as the excavator's estimate of probable age.

At the radiocarbon laboratory (Fig. 9.12), after the sample is further cleaned and purified, one of two procedures may be followed. In the conventional method, developed in the late 1940s by Willard F. Libby, the amount of ^{14}C is detected by Geiger counters that measure the rate of beta particle emission from the sample, usually for a period of 24 hours. The most recent refinement uses accelerator mass spectrometry (AMS), which allows the physicist to directly measure the amount of ^{14}C in a sample. Although fewer laboratories are equipped to use the newer AMS technique, it offers significant advantages, since it is nondestructive and dates can be obtained from much smaller samples. This means that items such as seeds, which are too small for the conventional method, can be dated and not destroyed in the process. Results obtained from either method are then converted to an age determination. Besides reporting the determinations to the original excavators, many laboratories also publish their "dates" in a specialized journal called *Radiocarbon*.

Radiocarbon age determination has revolutionized both archaeology and geology. It provided the first means of relating dates and sequences on a worldwide basis, because, unlike varves, style dating, and other methods available at the time, it did not rely on local conditions. The great

Table 9.6   Present Proportions of Carbon Isotopes on Earth

Isotope	Percentage of Carbon on Earth
^{12}C	98.85
^{13}C	1.15
^{14}C	.000 000 000 107 (1.07×10^{-10})

wave of enthusiasm it generated, however, led to uncritical acceptance and overconfidence in the precision of radiocarbon "dates." Although radiocarbon age determination is still the most popular method and among the most useful of all dating techniques available to the archaeologist, it does have a number of limitations that must be clearly understood to assess the reliability of radiocarbon "dates."

The first limitation derives from the small amount of ^{14}C available for detection (Table 9.6). For the conventional method, after seven half-life periods, or about 40,110 years, the beta particle emission rate is so low (about 0.1 cpm/g) that detection above normal background radioactivity has until recently been impossible. Thus, most laboratories figure that 40,000 years is the upper limit to radiocarbon age determination. Under special circumstances (and at extraordinary expense), the time range of radiocarbon dating can be extended to about 70,000 years by a technique known as "isotopic enrichment." The AMS method offers the possibility that dating can be carried back to about 100,000 years, because the radiocarbon is directly identified, which allows far smaller amounts to be detected.

The second factor that limits radiocarbon age determination is the built-in uncertainty inherent in all radiometric techniques. The decay of a given atom of ^{14}C into ^{14}N is a random event, so both the beta particle emission rate of a measured carbon sample and the half-life by which its age is then calculated are no more than averages and estimates. As an illustration of this difficulty, Table 9.7 lists several determinations for ^{14}C half-life. Most authorities today, however, accept the Cambridge estimate of 5730 ± 40 years as the most accurate; the Libby dates can easily be converted by multiplying them by 1.03. But any reported half-life and any calculated radiocarbon "age" expresses the built-in imprecision of the techniques by giving a time range rather than an exact date. Thus a radiocarbon age of 3220 ± 50 years B.P. ("before present"—which, for radiocarbon dates *only,* means before 1950) means *not* that the analyzed sample died 3220 years ago but that there is a 67 percent probability—2 chances in 3—that the original organism died between 3170 and 3270 years before A.D. 1950. The probability that a reported range includes the right

Table 9.7 Selected Half-Life Determinations for ^{14}C

Estimate Source	Half-Life (in years)
Libby (1949)	5568 ± 30
Radiocarbon journal	5570 ± 30
Cambridge (1958)	5730 ± 40
New average (1961)	5735 ± 45

"date" can be improved to 97 percent by doubling the " ± " range—in this case from 50 to 100 years on either side of the central date; but for consistency, most reported dates use the 67 percent figure.

One consequence of these considerations is that a radiocarbon "date" is incomplete without a range figure and a statement of the particular half-life used in its calculation. Another implication is that an isolated age determination is weak evidence for chronological placement: Any given date has 1 chance in 3 of being wrong. Clusters of mutually confirming dates give much stronger evidence that the indicated age is correct.

A third limitation to the radiocarbon technique is the documented fluctuation of past levels of ^{14}C on earth. For instance, we know that the proportion of ^{12}C to ^{14}C has greatly increased since the 19th century because of the release of large amounts of fossil carbon from the burning of coal, oil, and gas. And, since the mid-20th century, the amount of ^{14}C has increased because of nuclear explosions. But neither of these effects should produce error in radiocarbon determinations if prior levels of ^{14}C remained constant. However, measurements of radiocarbon "dates" for wood samples whose ages were determined by dendrochronology have shown that fluctuations *did* occur in the past, probably because of differences in cosmic ray bombardment rates. The result is that beyond about 1500 B.C., radiocarbon age determinations begin to furnish dates that are increasingly out of line (Fig. 9.13).

At 1500 B.C., radiocarbon age determinations are about 150 years too young; by 4000 B.C., radiocarbon "dates" are about 700 years too young. The solution to this problem has emerged from the same source that exposed the error—dendrochronology. Extensive radiocarbon testing of known-age samples of wood, taken from specific growth rings of trees, has enabled investigators to define a correction factor for radiocarbon dates (Table 9.8). Use of a calibration formula allows a date given in radiocarbon years to be corrected to a more accurate time value. The correction tables are limited by our ability to secure known-age samples of wood; but use of the oldest living tree, the bristlecone pine found in southeastern

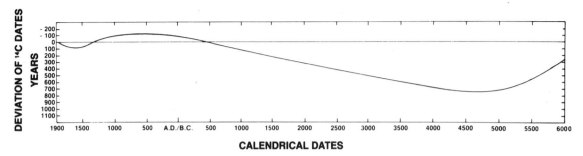

FIGURE 9.13 A representation of the discrepancy between the ideal ¹⁴C chronological scale (straight line) and a plotted series of samples, dated by radiocarbon analysis, whose age was independently determined by dendrochronology. The discrepancy is due to past fluctuations in the amount of ¹⁴C on earth. (After Michael 1985.)

California, has enabled scientists to extend the correction range back to 10,000 years B.P. (Fig. 9.14).

The final limitation to radiocarbon dating lies with the archaeologist: Any radiocarbon date is only as meaningful as the evaluation of the archaeological context from which it came. Charcoal from disturbed deposits—that is, from secondary contexts—will furnish dates, but these may have no bearing on the ages of associated materials. To use charcoal to date associated materials indirectly, the archaeologist must establish that all were actually deposited together.

Table 9.8   Examples of ¹⁴C Date Corrections

¹⁴C Date	Range or Midpoint for Corrected Date
A.D. 50	A.D. 130–110
A.D. 40	A.D. 130–110
A.D. 30	A.D. 110–90
A.D. 20	A.D. 100
A.D. 10	A.D. 90
A.D. 1/1 B.C.	A.D. 70
10 B.C.	A.D. 70
20 B.C.	A.D. 70
30 B.C.	A.D. 60
40 B.C.	A.D. 60
50 B.C.	A.D. 50

SOURCE: After Ralph, Michael, and Han 1973, Table 2.

FIGURE 9.14 The bristlecone pine, found in the White Mountains of California, is the longest-living tree species known and is the key to increasing the accuracy of age determinations using the radiocarbon method. (Photo by Henry N. Michael, courtesy of the Museum Applied Science Center for Archaeology, The University Museum, University of Pennsylvania.)

These considerations are serious ones that must be kept in mind in assessing chronological frameworks based on radiocarbon age determinations. But they are meant only as cautions, not as discouragement: Radiocarbon dating still provides archaeologists with one of their most valuable tools for establishing the age of archaeological materials. In fact, recent revisions and refinements in the radiocarbon technique have provided what Colin Renfrew has called the "second radiocarbon revolution." The first revolution was the development of a dating method that gave a uniform means to develop absolute chronologies applicable anywhere in the world; the second has been the realization of the archaeological implications, particularly in the Old World, of the dendrochronological calibrations that have revised many of the most ancient radiocarbon determinations, making them still older.

Before radiocarbon dating was available, Oscar Montelius, V. Gordon Childe, and others had used dating techniques based on stylistic and form comparisons to interrelate European and southwest Asian archaeological

Radiocarbon calibration: Revision of Old World sequences

sequences. Whenever a question arose about the source of an invention or innovation—such as copper metallurgy or the construction of megalithic (monumental stone) tombs—the usual assumption was that it had come from "civilized" southwest Asia to "barbaric" Europe. The first sets of radiocarbon dates seemed to support the chronological links based on those assumptions. Now, however, calibrated radiocarbon dates indicate that many of the interrelated elements, such as megalithic architecture, which had been considered the result of southwest Asian influence, actually occurred earlier in Europe! The traditional belief in a southwest Asian "monopoly" on innovation and cultural advance has been tossed aside, and archaeologists are now seriously reexamining interpretations of long-distance communication in the Old World in the last few millennia B.C.

Uranium Series Age Determination

Although a variety of radiometric age determination techniques have been developed (see Table 9.4), many of these are based on radioactive isotopes with half-lives that are too long to be of practical use to the archaeologist. For example, the half-lives of the two isotopes of uranium, ^{235}U and ^{238}U, provide dating techniques useful to geology rather than archaeology. But two daughter isotopes produced in the process, thorium (^{230}Th) and protactinium (^{231}Pa), have half-lives short enough to be used in archaeological age determination. The range for such dates is about 50,000 to 500,000 years, which generally lies outside the radiocarbon age span. Soluble in water, the uranium daughter isotopes may be deposited in limestone caves within the calcium carbonate that composes the familiar stalactites and stalagmites. Upon deposition, the radiometric clock is started, and the amounts of these uranium daughter isotopes then indicate the age of the calcium carbonate deposit. If such deposits are associated with bones or artifacts of early humans, as at several cave sites in Europe, they may be dated, providing indirect dates for the archaeological materials.

Potassium–Argon Age Determination

Another radiometric technique, **potassium–argon (K–Ar) age determination,** has been particularly helpful to archaeologists by yielding dates for the geological formations associated with fossil remains of early hominids. The original potassium–argon technique is based on the radioactive decay of a rare isotope of potassium (^{40}K) to form argon (^{40}Ar) gas. The half-life of ^{40}K is 1.31 billion years, but the method can be used to date materials as recent as 100,000 years old. The technique is used principally to determine ages for geological formations that contain potassium. The basic principles of radiometric age determination, already described for the radiocarbon method, are used with a rock sample to measure the ratio of ^{40}K to ^{40}Ar. With this information, the original amount of ^{40}K present can be determined; this figure and the ^{40}K half-life enable the investigator to calculate the time interval that has passed since the rock was formed.

Obviously, this method can be used only with rocks that contained no argon gas when they were formed; otherwise, the higher amount of ^{40}Ar would distort the calculations, producing a date far too old. For this reason, volcanic formations are best suited to the technique: The high temperatures characteristic of volcanism drive off accumulated argon in the process of forming the new rock. A complementary problem is that some minerals naturally lose ^{40}Ar through time, again distorting the measurements and producing an age determination that is too young. Examples include mica (which loses up to 20 percent of its ^{40}Ar) and feldspar (15–60 percent loss). As a result, only geological formations that retain ^{40}Ar can presently be used for reasonably accurate age determinations. Deposits of consolidated volcanic ash (tuff) are ideal candidates for this dating technique, because they contain no residual ^{40}Ar but do retain that produced by the decay of ^{40}K.

As noted above, the K–Ar technique has been particularly helpful in dating geological formations associated with the remains of fossil hominids and Lower Paleolithic tools. When Louis and Mary Leakey found the remains of *Zinjanthropus,* an early hominid now included in the genus *Australopithecus,* in Olduvai Gorge of Tanzania, they were able to assign the bones an age of about 1.75 million years on the basis of K–Ar dating of the volcanic tuff beds in which the remains were found. At the time (in the early 1960s), 1.75 million years was a much earlier date than most people were willing to accept for such a close evolutionary relative; so the Olduvai tuffs were subjected to another round of tests. These tests upheld the first set of dates, and thus an important chronological marker was set. More recently, K–Ar dates have been determined for tuffs associated with early hominid finds in the Lake Turkana/Omo Valley area on the border between Kenya and Ethiopia, extending the chronology of hominid existence back further than 2 million years.

A refinement of the K–Ar technique has been developed, which uses the ratio of ^{40}Ar to ^{39}Ar to calculate the age of the rock sample. Although this procedure is more complicated and expensive than the original one, it allows several age determinations to be made from each sample, thus increasing the reliability of the "date."

K–Ar dating: Olduvai Gorge, Tanzania

Fission Track Dating

The fission track method determines ages based on the natural splitting (fission) of ^{238}U atoms present in obsidian and other glassy volcanic materials, which leaves traces called *fission tracks.* These tracks can be detected by treating a prepared rock sample with hydrofluoric acid and then observing its surface under magnification (Fig. 9.15). Since fission tracks are erased if the mineral is heated above a critical temperature, the density of ^{238}U fission tracks is proportional to the time elapsed since the sample was last heated above this temperature. To assign an actual date, however, the analyst must also know the ^{238}U content of the mineral; this is measured

FIGURE 9.15 Photograph of fission tracks in obsidian, indicated by arrows, after etching with hydrofluoric acid. The other marks are scratches and bubbles. (Reprinted from *Dating Techniques for the Archaeologist,* edited by H. N. Michael and E. K. Ralph, by permission of The MIT Press, Cambridge, Massachusetts. Copyright © 1971 by the Massachusetts Institute of Technology.)

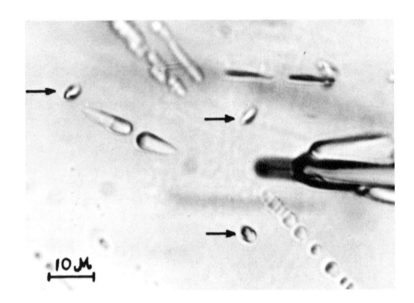

Fission track dating confirms Olduvai K–Ar dates

by bombarding the sample with a known dose of ^{238}U radiation. Once the ^{238}U content is known and the density of fission tracks determined, the analyst correlates the sample's fission track density with its estimated ^{238}U fission rate to assess its age. This age usually represents the time the rock was formed.

Like potassium–argon (K–Ar) age determination, the fission track method is most suitable for samples of great age: A sample usually requires at least 100,000 years to accumulate tracks dense enough to be measurable. Fission track dating has, for instance, been applied to pumice samples from Bed I at Olduvai Gorge, Tanzania—the same geological formation discussed with regard to K–Ar dating. Such dating by multiple methods is not redundant: Independently determined mutually confirming dates greatly increase the confidence the archaeologist can place in their reliability. At Olduvai, the **fission track age determination** for the pumice from Bed I was about 2 million years, well within the K–Ar range of 1.75 to 2.35 million years.

ARCHAEOMAGNETIC AGE DETERMINATION

Archaeomagnetic age determination relies on the fact that the earth's magnetic field varies through time, and that therefore the location of the magnetic north pole changes position. The location of magnetic north shifts in the horizontal plane, expressed as the *declination* angle, as well as vertically, expressed by the *dip* angle; the course of these shifts over the past few hundred years has been determined from compass readings pre-

FIGURE 9.16 Age determinations based on archaeomagnetism: (left) Careful collection and recording in the field are essential. One sample has been removed and preserved in the small square container to the left (above the leveling device); another is about to be removed (behind the compass). (right) The specialist measures and analyzes magnetic alignments in the laboratory later by replicating the original orientation of the sample. (Photo (l) Santa Barbara Project, Honduras; photo (r) M. Leon Lopez and Helga Teiwes, © 1967 National Geographic Society.)

served in historical records. Certain mineral compounds, such as clay, contain iron particles that may align to magnetic north just as a compass does. This occurs most readily when clay is heated above its *Curie point*—the critical temperature at which the particles lose their previous magnetic orientation. When the minerals cool again, the new magnetic alignment of the ferrous particles is "frozen" in the clay body. Thus if a sample of baked clay is not disturbed, it will preserve the angles of dip and declination from the time when it was heated. By using known-age samples of such fired clay, such as hearths dated by radiocarbon associations, archaeologists can trace the location of the magnetic pole into the past. Once enough archaeomagnetic samples with associated radiocarbon dates have been analyzed, the variations in angle of dip and declination can be matched to a time scale, allowing newly discovered fired-clay samples to be dated directly, using the archaeomagnetic data alone (Fig. 9.16).

This method has proved very useful, but its reliability depends on two factors. First, the magnetic variation calibration must be worked out separately for different geographical areas, because declination and dip angles are a function of the magnetic sample's location in relation to the magnetic north pole. Such areal calibrations have been done in several regions: the southwestern United States (where the method was first developed), Mesoamerica, Japan, Germany, France, and England.

Second, the successful application of the method relies on the availability of *undisturbed* fired-clay samples: If the clay has been moved, its original declination and dip angles can no longer be measured and its archaeomagnetic value is lost. Thus features such as burned earth floors and hearths can be used, both to extend the archaeomagnetic sequence back in time (if their position in time can be given by associated radiocarbon dates) and as samples for age determination once a local calibration sequence exists. Pottery vessels, however, are not appropriate for archaeo-magnetic dating unless they remain demonstrably in their original positions as fired.

Because of the importance of precise positional controls, archaeomagnetic samples must be collected by a specialist. First, the orientation of the burned surface is determined by accurate compass and level readings. Next, a series of samples is physically removed. Using the compass-and-level data, the specialist duplicates the undisturbed orientation of the samples in the archaeomagnetic laboratory, where accurate measurements of the magnetic alignments are made. An experimental technique, based on measurement of magnetic intensity, has the potential for dating pottery and similar artifacts.

CALENDRICAL AGE DETERMINATION

Any artifact or feature that bears a calendrical notation carries an obvious and direct date, and materials associated with such an artifact or feature can be dated indirectly. But **calendrical age determination** is not always an absolute date. Some calendar systems lack a "zero point," consisting instead of recurring cycles that repeat endlessly through time. An illustration from our own calendar is "22 October '77," a date that recurs every 100 years. Such calendrical notations allow relative age determinations within the limits of the cycles used. Most ancient calendar systems, however, do provide absolute dates, for they have a fixed zero point similar to our calendar. These calendar systems yield absolute age determinations—provided, of course, that the notations can be deciphered and the calendar correlated to a known, standard system such as our own Gregorian calendar.

Because calendar notations are records, they are most often associated with cultures that used writing systems and that are therefore historically known. This is especially true in the Old World, where the calendrical records of civilizations such as ancient Egypt have greatly aided in constructing a basic chronology of past events. In the New World, calendrical systems based on a recurring cycle of 52 years were widespread within Mesoamerica at the time of the Spanish Conquest in the 16th century. These cyclical systems have allowed archaeologists to reconstruct short-term, relative calendrical chronologies for areas such as the Valley of Mexico and Oaxaca, in some places extending back from the conquest for several hundred years. This is done by moving back in time from the date of the conquest, which provides a link between European and Meso-american calendars. Successively older 52-year cycles can then be linked by keying in certain prominent individuals or events mentioned in accompanying "historical" texts recorded in pictographic writing.

In contrast, one Mesoamerican civilization—the Maya—possessed an absolute calendrical system based on a fixed starting point, along with a true writing system using hieroglyphs. This calendrical system, known as the Maya "Long Count," was in use until about 600 years before the Spanish Conquest; it was used in the approximate period A.D. 1–900, and probably earlier as well. Unfortunately, the Long Count was not still in use when Europeans arrived, so direct correlation with the Gregorian calendar is impossible. Nevertheless, by working with the information available in the abbreviated (cyclical) system in use in the 16th century as well as with the ancient calendrical inscriptions, specialists in Maya calendrics deciphered the basic concepts of the Long Count by the beginning of the 20th century, thus giving archaeologists a relative method of dating inscribed Maya monuments and associated materials.

Over the years, a number of attempts have been made to correlate the Maya Long Count with the Gregorian calendar. Until recently, two of these proposals—the Goodman-Martinez-Thompson (or GMT) correlation and the Spinden correlation—appeared to be the best overall candidates, but scholarly opinion was divided on which was correct. Since the two systems differed by about 260 years, a significant disparity arose in attempts to use them to convert the relative Maya chronology into an absolute one.

The archaeological excavations at Tikal, Guatemala—the largest known Maya site—presented an opportunity to test the competing correlations. Several of the stone temples at Tikal contained door lintels and roof beams made of *zapote*, a sturdy wood that had survived the ravages of time. Furthermore, the structures were associated with dates in the Maya Long Count system, some of them actually carved into the wooden lintels. It was proposed that a series of wood samples from the roof beams be subjected to radiocarbon age analysis. In selecting the samples, the archaeologists used the outermost rings of the wood to obtain dates as close as possible to the cutting date—and presumably to the construction date of the structure. The results of the radiocarbon analysis would thus provide evidence to decide between the Spinden and the GMT correlations.

The radiocarbon age determinations for the Tikal wood samples clustered strongly in favor of the GMT correlation (Fig. 9.17); as a result, the GMT correlation is the one generally used in Maya studies today. This determination has effectively converted the Maya calendrical system into a method of absolute dating. The zero point of the Long Count has been fixed at 3113 B.C., and the date for the earliest Tikal monument can be interpreted as A.D. 292 in the Gregorian system.

Ancient calendrical systems are widely distributed among Old World civilizations, including Egypt, Mesopotamia, India, and China. It has even been claimed that Bronze Age European societies possessed sophisticated astronomical knowledge of the kind necessary to produce an accurate calendar based on the solar cycle. For example, Gerald Hawkins has proposed that astronomical alignments at Stonehenge allowed its users to identify, record, and predict celestial events. Unfortunately, such a calendar was not associated with recorded dates and thus cannot be used by archaeologists to establish chronological controls.

Calendrical dating: The Maya correlation question

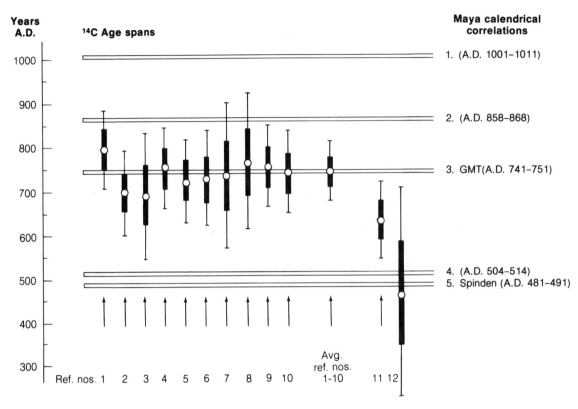

FIGURE 9.17 In this chart, the circles represent the midpoints of radiocarbon age ranges for 12 wood samples from Tikal, Guatemala, linked to Maya calendrical dates. The thick vertical lines indicate the single standard deviation for each "date" (67 percent probability that the actual date is within the range) and the fine lines, a double standard deviation (97 percent probability). The horizontal bars indicate where different correlations of Maya and Gregorian calendars predict the ¹⁴C dates to fall; these samples support strongly correlation 3, the GMT system. (After Satterthwaite and Ralph, reproduced by permission of The Society for American Archaeology, adapted from *American Antiquity* 26:176, 1960.)

EVALUATING AGE DETERMINATION METHODS

The age determination methods discussed in this chapter, as well as new methods and those yet to be developed, benefit the archaeologist by aiding in the control of the temporal dimension of data. Yet all these methods retain inherent limitations that the archaeologist must take into account before applying them to structure data temporally with any degree of confidence. Some of these limitations are inherent in the archaeological data: Demonstration of valid context of the sample being dated is always required, along with its association with the archaeological material that is being fixed in time. Other methods are so restricted in either time or space that their successful application is extremely limited. For instance, a calendrical correlation is good only for areas in which the given system was in use, and dendrochronology has been a prime dating tool only in the southwestern United States. As we have noted, most of the methods reviewed involve inherent inaccuracies that cannot be erased with our present capabilities. The prime example is that of the statistical probabilities inherent in radiometric methods, so that all age determinations by these techniques are expressed in time ranges with error factors.

Because of the built-in inaccuracies of most (or all) methods of age determination, the archaeologist must be wary of temporal schemes that rely on a single method or on just a few individual dated samples. A sequence based on a dozen dated samples is obviously better than one based on three. A sequence based on age determinations that are internally consistent is more likely to be valid than one with inconsistent results. The most obvious criterion here is that samples that can be arranged into a relative sequence on the basis of stratigraphic relationships should produce absolute age determinations that are consistent with the relative scheme.

The greatest degree of confidence in any chronological scheme arises from correspondence or agreement among results derived from many independent sources. If results from stratigraphic, seriational, radiocarbon, and archaeomagnetic analyses all produce the same sequential arrangement, chances are good that the arrangement is accurate. As we have seen, archaeologists often check the results of one kind of age assessment against those from another source. Thus the potassium–argon date of Olduvai Bed I, which first appeared to be older than most researchers would accept, was subsequently supported by fission track analysis as well as by further potassium–argon tests.

Increasingly, comparisons among age determination methods are being used to improve the accuracy of the methods themselves. Archaeomagnetic dating has been developed by using known-age samples of baked-clay surfaces; these surfaces are usually dated by radiocarbon determinations of associated charcoal samples. At least one major error inherent in the radiocarbon method has been corrected by using samples of trees, whose ages were determined by dendrochronology, to discover the correction factor for fluctuating ^{14}C levels in the past. And radiocarbon results have helped archaeologists to settle on the best of competing calendrical correlations used in the Maya area of Mesoamerica.

EXPERIMENTAL METHODS

New methods of determining the age of materials are being developed all the time. It is hoped that some of these, when refined, will prove useful for application to archaeological situations, as with the archaeomagnetic intensity method mentioned previously. We will briefly discuss three other experimental methods that may eventually be refined sufficiently to become commonplace in archaeology.

Aspartic Acid Racemization

Aspartic acid racemization depends on cumulative changes in a particular amino acid, aspartic acid, in the bone after the animal has died. The process of change is called *racemization,* and the principle behind the dating technique is that if the investigator knows the racemization rate and can measure the extent of racemization in a particular sample, she or he should be able to calculate the date the organism died (potentially for measuring ages in the range between about 5000 and 100,000 years).

The original test for the dating technique was based on some human bones from southern California, which by their geological context were suspected of being among the oldest human remains in the New World. There are problems with aspartic acid racemization dating, including the fact that the racemization rate depends on the temperature of the bone. Like obsidian hydration rates, racemization rates are area-specific and depend on local climate conditions. To correct for this, the aspartic acid analyses were "calibrated" using bones dated by radiocarbon analysis, to determine a local correction factor for the general aspartic acid racemization equation. The results of the calibrated racemization analyses indicated that several of the California samples were far older than previously suspected; SDM 16704 or "Del Mar man" was assigned an age of 48,000 years, and another, from Sunnyvale, was dated to 70,000 years before the present.

However, when some of the oldest bones dated by aspartic acid analyses were radiocarbon dated using the AMS method (see above), significantly more recent dates were produced. In these tests, the age of the Del Mar sample was revised downward from 48,000 to 8300 B.P., and the date of the Sunnyvale specimen was reduced from 70,000 to 11,000 B.P.

Problems such as these indicate that aspartic acid racemization is still an experimental dating technique. Other difficulties also exist, such as determining whether the bone has lain in a deposit subject to leaching. But, for a number of reasons, its potential utility remains important. First, it is a direct dating technique and thus does not rely on establishing the association of the bone with other datable material. Also, although the analysis is destructive, only a few grams of bone need be analyzed. In its most recent application, aspartic acid racemization has shown great promise in dating shell artifacts.

Thermoluminescence

Many crystalline materials, such as ceramics or glass, "trap" electrons released by the natural radiation present in the material. These trapped

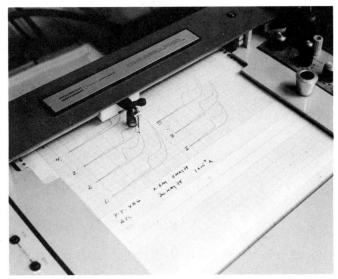

FIGURE 9.18 To determine age by thermoluminescence, (left) the sample is heated in a closed container and (right) the stored energy is released, measured, and recorded graphically. (© Nicholas Hartmann, MASCA, The University Museum, University of Pennsylvania.)

electrons accumulate through time, to be released as light energy (**thermoluminescence** or **TL**) when the substance is heated above a critical temperature (400° to 500° C for ceramics). Thus, in theory at least, researchers can determine the time elapsed since a given material, such as pottery, was last heated above this critical temperature. The investigator simply heats the sample and measures the amount of energy that has accumulated (Fig. 9.18). The original heating of the pottery (during the firing process, for example) would have released all previously stored TL energy in the clay, thus "setting the clock at zero" and starting anew the process of trapping TL energy. The measured energy release can be converted into an age measurement by comparing it with a table of energy accumulation rates.

Note that the TL method does not necessarily measure the time elapsed since the pottery was fired—it just measures accumulated energy from the last time the pottery was heated above the critical temperature. If, for example, pottery was stored in a building that burned down, that blaze might have reached the temperature required to reset the TL clock.

Unfortunately, use of this principle as an absolute dating method has encountered difficulties. In the first place, a specific rate of energy accumulation must be determined for each locale, and the capacity for given sample materials to retain that energy must also be established. Variables in the equation include both the site location—since background radiation is not constant from place to place—and the specific characteristics of the clay or other material being dated. These factors can be controlled by using a series of samples with different known ages, from a single site, to establish the accumulation rate and retention capabilities of the materials being analyzed. Once this is done, the method can assess the *relative* date of samples. In some cases, accurate *absolute* determinations have also been made, especially with glazed ceramics having uniform compositions, such as porcelains.

The TL method is still experimental, but cross-checks with associated radiocarbon dates are being used to calibrate TL accumulation rates and help refine the method into a reliable means of acquiring absolute dates. As TL becomes a more trustworthy index of age, it may become a very important method of age determination: Not only is it rapid and inexpensive, but it also provides direct dates for one of the most common of all archaeological finds, pottery.

Electron Spin Resonance

A variant of TL is also being developed, called **electron spin resonance** (**ESR**) and based on the number of electrons within shell and bone that can be measured when a sample is placed in a strong magnetic field. Unlike TL, this procedure does not destroy the sample, and it requires less than a gram of material for analysis. But thus far it is not as accurate as TL, although its promise for dating bone and shell beyond the range of radiocarbon makes its future potential highly significant.

SUMMARY

Before archaeologists can begin to reconstruct the past, the age of recovered data must be determined. Essential questions about the human past, such as cause and effect relationships, or the determination of the contemporaneity of archaeological remains, rest on the determination of age and the construction of temporal sequences.

A variety of techniques are available to the archaeologist to determine the age of recovered data, either directly (by dating the artifact, ecofact, or feature itself) or indirectly (by its association with other material that can be dated). Absolute (or chronometric) dating refers to the establishment of age in calendrical years or years before present (B.P.). Relative dating refers to establishing the age of an artifact, an ecofact, or a feature in relation to another (older, younger, or the same age).

Traditionally, archaeologists have used a series of relative dating techniques, including stratigraphy, stylistic and frequency seriation, and sequence comparison (or cross-dating). Geological associations of archaeological materials may provide relative dates (for example, by the application of geochronological sequences) or absolute dates (for example, in associations with glacial varves). Geochemical processes can yield absolute dates, best exemplified by the direct dating of obsidian artifacts using hydration rates. Floral and faunal remains can be dated by a variety of means, which may directly or indirectly determine the age of archaeological remains. Associations of archaeological data with extinct plant or animal fossils can furnish indirect dates. Dendrochronology, or tree-ring dating, often yields absolute dates, provided the wood sample can be linked to a master tree-ring sequence. The relative age of bone can be determined by various methods that detect chemical change in bone tissue after death. A series of radiometric methods are based on the process of radioactive decay of unstable isotopes. The most useful of these for archaeology is radiocarbon dating, since it relies on an isotope of carbon (^{14}C) present in all living tissue; the new AMS refinement allows nondestructive dating of smaller samples than the conventional method. Other radiometric techniques include uranium series dating, used to date cave deposits, and potassium–argon dating, valuable in determining the age of very old geological deposits; both provide indirect dates for associated archaeological remains. A related absolute method is the dating of glass materials by fission tracks. Preserved traces of ancient magnetic orientations, fossilized in burned hearths or similar features, can be absolutely dated, provided the samples can be correlated to known-age magnetic sequences. Finally, in dealing with ancient societies that developed and recorded calendrical notations, dating can be accomplished (directly or indirectly), as long as the ancient calendrical system has been deciphered.

A variety of experimental techniques promise to improve the archaeologist's ability to directly or indirectly date materials from the past. One of these, aspartic acid racemization, has the potential of producing absolute dates from bone and shell. The analysis of ceramics and glass materials by thermoluminescence and shell and bone by a similar process (electron spin resonance) are also potentially important for the direct dating of artifacts and ecofacts.

The various methods of age determination now available can lead to accurate control of the time dimension for archaeological data, provided that the archaeologist is aware of each method's shortcomings and that, whenever possible, two or more methods are used to cross-check the sequence to produce an internally consistent chronological order.

GUIDE TO FURTHER READING

Dean 1978; Orme 1982; Taylor and Longworth 1975; Zeuner 1958
Archaeological Age Determination
Stratigraphy: Harris 1975, 1989; Jennings 1957; Rowe 1961b
Seriation: Ascher and Ascher 1963; L. R. Binford 1961; Brainerd 1951; Deetz and Dethlefsen 1967; Dethlefsen and Deetz 1966; Ester 1981; Ford 1962; Graham, Galloway, and Scollar 1976; Harrington 1954; Hole and Shaw 1967; LeBlanc 1975; Marquardt 1978; Meighan 1959; Noël Hume 1979; Petrie 1901; Robinson 1951; Schrire et al. 1990
Sequence Comparison: Deetz and Dethlefsen 1965; Ehrich 1990; Krieger 1946; Patterson 1963; Taylor and Meighan 1978

Geological and Geochemical Age Determination

Geochronology: Giddings 1966, 1967; Salwen 1962; Steen-McIntyre 1985; Zeuner 1958

Varve Accumulation: Flint 1971; Zeuner 1958

Obsidian Hydration: Allen 1989; Friedman and Smith 1960; Friedman and Trembour 1978, 1983; Goodwin 1960; Michels and Tsong 1980

Faunal and Floral Age Determination

Dendrochronology: Baillie 1982; Bannister 1962, 1970; Bannister and Smiley 1955; Stahle and Wolfman 1985; Stallings 1949

Bone Age Determination: McConnell 1962; Oakley 1948, 1970; Weiner 1955

Radiometric Age Determination

Radiocarbon Age Determination: Arnold and Libby 1949; Bennett et al. 1977; Bowman 1990; Browman 1981; Gowlett 1987; Hedges and Gowlett 1986; Klein et al. 1982; Libby 1955; Michael 1985; Muller 1977; Nelson, Korteling, and Stott 1977; Ralph and Michael 1974; Ralph, Michael, and Han 1973; C. Renfrew 1971, 1973a; Stuiver 1982; Taylor 1987; Taylor et al. 1989

Potassium–Argon Age Determination: Carr and Kulp 1957; Curtis 1975; Evernden and Curtis 1965

Fission Track Dating: Watanabe and Suzuki 1969; Zimmerman 1971

Archaeomagnetic Age Determination

Aitken 1960; Tarling 1985; Wolfman 1984

Calendrical Age Determination

Houston 1989; Morley, Brainerd, and Sharer 1983; Satterthwaite and Ralph 1960

Experimental Methods

Aspartic Acid Racemization: Bada and Helfman 1975; Biscott and Rosenbauer 1981

Thermoluminescence: Aitken 1985; Fleming 1979; Mazess and Zimmerman 1966

Electron Spin Resonance: Aitken 1990; Schwarcz et al. 1989

CHAPTER TEN

ANALYSIS OF ARTIFACTS

Lithic Artifacts

Lithic Technology

Analysis of Lithic Artifacts

Ceramic Artifacts

Pottery Technology

Analysis of Pottery

Metal Artifacts

Metal Technology

Analysis of Metal Artifacts

Organic Artifacts

Organic Material Technology

Analysis of Organic Artifacts

Artifacts and Sampling

Summary

Guide to Further Reading

> Those less familiar with [the Paleolithic] should be surprised . . . to discover how much latent information of an entirely human kind awaits discovery amongst the dull old stones and bones.
>
> *Derek Roe, "Introduction: Precise Moments in Remote Time," 1980*

In the next three chapters we will examine the various studies archaeologists commonly use to analyze each category of archaeological data: artifacts, ecofacts, and features. Since each broad category encompasses a variety of archaeological remains, our discussion will emphasize only the forms of data most commonly encountered by archaeologists. For example, in this chapter on **artifacts** we will examine lithic tools and pottery in some detail but will only briefly discuss other forms of artifactual data, such as those composed of metal and various organic substances.

In discussing each kind of archaeological data, our principal goal will be to examine the most important kinds of studies appropriate to that data type and to consider the uses the archaeologist may have for the results of these analyses. We will emphasize the characteristics of each kind of data that differentiate it from the others, to show the ways each type of data can most effectively contribute to an understanding of past behavior.

By organizing the three chapters according to categories of data, we do not intend to imply that either the data categories or the resulting analyses are determining factors in guiding archaeological research. On the contrary, throughout this book we have stressed the importance of the *research problem* as the most important factor determining the course of archaeological research. Thus, in a given instance, the recovered quantities and relative importance of artifacts, ecofacts, and features are usually determined by the specific research problem and the research design chosen to investigate that problem. In the same way, the choice of **classification** method and the uses to which classification is put also depend on the research objectives. In other words, problem-oriented archaeology seeks both to define relevant data and to indicate appropriate data analysis procedures to reach conclusions relevant to the original research objectives.

LITHIC ARTIFACTS

Lithic technology refers to the manufacture of tools from stone. Stone tools were undoubtedly among the earliest used by human societies; in fact, their use predates the evolution of modern *Homo sapiens* by more than a million years. The first stone tools used by the ancestors of modern humans were probably unmodified rocks or cobbles, used only once for tasks such as hammering or pounding. But lithic technology has its roots in the first attempts to *modify* and *shape* stone to make tools.

There are two basic kinds of lithic technology: One entails the fracturing or flaking of stone (chipped-stone **industry**); the other entails the pecking and grinding or polishing of stone (ground-stone industry). Because **chipped-stone artifacts** are the oldest preserved traces of culture and technology, archaeologists have used them to name the earliest period of cultural development, the **Paleolithic** (Old Stone) period. In this traditional scheme, the later development of a stone technology involving grinding signals the advent of the second developmental age, the **Neolithic** (New Stone) Age. **Ground-stone artifacts** did not, of course, replace chipped stone; rather, the two technologies coexisted for several thousand years in both the Old and the New Worlds. Of the two, chipped stone is usually more commonly encountered by the prehistoric archaeologist, and it will be emphasized in the following section.

Lithic Technology

Stone tools are made by exploiting the inherent physical properties of certain classes of stone. Chipped-stone technology takes advantage of the characteristics of several hard, nonresilient, and homogeneous minerals. When struck, these materials fracture in a uniform manner and not according to any natural planes of cleavage in the rock. The most commonly exploited stone types possessing these characteristics include flint or chert and obsidian (a natural volcanic glass). When the surface of one of these materials is struck a sharp blow—usually from another, harder stone—the shock waves spread through the struck stone (called a **core**) in a cone-shaped pattern, producing a conchoidal fracture that detaches a fragment called a **flake.** The flake can be recognized by its **bulb of percussion** on the inside or bulbar surface (Fig. 10.1). Below the bulb of percussion, one can usually detect faint concentric rings or ripples marking the path of the radiating shock waves from the blow that produced the flake. The core will show a corresponding concave surface, or *flake scar,* marking the site of the flake's detachment, including a small depression, or **negative bulb of percussion,** immediately below the point at which the blow was struck. Chipped-stone tools are produced either by removing flakes to give a sharp edge to the core (core tools) or by utilizing one or more of the detached flakes (flake or blade tools).

Chipped-stone tools may be made by a variety of techniques. Some of these have been inferred from traces left on the tools themselves, others from ethnographic observations of peoples still manufacturing stone tools, and still others through archaeologists' experiments in duplicating the ancient forms. Some of these techniques are as old as the origins of stone tools; others represent later refinements during the long development of lithic technology. We shall briefly summarize some of the more important techniques.

The shape and size of the flake detached from a core depend on the

FIGURE 10.1 Terminology used in describing lithic core, flake, and blade tools, reflecting manufacturing technology. (After Oakley 1956. By courtesy of the British Museum [Natural History]).

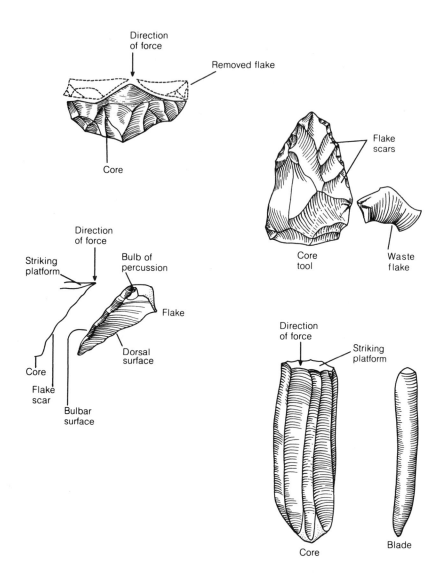

physical characteristics of the stone itself, as well as the angle and force of the blow and the material used to strike the blow. Short, rather thick flakes are produced by striking the core with a hammerstone or by striking the core against a fixed stone called an *anvil*. The earliest widely recognized stone artifacts, the Oldowan tools of East Africa, were produced by these **direct percussion** methods during the lower (earliest) part of the Paleolithic period more than two million years ago. Later, other materials such as antler were used in direct percussion (Fig. 10.2a).

A basic refinement of the percussion technique used in forming both core and flake tools is the **indirect percussion** technique, which involves

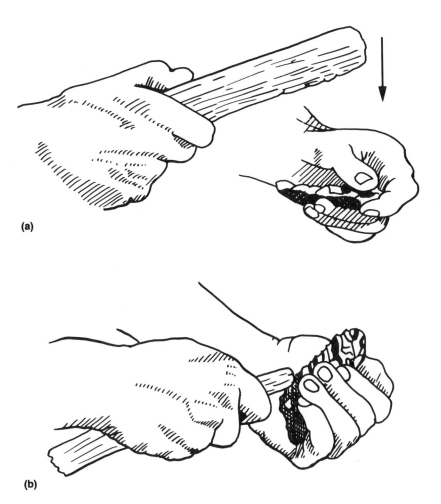

FIGURE 10.2 Manufacturing techniques for chipped-stone tools: (a) direct percussion using an antler, (b) pressure flaking using an antler.

(a)

(b)

placing a punch made of bone or wood between the core and the hammerstone. The punch softens the resultant blow, producing a longer, narrower cone of percussion and, therefore, longer, thinner flakes. A further refinement makes its appearance in the Upper Paleolithic. This technique is **pressure flaking:** Instead of either direct or indirect percussion, it uses steady pressure exerted on a punch to detach flakes from the core (Fig. 10.2b). Either indirect percussion or pressure flaking is used to make long, thin, parallel-sided flakes called **blades.** True blades produced from prepared cylindrical cores are typical of the Upper Paleolithic in the Old World and of much of the pre-Columbian era in the New World.

To increase the manufacturer's (or **knapper's**) control over the flaking process, the core may be "prepared" by shaping the **striking platform,** or surface to be struck. This is done by splitting the core or by removing a *lateral flake*—one at a substantial angle to the other flakes to be detached. This preparation gives the striking platform a relatively flat and smooth

FIGURE 10.3 Stages in the manufacture of flake tools using the Levallois technique. Flakes were carefully removed from the sides and top of the core (a, b); a flake was then removed from one end to form a platform (c) for the final blow, which detached the ready-to-use flake (d, e). (After Bordaz 1970.)

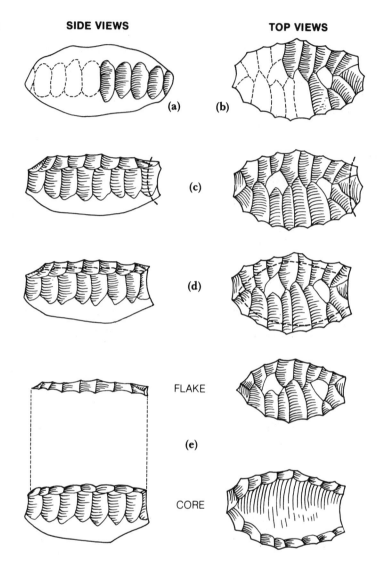

SIDE VIEWS   **TOP VIEWS**

(a)   (b)

(c)

(d)

FLAKE

(e)

CORE

surface, allowing the knapper to strike off longer and thinner flakes than would be possible from an unprepared core. One sophisticated technological development of the Paleolithic was the **Levallois technique,** in which cores were carefully preshaped so that when a single, large flake was removed, it had a predetermined, well-controlled shape (Fig. 10.3).

Once a flake or blade tool has been detached, it may be ready for use as a cutting or scraping tool (as Levallois flakes or blades), or it may need further modification for particular use. For example, edges too sharp to be held in the hand were often dulled by battering them with stone hammers.

Edges that required strength and durability rather than sharpness, such as those on scrapers (see Fig. 8.8, p. 295) were usually **retouched,** or secondarily flaked by pressure techniques to remove small, steep flakes. Skillful pressure flaking can sometimes completely alter the shape of a flake, for example, producing barbed or notched *projectile points* and miniature forms (microliths). One of the high points of pressure flaking skill is represented by the so-called eccentric flints and obsidians produced by Classic Maya craft workers (Fig. 10.4).

Archaeologists have traced the development of chipped-stone technology through a span of two million years. During that time, new techniques and forms gradually emerged that increased both the efficiency of tool production and the available inventory of tool forms. By the Upper Paleolithic period, however, a new lithic technology was also being developed—the shaping of harder, more durable stone by pecking and grinding it against abrasives such as sandstone. These tools, which took the form of axes and adzes, had more durable edges than their chipped counterparts and were thus more efficient for such tasks as cutting trees and splitting lumber. Ground-stone techniques were also used to shape large basins (**querns** or **metates**) used for grinding grains and other tasks.

Analysis of Lithic Artifacts

Traditionally, most **analysis** of lithic artifacts involved a classification based on form, often using assumed functional labels such as "scrapers" and "spokeshaves." The overall shape of stone artifacts usually provided **form types** that could be described by their outline, profile, and dimensions. The earliest and best-known classifications of this sort, made in Europe during the 19th and early 20th centuries, still serve as the basic reference classifications for Paleolithic chipped-stone tools. Particular forms, such as the Acheulian hand-axe and the Levallois core and flake, were isolated as "type fossils" or *fossiles directeurs* of specific time periods and cultures. More recently, François Bordes, Denise de Sonneville-Bordes, and James R. Sackett have been among the leaders in refining form classification, specifying more precisely the sets of criteria that distinguish among form types.

In fact, lithic typologies based on overall form have largely given way to more sophisticated attribute analyses based on criteria selected as indicators either of manufacturing technology (**technological types**) or of actual use (functional types). Stone tools are particularly well suited to such analyses and classifications, because stoneworking and stone use are progressively *subtractive* actions: Each step in the shaping and use of stone tools permanently removes more of the stone.

Technological Analysis   With chipped-stone artifacts, clues to most steps in ancient manufacturing and use processes are preserved—and can be

FIGURE 10.4
Chipped-flint effigy produced by skillful pressure flaking (Late Classic Maya). (Photo by José Lopez, courtesy of Administración del Patrimonio Cultural de El Salvador.)

detected—in flake scars, striking platforms, and other identifiable attributes. For instance, the length-to-thickness ratio of flakes (or of flake scars on a core) may indicate whether the piece was formed by direct percussion, indirect percussion, or pressure flaking. Even manufacturing mistakes are preserved: *Hinge fractures,* for example, indicate that the flake removal process was incorrectly carried out or that a flaw in the stone caused the flake to snap off abruptly. By analyzing the full range of lithic material, both artifacts and workshop debris, the archaeologist can reconstruct most or all of the steps in tool manufacture.

Significantly, the workshop debris—nontool by-products of chipping, called **debitage**—was usually ignored by traditional classifications that focused only on the forms of finished tools. Debitage, however, can include a wide range of technologically informative materials, from primary flakes that were hammered away to remove the outer weathered layer of the stone, to trimming flakes removed in preparing the form of the core for production of uniform flakes or blades, to the tiny secondary flakes that are the by-products of retouching a blade or flake. In analyzing the chipped-stone artifacts from Chalchuapa, El Salvador, Payson D. Sheets used technological criteria as his basis for classification. By attending to the technological "clues" preserved in the full range of chipped-stone materials, he was able to reconstruct the chain of manufacturing steps used by pre-Columbian lithic craft workers during a span of some 2000 years (Fig. 10.5).

Nicholas Toth's analysis of the manufacturing sequence for Oldowan artifacts suggests that, in this instance, traditional tool and debitage identifications might be reversed. That is, the cores have usually been considered the important Oldowan tools, but their final shapes depended less on intentional design than on simply how many flakes had been removed from them. The flakes themselves, far from waste products, were probably at least as important as the cores in the overall tool kit. In a similar vein, Joan Gero and others remind us that, of the stone tools observed in use in recent times, the great majority have been simple flakes, produced quickly for on-the-spot use; the technically more complex lithic tools have tended to dominate archaeologists' perception and study, but these are often greatly outnumbered by much simpler implements.

To test and refine reconstructions of ancient tool manufacture, lithic specialists such as François Bordes and Don Crabtree used experimental duplication of ancient chipped-stone technology. Through these experiments, and through their training of other archaeologists in the techniques used to manufacture stone tools, lithic specialists have increased the sensitivity with which ancient manufacturing practices can be analyzed, as well as proposing alternative methods that may have been used in the past.

Petrological examinations of **thin-sections** of stone are sometimes useful in establishing the source of the raw material. Petrology is the scientific study of rock, and a thin-section is a specially prepared slice of a stone. When first cut, the section is a few millimeters thick, but after it is fixed to

Technological classification of chipped-stone artifacts: Sheets's work at Chalchuapa, El Salvador

Technological classification of chipped-stone artifacts: Toth's reanalysis of Oldowan tools

Experimental lithic technology: François Bordes and Don Crabtree

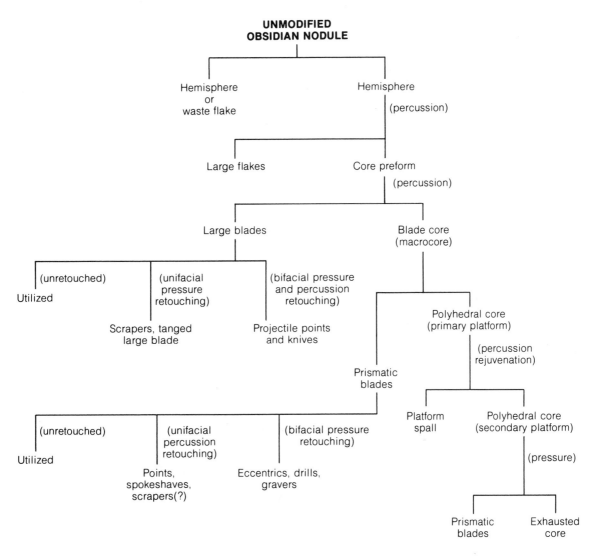

**UNMODIFIED
OBSIDIAN NODULE**

Hemisphere
or
waste flake

Hemisphere
(percussion)

Large flakes

Core preform
(percussion)

Large blades

Blade core
(macrocore)

(unretouched)

Utilized

(unifacial
pressure
retouching)

Scrapers, tanged
large blade

(bifacial pressure
and percussion
retouching)

Projectile points
and knives

Polyhedral core
(primary platform)

(percussion
rejuvenation)

Prismatic
blades

Platform
spall

Polyhedral core
(secondary platform)

(unretouched)

Utilized

(unifacial
percussion
retouching)

Points,
spokeshaves,
scrapers(?)

(bifacial pressure
retouching)

Eccentrics, drills,
gravers

(pressure)

Prismatic
blades

Exhausted
core

FIGURE 10.5 A technological classification representing manufacturing steps used in production of chipped-stone artifacts at Chalchuapa, El Salvador. (Courtesy of Payson D. Sheets.)

a glass slide, its thickness is reduced to about 0.03 mm, at which point most of the minerals in the rock are transparent. By examining the thin-section through a special microscope, the analyst can describe the size, shape, and other characteristics of the minerals in the stone. Comparing **quarry** samples with artifact samples, petrologists can sometimes identify distinctive quarry "signatures"—particular patterns of constituent minerals that come from one source alone. Some sources do not have distinctive signatures, however; a petrological study of flint axes in England, for example, was unable to distinguish among different flint bed sources, although the same study defined more than 20 source groups for axes made of stone other than flint.

Diagnostic trace elements within lithic materials such as obsidian can be identified and measured by neutron activation or similar analyses. The use of these techniques for detection of raw material sources has allowed archaeologists to reconstruct ancient exchange networks in many parts of the world (see Chapter 15).

Functional Analysis We have already mentioned that in Europe and elsewhere, inferred function was often a primary criterion for lithic classifications; one common distinction was between supposedly "utilitarian" objects (those with domestic or household uses) and "ceremonial" objects having ritual or nondomestic uses. This division could sometimes be validated when applied to artifacts from secure contexts, such as tools from household living floors as opposed to those from burials. But the distinction was often misused: Many analysts succumbed to the temptation to associate elaborate forms with "ceremonial" uses and simpler shapes with "utilitarian" uses, even in the absence of good contextual data. For example, a class of perforated ground stones found in prehistoric North American sites were first named "bannerstones," because they were thought to be decorations for ceremonial staffs or the like. We now know that, however fancy, these stones were quite utilitarian, used as weights for the ends of spear-throwers, to increase the force of the throw. Most modern archaeologists recognize that even artifacts from secure "ceremonial" contexts, such as burials, may once have served multiple functions, including "utilitarian" ones, before their final deposition in a burial or cache.

Early classification of chipped-stone artifacts: A. V. Kidder at Uaxactún and Pecos

A. V. Kidder, one of the pioneers in the analysis of New World chipped-stone artifacts, used this functional dichotomy as the basis of his 1947 classification of chipped-stone tools from the Maya lowland site of Uaxactún. After segregating the Uaxactún collection into presumed "ceremonial" and "utilitarian" categories, Kidder subdivided artifacts in each class further according to raw material (obsidian versus chert) and finally form. Kidder's earlier study (1932) of lithic artifacts from the Pecos site in the southwestern United States ignored this functional entanglement. The Pecos study, based uniformly on kind or degree of flaking and form, is usually regarded as the first systematic (or "modern") classification of chipped-stone artifacts in the New World.

More recently, lithic analysts have sought to identify artifact function through detailed **attribute** study. Increasingly, they examine specific characteristics of form, such as angle of the cutting edge, as well as attributes of wear resulting from use—microscopic fractures, pitting, or erosion of the edge—to establish the range of tasks once performed by stone implements.

The interpretation of what function these attributes indicate is, as we shall argue in Chapter 13, based on analogy—comparison of the attributes of the archaeological materials with those of modern forms whose function is known. Some of the analogs—the sources for inter-

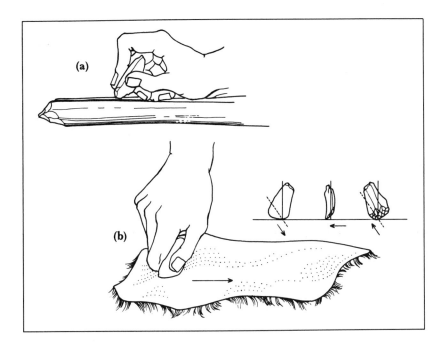

FIGURE 10.6 Determination of the function of chipped-stone end-scrapers: (a) traditionally archaeologists had speculated that these were used as engravers for bone or wood; (b) later researchers inferred that they were used as scrapers, based on comparison of wear patterns with those resulting from experimental use. (After Semenov 1964. Reprinted by permission of Barnes & Noble Books, Totowa, New Jersey.)

pretation—are drawn from ethnographically observed stone tools: For example, ancient projectile points, including "arrowheads" and spearpoints, are identified by the similarity of archaeological forms with modern forms used as projectile points.

Other analogs are provided by imitative experiments in which archaeologists make stone tools and use them to chop, scrape, slice, whittle, or saw various materials, such as meat, bone, and wood. After the experimental tool is used, its edges are examined microscopically to detect the pattern of wear resulting from each kind of use. Distinctive wear "signatures" can be identified in some cases; these can be used to infer ancient tool uses when archaeological specimens show similar wear patterns.

For example, in studying Upper Paleolithic end-scrapers (see Fig. 8.8, p. 295), S. A. Semenov found scratches and luster along the edges that had been retouched to a steep angle. The consistent direction and shape of the scratches or striations indicated the direction in which the tool had been moved, while the luster suggested that it had been used on relatively soft organic materials. From these inferences, Semenov reconstructed that the tools had indeed been used as scrapers, specifically for cleaning animal skins (Fig. 10.6).

Since Semenov's research, Lawrence Keeley, Robert Lawrence, Nicholas Toth, and others have extended and refined the identification of use-wear "signatures" on lithic artifacts of varied shapes, ages, and materials.

Use-wear analysis: S. A. Semenov

In some cases, residues left on working edges also provide clues to ancient function. A well-known example is the interpretation of silica residue as an indicator that an artifact was used as a sickle to cut grain or other plants containing silica. The presence of such a silica sheen has been sought as evidence of crop harvesting for sites believed to have been occupied during early stages of the development of grain agriculture. Thomas Loy has shown that stone weapons may preserve traces of blood from their prey. He has identified blood residues from a variety of mammals—including grizzly bears, rabbits, and humans—on the cutting edges of Canadian stone tools between 1000 and 6000 years old.

Ground-stone tools can also preserve clues to manufacture and use, but when both of these processes involve grinding, many of the traces necessarily are "erased." Whether because of this decreased information potential or simply because chipped stone is more common, ground stone has traditionally received less analytic attention—a situation that we hope will change. One analysis that is often fruitful is examination of residues, to see what was cut with or ground on the implement in question. For example, a quern or mortar could have been used to grind food or, alternatively, to grind pigment materials; only analysis of residues or wear will tell.

CERAMIC ARTIFACTS

Ceramics is a blanket term that covers all industries in which artifacts are modeled or molded from clay and then rendered durable by firing. In addition to pottery, this overall category includes production of ceramic figurines (three-dimensional representations of animals, humans, or other forms), musical instruments (such as flutes or pipes), articles of adornment (such as beads), hunting or fishing implements (such as clay pellets and fish line weights), spindle whorls (used for spinning thread or yarn), and even building materials (such as bricks and roof tiles). Although clay figurines—such as the "Venus" figurines of the Upper Paleolithic in Europe (see Fig. 16.3, p. 517)—appear to be the earliest known form of ceramic technology, pottery is undoubtedly the most abundant and widespread kind of ceramics.

Pottery can be defined as a separate ceramic industry because of its unique body of manufacturing techniques as well as its specialized function: providing containers for a wide range of solid and liquid substances. Archaeological evidence throughout the world indicates that pottery originated with humanity's first attempts at settled life, usually associated with new subsistence adaptations such as coastal fishing and gathering or, inland, experiments with agriculture. In southwest Asia, Southeast Asia, and South America, pottery appears very early in the record of settled communities; it developed as part of a more complex, expanding technology that was fostered by the relative stability of settled village life. Pottery was and still is used to transport, cook, and store a wide range of solid and liquid foods, as well as to contain other supplies. But as societies became increasingly complex, pottery also assumed other specialized functions, including ritual uses as burial urns and incense burners.

Compared with the age of the chipped-stone industry, pottery's 10,000-year history seems short. But from the time of their first known occurrence, in the Jomon culture of Japan, pottery vessels have been used by most of the world's settled communities, and this widespread and common occurrence, combined with extreme durability and capacity for great variety in form and decoration, makes pottery one of the most commonly analyzed and useful kinds of artifacts available to archaeologists. The traditional importance of the "infamous potsherd" in archaeological research can hardly be overstressed; at least one unabridged dictionary even gives as its *definition* of potsherd "a broken pottery fragment, esp. one of archaeological value."

Pottery Technology

Pottery, like other ceramic artifacts, may be made from a wide variety of clays. *Clay* is a general term for any fine-grained earth that develops plasticity (the capacity to be molded and shaped) when mixed with water. Clays are often water-laid soils; they vary in consistency according to grain size, degree of sorting, and chemical composition. The finest quality clays contain *kaolinite* (hydrated aluminum silicate), whose particles are as small as 0.05 microns (0.00005 mm) in diameter.

Pottery is manufactured in a variety of ways throughout the world, ranging from simple household hand-production to modern factory mass-production methods. Because the bulk of prehistoric pottery was produced by rather simple means, we will briefly describe the general manufacturing process as it is carried out by small, family production units in many parts of the world to this day.

First, the potter must acquire the proper clay, either by mining it or by purchasing it from a supplier. Then the potter processes and prepares the clay to assure its purity and uniformity. Because clay is often collected dry or allowed to dry out, it must be pulverized and mixed with water until it reaches the proper consistency for forming vessels. The moist clay must then be thoroughly kneaded (or wedged) to drive out air bubbles and create a uniform, plastic mass. The plasticity of moist clay is what gives it practical value. But another property of clay is that as it loses water during drying and firing, it shrinks and is subject to cracking or breaking. As part of the clay processing, then, nonplastic substances that retain their shape and size—called **temper**—may be added to reduce shrinkage and lessen the chance that the completed vessel will break during drying or firing. Common tempering agents include sand, ground shell, volcanic ash, mica, ground pottery sherds, and organic materials (such as grass). Some clays already contain these or similar substances and thus do not require the addition of temper.

Once processed, the clay is ready for forming. There are three basic techniques for making pottery from clay: hand forming, mold forming, and wheel forming. These techniques may be used separately or combined. Hand-forming methods undoubtedly represent the oldest kind of pottery technology; they are usually associated with small-scale production by part-time specialists for immediate household uses, or sometimes for limited markets outside the family. Mold- and wheel-forming techniques, because of their potential for mass production, are often associated with full-time specialist potters who manufacture their vessels for widespread market distribution.

Hand forming involves modeling a vessel either from a clay core or by adding coils or segments and welding the junctures with a thin solution of clay and water (Fig. 10.7a). Mold forming is commonly used not only to make pottery but also to mass-produce small clay artifacts such as figurines and spindle whorls. For simple forms, such as open bowls, molds may form the entire vessel; with more complex pottery shapes, such as jars, molds can be used for one part, such as the rounded base, whereas the upper portion is hand formed.

Wheel forming is the most common means of mass-producing pottery vessels. A relatively recent invention—appearing sometime before 3000 B.C. in southwest Asia—this technique is the most common throughout the world today. The true *potter's wheel* is used to form the vessel by manipulating a rapidly rotating clay core centered on a vertically mounted wheel, powered by the potter's hands or feet or by auxiliary sources. The forming process is similar to the turning of wooden or metal forms on a lathe, except that the principal tools used in forming pottery are the potter's hands. A similar technique, often called the *slow wheel,* uses a concave basal mold that is allowed to rotate freely on a flat platform, somewhat like a toy top. However, the slow wheel is not fixed to an axle as is the true potter's wheel, so it cannot be rotated fast enough or with enough stability to produce the "lathing" effect of the potter's wheel.

Once the vessel is formed by any of these methods, its surface is usually smoothed with a wet cloth, a sponge, or the palm of the hand to create a uniform, slick surface. An overall coating with a thin clay solution (**slip**) may be applied, by dipping or brushing, to give the surface a uniform texture and color (Fig. 10.7b). Special clays are often used for slipping because of their ability to impart a particular color on firing. Other slips or paints may be used to decorate the vessel in a variety of painted patterns and colors. Specialized slips that actually turn to glass (vitrify) during high-temperature firing are called **glazes.** The vessel may also be further modified or decorated by modeling, either adding clay (welding appliqués) or subtracting clay (incising, carving, cutting, and so on) (Fig. 10.7c). As the clay begins to dry, it loses its plasticity. When it cannot be further modeled but is still somewhat moist to the touch, it is described as **leather hard.** Leather-hard clay can still be carved, incised, or punctated. At this

FIGURE 10.7   Selected steps in pottery manufacture: (a) hand-forming vessels (Chinautla, Guatemala); (b) applying a slip (Senegal); (c) decorating the vessel shoulder by incising with a shell (Senegal); (d) firing pottery in an open kiln (Chinautla). (Photos b and c courtesy of Olga F. Linares; photos a and d by author.)

FIGURE 10.8 Pottery style classification: vessels from the Southwestern United States representing four different pottery types defined by painted decoration. (After Carlson 1970.)

stage the vessel's surface may be polished by rubbing it with a smooth hard object such as a beach pebble. The effect of polishing is to compact the surface and give it a lustrous gloss.

After decorating and drying, the pottery vessel is ready for firing. Firing transforms clay from its natural plastic state to a permanent nonplastic one. During the firing process, clay may pass through as many as three stages: Dehydration, or loss of water, occurs at temperatures up to about 600° C; oxidation of carbon and iron compounds in the clay takes place at temperatures up to about 900° C; and, finally, **vitrification** occurs at temperatures above about 1000° C. Vitrification fuses the clay so that the vessel walls lose their porosity and become waterproof.

The place where pottery is fired is called a *kiln*. The oldest and simplest kiln is an open fire, specially prepared to ensure the proper and even temperatures required by pottery (Fig. 10.7d). Open kilns can usually attain temperatures within the oxidation range, but they cannot reach the threshold point of vitrification. Closed kilns, which are usually specially constructed ovens, are necessary to vitrify pottery. Glazed pottery is actually fired twice in closed kilns: The first process, bisque firing, dehydrates and oxidizes the clay; then, after the vessel cools, glaze is applied, and the vessel is fired again to vitrify the glaze. The earliest glazed pottery appears to have been produced in China by 1500 B.C.

Analysis of Pottery

The archaeologist uses a variety of approaches to analyze pottery; the methods used in any given study depend on the objectives of that study. We will consider each of the three broad approaches discussed earlier—studies based on **stylistic attributes, form attributes,** and **technological attributes**—and discuss the major applications of each.

Stylistic Analysis Traditionally, stylistic analyses of pottery have received the greatest emphasis by archaeologists (Fig. 10.8), probably because pottery lends itself to such a variety of stylistic and decorative treatments—painting, appliqué, incising, and so on. This underlying "freedom of choice" in pottery style leads archaeologists to assume that stylistic regularities represent culturally guided choices rather than technological or functional limitations. Pottery styles have been used to trace ancient social and cultural links in time and space, and stylistic classification remains one of the most important methods of analyzing ancient pottery collections.

In many cases, pottery collections have been classified into types on the basis of the most readily observable style characteristics, usually color. However, such classifications tend to provide only very broad and general type categories, such as "red ware" and "gray ware" and to lack precision in defining the criteria used to separate one type from another. Most unfortunately, for many years and in many parts of the world, pottery analysts made no attempt to standardize the procedures, nomenclature, or criteria used in defining pottery types on the basis of stylistic attributes; instead, each pottery analyst worked independently. The lack of comparability among analyses greatly reduced their usefulness for making fine temporal distinctions, intersite comparisons, area syntheses, reconstruction of trade networks, and other higher-level generalizations. The situation was similar to that in other early scientific attempts to classify complex phenomena, such as the beginnings of biological classification: Individualistic classification schemes tended only to compound a chaotic situation, until agreement on a single set of procedures emerged.

In several areas of the world, archaeologists have begun to standardize their approaches to defining **stylistic types.** One example of this process is the development and spread of a particular classification method known as **type-variety-mode analysis.** This analysis is based on the definition of minimal attributes and the determination of the way sets of attributes combine to form a hierarchy of typological units called *modes, varieties, types,* and *groups.* It originated in classification systems based on types and varieties, developed in both the southwestern and the southeastern United States. However, in its modern application, the method combines those considerations with use of the **mode** concept developed by Irving Rouse, an approach that is often used as a separate means of classification in some geographical areas. The type-variety-mode method was eventually extended into the Maya area of Mesoamerica as a solution to the classificatory chaos that prevailed in that region.

In this approach, definition of attributes within a given pottery collection, as well as the eventual definition of typological units, is based on visual and tactile examination of each sherd or vessel in the sample. Although the type-variety-mode method emphasizes stylistic attributes as those most readily recognized and manipulated by the ancient potter, form and technological attributes may be used as secondary criteria to help in the definition of types.

This hierarchical classification, from modes to varieties, types, and groups reflecting different degrees of variability in attribute clustering, may reflect the ancient potter's social system. That is, it can be used as a behavioral classification (Chapter 8; Fig. 8.12, p. 300). Thus, the minimal cluster of attributes—the variety—may represent the work of individual potters or small groups of potters closely related in time (a family of potters descending over several generations) or space (a family of potters during a short time interval). The type corresponds to the next level of social organization, usually a group of family units such as a neighborhood, a settlement, or a village. Finally, the ceramic group reflects a larger social unit, such as an area of several villages, a town, or even an entire region. The kinds of organizational units vary from one society to another, but the general hypothesis is the same: that the levels of pottery classification correspond to levels of ancient social organization in each situation. Moreover, characteristics of the pottery classification provide insights into the nature of the ancient social and political system. For instance, a great profusion of varieties for each type may indicate considerable freedom of expression for individual potters, the result of a noncoercive sociopolitical system. On the other hand, more restricted types—each with few varieties—might reflect a more rigid and tightly controlled system.

As an analytic tool, the type-variety-mode method has been most effective in encouraging consistency in classification and description of pottery collections in areas in which it is in use. Nevertheless, the validity of the specific behavioral assumptions that underlie the method has yet to be thoroughly tested by long-range studies of contemporary pottery-producing communities. The point is, rather, that by encouraging production of comparable type descriptions, type-variety-mode analysis has facilitated recognition of time–space patterns in pottery. The behavioral interpretation of such patterns is a separate question, which will be taken up again in Chapter 13.

Form and Function Analysis   The analysis of pottery on the basis of vessel form is perhaps not as common as that based on stylistic attributes. However, form attributes may be combined with stylistic classifications (such as those in the type-variety-mode method) to assist in the definition of types. And because of the capacity of clay to take a wide variety of shapes, differences in form among pottery vessels should represent the potter's choices rather than technological limits, although constrained by functional considerations.

Initial classifications of vessel form are usually based on the consistent clustering of overall vessel shapes or on clustering of component shape attributes, such as form of vessel lip, neck, shoulder, or base (Fig. 10.9). When possible, classifications based on overall vessel form may be compared with vessel shapes still used in the area under study. These classifications often produce rather broad categories or form types, such as bowls, platters, or jars. Detailed studies of each component attribute of vessel form often produce finer, more narrowly defined categories. The broader classification has greater utility in proposing relationships between vessel form and function, whereas the more detailed approach is often better for defining spatial relationships and temporal distinctions. Since we have already discussed spatial and temporal applications under stylistic classifications, we will restrict our discussion here to the question of functional implications. The discussion will also include other means of assessing vessel function.

Ancient vessel function may be determined in several ways. The archaeologist may recover direct evidence of function in association with pottery, such as residues from food storage. In such cases, it may be possible to reconstruct a great deal about ancient patterns of pottery usage. Such remnants may be present in visible quantities or may be discovered through microscopic analysis. One promising technique, lipid analysis, allows the identification of fatty residues ("lipids") from foods or other sub-

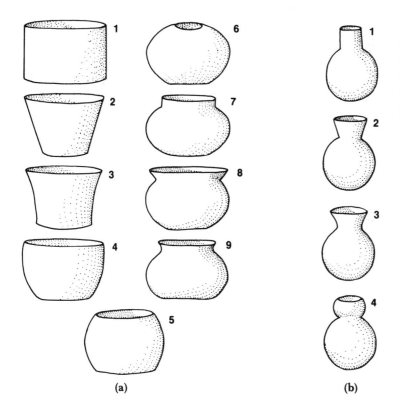

FIGURE 10.9 An example of pottery form classification: (a) nine defined bowl categories, (b) four defined jar categories. (After Sabloff 1975.)

(a)

(b)

stances that were absorbed into the matrix of unglazed pottery during use (the same technique can be used on nonporous artifacts such as obsidian and flint cutting tools). A small sample of the vessel is removed and tested by a series of analyses that separate lipids by their composition, thus identifying their original source. Lipid analysis can distinguish marine, animal, and vegetal residues, thus revealing what the vessel originally contained (vessel function) and whether it had a single use or multiple uses. This evidence can then be used to help reconstruct ancient diet, and discover variations in food use in space and time. Vessels that lack food residues but that have burned and blackened exteriors may still be identified as cooking containers. Conversely, pottery that has interior food residues but lacks exterior burning might be interpreted as cooking vessels utilizing internal heat sources such as heated stones, or perhaps as vessels for storing or serving food. Other residues, such as incense resins, grain pollen, or unfired clay can also help in identification of function—for example, as incense burners, storage jars, or potter's equipment.

Direct evidence of function may not be present, and ancient use must be inferred from analysis based on vessel form. The use of general shape—

function analogs is common in archaeological studies. For instance, vessels with necks are assumed to have been used for storing and dispensing liquids, as they are today in most areas of the world without running water; the restrictive neck helps to control spillage and reduce waste. Smaller jars with narrow necks are usually interpreted as vessels for carrying liquids, and larger, wider-mouthed vessels are usually seen as stationary water storage jars. But although function is an important determinant of form, other factors (such as technological limitations, properties of the clay being modeled, and cultural value orientations) all influence vessel shape.

A functional distinction is commonly drawn between utilitarian (domestic) and ceremonial pottery; this distinction may be based on direct evidence from vessel provenience and from associated residues, or it may be inferred from vessel form. Such categorizations assume that an ancient distinction existed among vessel forms, so that certain shapes were associated with ceremonial uses and others with domestic tasks. Some of these classifications, involving the degree of vessel elaboration or decoration, assume that more elaborate pottery forms were associated with ceremonial or higher-status activities, whereas simpler pottery was used for lower-status and domestic activities. As we noted in discussing lithic analysis, such an equation of form elaboration with ritual use is not always justified, and it should be made only when other evidence, such as association of particular elaborate forms with ritual contexts, so indicates.

The archaeological provenience of the pottery may also allow the investigator to determine past uses. Vessels found in tombs or associated with burials are usually regarded as ritual paraphernalia used in funerary rites. Other ritual uses include constructional offerings or caches found in ancient structures; these are comparable to the cornerstones of modern buildings. In pre-Columbian Mesoamerican sites, for instance, pottery often appears to have been part of dedicatory offerings or containers for offerings placed within a building platform; an example of such a dedicatory cache from the site of El Portón in Guatemala was described in Chapter 7. However, the archaeologist must be cautious in assigning single functions to the pottery vessels. For instance, funerary vessels often show traces of prior use, indicating that they served different purposes before their final ritual function. Determination that pottery vessels had multiple uses and were recycled is often not possible, but this complicating factor should be kept in mind in interpreting vessel functions.

Technological Analysis   The manufacture of pottery involves a complex technology consisting of a series of operations performed by the potter. This technology includes the acquisition and preparation of raw materials (clays, tempers, pigments, wood for firing, and so forth), the shaping and decoration of the vessels, preparation for firing, and the actual firing process. An analysis of ancient pottery remains may reveal clues about the manufacturing methods used. But, in contrast to a subtractive technology such as the manufacture of stone tools by chipping and flaking, pottery involves a plastic, additive technology. Manipulation of the clay in the later stages of manufacture may thus obliterate the diagnostic markings and features left by earlier stages. For this reason, archaeologists usually cannot completely reconstruct the manufacturing process solely by examining the traces provided by the archaeological record. The only way to overcome this difficulty is to use analogy with documented instances of pottery production today. In this way, new clues may be recognized by observing actual production procedures and matching those with similar features on ancient pottery. In addition, manufacturing steps that leave no trace may be proposed or inferred for a better understanding of ancient technology.

Unfortunately, only a relatively few technological studies of pottery have been completed; more research of this kind is needed. One of the most common technological studies done by archaeologists involves analysis of firing conditions. Ancient firing procedures may be inferred from observable characteristics of the finished product. If the vessel surfaces are vitrified or glazed, for example, the pottery was fired at a temperature in excess of about 1000° C, probably in an enclosed kiln. Complete oxidation may be diagnosed from a uniform color in the interior clay (paste): If the paste has a dark core (usually dark gray or black), chances are that the firing was insufficient to oxidize the vessel fully. Blotchy surface discolorations on the vessel, called *fire clouds,* are typical of open firing methods. The overall color of the vessel may also be affected by firing conditions: For instance, insufficient oxygen can produce *smudging* or blackened surfaces.

The outstanding pioneering work in archaeological pottery technology was done by Anna Shepard. She conducted studies of the manufacturing processes used in several pre-Columbian wares by detailed analyses of sherd pastes. These efforts included the definitive study of plumbate ware, the only prehistoric vitrified pottery produced in the New World. In most areas of the world, technological analysis is made more difficult by the paucity of reported discoveries and systematic excavations of prehistoric manufacturing and kiln sites. Unfortunately, physical evidence of pottery manufacturing activity is often difficult to find. Open kiln sites may vanish or be hard to distinguish from hearths or other burned areas. Evidence of ancient production can occasionally be inferred from the discovery of tools and materials used in pottery manufacture. For example, the excavations at Chalchuapa, El Salvador, revealed an array of indirect evidence for pre-Columbian pottery production, including lumps of unfired clay, small stone palettes for grinding pigments, pieces of unprocessed hematite pigments, and small polishing stones. However, the inherent difficulties of reconstructing ancient pottery technology reinforce the need for thorough ethnographic treatments of contemporary production that can be used as analogs for archaeological interpretation.

Technological analysis of pottery: Anna Shepard and plumbate ware

Indirect evidence of pottery manufacture: Chalchuapa, El Salvador

METAL ARTIFACTS

The complex technology involved in the extraction of metal from ores and the production of **metal artifacts** is called *metallurgy*. The earliest traces of this technology are found in the Old World—specifically in southwest Asia—where between 8000 and 9500 years ago people began to shape copper into simple tools and ornaments. These first metal artifacts were **cold hammered,** probably with stone tools. Within several millennia, however, copper was being extracted from ores by the use of heat and cast into a variety of forms. An independent tradition of metalworking appeared in the New World, marked by use of cold-hammered copper in the upper Great Lakes region by 2000 B.C. and somewhat later by the development of more complex metallurgy in the Andes of South America, lower Central America, and Mesoamerica. Since that time, metallurgy has developed and spread throughout the world, almost completely replacing lithic technology. Today, of course, sophisticated metal technology has become an essential part of our complex civilization.

Metal Technology

Prehistoric metallurgy was based on three hard metals—copper, tin, and iron—and, to a lesser degree, on two rare or precious metals, silver and gold. Because the development of metal technology followed a fairly regular sequence, gradually replacing the two established lithic technologies in the Old World, 19th-century archaeologists found it convenient to classify the "progress" of Old World civilization with labels referring to the successive "ages of metal." Thus, the first metal to be used gave its name to the Copper Age, or Chalcolithic. The alloy of copper and tin that was produced in later times gave its name to the Bronze Age, which was followed ultimately by the Iron Age.

Since the 19th century, archaeologists have learned a great deal more about the origin and development of prehistoric metallurgy. As a result, the course of technological innovation can now be traced not only in southwest Asia but also in Southeast Asia, China, Africa, and the New World. The picture is by no means complete; for instance, recent discoveries in Non Nok Tha and Ban Chiang in Thailand have generated new—if controversial—support for the hypothesis that tin bronze metallurgy developed as early in Southeast Asia as in its traditionally assigned home, southwest Asia.

Origins of bronze metallurgy: New evidence from Thailand

The sequence of metallurgical development is still best known for southwest Asia, however. In that area, the first uses of metal, sometime before 7000 B.C., involved cold hammering of native copper. (The term *native copper* refers to the metal's occurrence in an uncombined form, so that relatively pure supplies can be collected or extracted simply.) Copper is malleable enough to be shaped by hammering, but the progressive pounding cracks and weakens the metal. **Annealing**—heating and slow cooling—"heals" the cracks and stresses produced by hammering, providing renewed strength to the metal tool.

Before 4000 B.C., copper was being melted and cast in molds into a growing variety of desired shapes, from axe heads to spear-points, swords, and ornaments. At the same time, intense heat was used to **smelt** copper from ores, thereby greatly expanding the range of sources for the raw material. At first only weathered, surface (oxidized) ores were mined, but by about 2500 B.C., deeper-lying and harder-to-reach sulfide ore deposits were also being used; their exploitation indicates the increased importance of copper technology and copper artifacts.

Another significant advance involved deliberate production of metal **alloys.** Most scholars believe that experimental attempts to remove impurities from copper led to the discovery or the realization that some of the "impurities" were beneficial. Most notably, inclusion of small quantities of tin or arsenic in copper formed a new metal combination or alloy, *bronze*. Bronze has several advantages over copper: Not only is its melting point lower, but it also cools into a harder metal capable of retaining a sharper, more durable edge. Further hammering, after cooling, hardens it even more. Other copper alloys can be made, but many are brittle, and tin bronze is not. The problem is that tin is relatively scarce. There are no verified major sources of tin in southwest Asia, and a great archaeological controversy has arisen over the origin of the tin exploited by southwest Asian metallurgists. But bronze was certainly being produced in southwest Asia by about 3000 B.C. As noted above, Southeast Asia has recently yielded some very early bronze artifacts, including daggers and axe heads, which may date to 3500 B.C. And Southeast Asia is known to be rich in tin ores. Whether the two postulated "homes" for bronze metallurgy represent independent invention and, if not, which one first developed the technology remain intriguing research questions. Whatever its origins, bronze metallurgy spread swiftly (Fig. 10.10). Some of the most sophisticated products of bronze casting were created in China during the Shang Dynasty, extending from about 1500 to 1027 B.C.

Iron metallurgy was the next major development in metallurgical technology. Meteoric iron was known and used during the Bronze Age, but in the later part of the second millennium B.C., ironworking displaced bronze casting as the principal metallurgical means of tool production. The change was more than one of material; ironworking is also a more complicated technology. Iron melts at 1537° C: Chinese and possibly South Asian metallurgists were able to melt iron during the first millennium B.C., but there is no evidence for *cast iron* production in ancient southwest Asia. The principal iron output of the southwest Asian furnaces was a spongy mass called a *bloom*, which was then reheated in a forge and hammered by a blacksmith to shape the tool, increase the metal's strength, and drive out impurities. Even so, forged iron is relatively soft. Use of a charcoal fire for the forge, however, introduces carbon and strengthens the iron, producing carburized iron, or *steel*, a much harder and more durable

FIGURE 10.10 A grouping of bronze vessels from the first millennium B.C. found in a tomb chamber at Gordion, Turkey. (Courtesy of the Gordion Project, The University Museum, University of Pennsylvania.)

metal. By the end of the second millennium B.C., southwest Asian blacksmiths were making "steeled" iron tools, and the Iron Age was under way. Further technological advances increased the strength of the steel even more: For example, **quenching**—rapid cooling of the carburized iron in water—adds strength, although it increases brittleness. But, as metallurgists discovered by the beginning of the fourth century B.C., **tempering**—reheating the iron to a temperature below 727° C—offered a solution to the brittleness introduced by quenching.

The most sophisticated metallurgical technologies in the New World were developed in South America and lower Central America. Although their craft was based on copper and the soft precious metals (gold and silver), Andean metalsmiths also worked with a variety of alloys, including bronze, and sophisticated surface plating techniques. These metalworking traditions developed during the first millennium B.C., although their origins lie in even earlier times. The Moche period (ca. A.D. 100–700) represented the peak of Andean metallurgy, for much of the Chimú (ca. 1150–1476) and Inka (ca. 1476–1534) metalworking was derived from Moche technology. This indigenous metallurgical tradition and the allied technologies in northern South America, Central America, and Mexico were replaced by European iron- and steel-based technology after the Spanish Conquest.

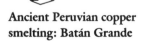

Ancient Peruvian copper smelting: Batán Grande

New World metallurgy was based on a variety of techniques. Recent excavations at Batán Grande, Peru, directed by Izumi Shimada, have revealed well-preserved production facilities for smelting copper ores using a series of small fire pits. Once obtained, copper and copper alloys were usually worked by hammering and annealing (heating) in the Andean area. Sheet metal was shaped and joined by further hammering and annealing to create three-dimensional objects. Farther north, in Central America and Mexico, mold casting was the principal metalworking technology. Using the **lost-wax process** (also known to Old World metallurgists), the metal-smith first created the desired shape in wax and then formed a ceramic mold around it. Molten metal poured through holes in the mold melted away the wax, leaving metal in its place—hence the name of the technique.

A common alloy used throughout these regions was composed of copper and gold (and sometimes silver as well) and was known as *tumbaga*. As the analyses conducted by Heather Lechtman have shown, Andean metalsmiths also developed techniques to ensure that the surfaces of these alloys were pure gold. This was done by a technique known as **depletion gilding,** whereby a tumbaga object was treated with chemicals that removed the copper (and silver) at the surface. Once polished, the remaining surface of glittering gold disguised the fact that the underlying alloy was mostly copper, containing only from 40 percent to as little as 12 percent gold. Lechtman's experiments also indicate that some Andean copper objects were plated with thin coatings of gold or silver by electro-chemical means.

Overall, it is significant to note that metallurgy in the Old World functioned quite differently from New World metalworking, which was related much more closely to social and ideological concerns. In contrast to the Old World, where metals were developed to serve agricultural, warfare, and transportation technologies, and therefore emphasized characteristics necessary for those uses (strength, hardness, durability, edge retention, and the like), New World metals were primarily used for status objects and symbols of supernatural authority (Fig. 10.11). In the Andes, gold represented the "sweat" of the sun, and silver was the "tears" of the moon. Thus, it is not surprising that New World metallurgy emphasized techniques that enhanced the gold and silver content of metal surfaces.

Analysis of Metal Artifacts

Metal artifacts have been found in archaeological contexts from southwest Asia to Southeast Asia, and in Europe, Africa, and the Americas. Archaeological analyses have varied with the geographical area, in accord with differing research priorities. Because metal—especially molten metal—is a plastic, malleable material, it, like pottery, is particularly suited to stylistic analyses and classifications. Such studies have been done; one example is the classification of bronze *fibulae* or "safety-pin brooches" from La Tène sites of Iron Age Europe (Fig. 10.12). Other studies have focused on the form of metal artifacts and on functional attribution based on variation in form, similar to studies done for stone and ceramic artifacts.

A more general focus in studies of metal artifacts, however, is on analyses that aid in reconstructing ancient technology. Classifications divide the metal industry into subindustries according to the metal being worked.

FIGURE 10.11 New World metallurgy: pre-Columbian gold breast plate from Ecuador. (Courtesy of The University Museum, University of Pennsylvania.)

More technical analyses are then performed, including constituent analysis and microscopic examination of the metal structure; these studies help the archaeologist to understand the range of technology involved in production of the pieces, from procurement of raw materials to formation and refinement of the final product. Constituent analysis, for example, can not only identify the metals and nonmetallic materials present but also specify the metal sources. Examination of the microstructure of an artifact may yield clues to the precise techniques used in its production—hammering, annealing, quenching, and so on.

A complicating factor in these analyses is that metallurgy, like pottery, is an additive and correcting process in which mistakes can to some extent be covered and "smoothed away" by subsequent treatment. Unlike pottery, however, in which firing permanently alters the raw material, metal artifacts can also be melted down and the "raw material" reclaimed and reused. Such recycling may, for example, account for a relative lack of bronze artifacts early in the Iron Age: The expected number of pieces may actually have been produced, but their material might have been reclaimed, so that it entered the archaeological record only after its recycling ended, an unknown period of time after the original smelting.

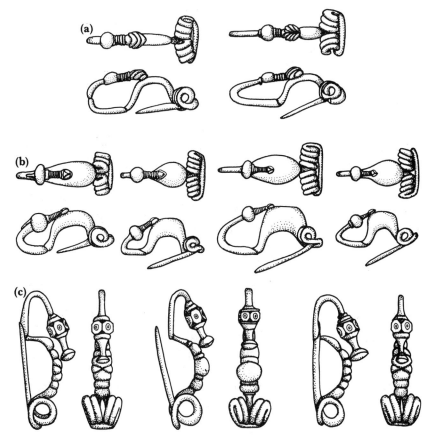

FIGURE 10.12 Three hypothesized stylistic types of bronze fibulae from an Iron Age grave at Münsingen, Germany. (After Hodson 1968.)

ORGANIC ARTIFACTS

A variety of artifacts are made from organic materials such as wood, plant fibers, bone, antler, ivory, and shell. Such items are known to be important and are sometimes even numerically dominant in the tool assemblages of some modern societies, such as the Inuit (Eskimo), and were probably among the earliest kinds of artifacts made and used in the human past. They are quite susceptible to decay, however, and thus are encountered by archaeologists only under special conditions.

Other kinds of organic materials have also been used to produce artifacts, of course: Paper, leather, gourds, and many more have been exploited, and many have special technologies associated with their production and use. However, we shall restrict discussion here to the most frequently encountered artifact categories: bone and related materials (such as antler and ivory), wood, plant fibers, and shell.

Organic Material Technology

Animal skeletons have been proposed as the raw material for some of the earliest tools. Raymond Dart, one of the discoverers of the early hominid form *Australopithecus*, hypothesized that this relative of modern human-kind used tools made from the long bones and jaws of gazelles, antelopes, and wild boars. The principal body of evidence for this **osteodontokeratic** ("bone-tooth-horn") technology was the material found with the austra-lopithecine remains in Makapansgat cave, in the Transvaal of South Africa. Other scholars, however, have argued that the Makapansgat remains may represent nothing more than a food refuse deposit, accumulated by car-nivores such as hyenas or leopards as well as (or even instead of) hominids.

Most specialists now favor the latter explanation for the African mate-rial, but a similar debate still rages concerning the possibility that some of the earliest human settlers in the Americas may have used bone rather than stone for tools. Arguments about New World uses have centered on whether the **spiral fracture,** a break curving along and around the bone (Fig. 10.13) that yielded sharp-edged bone fragments, could have come only from a human blow. Some analysts believed that to be the case, but most now argue that the same fracture would be produced when a bone is trampled by large animals such as bison.

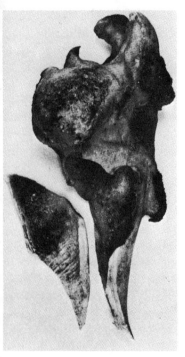

FIGURE 10.13 Bison limb bone showing a good example of a spiral fracture. (From Johnson 1985, by permission of Academic Press. Photography by Nicky L. Olson, Museum of Texas Tech University.)

These controversies over interpretation have given rise to a productive line of research aimed at distinguishing bones modified by human acts from those modified by nonhuman agents. We will consider this complex question again in Chapters 11 and 13, when we discuss animal bones as food remains and when we consider interpretive issues in general.

Despite the controversy over the origins of bone tools, there is no doubt that by the Upper Paleolithic, people were making artifacts from a variety of animal parts. In both the Old and the New Worlds, bone was split and carved with stone tools to form projectile points, fishhooks, and other tools (Fig. 10.14). It was also used to make articles of adornment, such as beads. Antler, usually from deer, was split or carved to make pro-jectile points, especially barbed points for spears or harpoons. In the Arc-tic, the prehistoric tradition of carving ivory with stone to make harpoons and other artifacts has survived into historic times.

The technology involved in the production of bone, antler, and ivory tools is subtractive, like stoneworking. Technologically, the simplest such tools were those that involved *no* form modification, such as an animal bone used as a club. The next technological level would be breaking the bone to produce a sharp or jagged edge. Many forms, however, involved working with other tools. The earliest finds suggest that such work was first confined to chipping and cracking, but by the Upper Paleolithic, the production of controlled forms of bone, antler, and ivory tools shows great variety and sophistication; some forms even have engraved decora-tion. This development corresponds with the Upper Paleolithic prolif-eration of functionally more specialized stone tools, such as gravers and burins with edges used to shape or decorate bone or other organic materials, as well as with the beginnings of art and—according to Alexander Marshack—of symbolic notation.

Like those made of bone, antler, and ivory, wooden artifacts are highly perishable; thus the precise origins and antiquity of woodworking are obscured by lack of preserved evidence. Lower Paleolithic wooden tools have been reported from waterlogged sites in Africa, however, and spear-points from sites at Clacton, England, and Lehringer, Germany, testify that woodworking technology existed by the Middle Paleolithic in Europe. Woodworking, too, is a subtractive industry, achieving the desired artifact shape by scraping, engraving, breaking, and so on. Indirect evidence of woodworking is preserved more often than the wood itself, in the form of certain stone tools—those we call *scrapers, spokeshaves,* and *gravers*—that could have been used to manufacture wooden tools. (Some of the lithic use-wear studies noted earlier are helping to identify more firmly when these stone tools really were used as woodworking implements.) Fire, too, may be used in the production of wooden tools; for instance, the points of digging sticks are hardened by controlled exposure to fire.

Plant and animal fibers, such as reeds, cotton, sinews, and wool, provide raw materials for making baskets, cords, nets, and textiles. All these products occur commonly around the globe, and although we can document their having been made for at least the last 11,000 years, surely this is only a minimum estimate of their antiquity. The evidence for these technologies includes finished baskets, cords, and textiles, most often in very fragmentary form, and indirect representations such as cord or cloth impressions decorating pottery surfaces. Indeed, the name given to the oldest known ceramic vessels—Jomon—refers in Japanese to their cord-impressed surfaces.

Both the organic pieces and their impressions can yield information on manufacturing techniques. For example, cord or thread, made of multiple twisted strands of fiber, may be identified according to the direction in which it was twisted or *spun*. Those twisted to the spinner's right are called *S-angle,* because fibers slant from upper left to lower right, like the middle part of the letter S. Likewise, cords twisted to the spinner's left are called *Z-angle,* since the slant of the spinning resembles the upper right to lower left angle of the letter Z. Baskets (Fig. 10.15) may be identified as **twined, coiled,** or **plaited** depending on whether the basketmaker wove the stitch (the *weft*) horizontally (twining) or vertically (coiling) through the stationary element (the *warp*), or whether stitching proceeded in both directions at once (plaiting). Ancient weavers and basketmakers achieved many complex forms and designs, sometimes showing development of their work as an art—when archaeologists have the good fortune to recover enough of these fragile remains to discover the artisans' skills.

Shell artifacts have been found the world over, including in Neolithic Egypt, where they were the raw material for some fishhooks. Certain shells are appropriate for cups or spoons, and in areas where stone is scarce, they

FIGURE 10.14 Bone harpoon heads from Alaska, with flint inserts, illustrate one kind of artifact fashioned from organic materials. (Courtesy of The University Museum, University of Pennsylvania.)

FIGURE 10.15 A coiled basket from Antelope House, Arizona, well preserved despite its 1000-year age. (After Adovasio 1977.)

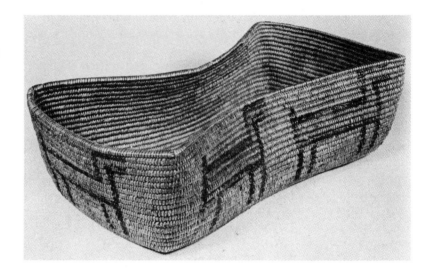

have occasionally been used as adze blades or other such tools. Shells are also used for adornment; in cultures such as the Hohokam of the American Southwest, the technology of shellworking includes the craft of etching designs into the surface of the shell by delicate application of a corrosive agent to eat away selected areas, leaving others in relief to form a decorative design (Fig. 10.16).

Analysis of Organic Artifacts

A fundamental kind of analysis performed on organic artifacts is identification of the material—including the biological species from which it was made. Such analysis yields information on the range of biotic resources exploited by an ancient society and may give clues to communication links with other areas, for instance, when shell artifacts at an inland site are found to be marine (saltwater) species. We will consider the "ecofactual" aspect of organic artifacts in more detail in the chapter on ecofacts.

Most classifications of organic artifacts are based on criteria of form (Fig. 10.17). Sometimes these form taxonomies have stylistic overtones, but more often they involve functional inferences, and the types may be labeled with assumed functional names. For example, the well-known artifact assemblages of the European Upper Paleolithic, especially the Magdalenian, include a great variety of barbed bone projectile points, almost always referred to as "harpoons." The dangers of such unsupported functional labeling have already been noted: It provides convenient names—and easy ways to remember—the formal types, but does not establish the actual function of these artifacts.

ARTIFACTS AND SAMPLING

Artifactual studies can involve sampling strategies at two points: data collecting and data analysis. Sampling in data collection procedures has been discussed in previous chapters, but we shall note again here that excavation planning can be organized to facilitate artifact studies. For example, an archaeologist who wished to investigate the range of pottery forms used by an ancient community would want to maximize the variety of functional contexts investigated. Different vessel forms might well be found in burials as opposed to domestic situations, and excavation of midden deposits would increase the quantity of material available for analysis.

Whether the archaeologist analyzes all or only part of the artifact collection obtained depends on two factors—the size of the artifact collection

FIGURE 10.16 An example of a Hohokam decorated shell from Arizona (ca. A.D. 800–1200). The design was etched with acid from a saguaro cactus. (Arizona State Museum Collections, University of Arizona.)

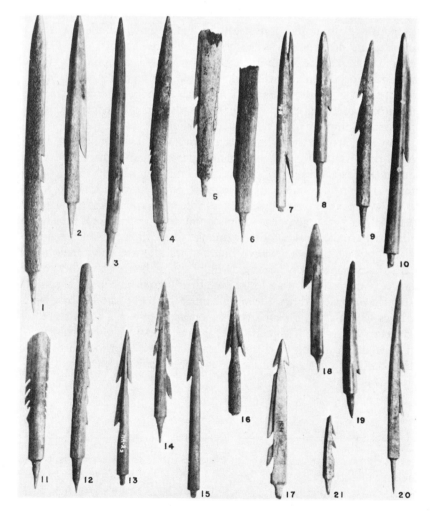

FIGURE 10.17 Classification of bone projectiles from Cape Denbigh, Alaska. (From *The Archaeology of Cape Denbigh* by J. L. Giddings, Brown University Press, © 1964 Brown University.)

and the expense of the analysis, in time or money or both. Generally speaking, the closer to total sampling researchers can get, the more confidence they can have that the results of the analysis can be generalized to the whole collection.

Some artifact categories contain so few items that examination of all pieces is both desirable and easily feasible. Such a situation is more often associated with organic artifacts than with stone, ceramic, or metal ones, since the organic remains are least likely to survive. The reverse situation—more artifacts than can possibly be studied—is most often true for stone and ceramic collections; for instance, Kidder calculated that more than 1,000,000 sherds were recovered during his excavations at the highland Guatemalan site of Kaminaljuyú. In such cases, sampling in analysis is usually necessary.

The fundamental question in designing a sampling program concerns representation: Of what is the analyzed sample to be representative? Randomized sample selection increases the probability that the sample is representative of the population from which it is drawn. But how are the sample units defined? One can choose individual artifacts, but George Cowgill suggests using provenience units—lots—as sampling units, and then analyzing all artifacts within the selected lots. In this way, the archaeologist can examine the full range of materials from the same context. Since laboratory processing deals with the materials in provenience groups, using these as sampling units also makes drawing the sample easier.

Drawing samples for technical laboratory analyses is somewhat different. If the analyses require consultant experts and specialized laboratory equipment, expense usually places strict limits on sample size. For example, thin-sections, radiocarbon analyses, and neutron-activation analyses are so expensive that it is seldom feasible to do more than a few dozen such analyses per project. The sampling unit for such studies is usually the individual artifact, and random sampling is less often possible or appropriate. For example, researchers would not want to use whole artifacts for a destructive analysis. The objectives of research may also dictate the choice: If the analysis seeks to indicate the range of raw material sources exploited in ancient times, the sample units should be selected by characteristics—such as visible differences in stone type—that seem to reflect maximum variability. The point here, as in all questions of sampling, is to know what the sample is meant to represent, and then to structure the sampling design to make the sample as representative of the target population as possible.

SUMMARY

In this chapter we have reviewed in some detail the analysis of artifacts—as the first of three categories of archaeological data. Artifacts are portable items whose form is partially or wholly the result of human activity. Archaeologists begin the analysis of artifacts by dividing them into a series of industries defined by shared raw materials and manufacturing techniques. The artifact industries most commonly encountered by archaeologists are chipped stone, ground stone, and pottery. Industries of various metal and organic materials are somewhat less likely to survive the ravages of time and, therefore, are less often encountered in most archaeological situations.

The physical characteristics and original manufacturing techniques used in each artifact industry influence the kinds of analyses employed by archaeologists and other specialists. Beyond this, the choice of analysis technique applied in each case is determined by the research goals and the specific questions being asked of the data.

Chipped-stone tools are the result of a subtractive production process that often preserves in the archaeological record evidence for most, if not all, the steps taken during the original manufacturing behavior. This makes technological analysis of chipped-stone industries both feasible and rewarding for understanding this kind of ancient behavior. Functional analysis is also especially useful in reconstructing past activities when the analysis is based on detectable use-wear and residues. In contrast, pottery making is an additive process, so that technological analysis for this industry is often more difficult and limited in scope. But clay is a plastic and easily manipulated substance that can be shaped and decorated in a variety of ways, thus lending itself to stylistic classifications that define fine-grained variations in both time and space. Pottery vessel shapes and the identification of residues in and on the vessels are used to infer function as a basis for reconstructing ancient activities. Metal artifacts, like pottery, present characteristics and opportunities for technological, stylistic, functional, and constituent analyses. Artifacts made from organic materials, in contrast, are most often classified by form as a basis for functional inferences. Constituent analyses of most kinds of artifacts can identify sources of raw material and allow the reconstruction of past trade and distribution systems.

Regardless of the artifact industry under scrutiny, or the kind of analysis applied to that category, the archaeologist must ensure that the sample being studied represents the full range of ancient behavior in the record, to develop an accurate reconstruction of the past.

GUIDE TO FURTHER READING

Allen 1989; Beck 1974; Brothwell and Higgs 1970; Carter 1978; Henderson 1989; Hodges 1964; Joukowsky 1980; Lambert 1984; McNally and Walsh 1984; Noël Hume 1969; Sayre et al. 1988; Shott 1989b; Tite 1972; Vandiver et al. 1991

Lithic Artifacts
J. Adams 1988; Bordaz 1970; Bordes 1968; Clay 1976; Cotterell and Kam-

minga 1987; Crabtree 1972; Fladmark 1982; Flenniken 1984; Gero 1991; Gurfinkel and Franklin 1988; Hayden 1979; Henry and Odell 1989; Hester and Heizer 1973; Jelinek 1976; Johnson 1978; Keeley 1974, 1977, 1980; Keeley and Toth 1981; Kidder 1932, 1947; Lawrence 1979; Loy 1983; Meeks et al. 1982; Moss 1983; Oakley 1956; Roe 1985; Sackett 1966, 1982; Schiffer 1976; Semenov 1964; Sheets 1975; Swanson 1975; Torrance 1989; Toth 1985; Tringham et al. 1974; Wright 1977; Young and Bonnichsen 1984

Ceramic Artifacts

Arnold 1985; M. Bennett 1974; Bishop, Rands, and Holley 1982; Bronitsky 1989; Cunliffe 1984; Gibson and Woods 1990; Gifford 1960, 1976; Glover and Griffiths 1989; Kingery 1985, 1986; Matson 1965; Nelson 1985; Plog 1980, 1983; Rice 1977, 1987; Rye 1981; Sabloff and Smith 1969; Shepard 1971; Smith, Willey, and Gifford 1960; Stoltman 1989; Whallon 1972

Metal Artifacts

Bayard 1972; Benson 1979; Bray and Seeley 1989; Lechtman 1976, 1984a, 1984b; Maddin 1988; Maddin, Muhly, and Wheeler 1977; Rothenberg 1990; Rowlands 1971; Schmidt and Avery 1983; Shimada 1981; Shimada, Epstein, and Craig 1982; Shimada and Merkel 1991; C. S. Smith 1973; Thompson 1970; van der Merwe and Avery 1982; Wertime 1973; Wertime and Muhly 1980; Wertime and Wertime 1982

Organic Artifacts

Adovasio 1977; L. R. Binford 1981b, 1985; Brain 1981; Coles 1984; Dart 1949, 1957; Giddings 1964; Hurley 1979; Jakes and Angel 1989; Johnson 1985; Kent 1983; M. E. King 1978; Read-Martin and Read 1975; Rowell and Barbour 1990; Ryder 1983, 1984; Stanford, Bonnichsen, and Morlan 1981

Artifacts and Sampling

Carr 1985; Cowgill 1964; Kidder 1961; Mueller 1975

POTTERY IN THE HIGH TECH LAB

Ronald L. Bishop

Ronald L. Bishop earned his Ph.D. from Southern Illinois University and is currently Senior Research Archaeologist at the Conservation Analytical Laboratory of the Smithsonian Institution. Both at the Smithsonian and earlier at Brookhaven National Laboratory, Bishop has been at the forefront of development of increasingly sophisticated methods for physico-chemical characterization of the raw materials from which artifacts are made. He is best known for his studies of ceramics and jade.

Sometimes I am struck by the sounds—the clicking of relays and the deep gulping noises of diffusion pumps—that indicate that laboratory instruments are alive and maintained. It is a marked contrast to another life in Central America, where insects and birds offer a chorus of sound, punctuated at times by the territorial call of howler monkeys. Archaeology and my interest in the functioning of ancient exchange systems have allowed me to live a somewhat schizophrenic existence, one that embraces both life in the field and in the high tech laboratory.

I am particularly interested in the relationships that existed among different sectors of Maya sites, such as residential units and the public or elite structures, and the relationships of one site to another. Specifically, I have wondered how the distribution of tangible remains in the meager archaeological record could give an indication of how goods, services, and ideas flowed between different social groups. One avenue of investigation I decided to pursue is the way in which raw materials and finished items are acquired and distributed.

Attention to exchange or trade as important forces in the evolution of societies intensified during the 1960s, fueled in part by decades of research that had roughed out the developmental history of a major part of the world. Another significant factor in this changing focus was the development of new technology for identifying the composition of raw materials.

The work of Robert Rands, an archaeologist at Southern Illinois University at Carbondale, exemplified many of the new concerns with trade and exchange. He sought to determine the relationship of the major ceremonial Maya center of Palenque to the minor centers that surrounded it by using traditional and technologically advanced analyses.

The subject of his analysis at Palenque was the pottery, which was ravaged by time and nature. The soft-fired, sand-tempered pottery had been attacked by a thousand years of heavy rain and acid soils to the point where little surface finish remained. Rands was forced to use characteristics of the ceramic paste—the kinds and amounts of tempering materials—along with variation in vessel form and type of plastic surface decoration to reconstruct changes in the ceramic sequence and to determine what pottery was made locally and what had been imported. In the early 1970s, as part of his investigation, he sent samples to Brookhaven National Laboratory for chemical analysis by a then relatively new technique called instrumental neutron activation. This analytical tool for archaeology detects minute differences in the elemental composition of the ceramics, and Rands hoped that it would be useful in providing new insight into the systems of Palenque ceramic production and distribution.

(continued)

(continued)

Rands's study rekindled in me an earlier interest in the physical sciences. With his assistance, I left archaeological field work in the southern Mexican jungle in 1973, went home, repacked my clothes, and began a year of study at Brookhaven National Laboratory. I embarked on a future that was marked not only by training in nuclear chemical instrumentation, but also in geochemistry, statistics, and computer applications as well, all of which have proven indispensable in a multidisciplinary study of archaeological materials.

At the heart of all empirically based studies documenting the movement of a material or artifact from one location to another is the notion of characterization. Using techniques borrowed from the physical or natural sciences such as chemistry, petrography, and so forth, scientists can determine, or characterize, a set of physical attributes that differentiates one material from all others. The success of characterization of archaeological materials relies on the principle that objects such as obsidian, pottery, jade, chert, and so on from a specific source are more similar to others from that source than to objects produced from other sources. For example, the composition of the ceramic paste of a piece of pottery from a specific clay deposit will be more similar to other pottery from that clay bed than it will be to pottery made from a different deposit of clay. Data from the Palenque research illustrates this general principle well.

Large cylinders used to support ceramic incense burners are numerous about the ceremonial center of Palenque and have been recovered with less frequency at certain smaller sites in the surrounding area. Ornately decorated with symbols of the supernatural, the stands were an important component in the ritual paraphernalia of Palenque. Macroscopically, they are of the same paste that has a long tradition in certain other Palenque ceramics. Interestingly, however, conical vessels that fit into the open top of the burner stands are made of a different paste. An important piece of information concerning Palenque's trading relationships and the geographical extent of Palenque's religious influence would be gained if we could determine the number and locations of places where these ritual components were made.

We characterized the pottery at Palenque and the surrounding sites through chemical determination of elemental abundances in the ceramic pastes. Using statistical analysis, we found several groups of pottery to be internally consistent in chemical composition and separable from other, similarly formed groups. But did these chemically and statistically derived groups reflect anything more than mathematical gamesmanship?

To find out, we examined each group for relative homogeneity of such attributes as site provenience, form, paste color, and the kind and abundance of minerals present. Gratifyingly, the groups appeared to show cohesiveness in regard to these other attributes and, importantly, when the proveniences were inspected, six of the seven groups showed rather specific geographic locations, with distributions north, south, east, and west of Palenque; two groups were almost exclusively of Palenque provenience and were inferred to have been produced at the site.

Against this background of characterized red-brown medium to fine sand-tempered pottery, we compared the chemically derived profiles for the region's incense burners and burner stands. Approximately 80 percent of all of the ornate incense burner stands "matched" one of the two groups of ceramic presumed to have been made at Palenque—regardless of where the stands had been recovered. Interestingly, the conical inserts for the burner stands did *not* match the Palenque groups but were more like the groups of pottery from the plains to the north.

We now had part of the information that we sought. It appears that Palenque was involved in the production of ceramic materials that functioned within a ritual context. Some of these items were exported to the smaller sites in the surrounding area, perhaps as markers of Palenque's ritual importance. Among the items that were imported were the conical inserts, linking the smaller sites to the major center; whether the linkage was by ritual inclusion, trade, or tribute remains unknown. Looking at similar information about other ceramics analyzed from the study area, we found that several kinds of utility ceramics were produced at the outlying population centers and were obtained by the inhabitants of Palenque. Taken together, we were able to infer with considerable certainty that the production and distribution of ritually-charged Palenque-produced ceramic materials can be observed to have a greater distribution in the region than exists for the more utilitarian products. The detailed changes in this pattern over time are still under investigation.

For any material of interest, the technique chosen for characterization depends on the specific questions being asked. I have focused primarily on one aspect of pottery: composition. The archaeological meaning of that composition, however, is found only within the context of other information. There is a long way to go from simply showing that a particular object was made of material from Source X to showing its importance in the movement of goods, services, and ideas. Indeed, studies of trade or exchange, production and distribution, and the use of techniques from the physical sciences constitute but one part, albeit an integral one, of archaeological investigation.

CHAPTER ELEVEN

ANALYSIS OF ECOFACTS

Floral Remains

Species Identification

Floral Analysis

Nonhuman Faunal Remains

Species Identification

Faunal Analysis

Human Remains

Inorganic Remains

Ecofacts and Sampling

Summary

Guide to Further Reading

It may come as a surprise to some that most of the behavioral ideas regarding our ancient past are dependent on the interpretation of faunal remains and depositional context—not . . . stone tools.

    Lewis R. Binford, Bones: Ancient Men and Modern Myths, *1981*

Unlike artifacts, **ecofacts** are archaeological data that do *not* owe their form to human behavior. For the most part, they are the residues of human subsistence. Quite obviously, the acquisition of food is an essential and fundamental activity, but to archaeologists, the kinds of subsistence activities and their changes through time are crucial keys to reconstructing past societies and their evolution through time.

Ecofacts provide the primary evidence for such studies. Examples include plant and animal remains and soils found in archaeological deposits. Although they are "natural," essentially unaltered objects, ecofacts can still give us important information about past human societies. For instance, at the Olsen-Chubbuck site in southeastern Colorado, a series of bison skeletons was revealed in association with some stone tools, all strewn along the base of a ravine (Fig. 11.1). The site represents the remains of human food-procurement behavior some 8500 years ago. The location and arrangement of both ecofacts and artifacts have been used to infer a good deal about hunting strategy (how and from what direction the animals were being driven over the ravine edge, including which way the wind may have been blowing), butchering techniques (how the carcasses were dismembered, which bones were stripped of meat on the spot and which were carried off to the presumed "camp" site), and yield (how much meat and by-products were available from the kill).

Ecofacts can also tell us about noneconomic activities such as ritual. **Analysis** of the heavy concentration of pollen found scattered over Burial IV in Shanidar cave, northern Iraq, implies that when this Neanderthal man was buried some 60,000 years ago, his survivors covered him with flowers, including daisies, cornflowers, and hollyhocks. Further, because such flowers now bloom locally in May and June, one can infer that the burial probably took place at that time of year.

Most frequently, however, ecofacts are used to reconstruct the environment in which past societies lived and the range of resources they exploited. Grahame Clark and his coworkers analyzed pollen samples from Star Carr, a 10,000-year-old **Mesolithic** site in northern England, and inferred that the surrounding area was largely covered by a forest of birch and pine; the presence of pollen from plants that thrive in open areas points to localized clearings, one of which was the site of Star Carr. By examining both the plant remains and the abundance of antlers of red deer, roe deer, and elk that were recovered, the original investigators and later analysts could establish the times of year the site had been occupied.

Interpretation of ecofacts: The Olsen-Chubbuck site, Colorado

Pioneering environmental reconstruction: Grahame Clark at Star Carr, England

FIGURE 11.1 Remains of bison killed and butchered by hunters some 8500 years ago, excavated at the Olsen-Chubbuck site, Colorado. (Reproduced by permission of the Colorado State Museum and the Society for American Archaeology, from *Memoirs of the Society for American Archaeology* 26:ix, 1972.)

This interpretation has relied mainly on comparing the distribution of antlers broken from the animals' skulls with those that had simply been collected after being shed naturally, and correlating these data with the known seasonal cycles of deer antler growth and shedding. The work at Star Carr was a landmark, showing the wealth of interpretation that could be gained from ecofactual data.

The first step in analysis of ecofacts, like artifacts, is classification. Artifacts may be classified in a number of ways—all of them involving effects of human behavior on the artifact. Clearly, the classification of ecofacts must use different criteria. Classification of ecofacts begins with sorting into gross categories: **organic ecofacts** (plants and animals) and **inorganic ecofacts** (soils). Specimens are then further identified, usually by specialists, within classificatory schemes borrowed from botany, zoology, and geology. Once these preliminary steps are completed, ecofacts may be classified according to properties that might relate them to past human societies. For example, some plants and animals are available for harvesting only at limited times of the year; these, as the Shanidar and Star Carr cases indicate, may be used to determine seasonality of exploitation. Animals can also be studied in terms of the amounts of meat they would yield and therefore the size of the human population they could support. Similarly, soils may be classified by their relative potential fertility under given kinds of agricultural exploitation.

FLORAL REMAINS

Plant remains in archaeological contexts include two basic categories: microspecimens (pollen and phytoliths—defined and discussed later) and macrospecimens (seeds, leaves, casts or impressions, and so forth). Although pollen is often durable and remains in the archaeological record, other **floral ecofacts** survive far less often (they may be preserved in extremely cold, dry, or wet conditions). Indirect evidence of plant use can also be gleaned from such sources as pictorial representation—Egyptian murals illustrating growing wheat or brewing beer are examples. But here we wish to deal with archaeological plant remains and how they are studied.

Species Identification

Once recovered, usually by flotation or similar means, floral specimens are packed in sealed containers in the field to prevent contamination. They are then sent to either a consulting botanist, such as a palynologist, or a botanically trained archaeologist for microscopic examination and species identification. Microspecimens, including pollen and opal phytoliths (discussed below), always require a specialist's eye, but macrospecimens, such as maize cobs, often can be identified in a preliminary way in the field. Some illustrated manuals give the range of species known in a given area, but the archaeologist may find it useful to collect and identify seeds, leaves, and flowers of plants currently present in the locality, for direct comparison.

As a part of the identification process, many plants are categorized as wild or domesticated. The **domestication** of plants in the Old and New Worlds was a significant cultural development, giving people more direct control over the quantity and quality of their food supply. Accordingly, a good deal of study has been done on when, where, and how the domestication process was carried out. Since domestication is a gradual effect of repeated selection for desired traits—for example, larger or faster-growing strains are deliberately replanted and nurtured—there is no single "original" domesticated maize cob or wheat kernel. Rather, one

FIGURE 11.2 Two types of wheat: On the left, a wild form; on the right, a more domesticated one. Domestication resulted in an increase in the number of grains and a decrease in the brittleness of the junction between the *glume* and the *rachis*. The tougher junction prevented the grain from being released before threshing.

can discern trends in form from "fully wild" to "fully domesticated." In the Old World, for example, wild forms of wheat were characterized by a brittle **rachis** (stem) and a tough **glume** (the strands holding the grain) (Fig. 11.2). If the rachis is brittle, the mature plant can spread its seed easily to produce the next generation. A brittle rachis is unfavorable to human gathering, however, for it breaks when the plant is jarred by being harvested, and the seed is lost. Similarly, a tough glume protects the wheat kernel until it germinates, but it also makes the wheat more difficult to thresh, to yield the kernels for human consumption. It is not surprising, then, that in the course of wheat domestication, the brittle rachis and tough glume were selected *against;* selection favored forms that were easier both to harvest and to thresh. Other examples include the trend in New World maize domestication to larger size—more and longer rows of kernels (Fig. 11.3).

Once the botanical identification of species and domestication status has been made, the specimens can be further classified or grouped in a number of ways. Except for special laboratory procedures, floral analyses fall into three categories: what forms are present, what special traits these forms possess, and in what contexts they were found.

Floral Analysis

Simple tallies of presence/absence and relative abundance of the various forms represented at a site (or other archaeological unit) can suggest interpretations. For example, the relative abundance of wild as opposed to domesticated plant forms may indicate relative reliance on food collection as opposed to food production. The parts of the plants represented, such as macrospecimens as opposed to microspecimens, may sometimes be important: Pollen is commonly carried by wind (as hay fever sufferers know all too well!) and may be introduced to an archaeological deposit accidentally without signifying deliberate ancient exploitation of the species represented. The identification of pollen species is a task of **palynology,** the area of botany devoted to pollen studies. Macrospecimens, on the other hand, are more likely to represent human exploitation. Yet caution is always necessary in interpreting such tallies, since observed presence and absence or relative abundance figures are always affected by sampling design and differential preservation. For example, cacao pollen is most unlikely to be preserved in the tropical soils in which this tree was grown.

As the last statement suggests, a major problem with floral analysis concerns preservation and recovery of the data. Because they are organic, macrospecimens and even pollen are usually subject to decay. As we have noted, permanently dry, wet, or cold deposits preserve floral material in greater abundance, and flotation processing and deliberate pollen sampling have improved recovery rates for what has survived. Since 1970, however, new emphasis has been placed on a more durable kind of plant residue—**opal phytoliths.** Their name comes from words for "plant" and "stone," and that is what they are: microscopic silica bodies formed naturally in living plants. The particular phytoliths vary among species. Opal phytoliths have been identified by specialists in deposits up to 60 million or 70 million years old. When recovered from archaeological deposits—all of which are much younger than that—they have provided a rich source of information (and sometimes the only one) on the ancient utilization of plants. For example, phytoliths were the only floral clue to the early presence of domesticated maize at Real Alto, in Ecuador, at about 2300 B.C. And phytoliths were among the residues found on stone tools from Hinds Cave, in southwest Texas; these residues helped Harry Shafer and Richard Holloway identify the use of the stone tools in plant processing 2000 to 5000 years ago.

Archaeologists can compare what is known of special growing requirements or other characteristics of the plants they have found to glean interpretive data. Some plants reflect very specific climatic conditions; others indicate conditions of open or forested vegetation cover. The latter factor was used at Star Carr to reconstruct the environmental surroundings of the site. More broadly speaking, palynological studies have used such properties to reconstruct climatic changes in temperate Europe for the millennia following the final retreat of the glaciers, and to trace (by evidence of large-scale deforestation) the advent of land-clearing practices and cultivation (Fig. 11.4). Other specific plant characteristics can also provide clues to whether and how the plants were used. For example, plants have various effects on the human body when ingested: Certain plants are known to be edible, others poisonous, hallucinogenic, or medicinal. Solecki has suggested that because many of the pollens found with Shanidar Burial IV are from flowers used medicinally today, such properties may have been appreciated in ancient times. He speculates that the flowers may indicate that the dead man was a shaman or curer.

Another dimension in the study of floral ecofacts is the context in which they are found. The Shanidar IV context suggests the ideological or symbolic use of plants. Indeed, the only sure indication that a plant was a food resource is contextual—finding it in the gastrointestinal tracts of mummies or bog corpses, or in human **coprolites** (preserved feces). Food remains and residues may also be found adhering to the interiors of food storage vessels or to preparation surfaces such as grinding stones. Of course, vegetal food remains may occur in other contexts, but in such cases their interpretation as "food" depends less on context than on whether the item is a known or probable food item, such as maize or barley.

The excavation of ancient agricultural fields at Pulltrouser Swamp, Belize, provides an example of the importance of ecofactual identification in reconstructing ancient subsistence activities (also see Chapter 14). Excavations at Pulltrouser Swamp revealed maize pollen and a carbonized maize stem fragment, along with cotton and amaranth pollen. Although the evidence supports the idea that the fields were used for ancient maize

FIGURE 11.3 Comparison between a reconstructed early maize cob on the left, and domesticated maize on the right. Over time, selection favored more and longer rows of kernels.

Reconstructing ancient subsistence: Pulltrouser Swamp, Belize

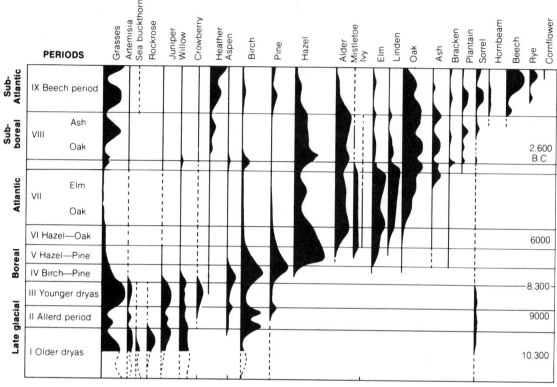

FIGURE 11.4 Simplified pollen sequence in postglacial Denmark, used to reconstruct climatic changes by inference from vegetative changes. Because the different species shown here are sensitive to climatic factors, shifts in frequency of pollen indicating thick forests as opposed to open grasslands point to ancient changes in climate. (After Dimbleby 1970.)

agriculture, the question of whether cotton and amaranth were also cultivated remains unresolved, since it could not be determined whether those two kinds of pollen were from wild or domestic varieties.

NONHUMAN FAUNAL REMAINS

Animal remains in archaeological contexts take a number of forms, from whole specimens, such as mummies, to partial ones, such as bones or coprolites. Bones and teeth, the most commonly recovered **faunal ecofacts,** have received the most attention. Human exploitation of animals, like human use of plants, may often be inferred from indirect archaeological evidence—perhaps the most famous being the Paleolithic cave murals of western Europe. But we shall confine discussion here to physical remains of actual animals.

As we noted in Chapter 10, a fundamental analytic and interpretive issue regarding faunal remains is the extent to which animal bones and other materials defined as ecofacts actually reflect human activity. Artifacts and features are by definition products of human behavior and are thus automatically pertinent to the study of the human past. Ecofacts, on the other hand, usually possess no overt evidence of human activity, or, if they do, such evidence may be extremely subtle or difficult to assess. Thus it is certainly possible that some animal bones, plant remains, pollen, and other ecofactual materials found in archaeological situations, even when associated with artifacts and features, owe their presence to entirely nonhuman agencies such as animal activity, wind, or water deposition. The key is obviously to recognize the distinction between human and nonhuman activity in cases of apparent ecofact associations.

The ability to make such a distinction comes from the field of **taphonomy.** This is the study of what happens to the remains of a plant or an animal after it dies, and one book on the subject is appropriately named *Fossils in the Making.* Archaeologists involved in taphonomic research seek to specify how human acts, such as hunting, butchering, or toolmaking, are reflected in bone and how they can be contrasted with effects of other agents.

Taphonomic studies: Distinguishing human from nonhuman activity in Africa

For example, as we noted in Chapter 10, Raymond Dart used the pattern of occurrence of nonhominid bones—how they were broken, what elements were present, and how they were deposited—to argue that these bones were tools used at the South African site of Makapansgat more than a million years ago. But were they? The lack of reference material to answer that question was one of the chief issues that led archaeologists to taphonomy. Innovative research by scholars such as C. K. Brain and Lewis Binford uses contemporary observations to identify how bone deposits produced by modern human hunting groups contrast with those resulting from other activities, such as the feeding of carnivores. This kind of detection allows archaeologists to begin to identify differences in prey animal bone mutilation or breakage patterns and the kinds and patterning of body parts that ultimately are deposited. For instance, some investigators have attempted to differentiate butchering marks made by human tools from the marks left by carnivore teeth.

As a result, archaeologists now fully appreciate that many bone assemblages (and, by implication, other ecofacts) that have been treated as the result of human activity may actually represent nonhuman actions. It is evident that nonhuman causes can produce bone modifications that mimic the signs archaeologists draw on to detect ancient human use. For instance, a large accumulation of animal bones in Shield Trap Cave, Montana, studied by James Oliver, resulted from accidental falls into the 14 m deep pit over a span of several thousand years. Oliver's examination of these bones revealed characteristics, including polish, abrasions, and percussion breakage and flaking, that could well be mistaken for human boneworking.

Taphonomic studies: Shield Trap Cave, Montana

The critical lesson of recent research on this issue is clear: When dealing with possible ecofacts, archaeologists are obliged to document completely all possible evidence of form, context, and association, and to test this evidence against propositions of both human and nonhuman causation, before concluding that the materials are ecofacts and thus relevant for making inferences about past human activity. In cases such as the Olsen-Chubbuck site (see Fig. 11.1), for example, the evidence of human intervention is much more obvious.

Species Identification

The first step in analysis of animal remains, like plant materials, is classification. Detailed identifications are best done by zoologists or zooarchaeologists, but most archaeologists can learn to distinguish the bones and teeth of common animals such as dogs and deer. Illustrated taxonomic manuals have been prepared for bone identification in specific areas, including Europe and North America, but more are needed, especially for animals other than large mammals. The best aid to species identification is a good comparative collection. However, such collections require much time and work to assemble, as well as a sizable and secure storage and study space. It may also be difficult, impossible, or ethically undesirable to obtain skeletons of rare, protected, or extinct species. For these reasons archaeologists usually rely on specialists who have access to established comparative collections. Once identified, the animal remains can be examined in terms of their inferred impact on the archaeological situation under study.

Faunal Analysis

Archaeologists attempt not only to determine what kinds of animals were being exploited but also to establish the proportions of adults to juveniles and, for some adult animals, of males to females. Tallies of this kind have been used as evidence for the very beginning of animal domestication, before bone changes due to selective breeding can be detected. In this case, the presence of large numbers of young animal remains may indicate direct access to and control of a herd, or selective culling before breeding age to "weed out" certain characteristics. In other cases, the presence of young animals may point to use of the site in the season when the young animals would have been available. In contrast, Smith and Horwitz found changes in the bone mass of sheep and goats from sites of the third millennium B.C. in Israel. The specific changes suggested that older females were present in greater numbers in later periods, and from this change in herd composition the analysts inferred a rising emphasis on milk production.

Bone mass and herd makeup: Smith and Horwitz and early dairy farming in Israel

Archaeologists can also examine the parts or traces of animals present at a site. At Star Carr, the occurrence of stag antlers gave evidence not only of season of occupation of the site but also of the range of antler "raw materials" that were desired by or acceptable to the site's occupants. At Olsen-Chubbuck, study of presence/absence of various skeletal elements led to inferences about aspects of butchering techniques by indicating which parts of the animals were taken back to the residence area for more leisurely utilization. And at Tikal, Guatemala, the accumulation of layers of bat guano in buildings indicated intervals of human abandonment of those buildings.

One very basic manipulation in the analysis of animal remains is calculation of the **minimum number of individuals (MNI)** represented. Bones are categorized by species and *element* (skeletal part), such as left bison ulnae, as well as age and sex if identifiable. The element category represented by the largest number of remains indicates the minimum number of individuals of that species that could be represented by the collection. That is, if for (adult) bison there are five right lower jaws, one left heel bone, and three left shoulder blades, the bones had to come from at least five bison. The MNI does not tell how many animals were ever present or exploited, but it does indicate that *at least* a certain number were represented. The MNI is important in the weighting of species representations: If the researcher simply counted bones, a complete skeleton of a single animal of one species would give a vastly higher count for that species than one or two bones each from several animals. Regardless, as studies by Donald Grayson have demonstrated, there can be problems with MNI calculations. Although MNI probably remains the best technique, one should be aware of the potential pitfalls, including the tendency for highly fragmented bones to produce inflated estimates, along with the general problem we have already discussed of confusing nonhuman utilized bone with specimens that do reflect human activity.

Special characteristics of animals may lead to specific interpretations. Some small animals, such as snails, are very sensitive to climate and thus can serve as indicators of local climatic change or stability. An increase in white-tailed deer could signal an increase in cleared areas or a decrease in local forest cover. Presence of large mammals as prey often indicates organized group hunting practices, and herd animals require different hunting tactics from solitary animals. Ideological interpretations may also be made from faunal evidence. For example, the swift fox has a rich pelt that was ethnographically known to be prized by the Fox society of Skidi Pawnee of Nebraska. As B. Miles Gilbert has suggested, the presence of the bones of this fox in archaeological sites of that region might suggest that the ideological association of these pelts was present in prehistoric times as well.

Ideological behavior reconstruction: B. Miles Gilbert's analysis of fox remains

Contextual associations can be related to various kinds of human–animal relations. For example, the occurrence of mummified cats in ancient Egypt and jaguar remains in elite Maya burials reflect the recognized high symbolic status enjoyed by those animals in the two societies. Bones found in middens, on the other hand, are usually interpreted as remains of food animals or scavengers.

As part of the consideration of context, the archaeologist must be careful to distinguish, as far as possible, which animals are related to human presence and exploitation and which are not. For example, burrowing animals such as gophers or opossums found in graves may have gotten there on their own, independent of the ancient burial. Other animals may simply take advantage of the shelter provided by occupation areas, such as bats roosting in abandoned Maya temples.

HUMAN REMAINS

One entire branch of anthropology—**physical anthropology**—is concerned with study of the biological nature of human beings. Some physical anthropologists study the observable biological characteristics of living people; others study human remains preserved in the archaeological record. We cannot here review the field of physical anthropology or discuss the course of human biological evolution, although the physical remains that give direct evidence for this evolution are recovered by archaeological techniques. All archaeologists should have some classroom and laboratory training in these subjects. Here we shall simply review some of the ways in which human remains from an archaeological context may further the understanding of the extinct society being investigated. Forms of human remains include mummies, fragmentary bones and teeth, and coprolites. Bones and teeth are the remains most often preserved, and they will receive the most attention.

Ethical issue: Archaeology and human remains

More than anything else encountered and studied by archaeologists, human remains raise significant ethical issues. This is most apparent when living descendants of the dead express their concerns about the excavation and analysis of skeletal remains. We will consider the professional responsibilities of the archaeologist in the treatment of human remains in our final chapter.

Analysis of human remains begins with identification of the particular elements (bones, teeth) present and of the number of individuals represented. Since people are often buried in individual graves, this may not be a difficult task, but mass graves or reused ones present special problems. All archaeologists should learn to identify human skeletal elements; illustrated manuals are available as field aids, but laboratory practice with skeletal collections is indispensable. Once the elements are identified, an assessment should be made of each individual's sex and age at death. Some skeletal elements are more reliable or easier to interpret in these assessments. For example, sex can be most readily judged from the pelvis, especially from the form of the sciatic notch. But other elements, including the skull and even the teeth, can be used when necessary. Because sexual differences do not appear in the skeleton until puberty, children's bones cannot be differentiated by sex.

Age can be assessed by a variety of means, including eruption sequence and degree of wear on teeth, fusion of the sutures between bones of the skull, and fusion of the ends (epiphyses) to the shafts (diaphyses) of limb

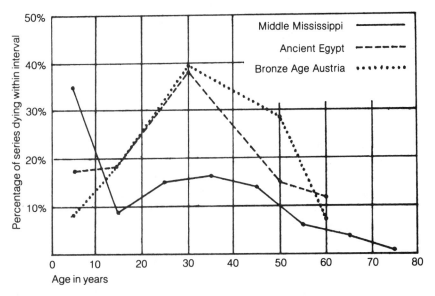

FIGURE 11.5 Comparative mortality profiles from selected ancient populations. Middle Mississippians, of the southeastern United States after A.D. 1000, were two to three times as likely to die before 10 years of age as were ancient Egyptians or Austrians of the Bronze Age several thousand years earlier. Once past childhood, however, members of all three groups reached a peak death rate between ages 25 and 35. (From Blakeley 1971; courtesy of Robert L. Blakeley and the *American Journal of Physical Anthropology*.)

bones. In some cases, correlation of these rates and sequences with specific ages depends on the population involved. For instance, children's tooth eruption sequences are broadly predictable, whereas tooth wear patterns depend on age and diet, since gritty foods wear teeth down faster than do other foods. Aspartic acid racemization (see Chapter 9) has been used to estimate individual age at death by comparing racemization among different parts of a single skeleton.

Once age and sex identifications are made, a number of other studies may be done. **Paleodemographic** analyses seek to understand the structure of the ancient population under investigation, including determination of the sex ratio and life expectancy (Fig. 11.5). Great difficulties are involved in trying to characterize a whole human population on the basis of the remains of a relatively few individuals who may have lived at different times in the history of an archaeological site. The necessary assumptions and concomitant pitfalls are presented in some of the writings listed in the Guide to Further Reading. As one example, suppose that a large number of young men were killed in battle and buried away from home; they would not be represented in their home burial population, so that, even if archaeologically excavated burials accurately represented the range of burials at the occupation site, they would not accurately represent the original overall population. Nevertheless, efforts at constructing life tables for archaeological populations have begun to reward paleodemographers by suggesting ways in which these populations may have been either similar to or different from modern populations. For instance, both Edward Deevey and Kenneth Weiss have attempted "histories" of human life expectancy; they find less difference among preindustrial populations than

**Isotope analyses as clues
to ancient diet: Mexico,
Peru, and Venezuela**

between them as a group and industrial populations—indicating that the cultural changes associated with industrialization had more effect on human longevity than did those associated with the advent of agriculture.

Recent analytical advances have made possible the reconstruction of some aspects of ancient diets from skeletal samples. One of these techniques involves the study of the carbon component remaining in human bone collagen. Because plants metabolize carbon dioxide according to different ratios of two carbon isotopes, ^{13}C and ^{12}C, they can be classed into three mutually exclusive groups. Such important foods as maize, sorghum, sugar cane, and millet, for example, belong to one major group, called C_4 plants, and spinach, manioc, barley, sugar beets, and peas belong to another, the C_3 group. Measurement of the ratios of these isotopes in human bone collagen can indicate which of these plant groups were used in the ancient diet. Based on this, Nikolaas van der Merwe and others have examined hundreds of skeletons from both Old and New World populations, seeking to trace both past dietary practices and their changes over time. Among the results of these studies is dramatic independent corroboration of the prevailing assumption that maize, a C_4 plant domesticated in Mexico and Peru, became a staple crop in North America between about A.D. 1000 and A.D. 1200. Analyses using skeletal remains from prehistoric Venezuela have supported a more controversial proposition concerning maize: Isotopic measurements imply that Andean maize, adapted to the tropical lowlands, had by A.D. 400 far eclipsed indigenous root crops such as manioc. It was this relatively protein-rich maize—rather than intensively cultivated manioc or other native forest plants—that provided the subsistence base for major population increases, inferred from the archaeological record, that culminated in the large, complex, chiefdom-level societies living in the Orinoco and Amazon floodplains when Europeans arrived.

The **stable carbon isotope analysis** of human skeletal material from Tehuacán, Mexico (see Chapter 6; also discussed in Chapter 14), by Farnsworth and his colleagues revealed that C_4 plants (possibly maize) composed 90 percent of the diet by 4500 B.C. and remained at that level for the remainder of the pre-Columbian era. This contrasts with the far lower estimates of plant use in the Tehuacán diet made by MacNeish, based on pollen counts. The discrepancy seems to be due to a sampling bias, in that the pollen samples came from dry caves that were occupied mostly by hunting and gathering bands, and where plant utilization could well have been relatively minor. In contrast, the stable isotopic analysis of the human skeletal sample more likely represents the complete dietary inventory of the Tehuacán population.

Other isotopes present in human skeletal remains provide clues for dietary reconstructions. Stable nitrogen isotope analysis reveals distinctions between reliance on marine and land-based food resources. Strontium isotope analysis can detect distinctions between meat and plant diets.

Human remains also yield information on the health and nutritional

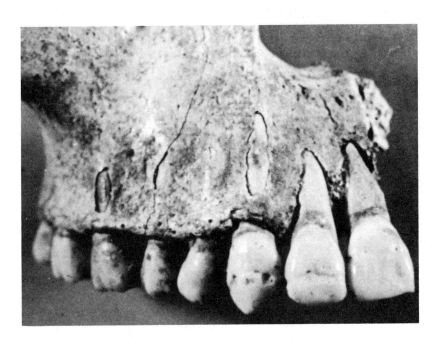

FIGURE 11.6 Right upper jaw of a young adult female with incomplete enamel formation that is especially visible on the second and third teeth from the right. This condition indicates malnutrition or other severe illness during growth, in this case, probably at about three to four years of age. (Courtesy of Dr. Frank P. Saul, Medical College of Ohio.)

status of the population under study. Not all diseases or injuries affect the skeleton, but many do. Obvious examples are bone fractures and tooth caries; other maladies, including arthritis, yaws, tuberculosis, and periodontal disease, leave tangible marks. (Of course, if mummified bodies are available for study, analysis can be much more complete, akin to a regular autopsy.) Nutritional problems may be detected in such forms as enamel hypoplasia, incomplete formation of tooth enamel during growth (Fig. 11.6). William Haviland has attributed differences in male stature at the Maya site of Tikal, Guatemala, to social class and concomitant wealth differences. The taller males, found in richer tomb burials, were probably also richer in life and thus able to secure better food supplies than could their shorter counterparts buried in less well made and less well furnished interments.

Human skeletal analysis: William Haviland at Tikal, Guatemala

Some cultural practices also leave their mark on skeletal remains, intentionally or otherwise. One intentional example is cranial deformation, practiced in pre-Columbian times in North, Central, and South America; in this custom the head is tightly bound until it takes the desired form (Fig. 11.7); the Chinese practice of binding girls' feet to make them smaller is comparable. Teeth are sometimes filed, or inlaid with stones, such as jade; again, the ancient Maya and their neighbors are examples.

In other instances, bones and teeth are modified by habitual behavior rather than intentional alteration. Police pathologists know this and, when trying to identify unknown skeletal remains, will use such alterations

FIGURE 11.7 Photograph of an artificially deformed skull from the Classic Maya site of Altar de Sacrificios, Guatemala, with a superimposed reconstruction of the individual's profile in life. The inset shows an individual with a similarly deformed skull painted on a pottery vessel from the same site. (Courtesy of Dr. Frank P. Saul, Medical College of Ohio.)

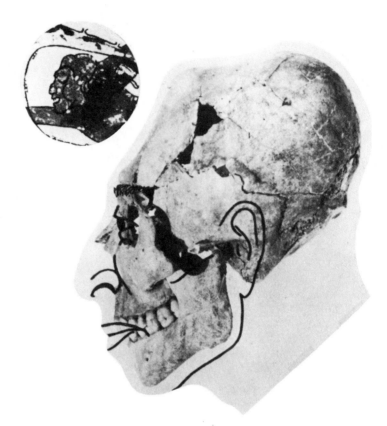

Human skeletal analysis: Tomb of the Eagles, Isbister, Orkney Islands

whenever possible as clues to occupation and other activities. The same clues can be used to infer some routine behavior patterns in ancient populations. For instance, prolonged and frequent strenuous activity will produce stronger and more pronounced muscle attachments on bone; such changes in Neanderthal skeletons imply that these ancient people engaged in more heavy tasks than do most modern individuals. A more specific kind of habitual behavior was inferred from skeletal remains more than 4000 years old, excavated at Isbister's Tomb of the Eagles, in Scotland's Orkney Islands (see Chapter 16 for a discussion of the tomb and its interpretation). Several skulls, mostly female, had marked depressions across the top, and on the back of the same skulls, neck muscle attachments were notably well developed. Such modifications would result from routinely carrying heavy loads suspended from a strap across the head, a method John W. Hedges says was still used in other parts of Scotland in recent times. Hedges cites further skeletal remains from Isbister that attest to another manner of burden bearing among this same Neolithic people. Localized osteoarthritis in ribs and neck vertebrae are consistent with the practice, known in Orkney in modern times, of supporting a load with a strap passed over one shoulder and under the other arm.

INORGANIC REMAINS

The most important inorganic ecofacts are the various soils uncovered by excavation. The soil in an archaeological deposit is more than just a matrix in which culturally relevant materials may be embedded. It is only in the last quarter century or so, however, that researchers have begun to recognize the importance of archaeological soils. Two principal aspects of soils should be examined: how the soil was deposited and of what it is composed. For both of these considerations, a specialist in **pedology** or **geomorphology** is the expert to consult. The archaeologist should be able to make basic field distinctions, such as recognizing various soil types (sand, clay, loam, and so on), and should know enough about the potentials of sediment analysis to be able to frame questions for the geomorphologist to answer.

The deposition of soil layers can result from human activities or from natural geological processes. One of the more easily identifiable distinctions, for example, is between water-laid silts, which are fine-grained and evenly deposited by flooding, and deliberately packed construction fills. In other cases, depositional "cause" is not so easy to determine. For example, natural deposits such as black manganese dioxide can sometimes resemble hearth lines; chemical tests of the soil can often resolve these questions.

One productive line of such testing is phosphate analysis. Phosphorus is an important part of food, refuse, feces, and other substances common in human settlements, and it normally forms relatively large amounts of phosphate compounds in soils of occupied areas. Unlike other commonly accumulated chemicals (such as nitrogen), however, the phosphates tend to stay put in the soil. Phosphates therefore constitute stable and reliable markers of human presence, even when artifacts and other more obvious signs are absent. Robert Eidt has described two useful and complementary phosphate analyses. The first is a rapid field test, requiring 50 mg (less than 1/500 of an ounce!) of soil and a few minutes' time, to determine whether human occupation is indicated at all. The second procedure requires several days' testing in a laboratory, but it seems capable of discriminating among specific categories of land use, for example, cultivation versus residence.

Phosphate analysis: Detecting human residues

It is basic to stratigraphic evaluation to distinguish between natural and cultural origins for all deposits encountered. But in some cases, the soils have a particularly dramatic story to tell. For example, on the island of Thera (now called Santorini) in the Aegean, an earthquake destroyed the town of Acrotiri. In Chapter 4 we discussed the explosion of the volcano on that island, in about 1500 B.C., and the way that event completely disrupted local human occupation. However, excavations at Acrotiri have established that a considerable time elapsed between the earthquake and the volcanic explosion, since a thin humus layer (the result of natural, gradual soil formation processes) was found between the remains of the fallen abandoned buildings and the material ejected from the volcano.

Soil analysis: Thera and volcanic activity

Indeed, two distinguishable eruptions apparently took place—a small one followed by the catastrophic one. The "warning" provided by the smaller eruption probably allowed most of the residents of Thera to leave: The excavations at Thera are relatively lacking in human remains—compared, for instance, with Pompeii, where the residents had no time to flee before the eruption of Vesuvius in A.D. 79 (see Figs. 4.9, p. 124, and 7.17, p. 260).

Sediment analysis should also include consideration of the basic structure and properties of the soil. For example, soil pH, a measure of alkalinity or acidity, is a critical factor in determining whether organic materials are likely to be preserved: The absence of visible organic remains may result from lack of preservation rather than lack of deposition.

Soil characteristics were observed by ancient inhabitants as well as modern investigators. Soil surveys in many areas of the world have indicated that, for example, occupation by agriculturalists correlates well with the distribution of well-drained and fertile areas. Fertility potentials must be tested, however, not simply assumed. For example, volcanic ash is generally a fertile parent material for agricultural soils. But the ash fall from the eruption around A.D. 200 of Ilopango, traced by Sheets and his associates in what is now El Salvador, blanketed the area with an infertile layer that would have *decreased* local agricultural production capacities for as long as several centuries.

ECOFACTS AND SAMPLING

Sampling strategies in ecofact analysis can be considered in two senses: the sample recovered and that actually studied. Because pollen is small and often wind-borne, it can be recovered from most locations in a site. A systematic sample of pollen cores can be designed to give a broad picture of horizontal (spatial) or vertical (temporal) distribution and variability in the pollen species. The same samples can be used simultaneously to recover phytoliths. Collection of supplementary samples, from grinding-stone surfaces or from abdominal areas of human burials, for instance, can help answer specific questions about use of plant materials.

Soil, like pollen, can be sampled systematically from most parts of a site. Plant macrospecimens, animal and human remains, and other inorganic remains (stone, minerals, and so on) are usually less continuously distributed within a site, so their collection or observation tends to be dependent on what areas of the site are excavated. Sometimes the archaeologist tries to predict their occurrence, for example, by excavating a likely or known trash dump in an attempt to enlarge the sample of bone and plant remains. As we noted in Chapter 6, MacNeish's excavations in the Tehuacán Valley of Mexico were oriented to sites in which the perishable remains required for documentation were most likely to be preserved. But stable carbon isotope analysis of human bone from Tehuacán indicates that the resulting conclusions underestimated the percentage of plants used in the ancient diet. Presumably the emphasis on sites with preserved plant remains gained a sample not fully representative of the subsistence activities in the Tehuacán Valley.

In many situations, however, recovery patterns for ecofacts are the same as those for artifacts, and how representative—statistically or otherwise—the sample is depends on how representative the excavation units are relative to the site as a whole.

Once the ecofactual remains are found, a second sampling decision must be made concerning what portion will actually be studied. Again, pollen and soil samples differ from other kinds of data. Lack of funds may preclude study of all such samples taken. Decisions on "subsampling" depend on the research questions being asked. What is the sample supposed to represent? For instance, to reconstruct the sequence of climate and vegetal environment in a long-occupied site, a sequence of cores from a single deep, stratified excavation unit may be studied. These samples will be further "sampled" in the process of analysis: Only a small fraction will actually be put under the analyst's microscope for a count of pollen grains and species represented.

Sampling of organic ecofacts other than soil and pollen usually involves inspection of all recovered items; in most cases, only unidentifiable fragments are not examined further.

SUMMARY

Ecofacts are natural items that are nonetheless relevant to the interpretation of past human behavior. The various categories of ecofacts—plant, animal, human, and inorganic remains—can be analyzed to yield culturally meaningful information. Floral remains include both microspecimens (pollen and phytoliths) and macrospecimens (seeds, plant fragments, and impressions). Faunal remains include mummified, skeletal, and coprolite materials, either whole or fragmentary. Once species have been identified, the analysis of both floral and faunal samples can yield information on ancient environmental conditions, subsistence techniques, diet, and other activities (medical, ritual, and mortuary behavior, for example). Human remains provide direct evidence about the nutritional and health status of ancient populations—information vital not only to understanding the past but also to modern society (in studies of the origins and evolution of human disease, for example). Inorganic remains, especially the analysis of soil matrices, can yield clues to the presence or absence of past human activity and information about ancient land use and environmental conditions.

The analysis of ecofacts often raises one of the most crucial problems facing archaeologists—distinguishing between human and nonhuman exploitation of resources. Perhaps the most difficult aspect of this problem is differentiating human from nonhuman agents of bone modification, a dilemma often encountered in the study of the activities of the earliest humans. The rising importance of taphonomic research reflects archaeologists' increasing efforts to solve this dilemma. Despite such problems, ecofactual data can be crucial to the reconstruction of ancient environments, subsistence, and related economic activities.

GUIDE TO FURTHER READING

Allen 1989; Andresen et al. 1981; Beck 1974; Bray 1976; Brothwell and Higgs 1970; Butzer 1982; Callen 1970; Carter 1978; Clark [1954] 1971, 1972; Henderson 1989; Higgs 1972, 1975; Lambert 1984; Shackley 1981; Solecki 1975; Wheat 1972

Floral Remains

Bryant and Holloway 1983; Dimbleby 1967, 1985; Ford 1979; Hastorf and Popper 1988; Leroi-Gourhan 1975; McWeeney 1984; Pearsall 1989; Pickersgill 1972; Piperno 1988; J. M. Renfrew 1973; Rovner 1983; Shafer and Holloway 1979; Solecki 1975; Turner and Harrison 1983; Ucko and Dimbleby 1969

Nonhuman Faunal Remains

Baker and Brothwell 1980; Behrensmeyer and Hill 1980; L. R. Binford 1978, 1981b; Bonnichsen and Sorg 1989; Brain 1981; Casteel 1976; Chaplin 1971; Claasen 1991a, 1991b; Clutton-Brock and Grigson 1983, 1984; Crabtree 1990; Davis 1987; Gifford 1981; Gilbert 1973; Grayson 1979, 1984; Haynes 1983; Hecker 1982; Hess and Wapnish 1985; Hillson 1986; Johnson 1985; Klein and Cruz-Uribe 1984; Koch 1989; Mori 1970; Olsen 1964, 1971, 1979, 1985; Perkins and Daly 1968; Potts 1984, 1986; Potts and Shipman 1981; Read-Martin and Read 1975; B. D. Smith 1974, 1983; Smith and Horwitz 1984; von den Driesch 1976; Waselkov 1987; Wheat 1972; Wheeler and Jones 1989; Wilson, Grigson, and Payne 1982

Human Remains

Angel 1969; Bass 1986; Brothwell 1971, 1981; Brothwell and Sandison 1967; Buikstra 1976, 1981b; Buikstra and Cook 1980; Buikstra and Konigsberg 1985; Cohen and Armelagos 1984; D. Cook 1981; S. Cook 1972; Deevey 1960; DeNiro 1987; Farnsworth et al. 1985; Gilbert and Mielke 1985; Goodman, Thomas, Swedlund, and Armelagos 1988; Hart 1983; Haviland 1967; Hedges 1984; Horne 1985; Huss-Ashmore, Goodman, and Armelagos 1982; Orter and Putschar 1987; Petersen 1975; Price 1989; Price, Schoeninger, and Armelagos 1985; Rogers and Waldron 1989; Roosevelt 1980; Shipman, Walker, and Bichell 1985; Sillen, Sealy, and van der Merwe 1989; Ubelaker 1984, 1989; van der Merwe 1982; Ward and Weiss 1976; Weiss 1976; White 1990; Wing and Brown 1979; Zubrow 1976

Inorganic Remains

Cornwall 1970; Doumas 1974; Eidt 1977, 1985; Gladfelter 1977, 1981; Money 1973; Rapp and Gifford 1985; Shackley 1975, 1981; Sheets 1971; Sjoberg 1976; Stein and Farrand 1985

Ecofacts and Sampling

Bryant and Holloway 1983; Carr 1985; Claasen 1991b; Grayson 1981, 1984; Hastorf and Popper 1988; Pearsall 1989; Piperno 1988; Rovner 1983; van der Veen and Fieller 1982

CHAPTER TWELVE

ANALYSIS OF FEATURES

Constructed Features

Materials and Technology

Form and Location

Style

Cumulative Features

Features and Sampling

Summary

Guide to Further Reading

Archaeologists can trace a trail of apparent refuse concentration from the present back to a time around 2 million years ago. The younger segments of the trail include substantial ruined structures, food remains and artifacts. . . . Material remains localized at relatively recent settlements are generally attributed to familiar kinds of human activity, but the significance of very old accumulations of stone and bones is more problematic.

> *Ellen M. Kroll and Glynn L. Isaac, "Configurations of Artifacts and Bones at Early Pleistocene Sites in East Africa," 1984*

Features, like artifacts, owe their form to human intervention, so it is not surprising that **analysis** of features is similar to that of artifacts. Formal, stylistic, and technological analyses are all appropriate approaches to the study of features. Two particular characteristics of features are important in analysis: location and arrangement. But artifacts can be moved, whereas the characteristics of features are destroyed by removal. For example, when a multistory house collapses, features from the upper floors, such as hearths or meal-grinding apparatus, may still be inferred from their disarrayed components (Fig. 12.1), but the original form, placement, and arrangement of the feature can only be estimated.

Archaeologists attempting to understand the significance of a particular feature make use of provenience, association, and context, as they would for understanding an artifact. The difference is that intact features directly indicate the original makers' and users' intentional placement, whereas the locational aspects of artifacts are used to infer (by determination of context) whether a use-related placement has been preserved. Features are most valuable in understanding the distribution and organization of human activities, for they represent the facilities—the space and often some stationary equipment—with which these activities were carried out.

Features may be composed of arrangements of artifacts or ecofacts. Such arrangements become features when the provenience and associations of such portable remains reflect ancient activities. For example, in the archaeologically rich Koobi Fora area of the east shore of Lake Turkana, in northern Kenya, Site FxJj50 is a scatter of stone artifacts and broken bones revealed over roughly 170 m² of clearing excavation. The matrix in which the materials were found is 1.5 to 1.6 million years old. But, if the clusters of stone and bone fragments were indicative of human activities, they ought to belong to a much narrower time span than that, ideally one even shorter than a single human life. Archaeologists Henry Bunn, Glynn Isaac, and their colleagues thus had to establish that the materials were truly associated with one another, rather than the result of either a series of separate activities spread over many years' time or rearrangement by floodwaters at this riverbank location. They had to demonstrate that Site FxJj50 was, in fact, a meaningful archaeological feature.

Artifact and ecofact clusters as features: Bunn and Isaac at Koobi Fora, Kenya

FIGURE 12.1 Features may often be identified, even after disturbance: (left) an intact mealing bin, where stones were set for grinding grain, in a prehistoric pueblo from the southwestern United States; (right) a feature presumed to be a collapsed mealing bin, the disturbance seemingly resulting from destruction of the building's roof or upper story. (Photo [l] by author; photo [r] by M. Thompson, Arizona State Museum, University of Arizona.)

To do so, they examined several kinds of evidence. In addition to plotting provenience of each artifact and ecofact, they did a **conjoining study,** fitting together the flakes that had been progressively removed from a single core. When lines were drawn connecting the proveniences of conjoinable pieces, the resulting web of linkages suggested that the scatter was indeed a single complex feature (Fig. 12.2) and represented a single set of activities. Bone pieces, too, were conjoined, with the same resulting interpretation. Moreover, taphonomic studies of the weathering on bone remains indicated that those remains had lain exposed for little more than a year at most, before burial by flood-laid soils.

Taken together, these inferences established the site as a feature and gave greater weight to behavioral interpretations concerning the distribution of activities represented. Toolmaking was concentrated in two parts of the site, and the relative intensity at one suggests a particularly attractive work location—quite probably in the shade of a large tree, long since disappeared. Butchering took place at Site FxJj50, too, revealed by stone-tool cut marks on the bone and careful breakage patterns pointing to extraction of marrow from the interior cavity of limb bones. Although some damage seen on the bones was caused by nonhuman carnivores, the data that establish Site FxJj50 as an archaeological feature emphasize that the ancient behavior reflected there was principally that of very early humans.

Although much information can be gained from study of individual artifacts and ecofacts, it is study of their context and associations that allows the fullest range of interpretations about ancient behavior. This point was stressed in Chapter 4, but we raise it again here to emphasize the special interpretive value of features. Recognition of an archaeological feature—such as a hearth, burial, workshop, house, or midden—depends on identifying that items were positioned or arranged by people in ancient

FIGURE 12.2 Glynn Isaac examines artifacts restored to their original horizontal positions at Koobi Fora Site FxJj50, showing the overall distribution of ancient debris scatter. (Photograph Peter Kain: copyright Richard Leakey.)

times. When a feature is found intact, it necessarily contains and provides information on context and association. For this reason, features are of particular interest to archaeologists.

Unfortunately, no single comprehensive system has been developed for categorizing features for study. The "industry" categories of artifacts or the species classifications of ecofacts have no analogs in feature analysis. Most studies isolate particular kinds of features, such as hearths, burials, or houses, but do not consider the entire range of forms or functions that features may take. With the growth of settlement pattern studies (see Chapter 15), a wider range of feature types is being considered, but there is still a tendency to focus on one or a small number of specific form-functional types.

In Chapter 4 we distinguished between simple features and composite ones. Here we shall divide features into two somewhat different categories that have possible behavioral implications: constructed features and cumulative features. **Constructed features** are those that were deliberately built to house or facilitate some activity or set of activities. They may provide an enclosed shelter, such as a house, or they may simply define or create an area appropriate to specified activities, such as agricultural terraces or a boat-docking pier. **Cumulative features** include entities that do not seem to have a planned structure to them. They may grow by accretion, as **middens** or workshops do, or by subtraction, as **quarries** do.

CONSTRUCTED FEATURES

Constructed features were built to provide a space or facility for some activity or set of activities. Examples range from simple windbreaks to elaborate houses and temples, from burials and tombs to roadways and fortification walls, and from artificial reservoirs and stone-lined hearths to agricultural terraces and irrigation canals. The important criterion is that there is some construction that formally channels the ongoing use of space. Classification and analysis of constructed features may examine attributes of form, style, technology, and location, or combinations of these attributes.

Materials and Technology

Technological analyses include consideration of the materials used in the construction and the ways these were put together. When complex architecture is involved, for example, in the construction of imposing features such as the Egyptian pyramids, analysis may require intricate study. The technological analysis of such features usually yields data not only about the physical act of construction, such as the use of particular materials and the sequence of their incorporation in the growing structure, but also about related social aspects of the construction process. At Quiriguá, Guatemala, for example, as the elite center grew in size and grandeur, so did the variety of stone resources its residents drew upon for construction materials. In the earliest constructions, soils and cobbles from the floodplain and the adjacent river were predominant. Subsequent use of successively more distant resources, including rhyolite, sandstone, schist, and marble from sources 2 to 7 km away or more, suggests growing wealth and power in the hands of those who were commissioning the construction projects. In some sites of the Moche Valley in Peru, the adobe brick construction was found to consist of discernibly discrete fill units; each multibrick unit bore a distinctive label, which Michael Moseley has inferred to represent a maker's mark. Each work force responsible for supplying a certain number of bricks could thus verify that its proper contribution had indeed been made.

Even structures built of perishable materials, such as wood, can be detected by their remains and yield information about size, materials used, and methods of construction. In excavating the Howlett Hill site, south

Changes in construction materials: Quiriguá, Guatemala

Evidence of task groups: Moche Valley, Peru

Construction techniques: Howlett Hill, New York

FIGURE 12.3 In this view of the Howlett Hill site, modern stakes have been set into the original postholes to outline the exterior and interior walls of the Iroquois long-houses. The larger house is more than 300 feet long, with 16 hearths along its central corridor. (Courtesy of James A. Tuck.)

Solutions to construction problems: Swiss lake dwellings and Mohenjo-daro, Pakistan

of Syracuse, New York, James Tuck exposed the remains of four long-houses, dated to about A.D. 1380–1400. Built by the Iroquois, and revealed by the pattern of postmolds left by the original construction (Fig. 12.3), the largest of the Howlett Hill houses was longer than a football field, an incredible 334 feet long by 23 feet wide. The postmold pattern indicates that the outer wall was originally framed with 3-inch posts set about a foot into the ground. Two alignments of larger posts, 8–10 inches in diameter, defined a central corridor that ran along the interior axis of the building and must have supported the long-vanished roof. A single doorway was found midway along the western side of the long-house. From its size, Tuck estimated that between 150 and 200 people once occupied the structure.

Different builders choose different technological solutions in response to similar constructional or engineering problems. This can be illustrated by comparing, for example, Neolithic lake dwellings in Switzerland with urban constructions of the late third and early second millennia B.C. at Mohenjo-daro in the Indus valley of Pakistan. Ignoring rather gross differences in construction scale, building materials, and precise setting, we can note that in both cases structures were set on saturated, unconsolidated, and ultimately unstable land. The builders of the lakeside dwellings enhanced the stability of their structures by driving support pilings into the ground beforehand (Fig. 12.4) to keep load-bearing elements from sinking uncontrollably into the ground. At Mohenjo-daro, on the other

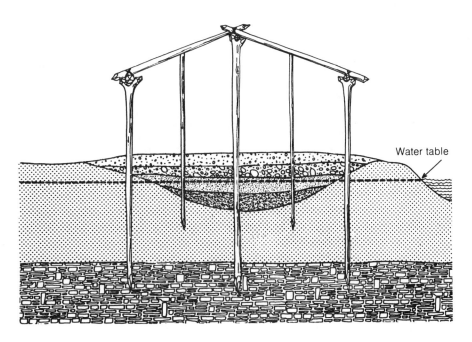

Water table

hand, the strategy—or perhaps the *post hoc* solution—seems to have been periodic leveling, repair, and renovation rather than prevention (Fig. 12.5).

These specific technological solutions in feature construction are certainly influenced by availability of raw materials for building and by other environmental considerations. For example, at Mohenjo-daro and other sites of Harappan civilization, earth was the most abundant resource and was—not surprisingly—the primary construction ingredient. Because of threats of flooding as well as a generally high water table, the builders fired the earth into bricks so that it would resist erosion. In a much different setting—the Orkney Islands off the northeast coast of Scotland—thin soils and the rarity of wood led ancient people to construct houses and many furnishings in stone. Because of this extensive use of stone, houses more than 4000 years old in sites such as Skara Brae and Rinyo preserve a remarkable array of usually rare items, such as bed platforms and cupboards. As can be seen in Figure 12.6, these features yield a rich view of ancient provisions for domestic comfort.

A mutual influence between technology and raw materials is also illustrated by the roads and bridges of the Inka. In the mid-1400s, the Inka expanded rapidly from their home in the south-central Andes of Peru, and one of the hallmarks of their empire was the system of roads established to unite distant quarters with the capital at Cuzco. There were no wheeled vehicles at the time, and all traffic was by foot. But the roads were critical

Technology and environment: Mohenjo-daro, Pakistan, and Skara Brae, Scotland

Mutual influence of technology and materials: Inka roads and bridges of Peru

FIGURE 12.5 At Mohenjo-daro, Pakistan, the remedy for slumping construction caused by water-saturated soils was to level the old wall and build over it. (Courtesy of George F. Dales.)

FIGURE 12.6 House 1 at Skara Brae, in the Orkney Islands of Scotland, provides a good illustration of features. Not only is the house itself a complex feature, but its furnishings are features too, from the bed platforms at upper left to the stone hearth at center and cupboard at upper right.

for effective rule of an empire spanning more than 4300 km, from modern Ecuador south to Chile. These roads crossed diverse kinds of terrain, from flat desert to steep, rugged mountains. Sometimes, in the arid plains, the roads were no more than cleared lanes, with stone debris pushed aside and thus defining the edges. In other places, construction investment was more elaborate, providing stone-paved surfaces or sidewalls built of earth or stone up to the full height of a person. Steep slopes required zigzag routes or steps. But perhaps the biggest obstacle was water. Shallow watercourses could be spanned by roadbeds pierced with one or multiple culverts or drains. Some rivers were crossed with log bridges: These tended to be associated with narrow streams, however, since logs longer than 14 m were rarely available. For longer spans, and especially ones crossing the spectacular, deep Andean gorges, the solution was neither wood nor stone but woven suspension bridges.

Modern bridges of this form are common and often quite imposing sights; they are built with steel suspension cables. The Inka, however, used the materials and traditional technologies available to them, making bridges of woven plant fibers. The fibers were braided into ropes and cables, sometimes as thick as a human body, and were attached to stone-masonry abutments built on each side of the river. Bridge floors were then covered with branches and wood. These bridges could span gaps as wide as 45 m. Although they swayed terribly in the wind and had to be replaced every couple of years, they were sufficiently strong and wide for Spanish horsemen to cross them two abreast. The most famous of these woven bridges, over the Apurimac River, was renovated repeatedly in historic times. It finally fell in 1877, though it lives on in Thornton Wilder's novel *The Bridge of San Luis Rey*. No Inka suspension bridges survive intact to-day, but some of their stone abutments are still visible.

Inka roads and bridges have been traced for roughly 23,000 km. Many other ancient societies also built roads with varying degrees of technical elaboration—and not just the Romans, whose accomplishments in this regard are so famous. In the Americas, over 200 km of roads have been traced in arid northwestern New Mexico, linking pueblo sites of Chacoan culture around A.D. 1000. Most of these were simply lanes cleared of stone and other debris. The Maya, on the other hand, built elaborate raised avenues of limestone rubble coated with brilliant plaster, sometimes joining sections of a single site and sometimes connecting distant communities. Of these roads, the earliest known ones, at El Mirador in Guatemala, probably date to A.D. 100 or before.

Among the oldest known preserved roadways are the wooden tracks used to cross bogs and other wetlands in Europe. Such wooden features have often been remarkably well preserved by their permanently wet settings. An example is the Eclipse Track in the Somerset Levels, southwest England, which dates to 1800 B.C. (Fig. 12.7). The oldest known road in the world was found in the same peat bog levels and dates to around 4000 B.C. This is the Sweet Track, named for its 1970 discoverer, Raymond Sweet, and investigated by John Coles and his colleagues over a decade's time (Fig. 12.8). Although at first glance it appears simple in form, the Sweet Track yielded a complex wealth of information about technology and other aspects of life in Neolithic Somerset. The track was built as a footpath to allow local residents to cross waterlogged terrain. First, the

Preserved wooden roadways: Somerset, England

FIGURE 12.7 The Eclipse Track, preserved in perennially saturated ground in Somerset, England. Despite the relatively fresh appearance of the wooden construction elements, this feature dates to 1800 B.C. (By permission of John M. Coles.)

line of the path was laid out and marked among the high reeds of the swamp. Meanwhile, beyond the swamp, trees such as oak, ash, and elm were felled to provide raw material for the planks, rails, and pegs used in construction. A line of thick, round rails was laid along the marked path, and pairs of long sharpened pegs were driven, at an angle and point down, into the soggy earth along that line. Each pair of pegs formed an upright "X" across and resting on the rail, the rail preventing the pegs from sinking into the soft wet ground. Finally, the track's walking surface was formed by a line of planks that was wedged flat into the upper "V" portions of the crossed pegs.

Radiocarbon dating yielded the age of the track, and extensive use of dendrochronology as a relative dating technique showed almost all the plank wood came from trees cut in the same year. Furthermore, the lengths identified as repair pieces had been cut no more than 11 years after the original construction, suggesting the Sweet Track was built, used, and abandoned well within the span of a single lifetime. The finished path ran for 1.8 km and was only about 30 cm (slightly under 12 inches) wide, with no widened areas for passing. When ancient pedestrians bumped into one another or slipped, they (then as now!) dropped things. Not surprisingly, excavations adjacent to the Sweet Track have recovered a rich array of implements from everyday use, and a good number of these—such as

paddles, wedges, a spoon, a comb, and a carved bowl—were made from wood, rarely preserved beyond such bog environments. As we shall discuss in Chapter 14, the Sweet Track investigations also yielded complex and important information on the local environment of 6000 years ago, as well as evidence of ancient land-management practices. All in all, so many things have been learned from investigation of the Sweet Track that its being the oldest known road is almost the smallest part!

Except for the Sweet Track, the examples of construction technology cited to this point have tended to represent imposing and complex construction features. They have been chosen to give some idea of the range of construction techniques and materials that people used in the past. But smaller and seemingly simpler features can be subjected to technological analysis just as productively. One example is a series of wells lined with pottery tubes at the Classic Maya site of Quiriguá. Although small—about 50 cm across and extending roughly 2 m below ground surface—these residential features required a moderately complex set of steps for their creation. A fired-clay tube was made and set over a large vessel buried in a special pit surrounded by sand and small stones, which acted together to filter the groundwater entering the well. The water entered through five holes in the large vessel at the base of the tube. Each of the holes had also been packed carefully with stone, to keep sand and dirt from getting into

Smaller constructed features: Pottery wells at Quiriguá, Guatemala

the well. Then all a Quiriguá inhabitant had to do was lower a small jar on a rope into the well and pull up clean, fresh water. There was certainly no local water shortage at this site, for the Motagua River was at most a few hundred meters away. But the well water was handy, as well as cleaner and healthier, and obviously the labor expenditure was worthwhile to the ninth-century residents of Quiriguá.

The Quiriguá wells may be smaller than the houses and roads described earlier, but they are at least as complex technologically as other constructed features we have cited. Features need not be large *or* complex, however. Indeed, archaeologists more commonly encounter small and simple features such as burials and hearths. Although these are just as much the products of deliberate construction as highways, temples, or castles, they may be quite simple technologically. Large, elaborate tombs, in specially prepared chambers—such as the glamorously rich tombs of Egypt's Tut-ankh-amun or China's Emperor Qin—loom large in our minds. Around the world and through the ages, however, the majority of human interments have surely been little more technologically elaborate than a shallow depression into which the deceased was placed. And hearths are certainly deliberately constructed, although they may have involved simply laying wood or other fuel materials in an arrangement to facilitate their burning. As suggested by the quotation that opens this chapter, activities from the bulk of human prehistory are likely represented in features reflecting relatively simple technologies.

Form and Location

Functional association of structures: Hill at Broken K, Arizona, Movius at the Abri Pataud, France, and Roosevelt at the mouth of the Amazon

Perhaps a clearer idea of the range of things that constitute constructed features can be given by considering studies of form and location. Studies of form usually pertain to particular categories of features, such as rooms, structures, hearths, or burials. Formal attributes that have been studied include size, shape, and arrangement of constituent parts. For example, James Hill has argued that at least two gross categories of room size are distinguishable at Broken K, a 13th-century Pueblo site in east-central Arizona. Using associated artifacts for each room type, he asserts that larger rooms were for habitation and domestic activities, and smaller rooms were storage facilities (see Fig. 4.19, p. 139). For the Abri Pataud, a rock shelter in southern France that has yielded cultural remains from about 32,000 to about 18,000 years ago, Hallam Movius has studied changes through time in the size, shape, and number of hearths within the shelter. He has used his analyses to suggest that marked differences existed from one period to another in the size and composition of resident social groups. Specifically, he associates larger hearth areas with larger, more communally organized living units, whereas smaller, more numerous hearths imply a smaller-scale residential social group. Anna Roosevelt took a similar approach in her inferences about social group size and composition in a pre-Columbian town on Marajó Island, at the mouth of the Amazon. As we discussed in Chapter 6, remote sensing identified a series of magnetic anomalies (see Fig. 6.27, p. 221), and Roosevelt identified these as hearths; she related these hearths to family groups through analogies with modern South American situations.

In the same vein, a number of people have studied house form and location to make inferences about the residents. The sheer size of a house may be an indicator of how many people lived there, but, when considered together with the kinds of materials used, how much labor is implied in the kinds of materials used, how much labor is implied in the kinds of walls and roof, and location relative to civic centers or other "desirable" areas, a house's form can contribute to inferences about the social status of its occupants. For example, the smallest houses at 10,000-year-old Aïn Mallaha, in Israel, provided only 5 to 7 m² of floor space and were big enough to shelter only one person. The largest house, however, covered 64 m², was unusually well made, and was finished with plaster. Kent Flannery therefore suggests that it may have been the residence of the head of the compound. In the much more complex Maya society, at Tikal, in the seventh to ninth centuries, William Haviland found that the basic form of residences was similar across the social continuum from elite to commoner. But houses were notably larger, more elaborate, and better situated for those with more wealth and power, and what was most probably the ruler's compound was a truly palatial architectural complex right in the core of the civic center.

Residence size and status: Flannery on Aïn Mallaha, Israel, and Haviland on Tikal, Guatemala

Even unimposing and seemingly mundane construction features can have great interpretive significance. Consider, for example, bedrock mortars of the western Sierra Nevada of California. These features are roughly circular depressions, of various sizes, formed artificially in granite outcrops or huge boulders. They are often found in clusters and frequently are associated with unshaped stream cobbles of about the same diameter as the depressions. These depressions and cobbles are mortars and pestles, used together for pulverizing seeds and other plant materials. In this case, the mortars are known to be where women of the Mono and related Native American groups prepared such foods as acorn flour, a staple of ancient and historic diet in this area (Fig. 12.9). Although these features have been recognized for many years, Thomas L. Jackson's recent analyses have provided a number of new and significant insights about the nature and role of bedrock mortars in Mono society. Archaeologists had previously argued that the variation in mortar depths was likely due to differential wear: The longer a mortar was used, the deeper it got. Jackson questions the technological likelihood of this inference and also cites accounts of Mono women, who describe mortars as being of three deliberately distinct depths, each for use in a different phase of the acorn processing. Beyond simple recognition of an emic classification of these features (see Chapter 8), however, Jackson's combined archaeological and ethnographic study shows bedrock mortars as keys to understanding Mono society and economy. In particular, the location, spacing, and associations of these

Ancient socioeconomic organization: Jackson and the bedrock mortars of east-central California

FIGURE 12.9 Mono woman, photographed ca. 1918, using a cobble pestle to pound berries in a bedrock mortar. (Photograph by E. W. Gifford, courtesy of Lowie Museum of Anthropology, The University of California at Berkeley.)

Archaeoastronomy: Stonehenge, Big Horn Medicine Wheel, and Group E buildings

"fixed production facilities" defined emic divisions in the landscape. Sites with high densities of mortars were spaced regularly across the landscape, and spacing was geared to relative density of acorns at different mountain elevations. Such site distribution, in Jackson's words, "suggests that the facilities were situated to accommodate systematic annual movements across the landscape to collect and process, primarily, the acorn resource" (1991:312). Because the mortars are known to have been made and owned by Mono women, the site distribution also leads to a new appreciation for the central role of women's activities and decision making in structuring Mono life.

In keeping with the growing attempts to deal with the ideological realm of ancient behavior (see Chapter 3), features are increasingly being examined for clues to past symbolic meanings, in addition to their technological and social significance. Thus, the internal arrangement, elaboration, and orientation of features may be used to infer aspects of ancient idea systems. The clearest and most enduring example is the range of features that have been studied as astronomical observatories. Gerald Hawkins published a number of essays describing his analyses of the astronomical alignments found in the components of Stonehenge, interpreting the range of observations that could have been made from this Bronze Age station. Many of Hawkins's specific conclusions have been discredited, but his work helped inspire other scholars to examine other monuments to see if their arrange-

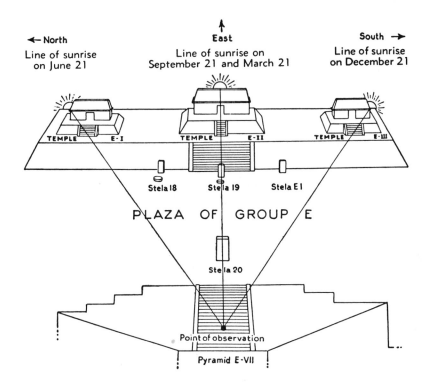

← **North**
Line of sunrise
on June 21

↑
East
Line of sunrise on
September 21 and March 21

South →
Line of sunrise
on December 21

TEMPLE   E-I

TEMPLE   E-II

TEMPLE   E-III

Stela 18   Stela 19   Stela E I

PLAZA   OF   GROUP   E

Stela 20

Point of observation

Pyramid E-VII

FIGURE 12.10 Archaeoastronomy: Group E at the Maya site of Uaxactún, Guatemala. Observers on top of Pyramid E–VII could use the buildings to the east, Temples E–I, E–II, and E–III, to track the seasonal positions of the sun. (Reprinted from *The Ancient Maya,* Fourth Edition, by Sylvanus G. Morley and George W. Brainerd; rev. by Robert J. Sharer, with the permission of the publishers, Stanford University Press. © 1946, 1947, 1956, 1983 by the Board of Trustees of the Leland Stanford Junior University.)

ments suggest similar use. Most of the features under investigation are horizon markers, where the rise and set points of the sun, moon, and various other stars, planets, and constellations can be charted. These features can range in form from the circular "henge" sites of the British Isles to stone circles called "medicine wheels"—such as the Big Horn Medicine Wheel in the western Great Plains of the United States and Canada—or even to special building complexes of the Classic Maya such as Group E at Uaxactún, Guatemala (Fig. 12.10). More will be said about **archaeo-astronomy** and other symbolic approaches in Chapter 16.

Arrangement, elaboration, and location have also been fruitfully examined for other types of constructed features, such as burials. For example, both the location of a burial and elaboration of its contents may be taken as indicators of wealth, social status, and sometimes the occupation of the deceased. In Chapter 11 we mentioned the instance of Shanidar cave, where a Neanderthal was buried with flowers. Frequently the analysis of an assemblage of contemporary burials will indicate marked differences in the variety and quality of goods included with the interments. The Royal Tombs of Ur and the tomb of the Emperor Qin, the unifier of China, are obvious illustrations of formidable wealth and power distinctions; the latter tomb even contains a full, life-size army modeled in clay (see Fig. 1.1, p. 9).

Ritual offerings other than burials can also be analyzed as deliberately constructed features. For example, in many societies, erection of a new building was often accompanied (and ritually legitimized) by inclusion of a *cached*, or ceremonially interred, deposit (see Fig. 7.6, p. 248), rather like the cornerstones laid at dedications of new buildings in our own society. Sometimes these building caches are fairly simple in content; at other times they are far more complex. For example, a small but ritually important structure built about A.D. 500 at Quiriguá, Guatemala, merited a small but lavish dedicatory deposit. Its contents were three pairs of ceramic vessels, each containing pieces of worked jadeite, all set in a specially prepared masonry chamber. But not only does this illustrate a dedicatory **cache** for a building, its characteristics also allow archaeologists to infer its specific meaning. The form of the carved human figures and the triangular arrangement of the jadeite artifacts suggest they were intended as symbolic substitutes for sacrificial human burial. This is because the same triangular arrangement of sacrificed human burials, each associated with new buildings, has been excavated at the site of Kaminaljuyú in the Guatemalan highlands southwest of Quiriguá.

Inferring meaning of caches: Quiriguá, Guatemala

Location of constructed features can be relevant to particular research questions. For example, location of burials in special mortuary structures or elite areas, such as the North Acropolis of Tikal, Guatemala, or the Great Pyramids of Egypt, may indicate special social status and privilege. Study of locations of these or other particular kinds of features may suggest factors involved in siting or placement decisions, such as preference for elevated ground or proximity to water sources in locations of houses. With the increased use of quantitative methods and with the adoption of analytic techniques from fields such as geography, archaeologists are beginning to study locational attributes more thoroughly and to specify more rigorously whether the locational choices observed are due, in fact, to human preferences and decisions or to chance. We shall discuss this topic further in Chapters 15 and 16.

Style

Finally, constructed features may be analyzed by attributes of style or decoration. The idea of architectural style comes readily to mind in this regard. Archaeologists working with remains of classical Greek and Roman civilizations have paid more attention to architectural style than have archaeologists working in most other areas. But stylistic analyses have been made elsewhere. George Andrews and David Potter have done studies in the Maya area, and distinctions have been made among styles in the ancient pueblos of the southwestern United States. For example, there are notable differences between the architecture of the Mimbres area of western New Mexico and the Chacoan area in northwestern New Mexico at and after approximately A.D. 1000. Some of these are surely due in part to

Stylistic variation in masonry: Mimbres and Chaco areas, New Mexico

availability of building resources: Whereas the Chacoans built with stone slabs easily gained from adjacent sandstone formations, the Mimbres people used river cobbles set in thick mud mortar. On the other hand, such an approach does not explain why the specialized ceremonial chambers, or **kivas,** were rectangular in the Mimbres area and round in the Chacoan region. And within the Chacoan area, masonry style shows stylistic variation, perhaps as a result of changing preferences through time.

CUMULATIVE FEATURES

Cumulative features are those that are formed by accretion rather than by a planned or designed construction of an activity area or facility. Examples include middens (see Fig. 4.15, p. 132), quarries (which "grow" by subtraction of the exploited resource, sometimes accompanied by an accumulation of extracting tools), and workshop areas. We have already seen how conjoining studies helped define a cumulative workshop feature at Koobi Fora.

Conjoining studies also aided interpretation of the features defined by some 16,000 lithic artifacts at Meer II, a 9000-year-old campsite in northern Belgium. In horizontal extent, Meer II was little greater than the exposed area at Koobi Fora Site FxJj50, but its artifacts were dispersed vertically through nearly 50 cm of deposit. Enough of the Belgian site's lithics could be refitted, however, to argue that this site, too, was a single complex feature—and still essentially intact. Evidence on manufacturing sequences among the conjoinable pieces was combined with details of their movement across the site (as shown by widely separated proveniences for conjoins) to show spatial relations between making and using the stone tools. When data were added concerning general debris density, hearth location, and wear patterns on the tools, a convincing and fairly detailed map of overall activities could be created. This showed a domestic area in the southwest, where hide processing and bone and antler working took place around a hearth. To the northeast, a smaller hearth served as the focus for rough bone and antler working, probably preliminary to the work done in the domestic area. From wear patterns, Daniel Cahan and Lawrence Keeley could even argue that the bulk of the rough work was done by a right-handed person, with a left-hander working alongside for perhaps a shorter time.

Although stylistic analysis is clearly inappropriate here, cumulative features can be analyzed according to attributes of form, location, and sometimes technology. Formal attributes include, for example, size and content. Because we are dealing with accumulated entities, size can indicate either the duration or the intensity of use. For example, a trash deposit will be larger if it is used longer but also if it is used more frequently. It is not always possible to distinguish the relative importance of these two factors in cumulative features; but, when distinctions are possible, long-term

Artifact clusters and features: Cahan and Keeley at Meer II, Belgium

stratified middens are particularly valuable to the archaeologist because they yield evidence concerning the temporal span of occupation at a site.

Analysis of the location of cumulative features may give information on the distribution of ancient activities. For example, distribution of quarry sites relative to living sites might indicate how far people were willing to travel to obtain stone raw materials; the location of workshop areas reveals the distribution of manufacturing activities within or among settlements. Locational questions will be discussed in more detail in Chapters 14 and 15.

**Cumulative features:
Copper mines of Rudna
Glava, Yugoslavia**

Cumulative features, because they are unplanned accretions of artifacts and other materials, have different technological attributes from constructed features. That is, cumulative features were not "built," but they may still yield technological information. For example, quarries may preserve extraction scars as well as abandoned mining tools, and these may indicate how the materials were removed. At the ancient copper mines of Rudna Glava, in eastern Yugoslavia, miners 6000 years ago lit small fires to heat the ore veins; when the rock was hot, they threw water on it, cracking the deposit. Then they picked and pried away the desired ore with stone mauls and antler picks. Ancient water pots, mauls, and picks have been found in a number of abandoned mine shafts at the site (Fig. 12.11). Earlier in this chapter we cited the inferences that could be drawn about workshop activities from the short-term accumulations at Koobi Fora Site FxJj50, in Kenya, and Meer II, in Belgium. Similarly, artifacts from a midden—molds, bowl sherds containing unfired clay or pigments, and so on—may indicate the nearby presence of a pottery production area and aid in outlining the technology involved in its use.

FEATURES AND SAMPLING

Two kinds of sampling are involved in the study of features: one governing data collection, the other for data analysis. In most cases, all recovered features are analyzed, because their numbers are small enough so that consideration of all examples is possible as well as desirable.

In planning a data recovery strategy, it is sometimes possible to anticipate roughly the number and variety of features that will be recorded. For example, in the southwestern United States, the preservation of pueblo sites (such as Broken K, mentioned earlier) is such that wall lines are usually visible on the surface. The archaeologist can then design sampling strategies that stratify along known dimensions of formal or locational variation, such as room size and shape or location in one or another part of the overall site. At Hatchery West, Lewis Binford and his colleagues wanted to maximize feature recovery, so they peeled away the plow-disturbed zone over the whole "site area" (see Chapter 6) and proceeded to record all features revealed.

In many situations, however, the number and range of features that will

FIGURE 12.11 The abandoned shaft of the ancient copper mines at Rudna Glava, Yugoslavia, still contained vessels used in the quarrying process 6000 years earlier. (After "The Origins of Copper Mining in Europe" by B. Jovanovič. Copyright © 1980 by Scientific American, Inc. All rights reserved.)

be recovered is impossible to predict. At deeply stratified southwest Asian *tell* sites, for example, surface remains may provide clues to the uppermost features but not to those in earlier, deeper levels. In such circumstances, the archaeologist may attempt to recover a variety of features by excavating in a varied set of locations within the site.

Once again, the paramount concern in sampling is the goal of the sample: What is it to represent? Once this has been decided, the archaeologist can design a sampling procedure accordingly.

SUMMARY

Features are nonportable artifacts that preserve in their form and location a record of the spatial distribution of past human activities. Some features are deliberately constructed to house certain activities, whereas others simply represent the accumulation of occupational debris. Because features owe their form to human behavior, they can be analyzed in somewhat the same way as artifacts. In addition, they provide information on the ways ancient societies organized the use of space.

Many features were deliberately constructed to channel use of space. The various technologies used in their creation are related to characteristics of their environmental setting. Whereas some ancient construction technologies were quite sophisticated and complex, most constructed features from humanity's prehistoric past were probably made fairly simply. The attributes of form and location of constructed features yield valuable inferences about past human behavior and culture. In addition, features, like artifacts, can exhibit variation in style, and these can provide important markers of age or cultural identity.

Many features are not the result of deliberate manufacture but result instead from either gradual accumulation of artifacts and ecofacts or progressive deletion of materials. Workshops and middens are examples of the first kind of cumulative feature, and mines and quarries exemplify the other kind.

Sampling of features takes place during data collection and data analysis. The number and variety of features recorded depend both on the predictability of their discovery (how easy they are to find) and on the questions the researcher wants to answer with them. Because the number of features actually recovered is generally small, archaeologists usually analyze all of them.

In Chapters 10–12 we have explored the kinds of information that can most appropriately be sought from each class of archaeological data. In the next five chapters we will change our perspective to consider how combining analyses of different kinds of data can reveal structure and meaning in the archaeological record.

GUIDE TO FURTHER READING

Bunn et al. 1980; Cahan and Keeley 1980; Cahan, Keeley, and Van Noten 1979; Clarke 1977; Hietala 1984; Kroll and Isaac 1984; Kroll and Price 1991; Toth 1985; Van Noten, Cahan, and Keeley 1980

Constructed Features

Ashmore 1980; Aveni 1989; Barnett and Hering 1986; Biddle 1977; Chippindale 1986; Coles 1984, 1989; Coles and Coles 1989; Cordell 1979, 1984a; Dales 1966; Davies 1987; Donnan 1964; Eddy 1974; Flannery 1972b; Flannery and Marcus 1976a; Forbes 1963; Hastings and Moseley 1975; Haviland 1982; Hawkins 1965; Heggie 1981; Hyslop 1984; Jackson 1991; Kidder, Jennings, and Shook 1946; Matheny 1976; Mendelssohn 1971; Morley, Brainerd, and Sharer 1983; Moseley 1975; Movius 1966; Müller-Beck 1961; Netting 1982; Roosevelt 1991; Smith 1978; Thompson and Murra 1966

Cumulative Features

Anderson 1978; Betancourt, Van Devender, and Martin 1990; L. R. Binford 1978; Bunn et al. 1980; Cahan and Keeley 1980; Ericson and Purdy 1984; Hatch and Miller 1985; Holmes 1900; Jovanovic 1980; Kintigh and Ammerman 1982; Kopper and Rossello-Bordoy 1974; Longworth 1984; Whallon 1973, 1974, 1984

Features and Sampling

Binford et al. 1970; Carr 1985; Hill 1967, 1970; Sharer 1978

CHAPTER THIRTEEN

ANALOGY AND ARCHAEOLOGICAL INTERPRETATION

Analogy serves to provoke certain types of questions which can, on investigation, lead to the recognition of more comprehensive ranges of order in the archaeological data.

Lewis R. Binford, "Smudge Pits and Hide Smoking: The Use of Analogy in Archaeological Reasoning," 1967

Careful analysis . . . may lead to precise definition of significant and comparable technological elements. However, these techniques do not, by themselves, interpret prehistory. Such interpretation depends upon ethnographic analogy.

Keith M. Anderson, "Ethnographic Analogy and Archaeological Interpretation," 1969

Now that we have described how archaeologists construct the essential chronological frameworks for their data, we can move fully into the final step in archaeological research—synthesis and interpretation. By **synthesis,** we mean the process of reassembling the data that have been isolated, described, and structured by analysis. In this chapter we consider how the archaeologist combines the analyses of different data categories (artifacts, ecofacts, and features) across dimensions of time, space, and function to interpret those data.

Interpretation is the meaning the archaeologist infers from analyzed and synthesized data. In other words, as in any science, the end product of research is *explanation and understanding*—the attempts to answer questions such as *what* happened in the past, *when* it happened, *where* it happened, *how* it happened, and *why* it happened. In reality, interpretation goes on all the time, from the outset of problem formulation. But at this point, we are concerned with how archaeologists view their assemblage of analyzed and synthesized data and with the methods and theoretical frameworks they use to do so.

These various aspects of interpretation can be briefly illustrated by James Deetz's study of the 18th-century Arikara. In this case, the archaeological data, once collected and analyzed, were used first to describe *what* took place in the past: Changes in certain pottery styles were detected by classification methods. Specifically, the data showed an initial set of "standardized" pottery styles, or regular associations between attributes of form and decoration. This situation was followed in time by a more variable and less predictable assemblage and then by a new "standardized" set of styles. *When* these changes took place was revealed in various methods of age determination, including indirect dating by association with European trade goods of known age. *Where* the changes took place was identified by the spatial distribution of the sources of the pottery styles under study, in the middle Missouri River region of South Dakota.

Once the questions of what, when, and where had been answered, a

Aspects of interpretation: James Deetz and the Arikara study

correlation between Arikara residence patterns and mother–daughter transmission of pottery-making knowledge was used to explain *how* the changes took place. By using ethnographic data, Deetz postulated that residence in ancient Arikara families was matrilocal, with a husband coming to live in his wife's house, so that over time several generations of women would remain living in a single location. Pottery production was women's work, and a girl would learn from her mother and grandmother the proper ways of making vessels. Thus matrilocal residence would foster pottery styles that remained consistent and recognizable within a single residential area. A change in residence pattern, however, would tend to disrupt the consistency of pottery production by breaking up the women's groupings. Such a change in residential groups, Deetz argued, is exactly what accounted for the dissolution of 18th-century Arikara pottery styles. The reasons *why* these changes in pottery styles took place were postulated to be changes in residence rules, which in this case could be traced to disruptions brought about by contacts and conflicts with Europeans and other neighboring peoples—conflicts attested by documentary accounts as well as by archaeological evidence of fortifications.

In this case, the descriptive interpretation (what, when, and where) followed fairly directly from the data analysis: The artifacts were classified so that they revealed changes in time and space. The explanation and understanding aspect of interpretation (how and why) rested on the application of analogy, which in this case could be at least partially supported by historical information. As we shall see, prehistoric archaeological interpretation is almost always based on some kind of analogy. The rest of this chapter will be devoted to discussion of this vital interpretive tool.

USING ANALOGY IN INTERPRETATION

There is a basic paradox in archaeology: The archaeological record exists in the present, while the archaeologist is concerned with the past—specifically the past human behaviors that created that record. Since events in the prehistoric past cannot be directly observed, the archaeologist can only reconstruct them from the material evidence recovered. To guide these critical links between the material record and past behavior, the archaeologist applies middle-range theory (described in Chapter 1). These theoretical links are based on **analogy**—a form of reasoning in which the identity of unknown items or relations may be inferred from those that are known. Reasoning by analogy is founded on the premise that if two classes of phenomena are alike in one respect, they may be alike in other respects as well. In archaeology, analogy is used to infer the identity of and relationships among archaeological data on the basis of comparison with similar phenomena documented in living human societies.

This is not to say that analogy underlies all archaeological reconstruction. Historical archaeology can often rely on documentary sources to identify and interpret archaeological remains. In protohistorical situations, later historical information is sometimes projected back in time to assist archaeological reconstructions. Deetz's Arikara study is an example of this method (an application of the direct historical approach, discussed in Chapter 2 and on page 000). But in clear-cut prehistoric situations, without direct links to historical information, the archaeologist must rely on inferences based on analogy.

On the most basic level, analogy allows the archaeologist to identify the remains of past human behavior as archaeological data. For example, the archaeologist does not observe the ancient human activity that produced an Acheulian hand-axe, a Paleolithic stone tool produced in Europe thousands of years ago. Hunters and gatherers in several parts of the world continue to make and use similar chipped-stone axes. The behavior associated with the manufacture and use of these tools has been recorded by ethnographers and other observers. Because of the similarity in form between the Paleolithic artifacts and the ethnographically observed examples, the latter serve as *analogs* for identifying Paleolithic hand-axes as ancient tools and, by extension, allow reconstruction of relevant manufacturing and use behavior associated with the ancient tools (Fig. 13.1).

Artifacts are not the only materials identified by use of analogy. Archaeological features, too, are recognized as the products of human behavior by use of such reasoning. In many cases, the archaeologist's use of analogy to identify a feature such as a building foundation or a burial is not a conscious process. Because these features are so familiar, the professional archaeologist seldom pauses to reflect that analogy is involved in recognizing a line of masonry as a building foundation. An automatic association takes place from everyday experience, where masonry foundations support modern buildings, to the archaeological feature; this process makes the identification. But often the archaeologist will encounter a feature or an artifact that is not familiar; in such cases, identification by analogy becomes most clearly a conscious, rational process.

Analogy in interpretation: Binford's hide pits

A good example of detailed analogical reasoning is Lewis Binford's study of a certain category of pits encountered in sites of the middle and lower Mississippi River valley and adjacent areas after A.D. 1000. The pits in question are always fairly small, averaging about 30 cm or less in length and width and slightly more than that in depth. They contain charred and carbonized twigs, bark, and corncobs, and they are found around houses and domestic storage areas, never near public buildings. The one sure interpretation concerning the nature of these pits was that the charred contents had been burned in place, in an oxygen-starved atmosphere that must have produced a lot of smoke. So the pits were labeled "smudge pits." Further interpretations offered for these features, however, included corncob "caches" or facilities for creating smoke to drive away mosquitoes.

In seeking a firmer interpretive base from which to establish the nature of these smudge pits, Binford went through the ethnographic literature on modern Native American groups in that area. These accounts included descriptions of hide-smoking procedures in which an untanned deerskin was tied as a cover over a small hole. A smoldering, smoky fire was then set in the hole and allowed to burn until the hide was dried and toughened, ready to be sewn into clothing. Binford pointed out that whenever the ethnographic accounts offered details on the form and contents of the hide-smoking pits, these details corresponded well with equivalent attributes of the archaeological smudge pits. Because there was a high degree of correspondence in *form* between ethnographic and archaeological examples, because the *geographical* areas involved were the same, and because a good case could be argued for the *continuity* of practices in that area from the archaeological past (after A.D. 1000) to the time of ethnographic observations (1700–1950), Binford argued—by analogy—that the archaeological smudge pits represented facilities for smoking animal skins.

More precisely, Binford offered the analogical interpretation as a hypothesis to be tested: If this identification were correct, other ethnographically described correlates of hide-smoking activities should also be found associated with the archaeological smudge pits. For example, since the ethnographic accounts noted that tanning activities occurred between, rather than during, peak hunting seasons, the sites with this kind of smudge pits should be spring–summer camps, not hunting camps.

The more correspondences are found between the ethnographic and the archaeological data, and the more strictly the specific attributes identified refer to a particular kind of feature—in this case, hide-smoking pits rather than any other kind of smudge pits—the stronger the analogical interpretation.

FIGURE 13.1 Manufacture of chipped-stone tools in Ethiopia. Lithic technology survives today in several parts of the world, providing analogs for understanding similar technologies in the past. (Photo by James P. Gallagher.)

MISUSE OF ANALOGY

Analogy has not always been used correctly, and its improper use has led to erroneous reconstructions of the past. The smudge pits example above illustrates a proper use of analogy. But, before examining in more detail the ways analogy *should* be used, we need to explore some of the errors that have resulted from its improper use in interpretation.

In the 19th century, when (as we saw in Chapter 2) anthropology was dominated by a theory of **unilinear cultural evolution,** living "primitive" societies were often equated directly with various postulated stages of the proposed evolutionary sequence (Fig. 13.2). These stages were defined by technological attributes (Stone Age, Iron Age, and so on), and each stage supposedly had its corresponding developmental level of social system, political organization, and religious beliefs. By means of these combined technological, social, and ideological attributes, living societies could be ranked in their progress along the evolutionary scale.

FIGURE 13.2 Lewis Henry Morgan's unilinear stages were used to equate past and present societies on a scale of evolutionary progress.

Stage		Examples of associated technological innovations
Civilization		Alphabet and writing
BARBARISM	Upper	Iron tools
	Middle	Plant and animal domestication
	Lower	Pottery
SAVAGERY	Upper	Bow and arrow
	Middle	Fishing and fire
	Lower	Fruit and nut subsistence

(Direction of unilinear evolution ↑)

Since technological attributes were weighted so heavily in this classification scheme, it was often relatively easy to link evidence of prehistoric technology gained from the archaeological record with the traits used to define the various evolutionary stages. Given their assumption that cultures everywhere had followed the same single course of development, Lewis Henry Morgan and other unilinearists found it easy to assign "appropriate" social and ideological traits to a particular prehistoric culture whose technological level was known. Living societies whose technology was similar to that inferred from archaeological evidence for a past culture were used as exact analogs for the reconstruction of the entire prehistoric culture. For instance, living societies still using stone tool technologies, such as the Australian Aborigines, were used as analogs to reconstruct Paleolithic hunting societies that lived in Europe tens of thousands of years before. Technology simply provided a convenient, nonperishable link between the "known" world of today and the "unknown" of the prehistoric past.

It should be obvious that this kind of analogy is suspect, since it is founded on only one criterion—technology—and ignores other variables, such as time, space, and environmental conditions. In linking the Australian Aborigines with European Paleolithic peoples, for instance, the analogy disregards a temporal separation of more than 10,000 years and a spatial separation of over 10,000 miles. Recent research has made it clear that we cannot use the single trait of "hunting" to predict the forms the rest of the culture will take. Yet this is essentially what the 19th-century unilinear evolutionists attempted to do.

Because of such simplistic reliance on limited criteria, usually technology, the wide-ranging analogies associated with the 19th-century unilinear cultural evolutionists are generally not accepted today. However, simplistic analogies are not confined to the literature of the 19th century; similar careless equations between living cultures and those of the past may be found in some archaeological publications of the 20th century. And the general analogy between the hunters of the European Paleolithic and certain contemporary peoples still occurs—most recently in popular accounts of the discovery of the Tasaday tribe in the Philippines, which described this isolated society as a "Stone Age tribe."

The obvious abuses of analogy in reconstructing the past have led to reactions, both by cultural anthropologists and by archaeologists, against the use of this method of reasoning. Much of the criticism of analogy has centered specifically on the use of ethnographic studies as analogs for archaeological interpretation. The most extreme critics would eliminate ethnographic analogs as sources for the reconstruction of the past. They reason that every culture is unique, and therefore no single trait from one society can be equivalent to one from another society. According to this argument, the fact that small triangular chipped stones are used as projectile points in one culture does not mean that similar artifacts have the same function in another; they might be used as articles of adornment, counters in a game, or even ritual symbols. As a result, the identification of an artifact or a feature in an ethnographically observed culture cannot be used to identify any similar artifact or feature found archaeologically.

If archaeologists accepted this position, they would not be able to identify or interpret their data and reconstruct the events of the past. The archaeologists would merely collect and describe relics without identifying how they were made or what they were used for. More important, the data could not be synthesized to reconstruct the past. Fortunately, this extreme argument against any use of analogy rests on a false premise—that cultural characteristics are unique. Although each cultural system is unique (as a culture), systems do share characteristics in varying degrees. It is true that any given cultural trait, such as a projectile point, may have many uses, and these uses may vary from society to society. However, to accept the position that the traits of one culture are *in no way* comparable to those of another is to deny the patterned regularities of human behavior described by countless ethnographers, historians, and other observers. Archaeologists can validly identify certain small triangular chipped-stone artifacts as projectile points, because this identification is based on myriad cases of observed human behavior associated with the bones of game animals. Even though the use of analogy in archaeological interpretation has the potential for error, rather than rejecting analogy as a method, the archaeologist needs to maximize its usefulness by recognizing and avoiding the sources of error.

These considerations highlight a useful distinction between specific and general analogy: **Specific analogy** refers to specific comparisons within a given cultural tradition; **general analogy** refers to generalized comparisons that can be documented across many cultural traditions, based on the principle of *uniformitarianism* (that all human behavior is motivated by the same need satisfactions; see Chapter 3).

SPECIFIC ANALOGY

Some very general analogies—such as the identification of human bones in a pit as a human burial—require little defense. But for more detailed interpretations, the archaeologist must be prepared to defend the appropriateness of a given specific analog on three grounds: cultural continuity, comparability in environment, and similarity of cultural form. In the smudge pits example described above, Binford was able to substantiate all these factors in his analogy.

Cultural Continuity

The degree of cultural continuity between the prehistoric society and the society being used as a specific analog is an important and obvious factor. In most cases, the greater the degree of cultural continuity, the more reliable the analogy will be. In the southwestern United States, for instance, there is considerable evidence that the contemporary Native American societies documented by ethnographic and historical accounts are the direct descendants, both culturally and biologically, of local prehistoric (pre-16th-century) occupants (Fig. 13.3). This link allows the archaeologist to draw frequent and reasonable analogies on the basis of living societies to interpret southwestern prehistory. Studies by James Hill and William Longacre that, like Deetz's Arikara study, examine ceramic data as a reflection of prehistoric social organization rely on this continuity of southwestern occupation to support their analogical reconstructions of pottery production and residential patterns (the Hill and Longacre studies are considered in Chapter 15).

In the New World, situations with maximum continuity fostered development of the **direct historical approach,** a method of reconstructing prehistoric societies by progressive extension of analogies back through time. This method, described in Chapter 2, first involves identification of sites occupied by documented groups: This step establishes the crucial link between prehistoric past and documented "present." Then earlier sites are located and examined. If similarity of the material remains continues to be evident through the series of increasingly earlier settlements, then continuity of other aspects of culture is also posited. Of course, the links diminish as the archaeologist goes further back in time, because no society remains unchanged for long. We will discuss the direct historical approach in more detail in Chapter 17 when we consider culture historical reconstruction.

Consider, as a contrast, the degree of cultural continuity between contemporary English society and that of England's prehistoric past. The issue is not simply that the historic period is five times as long in England as in the southwestern United States, but also that during that history the known changes and upheavals in the local way of life make it difficult to justify analogies between contemporary industrialized society and Bri-

FIGURE 13.3 Cultural continuity, in the southwestern United States, for example, is an important criterion for using ethnographic studies as analogs for understanding ancient societies. The photographs above were taken around the turn of the century and show (top) an overall view of Oraibi Pueblo, Arizona, and (bottom) a room with equipment for preparing meals. Compare (b) with the mealing bin in Fig. 12.1, p. 403. (Field Museum of Natural History, [t] Neg# A185, [b] Neg# A246, Chicago.)

tain's prehistoric past. On the other hand, analogs for prehistoric England *are* provided by historical documents that reduce the temporal separation between the present and the prehistoric past. The use of 2000-year-old Roman historical sources has been of great benefit in interpreting the archaeological evidence from Celtic sites of Iron Age England. A classic

Use of historical analogs: Wheeler at Maiden Castle, England

FIGURE 13.4 Historic accounts complemented information from archaeological excavations to reconstruct ancient life and events at Maiden Castle, Dorset. In spite of earthen fortifications, the settlement was stormed and sacked by Roman troops under Vespasian about A.D. 47. (Ashmolean Museum, Oxford.)

study in this regard is Sir Mortimer Wheeler's reconstruction of events at Maiden Castle, in Dorset, England, a first-century A.D. Celtic fortified settlement besieged and captured by an invading Roman army (Fig. 13.4). A Roman account of the conquest provided Wheeler with the means not only to interpret the archaeological evidence of the military action but also to reconstruct aspects of daily life in Celtic England.

But as the time span between the analog and the archaeological data increases, the chances for other variables to distort the reconstruction also increase. The Roman historical sources just mentioned have also been used in attempts to interpret aspects of the more distant past in England. However, conditions in Celtic England at the time of the Roman invasion may not be a reliable gauge of conditions several thousand years earlier. For instance, the popular (and erroneous) belief that Stonehenge was a center of druid worship is based on Roman accounts of Celtic religion, yet Stonehenge was built and used more than a thousand years before the Roman Conquest.

Comparability of Environment

Successful specific analogs also depend on the control of another important variable, comparability of environment. The relationship between environment and culture will be discussed in Chapter 14, but here we note that an analog drawn from a society living in an environment different from that of the prehistoric society will be less reliable than one based on a society in a similar environment. It would obviously be difficult to maintain that Inuit ("Eskimo") culture, which is adapted to an arctic environment, could be used to reconstruct Paleolithic societies in temperate Europe. A more valid application of analogy would be to use aspects of the Inuit adaptation to the arctic environment in reconstructing prehistoric life along the northern coasts of Europe during the close of the last glacial period, when this area did possess an arctic environment. If we make the assumption that a given culture is adapted to its natural and social surroundings, then similar conditions of relative abundance or deficiency in natural resources—water, good soils, game animals, and so forth—will provide similar social opportunities and limitations. For example, desert-dwelling societies are generally best used as analogs for prehistoric communities that lived in arid environments, where the water supply was a constant and central concern. Likewise, groups living in tropical climates provide models for ancient societies in similar settings: Archaeologists studying the Maya, whose civilization flourished in the tropics of Guatemala and adjacent areas in the first millennium A.D., have sought analogs in areas with like tropical settings, from modern Central America to West Africa and Southeast Asia.

Of course, the technological variable remains important, too, despite its abuse in the 19th century. As we have pointed out, the relationship between technology and environment is a fluid one. For example, similar environments encourage some similarities in technology: Areas having fish as the primary food resource will foster development of fishing gear—hooks, spears, fishing boats, and so on. But technological changes can redefine environments. In Chapter 2, we cited the case of the Great Plains of the United States, where the European introduction of the horse as a means of transport increased the mobility and hunting range of the Native American people in the area, effectively redefining the available food resources. The same innovation affected their social organization—by increasing mobility—and their capacity to wage war on neighboring groups.

Similarity of Cultural Form

A final consideration in analogy is the question of cultural comparability, which, in turn, includes a series of variables—some defined more objectively, others quite subjectively. The first criterion to consider is relative cultural complexity. To be successful, a specific analogy should involve a society that possesses the same degree of overall complexity as that indicated for the prehistoric situation. Cultural complexity is usually defined on the basis of the contemporary multilinear evolutionary scheme, discussed in Chapters 3 and 17. Thus, for example, the interpretation of data from prehistoric hunting and gathering societies should be based on analogs drawn from documented hunting and gathering peoples, rather than from groups that possess a greater or lesser degree of complexity. Other criteria of comparability should be considered also. For instance, some societies tend to resist change and to place a high value on preserving traditional ways. As a general rule, analogies based on such tradition-bound societies tend to be more useful in archaeology than those involving societies that have experienced rapid and drastic changes. For example, in Southeast Asia, conservative highland tribal groups provide more likely analogs for local prehistoric reconstructions than their urbanized neighbors in Bangkok. In a related way, some societies tend to resist outside influences, whereas others are open and receptive to external influences. It is often preferable to choose analogs from societies that tend to be resistant to external influences, since distortion resulting from externally induced change is less likely.

As long as the archaeologist is aware of these variables and can isolate and control them in using specific analogy to deal with the prehistoric data, the resulting interpretation will be not only more complete but more accurate as well.

GENERAL ANALOGY

In recent years some of the fundamental assumptions underlying general analogies have increasingly been challenged by detailed observations of the actual use of artifacts, ecofacts, and features, and how such use reflects behavior. The goal of these **actualistic studies** is to build a reliable set of general analogs for archaeological interpretation—a body of middle-range theory that relates material remains to behavior regardless of the specific cultural setting. Like specific analogies, however, general analogies applied to reconstruct past behavior must be subjected to rigorous examination. For example, as Richard Gould and others have pointed out, the basic idea that prehistoric human behavior has analogs in the historical or ethnographic present must be tempered by consideration of physical conditions in the more remote past, both in the environment and in the populations, that no longer exist. Even in the more recent past, archaeologists cannot be sure that the known analogs cover the full range of ancient behavioral variation and idiosyncrasy. As we have seen in Chapter 3, postprocessual archaeologists have questioned the use of general analogies because of potential differences in belief and value systems from one culture to another (denial of the principle of uniformitarianism).

Gould stresses the importance of actualistic studies in specifying the

FIGURE 13.6 Contact sites, such as Cuzco, Peru, offer a direct link between history and the prehistoric past. This photograph shows the incorporation of prehistoric buildings (note the large, finely cut blocks made by Inka stonemasons) in modern structures along a street in Cuzco. (Courtesy of The University Museum, University of Pennsylvania.)

from the Spanish Conquest in the 16th century (Fig. 13.5). Many of these were written by soldiers, missionaries, and administrators from Spain; they include accounts by eyewitnesses such as Fray Bernardino de Sahagún, Bernal Diaz del Castillo, and Hernán Cortés himself. Others were written by native chroniclers, trained by the Spanish to translate and record aspects of their vanishing way of life.

The use of historical sources may enable the archaeologist to identify *contact sites*—sites occupied by a prehistoric people at the time contact was made with a people possessing a historical tradition. Examples include Maiden Castle, England, documented in the Roman histories, and Cuzco, Peru, recorded in the Spanish Conquest accounts (Fig. 13.6). Contact sites provide the archaeologist with a starting point for interpretation using the direct historical approach.

Ethnographic studies of living human societies are probably the most common source of archaeological analogs. Since they are written by professional anthropologists, ethnographies are generally more relevant and useful to the archaeologist than other sources. However, the overall quality of ethnographic accounts varies considerably. Usually there is some information of use to archaeologists, but, since ethnographers pursue their studies for their own theoretical interests, the data are often not presented in ways that relate behavior to material remains—that is, in ways that facilitate archaeological analogy. Binford was able to find descriptive accounts that related hide-smoking behavior to smudge pit features. But, as

Richard Gould points out in summarizing the ethnographic resources for the Australian Aborigines, the elaborateness of the kinship and ceremonial side of aboriginal life has so impressed most observers that, until recently, ethnographic descriptions of the Aborigines have focused on these particular aspects of culture, seldom relating them clearly to settlement patterns, subsistence behavior, and associated material remains.

Ethnoarchaeology

Situations in which ethnographic data cannot be related directly to archaeological remains are common enough that archaeologists are increasingly becoming trained to participate actively in ethnographic studies. Of particular concern in such projects are clear statements of relationships between those aspects of culture that are likely to be archaeologically preserved (durable material remains) and behavioral systems that are likely to be archaeologically "invisible." **Ethnoarchaeology** is the term for these studies, which are based on observations made within living societies.

Ethnoarchaeology: Nicholas David's study of Fulani pottery use

A primary focus of ethnoarchaeological attention is the way material items enter the archaeological record: What gets thrown away, how often, and why? Nicholas David has presented detailed data on Fulani compounds in West Africa, including information of the average life expectancy of various types of pottery vessels. His figures indicate, for example, that vessel types that suffer more frequent breakage—and must be replaced more often—will be overrepresented in any archaeological assemblage relative to their numbers in a Fulani household during use. If specific forms reflect specific functions, then this finding serves as a caution for direct analogical reconstruction: The *range* of pottery (and, indirectly, its uses) may be accurately recovered archaeologically, but archaeological frequency of form types should not be taken as a direct index of the relative emphasis placed on various activities (cooking, storage, or whatever).

Ethnoarchaeology: Longacre and Ayres's Apache *wickiup*

Other studies treat occupied or recently abandoned settlements as archaeological sites, comparing what would be preserved archaeologically with what is present ethnographically. David's Fulani work includes this kind of consideration, as does Karl Heider's description of New Guinea settlements. A well-known example of "checking" archaeological observation and interpretations against ethnographic information is a study done by William Longacre and James Ayres. Taking a recently abandoned Apache *wickiup* (a small domestic structure) as an archaeological site, they recorded the visible artifacts, ecofacts, and features and their spatial relationships (Fig. 13.7). Then, using an Apache ethnographic analogy, they interpreted the material data as indicating the residence of a nuclear family—husband, wife, and unmarried children—in which there was a sexual division of labor, with female-associated activities predominating. The associations of distinct artifact and feature assemblages in different locations were also interpreted by analogy with modern Apache use of

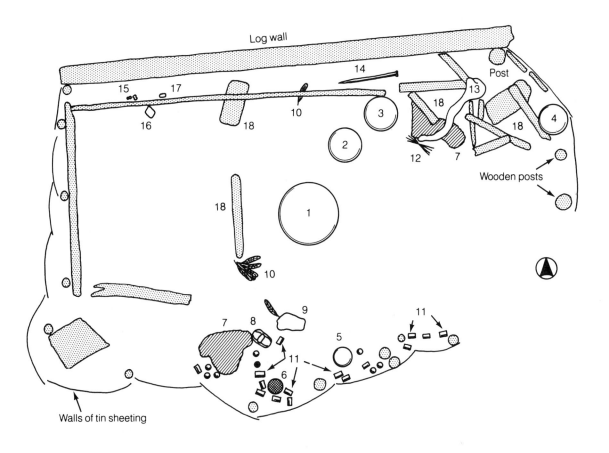

Log wall

14

Post

15   17
16   18
10
18
13
18
3
2
12   7
18
Wooden posts
4

18
1

10

9
11
11
7   8
5
11
6
11

Walls of tin sheeting

Key:

1	Wash tub over hearth	10	Turkey feathers
2	Wash basin	11	Tin cans
3	Enameled pail	12	Twigs
4	Milk can lid	13	Plastic sheeting
5	Tin can pail	14	Iron spike
6	Can of nails	15	Vertebrae
7	Burlap	16	Wallet
8	Grinding stones	17	Rawhide
9	Bread wrapper	18	Boards

FIGURE 13.7 Investigation of recently abandoned sites, such as this modern Apache *wickiup*, allows the archaeologist to test interpretation of the physical remains by interviewing informants who can describe the actual behavior associated with material remains. (After Longacre and Ayres 1968.)

such assemblages: The *wickiup* structure itself had been a storage and food preparation facility, perhaps also serving as sleeping quarters during bad weather. Some cooking had also taken place outdoors, as attested by the hearths near the *wickiup*. After making these interpretations, Longacre and Ayres consulted a local Apache resident who was a friend of the former occupants, and they were able to confirm the majority of their archaeological interpretations. Although the research was reported to give evidence for the behavioral structure reflected in spatial associations of archaeological data, it also serves as a reminder of the kinds of ethnographic observations that must be made—relating particular activities to the associated material remains—if ethnographic studies are to be maximally useful to archaeologists.

Ethnoarchaeology: The Makapansgat controversy

Several investigations have involved observation of "midden production," especially the accumulation and relative preservation of animal remains. Motivated at least in part by the controversy surrounding the bone assemblage from Makapansgat cave, discussed in Chapters 10 and 11, these studies have sought to determine the kinds of food-animal bones that wind up in and are preserved in trash deposits. At issue in the Makapansgat case is whether the array of nonhuman bones found in the cave represents elements selected by hominids for use as tools or simply an accumulation of a carnivore's food refuse. As we noted in Chapter 11, Raymond Dart has argued that the set of elements found reflects deliberate hominid selection; using as illustrations some pieces whose original form had clearly been altered, he posited that the bones were the remains of an osteodontokeratic (bone-tooth-horn) toolmaking tradition. Many have taken issue with this position, arguing that Dart did not have the appropriate comparative base—the specific analogs from modern carnivore lairs and from modern cultural middens—to make his interpretation. Among the observational studies that have been done in response are C. K. Brain's study in Southwest Africa of what elements of goat bone survive in modern Hottentot middens after the goats are eaten by the local people and the bones have been exposed to scavenging dogs; documentations by Gary Haynes (among others) of bone breakage or other modification patterns resulting from trampling by other animals, some of which may mimic the diagnostics of human modification (see p. 389); and Lewis Binford's studies of what sheep bone elements survive in Inuit and Navajo camps of North America. The results of these studies have tended to contradict Dart's arguments, indicating instead that the Makapansgat assemblage could well be the remains of ancient food debris, in which the "selection" of parts preserved is a result of natural transformational processes.

Wear and breakage patterns on bone have also been examined, especially with respect to the issue raised in Chapter 11 concerning the distinctions between bone "middens" created by human activity and those produced by animals. Electron microscopes have been used to scan marks made by various agents, such as carnivore teeth and stone tools, to define the diagnostics of human utilization of bone. These criteria may then be applied to archaeological samples to identify evidence of human activity. Although the distinctions may not always be clear-cut (they were not in the Haynes study mentioned above), the recognition of what appear to be tool marks on bones from ancient sites such as Olduvai Gorge has supported arguments that early hominids were the meat eaters. Occasional overlaps of marks not from tools suggests, however, that our ancestors did not have exclusive right to these prey animals, and indeed may have scavenged food killed by carnivores.

Experimental Archaeology

The final source of archaeological analogy is **experimental archaeology,** based on observations made under artificially controlled conditions. Although these have a long history in archaeology, only recently have they begun to reach their full potential as a fundamental source of interpretive analogy. Early experiments often involved using actual archaeological materials, such as cutting tools and musical instruments, in an attempt to discover their ancient functions. Such experiments continue, but in many cases experimental archaeology has been redefined, with the goal of providing analogs for a broader range of behavior—manufacture, use, and deposition—associated with archaeological materials.

Experimental work with stone artifacts is particularly well known. Don Crabtree and François Bordes have been leaders in reconstructing the techniques used to manufacture stone tools, by experimental stone chipping or "knapping" designed to duplicate the archaeologically recovered forms. S. A. Semenov, Lawrence Keeley, and others have pioneered in studying the wear patterns produced on stone tools by various kinds of use (slicing, chopping, and so on). Some studies examine the relative efficiency of different technological systems, indicating how much time and effort each one requires to accomplish the same task; an example is the experiments by Stephen Saraydar and Izumi Shimada comparing steel and stone tools for felling trees and planting crops. Similarly, archaeologists have fired pottery, smelted copper, caught fish, and done many other activities to provide experimental analogs for interpreting past behavior associated with ancient artifacts.

Experimental archaeology: Production and use of artifacts

Features, too, have been studied by experiment. For example, imposing structures such as the Egyptian pyramids and Stonehenge have inspired projects aimed at calculating the labor force needed for their construction. A famous Danish experiment at Roskilde reconstructed an Iron Age house, which was then burned and excavated. At Overton Down, England, an earthwork was built in 1960 that duplicates prehistoric constructions (Fig. 13.8). Test excavations at preset intervals since that time, most recently in 1976, have documented gradual transformations in the form of the earthwork. While the building was in progress, the Overton Down project also enabled investigators to compare ancient and modern tool efficiency; ancient tools such as antler and bone picks and shovels were found to be nearly as productive as their modern counterparts. A number of presumed storage features, from earthen pits in England to *chultun* chambers hollowed out of the limestone bedrock of northern Guatemala, have been filled with grain, water, and other such supplies to see how well they actually served their postulated function.

Experimental archaeology: Production and use of features

Possible environmental constraints on ancient cultures have been examined in a number of ways. For instance, experimental attempts to duplicate ancient agricultural practices have been made in a number of areas, from the Yucatán peninsula to the Negev desert of Israel. Energy spent in

Experimental archaeology: Agriculture and sea travel

FIGURE 13.8 The experimental earthwork at Overton Down, Wiltshire, was created to supply information on behavioral as well as transformational processes involved in the formation of similar archaeological features in England. (By permission of the British Association for the Advancement of Science.)

Experimental archaeology: Community living

preparing, planting, and maintaining agricultural plots can be compared with final food yield, sometimes over a series of planting and harvesting cycles, to arrive at a more precise idea of how large a population a given area could have supported under that agricultural system. The influence of the sea on settlement of the Polynesian islands of the Pacific has also been examined experimentally. Best known is Thor Heyerdahl's dramatic trip aboard the raft *Kon-Tiki,* sailing westward to Polynesia from South America. More recently, Ben R. Finney has sailed in both directions between Hawaii and Tahiti—a distance of more than 5000 km each way—in reconstructed duplicates of traditional Polynesian canoes. Heyerdahl's voyages indicate that occasional ancient contacts between South America and the Pacific Islands were at least possible. Finney's more focused experiments aimed at discovering to what extent traditional craft could sail into, as well as with, the wind; the success of his canoes at doing both implies, by analogy, that prehistoric communication among people on the far-flung islands of Oceania was at least partly under human control, not due solely to drifting canoes sailing wherever the seas and winds would take them.

The most elaborate experimental studies—and the least often manageable—involve reconstruction and maintenance of a community under ancient conditions. Archaeologists dealing with recent, historically documented periods are in a better position to do experiments of this kind. Plimouth Plantation in Massachusetts and Colonial Pennsylvania Plantation in eastern Pennsylvania are examples of "reconstituted" colonial American communities (Fig. 13.9); in these projects, crops have been raised, food cooked, buildings heated, and tools produced, all according to colonial customs. The experience provided is comparable to that of

FIGURE 13.9 The Colonial Pennsylvania Plantation is an example of experimental archaeology, in which past conditions and behavior are recreated to understand more fully what life was like in the past. (Courtesy of the Colonial Pennsylvania Plantation, Edgmont, Pa.)

ethnoarchaeology, for the archaeologist has the opportunity to observe and record the behavior associated with the material "remains." Granted, these reconstructed communities are somewhat more artificial than the communities studied by the ethnographer. But, by putting the material remains back into a working social system, they do provide insights and interpretive analogs not available from documents or other sources alone.

A last category of experimental archaeology involves study of what happens to archaeological materials on deposition. These experiments consider the transformational processes discussed in Chapter 4. Although these processes do not always involve human behavior, they are relevant to the interpretation of human behavior. For example, Glynn Isaac and his colleagues have sought to outline details that will help in distinguishing whether stone tool scatters in riverbank locations are intact sites or just the cumulative effects of artifacts being washed downstream from their original deposition points. To accomplish this, they set out a series of systematically arranged artifact scatters in the valley of a stream feeding into Lake Magadi, Kenya; then they returned annually to chart the artifact positions in these experimental analogs. Archaeologists have also made controlled observations of various kinds of preservation and destruction, including the burning of experimental houses of various materials, burial of hair under different soil conditions, and exposure of bones to weather and scavengers. Some of Lewis Binford's or Gary Haynes's work on bone preservation, cited earlier, fits here, for it has crossed the line from "detached" ethnographic observation to the deliberately arranged and controlled situation of an experiment. During construction of the Overton Down earthwork, a series of organic and inorganic remains were incorporated in it. Sample excavations are scheduled to take place at predetermined intervals over the next century to see how the processes of transformation have affected the preservation and recovery of these or-

Experimental archaeology: Deposition of artifacts

ganic and inorganic remains. For example, excavations in 1962, 1964, 1968, and 1976 have documented deterioration of textiles, but little change in pottery.

SUMMARY

Analogy provides the foundation for archaeological interpretation. Because past behavior can no longer be directly observed, the archaeologist must rely on analogy to interpret the behavioral significance of recovered material data. Both specific and general analogy are used for this purpose. Reasoning by analogy has not always been correctly applied in archaeological situations, but researchers can follow a number of guidelines to keep its use within proper bounds. They must consider continuity of occupation, similarity of setting, and comparability of cultural forms between the archaeological situation and its proposed analog. The more links they can establish between the two situations in these respects, the stronger will be the case for using the analog to interpret the archaeological remains. The sources for archaeological analogs are history, ethnography, ethnoarchaeology, and archaeological experiments.

Analogy is the basis for both description (what, when, and where) and explanation (how and why) of the past. Although inference based on analogy usually provides the crucial link between archaeological data and ancient behavior, to be meaningful these data must be placed within a cultural framework. In the following three chapters, we will discuss how archaeologists reconstruct the technological, social, and ideological realms of culture.

GUIDE TO FURTHER READING

K. Anderson 1969; Ascher 1961a; L. R. Binford 1967; Deetz 1965
Using Analogy in Interpretation
Ascher 1961b; Behrensmeyer 1984; L. R. Binford 1967, 1972b; Chang 1967; Coles 1973; Gould 1969, 1978, 1980a; Gould and Watson 1982; Haynes 1983; Hester and Heizer 1973; Hodder 1982c; Jewell 1963; Jewell and Dimbleby 1968; Johnson 1978; Lee and DeVore 1968, 1976; Longworth 1971; McIntosh 1974; Morgan 1877; Munsen 1969; Potts 1984; Potts and Shipman 1981; Shipman and Rose 1983; Steward 1942; Stiles 1977; Wauchope 1938; Wheeler 1943; Winterhalder and Smith 1981; Wylie 1985; Yellen 1977
Sources for Analogy
L. R. Binford 1981b, 1985; Blumenschine 1986; Bordes 1969; Brain 1981; Bunn 1981; Callender 1976; Crabtree 1972; Dart 1957; David 1971; Diaz del Castillo [1632] 1956; Finney 1977; Fowler 1988/89; R. A. Gould 1980a; Gould and Schiffer 1981; Graham 1985a; Haynes 1983; Heider 1967; Heyerdahl 1950; Isaac 1967, 1984; Johnson 1985; Jones 1980; Keeley 1980; Longacre and Ayres 1968; Newcomer and Keeley 1979; Puleston 1971; Saraydar and Shimada 1973; Schrire 1984; Semenov 1964; Wheeler 1943

LETTING LIONS SPEAK FOR FOSSIL BONES

Robert J. Blumenschine

Currently an Associate Professor at Rutgers University, Blumenschine spent 11 months in the Serengeti National Park and Ngorongoro Crater, Tanzania, studying modern scavenging behavior of African plains animals. On the basis of this data, he offers the following picture of the foraging behavior of early hominids.

January 2: I hear the distant, raucous yipping of spotted hyenas, a sure indication that ownership of a carcass is being contested. At 0729 I locate the carcass two kilometers away, an adult zebra that had apparently been killed by the two adult and five cub lions still largely in possession of it. Circling with lowered heads at a safe distance of at least 10 meters are some of the 34 spotted hyenas awaiting their turn. . . . The carcass is completely defleshed save small scraps, and the male lion, accompanied by the cubs, chews slowly on some skin, keeping his eyes on the braver (hungrier) hyenas. At 0755 . . . the full-bellied lioness and cubs leave and the bloated male soon follows at 0800. Immediately the hyenas rush in on the minimal edible remains, and after seven

minutes of frantic action, these are dispersed into a number of anatomical segments among several groups of hyenas. By 0845, most of the carcass is finished, with only fragments of bone remaining. . . . With consumption complete at 0920 and no feeding opportunity remaining for other scavengers, I continue to Reedbuck Gap in the hope of finding that the lions of the Maasi Pride, too, had made a kill.

The above excerpt from my field notes in Tanzania's Serengeti National Park represents the work not of a wildlife biologist, but of an archaeologist attempting to learn how to elicit information from animal ecofacts at early archaeological sites. Specifically, the study I undertook addressed the question of how our earliest meat-eating and stone-tool-using ancestors acquired animal foods: Was it through hunting, scavenging, or a mix of the two?

My work is characteristic of the growing numbers of archaeologists who are temporarily setting aside their trowels and climbing out of their trenches into the present day to observe how and why

the artifacts and ecofacts they find take on the forms and interrelationships they do. These traditionally nonarchaeological studies can be labeled broadly as *actualistic studies*. These studies of actual, modern-day use of artifacts and ecofacts permit empirical data rather than personal preconceptions to guide interpretations of the often fragmentary, incomplete, and mute archaeological data.

Lewis Binford calls actualistic studies "middle-range research," for they establish a link between empirical data and theory. Binford aptly likens these studies to the animal tracker attempting to identify an animal by its footprint: After seeing a bear walk (the activity) and in so doing leave a footprint (the physical trace), the tracker can henceforth infer the former presence of a bear from its footprint only.

My actualistic research in the Serengeti was concerned with linking the manner by which nonhuman predators and scavengers use carcasses (the walking bear) to the types and conditions of bones re-

(continued)

(continued)

maining after consumption of the carcass (the footprint). By so doing, I hoped to be able to determine the archaeological signatures, as written in the bone remains, of hunting and scavenging. Stated in the extreme, scavenging implies that meat is obtained on an irregular basis and in quantities too small to effect major adjustments in foraging strategies or social organization. Hunting, on the other hand, implies that meat is acquired frequently and in large amounts, thereby representing a staple of subsistence; hunting also possibly requires a mode of social organization more similar to that of modern hunting-and-gathering humans than to that of our ape relatives.

Early attempts to assess how our ancestors foraged for animal foods relied mostly on intuition. It was not until 1975 that Elizabeth Vrba of the Transvaal Museum, South Africa, first proposed criteria for distinguishing hunting and scavenging archaeologically on the basis of general patterns of predation and scavenging by modern carnivores. Since then, several other researchers have tackled the question actualistically, and my study represents one of the most recent attempts.

In addition to searching for archaeologically useful bear-and-footprint signatures of hunting and scavenging, my research also centered on assessing the ecological contexts (habitat type, season, etc.) in which carcasses would be most available to a hominid-like scavenger. The latter tack was necessary because physical, archaeologically visible traces of scavenging are highly variable and dependent on the availability of carcasses and the pursuant degrees of competition for them.

I found the intensity of competition for carcasses changed markedly but predictably with season and habitat type. Very high levels of competition occur mainly during the rainy season, when natural mortality among prey animals is low or nil. Competition is also usually high in open plains and lightly wooded habitats, where spotted hyenas, the most thorough carcass consumers, are plentiful and quick to scavenge any carcass they do not kill themselves. In these situations, predators and scavenging hyenas tend to consume carcasses completely, leaving little if any food for other scavengers.

I identified two contexts of low competition for carcasses that our ancestors might have encountered and taken advantage of. One occurs during the height of the dry season when accompanying high levels of drought-related mortality among prey animals produce a glut of carcasses for all scavengers. The second is also a dry-season phenomenon, when temporary water holes dry up and prey animals are forced to drink at perennial, well-wooded rivers and lakes (riparian woodland); when they come to drink, lions regularly ambush them. Lions typically consume most, if not all, the flesh of small-cow-sized and larger prey such as adult wildebeest and zebra, but, because of their relatively weak jaws, they leave the bone-covered brain and marrow of the limbs untouched. The regular and predictably located remains are usually not scavenged by spotted hyenas for at least a day or two, if at all, because hyenas show a strong aversion for entering riparian woodlands, apparently wary of encountering lions.

These two good-quality, low-competition opportunities for scavengers existed in East Africa during the time our ancestors first ate foods from large animals. Did early hominids take advantage of either scavenging opportunity? All known earliest archaeological sites where evidence of carcass processing has been found were once riparian woodland settings. A regular source of scavengeable food from lion kills, then, probably occurred within close proximity to the archaeological sites during the dry season. Although the remains do not seem to constitute much of a meal, the calorically rich marrow bones and the brain would represent an important seasonal supplement to a diet based on plant foods.

Given this, we can now ask the question of whether the composition of these earlier archaeological bone assemblages is consistent with scavenging in the modern-day context I have described. Here are some preliminary findings. First, the types of animals most commonly represented at the earlier sites are the wildebeest- and zebra-sized animals that are the most common dry-season prey of modern lions. Second, the edible parts of the animals most commonly abandoned by modern lions and available to a riparian-based scavenger (marrow bones and the brain) are precisely those that dominate the skeletal part inventories of the archaeological bone assemblages (highly fragmented limbs and skulls). If hunting had been practiced, we might expect to find many smaller, more easily subdued animals, and more body parts, that is, including the parts available only to hunters.

Were early hominids hunters or scavengers? At present, the answer is inconclusive. Despite the evidence for scavenging that I have cited, other archaeological evidence has been argued to be more consistent with hunting. Indeed, a mixed hunting *and* scavenging strategy might have been practiced. The observations on modern carcass use and availability do provide unambiguous expectations for what scavenging and hunting should look like archaeologically. As Binford has said, science is a method for identifying and correcting our ignorance. Actualistic research, designed and carried out in conjunction with careful excavation, permits archaeologists to operate scientifically.

CHAPTER FOURTEEN

TECHNOLOGY AND ENVIRONMENT

Humankind's ability to modify elements of its environment into a range of usable tools was undoubtedly one of the principal behavioral traits that contributed to the success of the genus *Homo* during the Pleistocene.

Nicholas Toth and Kathy D. Schick, "The First Million Years: The Archeology of Protohuman Culture," 1986

In Chapter 9 we discussed methods for arranging archaeological data in time, and in Chapters 10–13 we outlined the ways archaeologists reconstruct the human behavior behind those data. The intent in those chapters was to present the range of approaches from which an investigator could choose. Now we are ready to examine spatial distributions, to see how the spatial combinations of individually interpretable artifacts, ecofacts, and features may be used to reconstruct specific ancient behavior patterns. In doing so, we reemphasize the problem orientation that guides archaeological research: Archaeologists set out to answer particular questions about ancient ways of life, and discussion in this and the following **synthesis** chapters illustrates how archaeologists reassemble the data they have collected and analyzed to answer those questions.

In a sense, spatial distributions appear to furnish data automatically ready for **interpretation:** Plotting finds on plans and maps, for example, is an essential part of the data collection process, and it presents arrays of data that seem to be in association with one another. But, until the artifacts, ecofacts, and features are described, individually analyzed, and sorted in time, archaeologists do not know which parts of the observed spatial picture are remains of *related* activities. Past behavior cannot be reconstructed until the archaeologist knows which bits of evidence go together in time and which are from different periods: Contemporaneous data clusters must be distinguished from sequential ones. The former give information about behavior and human interaction **synchronically** (at one point in time), and the latter allow the archaeologist to look **diachronically** at continuity and change in behavior. By combining evidence from artifacts, ecofacts, and features, the archaeologist can infer how past societies functioned, both synchronically and diachronically.

Archaeologists usually use three broad categories—the technological, the sociopolitical, and the ideological—to classify the uses to which artifacts could be put. In the next three chapters we shall use a similar categorization to organize our discussion of the reconstruction of past culture and behavior. In this chapter we will look at **technology,** the means by which human societies interact most directly with the natural **environment.** Technology consists of the set of techniques and the body of information that provide ways to convert raw materials into tools, to procure and process food, to construct or locate shelter, and so on. Because technology relates so closely to the natural environment, our discussion of technology will also examine the ways archaeologists reconstruct ancient environments. As we have seen, these concerns make technology the focus of archaeological research guided by a cultural materialist view of culture.

After examining technology in this chapter, in Chapter 15 we will examine **social systems,** which assign roles and define relationships among people. Kinship organization, political structure, exchange networks, and the like are all facets of the way people organize themselves and their social interactions. Finally, in Chapter 16 we will turn to **ideological systems,** which encompass the belief and value systems of a society. Religious beliefs come most readily to mind as examples of ideological systems, but art styles and other symbolic records also provide information about the ways human groups have codified their outlook on existence.

The distinctions among these three categories of human activity should not be taken as strict or inflexible boundaries. For example, exchange systems serve to move tools and raw materials, thus acting as part of the technological system as well as reflecting (and affecting) social relations. The categories simply represent broad and convenient distinctions among general kinds of cultural behavior: behavior relating people to the physical environment, relating people to one another, and relating people to ideas.

Although, traditionally, all archaeologists have used technology as the starting point in their analyses, the most overt emphasis on this approach is associated with cultural materialism, which sees technology as the driving force behind the social and ideological aspects of culture. More recently, however, the postprocessual approach has reversed this relationship by taking ideology as the template that shapes both society and technology.

CULTURE AS ADAPTATION TO ENVIRONMENT

One definition of culture commonly used by archaeologists today is that of Leslie White: **Culture** is the extrasomatic (nonbiological) means by which people adapt to the physical and social environment. *Technology* is the part of culture most intimately linked with the physical environment, for it is the set of activities and knowledge that allows people to convert natural resources into tools, food, clothing, shelter, and whatever other products and facilities they need and want. Specific techniques for converting natural resources usually require a corollary set of specific tools. A simple but illustrative comparison can be made between a stone tool technology, with its array of artifacts of stone, antler, and so on, and our contemporary technology, with its computers, transistors, and an incredible diversity of equipment made of metals, plastics, and other materials. Development and innovation in tools go hand in hand with development and innovation in technical knowledge. Our landing on the moon in 1969 would not have been possible without sufficient elaboration in theories of aerodynamics since the time of the Wright brothers, along with increasing sophistication in knowledge of the physical properties of outer space and development of materials capable of withstanding the special rigors of space travel. Technology, then, consists of the knowledge, techniques, and associated equipment that allow human societies to exploit their environment.

A related but crosscutting term is **economy,** which refers to the provisioning of society. An economy is broader in scope than 20th-century use of the term implies: Prices, wages, international markets, capitalism, and so on are very specific characteristics of the present-day Western economy. In its broader sense, however, economy refers to the range of processes and mechanisms by which adequate food, clothing, and shelter are provided to all members of a society. Economic considerations include technological ones: How is food procured? How are houses built? But economy also includes social organizational aspects, such as controls exerted over the distribution of resources through the society. We will take up such social aspects of economy in Chapter 15.

Technology mediates human interaction with the environment in many ways. People build shelters and make clothing to protect them from heat, cold, rain, wind, and snow. They make baskets to help in collecting plants, fashion spears and arrows to kill food animals, and dig irrigation ditches to provide water for crops. The precise techniques and equipment used for a given task in a given time and place depend on past accumulation of technological knowledge. They also depend on the nature of the environment and the raw materials it supplies; for example, we do not find wooden houses in a treeless part of the world.

Chapter 3 mentioned that one of the current theoretical frameworks in anthropology is **cultural ecology.** Human ecology includes interaction with a social environment. The relations between technology and environment are complex and interactive. For example, an innovation in technology may redefine the nature of the exploitable environment. The ecological questions asked by archaeologists center on which aspects of the range of environmental resources a prehistoric society recognized as available, and which available resources it used. To answer these questions, archaeologists must reconstruct not only the nature of the techniques and equipment used by the past society but also the nature of the environment that could be exploited. In terms of research, the most common meeting ground for these approaches is the issue of subsistence technology: What resources were available for food? What did the society choose to eat, and how did it acquire and process those resources? Here we shall discuss, first, some ways of reconstructing technology, then some means of reconstructing past environments, and finally the way information from both can be combined to outline prehistoric subsistence systems.

RECONSTRUCTING TECHNOLOGY

In Chapter 10, as part of the discussion of particular artifact industries, we presented specific information about the technologies involved in production and use of various kinds of artifacts. This information, focusing on the analysis of individual artifacts, enables the archaeologist to answer specific questions about how stone tools or pottery vessels were made. At this point we want to ask different questions. Most broadly, we want to know what technologies were available to a given group by which it could produce tools, facilities, and other manufactured products. In a specific research project, the question is usually phrased in more concrete terms, such as: Was metallurgy practiced by the occupants of this site (or region)? To answer such a question, we must ask another: What is the evidence that indicates the presence of a given technology?

Countless specific technologies could be discussed; the surveys in Chapters 10 and 12 touched only the most common products of human manufacture and use. Here we shall consider four categories of technology: food procurement, tool production, feature construction, and transportation.

Food Procurement

Food procurement is obviously the most basic of all human technologies. For those archaeologists who utilize deterministic cultural models, such as cultural materialism (see Chapter 3), the overall evolutionary capabilities of each society are seen to be conditioned by the efficiency of food production, and changes in such production are considered the keys to understanding the process of cultural evolution. Thus prehistoric subsistence systems are the central focus of most cultural materialist investigations.

Specific means of food procurement may be indicated by many kinds of archaeological data; we shall discuss only a few illustrative examples. To reconstruct food procurement and processing techniques, the archaeologist begins with a knowledge of the procedures and equipment used in various systems. For example, hunting and gathering involve different kinds of knowledge and tools than does agriculture, and irrigated fields are technologically distinct from crop production that relies solely on rainfall. An archaeologist usually forms a working hypothesis about which subsistence technologies the prehistoric people being studied were likely to have used; this hypothesis is tested against the recovered evidence.

Projectile points, for instance, are usually taken as evidence of hunting; discovery of these points in association with slaughtered animals, for instance, in the Olsen-Chubbuck, Lindenmeier, or Folsom kill sites mentioned in previous chapters, clearly reveals the prehistoric subsistence technology. Other hunting technologies, however, leave little in the way of artifactual traces: Hunting by means of trapping, for example, may involve digging a hole, putting upright sharpened stakes or other such lethal devices inside, and camouflaging the hole so the animal will fall through the surface cover to its death. Remains of such traps, or of snares or nets, are seldom preserved; the technology in such a case is usually reconstructed by analogy with modern hunting techniques used by inhabitants in the same area or a similar one. Artifacts indicative of other food procurement or processing technologies include querns or grinding stones used to grind seeds and grain, sickles or scythes used to harvest grains, and fishhooks or harpoons used to catch seafood.

Ecofacts can provide direct evidence of ancient diets. Bone, shell, and plant remains found in residential middens, for example, are good clues to the kinds of foods eaten by the ancient occupants of a site and can suggest the technologies that would have been required to procure and process them. As noted in Chapter 11, however, human coprolites or the contents of preserved digestive tracts (in mummies, for example) provide more conclusive indications that a particular item was actually eaten. Likewise, ^{13}C–^{12}C analysis of bone was cited as directly indicative of diet content. Such analysis can also suggest interpretations of procurement technology, such as the inferred early Amazonian maize cultivation described in Chapter 11. Another application of the same kind of analysis has contradicted traditional views on food procurement strategies for societies living in the vicinity of Cape Town, South Africa, between 2000 and 4000 years ago. The usual view was that people moved seasonally from the coast to inland areas and back, taking advantage of different food resources in the two zones. Judith Sealy and Nikolaas van der Merwe found, however, that the carbon content of human skeletons from these zones reflects contrasting diets, and they could convincingly identify the two diet types with, respectively, sea and inland food resources. The skeletal data thus indicate that, contrary to the prevailing model, people ate foods predominantly from only one of the two zones, and most likely did not move back and forth between them.

Alternation vs. stability in diet: Sealy and van der Merwe and isotopic studies

Features, too, sometimes yield information about ancient food procurement and production systems. For example, some prehistoric animal pens have been tentatively identified in the archaeological record, and ancient granaries have been found at a variety of sites. Irrigation facilities, from simple ditches to elaborate canals (Fig. 14.1), and artificially constructed fields provide evidence of crop production and water management technologies.

Sometimes even seemingly obvious food remains may be misleading, however. Shell heaps are a case in point, as common archaeological features along rivers and coastlines the world over. Cheryl P. Claasen and others caution that archaeologists too readily assume that these are always or only the residues of meals. In some ethnographic cases, for example, mollusks are used as fish bait, not human food, but the shells left behind won't tell us that directly. More dramatically, Claasen has recently reinterpreted a whole category of shell-bearing sites, the mounds of the Shell Mound Archaic. These prominent features were formed along major waterways of Kentucky, Tennessee, and Alabama more than 3500 years ago. They have usually been interpreted as dumps from shellfish consumption, and as marking places where people lived. Claasen, however, points to—among other things—the large density of human burials within the mounds (1.2 individuals per cubic meter!) and the lack of evidence of

Interpreting the "obvious": Claasen on shell mounds

FIGURE 14.1 This system of prehistoric canals (indicated by black lines) near modern Phoenix, Arizona, is evidence of the sophistication of ancient Hohokam agriculture. (After Haury 1945.)

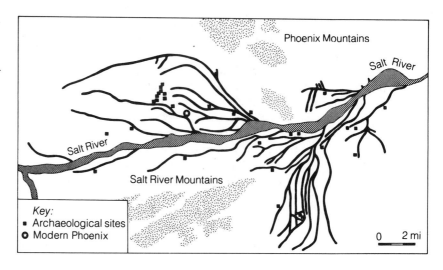

adjacent habitation, and instead suggests the mounds were ritual sites, constructed specifically as burial places. Some of the shellfish may have been eaten, but limiting interpretation to subsistence potentially misses a good deal of understanding about the society that produced such mounds. Besides weighing what the mounds might (or might not!) indicate about food practices, we must also consider possible implications for behavior representing social and belief systems.

We shall discuss food procurement and production technology again, when we discuss subsistence systems as a whole at the end of this chapter. But, as a different kind of reminder of the need for critical evaluation of evidence, we would like to discuss briefly the food techniques and strategies attributed to the earliest known cultures and changes in interpretation that have taken place on this subject in recent years.

Hunting by Oldowan tool users: Reevaluation of a traditional model

Traditionally, archaeologists had argued that users of the Oldowan and other early tool assemblages, between one and two million years ago, had gained their food from hunting and gathering, more or less as some modern human societies still do. Sites with stone tools and broken animal bones were commonly accepted as camps where killed game was brought, as whole or partially butchered carcasses, to take meat off the bones and remove rich marrow from inside them. In Chapters 10 and 11, however, we noted that reexamination of the animal bones themselves has suggested that their breakage and deposition were not always the results of cultural behavior. Archaeologists such as C. K. Brain, Henry Bunn, Pat Shipman, Robert Blumenschine, Gary Haynes, and Lewis Binford have sought, from varied perspectives, to specify the characteristics that distinguish remains of human hunting behavior from bone assemblages accumulated by other means—such as kills made by lions or other carnivores, or carcasses exploited by scavengers after the original predator has abandoned them.

These archaeologists have asked, for example, which parts of the food animal's skeleton are most likely to be found in each kind of case. How can butchering marks left by stone tools be reliably distinguished from pits and scratches on bone caused by lion, hyena, or other carnivore teeth? How do breaks to obtain marrow contrast with breaks when bones have been trampled by other animals? How does wear on stone tools used for cutting meat and sinew differ from wear caused by other uses?

Examination of a wider range of bone assemblages as analogs—including bones from animals killed by modern hunters, as well as animals who fell prey to lions, wolves, or even disease—has gone hand in hand with microscopic and other analyses of tool wear and bone damage attributable to known causes. For example, Robert Blumenschine and Marie Selvaggio have experimentally broken marrow-rich animal bones with a stone hammer and anvil and have found that the resulting percussion marks are similar to but still distinct from tooth marks. They suggest that because analysts had not previously been able to differentiate the two kinds of marks, scientists had missed key evidence that our early ancestors did exploit marrow as a food resource. Obvious cut marks were not required to indicate hominid interest in the bones.

Analysts have also set aside the assumption that the food procurement behavior of these early hominids, whose brain size and structure were quite different from those of modern humans, necessarily resembled that of any living people. With this new perspective, and with reference to new interpretive analogs, archaeologists used the spatially clustered evidence of individually examined artifacts and ecofacts to reassess the activities represented by the early sites and to reinterpret the food procurement technology these data are believed to reflect. One example of the result is Richard Potts's proposal, described in Chapter 13, that sites in Olduvai Gorge were not campsites but storage points for stone tools used to process carcasses periodically discovered nearby.

Indeed, although there is still disagreement over details, most archaeologists familiar with these early data sets now reject the idea that our ancestors in this period gained meat exclusively from hunting. Meat was likely part of the diet, but it is clear that the meatiest body parts were often not available. Stone tool butchering marks sometimes overlie—and therefore were made after—carnivore tooth marks, and sometimes percussion marks alone testify to hominid involvement, to gain nutrient-rich marrow from broken bones. The implication is that these early tool users did not always have sole or even first access to the game. Spatial combinations of such evidence within a series of sites have thus led to a picture rather different from the traditional view: We now believe that meat procurement technology in the earliest known cultures relied at least partly on scavenging—by taking advantage of kills made by other predatory animals or by disease.

FIGURE 14.2 This partially reconstructed ceramic vessel from Peru incorporates information on architectural form and construction through a three-dimensional model of a small thatched building, while the body of the vessel itself appears to represent a supporting platform. (Courtesy of The University Museum, University of Pennsylvania.)

Tool Production

Tool production technologies include the manufacture of all kinds of artifacts, from weapons to clothing, storage containers, and transport vehicles. Again, the archaeologist starts with a working model of the way the ancient society may have functioned and what tools and other artifacts it produced. Evidence for or against this preliminary view may come from several sources. The most direct evidence is the manufactured products themselves. Artifacts made by some techniques, especially those produced by subtractive industries such as stone knapping, are more apt than others to preserve marks indicative of how they were made. Sometimes the archaeologist is fortunate enough to encounter artwork or three-dimensional models that indicate graphically how certain products were made (Fig. 14.2).

One extremely valuable form of technological evidence is provided by remains of workshops. These are particular, activity-specific clusters of artifacts, sometimes including specially constructed features such as kilns, that preserve a variety of details about manufacturing processes. Workshop features are of as many kinds as there are different manufacturing technologies; how formalized the area is depends on how specifically isolated the activity was. For example, flint knapping might have been carried out at various locations over time, so that a number of casual chipping stations might be found in a given area of occupation. Activities that require specialized facilities, however, such as iron metallurgy, which needs intense and controlled heat, are more likely to have easily identifiable areas set aside as workshops. In a workshop, the archaeologist would expect to find a variety of manufacturing remains, including raw materials, partially finished artifacts, mistakes (such as pottery vessels that cracked during firing), debris (such as stone debitage), and any special tools or facilities needed for production. For example, a pottery workshop might include lumps of unfired clay, pigment in bowls or on the grinding surfaces of small mortars, broken sherds or other tempering materials, molds and stamps used in forming or decorating the vessels, small pebbles for polishing vessel surfaces, and perhaps the remains of a kiln. Each kind of workshop may have a specialized set of associated materials; the archaeologist specifies the particular elements expected for each kind, on the basis of a background knowledge of manufacturing technologies.

Feature Construction

Evidence of the technology involved in the construction of features, from storage pits to houses to the pyramids of Egypt, is most readily gleaned from the constructed facilities themselves. In Chapter 12 we discussed, for example, features as varied as Mono bedrock mortars in California, the remains of the Sweet Track in southwest England, and those of Iroquois longhouses at Howlett Hill, New York. Similarly, other constructed features preserve information about the kinds of materials used and the engineering skills possessed by past societies. For instance, prehistoric earthen mounds of eastern North America sometimes preserve outlines of the individual basketloads of soil with which they were built; one example is the mounds of Cahokia, Illinois, of around A.D. 1000. And the Inkas of 15th- and 16th-century Peru are renowned for the precision with which they cut and fitted huge stone blocks to construct settlements such as Cuzco or Machu Picchu. Studies by Jean-Pierre Protzen, Susan A. Niles, and others have documented Inka architectural technologies. The finest blocks were carefully shaped to fit, sometimes given bevelled edges for light and shadow effects (Fig. 13.6, p. 435), and sometimes so flat the seams between blocks are scarcely visible. Such exquisite stonework was reserved for the most important Inka buildings, in the capital at Cuzco and in the most sacred precincts of the larger satellite sites. But, as we saw in Figure 13.6, some of these blocks have been retained or reused in modern buildings.

Transportation

The technology of transportation refers to the knowledge and techniques used for moving goods and people. This is a direct interaction with the physical environment, because it affects the relative ease with which people can get about in that environment. For example, people can move more things farther and more easily if they have wheeled vehicles and beasts of burden than if they must walk and carry everything themselves. Roads and bridges, discussed in Chapter 12, likewise facilitate movement of people and goods across the landscape.

Transport technology, in these senses, obviously affects the range of territory (and resources) that a group of people can conveniently tap. Changes in transportation technology can even redefine the landscape. For example, large bodies of water can be obstacles to transportation, but when boats or even rafts are available, water transport routes may be preferable to land routes. Indeed, much of the trade in obsidian throughout the ancient Mediterranean world was carried by ship.

Direct evidence of the transportation technologies available to ancient people may sometimes be found in artifacts, ranging from horse trappings to actual wheeled vehicles to models or toys of boats or carts. For example, ancient shipwrecks have furnished data, unavailable through historical or other sources, concerning techniques for construction and operation of seacraft in various eras. The waterlogged environment of Florida's wetlands has preserved otherwise highly perishable wooden dugout canoes; more than 100 of these Native American canoes have been found so far, two of which are more than 3000 years old.

Occasionally, pictorial representations of transportation techniques are available, such as scenes of dignitaries being carried on litters. Frequently,

Indirect evidence of transport: Obsidian at Franchthi Cave and in the Maya Lowlands

however, evidence of transport is even more indirect. The earliest indications of Mediterranean seafaring, for example, consist of obsidian debris from deposits more than 8000 years old, in Franchthi Cave, near Porto Cheli in southeastern Greece. The obsidian originally came from the island of Melos, 120 km away across open water, and it could have reached the mainland only by boat. Similarly, in the Maya area, Norman Hammond has used the distribution of obsidian artifacts from the Ixtepeque source in the highlands of Guatemala to infer that finished goods, raw materials, or both were moved by canoe along the coast of the Yucatán peninsula (Fig. 14.3). Canoe travel was known to be important in this area at the time of Spanish contact in the 16th century, but—unlike the unusually favorable situation in Florida—actual remains of canoes are unavailable here and evidence for their earlier occurrence is confined to such indirect indications.

RECONSTRUCTING ENVIRONMENT

If technology is the means by which society interacts with the natural environment, how can the archaeologist discover what the ancient natural environment itself was like? Archaeologists seek two kinds of data to reconstruct ancient physical environments. The first is observations of the modern landscape, including topography and the range of biotic and mineral resources. The second is collection of ecofactual data, either from archaeological deposits or from other deposits within the zone under study. Such data give the archaeologist evidence about whether—and how—the area may have been different, in terms of resources, in ancient times from the way it is today. Combining these two approaches, the archaeologist, usually in consultation with other specialists, attempts to reconstruct the nature of the environment in which the ancient society lived.

Observations of Modern Environment

Observation of the modern environment entails recording the range of resources the archaeologist considers of potential use to local occupants. These resources include water supplies, game animals, edible plants, fertile soils for agriculture, suitable stone for tool production, and wood or other materials for house construction. In describing observed resources, the archaeologist must note two kinds of distributional limits: seasonality and distance from occupation areas. That is, some of the resources, such as migratory game animals or intermittent streams, might be available only part of the year, and this fact limits their exploitation. In addition, resources are seldom spread evenly over the landscape: Good chipping stone occurs in discrete, if sometimes large or abundant, deposits; edible plants may be restricted to certain elevations or distances from water sources. Various combinations of resources define **microenvironments,** which of-

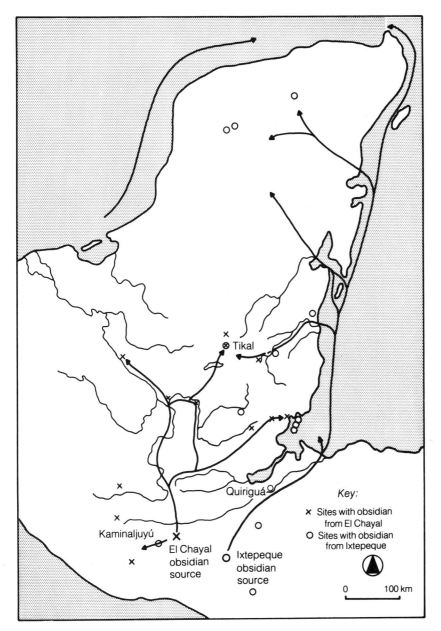

FIGURE 14.3 Obsidian from two known sources in highland Guatemala is distributed among lowland Maya sites in a pattern that suggests an overland route for exchange from the El Chayal source and canoe-oriented routes for transport from the Ixtepeque source. (After Norman Hammond, from *Science,* vol. 178, p. 1093. Copyright 1972 by the American Association for the Advancement of Science.)

Key:
× Sites with obsidian from El Chayal
O Sites with obsidian from Ixtepeque

0   100 km

Tikal

Quiriguá

Kaminaljuyú

El Chayal obsidian source

Ixtepeque obsidian source

fer varying opportunities for exploitation. Although observations and descriptions of local resources are usually best made by the archaeologist or a specialist, quite detailed information can sometimes be obtained from published works, such as guides to local soils, flora, and fauna. Supplementary information can often be obtained from local inhabitants, who may know from personal experience when and where food and other resources are available.

The area to be observed may be defined in several ways. If the archaeological universe is a single site, the observations on the natural environment are usually made for a larger zone surrounding the site, on the assumption that people would exploit resources close to home. In studies taking a regional approach, such as a project focusing on occupation and exploitation of a valley, the resource area to be studied will usually coincide with the archaeological universe. In neither case can the archaeologist automatically assume that the observed area represents the zone exploited by prehistoric people, but if local supplies were preferred to those farther away, the observed zone should coincide with at least part of the anciently exploited area. Paleoecological finds may substantiate the nature of local exploitation.

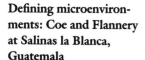

Defining microenvironments: MacNeish at Tehuacán, Mexico

Examples of various modern observational approaches are easy to find. For instance, in the Tehuacán Archaeological–Botanical Project, the resource area recorded was the same as that in which archaeological remains were recorded. The overall goal of the project was to trace the development of agriculture in the New World; the Tehuacán Valley, in the Mexican state of Puebla, was chosen as the research location partly because it contained a number of dry caves that seemed to promise the climatic conditions under which maize (corn) and other domesticated plants would be preserved. At the same time, however, Richard MacNeish and his colleagues needed to determine the range of food resources available to the ancient residents of the Tehuacán Valley to outline the conditions under which they increasingly chose food production over food collection as their subsistence base. To get this information, the investigators surveyed the Tehuacán Valley and divided it into four microenvironmental types, each with a set of seasonally or perennially available resources. Combining this information with analysis of ecofactual materials recovered from the various archaeological sites, MacNeish and his coworkers were able to reconstruct the subsistence-related migrations of ancient human populations within the valley, postulating their movements in search of shifting food resources as the seasons passed (in Chapter 11 we noted how more recent stable isotope analysis of human bone has contradicted some of MacNeish's dietary findings based on plant remains). In a later project, MacNeish and his colleagues were able to apply the same approach to study the ancient subsistence system in the Ayacucho Basin of Peru (Fig. 14. 4).

Defining microenvironments: Coe and Flannery at Salinas la Blanca, Guatemala

A related approach was taken by Kent V. Flannery and Michael D. Coe in their study of the Ocós region of south coastal Guatemala. Instead of a universe nicely circumscribed by topography, such as a valley, however, they were dealing with a broad expanse of coastal floodplain. To sample the range of resources in the vicinity of the site of Salinas la Blanca, they examined a transect of land extending inland from the Pacific Ocean through Salinas la Blanca, over a linear distance of about 15 km. This

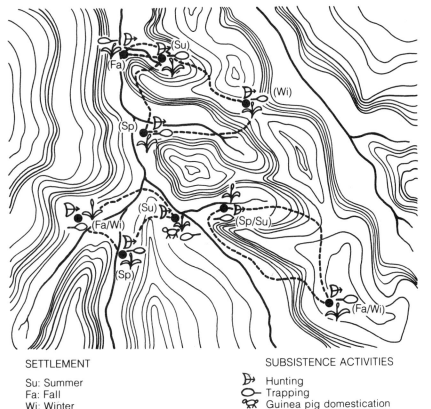

FIGURE 14.4 Synthesis of archaeological data from the Ayacucho Valley of Peru has led to postulation that ancient populations moved seasonally among sites to exploit different subsistence resources. (After MacNeish, Patterson, and Browman 1975.)

SETTLEMENT

Su: Summer
Fa: Fall
Wi: Winter
Sp: Spring

SUBSISTENCE ACTIVITIES

Hunting
Trapping
Guinea pig domestication
Plant collecting

transect provided a cross-section through eight microenvironmental zones, each roughly parallel to the Pacific coast and each contributing different resources to the wealth available to local occupants (Fig. 14.5).

A third approach, developed by Claudio Vita-Finzi and Eric S. Higgs, is called **site-catchment analysis.** In reviewing studies of modern agriculturalists, Vita-Finzi and Higgs noted that exploitation areas tend to be limited to zones of 4 to 5 km around the home base; for hunters and gatherers, the radius is about 10 km. For purposes of data collection, however, and to adjust such straight-line distances to the vagaries of specific local topography, they defined their observation areas as those lying within one hour's walk of a hunter-gatherer camp. These zones are the site-catchment areas. Within a site-catchment area, distances are considered insignificant in differentiating resources as more or less accessible; overall proportions or abundance of arable and nonarable land are recorded, as well as other resources. Examination of the site-catchment areas of a series

Defining microenvironments: Vita-Finzi and Higgs in Israel

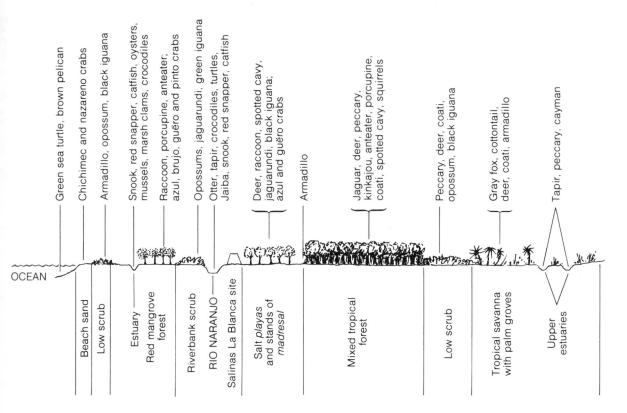

FIGURE 14.5 This idealized transect inland about 15 km from the Pacific Ocean shows the diversity of resources available to the prehistoric residents of Salinas la Blanca, Guatemala. (Redrawn and modified by permission of The Smithsonian Institution Press from *The Smithsonian Contributions to Anthropology*, vol. 3; *Early Cultures and Human Ecology in South Coastal Guatemala*, by Michael D. Coe and Kent V. Flannery, Smithsonian Institution, Washington, D.C. 1967.)

of occupation sites in Israel—including Nahal Oren, El Wad, Kebarah, and Iraq el Baroud—led M. R. Jarman, Vita-Finzi, and Higgs to conclude, among other things, that the amount of arable land was too slight for agriculture to have played a significant part in the food procurement strategies of the ancient occupants.

Many applications of **Geographic Information Systems (GIS),** as described in Chapter 6, have involved research on ancient human use of the landscape. The advantage of GIS in such work is that it permits storage and sophisticated manipulation of large, complex data sets, on a scale not possible without computers. For example, in 1973 (pre-GIS), Leonard Williams, David Hurst Thomas, and Robert L. Bettinger had outlined the environmental characteristics they believed had most concerned the ancient Shoshoneans of central Nevada. "Favorable" characteristics included proximity of water and location within a zone of piñon-juniper trees, and Williams and his colleagues predicted that the Shoshoneans had required five of seven "favorable" traits before they would settle in a place. Sixty-three (97 percent) of the 65 sites they discovered met the requirement.

Kenneth Kvamme later pointed out, however, that it might be that 97 percent of all locations in the study area met the requirement and that the criteria Williams and his coworkers specified might not have been significant to ancient Shoshoneans at all. With GIS, Kvamme was able to do further research that his predecessors could not have and, by computer, examined 10 (not 7) criteria for 19,000 locations (with and without sites) in the original study region. About 50 percent of the area met the "favorable" requirements but contained more than 95 percent of the known sites—suggesting much more strongly that Williams, Thomas, and Bettinger's inferences about Shoshonean land use were right. GIS is indeed a powerful tool, and we will have more to say about it again in Chapter 15.

Building environmental data bases: GIS

Collection of Ecofacts

The complementary perspective for reconstructing ancient environments is analysis of paleoecological data. In Chapter 11 we indicated some of the ways ecofacts in archaeological deposits could yield paleoecological information. For instance, pollen samples can indicate the variety of past local vegetation, which in turn indicates whether the surrounding area was open grassland or forested land with clearings, like the vicinity of Star Carr. Changes in vegetation cover can be determined from stratified pollen cores; in the example from Chapter 11, changes through time in pollen profiles were used to trace the course of extensive land clearing that the investigators argued was evidence of the spread of agricultural practices.

Pollen and small animals such as snails or insects are also useful and sensitive indices of environmental conditions. Their presence or absence may reflect local climatic continuity or change in temperature and humidity. In excavation of the Sweet Track, the prehistoric roadway described in Chapter 12, John Coles and his colleagues retrieved a number of finds indicative of the ancient environment of the Somerset Levels. One kind of beetle they found, *Oodes gracilis,* occurs today only in areas with warmer summers and colder winters than those of modern Somerset, so the builders of the Sweet Track likely experienced a similarly greater temperature range 6000 years ago. Raft spiders and whirligig beetles were also found in the Sweet Track peat, and knowledge of their modern habitats attests to the presence of open water adjacent to the ancient roadway, for at least part of its extent.

Beetles, spiders, and wood: The environment of the Sweet Track in Neolithic times

Finds from the Sweet Track told of other aspects of the ancient environment as well, including its modification and management by people of Neolithic times. Specifically, Coles has identified the earliest known woodland management system in the world, evident in a practice called *coppicing.* Coppicing involves selectively cutting trees to encourage growth of new shoots from the stumps. The long, straight shoots can themselves be cut easily within a few years' time, encouraging further new growth, and cyclically replenishing the supply of desirable wood. The wood used for the Sweet Track pegs (the cross-pieces supporting the road-surface planks) were just such shoots from coppiced stands of hazel, ash, and other trees.

Paleoecological materials need not come from the archaeological deposits themselves. For example, in the Fenlands Research Project, of which the investigation of the Mesolithic site of Star Carr was a part, paleoenvironmental studies were conducted over a broader area as part of a coordinated effort between archaeologists and other scientists to reconstruct the natural history as well as the cultural prehistory for the area. We noted in Chapter 9 that something of the paleoenvironment associated with Ertebölle sites in southern Finland was reconstructed by varve analysis, which elucidated the sequence of ancient shorelines and thereby indicated where the shore stood in relation to Ertebölle occupation (and vice versa). Recent analysis of sediment accumulations in the Aegean have similarly demonstrated that many "inland" sites, such as Pella in Macedonia (northern Greece), were much nearer the coast during their ancient occupation (Fig. 14.6): Sedimentation has filled in many shallow bays, moving the shoreline away from sites that were once coastal. In contrast, rises in sea level in the last 15,000 years progressively submerged a 70-km-wide strip of Peruvian coastline. Michael Moseley has argued that coastal occupation very likely began before the sea stopped rising about 5000 years ago, but these sites are now underwater and therefore remain unknown.

Paleoecological data may indicate that local environmental conditions in ancient times were similar to those found today near the site or sites being studied, or they may suggest that resources were different from those available today. Either way, they define the environmental framework within which the past society functioned. Unless they come from archaeological contexts, however, these data tell us only what resources were *available* to be used, not necessarily whether the ancient inhabitants actually used them. Whether past local occupants thought it appropriate—or had the technology—to smelt copper from ores or to grow crops on arable land can be determined only by combining data on paleoecological potentials with the technological and ecofactual data from archaeological contexts indicating what resources were actually exploited and how they were used. To illustrate such reconstruction, we shall consider the study of subsistence systems.

RECONSTRUCTING SUBSISTENCE

All organisms need water and nourishment to survive; no one need be reminded of that. All human societies, then, must have a set of customs—a part of the culture—that deals with the technology of supplying food and water to members of the society. The specific technology depends on two factors: the food and water resources available in the environment, and the choices the society makes about what it can or ought to consume. In most cases, many times more edible resources are available to a society than it is

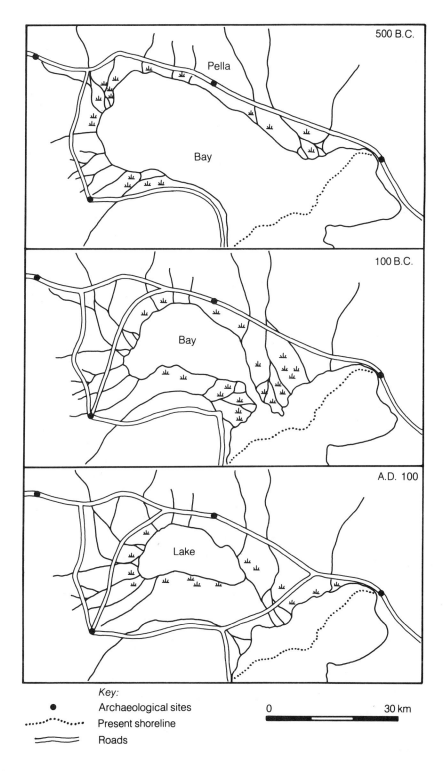

FIGURE 14.6 Gradual silting in of coastal bays has moved the shoreline away from sites such as Pella, Greece, originally founded near the water's edge. (After Kraft, Aschenbrenner, and Rapp, from *Science,* vol. 195, p. 943. Copyright 1977 by the American Association for the Advancement of Science.)

Key:

● Archaeological sites

•••••••• Present shoreline

═══ Roads

0   30 km

able or considers appropriate to eat. Our own society generally views insects as inedible, but in many parts of the world nutritious grubs and other insects are eaten with great gusto. In addition, a particular society may not have the technological capacity to exploit all food resource potentials. For example, the "breadbasket" of the United States—the area of the Great Plains—was always fertile, but sowing crops was an arduous enterprise before introduction of tools that could cut easily through the matted root system of the natural grass cover.

The point of these illustrations is that cultural adaptation to a given environment results from both the availability of resources and the ways people exploit those resources. Environment does not determine culture, even the subsistence aspect of it, but it provides a flexible framework within which a culture operates. Similarly, culture does not determine environment, but cultural values and technological capacity may define the extent to which available resources are exploited.

Reconstructing ancient subsistence systems, then, requires knowledge of two reciprocal kinds of data. First, the archaeologist must be able to reconstruct the past environment and determine what the potential resources were. Second, he or she must reconstruct the technological capabilities of the society and then determine which of the potential resources and technological abilities were actually, actively exploited in the past.

Potential Resources

To specify the subsistence potential of past environments, the archaeologist must go beyond a mere list of the edible plants and animals that were locally present or that could have been raised. The characteristics of these organisms must also be considered: The animals may migrate with the seasons, or fruits and nuts may be present only during parts of the year, or local rainfall and soil fertility may be adequate to support one kind of crop and not another. Detailed analyses, taking these characteristics into account, attempt to estimate the **carrying capacity** of a given area—the number and density of people it could sustain. Carrying capacity is not a fixed or magic number, however; we shall discuss the flexibility of this calculation in a moment.

Carrying capacity calculations can include a number of considerations. For example, Bruce D. Smith and others have discussed ways of measuring how much meat is available in an area: Such figures as annual productivity and biomass, calculated from modern wildlife studies, indicate the number of animals that can be expected per year within a given zone, and then how much meat could be obtained from them. J. R. Harlan has measured experimentally the productivity of wild wheat stands in the Near East, in terms of the amount of effort required to supply a family with grain. Soil fertility has been tested under a number of conditions. For example, researchers have planted experimental maize plots in Mesoamerica and then

Carrying capacity: Smith on animal protein and Harlan on grain yields

FIGURE 14.7 Construction of stone-enclosed fish ponds, such as the one shown here, was one of the methods used by ancient Hawaiians to augment their food supply. (Photo courtesy of Marshall Weisler, University of California, Berkeley.)

measured the crop yields over a number of years, as nutrients are progressively removed by successive crops. From these tests, maximum yields per unit of land are computed, as are the reserve lands that must be available to substitute for an exhausted plot while it lies fallow to recover nutrients and fertility. To calculate carrying capacity from such figures, researchers must first assess the amount of meat protein or grain each person would require per year; then they can determine how many people could be supported by the potential resources present.

As we noted above, however, carrying capacity is not a constant figure. If a resident group changes its definition of what is an acceptable (or desirable) food, it moves certain species into or out of the category of available food resources and changes the carrying capacity of the area. Soil fertility and other measures of agricultural potential are particularly hard to control, for carrying capacity is also partly dependent on the particular agricultural technology used. Shortening of the fallow period, even to the point of continuous planting, and addition of fertilizers are among the ways crop yield can be increased or maintained. Patrick V. Kirch has outlined the sequential measures taken by ancient Polynesians, in Hawaii and elsewhere, to increase the islands' food yields. Specific measures varied with time and location. In the Hawaiian Islands, alone, those documented include reducing or eliminating fallow time in unirrigated stone-bordered fields, adding irrigation water to other fields, creating groves of breadfruit trees, and constructing artificial fishponds (Fig. 14.7). Although population growth surely stimulated some of this intensification, Kirch argues that creation of a surplus for use by expansively powerful chiefs was also a potent spur.

Changing carrying capacity: Kirch on ancient Polynesia

Technological Capabilities

Next let us consider the cultural component in reconstructing subsistence: technology. We have already discussed some of the ways archaeologists reconstruct ancient food procurement technologies. The archaeologist determines what alternatives were available, and which ones were used, by specifying what artifacts, ecofacts, and features should reflect particular subsistence strategies; the data actually recovered are then analyzed to see what practices are indicated. For example, grinding stones do not in themselves unequivocally imply the deliberate growing of domesticated grain. But a complex of data including grinding equipment, grain storage facilities, and—preferably, of course—the remains of identifiable domesticated plants does indicate at least partial reliance on grain agriculture for subsistence.

Several other, indirect indices of subsistence activities should be mentioned. For instance, evidence of seasonality of site residence attests to population movement in response to seasonal availability of food resources (see Fig. 14.4), as opposed to a permanently settled population exploiting resources within a fixed, smaller area. The latter pattern, called *sedentism,* need not, however, imply agriculture: For example, the environment around the site of Monte Verde, in southern Chile, seems to have included such a diversity and abundance of nearby food resources that its residents could live in one place the year around and subsist by collecting wild food resources (see Fig. 14.5). The Pacific coast of the northwestern United States seems to have provided a similarly generous habitat, especially in its fish resources, so that sedentism was easily feasible without agriculture.

Selectivity—food choices—can sometimes be reconstructed too. Bruce D. Smith has shown that the proportion of white-tailed deer, raccoon, and turkey represented in faunal assemblages of sites in the middle Mississippi Valley are out of line with the amounts that would be expected on the basis of their contributions to the potential biomass available for hunting. In other words, there are many more remains of these three kinds of animals, relative to other species, than there should be if the prehistoric hunters were simply killing prey indiscriminately to fill the quota of meat they needed to eat. Smith therefore suggests that these three animals were actively sought and preferentially selected above other prey as food sources.

Subsistence systems: The Classic Maya

Finally, some aspects of the archaeological record (or inferences based on it) can serve as "checks" on reconstruction of subsistence systems. Specifically, reconstructions of population density can indicate whether the reconstructed subsistence pattern would have been feasible. Models of ancient Maya food production provide a case in point. Traditionally, the prehistoric Maya were believed to have subsisted primarily by slash-and-burn, or *swidden,* agriculture, growing maize and other crops in a rotating system of fields without fertilizers or irrigation. Today, the Maya rely on such a system to produce most of their food, and artifacts as well as symbolic representations of maize seemed to underscore its central importance in ancient life too.

As we noted earlier, carrying capacity is a flexible figure. But in the 1960s, as more careful and extensive surveys pieced together a picture of unexpectedly dense populations for the Classic Maya, archaeologists realized that maize swidden agriculture simply could not have supported these communities. A reevaluation of the evidence for Maya subsistence has consequently taken place, including suggested alternatives and a search for new evidence. It now appears that Classic Maya food production and procurement strategies varied greatly in time and space, and possibly as a function of social status. The search for new evidence and alternative subsistence models has led, among other things, to the discovery and recognition of irrigation features and artificially raised and enriched field systems. Dennis E. Puleston has argued repeatedly and forcefully that a significant part of the prehistoric Maya diet was supplied by fruit and nut trees and by produce from kitchen gardens outside the houses. None of these new interpretations is contradicted by previous evidence of artifacts, ecofacts, and features, but scholars now see that the model into which they were previously incorporated was too narrow and simplified.

SUMMARY

We have begun to examine how spatial clusters of individually analyzed artifacts, ecofacts, and features may be used to reconstruct and interpret ancient behavior patterns. Previous chapters have focused on varieties of data and of analyses, outlining the ranges of interpretations to which each kind could be applicable. In this and the following chapters, the emphasis shifts to the interpretations themselves and the ranges of data and analyses that can serve as evidence for them. The shift underscores both the importance of a problem orientation and how an archaeologist's ability to discern and understand particular categories of ancient behavior depends on having acquired and analyzed data pertinent to that behavior.

Human activities can be divided into three broad areas—technology, social systems, and ideology. This chapter has focused on the first of the three. Technology is that part of culture most intimately related to the physical environment. It is the set of techniques and knowledge through which people modify natural resources into tools, food, clothing, and shelter. These techniques are best understood in the context of cultural ecology, which recognizes that relations between culture and environment are complex. That is, the environment provides the range of resources available for people's use, but culture (through choices and capabilities) defines which resources are actually used. As a result, understanding ancient technology requires study not only of cultural remains but also of the environment in which they were used.

To illustrate reconstruction of technologies, examples were described from four different kinds of technology: food procurement, tool production, feature construction, and transportation. In each case, individually analyzed artifacts, ecofacts, and features are all valuable as evidence, but reconstructions are most solid when they can rely on combinations of such evidence, as recent reevaluations of early food procurement practices do.

Reconstructing ancient environments entails observations made on the modern landscape and its now-visible resources, such as good chipping stone, abundant fresh water, or fertile farming land. But it also requires attention to possible differences in ancient times, for which archaeologists collect ecofactual data. Examples include plant and small animal remains, which may suggest climate or vegetation changes, and sedimentary evidence, which can reveal changes in the shape of the landscape.

Reconstruction of subsistence systems provides a particularly good illustration of the interrelations of technology and environment. Carrying capacity is an estimate of the size of population that could potentially be supported by the food resources in a particular environment. But, for human populations, the range of resources available depends in significant part on both cultural preferences in diet and technological capabilities for harvesting the resources. Examination of carrying capacity along with actual remains of subsistence technologies provides archaeologists with dual avenues for reconstructing ancient population size as well as patterns of behavior. Overall, by reconstructing ancient subsistence systems and revealing how they changed through time, archaeologists gain a significant understanding of how and why human societies have evolved toward greater complexity.

GUIDE TO FURTHER READING

Culture as Adaptation to Environment
Butzer 1982; Clark 1952; Hardesty 1980; Higgs 1972, 1975; Jochim 1979; Kirch 1980, 1984; Netting 1977; Wilshusen and Stone 1990

Reconstructing Technology
L. R. Binford 1978, 1981b, 1985; Blumenschine 1986; Blumenschine and Selvaggio 1988; Bunn 1981, 1983; Coles 1984; Diamant 1979; Gasparini and Margolies 1980; Gibson and Woods 1990; Graham 1985b; Hammond 1972; Haury 1945; Hill 1979; Isaac 1983, 1984; Johnstone 1980; Jones 1980; Klein 1973; Niles 1987; Oakley 1956; Potts 1984; Protzen 1986; Sealy and van der Merwe 1986; Shipman 1981, 1986; Toth and Schick 1986; Wheat 1967, 1972; Wilmsen 1970, 1974

Reconstructing Environment
Allen, Green, and Zubrow 1990; Aronoff 1989; Butzer 1964, 1982; Clark [1954] 1971; Coe and Flannery 1964, 1967; Courty, Goldberg, and Macphail 1989; Findlow and Ericson 1980; Folan et al. 1983; Jarman, Vita-Finzi, and Higgs 1972; Kraft, Aschenbrenner, and Rapp 1977; Kvamme 1989; MacNeish 1964a; MacNeish, Patterson, and Browman 1975; Moseley 1983; Rapp

and Gifford 1985; Roper 1979; Scarre 1984; Shackleton, van Andel, and Runnels 1984; Shackley 1985; Stein and Farrand 1985; Vita-Finzi and Higgs 1970; Wertime 1983

Reconstructing Subsistence

Barker 1985; Beadle 1980; Cavallo 1984; Chang and Koster 1986; Claasen 1991a, 1991b; Clutton-Brock and Grigson 1983, 1984; Davis 1987; Farnsworth et al. 1985; Flannery 1982; Gilbert and Mielke 1985; Glassow 1978; Green 1980; Grigson and Clutton-Brock 1983; Harlan 1967; Harris and Hillman 1989; Harrison and Turner 1978; Hassan 1978, 1981; Higham 1984; Kirch 1980, 1984; Lee 1968; Lyman 1982; Monks 1981; Price 1989; Robertshaw and Collett 1983; Roe 1971; B. D. Smith 1974, 1983; Smith 1976; Struever 1971; Ucko and Dimbleby 1969; van der Merwe 1982; Waselkov 1987; Wing and Brown 1979; Winterhalder and Smith 1981

DAWN OF A NEW STONE AGE IN EYE SURGERY

Payson D. Sheets

A Professor at the University of Colorado, Sheets has adapted prehistoric obsidian technology to produce extremely sharp implements for modern surgery. He began this work nearly a dozen years ago, and he and an eye surgeon have since formed a corporation to develop and market obsidian scalpels.

Occasionally, archaeological findings can be applied to today's world and improve modern life. Archaeologists have rediscovered prehistoric crops and agricultural technologies that are no longer used but have considerable value for contemporary society. Ancient remedies, too, have been found that can help cure illnesses. This is an account of the rediscovery of an ancient technology for making stone tools that died out centuries ago but has an unexpectedly important potential for improving modern medical treatment.

Beginning in 1969, as a young graduate student, I participated in the Chalchuapa Archaeological Project on the edge of the Maya area in El Salvador. Beyond supervising several project excavations, I was responsible for the analysis of the ancient stone tools—composed mostly of obsidian (volcanic glass)—as part of my doctoral dissertation. In my work I discovered that most previous studies classified stone tools by their shape. I did likewise, but I also wanted to contribute something different, so I kept looking for a new angle from which to analyze the Chalchuapa stone artifacts.

In 1970 I excavated a workshop at Chalchuapa where I recovered the remains of ancient obsidian tool manufacture. From the workshop debris I figured out the various techniques, and their sequence, that had been used by the ancient Maya knappers to make chipped-stone tools. I also identified errors made during this process and how the ancient craftsmen corrected them. These data provided the new angle I was looking for—an analysis based on the ancient tool-making technology.

The reconstruction of past behavior, within the structure of the obsidian tool industry, was the first step in developing modern surgical blades based on an ancient technology.

The following year I attended Don Crabtree's training program in lithic technology so that I could learn how to make stone tools. I learned to duplicate the ancient Maya technology, including how to make tools and cores by percussion (striking the stone with strong blows to detach flakes) and long, thin obsidian blades by pressure (slowly increasing force applied to a core to detach flakes). Don suggested that the replicas of the ancient blades would be excellent surgical tools and that I should experiment with the technology to see if I could make scalpels that would be acceptable to surgeons. But I was unable to follow up these suggestions; after writing my dissertation, earning my Ph.D., and finding a teaching position at the University of Colorado, I embarked on a new research project in the Zapotitán basin of El Salvador. But by 1979 the guerrilla warfare in El Salvador made the area too dangerous to continue research, so I then had the time to explore the possibility of adapting obsidian blades for modern surgical use.

Meanwhile, Don had gone ahead and provided a dramatic demonstration of the obsidian blade's utility in surgery. Since he had undergone two thoracic operations in 1975, he had made obsidian blades for his surgeon to use. The operations were very successful, and his surgeon liked the obsidian blades for their ease in cutting and the improved healing of the incisions.

But before obsidian scalpels could find wide use in surgery, a series of problems had to be resolved. The first problem was to determine how sharp the obsidian blades were and how they compared with the various scalpels already used by surgeons. The answers came from examining the edges of obsidian blades, other kinds of stone (chert and quartzite), razor blades, and surgical scalpels under the tremendous magnification of a scanning electron microscope (SEM).

The results showed that the dullest edge belonged to a percussion flake made of chert. The quartzite flake was much sharper, having an edge 9.5 times sharper than the chert flake. I had expected the stainless steel surgical scalpel

to be sharper than the razor blade, but the results were the opposite. The scalpel was only 1.5 times sharper than the quartzite flake. The razor blade, a standard Gillette stainless steel double-edged blade, was 2.1 times sharper than the surgical scalpel. This was a surprise to me, but not to surgeons, who often use razor blades for operations by adapting them with "blade breakers," small devices that snap razor blades into segments for surgical use.

Most significantly, the obsidian blade was far sharper than any of these edges. Depending on the edge being measured, the obsidian was *100 to 500 times sharper* than the razor blade and thus was 210 to 1050 times sharper than the modern surgical scalpel!

By 1980 I was ready to see if there was any application in modern surgery for such sharp cutting edges. After calling several prominent eye surgeons, I reached Dr. Firmon Hardenbergh of Boulder, Colorado. The more I described the astounding sharpness of the obsidian edge, the more interested he became. He decided to use one of these blades for eye surgery. The results were quite successful, for the sharper edge did less damage to the tissue and the cleaner incision facilitated healing. And, very importantly, there was less resistance to the blade, so the eye moved far less, allowing the surgeon to make a more accurate incision.

Since that time obsidian blades have been used in other kinds of operations. Healing was usually faster, scarring was reduced (sometimes dramatically so), and often the pain during recovery was reduced or almost eliminated. Once the full research and development program for eye surgery is completed, Dr. Hardenbergh and I plan to modify the blades for use in general surgery and in specialized applications such as plastic surgery and neurosurgery.

We needed to compare the use of obsidian and steel scalpels. We did this by experimental cutting of muscle tissue with both kinds of blades and then examining the incisions with the SEM. The differences were dramatic. The metal blades tore and translocated large amounts of tissue, leaving the ragged edges of the incision littered with displaced chunks of flesh. The obsidian cut was strikingly crisp and clean.

We have improved the blades greatly from their early form in 1980; they are now more uniform in shape and are fitted with well-formed plastic handles. But they still must be made by hand, replicating the ancient Maya technology. The next step will be to engineer a transformation from a traditional handicraft to a modern manufacturing system. Because shapes of cores vary, each blade has to be individually planned and detached, and each blade varies in

(continued)

(continued)

length and shape. This technology is not adequate for manufacturing large numbers of standardized surgical scalpels.

Part of the manufacturing problem has been solved by designing a metal mold into which we pour molten glass, producing uniformly shaped cores. This process also eliminates the impurities and structural imperfections present in natural obsidian, and it allows us to vary the glass chemistry to maximize desirable properties such as color and edge toughness. We have also designed a machine to detach the blades from the core, and this device is being tested and refined. These improvements in manufacturing have resulted in more consistent blades, but more work needs to be done to fully automate the process and produce precisely uniform obsidian surgical scalpels every time.

Once the blades are in production and are readily available to surgeons, they will have the advantage over even the sharpest scalpel presently used, the diamond blade. Based on present tests, our obsidian blades are just as sharp as diamond blades—in fact they are up to three times sharper. But diamond blades are extremely expensive, costing several thousand dollars apiece, and they are tiny, with only 3 mm of cutting edge. Obsidian scalpels will cost the surgeon only a few dollars each, and the blades can be as long as needed. Fortunately, the ancient Maya have shown us the way not only to sharper and cheaper scalpels, but to surgical instruments that have very real benefits for the patient in reducing trauma, scarring, and pain. In these ways the past has provided a very real improvement to the present.

CHAPTER FIFTEEN

SOCIAL SYSTEMS

Exchange Systems

Recognition of Trade Goods

Exchange Models

Settlement Archaeology

Activity Areas and Buildings

Communities and Settlements

Regions

Population Reconstruction

Social Implications from Burials

Evidence of Social Groupings

Ceramic Sociology

Ancient Assertions of Social Identity

Summary

Guide to Further Reading

The past twenty years have seen a fundamental change in the objectives, the methods, and in particular the aspirations of the archaeologist. Nowhere is this clearer than in the approach to the study of what has been termed "social archaeology," that is[,] the reconstruction of past social systems and relations.

Colin Renfrew, "Social Archaeology, Societal Change and Generalisation," 1984

Traditionally, archaeology has emphasized technological data, so that is where we began our discussion of **synthesis** and interpretive reconstruction in Chapter 14. As we noted in that chapter, the effective scope of archaeology has expanded significantly in recent years, and, as the opening quotation indicates, one hallmark of this development has been an increased concern with the reconstruction of past **social systems.** After all, we cannot fully understand the things people did unless we know how they organized themselves to do them. Emblematic of this expanded interest was the publication of *Social Archeology: Beyond Subsistence and Dating,* edited by C. L. Redman and his colleagues. Although this collection of essays was more a consequence than a cause of the broadening of scope within archaeology, the book discussed new goals and challenges for archaeologists in entering the social dimension of the past. More recently, postprocessualists have given particular attention to reconstructing how ancient societies were organized.

In this chapter we will explore some of the ways past social systems may be reconstructed. The discussion will also include reminders of how the three broad categories of data—the technological, social, and ideological realms—are related. These categories provide useful ways of breaking down human behavior for easier study, but we must not forget that in any culture, all three form a unified and interrelated whole.

Every society distinguishes among its members by assigning various roles and statuses. The most fundamental distinctions are those based on age and sex differences, but most human groups organize social interaction along a number of other lines as well. Kinship studies, a well-known part of anthropological research, have revealed the great variety of ways people have developed for naming relatives, reckoning descent, governing what family members a person lives with, and so on. Principles of social organization extend beyond consideration of family organization, however, to include the ways power is channeled (political organization) and who controls production and distribution of wealth and other resources (economic organization), among other things.

As we have just noted, the most fundamental ways of distinguishing among members of a society are by age and gender. These aspects of personal identity would seem, on the surface, to be automatic—one is inevitably a child or an adult, a male or a female. But in fact, even these "universal" categories are quite flexible, subject to negotiation and redefinition within different cultures. For example, in our society, we distinguish various age categories—principally citing age in years as the defining criterion—from "baby" to "child," "teenager," "young adult," "middle-aged adult," and "senior citizen." In other cultures, however, distinctions are often based on developmental transitions, perhaps the most obvious of which is attainment of puberty, and with it the ability to produce children, which can occur within a fairly wide range of chronological ages. Similarly, gender ascriptions can vary within and across cultures, such that in Nuer culture of East Africa, an older woman, past child-bearing age, may marry a younger one and thereby legitimatize the second woman's children; in this case, the first woman fills the more usual legal role of a male.

Not only do the definitions and boundaries of these basic role categories vary, but so does the behavior deemed appropriate, and the prestige and power available to each. Rarely, for example, do children conduct affairs of state, and prestige is accorded them most often in societies with inherited status differences more generally (such as those that recognize royal or chiefly families). Identifying activities appropriate to and prestige accorded by gender is somewhat trickier, and many have argued that archaeologists have tended (if often unconsciously) to project Euro-American gender roles and relative statuses to all other societies, regardless of evidence sometimes to the contrary. Joan Gero, for instance, has examined lithic manufacture and its study by archaeologists; she concludes that there is a strong tendency to assume that stone tools are and were made by men, and there has been nearly as strong a tendency for archaeologists analyzing ancient stone tools to be male. (To some extent, the latter reflects the preponderance of men as archaeologists until recent decades [see Chapter 1].) Looking at the ethnographic record, however, Gero notes that women frequently use and manufacture their own chipped-stone implements. According to ethnographic observations, these tools tend to be technologically simpler, more expedient (produced on the spot, for immediate use), used for domestic tasks, and discarded relatively soon. Men are, Gero asserts, more often the makers of more elaborate, bifacially worked tools, and the ones associated with hunting or ritual activities. But in sheer volume, the archaeological record of stone tool manufacture and use most likely represents women's, rather than men's, activities. Ancient women were perhaps more autonomous and less dependent on men than we have tended to assume. Indeed, in Thomas Jackson's study of California bedrock mortars, discussed in Chapter 12, we saw how it was the activities of women, making and using these flour-grinding facilities, that governed movement of the Mono and other groups across the landscape with the seasons. Emergence of an emic perspective in archaeology, associated with postprocessual (and especially feminist) approaches, has led archaeologists to presume less etic consistency across cultures and to look at the archaeological record with somewhat more critical eyes.

Ethnographers and social anthropologists have revealed a great deal about the various ways people in living societies are categorized and organized to handle the distinctive problems associated with particular societies or activities. Much of the evidence for social structure is intangible, however, such as attitudes of respect and deference or linguistic taxonomies of social relationships. For this reason, archaeologists have tried to develop more sensitivity to aspects of material remains that may contain clues to past social organization. In this chapter we shall discuss five approaches now in use to reconstruct past social relationships and social structure: exchange systems, settlement archaeology, population reconstruction, human burials, and artifacts as emblems of social identity.

EXCHANGE SYSTEMS

We begin our discussion with study of exchange systems because they are so closely linked with **economy** and other topics discussed in the previous chapter. **Exchange systems** are the means by which human societies acquire goods and services not normally available to them locally. Exchange includes **trade,** gift giving, tribute, and any other means of moving objects from one person or group to another. A common distinction is drawn between local and long-distance exchange.

All forms of exchange are ways of drawing on technologies and environmental resources at a distance. Instead of repeating the methods and interpretations discussed in Chapter 14, however, here we wish to emphasize the social aspects of providing goods and services. Organization of who does the tasks and who gets to consume the products is important at the local level too, of course, but the organizational issues are perhaps more obvious in dealing with trade and exchange networks.

With development of these systems, trading ventures and other institutions arise to handle repeated cooperative and peaceful exchanges between two or more parties. Of course, there are other means to acquire nonlocal goods and services: Foraging expeditions may be used to collect materials from distant sources, and raids or military conquests often plunder foreign lands for wealth and slaves. The latter means present a contrast to trading systems in that they obviously do not involve either cooperation or two-way exchange. The archaeologist may have difficulty distinguishing exchanged goods from those acquired by other means, but the distinction is important for at least two reasons. First, the recognition of exchange in the archaeological record leads to the reconstruction of past economic systems, and, since such systems are basic to all human societies, by extension this contributes to an understanding of the organization of entire ancient societies. Second, since cooperative exchange between individuals and between societies provides a primary means for the transmission of new ideas, recognition of exchange leads the archaeologist to an understanding of culture change.

In this section we will discuss the ways in which archaeologists identify ancient trade goods and reconstruct exchange systems. Before doing this, however, we will briefly outline some of the characteristics of exchange systems as determined from ethnographic and historical examples.

Most anthropologists distinguish two basic forms of exchange; often both can be found within a single economic system. **Reciprocal exchange** refers to simple, direct trade between two parties; "payment" may be made through barter, in services, through indentured labor, or in monetary units. **Redistributive exchange** is more complex and indirect, involving a third party or an institution that collects goods or services, such as surpluses, tribute, duties, or taxes, and reallocates the accumulated wealth to others. Reciprocal exchange is found in all human societies, but redistributive exchange is usually associated with more complex, socially stratified societies. In these societies, the allocating authority—be it chief, king, or centralized bureaucracy—usually has the right or power to retain a portion of the collected goods and services that pass through its hands. Colin Renfrew has outlined ten forms of resource acquisition. The simplest is direct access to resources; of the rest, two involve reciprocal exchange and the remaining seven involve redistribution (Fig. 15.1).

Although human exchange systems transfer goods, services, and ideas, by necessity archaeologists deal directly only with the tangible products of trade, usually recovered as artifacts and ecofacts. These data are traditionally divided into two classes: utilitarian and nonutilitarian items. Utilitarian items include food, tools for acquiring, storing, and processing food, weapons, clothing, and other materials. Nonutilitarian items include gifts, ritual goods, and prestige goods. These distinctions can be interpretively important. For instance, utilitarian goods frequently end up in the hands of a broad range of consumers, whereas prestige items are often fewer in number and restricted to consumption by the wealthy and powerful. They may even point to the presence of special groups of artisans for their production or special networks for their exchange.

By considering such distinctions, the archaeologist attempts to reconstruct both the inventory of trade goods and the mechanism of exchange, examining the relative amounts as well as the spatial distribution of recovered trade items. But before such **interpretation** can begin, the archaeologist must be able to separate trade goods from local goods in the archaeological record and to distinguish ancient acquisition, manufacture, and use behavior.

Recognition of Trade Goods

The identification of trade goods in archaeological situations is based on a variety of classification procedures. The archaeologist must determine the source locations for the raw materials of both artifacts and ecofacts, the manufacturing place for artifacts, and areas of use for both artifacts and ecofacts. Area of use is inferred to be the site of discovery if the evidence

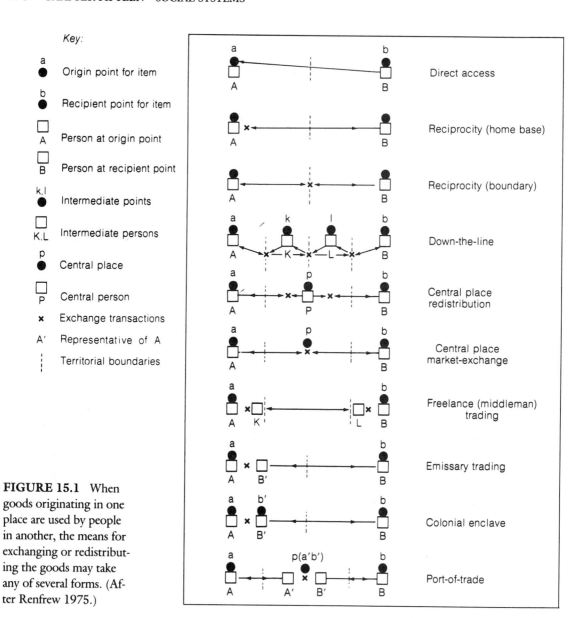

FIGURE 15.1 When goods originating in one place are used by people in another, the means for exchanging or redistributing the goods may take any of several forms. (After Renfrew 1975.)

is found in primary context. Places of manufacture are reconstructed directly by discovery of workshop sites or indirectly from recovery of manufacturing debris in other associations, such as middens. Sources of raw materials are determined by identification of ancient quarries, mines, and other acquisition areas. Figure 15.2 presents the relationship of these identified **activity areas** to the reconstruction of ancient trade.

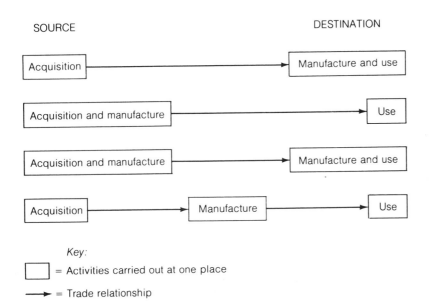

SOURCE

DESTINATION

Acquisition ──────────────────→ Manufacture and use

Acquisition and manufacture ──────────────────→ Use

Acquisition and manufacture ──────────→ Manufacture and use

Acquisition ──────→ Manufacture ──────→ Use

Key:
☐ = Activities carried out at one place
──→ = Trade relationship

FIGURE 15.2 Exchange or trade may take place at any point during the behavioral cycle of acquisition, manufacture, and use of resources. The archaeologist attempts to determine the location of each of these activities.

In dealing with ecofacts, such as floral and faunal remains, the archaeologist need identify only the source and use areas. For instance, marine materials may be recovered from a site located far inland, or bones of lowland-dwelling animals may be found at a site in a highland region. In both cases, the demonstration of trade rests on the biological identification of plant and animal species, recognition that a recovered ecofact is nonlocal in origin, and subsequent identification of its probable source area (Fig. 15.3).

Artifacts often present a much more complex problem (Fig. 15.4). Because artifacts are products of human manufacture or modification, the

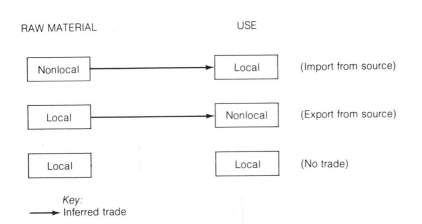

RAW MATERIAL

USE

Nonlocal ──────────→ Local   (Import from source)

Local ──────────→ Nonlocal   (Export from source)

Local   Local   (No trade)

Key:
──→ Inferred trade

FIGURE 15.3 Identification of exchange of ecofacts depends on recognition of species that have been removed from their natural habitats.

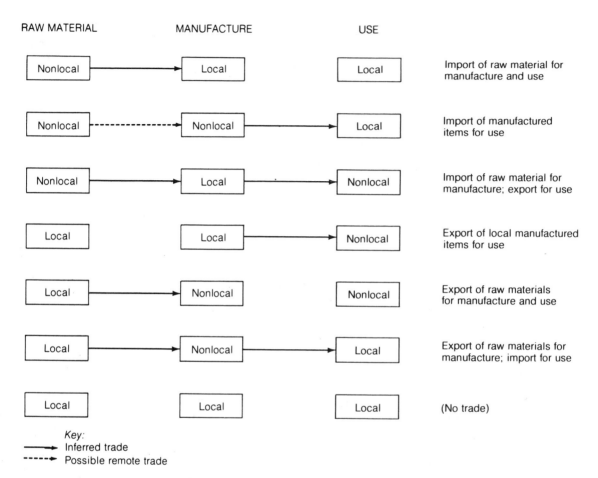

RAW MATERIAL	MANUFACTURE	USE	
Nonlocal	Local	Local	Import of raw material for manufacture and use
Nonlocal	Nonlocal	Local	Import of manufactured items for use
Nonlocal	Local	Nonlocal	Import of raw material for manufacture; export for use
Local	Local	Nonlocal	Export of local manufactured items for use
Local	Nonlocal	Nonlocal	Export of raw materials for manufacture and use
Local	Nonlocal	Local	Export of raw materials for manufacture; import for use
Local	Local	Local	(No trade)

Key:
→ Inferred trade
----→ Possible remote trade

FIGURE 15.4 Exchange of artifacts may involve trade in raw materials, manufactured goods, partially manufactured goods, or some combination of these.

archaeologist must identify not only the source of raw materials and the location of use but also the place of manufacture. Manufacture itself may involve several steps, each carried out at a different location. For instance, mineral substances such as flint or obsidian are sometimes manufactured into tools right at the quarry site and then traded as finished tools. In other cases, the raw material is traded first and then manufactured into tools at its destination. Or manufacture may be carried out at both source and destination: Tool "blanks" may be roughed out at the quarry, traded, and converted into finished tools at the final destination. Other variations are also possible, such as manufacture at a point between source and destination. The archaeologist may even distinguish between original manufacture and reworking, if artifacts were modified for secondary uses.

The identification of local as opposed to imported artifacts may be made by either stylistic or technological (constituent) classification. **Stylistic types** (Fig. 15.5) have traditionally been used to distinguish certain

FIGURE 15.5 Some nonlocal artifacts can be distinguished as imports because of their style. These two seals are both about 4000 years old and are similar in style. Each depicts a humped bull with a brief inscription above its back. The seal on the left, however, comes from the Indus site of Mohenjo-daro, in Pakistan, where this style of seal is common and where stylistically related artifacts are also found. The seal on the right was discovered at Nippur, in Mesopotamia, where it is stylistically unusual, leading to the inference that it was imported. (Photo (l) courtesy of George Dales; photo (r) courtesy of McGuire Gibson.)

categories of traded artifacts, such as pottery. However, **stylistic attributes** (such as surface color and decoration) may themselves be unreliable criteria for differentiating local from nonlocal artifacts. This is because style attributes, along with most **form attributes,** can easily be copied by local manufacturers to mimic imported examples. This does not mean that either stylistic or form types cannot contribute to the reconstruction of ancient exchange systems. The impact of trade relationships, as expressed in the exchange of *ideas,* can often be gauged by the extent to which foreign elements are accepted and integrated into local styles and forms, whether these are expressed by pottery, architecture, or other evidence.

The most reliable means of identifying trade goods is technological classification based on **constituent analysis.** Constituent analysis identifies the chemical composition of the raw material (clay, metal, mineral, or whatever), using a variety of techniques ranging from microscopic visual inspection to sophisticated methods of analytic chemistry and physics, including optical spectroscopy, X-ray fluorescence, and neutron activation. The goal of these analyses is to identify characteristics unique or specific to material from a single source; this is often referred to as the "fingerprint" or the "signature" of the source. The choice of one analytic technique over another often depends on such factors as cost, precision of the identification needed, and whether the artifact sample may be destroyed by the analysis.

Constituent identification of trade goods is usually applied within a regional archaeological strategy. The environmental survey of a given region should include identification of potential sources of raw materials, such as mineral deposits, clay beds, metal ore deposits, and so forth. Samples of raw material from the potential sources are analyzed along with artifacts recovered archaeologically, using one or more of the techniques designed to reveal their chemical composition. The resulting characteristics of the samples are used to group the materials statistically according to their chemical "fingerprints." The artifact classes and the source classes are then compared to determine the probable sources of the raw materials for the artifacts under study (Fig. 15.6). Because the variability involved can be quite complex, the matches are often facilitated by using a computer. Constituent analyses such as these have been done for a variety of materials in a number of areas, including turquoise in the southwestern United States and northern Mexico, and soapstone (steatite) in Virginia, but most of the emphasis has been placed on obsidian.

Exchange Models

Exchange models allow the archaeologist to reconstruct ancient trade and its accompanying social interaction by examining spatial patterning from several perspectives, including simple presence or absence of certain trade items and quantitative patterns in their occurrence. Simple presence/absence plots show the distributions for one or more categories of traded artifacts and their identified raw material sources. Such maps may suggest quite readily the spatial range and even routes used in ancient trade systems.

Colin Renfrew has discussed a number of mathematical models for studying quantitative patterning in distribution of trade items. These are **distance decay** functions: The traded item occurs in smaller quantities with increasing distance from the source. In his original studies of obsidian trade in southwest Asia, Renfrew posited a down-the-line social model to account for the quantitative distribution. According to this model, each town successively farther from the source passes along only a certain proportion of the total goods received. The result is an exponential decline in the amount of material moving down the line.

Detailed attention to refinement of trade models has pointed out a number of factors differentiating among trade systems. For instance, Ian Hodder has distinguished two categories of distance decay effects, which Renfrew discusses in terms of *network* or down-the-line trade as opposed to areally more limited *supply-zone* trade. The first category involves multiple trade transactions and movement over long distances; the second, apparently associated with common, bulky items such as roof tiles, seems to involve single transactions and short trips to supply a specified local area.

Under some circumstances, the distance decay is marked from a location other than the manufacturing source. These places are redistribution centers, where goods are brought and stored before being distributed—sold, traded, or given away—to consumers. Whether redistribution centers handle one or many commodities, their existence is important, for they increase exchange interaction and accumulate more than their expected share of trade goods. To the archaeologist, they are therefore rec-

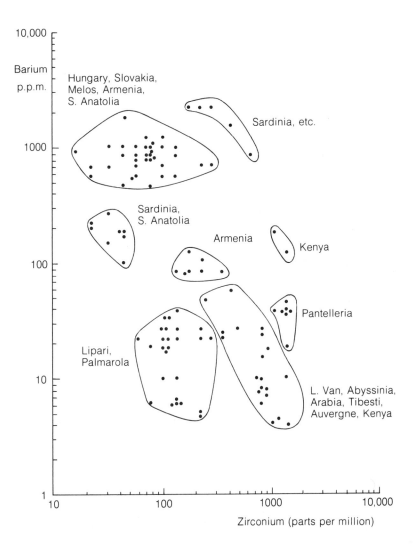

FIGURE 15.6 Graph of the amounts of zirconium and barium in obsidian specimens from several known sources in the Mediterranean area. The source groupings defined here can be more specifically "fingerprinted" by considering additional elements, such as iron and strontium. (After Cann and Renfrew 1964.)

ognizable in part because they produce bumps on the overall distance decay curves (Fig. 15.7).

Often a hierarchy of such centers develops, with the greatest volume and variety of goods and services located in the largest. As Renfrew notes, some of the increased accumulation in the higher-order centers may result from the role of these centers as marketplaces, but some may also be due to the greater personal wealth or prestige of their residents, who are thus able to bring in more imported goods. For example, Raymond Sidrys has demonstrated that the quantities of obsidian found in pre-Hispanic Maya sites are determined both by distance from the source and by stature of the site in a rough hierarchy of centers.

FIGURE 15.7 The amount of an exchange item reaching a specific destination decreases with the distance of that destination from the source. But the rate of decrease is not completely constant, and the presence of redistribution centers in particular disrupts the distance decay curve. (After Renfrew 1975.)

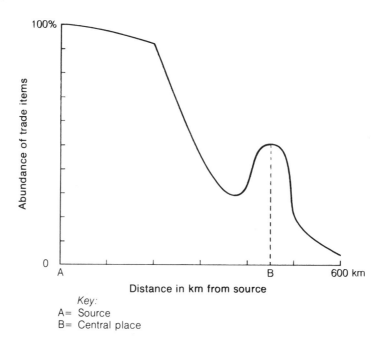

Key:
A = Source
B = Central place

Such a site hierarchy, however, reflects another means of inferring dimensions of ancient social systems—settlement archaeology—an area to which we now turn.

SETTLEMENT ARCHAEOLOGY

Settlement archaeology is the study of the spatial distribution of ancient human activities and occupation, ranging from the differential location of activities within a single room to the arrangement of sites in a region. Settlement studies use features and sites as their principal data bases. This does not mean that individual artifacts and ecofacts are not considered in such studies; however, since the focus is on understanding the distribution of ancient activities, the archaeologist doing settlement studies needs the locational information preserved by primary context, and features and sites retain such information intact.

The development of settlement archaeology has different roots in England and the United States, but in both cases it has involved attention to the way human occupation is distributed across the landscape. In England, the work of Sir Cyril Fox in the second quarter of the 20th century provided the stimulus for relating the distribution of archaeological remains to the distribution of environmental features. In the United States, the inspiration for settlement studies can be traced most directly to Julian Steward's research in the Great Basin area in the 1930s. Steward rec-

Pioneering settlement studies: Sir Cyril Fox in England, Julian Steward in the Great Basin of the United States, and Gordon Willey in the Virú Valley of Peru

ognized that patterns in the location of household residence could be understood as a product of the interactions between environment and culture—especially the combined cultural factors of technology and social organization. In other words, the spatial patterning of archaeological features that represented ancient residences could be analyzed to reconstruct past decisions about use of the environment, allocation of resources, social relationships, and the like.

One of the first research projects to apply Steward's ideas to strictly archaeological data was Gordon R. Willey's study of changing regional patterns of settlement in the Virú Valley of north coastal Peru. In 1954, the year after the Virú research was published, Willey organized a symposium on prehistoric **settlement patterns** in the New World. At that time, only sketchy formulations could be offered for the various regions covered; archaeological settlement research has greatly expanded since then, however, both in frequency and in sophistication, so that archaeological research in most parts of the world now includes investigation of settlement distributions.

In recent years much effort has been expended to develop more rigorous techniques for ferreting out structure in the spatial dimension of archaeological data. Part of this new emphasis has resulted from a theoretical reorientation to the view that the study of relations among artifacts, ecofacts, and features is at least as important and informative as the study of artifacts, ecofacts, and features themselves. But the change is due also to the increasing attention archaeologists now pay to other social sciences (especially **geography** and regional planning) that study human behavior in a spatial framework. Related to this is the growing use of statistical analytical techniques and mathematically based models for describing and analyzing all the dimensions of archaeological data. **Geographic Information Systems** (GIS; see Chapters 6 and 14) have proven powerful here as well.

The assumption underlying settlement archaeology is simple: The spatial patterning evident in archaeological remains results from and reflects the spatial patterning in ancient human behavior. Archaeologists usually analyze spatial patterns on three levels. The smallest level is that of activities within a single structure or on a single occupation surface, such as a cave floor. The next or intermediate level concerns the arrangement of activities and features within a settlement or site. The largest-scale studies examine the distribution of sites within a region.

Activity Areas and Buildings

At the smallest level of human settlement, archaeologists reconstruct the spatial organization of activities within a single structure—a dwelling or some other kind of building—or within a comparably small unenclosed space. Such a study may consist of delineating areas in which various activities were carried out, such as distinguishing food preparation areas.

The nature of the specific activities carried out in a given area is inferred by comparison of the archaeological remains with material remains of known activities. For example, hearths, fire-blackened jars, and grinding stones would indicate a cooking area. At this smallest level of settlement analysis, then, the archaeologist is attempting to understand how the prehistoric society divided up space into areas appropriate for particular activities.

Statistical analysis of activity areas

A number of archaeologists, including Robert Whallon, John D. Speth, and Gregory A. Johnson, have used statistical analysis of activity areas to differentiate artifact clusters and define distinct activity areas or "tool kits." These techniques have been used primarily on data from Paleolithic cave sites in the Old World, where tool kits are frequently difficult to sort out by visual inspection of artifact arrays as they are uncovered. The statistical approaches used in these studies go beyond impressionistic assessments of spatial clusterings of artifacts and other materials on occupation floors; rather, horizontal patterns and clusters are defined by statistical measures of spatial association.

At this "microsettlement" level of analysis, the most frequently studied feature is the dwelling. A number of scholars have examined the potential determinants for house form. Bruce G. Trigger's list of such factors includes subsistence regime (whether a society is sedentary or migratory); climate; available building materials; family structure; wealth; incorporation of special activities, such as craft production; ideology; security; and style. Although several of these factors are related to environmental variables, others have to do with the social system of the culture being studied. For example, societies in which people live in extended families, with several generations of family residing together, have larger house structures than those in which nuclear families (parents plus children) are the usual household unit. Some studies have attempted to relate particular dwelling forms to particular kinship structures. By studying dwelling forms in a number of ethnographically known societies, for example, John W. M. Whiting and Barbara Ayres examined the extent to which such characteristics as number of rooms or curvilinear as opposed to rectangular ground plans might be used to predict family organization. A frequently cited finding from their research is that curvilinear dwellings tend to occur in polygynous societies—societies in which a man may have more than one wife. This statistical association, though useful and suggestive for archaeological inference, should not be taken as an automatic predictor: Round houses do not invariably indicate that the prehistoric society was polygynous.

Increasing attention is being given to **household archaeology**—literally, the study of ancient households. In Garth Bawden's words, households are the "organizational denominators" of society, the elemental units that perform most primary functions of society, including production and consumption of food and other commodities, reproduction and child rearing, disposal of the dead, and decision making. Households, then, provide microcosms of a society as a whole. While archaeologists, like ethnographers, are coming to appreciate that the nature of individual houses and households can be quite variable and complex, the investigation of these units—houses being architectural and archaeologically observable features, households being social and indirectly inferred from the archaeological remains—is providing rewarding information on diverse aspects of ancient culture in areas such as Peru, Guatemala, Yugoslavia, Iran, and England. David Clarke's analysis of house compounds in Iron Age Glastonbury, cited in Chapter 4, illustrates clearly the multifaceted array of inferences that result from settlement study at this level.

Clarke's study of the various clusters of artifacts, ecofacts, and features in the seven compounds of the small community of Glastonbury, considered in conjunction with historical sources on Iron Age society in the British Isles, indicated that men's and women's work quarters were spatially segregated within the household grounds and that there were subtle gradations of power and wealth among household groups. In addition, the Glastonbury study suggested that the rounded architectural forms typical of these houses and compounds were conceptually related to the predominantly curvilinear La Tène art style that flourished at that time, demonstrating how household archaeology can approach ideological aspects of analysis—a subject we shall turn to in the next chapter. In other examples of household archaeology, analysts stress particular social, political, and economic variables: how the form and size of houses change over time; how location of craft or other production activities relates to the residential unit; how differences in status, wealth, or power can be discerned from the remains of houses and associated artifacts. We will examine another extended example of household archaeology in reviewing postprocessual interpretations in Chapter 17.

Household archaeology: Clarke's Glastonbury study

Buildings other than dwellings may be examined at this level of settlement study. For example, Izumi Shimada has identified a series of specialized metalworking complexes within the seventh-century A.D. site of Pampa Grande, Peru. No residential buildings are nearby, so it can be concluded that the metalworkers commuted from elsewhere in the city and were fed daily rations prepared in kitchens revealed by excavation at the workplace. The results attest to a complex organization of people and production in this Peruvian city of the late Moche culture.

Urban commuters of ancient Peru: Shimada's analysis of Pampa Grande

Research by Kent Flannery and Joyce Marcus has also shed light on ancient nondomestic structures. They have traced the development of "public buildings" in the Valley of Oaxaca, Mexico, during the last few millennia B.C. By public buildings they mean special structures to house communal rituals; they believe they can detect demarcation of public space as early as the fifth millennium B.C. at the site of Gheo-Shih (Fig. 15.8). The Gheo-Shih public space is a cleared lane, 20 m long and 7 m wide, whose cleanliness and lack of artifacts contrast markedly with the abundance of remains just outside its boulder-marked limits. By 1500 B.C. in Oaxaca, special buildings had been constructed as public spaces; as time

Analysis of public buildings: Flannery and Marcus at Oaxaca, Mexico

FIGURE 15.8 This stone-bordered lane at the site of Gheo-Shih, Oaxaca, Mexico, dates to the fifth millennium B.C. It may have been a dance ground and is believed to be a local forerunner of public spaces more formally defined later by increasingly elaborate architecture. (From Flannery and Marcus 1976, by permission of the authors and Academic Press.)

passed, these became larger, architecturally more elaborate, less accessible, and more diversified into recognizable types. Flannery and Marcus argue that this developmental record reflects, in part, the development of social relationships: The growth in size and elaboration and the tendency toward spatial segregation of these structures imply their association with a wealthy, elitist segment of society, and the increase in recognizable types attests to a diversification of social roles—perhaps of ritual specialists to manage and carry out the activities for which the buildings were constructed.

In settlement analysis at this level, archaeologists should also include outdoor areas. Although many activities do take place within buildings, many others, from stone chipping to public dancing, can be performed as well outdoors. In hot climates, in fact, the majority of activities that do not require privacy may be carried out in the open air, often in patio areas adjacent to houses. Thus archaeologists who look only at structures may miss much of the overall picture of life in the prehistoric society.

Communities and Settlements

Consideration of outdoor areas leads us to the next level of settlement analysis: settlement layout. The site is the unit of analysis here, especially sites that are considered residential communities (as opposed to kill sites, for example). At this level, archaeologists consider the articulation of individual "microunits" into the larger whole; this allows them to examine aspects of prehistoric social systems from a number of perspectives.

Social stratification, for example, is frequently inferred partly on the basis of evidence from settlement analysis. In the public buildings in Oaxaca just mentioned, structure size and architectural elaboration were interpreted as clues to differential wealth and power. At the Maya site of Tikal, Guatemala, archaeologists have found that houses are consistent in form throughout the site, but they range considerably in size, decoration, and relative use of perishable as opposed to stone construction materials. Larger, more substantial residences are assumed to have housed people who had more wealth or other means of controlling and acquiring goods and labor.

Aspects of social control can also be inferred from the regularity of settlement layouts. The site of Teotihuacan, Mexico, with its gridded streets and its orientation to the cardinal directions (see Fig. 6.34, p. 234), is a striking example of imposed planning—which implies the presence of a powerful elite able to command and direct the placement of structures and facilities over this broad expanse of land. Ancient Chinese political centers were laid out according to a plan whose basis was partly religious but whose execution required effective social control.

Concerns with privacy or security can also be detected. For instance, Richard W. Keatinge and Kent C. Day have described the complex urban center of Chan Chan, in the Moche Valley of Peru, as divisible into three components: houses of the poor, intermediate buildings, and monumental structures. The three categories reflect differences both of complexity and of regularity of arrangement. The monumental structures are the most complex and regular of all. They constitute a set of ten enclosures (Fig. 15.9) that have been interpreted as elite residential compounds. Given this interpretation, the articulation of elite with nonelite people of the area can be partially examined by looking at how the residences relate—or were allowed to relate—in space. Clearly the poorer areas were segregated even from the intermediate sections, but the monumental compounds were the most restrictive of all. Although they encompassed great amounts of space, each had only one or two entrances, allowing its occupants to control strictly with whom they would interact.

Besides social stratification, role differentiation and economic specialization can also be studied by using settlement data. For example, study of the distribution of workshop areas within a community might indicate whether these are associated with particular classes of people, whether they are segregated into specific quarters of the community, and so on. Some industries, such as flint knapping, might be "cottage industries," carried out by every family (or other social unit) to supply its own needs; within the same community, other industries might be carried out by skilled specialists. In developmental studies of the rise of urbanism, the criteria used to define urban status often include not only population size

Social organization: Keatinge and Day at Chan Chan, Peru

FIGURE 15.9 This portion of the map of Chan Chan, Peru, shows remains of (a) nonelite residential areas contrasting with (b) one of the ten elite walled enclosures with restricted access from the outside. (After Moseley and Mackey 1974.)

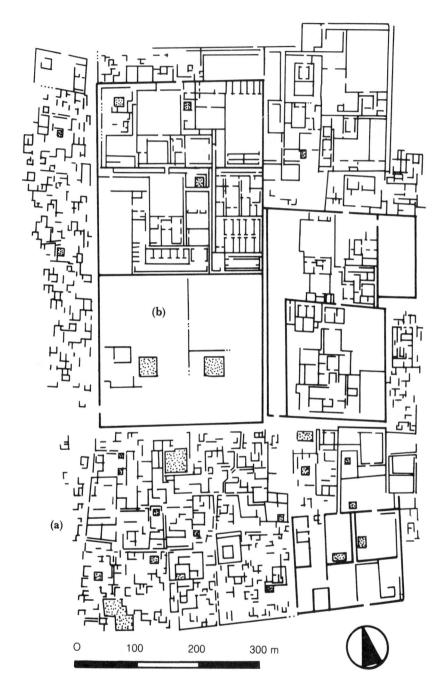

and density but also the existence of specialized craft production of a number of commodities.

Some scholars have attempted to correlate settlement layouts with kinship structures. In a pioneering study of this kind, Kwang-Chih Chang suggested that segmented village plans might be associated with segmented lineage (descent group) social organization. This research was the direct inspiration for the Whiting and Ayres study on residence shape. Like the latter study, Chang's work is suggestive but cannot be used as a strictly predictive model for interpretation of archaeological settlement remains, because we cannot yet demonstrate conclusively that this type of social system is the *only* source for such settlement patterns.

Kent V. Flannery has used house form and settlement layout to develop a hypothesis about the growth of village life and development of political organization. Specifically, he postulates that round houses and house compounds are less conducive than rectangular units to the addition of new units and the integration of larger numbers of people. He notes that in both Mesoamerica and southwest Asia, two major world centers in the development of agriculture and urbanism, the village of rectangular houses became the "standard" community organization.

House types and evolution of community organization: Flannery's comparison of southwest Asia and Mesoamerica

Regions

At the broadest level of settlement analysis, archaeologists consider the distribution of sites within a region. This can be approached in at least two ways. One is to reconstruct the function of each component in the settlement system and then to look at the various ways in which they may have been organized into an interacting social network. Another is use of spatial analysis techniques borrowed from fields such as economic geography. Whatever the approach taken, settlement analyses at a regional scale increasingly employ GIS to make more comprehensive and complex study possible.

Underlying the first approach is the idea, expressed by Chang and others, that the same settlement pattern can reflect a number of different systems of social relationships (Fig. 15.10). Richard MacNeish's Tehuacán subsistence cycle is one example of a particular view of settlement systems where different sites were used to exploit contrasting food resources according to their seasonal availability.

A different example is provided by analysis of Paleolithic sites, in France and elsewhere, having a Mousterian stone tool assemblage. These sites have been categorized into a number of Mousterian "types"; François Bordes, a leader in delineating variation in Mousterian artifacts, argued that the different sites reflected occupation of adjacent locales by contrasting social groups who used different styles of tool manufacture. Lewis and Sally Binford, however, have used statistical factor analysis of some of the tool assemblages to support their contention that the variability represents not "ethnic" difference but complementary sets of activities. The Binfords' analyses led them to posit that some of the occupations represented residential "base camps," whereas others represented hunting/butchering or other work camps. The contrast in the social interaction implied by the

Social differentiation vs. complementary activities: Bordes and the Binfords on Mousterian artifacts

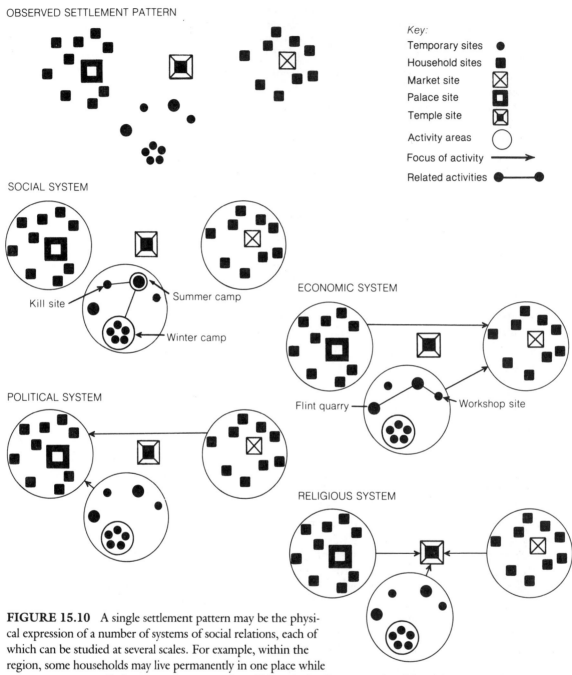

FIGURE 15.10 A single settlement pattern may be the physical expression of a number of systems of social relations, each of which can be studied at several scales. For example, within the region, some households may live permanently in one place while others move seasonally from one place to another. Although the diverse people of the region may all be governed from a single political capital, it need not be located in the same place as the economic hub or the ritual center. (Redrawn from K. C. Chang, *Settlement Patterns in Archaeology*, © 1972 by Addison-Wesley Publishing Company, Inc. Philippines copyright 1972 by Addison-Wesley Publishing Company, Inc.)

two interpretations is clear. In one view, the Mousterian occupations represented contrasting human social groups doing similar things; in the other, an undifferentiated overall group was simply dividing up activities according to appropriate locales. Again, the nature of individual parts of the settlement system must be examined to reconstruct the social system involved.

Analytic techniques originated by economic geographers have become increasingly popular in regional studies. These approaches tend to be based on regional spatial organizations and holistic perspectives. Many of the actual techniques, however, come under the term **locational analysis,** and a particularly important analytic model is that of **central place theory.** Underlying the latter theory—and other models derived from economic geography—is the assumption that efficiency and minimization of costs are among the most basic criteria involved in spatial organization of human activities. An individual settlement will be located in a position where a maximum number of resources can be exploited with the least effort; these resources will include not only aspects of the natural environment but also communication with neighboring groups. As the landscape fills with people, settlements will tend to space themselves evenly across it, and the most efficient pattern for spacing of communities is a hexagonal lattice. This is all in theory, of course: In practice, landscape variables such as steep topography or presence of uninhabitable areas—swamps and the like— break up the predicted pattern. Still, a reasonably close approximation of the hexagonal-lattice pattern has been observed in a number of situations both modern and ancient, including Ian Hodder and Mark Hassall's study of Romano-British towns (Fig. 15.11).

Given an already populated landscape, geographer Walter Christaller developed a model to describe the rise of cities; this is "classical" central place theory as first developed in Christaller's 1933 study of modern settlement in southern Germany. Briefly, the theory states that *central places* will develop within this lattice arrangement. These centers will provide a wider variety of goods and services than do surrounding smaller settlements. In fact, a hierarchy of central places will arise, with centers of equivalent level spaced equidistantly through the lattice (Fig. 15.11). Different lattices, reflecting different nesting patterns for the levels in the hierarchy, are more efficient for different goals; the three goals usually considered are movement of rurally produced goods, movement of centrally produced goods, and control of distribution patterns by centralized administration.

Central place theory has been of interest to archaeologists for describing regional settlement patterns; its primary application has been in studying the development of cities in the archaeological record. Although overall application of this model in anthropology has been made largely by social and cultural anthropologists, archaeologists studying areas of the world in which cities and civilizations emerged have also explored the model's potentials. In so doing, they have brought forth variations on

Applications of central place theory: Johnson on the Diyala Plains of Iraq, Blanton on Teotihuacan, Mexico

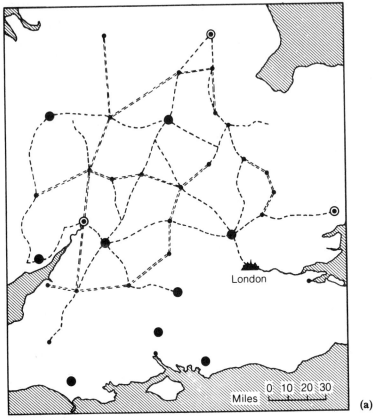

(a)

Key:
- ● Capital
- ◉ Colony
- • Lesser walled town

--- Road
=== Boundary of tributary areas

FIGURE 15.11 Romano-British settlement in the third century A.D.: (a) plotted on a conventional map, and (b) fitted to an *idealized* hexagonal lattice demonstrating central place theory. (After Hodder and Hassall 1971, by permission of the Royal Anthropological Institute of Great Britain and Ireland.)

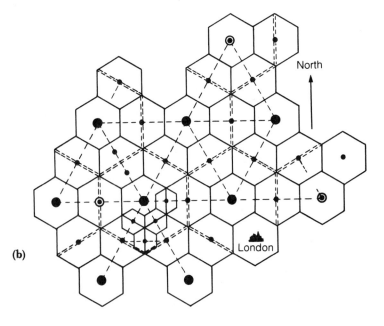

(b)

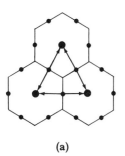 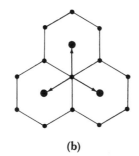

(a)   (b)   (c)

FIGURE 15.12 Central place models of settlement are usually divided into three idealized variants. In all three, a large center has direct access to six smaller settlements. The difference is: in (a), the transport landscape, each smaller settlement relates to two large centers; in (b), the marketing landscape, each smaller settlement is connected with three larger centers; and in (c), the administrative landscape, the smaller settlements interact with only one larger center.

Christaller's basic model. For instance, Gregory Johnson's study of the settlement lattice on the Diyala Plains of Iraq at about 2800 B.C. shows that it fits Christaller's model but, probably because of the existence of a series of roughly parallel watercourses, the lattice there is composed of rhomboids rather than hexagons. Other work, such as Richard Blanton's interpretation of the rise of Teotihuacan, shows what is called the "primate pattern," in which the highest-order central place absorbs the function of intermediate centers, growing in size and importance at their expense and interacting directly with much smaller settlements.

The value of central place theory and its variants is that, when an archaeological situation fits a particular variant, the theoretical model suggests the kinds of economic decision making and organization principles that may have been operating in the past society (Fig. 15.12). The model does not in itself explain what actually went on in the past, but it helps to suggest explanatory hypotheses to be tested.

Other locational and spatial analyses have been or are being developed to describe, compare, and understand settlement distributions. **Network analyses** examine routes of communication between settlements. In another technique, **Thiessen polygons** are imposed on a regional map by drawing perpendiculars at the midpoints between settlements; the areas included within the Thiessen polygons suggest the areas under the control of each settlement (in an approach comparable to Vita-Finzi and Higgs's site-catchment analysis, noted on p. 459) and provide a graphic indication of the equality or inequality of settlement spacing. This technique has been used in a variety of archaeological situations, including Hodder and Hassall's study of Romano-British walled towns and Norman Hammond's exploration of possible "realms" among the Classic Maya.

Colin Renfrew's study of Neolithic site forms and settlement patterns in several regions of England illustrates both the incorporation of these geographic approaches and the strong emphasis on reconstruction of social systems that has emerged in contemporary archaeology. The revised chronology of Neolithic Europe, resulting from the recalibration of radiocarbon dates (see Chapter 9, p. 331), has shown that the famous European "megalithic" sites, such as Stonehenge (Fig. 4.3, p. 117) and Avebury in

Use of distributional and functional data: Renfrew's study of the evolution of Neolithic society in England

England and Carnac in France, are in fact older than sites in the Mediterranean basin and southwest Asia that were previously assumed to be their prototypes. Simple mimicry of stone architecture found at sites in Egypt, in Greece, and on several Mediterranean islands can no longer explain the monumental construction of Neolithic Europe. Consequently Renfrew and other archaeologists have sought new models to account for the origins of these imposing sites.

Drawing on work by Andrew Fleming and others, Renfrew noted that the smaller, long, earthen burial mounds (barrows) of the early Neolithic (ca. 4000–3500 B.C.) were distributed in discrete clusters across the English landscape, each of which was dominated by a specialized type of larger earthen enclosure known as a "causewayed camp." These larger enclosures were evidently used for ritual purposes and as centralized places for exposing the dead to the elements. When the dead were reduced to skeletal remains, the bones were collected and taken to the smaller communal barrows for final burial. Renfrew used combined distributional and functional data to infer that the barrows represent localized landholding kin groups, united into a larger social system by means of a shared custom of treatment of the dead at centralized ritual facilities.

In later Neolithic times, by 3000 B.C., these spatial social units were each organized around a larger and different kind of ritual center. These are known as *henge monuments,* bounded by circular earthen enclosures, up to 500 m in diameter, with a large timber construction at the center. The most elaborate and famous of these is Stonehenge, notable because its central enclosure was built of stone on a monumental scale. Although the precise role of the henge sites seems to have changed from that of the earlier causewayed camps, they were similar regional ritual centers. But the growth of population size and social complexity can be inferred from estimates of labor investments for building these henge monuments. They were at least ten times greater than their earlier counterparts.

By adopting a regional geographic and settlement pattern approach, Renfrew developed a working model for population distribution and territorial integration in successive periods of British prehistory. The model explains the origins of the megalithic monument and related constructions as indigenous developments from known antecedents, rather than from distant prototypes. Beyond this, Renfrew argues that the significantly greater costs in human energy implied in these increasingly elaborate ritual sites suggest changes in the political and economic organization of Neolithic society.

Utility of GIS in settlement archaeology: Crumley, Marquardt, and Madry in Burgundy, France

GIS applications have opened great new potentials for settlement analyses at the regional scale. One recent example is an ongoing study, by Carole L. Crumley and her colleagues, of 2500 years of occupation—from the Celtic Iron Age to the present—of the Arroux valley region, in Burgundy, France. A multidisciplinary team has compiled a richly varied data base, digitizing into a Geographic Information System (GIS) information from published maps, aerial photographs, and satellite imagery. The resultant GIS incorporates records of geology, soils, rivers, climate, and road and settlement locations, as well as much derived information about the region's landscape. Derived information here refers to such topics as definition of watershed limits, calculation of optimal routes for human travel, or lines of sight to or from specified points in the region. Thanks in large part to the great degree of locational detail of the data base, its diversity in time frame and subject matter, and its storage in a GIS, the Arroux valley data has already begun yielding a wealth of insights into regional changes in Burgundian settlement and society. To cite one concise example, by combining information on site locations with data on soils, geology, elevation, groundslope, and climate, "it becomes clear that the warming climate of the Roman Optimum (approximately 250 B.C. to A.D. 250) drove Celtic settlement to higher elevations—where moist conditions continued to prevail—and opened lower elevations to Mediterranean vegetation and . . . Roman agricultural practices" (Crumley and Marquardt 1990:78). From other GIS analyses of the Arroux data, Scott Madry and Crumley found that ancient roads follow paths that remain in the line of sight of hillforts, steering away from areas hidden from protective view. These kinds of observations are certainly possible in a limited sense using traditional techniques of observation and analysis; with GIS, however, they can be documented (or refuted!) more thoroughly and confidently, with data on a regionwide scale.

A battery of techniques is now being tested for potential application to archaeological data; many of these involve the use of statistics. Locational models—along with exchange and other social systems models—have often been fruitfully subjected to **computer simulation studies,** for development and testing of hypotheses. Simulations allow archaeologists, for example, to outline their models concerning ancient resource requirements (such as water supplies and fertile soils), subsistence systems, population growth rates, and the like, and then ask the computer to indicate how the settlement landscape would look after a given amount of time, usually multiple centuries, under the provisions of the model. If the computer is also told about transformational processes leading to site destruction, archaeologists can assess how closely the known, modern site distribution approximates that predicted by the model. Using such an approach, David Clarke showed that the distribution of Danubian sites of the fifth millennium B.C. was similar to that projected by simulation when the model assumed that farmers, practicing shifting cultivation, moved their settlements at regular time intervals but randomly in space, within the zone of the best soils. Other simulations have allowed archaeologists to study conditions under which central places arise in a given landscape. More recently, Ezra Zubrow and Kathleen Allen have used GIS capabilities to simulate, respectively, European colonization and exchange networks in early historic New York. In general, the greatest value of these simulations is that they allow the analyst to incorporate large amounts of complex information and to manipulate that information experimentally.

They are also nondestructive. If the actual archaeological record were subjected to experiment, models and hypotheses could be tested only with new data collection. With simulations, however, the archaeologist can alter the working assumptions of his or her interpretations repeatedly, asking the computer each time to indicate what the product (settlement distribution or whatever) would be, until the simulated result most closely matches the observed archaeological remains.

POPULATION RECONSTRUCTION

In previous contexts we have noted that population figures may be important indices of such things as degree of urbanization, or they may serve as a check on the feasibility of a reconstructed model of an ancient subsistence system. Population estimates are derived from archaeological data in a number of ways. One is to estimate possible population from carrying capacity figures. This gives an approximation of population size—but, since it is based on carrying capacity estimates, the resulting figure cannot be used to "check" the feasibility of carrying capacity calculations.

Most reconstructions of population size and density have relied on settlement data. Specific approaches have included measures or counts of floor space, dwellings, middens, site areas, and available sleeping space. Perhaps the two most common approaches are dwelling counts and measurements of floor space. In the former, houses are identified and counted; then the archaeologist calculates the average family size per house and multiplies this figure by the number of houses, to compute the population size. The figure for average family size is obtained from local ethnographic or historical descriptions. Although the method is simple, demonstrating the appropriateness of the household size number presents a formidable difficulty. It can also be difficult—but no less necessary—to establish which houses were occupied at the same time.

One of the most frequently discussed means of estimating prehistoric population is Raoul Naroll's "floor space" formula. Compiling information from the Human Relations Area Files, an indexed compendium of ethnographic data from all over the world, Naroll found that in his sample of 18 societies, roofed space averaged 10 m^2 per person. This figure has been used to reconstruct ancient population figures in a variety of archaeological situations, but it has not, of course, gone without criticism. For instance, Polly Wiessner has suggested that the appropriateness of *any* constant figure should be reexamined. Personal space requirements, she asserts, are not likely to be the same among hunters and gatherers as among urban dwellers, and roofed space may not adequately reflect the space needs of people who spend the majority of their time outdoors. Using data from modern !Kung Bushman camps, for example, she calculates about 5.9 m^2 per person within the camp area as a whole; the amount of roofed space per person would be even smaller. Furthermore, within complex societies especially, wealthier folk tend to occupy more spacious

Estimating ancient population sizes: Ethnographic and archaeological approaches

homes than do their poorer neighbors, so that using a single figure to calculate space needs for the whole society may be inappropriate.

A logical offshoot of Naroll's work has been the calculation of sleeping space, which is a portion of total roofed space. Richard E. W. Adams has used this approach to compute the size of elite populations at the Maya site of Uaxactún, Guatemala, and René Millon has used it in his population estimates for the urban site of Teotihuacan, Mexico. Whatever approach is used, the critical factors in population reconstruction are, first, how precisely the archaeologist can measure the physical population index—floor space, number of dwellings, or whatever—and, second, how reliable a multiplier can be produced to convert the archaeological materials into counts of people.

Another approach to estimate ancient population is extrapolation from burial populations. The problem with this approach, however, is that excavated samples of human burials are seldom representative of the entire population, either statistically or demographically. And, even if they were, burial populations constitute the *accumulation* of dead persons over the period of occupation of the settlement, not just a census of the living populace at one point in time. When these qualifications are kept in mind, burial populations can provide valuable insights into ancient population size and structure. In fact, with the growth of "social archaeology," burials have won widespread attention as a unique source of evidence about ancient social organization.

SOCIAL IMPLICATIONS FROM BURIALS

Discoveries of ancient human remains have always attracted attention and interest, and burials are among the most widely known kinds of archaeological features. Analysis of these features has traditionally focused on their reflection of funerary customs and religious beliefs concerning death and the existence of an afterlife. This kind of study assumed central importance when variations among graves and their contents came to be viewed as indices of the social standing of the occupants during their lifetimes. It is obvious that elaborate and richly endowed tombs, such as those of Egypt's Pharaoh Tut-ankh-amun (Fig. 1.2, p. 11), Maya Tikal's Ah Cacau, or China's Emperor Qin (Fig. 1.1, p. 9), reflect the tremendous wealth and power of their occupants. But archaeologists such as Arthur Saxe, James Brown, Joseph Tainter, and Lewis Binford argued that the inferences made in these cases could be applied more broadly. That is, the range and social importance of an individual's roles and positions during life should be represented in the form and content of his or her interment. The effort (and other resources) spent in preparing and furnishing an interment should reflect the social rank of the individual. Considered as wholes, then, cemeteries and other burial grounds ought to serve as guides to ancient social structure.

Reconstructing social hierarchies from burials: Peebles and Kus at Moundville, Alabama

The most widely treated topic in this area continues to be reconstruction of social ranking. Studies of this type are best known for societies with marked social hierarchies. For example, in prehistoric North America, Christopher Peebles and Susan Kus have described analyses of more than 2000 burials from Moundville, Alabama, a major ceremonial center of Mississippian culture between about A.D. 1200 and A.D. 1500. From Peebles's computer-aided statistical analyses, they defined 12 groups of burials, which together indicated pronounced and hierarchical social ranking.

Cluster Ia consisted of seven individuals—all adults and probably all male—who were interred in the principal mound at the site. They were accompanied by the most elaborate, exotic, and therefore expensive goods found with any of the burials. These included axes made from imported, cold-hammered copper, which were rare items and perhaps used as symbols of office. The next most elaborate grave goods, still including some imported copper, were found with 110 individuals (Clusters Ib and II). When sex of adults could be established, these too were males, and the presence of children in this group suggests that whatever prestige or status it involved was **ascribed** (inherited) rather than **achieved** (earned during the individual's lifetime)—those who die as children usually have not lived long enough to achieve much status or prestige. Members of Clusters Ib and II were all buried in slightly less central positions. Somewhat more peripherally placed were another 251 men, women, and children (Clusters III and IV) who were buried in cemeteries near mounds. They were laid to rest with some fancy and imported goods, such as worked shell, but with nothing nearly as elaborate as those of Clusters Ia, Ib, and II. An additional 341 people (Clusters V–X) had simple bowls, jars, or even sherds as burial goods, and their graves were in increasingly distant areas. Finally, 1256 individuals were buried with no grave offerings at all—and sometimes apparently as sacrifices. The composite picture gained from this evidence is one of a social pyramid, with power and access to exotic resources vested in the hands of a very few, while, among other ranks, the greater the number of people in the rank, the fewer the resources at their command and, implicitly, the lower the rank (Fig. 15.13).

Rothschild and King study social ranking in ancient nomadic and sedentary societies

Analyses, by archaeologists such as Nan Rothschild and Thomas F. King, have shown that social distinctions may also be detected in the burial populations of societies generally thought to be more simply organized—and that perhaps the simplicity of their organization has been overdrawn. Rothschild examined the Mississippian cemetery site of Dickson Mounds, Illinois (ca. A.D. 1100–1250), and compared it with remains from the **Archaic** site of Indian Knoll, Kentucky (ca. 4150–2550 B.C.). Part of her intent was to test the idea that the earlier, Archaic society, with a mobile, hunting and gathering way of life, should have had a much simpler social structure, making many fewer and less elaborate social distinctions among its members, compared with the later, sedentary, agriculturalist Mississippians. For each site, burials totaled more than 1000, but examination focused on those with multiple grave goods—in each case,

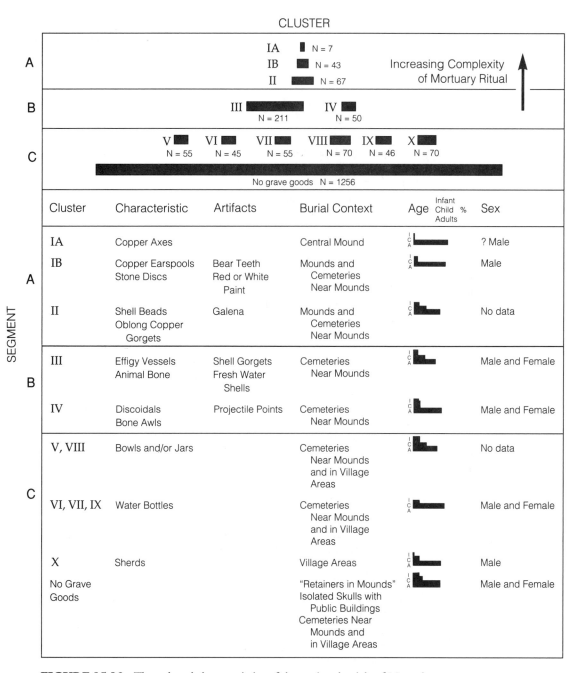

FIGURE 15.13 The cultural characteristics of the ancient burials of Mound-ville, Alabama, form distinct clusters that, taken together, define a social pyramid with few individuals at the top and increasing numbers at successively lower social ranks. (After Peebles and Kus 1977. Reproduced by permission of the authors and the Society for American Archaeology from *American Antiquity* 42:3, 1977.)

more than 680. Rothschild's statistical analyses confirmed significant differences between the two burial populations in the directions predicted. But Indian Knoll was not as thoroughly egalitarian, nor Dickson as completely hierarchical, as expected. In particular, for Indian Knoll, grave goods distinguished two social groups, perhaps ranked with respect to one another. And the presence of children in both groups suggests that membership was ascribed.

Prehistoric California Indians, too, were hunters and gatherers and are widely considered to have had egalitarian societies, lacking social ranking. But excavations at the 2000-year-old site Mrn–27 at Tiburon Hills, on the edge of the San Francisco Bay, yielded 44 burials whose distribution and grave goods suggest quite the contrary interpretation. Thomas King describes the findings as providing "strong evidence for social ranking":

> The cemetery was small but highly structured, consisting of a central cremation area containing very large quantities of nonutilitarian artifacts [in fact, 62 percent of total grave goods from the cemetery], an encircling group of male burials without associations, and a loose outer cluster of males and females with few artifacts, plus a few anomalies. The rich central area contained almost equal numbers of males, females, and children [the latter again suggesting ascribed status and inherited membership in the high-ranked group]. (King 1978:228)

These examples, from quite distinct and diverse societies, illustrate how both the contents and the collective arrangements of burials can be taken to indicate social structure. But interpretation is not always so straightforward. Initial optimism about the directness with which burials could be used to reconstruct social organization has been tempered by more critical assessments. Robert Chapman and Klavs Randsborg have summarized development of the more cautious perspectives. For instance, we know from ethnographic accounts that distinct segments of some societies are given final rites that do not involve actual burial (such as placing the corpse in a tree) and therefore do not leave graves or other common mortuary traces. And sometimes what appear to be contemporary differences in funerary treatments—and thus social differences—actually point to changes in practices through time. For these and other reasons, the archaeologist must be alert to the behavioral and transformational processes behind formation of a given series of burials and aware of what sample of the whole population is represented by the burials examined.

Human burials, of course, consist of more than graves and grave goods. Their main component (whether or not it has been preserved very well!) is the skeleton or other physical remains of an individual, and such remains provide other and unique kinds of information about the deceased. Some of these were outlined in Chapter 11, and one example there—from the Maya site of Tikal, Guatemala—indicated how systematic differences in physical stature of the skeletons correlated with richness of burial. That is, individuals buried in elaborate tombs were taller, and presumably better fed, than those found in simpler, poorer graves. Once again, those with access to better resources in life had richer resources lavished on them at death.

Jane Buikstra has argued that health profiles and other inferences from skeletal data can be adequately interpreted only by knowing where the sample fits within the overall population and range of burial practices. For example, she discusses the 25 individuals recovered from excavations at the Koster site, in the lower Illinois valley, and the 28 from Modoc rock shelter, farther south in Illinois. Each sample represents 3000 years of occupation in the Middle Archaic period (ca. 6000–3000 B.C.) and is clearly minuscule in proportion to the number of people who must have occupied the site. Moreover, each sample is heavily weighted toward individuals with pathological deformities, including imperfectly healed fractures, arthritis, and signs of interrupted bone growth (Harris lines) attributed to periods of stressfully poor nutrition. These pathologies have been interpreted by some as evidence of the "hard life" these Archaic gatherers and hunters must have lived. But Buikstra argues that the age distribution of the two skeletal series suggests (even more strongly than do the small sizes of the samples) that remains from Koster and Modoc are biased samples of the whole original population. They consist principally of older individuals (commonly afflicted with arthritis) and younger ones who had, perhaps, particular disabilities—in either case, individuals presumably incapable of performing a normal range of activities. She then makes an intriguing comparison with the partly contemporary Gibson site, a cemetery near Koster, containing primarily young and middle-aged adults of both sexes—and all lacking pathological problems, from either age or accident. The contrast and complementarity with Koster and Modoc is clear, for both health and age profiles. Buikstra therefore suggests, tentatively, that the physical afflictions of individuals interred in the Koster and Modoc sites do not point to hard times for the whole society. Rather, they are clues that distinctions were made in burial practices: Handicapped individuals were laid to rest in residential areas, whereas those capable of performing the full range of customary activities were buried in spatially distinct cemeteries. Infants and small children—unrepresented in any of the cited samples—may have been interred in still another (as yet undiscovered) setting. The point is that although human remains themselves yield unique and important information, that information can be interpreted only within the context of the society's mortuary customs and only by considering how the sample of individuals likely relates to the social and demographic whole from which they came.

Buikstra's study of sampling effects on reconstruction of ancient health status from burials

EVIDENCE OF SOCIAL GROUPINGS

The final aspect of reconstructing social behavior that we will consider here is the attempt to correlate artifact classes to specific social units, such as kin groups. Based on inferences similar to those used to define ancient activity groups and households, this approach seeks to link patterns in single or multiple artifact classes to identification of distinct social groups.

Ceramic Sociology

James R. Sackett coined the term **ceramic sociology** to describe social reconstruction based on pottery classification. Especially in the southwestern United States and southwest Asia, aspects of ceramic style have been analyzed to define the different social groups within a community that were responsible for pottery production. To paraphrase Sackett, the underlying assumption is that since standards and styles of pottery manufacture are socially transmitted, the social group within which such standards are taught should produce a consistent and recognizable style of pottery that can be distinguished from the styles produced by other, equivalent groups. In Chapter 10, in discussing the type-variety-mode approach to pottery classification, we noted a similar point: that the pottery types recognized by this classificatory method are believed to represent the products of discrete social groups. Most of what Sackett refers to as ceramic sociology, however, has dealt not with pottery types (or more inclusive classificatory units) but with the distributional study of individual design elements or stylistic modes.

Ceramic sociology studies: Deetz, Longacre, and Hill

The most cited studies under this heading are the pioneer analyses of James Deetz, William A. Longacre, and James N. Hill. Deetz was working with sites and pottery from the Arikara area of South Dakota; Longacre and Hill both worked in Arizona, at the sites of Carter Ranch and Broken K, respectively. All three scholars studied associations and co-occurrences of pottery design motifs to define the existence of the pottery-producing groups. In Deetz's study, the dissolution of recognizable styles through time was taken as indicative of the breakup of (family) production units: The distinctive styles had dissolved because communication and mutual reinforcement among the potters had been disrupted. Robert Whallon has made a similar analysis of prehistoric pottery in the Iroquois area. In the Southwest, Hill and Longacre studied the distribution of motifs with regard to provenience units of the pottery. The potters were believed, by ethnographic analogy, to have been groups of women; within these groups, pottery technology and standards were passed down from mother to daughter. From this premise, the correlation of distinctive pottery styles with particular sectors of the site was argued to reflect residential divisions in which several generations of women would remain together throughout their lives.

This approach has received many criticisms, both from archaeologists and from sociocultural anthropologists. Matters eliciting specific critiques ranged from the assumptions by which material data were connected to social attributes, to the methods of data collection and analysis, to consideration of the contexts from which the analyzed sherds came. For example, is there evidence that the potters were exclusively women and that they learned their stylistic preferences from no one but their mothers? Were all the ceramics studied made and used in the same household (or even the same community) in which the archaeologist found them? Despite these questions, few have suggested that the baby be thrown out with the bathwater. Rather, archaeologists have chosen to refine the analytic approach so that it may realize its potential for reconstructing aspects of prehistoric social organization. Ethnoarchaeological studies, in particular, are helping in that refinement by examining modern processes of pottery production, design sharing, innovation, and the like.

Ancient Assertions of Social Identity

Ethnoarchaeologists are also among those deeply involved in developing means to distinguish ethnic, religious, or other self-consciously proclaimed social identities. Traditionally, archaeologists have used pottery (or other artifact) type distributions as keys for identifying ethnic and other such groups. But actually plotting material cultural distributions for multiple kinds of artifacts found in the same general area shows that the limits of the plots are frequently different for different items. When this is done for artifacts used by modern societies, the materials are often poor indicators of known social boundaries. This finding does not negate the fact that such groups exist: Certainly most people have many identities—all at the same time—as members of national, linguistic, religious, ethnic, occupational, and other groups. The issue, archaeologically, is determining when these identities are likely to be proclaimed to others, what kinds of material items are probable media for identity statements, and how archaeologists can recognize those items.

Social groups often develop distinctive means of identifying themselves, to set themselves clearly apart from other groups with whom they are competing for resources. As a simple example, consider uniforms on sports teams: Wearing distinctive styles and vivid colors allows members of each team to easily distinguish "us" from "them," a key ingredient in scoring more points (the resources) and thereby winning. Individuals or groups also use emblems noncompetitively, to assert or emphasize their belonging to a larger group, for example, when they proudly wave a national flag in a local parade.

H. Martin Wobst has made the argument somewhat more generally: Distinctive costuming and other such readily visible cues make social interaction easier, allowing one to distinguish friend from foe and differentiating people who probably share one's values from those who hold contrasting beliefs. The more pronounced the contrasts, the more valuable the availability of visible distinctions. Hairstyles and clothes, for instance, have been effective clues to recent social identities among young people in our society, from hippies to preppies to punk rockers.

How do these ideas apply to archaeology? To answer that question, and

Contemporary and ancient indicators of social identity: The Kalahari San and Classic Maya

to seek ways of identifying ancient social groups, archaeologists have examined the social uses of style. Ethnoarchaeologists, such as Polly Wiessner and Ian Hodder, have sought to discover what kinds of artifacts and features carry information on social identity and how that information is conveyed. Wiessner found, for example, that uniformities in arrow styles among the Kalahari San of Botswana helped identify the users as well-adjusted, nondisruptive members of the local society. In San society, where cooperation and solidarity are valued and individualism is disruptive, these expressions of sharing an identity can be quite important.

Taking an ancient example—the Classic Maya—we can discern several material means by which identity was asserted. Archaeologists have long recognized striking uniformities over space and time in Maya material culture. Corbel-vault (false arch) architecture, sculptured stone monuments (stelae) with hieroglyphic inscriptions, and particular kinds of polychrome painted pottery are among the hallmarks usually cited. Two things are noteworthy concerning these attributes as a whole: They all pertain to the elite of this highly hierarchical society, and they are all publicly visible, at least to other members of the elite. The architecture and sculpture were located in prominent civic settings (see Fig. 5.6, p. 163). Even the pottery involved forms used in elite gift giving or, sometimes, serving food or drink on ritual occasions. When settlement archaeology led to expanding investigation of the whole economic range of society, it became increasingly clear that the material cultural uniformities defined an elite culture only. The commoners governed by this elite were associated with considerably greater variation in material culture through space and time. It seems, therefore, as David Freidel, Edward Schortman, and others have argued, that the Maya elite used these highly visible material styles as emblems proclaiming their membership in this select segment of a far-flung and otherwise diversified society.

Emblems can thus be considered symbols of group membership. Symbols are shorthand means of communicating often complicated ideas, and social identity is only one of an infinity of subjects that can be expressed symbolically. The use of symbol systems and their reconstruction archaeologically are broad topics, launching the discussion of ideological systems—the subject of Chapter 16.

SUMMARY

The reconstruction of past social systems has received growing attention from archaeologists in recent years. There are a number of ways by which clues to ancient social organization and structure may be sought. In this chapter we singled out several particular approaches.

Exchange systems are the means by which human societies gain access to nonlocal goods and services. Trade may be either reciprocal—direct exchange—or redistributive, in which goods are initially brought to a central location before disbursal to consumers. To reconstruct ancient trade, archaeologists must first recognize which goods are not local and thus represent exchanges with other places. Exotic ecofacts are identified as such when they are beyond their natural habitat or source area. Imported artifacts may be pinpointed by several means, including stylistic analysis and study of chemical composition, that show an item to be "out of place." Models for exchange systems have been derived from several perspectives, including spatial plots of the presence/absence of imported materials relative to sources, and quantitative study of abundance of these goods in different locations.

Settlement archaeology studies the spatial distribution of ancient human activities and occupation, at scales ranging from a single room to the sites throughout a region. Household archaeology has developed recently to study these fundamental units of society, in part as microcosms of the workings of society at large. Archaeologists also analyze individual nondomestic buildings and work areas. The layouts of whole communities are studied to determine how these different settlement scales indicate social status, economic specialization, and the like. At the most inclusive settlement scale, archaeologists examine how the multiple sites of a region testify to the social structure of the people who once lived there. Many models for understanding regional settlement systems have been derived from economic geography, and in using these and other approaches, archaeologists frequently turn to computers and statistics, prominently including GIS, as analytic tools.

Settlement archaeology also provides one of several avenues for reconstruction of the size and density of ancient populations. Estimates of carrying capacity furnish one means toward this end. At least as frequently, archaeologists use counts of some unit (house remains or square meters of floor space), estimate how many people are represented by each of the units, and then multiply the number of contemporary units by the estimated conversion factor. None of these methods is without problems, but when used cautiously and appropriately, each can offer insights into ancient demography.

Human burials are sometimes used for population size and density reconstruction, but in recent years they have served most often as the source of inferences regarding social structure. The basic assumption is that the effort invested in mortuary practices reflects the social standing of the deceased during life. Obviously, kings and emperors receive vastly more elaborate interments than do most of the rest of their societies. But even within supposedly egalitarian societies, some social differences can be detected by examination of burial data. Many analyses focus on the form of the grave and the grave goods or offerings, but characteristics of the skeletal remains themselves often yield insights on social distinctions.

Artifact analyses have been used to identify kin and other groups within ancient society. "Ceramic sociology" is the name given to studies that have attempted to distinguish kin groups by styles in pottery production.

Archaeological interest in other kinds of social identities—ethnic, religious, and the like—has led to reconsideration of the social uses of style; researchers are studying when people deliberately proclaim affiliation with particular social categories and how such proclamations may be recognized archaeologically.

GUIDE TO FURTHER READING

Binford and Binford 1968; Burnham and Kingsbury 1979; Claasen 1991a; Conkey and Spector 1984; Costin 1991; Gero 1991; Gero and Conkey 1991; Hill and Gunn 1977; Jackson 1991; McGuire 1991; Nelson 1991; Redman et al. 1978; Renfrew 1984; Trigger and Longworth 1974

Exchange Systems

R. M. Adams 1974; Bishop, Rands, and Holley 1982; Bray 1973; Cann and Renfrew 1964; Earle and Ericson 1977; Ericson and Earle 1982; Fry 1980; Harbottle 1982; Hirth 1984; Johnson 1973; Luckenbach, Holland, and Allen 1975; Polanyi, Arensburg, and Pearson 1957; Rands and Bishop 1980; Renfrew 1969, 1975; Sabloff and Lamberg-Karlovsky 1975; Wilmsen 1972

Settlement Archaeology

Aldenderfer 1991; Allen, Green, and Zubrow 1990; Aronoff 1989; Bawden 1982; L. R. Binford 1973; Binford and Binford 1966; Blanton 1976; Bordes and de Sonneville-Bordes 1970; Carr 1984; Chang 1958, 1968, 1972; Christaller 1933; Clarke 1972b, 1977; Crumley 1979; Crumley and Marquardt 1987, 1990; Cunliffe 1978; Flannery 1972b; Flannery and Marcus 1976a; Fox 1922; Hammond 1974; Haviland 1981, 1986; Hietala 1984; Hodder 1978a, 1978b; Hodder and Hassall 1971; Hodder and Orton 1976; Johnson 1972; Keatinge and Day 1974; Kent 1984, 1987, 1990; Kvamme 1989; MacNeish 1974; Madry and Crumley 1990; Millon 1973; Moseley and Mackey 1974; Parsons 1972; C. Renfrew 1973a, 1973b, 1983b, 1984; Sabloff 1981; Shimada 1978; Steward 1938, 1955; Trigger 1968b; Ucko, Tringham, and Dimbleby 1972; Whallon 1973, 1974, 1984; Whiting and Ayres 1968; Wilk and Ashmore 1988; Wilk and Rathje 1982; Willey 1953, 1956, 1983; Williams et al. 1985

Population Reconstruction

R.E.W. Adams 1974, 1981; Culbert and Rice 1990; Dickson 1980, 1981; Hassan 1978, 1981; Naroll 1962; Schacht 1981; Webster 1981; Wiessner 1974

Social Implications from Burials

Bartel 1982; Benson 1975; L. R. Binford 1971; Brown 1971, 1975, 1981; Buikstra 1981a; Chapman, Kinnes, and Randsborg 1981; Chapman and Randsborg 1981; Haviland 1967; T. F. King 1978b; O'Shea 1984; Peebles and Kus 1977; Rothschild 1979; Saxe 1971; Tainter 1978; Winters 1968

Evidence of Ancient Social Groupings

Allen and Richardson 1971; Conkey and Hastorf 1990; Davis 1985; DeAtley and Findlow 1984; Deetz 1965, 1968; Dumond 1977; Freidel 1979; Gifford 1960; Green and Perlman 1985; Hill 1966, 1970; Hodder 1978b, 1982b; Longacre 1970a, 1981; McGuire 1991; Plog 1978b, 1980, 1983; Pollock 1983; Sackett 1977, 1982; Schortman 1986, 1989; Shennan 1989; Stanislawski 1973; Trinkaus 1986; Watson 1977; Whallon 1968; Wiessner 1983, 1984; Wobst 1977

CHAPTER SIXTEEN

IDEOLOGICAL AND SYMBOL SYSTEMS

> If archaeologists want to understand cultural evolution . . . [they] cannot continue to treat ideology as static or passive. We must recognize that ideology can be a dynamic force, and we must seek new generalizations about its role in culture change.
>
> *Geoffrey W. Conrad and Arthur A. Demarest,* Religion and Empire, *1984*

The final dimension of archaeological **synthesis,** ideology, comprises a broad range of human behavior. But, because ideology is concerned with the nonmaterial realm of ideas, it is obviously the most difficult area about which to make inferences based on material remains. **Ideological systems** are the means by which human societies codify beliefs about both the natural and the supernatural worlds. Through ideology, people structure their ideas about the order of the universe and their place in that universe. They also specify the structure of their relationships with each other and with things and beings around them. Ideology is often equated with religion, but religious ideologies—dealing with the belief systems that underlie formal religions—are only one part of the ideological realm. A given society may manifest technological, social, political, and economic ideologies as well. As a consequence, a broader term—**cognitive archaeology**—is often used to encompass the study of these idea systems.

Until recently archaeologists have given scant attention to ideology, primarily for two reasons. First, since the traditional foundation of archaeology is material remains, it has often been assumed that the realm of ideas lay beyond the reach of archaeological inquiry. Second, ideologies, especially religious ideologies, usually have been viewed as conservative forces, explaining and justifying the status quo and therefore resistant to changes within a society. They are thus seen as passive and certainly not causes of cultural change. Because archaeology emphasizes the study of cultural change, ideology was not considered a productive area of investigation. In fact, it has often been assumed that ideology could be safely ignored, because it is both difficult to deal with and not important to the concerns of archaeology. Although the difficulty of inquiry into past ideologies remains, it is increasingly clear that ideology plays a significant role in cultural processes. In fact, as we have seen (Chapter 3), postprocessual archaeology argues that ideology, not technology, is the driving force within cultural systems.

For all these reasons archaeological interest in past ideological systems has greatly expanded in recent years. Today most would agree that if ancient ideologies are ignored, our **interpretation** of the past will be woefully biased and incomplete. Recent studies by archaeologists and allied scholars have documented how ideological systems help steer the course of ancient societies, by structuring daily activities and by contributing actively to both cultural stability and cultural change. The best evidence for these conclusions comes from cases documented by ethnographic, ethnohistorical, and historical data, counteracting the problem of reconstructing ideological systems from material remains alone. In fact, as we shall see, one of the avenues to the reconstruction of past ideologies is through the interpretation of symbolic systems and the decipherment of ancient notations and writing. Reconstructing idea systems for prehistoric cultures is rather more difficult, but it is still possible. In attempting to do so, archaeologists are especially concerned to seek an emic perspective, and not impose their own belief and value systems on these ancient societies.

In this chapter we will consider both areas of archaeological concern in dealing with ancient ideology. We will begin by looking at some of the approaches used to reconstruct ideologies from material remains and then turn our attention to the role of ideology in cultural change.

RECOGNIZING AND ANALYZING SYMBOLS

Ideologies are expressed most commonly through symbols. *Symbols* are elements that stand for something else, and more important, the relationship between the symbol and what it stands for is arbitrary. There is no necessary or obvious relationship between a yellow ribbon and an absent loved one, for example; yet, we have come to use such ribbons symbolically to tell others—including those loved ones when they return—that we care and want them back. Symbols are thus shorthand ways of conveying messages about often complex subjects. It is the arbitrariness and usual complexity that make symbols both rewarding to study and difficult to interpret, especially in the archaeological record.

Not all symbols are material, but many are. For example, singing one's national anthem and saluting one's national flag are symbols of patriotism that leave no archaeological trace. But the national flag itself is a material item, an artifact, and does leave a trace. The flag of the United States, for example, is a symbol that communicates many messages to the country's citizens, including not only patriotism but also a reminder of the 13 original colonies (the stripes), today's 50 states (the stars), and the nation as a whole and its political ideology (ideals of freedom, democracy, and so on). Like the Statue of Liberty or the White House, the flag is a material item that has come to stand for a complex of ideas. As a material symbol identified with the United States, it becomes the shorthand "stand-in" in expressions—from Veterans' Day parades to embassy flag burnings—of attitudes and feelings about the larger entity it symbolizes.

Ancient ideologies, too, were expressed by symbols and are preserved through material symbols. The difficulty in reconstructing past ideologies lies not in discovering those symbolic representations but in recognizing them as such and in assigning them an appropriate meaning. We have

Symbols and material symbols: National flags

already mentioned that archaeologists commonly divide artifacts into utilitarian and nonutilitarian or ceremonial classes. The latter category, although it appears to offer the kind of information needed to reconstruct ideologies, too often becomes simply a catchall for forms whose utility is not immediately apparent.

Some theoretical perspectives predispose archaeologists to look for symbols. A postprocessual approach, for example, leads archaeologists to define ancient cultures as meaningful constructions and worldviews, and therefore to view almost any part of the archaeological record as symbol-laden. Postprocessualists then adopt one or another specific method (see below) to identify and interpret meaning from the record.

A widely used guide to reconstruct past symbol systems involves information theory, in which (as we saw in Chapter 15) use of a particular style symbolically identifies group membership (Fig. 16. 1). In this view, some stylistically endowed artifacts and features are more likely than others to convey symbolic information; these are usually specifiable items, such as buildings, clothing, or jewelry, that are most visible to members of other groups. The problem here is that once some such items are identified as having symbolic content, other elements in the culture tend to be presumed to have such content also—as Martin Wobst has put it, they lose their "signalling innocence." As long as we keep this caution in mind, however, this and other perspectives provide a potential route to identifying symbols.

How do archaeologists recognize symbols? There are a number of clues that suggest that some aspect of the archaeological record had symbolic function and meaning. The first and most obvious is depiction, in which, for example, an object of clay takes the form of a animal, or an image of a person is painted or carved on a surface. Sometimes these depictions are quite realistic to the archaeological observer, but the history of art teaches us that "realism" is relative to emic cultural contexts. More abstract depictions or decorations are sometimes clearly charged with symbolic meaning, as in writing and notation (see below); at other times, abstract forms are considered simply "decoration," with no inference of symbolic meaning. How, then, do we decide when there is such meaning and when there is not?

The answer is not simple, nor is there a straightforward recipe for recognition of symbols, although some formal methods, such as structural analysis, have been adopted from cultural anthropology and linguistics. Some methods of symbolic interpretation resemble techniques used in decipherment of ancient languages, such as cuneiform or Maya **hieroglyphs.** This is a form of structural analysis based on the identification of patterned substitutions, where alternative elements appear in the same or similar contexts. As we shall see in the Thule and Isbister examples below, such structural analysis allows identification of meaningful elements in the archaeological record as well.

In addition, an archaeologist will look for either repeated or markedly

FIGURE 16.1 The distinctive style of these young gymnasts' uniforms is a symbol identifying them as members of the same team. (Stock, Boston/© Spencer Grant.)

anomalous and (in either case) deliberate associations that lack evidence of technological, economic, or other kinds of justification. For example, painted pottery bowls of the Mimbres culture of New Mexico are frequently found with a hole broken through the bottom of the vessel (Fig. 16.2). Although many such bowls have been looted, those that have been recovered archaeologically suggest that they are usually associated with burials. The regularity of the existence and placement of the vessel holes, and the apparently systematic association of the bowls with ritual contexts, together suggest strongly that this pattern of breakage had symbolic meaning. (Inference of that meaning will be treated below.)

A different kind of example is McGhee's study of Thule culture, described in Chapter 3. This is an illustration of structural archaeology, in which a series of systematic associations define substitution sets, or instances in which one item can symbolically substitute or stand for another. Recall McGhee's observation that in this prehistoric Canadian culture, arrowheads were made of antler, whereas harpoons were made of ivory. Lacking a technological explanation for such mutually exclusive association of material and form, McGhee considered the possibility these were symbolic expressions. He observed that arrows were used in hunting terrestrial game; such game was, in turn, the source of the raw material—caribou antlers—used to make the arrows. In parallel fashion, ivory is a product of sea mammals and becomes the weapons (harpoons) used to hunt them. This example of structural analysis illustrates how symbol

Identification of symbols using structural analysis: McGhee and the Thule culture

FIGURE 16.2 The hole in the base of this beautifully painted Mimbres bowl may mark its ritual "killing" before having been placed in a grave. (Photo courtesy of Steven LeBlanc.)

candidates can be identified. Inferring the meaning of the symbols so identified requires a further step, to which we will now turn.

If an archaeologist has identified an instance of symbolic expression, how is he or she to infer the meaning of the symbol? Again we would note that the strongest inference of meaning, of emic significance, occurs in historical contexts, where there are written accounts indicating what the symbols stood for. The information from historical or ethnographic documentation can be extended back into the past using the direct historical approach (Chapter 3), providing a means for both identifying symbols and gaining an understanding of their meaning in some prehistoric situations. Certain human or animal depictions (or even abstract representations) may thereby be identified as symbolizing particular deities. Depictions of many of the pre-Columbian deities of Mesoamerica, found in archaeological contexts, can be identified by name, and their particular characteristics inferred, based on documents written at the time of the Spanish Conquest.

Using specific analogy to determine meaning: Mimbres and Thule

In other cases, specific analogy (Chapter 13) can suggest the meaning of a symbol. The Mimbres bowls mentioned above date to about A.D. 1000, and are probably too old to make a cultural connection using the direct historical approach, but the specific symbolic meaning for the vessel holes has been derived from analogy with known Native American practices, wherein objects owned by or intended as mortuary gifts for the deceased were themselves ritually "killed" before being placed in the grave. In the case of pottery, this ritual "killing" often takes the form of breaking or punching a hole in the vessel. In the Thule example, McGhee consulted ethnographic accounts of the modern Inuit descendants, and found that the structural contrasts and equivalents he had identified were tied to fundamental dichotomies in Inuit life. Ultimately he established symbolic structural associations equating arrowheads and antler with not only terrestrial animals but also summer activities and men; ivory and harpoons were similarly related to sea animals, winter, and women. Elements in what could be called the "land" domain were complementary to—structural counterparts of—elements in the "sea" domain, and together they served to organize the constituents of Inuit (and, by analogy, Thule) life into an orderly and meaningful whole.

There are also many instances, however, where establishment of an appropriate specific analogy is difficult or impossible. As we shall consider below, interpretations of Paleolithic cave paintings or figurines fall in this category, because we are so far removed in time and cultural context that we cannot confidently link Paleolithic cultures with any recent or modern counterparts. In such cases, archaeologists sometimes call on more general analogy, or on theoretical expectations. Treatment of artifact or feature styles as symbols of group identity is one example.

In a structural analysis similar to that in the Thule example, John W. Hedges identified prehistoric social symbols for different ancient groups in the Orkney Islands of Scotland. Initially, Hedges's inquiries focused on the Neolithic chambered tomb at Isbister, whose construction and use date to about 3200–2400 B.C. Over the centuries, more than 300 individuals had been interred in this communal tomb. Along with the human remains were 725 bones of various birds, as well as more than 1000 from other animals. Among the animal remains, the species represented, plus evidence of butchery, suggest that many represented either tomb offerings or traces of mortuary feasting. The birds, however, were a different story. Some 97 percent of their bones were not from species likely to have been eaten but, rather, from birds of prey. And of these, 90 percent were from one particular species, the white-tailed sea eagle.

Examining faunal remains found in other chambered tombs in the Orkneys, Hedges discovered that in several of these cases, as in Isbister, one kind of animal seemed uniquely prominent and that the highlighted creature usually differed from one tomb to another. At Quanterness, for example, the focus was on songbirds, and at Cuween and Burray dogs had received special attention. The communal tombs were, then, the substitution frame identified by the structural analysis, and the specific animals in each tomb were the alternative elements inferred to have symbolic meaning. To interpret the meaning, Hedges could not invoke specific analogy, since Neolithic Orkney society had no close cultural descendants. He could, however, draw on information theory (see Chapter 15 and the beginning of this chapter) and general analogy. That is, Hedges had already noted that the distribution of various artifact styles suggested division of Neolithic Orkney society into a number of distinct groups, and argued that the locations of the chambered tombs seemed to correspond to different social groups. He then pointed to a widespread custom in which social

Using general analogy to interpret social symbols: Tomb of the Eagles, Isbister, Orkney Islands

groups use animals as emblems, to identify themselves as distinct from others. For the Isbister site—aptly nicknamed the "Tomb of the Eagles" —Hedges cited this custom as a general analogy, suggesting that the eagles were the emblems or symbols of the people that had buried their dead in that place. By this reasoning, songbirds would have served the same role for the populace of Quanterness, and dogs for the people using Cuween and Burray.

Using general analogy to interpret ancient value systems: Indian Knoll, Kentucky

Another example involving general analogy is provided by analyses made by Howard Winters, especially as reconsidered recently by James Hill, concerning ancient value systems at Indian Knoll, on the Green River in western Kentucky. Indian Knoll is a site of the **Archaic** period, occupied about 2500–2000 B.C. To pursue his analyses, Winters examined several artifact classes from the site with respect to various attributes, including relative abundance, raw material source, contexts of discovery, and quality and elaboration of manufacture. Items of higher value were expected to be (1) less commonly available (and therefore more rarely found archaeologically), (2) made from imported and, implicitly, more "expensive" materials, (3) recovered from contexts associated with higher social status (such as elite burials), and (4) more elaborate and better made. On these bases, Winters was able to argue both that items such as conch shells and copper artifacts were highly valued in Indian Knoll society and that the full range of artifacts considered together defined at least one dimension of the ancient value system.

Having considered some of the ways archaeologists identify and interpret individual symbols, let us look more closely at some specific examples of reconstruction, and at some interpretive cautions they raise. We will examine instances of three kinds of symbols here: abstract and depictive material symbols, writing and other record-keeping systems, and, in a more general perspective, entire past worldviews.

ABSTRACT AND DEPICTIVE MATERIAL SYMBOLS

Ambiguity in symbol identification: Ucko and figurines

It is one thing to discover a symbolic representation and another to interpret its intended meaning correctly, especially when the age of the objects removes them from the plausible reach of analogy. For example, figurines of human females occur abundantly in the archaeological record, beginning as early as the Upper Paleolithic in Europe. Often these have been interpreted as "mother goddesses" or as symbols for human fertility (Fig. 16.3). Peter J. Ucko, however, has argued that no grounds exist for assuming that *all* female figurines served the same purpose or represented similar meanings. Some, especially those portrayed as pregnant, may indeed represent fertility symbols or mother goddesses, but others might simply be children's dolls. The contexts in which the figurines are found

FIGURE 16.3 These two Upper Paleolithic figurines from Lespugue, France (a) and Willendorf, Austria (b) are usually seen as symbols of female fertility. (Photo of casts of originals, courtesy of The University Museum, University of Pennsylvania.)

are potential clues in this regard. Similarly, ochre and other red pigments have been discovered in human burials in many prehistoric cultures, the oldest one associated with Neanderthal interments of the Middle Paleolithic. The common interpretation has been that the pigment was painted on the corpse to symbolize blood or warmth and was connected with beliefs about an afterlife for the deceased. These interpretations are not illogical, but we have no way of verifying them or affirming that all associations of red ochre with burials represent the same belief. Both of these examples, of figurines and pigment use, illustrate that archaeologists must guard against simply assuming the relevance of interpretive general analogies (see Chapter 13).

A parallel observation involves a concern discussed at some length in Chapter 3, but particularly germane in the study of symbol systems. That is, the archaeologist must always be alert to the danger of making the most "obvious" interpretation simply by imposing his or her own culture on

Emics and etics: San rock art

FIGURE 16.4 A San rock art scene that was traditionally interpreted as people crossing a bridge but has been reinterpreted as a curing ritual, based on ethnographic information. (After Lewis-Williams 1986 © 1986 by The Wenner-Gren Foundation for Anthropological Research, all rights reserved.)

interpretations of ancient ones. As an example, consider the rock art of southern Africa. The paintings come from areas once occupied by San hunter-gatherers. The San of today, who now reside in a much smaller area of Botswana and Namibia, have no surviving tradition of painting. The rock art, however, has been studied by a number of non-San analysts, and its scenes are frequently described as depictions of life among the ancestral San. The painting in Figure 16.4, for example, is commonly interpreted as individuals crossing a rope bridge, and the scene takes on further importance because it constitutes the sole evidence for this kind of bridge making among the San. J. D. Lewis-Williams argues, however, that what to Western eyes appears to be a bridge crossing is more likely a curing ceremony. Interpreted in the context of modern San culture, the scene contains painted elements that correspond well with San shamans' descriptions of such ceremonies viewed while in a trance. The individuals near the center have, in this view, gone into a trance: The lines above their heads represent their spirits leaving their bodies (as they are said to do), while the dashed lines in front of the chest of one of them symbolize an active nosebleed (a side effect of the trance state). Other traits characteristic of curing sessions include the clapping women at left and the bent sticklike implements (probably flywhisks) carried by several of the men. And the bridge? Lewis-Williams notes that, among other things, the heads of the spikes holding the rope ends are facing the wrong way to serve that purpose, and he suggests that the "bridge" represents instead two shamans facing each other with outstretched arms. The extreme length of the arms reflects a feeling of elongation of the limbs and the "hairs" are depictions

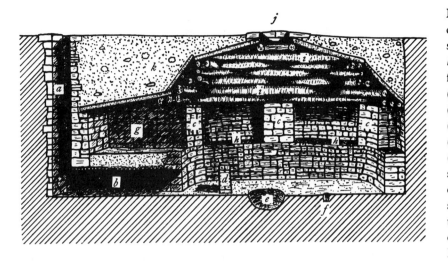

FIGURE 16.5 This cross-section view of a subterranean Puebloan *kiva* identifies several key features: (a, b) ventilator; (c) supporting pilasters; (d) air deflector to shield (e) the fire pit; (f) *sipapu;* (g) recessed area; (h) bench; (i) roofing; (j) smoke hole; (k) overlying earthen fill. (By permission of Smithsonian Institution Press from Bureau of American Ethnology, Bulletin 92, "Shabik'es-chee Village: A Late Basket Maker Site in the Chaco Canyon, New Mexico," by Frank H. H. Roberts. Smithsonian Institution, Washington, D.C., 1929.)

Symbols and analogy: The Pueblo kiva

of a tingling feeling, both commonly experienced in the trances. Whether or not Lewis-Williams's inferences are correct in all their details, his arguments point strongly to the importance of including consideration of the original cultural context when interpreting even what seem to be "obvious" representations from ancient life. How much more difficult it is, then, to identify and interpret more abstract or condensed symbolism.

Prehistoric ritual structures in the American Southwest provide a successful instance of such interpretation where religious ideology of modern Puebloan peoples was applied to interpretation of ancient architecture. The specific architectural form involved is the **kiva,** a kind of ceremonial chamber common to both modern pueblos and prehistoric Anasazi and Mogollon sites. The chamber as a whole is interpreted as a symbol for both the current Pueblo world and the story of its origin (Fig. 16.5). As described by Elsie Clews Parsons and other ethnographers (including Puebloans themselves), Hopi and other Puebloan peoples consider that the current world is the fourth in a series, and that passage from one to the next was accomplished by crawling through a hole in the sky in the older world—which was a hole in the earth of the next. In the kiva, this emergence hole is represented by a small hole or pit, called the *sipapu.* The floor is thus the earth, the walls of the usually circular chamber are the sky, and the domelike wooden roof is the galaxy or heavens above. In fact, for the people of Acoma pueblo, the word for galaxy means "beam above the earth." The hatchway through the roof serves as a smoke outlet as well as the door used by people. The ladder by which people enter and leave is equated symbolically with the rainbow, which likewise bridges earth and the heavens. The hatchway is also sometimes seen as another sipapu, through which people leave the primordial world of the kiva to enter the outside (actual fourth or current) world.

Material symbols can, of course, take the form of artifacts, ecofacts, or

Symbolic army buried with Emperor Qin, China

features. For example, pottery vessels and other artifacts might be deposited as a dedicatory cache before a building is constructed. Or a scepter and crown may symbolize a ruler's authority and power derived from supernatural sanctions. Symbolic use of ecofacts includes such ancient behavior as placing food offerings with the deceased, as provisions for an afterlife. Among the categories of archaeological data most frequently subject to symbolic interpretation are burial practices and mortuary goods. We have already noted the symbolic use of red ochre, and in Chapter 11 we described the use of flowers in at least one Neanderthal burial at Shanidar cave. Much attention has recently been focused on funerary practices as indices of social organization (Chapter 15). Among the social dimensions that have been so investigated are segregation of cemetery areas by rank or class, and reflection of wealth or occupational differences in assemblages of mortuary goods. Chiefs are often buried in areas separate from paupers, and grave goods in individual interments are frequently a gauge of the kinds of possessions the deceased had in life. Emperor Qin of China was buried with a full inventory of retainers, including an armed force—made of pottery, to be sure, but life-size and complete down to horse trappings and weapons. These are seen to be symbolic representations of his retinue in life, placed in his tomb to accompany him after death. Interestingly, Emperor Qin was apparently the first ruler in China to break with the tradition of sacrificing and burying human retainers; he appears to have chosen, rather, to be accompanied by life-size pottery figures as symbolic substitutes (Fig. 1.1, p. 9).

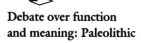

Debate over function and meaning: Paleolithic cave art

Although we have been discussing the symbolic use of artifacts, ecofacts, and features themselves, archaeologists also look for symbol and meaning in the decorations of artifacts and features. From the Paleolithic paintings in Lascaux cave to the abstractions of modern art, scholars have looked for meaning behind the human penchant for decorating things. Many of the cave paintings of the Upper Paleolithic had once been interpreted as symbols used in "sympathetic magic," a belief that depicting the images of animals acted to increase the abundance of game (Fig. 16.6). In addition, it was argued, the depiction of spears and arrows piercing the same animals assured the ancient hunters' success. In the 1960s, this functional view was largely replaced by the interpretations of symbolic meaning made by André Leroi-Gourhan. When he looked at sets of motifs rather than individual ones, Leroi-Gourhan identified what he believed were patterned scenes in structurally predictable locations, and argued that together these image assemblages reflected the underlying worldview of the Paleolithic people who created them. Peter J. Ucko and Andrée Rosenfeld, and more recently Margaret Conkey and Paul Bahn, have discussed such interpretations of these prehistoric paintings. They all contend that the paintings are too diverse and our links with Paleolithic peoples too tenuous for us to postulate a single framework for inferring meaning from cave art. Some of these paintings were obviously inaccessible, and thus may have been used for magic and ritual; others may have been the casual doodles of either adults or children. Pictorial symbols that are closer to

FIGURE 16.6 For over 100 years, scholars have sought the meanings that Upper Paleolithic cave paintings and sculptures may have had for the people who produced them. This view shows some of the beautiful paintings of Lascaux cave in southern France. (Reproduced from *Lascaux, A Commentary,* by Alan Houghton Brodrick, 1949, by permission of Ernest Benn Ltd., London.)

documented societies in time and space are more readily susceptible to interpretation. Once again, we see that consideration of the interpretive framework is absolutely critical.

WRITING, NOTATION, AND MEASUREMENT SYSTEMS

The most regularized codification of symbol systems is, of course, writing. And it is with writing that archaeologists enter the realm of historical documentation, vastly increasing the wealth of their interpretive resources. Writing systems were developed by many peoples all over the world, and not all have yet been deciphered. The scripts of the Indus and Maya civilizations are only now beginning to be "read" with any facility. The earliest writing in southwest Asia dates to at least 3500 B.C., and people were carving inscriptions in stone in Mesoamerica in the first millennium B.C. In both cases, the earliest records archaeologists have unearthed pertain to counting—in southwest Asia, to accounting records for business transactions, and in Mesoamerica, to counts of time.

The origins of Mesopotamian writing: Schmandt-Besserat's clay token hypothesis

Denise Schmandt-Besserat, for example, has argued that the distinctive *cuneiform* or wedge-shaped characters of ancient Mesopotamian writing are abstract renderings descended from earlier clay counters developed to keep track of business transactions. The clay tokens, found in great quantities at archaeological sites throughout southwest Asia, represented the number and kind of goods in a single sale or shipment. They were used by carefully sealing them in clay envelopes or *bullae* to guard against tampering. Useful as this system was, however, Schmandt-Besserat proposes that as the volume of commerce increased, this bulky record system was supplemented, first by pressing the tokens on the bullae, and later by depictions of the tokens impressed on clay tablets. Baking the tablets made these records tamperproof as well. In time this system of inscribing symbols on clay tablets evolved into cuneiform writing.

Paleolithic notation: Marshack's analyses

Notational systems seem to go back even further in time, perhaps 20,000 years earlier, according to the interpretations of Alexander Marshack. He decided to take a closer—indeed, microscopic—look at scratches and marks on Upper Paleolithic artifacts (Fig. 16.7). These marks had usually been ignored by previous analysts; in fact, they were sometimes left out of drawings of the artifacts because they were considered distracting! But Marshack detected regularity in such characteristics as the angle of nicking and the spatial patterning of groups of marks, and he has argued that these works might represent the beginnings of notational systems—the precursors of writing.

Marshack has further suggested that the subject of Upper Paleolithic notation was time, the passage of lunar months, seasons, or other observable time periods. This theme raises an area of archaeological inquiry that has seen a great deal of investigation in recent years—**archaeoastronomy,** or the study of ancient astronomical knowledge preserved in material remains. The most famous target of this concern has been the British site of Stonehenge (see Fig. 4.3, p. 117). As we noted in Chapter 12, astronomer Gerald Hawkins and others have argued that Stonehenge was constructed so that the alignments of its stones would chart the movements of the sun and other heavenly bodies through their seasonal cycles. Although some of Hawkins's specific claims have been disputed, and several dispelled, his widely popular book *Stonehenge Decoded* helped stimulate greater public as well as scientific interest in the study of ancient astronomies.

In recent years, a growing host of archaeological remains, from single

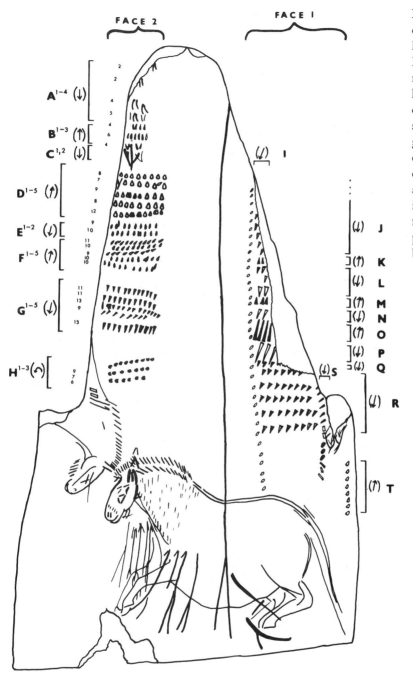

FIGURE 16.7 Alexander Marshack has postulated that some Upper Paleolithic engravings represent a form of record keeping. The notations on the La Marche bone, shown here, have been grouped (lettered brackets) according to differences in engraving tools and direction of engraving. (Marshack 1972, from *Science,* vol. 178, p. 822. Copyright 1972 by Alexander Marshack.)

buildings or other features to entire sites, has been identified as functioning, at least in part, as ancient astronomical observatories. Although such features are found throughout the world, most attention has focused on northwestern Europe and pre-Columbian America. The Maya, for example, have long been celebrated for their elaborate astronomical and calendrical records, and the Caracol of Chichén Itzá, Yucatán, and Group E at Uaxactún, Guatemala (see Fig. 12.10, p. 415), have been identified as probable observatories. Astronomer Anthony Aveni and others have reaffirmed the relation of these and other Maya constructions to ancient astronomical study. But, although the ancient Maya may have developed the most sophisticated astronomical and calendrical knowledge in pre-Columbian Mesoamerica, theirs was only one of multiple related traditions in that area.

Archaeoastronomy in North America: Big Horn Medicine Wheel, Cahokia, and Chaco Canyon

Ancient cultures of North and South America, too, left diverse traces of such traditions. In Chapter 12 we mentioned North American medicine wheel sites, such as the Big Horn Medicine Wheel in Wyoming. At Cahokia, in the Mississippi Valley across from St. Louis, Warren Wittry has identified postholes from a series of large circles of wooden posts, which he dubs "woodhenges." These circles range from 240 to about 480 feet in diameter, and Wittry believes they served as observatories, around A.D. 1000, for tracking the seasonal movement of the sun. Perhaps the greatest concentration and localized diversity of archaeoastronomical features in North America, however, is the set that has been identified in Chaco Canyon, New Mexico (Fig. 16.8), and associated (with varying degrees of certainty!) with its ancient Anasazi occupants of about A.D. 1000. Puebloan peoples today still charge one group member with daily observation of changes in the position of the sunrise, and a number of Chacoan sites may preserve earlier traces of this or related customs. In Pueblo Bonito, for example, there are several unusual corner windows in upper stories of the southeastern part of the apartmentlike site. They are believed to have served as sunrise observation stations (perhaps especially for the winter solstice), at which the observer either watched the sunrise through the window or noted where the light fell on the opposite wall within the room. At both Wijiji and Peñasco Blanco—located respectively at the east and west ends of the 15-km-long canyon—positions on the natural canyon rim that are best situated for observing winter solstice sunrise are also marked by sun symbols engraved on the rock face.

Many other sites, in the Americas and the Old World, contain archaeoastronomical evidence in varied forms, but time and the heavens were far from the only entities recorded by ancient peoples. They also kept track of more mundane events, as we have seen in the Mesopotamian clay token and cuneiform examples. Many societies have developed systems of standardized weights and measures to facilitate communication and efficiency in commercial transactions, building activities, and similar areas. Standardized weights have been recovered from sites in the Indus Valley, for example. Standard-sized bowls have been found at many sites in south-

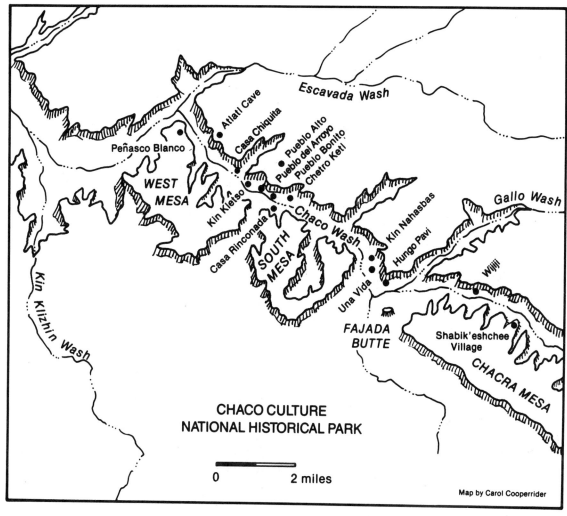

CHACO CULTURE
NATIONAL HISTORICAL PARK

0   2 miles

Map by Carol Cooperrider

FIGURE 16.8 Map of Chaco Canyon, New Mexico, showing sites mentioned in text. (Courtesy, School of American Research, map by Carol Cooperrider.)

west Asia and are interpreted as having been used for rationing uniform portions of food to day laborers. These kinds of evidence are, in effect, components of ancient recording systems and provide an insight into long-vanished cognitive frameworks.

Recording systems are obviously useful for more than counting or measuring. True writing systems provide the means for recording the full complexities of spoken languages. They are thus valuable to the archaeologist, since they have the potential to describe and record all aspects of human existence. Some specific early uses include accounts of the origins of the world and of human society. The Bible and the Epic of Gilgamesh record ancient and venerated ideologies about the nature of creation. Both ethnologists and archaeologists have begun to appreciate the wealth of descriptive social data contained in such accounts, including many details of daily life and social relationships as well as attitudes toward people, animals, and deities.

WORLDVIEWS

One of anthropology's most fundamental tenets is that there is no single, universal way of looking at the world. People of different cultures categorize their social and natural environment differently and hold different attitudes about raising children, burying the dead, respecting elders, extracting food from their surroundings, and so on. Through symbols, some of these beliefs are expressed concretely. But, as we have already argued, if archaeologists are to interpret prehistoric symbols, they must have some working model of the ancient ideology into which the symbols fit.

Roy Rappaport has described how ideological systems assure acceptance of social conventions or behavior. Each ideological system is composed of sacred propositions, or unchallenged beliefs or dogma, which guide and direct ritual, the activities that provide satisfying religious experiences. The inducement of religious experience in turn supports the original sacred propositions. Ideological systems sanctify, or provide a kind of noncoercive authority to, such things as rules of behavior, values, institutions, individuals, or even redistribution of goods and services. In applying this model to prehistoric Mesoamerica, Robert Drennan interprets various artifacts and features in the archaeological record as indications of the rituals used to sanctify and thus imbue with authority the institutions and offices associated with the rise of complex society. These ritual objects had several essential characteristics; they were exotic (derived from a distant source) and were therefore mysterious, or they incorporated shapes or symbols imbued with sacred meaning. As Mesoamerican society evolved, the institutions and offices intensified the rituals and the demand for ritual objects to support their authority, both of which led to concentrations of population in and around the ritual centers. Thus were born the first great population centers of Mesoamerica—the residences of the initial economic, political, and religious leaders who derived their authority from their own religious sanctity, their control over the ritual goods that expressed their power, and their conduct of rituals that provided religious experiences for the entire community, reinforcing their beliefs in the sacred propositions that were believed to govern the world.

The most reliable interpretations of symbols and worldviews, of course, can be made for situations in which ethnographic or historical records describe symbols *and* their meanings; next best are situations in which the ancient society is related to one for which there are such descriptions. The Puebloan kiva discussed earlier illustrated an interpretation of symbols through ethnographic information. Decipherment of the hieroglyphic writing of ancient Egypt has given us a richer and more reliable understanding of the symbolism and meaning incorporated in such items as funerary goods, the double crown of the pharaoh, and a sphinx. In any case, the key is to exercise caution and critical consideration of just what the evidence is for interpreting a symbol.

In Chapter 3 we described symbolic analyses by James Deetz and Henry Glassie of 18th- and 19th-century Anglo-American houses and their contents. As symbolic "guides" to worldview, houses and other forms of architecture have proved particularly intriguing subjects of study in a number of cultural settings. In Moslem Lamu, off the northern coast of Kenya, for instance, Linda Wiley Donley has outlined the arrangement of rooms and patterns of access between them. She has further shown how these combine with differential finishing, furnishing, and decoration in different rooms or stories and fortresslike construction of exteriors to symbolically remind owners, visitors, and resident slaves of the beliefs and values of the local version of Moslem Arab culture. In particular, purity and its protection are central concerns in Lamu. House architecture expresses this in several ways. It spatially isolates and thereby protects the purity of the freeborn women of the house. It also vividly segregates the servants from those being served and symbolically identifies the servants as possessions of the master by locating their living quarters with storage rooms, not other living quarters. Freeborn males are protected from contamination from various threatening activities—sexual intercourse, birth, preparation of corpses for burial, use of toilets—by confining these activities to tightly clustered and strictly bounded parts of the house and by placing charms, inscriptions, or other protective symbols at their entries (Fig. 16.9).

Comparable analyses have been made for houses in other cultures, and interpretations often portray the house as a compact description of the larger cosmos. We have described a similar situation for a ritual structure, the kiva of ancient and modern Pueblo culture—whose form (perhaps not incidentally) can be traced to earlier house forms. As for ritual structures more generally, social anthropologist Edmund Leach has asserted that essentially all the world's temples can be considered microcosms—material symbols expressing a culture's view of the universe in compact and condensed form. Indeed, many whole communities (and sometimes even multiple communities together) have been laid out, deliberately, as material descriptions of the cosmic order. Ancient Chinese cities, for example, were each established as a miniature version of the four-quartered world; each city, enclosed by its own wall, then became the center of the four quarters of the larger world—at least for its inhabitants and the supporting peasants living in the countryside beyond the wall.

John Fritz describes the cosmically guided organization of the 14th-century South Indian capital, Vijayanagara, and shows how this "cosmic map" helped reinforce the authority of the king. The residence of the king was in a grand compound just west of another monumental architectural

Worldview in Moslem Arab houses of East Africa: Donley's study of Lamu, Kenya

Worldview in Vijayanagara: Fritz's study of architecture, sculpture, and history

FIGURE 16.9 Seen now in the ruins of a Lamu house, this prayer niche was originally clearly marked as a holy place by its elaborate decoration and associated objects as well as by its distinctive shape. (After Donley 1982.)

compound that served as his official court. Just north of these two compounds, on the same north–south alignment as the wall separating them, was the temple to Rama, the divine Hindu hero-king. Sculptures on this and other public buildings depicted the king in his official duties and equated him symbolically with Rama. Likewise, the positioning of the palace, court, and temple linked the king spatially with this chief deity. On a larger spatial scale, these architectural monuments jointly defined the focus for the series of roads that encircled the city and for all the processions that passed along these roads. Documents of the period confirm the interpretations, for "inscriptions liken Vijayanagara to Rama's [divine] capital, Ayodha, . . . and contemporary literary texts enjoin kings to emulate the heroic activities of the Rama" (Fritz 1986:52). In all, the buildings, their arrangement, and their lavish sculptural decoration serve as powerful reminders of the authority of the king within this part of the Hindu world.

Use of material symbols to legitimate (and thereby support) authority is common in many complex societies, but again interpretation within a particular cultural context is critical. We noted Fritz's consultation of documentary descriptions as support for his reading of what the material symbols of Vijayanagara were meant to say.

A similar perspective has been proposed for ancient Maya sites, that is, that they were laid out as maps (or "cosmograms") of the universe as conceived by their inhabitants. Like Vijayanagara, most Maya settlements are too large for extensive excavation testing such propositions. Whereas Fritz and his colleagues used archaeological survey and historical data to explore the meaning of urban planning in southern India, the Copán North Group Project, one facet of a much larger program of investigations described in Chapter 5, chose excavation as a means to test one aspect of the meaning inferred for Maya city layouts. Specifically, two ruined masonry compounds were identified as marking "north" in the site plan, and were argued therefore to be a setting for activities the Maya associated with north, especially veneration of royal ancestors and associations with the heavens or afterworld where those ancestors were believed to live after death. The established pattern seen in other masonry compounds of similar age, size, and elaboration found throughout the site indicated they housed elite families who decorated their residences with sculptured portraits and carved texts celebrating the most prominent male residents. After death, these same prominent males were buried within their compounds in stone-lined graves accompanied by arrays of goods.

But in the North Group compounds the recovered sculpture dealt with a specific and famous former ruler of Copán, and with abstract themes of sacrifice and the heavens. Furthermore, the two most elaborate graves excavated in the North Group were of a rare pattern, double tombs in which a male and a female had been buried, most likely victims of human sacrificial rites (Fig. 16.10). Specific aspects of the symbol-rich North Group artifacts suggest the sacrifices were part of repeated rituals commemorating and deifying the dead rulers of Copán. Overall, the results of the test excavations show that the North Group differed from the usual pattern found in other elite compounds at Copán. This fact, and the specific results of the excavations, support the hypothesis that the North Group represented the ancient Maya concept of north as a sacred direction associated with royalty, death, and the afterworld. This, in turn, suggests that the layout of Copán as a whole was prescribed by very basic concepts of the structure of the universe.

On an even larger scale, Fritz has described possible meanings for the architecture of prehistoric Chaco Canyon (see Fig. 16.8), from the arrangement of individual architectural complexes and their spatial relations to one another. What he found was a series of symmetries and asymme-

Testing worldview at Copán, Honduras: The North Group Project

Worldview in prehistoric archaeological data: Fritz's analysis of Chaco Canyon architecture

FIGURE 16.10 The woman and man buried in this Classic Maya tomb were probably sacrificial victims whose death and interment were part of rituals associated with the North Group at Copán, Honduras. (Photo courtesy of the Instituto Hondureño de Antropología e Historia, Tegucigalpa.)

tries, which he interpreted as reflecting, respectively, symbolic equivalences and complementarities within the world as the Chacoans knew it. For instance, the north side of the canyon floor is occupied by the larger, more tightly organized (and more famous) towns, such as Pueblo Bonito (Fig. 16.11) and Chetro Ketl; across the Chaco Wash, on the south side of the canyon, are smaller sites, which are more haphazard in the appearance of their layout. This north–south asymmetry or complementarity can be contrasted with east–west equivalence: There are approximately equal numbers of town sites in the eastern and western halves of the canyon. The "dividing line" runs between Pueblo Alto, on the north rim, and a point on the south rim passing through the Great Kiva of Casa Rinconada, an architectural feature that is unique in other ways as well. Earlier in this chapter we cited the existence of winter solstice markers at both Wijiji and Peñasco Blanco; these functionally linked locations seem also to act as limits for the east and west ends of the canyon, respectively.

FIGURE 16.11 Aerial view of Pueblo Bonito, showing its location relative to the north rim of Chaco Canyon. (Photo by Paul Logsdon, 1982.)

Fritz and others have discussed the possible meanings of these (and further) equivalences and imbalances at Chaco. They *do* seem to be symbolic markers, serving at the same time to distinguish among and unify segments of the society. But interpreters disagree about whether the differences were economic, political, or religious—or some combination of these. We lack documents and tradition to help us interpret what clearly seem to be symbols here. Although there are strong continuities between prehistoric and historic Puebloan cultures, many aspects of 11th-century Chaco culture lack later parallels. One important attribute is clear, however: None of the material remains points to a single dominant central authority, as was the case in Vijayanagara (and many other complex societies). This is certainly in keeping with the sharing and deemphasis of individualism that are important values in the modern Pueblo worldview. Some analysts do point to Pueblo Bonito as the largest and therefore probably dominant town, but Chetro Ketl is a near mirror image in size, arrangement, and location.

The point here, however, is not whether there was a central authority in Chaco Canyon but rather that people in all cultures use symbolic expression widely in daily life, and usually individual symbols combine to express overall views about the nature of the universe and the place of human society in it. There is certainly no shortage of symbols, and often we can identify material symbols in the archaeological record. The key to a worldview, however, is in interpreting them. For that, cultural context must always be kept clearly in mind and appropriate analogies used.

IDEOLOGY AND CULTURAL CHANGE

The obvious difficulties in reconstructing ancient ideologies from material remains have helped support the assumption that these systems were unimportant in directing the course of cultural change. But this assumption has been successfully challenged by a series of studies combining archaeological and historical data that document the active role played by various ideological systems in the evolution of past societies. An excellent and representative case to demonstrate this is the rapid rise of the Mexica (or Aztec) nation of central Mexico in the 15th century, just before the Spanish Conquest. Although the interpretation that follows here relies principally on documentary sources, archaeological data—such as finds from excavations by Eduardo Matos Moctezuma and his colleagues at the Aztec Templo Mayor, cited in Chapter 1—are consistent with the central role of ideology in political affairs.

Ideology as a key to Aztec expansion: Conrad and Demarest

Although scholars differ in their interpretations, Geoffrey W. Conrad and Arthur A. Demarest have argued that several interrelated changes in the traditional religious ideology were instrumental to the success of two pre-Columbian societies, the Mexica and the Inka of Andean South America. Here we will limit discussion to the Aztecs and the case made by Conrad and Demarest for their expansion from a small tributary of several more powerful states to the dominant power in central Mexico. These authors see this change of fortunes as having been sparked by a reworking of their ideological system in the early 15th century. These ideological reforms were initiated by a few individuals toward limited political goals. Their purpose was to consolidate Aztec power at a time of threats from stronger local enemies. Once instituted, the changes had unforeseen effects that gave the Aztecs crucial advantages over not only their local competitors but also all the peoples of central Mexico. As a result, the Aztecs were able to expand their domain rapidly through a series of successful conquests. In the end, however, these same ideological changes produced severe economic and political problems within Aztec society. Failure to solve the problems led to a crisis that, in the view of Conrad and Demarest, would have destroyed Aztec society from within had not the Spanish hastened their demise.

What were these politically motivated ideological changes? They involved the reordering and intensification of preexisting forms to create a new and unified cult, organized and controlled by the state. This cult combined economic, social, and religious systems and provided a strong motivation for military conquest. At its core the new cult created an innovative view of the universe and the destiny of the Aztec people. According to this revised worldview, the sun (the Aztec patron deity and source of all life) was engaged in a daily struggle against destruction by the forces of darkness. Only by constantly feeding the sun with the source of its strength, the lives of human warriors, could the Aztecs save the universe from annihilation (Fig. 16.12). To support this new ideology and dem-

FIGURE 16.12
Graphic depictions such as this one attest to the Aztec practice of human sacrifice. (Neg. #292759 courtesy Department of Library Services, of the American Museum of Natural History.)

onstrate that they were the chosen saviors of the universe, the ruling elite leaders rewrote the history of the Aztec people and altered their myths explaining the cosmos.

Since the essential food for the sun could be secured only by taking warrior captives and sacrificing them, Aztec society became perpetually mobilized toward conquest. Of course, the practical benefits from this military expansion included considerable wealth, for tribute was extracted from vanquished enemies. But an essential motivation and key to the Aztecs' success as conquerors was ideological. Although both militarism and human sacrifice were practiced by all peoples of ancient Mexico, the Aztecs intensified the scale of both to an unprecedented degree. Convinced that they were chosen to perpetuate the universe, Aztec warriors fought with fanatic zeal, believing that they could not fail. Facing this new military fanaticism dedicated to conquest and human sacrifice, many of the Aztecs' enemies lost their will to resist and succumbed in terror.

The Aztecs' conviction of their destiny was reinforced by their initial successes. But soon those very successes produced an internal crisis. The huge increases in wealth and power gained from conquest led to greater economic and social distinctions within Aztec society, and this led to internal resentment and conflict. Moreover, fatal flaws in the new ideological system itself produced a more insidious crisis. The view of the universal struggle between sun and darkness required an infinite supply of enemy warriors, but the availability of this "nourishment for the sun" was soon threatened, as the numbers of opponents diminished. Actually, the Aztecs compensated for this by, in effect, encouraging rebellions against their authority: The conquerors did little to impose their control over the conquered peoples. The uprisings this policy produced gave the Aztecs new opportunities to capture additional warriors for sacrifice. But the consequences of inevitable defeats on the battlefield were more damaging to Aztec society. As the demands for human life and tribute mounted, the determination to resist the Aztec terror increased. Eventually the Aztecs confronted, first, enemies who could not be conquered and, finally, enemies who inflicted devastating defeats on their armies. To the Aztecs, these events meant that their universe was threatened, since the sun was being weakened by fewer human sacrifices. Compounding this threat, each military disaster weakened the confidence and will of the entire society, for military failures challenged the Aztecs' belief in their role as saviors of the universe. In sum, the ideology that led to a cycle of victories and confidence eventually yielded a cycle of defeats and demoralization.

Thus, Conrad and Demarest's interpretation illustrates how crucial ideology can be in the organization and motivation of human society. The Aztec ideological system guided and justified a military, economic, and political expansion that eventually dominated central Mexico. This development was due, in large measure, to a reformulated religious ideology created by a handful of their leaders. This is not to say that ideology should be viewed as the prime cause of cultural change. Certainly economic and other factors were also important in both the rise and the fall of the Aztecs. But history is full of examples of ideologies that have made significant contributions to the direction and development of society, including the rise and fall of nations. Archaeologists must heed the lesson of these examples. They cannot ignore the role of ideology if they wish to reconstruct the past as completely as possible.

SUMMARY

The final, and in a way the most challenging, realm of archaeological interpretation concerns ideology. Ideological systems are the means by which human societies codify their beliefs about both the natural and the supernatural worlds. Although investigation of this realm of ideas is often difficult, ideologies (religious, political, and other) are critical organizers of people's activities. Growing appreciation of the importance of ideology has therefore led archaeologists to increase the attention they give to its reconstruction and interpretation.

Symbols are elements that stand for something else, the relationship between a symbol and what it stands for being arbitrary. Symbols are therefore shorthand ways of expressing often complex messages, and material symbols are the traces through which we study ancient ideologies. Both material and other kinds of symbols are abundant in daily life, and the archaeological record is full of ancient material symbols. The problem is not one of encountering these but of recognizing them as such and interpreting them correctly. A number of methods, such as structural analysis, exist for identifying symbols. Interpretation of the emic meaning of symbols often depends on ethnographic analogy or historical documentation. Historical archaeology and ethnoarchaeology have given us particularly enlightening studies of symbols and their appropriate interpretation. They serve to remind us that archaeologists must continually be wary of the trap of reading the meaning of symbols from the perspective of their own culture. Every society has its own emic set of symbols, and the same or similar material expressions could well mean quite different things to societies with different cultural traditions.

The most regularized symbolic codes are writing systems, which allow the writer to communicate about virtually any topic. Other kinds of recording systems deal with more specific subjects. The earliest notational systems probably date to the Paleolithic, and a frequent subject of counting seems to have been astronomical events and cycles. Interest in this area has given rise to archaeoastronomy, the study of ancient astronomical knowledge preserved in material remains. Past cultures have also left evidence of systems they used to organize and keep track of economic transactions and other activities, by means of clay counters or standardized weights and measures. Some of these, in fact, have been suggested as the direct predecessors of formalized writing systems (which could deal with a variety of topics).

Taken together, the symbols of a society often outline its worldview—its overall description of the nature of the universe and people's relationship to the rest of creation. Analysts studying various cultures have observed that house and community forms and arrangements are particularly powerful symbols of a society's perspective about the way the world is organized.

Just as symbols are central to the conduct of everyday life, so they help guide people's behavior through time. Symbols and ideology are thus important in focusing and sometimes in giving rise to cultural change. Although they are certainly not the sole causes of such change, many cases of cultural transformation—including the rise of the Aztec and Inka empires—testify dramatically to the critical role ideology can play.

For all these instances, the key issue in reconstructing ancient ideological behavior, like any other ancient behavior, is the need to establish an appropriate interpretive framework. This leads to our next chapter and further consideration of the ways in which archaeologists establish the appropriateness of their interpretations.

GUIDE TO FURTHER READING

Gero and Conkey 1991; Hodder 1985, 1991a; Kehoe and Kehoe 1973; Rapoport 1982; Sears 1961; Willey 1962

Recognizing and Analyzing Symbols

Deetz 1977; Edwards 1978; Flannery 1976a; Hedges 1983, 1984; Hodder 1982a, 1982b, 1991a; LeBlanc 1983; Leone 1977, 1982, 1986; McGhee 1977; Schaafsma 1980; Winters 1968; Wobst 1977

Abstract and Depictive Material Symbols

Aveni 1975, 1980, 1981, 1982, 1989; Bahn and Vertut 1988; Baity 1973; Barnett and Hering 1986; Brodrick 1949; Brown 1971; Chippindale 1986; Conkey 1984, 1985, 1987, 1991; Cordell 1984a; Davis 1986; Dickson 1990; Ellis 1975; Hadingham 1984; Hawkins 1965; Heggie 1982; Leroi-Gourhan 1982; Lewis-Williams 1986; Parsons 1939; Renfrew 1983a; Roberts [1929] 1979; Sabloff 1982; Sieveking 1979; Ucko 1968, 1969; Ucko and Rosenfeld 1967; Williamson 1979, 1981; Williamson, Fisher, and O'Flynn 1977; Wittry 1977; Zeilik 1984

Writing, Notation, and Measurement Systems

Marshack 1972a, 1972b; Schmandt-Besserat 1978, 1992; Thom 1971

Worldviews

Ashmore 1991; Benson 1980; Donley 1982; Douglas 1972; Drennan 1976; Flannery and Marcus 1976b; Fritz 1978, 1986; Fritz, Michell, and Rao 1986; Glassie 1975; Leach 1983; Matos Moctezuma 1989; Rappaport 1971a, 1971b; Tuan 1977

Ideology and Cultural Change

Chang 1983; Conrad and Demarest 1984; Flannery 1972a; Freidel 1979, 1981; Leone 1982, 1986; Matos Moctezuma 1989; Miller and Tilley 1984; Puleston 1979; Willey 1962, 1976

THE ARCHAEOLOGICAL STUDY OF GENDER

Margaret W. Conkey

An Associate Professor at the University of California at Berkeley, Conkey is at the forefront of studies in gender and archaeology. She has worked as an archaeologist in the United States, Mexico, Jordan, France, and Spain. Her other major research interests include prehistoric images, social archaeology, hunter-gatherers, and material culture.

When compared with our sister subfields within anthropology, such as ethnography, archaeology is considered to be hard because archaeologists, some say, can't really "see" the past. The archaeological record, they say, is fragmentary and partial. Unlike ethnographers, who may spend months with living people on a day-to-day basis, archaeologists obviously can't see human behaviors and activities in the same ways that ethnographers can. Rather, archaeologists must *infer* aspects of the human past primarily based on material remains. However, ethnographers must infer what they are seeing, as well. They don't really "see" social structure, kinship, exchange networks, or social resistance; they infer these processes and categories. They use theories

about societies and cultures, about social relations and politics. And, they, like archaeologists, inevitably bring certain ideas and expectations with them when they study other people. Just because the ethnographer can see social interactions or tool-making or house-building doesn't necessarily make them any less susceptible to seeing what they expected or assumed. We are all subject to various kinds of biases and prejudgments. These are hard to avoid, given that we are all brought up in our own cultures, in our own ways of viewing the world. The various theories that anthropologists have about human behavior also predispose us to think about the people we study in certain ways. Is this a serious problem?

Certainly it can be. Bias has been shown to be particularly striking in the ethnographic and archaeological study of gender, especially the kind of bias that has overlooked or ignored the activities, roles, and perspectives of women. As this book goes to press, there seems to be a particular interest, albeit an embarrassingly delayed one, in the study of gender in archaeology. Ethnographers

took up gender and gender bias in the early 1970s. But what does it mean to study gender in archaeology? Why is it happening only now? What does this topic have to offer in terms of interpreting archaeological materials and understanding the past? Is this just a fad? Why didn't earlier researchers notice that their assumptions and their subsequent interpretations were biased? Obviously, this is a complicated set of issues, and there is now a burgeoning literature that takes up many of these questions. Since I have been fortunate enough to be part of an expanding group of scholars who have come to take gender in archaeology as a serious topic, I am convinced that archaeology has much to gain by an active engagement with this topic. Several reasons come to mind immediately.

First, although archaeology has always had something to say about men and women in past human societies, it is now clear that many of these observations were little more than extensions into the past of contemporary sex and gender roles (e.g., men go out and work; women stay at home and raise chil-

(continued)

dren). That is, much of what archaeology has had to say about men and women in the past has been biased and ethnocentric. This, in turn, has the effect of making these kinds of roles almost timeless, therefore "natural" and legitimate. Certainly these are among the many possible roles and activities for men and women, but rather than assume them, archaeologists must demonstrate them. Until the early 1970s much of the ethnography—data that archaeologists often draw upon for analogies—was biased as well. All too often, ethnographers' interpretations came from male informants and focused on male activities and actions. Thus, because women in many societies were often invisible or "muted" in both ethnographic and archaeological accounts, it is not surprising that the explicit focus on gender today is misinterpreted to be about women—about finding women, seeing women, and putting them back into the picture of human life.

But gender is about more than the heretofore invisible women. Gender is a social process; it is a way in which social categories, roles, ideologies, and practices are defined and played out. Usually these have to do with aspects of culturally perceived differences between males and females, but there can be more than two genders (men and women), and there can be many ways in which gender relations, roles, and identities can be

created and enacted. For archaeology to take up gender seriously, and in a way that is informed by the now-available theory about gender, means that there were probably all sorts of different ways men and women (and other possible genders) related to each other in the past societies we studied. Often these gender relations were central to the very ways in which past societies changed, such as when the various kinds of states developed in which former, usually kin-based, social relations were transformed into more economic and even class-based relations. And, for the social lives of hominid groups prior to the appearance of modern humans, we have to question whether gender—as a social and symbolic concept— even existed, at least in the ways we now think of gender. Thus, the idea of some primeval man-the-hunter, woman-the-gatherer society, where a symbolically recognized sexual division of labor was a part of daily life, is a simplistic and problematic idea that says more about what some would like the past to have been.

For archaeology to think seriously about gender means that we must recognize that there has been bias—that men are often credited with most of the important innovations and inventions; that men were the hunters, tool-makers, cave painters, priests, traders, etc.; or that men are at least four times as likely to be in stories about the

past and in illustrations of books and articles. But for archaeology to think seriously about gender also means that we need to think seriously about gender as a social and historical process.

The second exciting contribution that the archaeology of gender has to make is that archaeology is now thinking more about social and historical aspects of the past. The past several decades of archaeology have witnessed great strides in techniques and in theories about how people used or exploited their environments; what kinds of things stone tools were used to process, what kinds of plants were being selected for the development of agricultural societies, how irrigation systems were designed, and what individual humans ate, as based on the residues left in their bones. But archaeologists have not thought as much about the social lives of past peoples except in a most general sense, and they have often, in fact, left people out of the narratives we tell about the past. Often you can read about how "a population found itself exceeding the local carrying capacity of the environment and thus intensified its resource procurement strategies," but who makes such decisions? Who changes their daily activities to collect more shellfish, for example? Who accomplished other tasks that had to be done? Where are the men, women, and children who surely had tensions as well as agreements over how such "resource procurement strategies" got carried out?

Who, for example, asks one recent archaeological study, was responsible for providing the officials of the Aztec empire with the requisite cloth for tribute payments? In Liz Brumfiel's study of this phenomenon, she shows how some women developed different ways to meet the tribute demands, such as large-scale cooking and sale of foodstuffs in order to purchase cloth for tribute or in intensive weaving of cloth itself. The very changes and long-term processes that archaeologists have long been the best at studying are seen in more human terms when gender is taken up explicitly. People have always been social actors, making decisions, rearranging their lives with more or less success. Since the mid-1960s in our archaeological enthusiasm for understanding the large-scale processes and transformations in human ecosystems, we have all too often lost sight of the individuals, the factions, the social actions that were at work in the past.

Lastly, by considering gender explicitly—where and when we can—we have the possibility of knowing more about the past. This, after all, is a major goal of archaeology. For example, the takeover of certain rural areas of Peru by the Inka state is more than the expansion of a dominant polity. As Chris Hastorf has shown, with detailed data on plants, with changing diets from bone chemistry analysis, and using spatial studies on house patio activities, the Inka presence was accompanied by dietary changes that were different for men and women because of intensified production of corn by women which was probably made into corn beer and consumed mostly by men in the ritual feasting characteristic of Inka politics. To know this information is to know something more about how a major sociopolitical change was effected.

To make inferences about gender may not be a part of every archaeological research project and we may not always be able to attribute specific artifacts or actions to a specific gender. There is, however, much to be inferred about gender as a process without linking a specific tool with a man or a woman. Furthermore, in the relatively uncertain world of archaeology we know that there were men, women, and children in past societies. As with all of anthropology, archaeological accounts of human life provide cultural data that are good to think with. If we, as archaeologists, provide well supported and carefully reasoned alternative scenarios and situations, we can develop a more human view of the past as well as contribute to the wider scholarship that is generating increasingly dynamic understandings of gender, among other social processes. And, given the current gender tensions and issues in our own contemporary society, we may well learn a lot about the varieties and possibilities for social relations that could contribute to the necessary restructuring of our own societies.

CHAPTER SEVENTEEN

FRAMEWORKS FOR THE PAST

When the long task is finished . . . we must use our results for the solution of
those general problems of anthropological science without . . . which we can
never hope to arrive at valid conclusions as to the history of mankind as a whole.

   A. V. Kidder, An Introduction to the Study of Southwestern Archaeology, *1924*

. . . mature social science need not be practiced under the control of a single
monolithic paradigm but rather can develop in parallel under several different
paradigms . . . [this] allows us to take account of the unique complexity of the
subject matter of these fields by allowing us to consider many dimensions that
could not be encompassed within a single paradigm.

   Jane Kelley and Marsha Hanen, Archaeology and the Methodology of Science, *1988*

Any attempt on the part of the archaeologist to contribute to the larger problems
of cultural understanding was met with an astonishment like that in the classic
case of the "talking dog"; it was not what the dog said that was so amazing but
the fact that he could do it at all.

   Gordon Willey and Jeremy Sabloff, A History of American Archaeology, *1974*

In this chapter we will consider the most common approaches to explaining and understanding the archaeological record. As discussed in Chapter 3, this is done through several alternative but complementary archaeological frameworks: the culture historical, cultural processual, and postprocessual approaches. Each of these shapes the research process, from
formulation of the original questions to be asked, to defining the kinds of
data to be collected and how they are to be analyzed, and finally to the
application of appropriate interpretive frameworks. It should be made
clear that each of these frameworks is an abstraction of a continuum,
shaped by the individuals actually doing archaeology, many of whom in
fact combine aspects of these approaches in their work. Thus our definition of three frameworks is to some extent arbitrary and should be seen as
representing somewhat idealized points of view.

    The most traditional approach to archaeological interpretation is the
culture historical approach, based on a well-established research methodology and a **normative concept of culture.** This approach emphasizes
chronological and spatial ordering of archaeological data, followed by **interpretation** by means of descriptive **models** based on either specific or
general analogs, usually drawn from ethnography and history. The culmination of the interpretive process is a chronicle of events and general
trends of cultural change and continuity in the prehistoric past.

    The second established framework for interpretation is the **cultural
processual approach. Cultural process** refers to an understanding both

of how the parts of a culture work at one point in time (synchronic) and of how cultures change through time (diachronic) by explaining the causes of interactions and change. It is guided by one of several complementary cultural models—functional, ecological, and materialist (described in Chapter 3). The cultural processual approach represents the most explicit application of the **scientific method** to archaeology, using a specific and well-defined methodology in which both **multiple working hypotheses** and the kinds of data that will support or refute each are defined.

The **postprocessual approach** is still in the early stages of development, but it clearly contrasts with both of its predecessors in seeking an **emic,** or insider's, perspective on the past and using a **cognitive concept of culture.** Interpretation is aimed at understanding the past synchronically by discovering the meaning of specific events in the context of each individual culture, and diachronically by viewing culture change as the accumulation of multiple conscious decisions by purposeful individuals. This kind of understanding is the most difficult interpretive task facing the archaeologist. It is strongest when based on documented specific analogies and the **direct historical approach** originally associated with culture history, and becomes increasingly difficult and speculative as one moves further back into prehistory.

We reiterate that all these approaches are interrelated. The cultural processual approach is rooted in culture historical reconstruction, both in its development as a reaction to culture history and specifically as when hypotheses to be tested have been derived from culture historical models. Similarly, postprocessualism is related by its reaction to processualism, especially in its rejection of what it perceives as the biases inherent in an explicitly scientific approach focused on ecological and evolutionary processes. In a general way, however, each approach builds on its predecessor, and both cultural processual and postprocessual frameworks are built on a culture historical foundation, since it provides the temporal and spatial frameworks of prehistory.

CULTURE HISTORICAL FRAMEWORKS

As we have seen, the choice of a framework to guide archaeological inquiry influences all stages of the research process. In the case of the culture historical framework, interpretation is derived from the temporal and spatial **synthesis** of the archaeological data and is shaped by the scope of that synthesis. If temporal and spatial distributions encompass only a single site, interpretation is obviously restricted to that site. If the scope of the synthesis includes many sites covering an entire region, the resulting synthesis will be similarly broad.

However large or small the area covered, the analogs used for culture historical interpretation usually presuppose a normative view of culture.

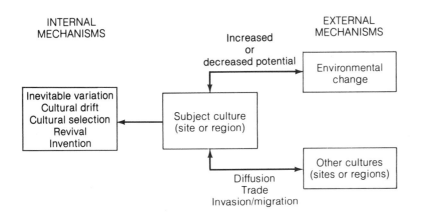

FIGURE 17.1 Culture historical interpretation is based on models that describe cultural change as proceeding from either internal or external mechanisms.

Normative analogs describe idealized rules or "templates" for the ways things were done—how pottery was made, what house forms were prescribed, and so on. For example, in the Southwest, in the Great Pueblo **phase** of the Anasazi **tradition,** people lived in apartmentlike dwellings, often nestled in cliff shelters, like Cliff Palace in Mesa Verde, Colorado. They also used black-and-white pottery of specific forms and types. These norms contrast with those of earlier and later phases and contemporary cultures of other traditions. Normative models are thus primarily descriptive, not explanatory, in that they identify and describe the variables of cultural change but do not attempt to describe the relationships among variables or identify the specific causes of change.

Some descriptive models used in archaeology are **synchronic,** identifying and describing what happened in the past at one point in time, or even irrespective of time (atemporal). Other descriptive models are **diachronic;** these identify and describe when past events occurred, emphasizing change through time. For example, Willey and Phillips's New World cultural stage model (Chapter 3) is diachronic and descriptive: It identifies and describes certain archaeological variables and their changes through time, to define the posited "stages" of New World culture history.

Because the culture historical approach emphasizes chronology and cultural change, most of the interpretive models used are diachronic, identifying and describing change in the archaeological record. However, some of these models also deal with situations involving cultural stability, or a lack of change through time. A more meaningful distinction, then, might be made between those diachronic models that emphasize the internal dynamics of culture and those that focus on external stimuli for change, whether cultural or noncultural in origin (Fig. 17.1). The principal internal cultural models include two sources of change (invention and revival) and three mechanisms to describe how change comes about (inevitable variation, cultural selection, and cultural drift). The primary

A descriptive model:
**Willey and Phillips's
New World synthesis**

external models include diffusion, trade, migration, and invasion or conquest—all cultural sources—and environmental change—a noncultural source. We will consider these models and indicate how each is used in culture historical interpretation.

Internal Cultural Models

The most general of the internal cultural models is often called the **inevitable variation** model. It is based on the simple premise that all cultures must change through time. One particular version of this model is the common thesis that all cultures experience growth and development analogous to that of a living organism: They grow, mature, and eventually die, a trajectory often referred to as the rise and fall of civilization. But the inevitable variation model is so simplistic and general that it is of little use in interpreting most archaeological situations. For instance, if we take the collapse of a specific civilization, such as that of Rome or the Maya, applying the inevitable variation model adds nothing to our understanding. We do not increase our understanding by saying that a civilization fell apart because it was destined to collapse. Of greater benefit to archaeological interpretation are internal cultural models that identify variables with which to describe the mechanisms of culture change.

How does this change come about? The human species is inquisitive and innovative. **Cultural invention** is the result of these human qualities; the term refers to new ideas that originate within a culture, either by accident or by design. All new ideas have their ultimate origin in such invention, of course; but to attribute to invention the appearance of a given trait in the archaeological record at a particular place, the archaeologist must demonstrate that the trait was not introduced from outside by trade or some other external mechanism. A specific example is the controversy over the early occurrence of bronze metallurgy in Southeast Asia. Proponents of an independent invention model point out that cast bronze artifacts now being found in Thailand rival those of southwest Asia in age. The counterargument, however, is that southwest Asia exhibits a full range of evidence for the local development of metallurgical technology: evidence of workshops and local sequential evidence of gradually increasing sophistication in metalworking techniques. To establish that Southeast Asia was indeed an independent center for the invention of metallurgy, future archaeological research there must uncover evidence equivalent to that in southwest Asia, documenting the *local prototypes* and *developmental steps* leading to the level of sophistication embodied in the artifacts found so far.

To contribute to cultural change, an invention must be accepted in a culture. Two general models, both founded on loose analogies to biological evolution, have been offered to describe mechanisms of acceptance, perpetuation, or rejection of cultural traits (Fig. 17.2). The first, **cultural selection,** mirrors the biological concept of natural selection. According

Old World metallurgy: Independent invention or diffusion?

Selective mechanism: Acceptance or rejection of centralized leadership

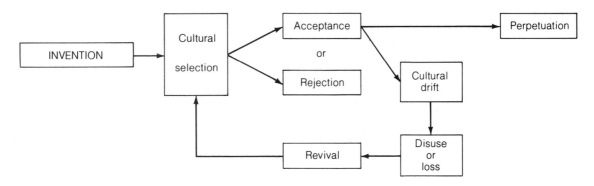

FIGURE 17.2 Internally induced cultural change is affected by the filtering mechanisms of cultural selection and cultural drift.

to the cultural selection model, societies that accept innovations that turn out to be advantageous tend to be more successful than societies that fail to accept such innovation. Conversely, societies that reject innovations that turn out to be nonadvantageous tend to be more successful than societies that accept such innovation. This tendency results in gradual and cumulative change through time. Selection can act on any cultural trait, whether in the technological, social, or ideological realm of culture. Whether a given trait is advantageous or not depends ultimately on whether it contributes to—or hinders—the survival and well-being of the society. For example, investment of power in a central authority figure may increase a society's efficiency in food production, resolution of disputes, and management of interactions with neighboring societies. If such centralization of authority leads this society to prosper, the trait of power centralization is advantageous and selection will favor its perpetuation. If, however, the society falls on hard times as a result of power centralization—perhaps because of inept leadership—authority is likely to become more dispersed again.

Selection also acts against innovative traits that are inconsistent with prevailing cultural values or norms. Generally speaking, technological inventions are more likely to be accepted than social or ideological ones, because they are less likely to conflict with the value system. A new form of axe head, for instance, usually has an easier path to acceptance than does a revised authority hierarchy or an innovative religious belief.

A related model, often labeled **cultural drift** (see Fig. 17.2), describes a complementary mechanism. In biological evolution, the term *genetic drift* describes an accidental fluctuation in gene frequency in which some genetic traits are lost by chance because the few members of the population who have them do not produce offspring and so do not perpetuate the traits. Like selection, this process results in change through time. But unlike selection, drift is random: The reason for trait loss is chance alone rather than active selection against a characteristic. Although genetic traits are passed on by biological reproduction, cultural traits are transmitted

Cultural drift in early Paleolithic tools: Sally Binford

Cultural revitalization: Wallace's model

Prehistoric revitalization: Late Classic Tikal

from one generation to the next by learning. Cultural drift, then, results from incomplete or imperfect cultural transmission: Because no individual ever learns all the information possessed by any other member of the society, some cultural changes through time have a random aspect. Sally Binford has suggested that cultural drift may be responsible for some of the variations in artifacts of early Paleolithic assemblages. That is, the accumulation of minor changes gives a superficial impression of deliberate stylistic innovation, but not until the Upper Paleolithic, or perhaps the Mousterian assemblages of the Middle Paleolithic, can definable zones of consistent and clustered stylistic types be discerned. Earlier variability (other than that related to artifact function and efficiency) may simply represent the cumulative effects of random cultural drift.

Another source for change is **cultural revival** of elements that have fallen into disuse. A number of stimuli may lead to revival of old forms, including chance discovery and reacceptance of old styles, reoccurrence of specific needs, and duplication of treasured heirlooms. One particular model relates revival to a coping response to stressful situations. Some kinds of stress elicit technological responses. For example, townspeople construct a fortification wall as a defense against siege. Other kinds of stress may elicit social or ideological responses. Cultural anthropologist Anthony F. C. Wallace has developed a model that describes rapid and radical cultural change in the face of stress. This revitalization model refers to situations in which members of a society perceive their culture as falling apart—as unable to provide them with an adequate standard of living. In revitalization, a leader emerges who revives old symbols associated with earlier periods of well-being, squashes those identified with the stressful situation, inspires positive and prideful identification with the society, and promises positive prosperity if people will adhere to the rules he sets down. The Ghost Dance phenomenon of 1890 was a revitalization response by Native American groups to the dissolution and devaluation of their culture by Euro-American contacts; other examples include the rise of the Black Muslim movement in the United States in the mid-20th century and the Communist revolutions in Russia and China. Some archaeologists believe that a revitalization movement can be detected at the Maya site of Tikal, where the rise of rival power centers in the seventh century A.D. threatened Tikal's previous political supremacy. A powerful leader emerged shortly before A.D. 700 and rapidly galvanized his followers into reasserting their self-respect and Tikal's importance. Among the means he used in this effort were revival of older symbols—including particular decorative motifs and genealogical reconstructions that recalled earlier heights of power and prosperity—and elaboration of previously minor symbols, such as a ceremonial architectural plan known as twin-pyramid groups, that were emblematic of Tikal itself. As noted in Chapter 16, interpretation of ideology and symbol systems is not easy, but a large and growing number of archaeologists argue that more attention should be given to reconstructing this aspect of ancient life.

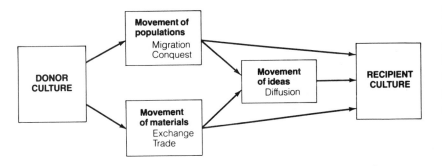

FIGURE 17.3 Externally induced cultural change, or acculturation, includes the mechanisms of diffusion, trade, migration, invasion, and conquest.

External Cultural Models

Once a change, such as that resulting from the acceptance of an invention, has occurred within a society, its utility or prestige may allow it to spread far beyond its place of origin. The spread of new ideas and objects involves a complex set of variables, including time, distance, degree of utility or acceptance, and mode of dispersal. Various modes of dispersal are well documented by both history and ethnography; these are often used as models for culture historical interpretation. They include the spread of ideas (diffusion), the dispersal of material objects by exchange or trade, and the movement of human populations through migration and invasion or conquest. The influences or changes within a given culture brought about by these external sources (Fig. 17.3) are collectively termed **acculturation,** especially when the impact is widespread and imposed.

Diffusion occurs under a variety of circumstances: Any contact between individuals of different societies involves the potential transmission of new ideas from one culture to another. When a given society is exposed to a new idea, that idea may be accepted unchanged, reworked or modified to better fit the accepting culture, or completely rejected. A classic ethnographically documented case of diffusion is the spread of the Ghost Dance movement among Native American groups in the late 19th century. Originating among the Paiute Indians in Nevada, the doctrine of the Ghost Dance of 1890 began primarily as a revival of traditional culture, brought about by the return of the "ghosts" of dead ancestors. As the movement spread east across the Great Plains, however, it was progressively modified by the various cultural groups that adopted it; finally, it came to incorporate an active and hostile rejection of all things associated with the white culture. Adherents of the movement's altered doctrine argued that sufficient purification of Native American culture (by purging the Euro-American traits) would increase the buffalo herds, restore ancestors to life, and drive away the whites—the source of troubles. Faith in the strength of the movement even led some to believe that the Ghost Dance shirts gave their wearers invincibility, a belief tragically disproved in the massacre

Diffusion documented: The Ghost Dance

at Wounded Knee. The Ghost Dance was not accepted by all Native Americans, however. Some groups, such as the Navajo, rejected the pan-Indian movement altogether because of their strong avoidance of the dead and fear of "ghosts." The Ghost Dance, then, illustrates widespread diffusion of an idea from one society to others, in which the idea was sometimes accepted without modification, sometimes modified, and sometimes rejected because it conflicted with existing cultural values.

The archaeological record contains numerous examples of ideas that have diffused over varying distances with varying degrees of acceptance. The 260-day ritual calendar of Mesoamerica is found in a wide range of cultural contexts; although specific attributes, such as day names, vary from one culture to the next, the essential unity of this calendrical system bespeaks long-term, continuing exchange of calendrical ideas among its users. In the Old World, the distribution of megalithic (large stone) monuments in Europe has traditionally been described as diffusion of an architectural idea westward from the cultures of the eastern Mediterranean in the third millennium B.C. As we saw in Chapter 9, however, recent revisions of radiocarbon dating techniques have indicated that the megalithic constructions in France and Spain are earlier than those in eastern Mediterranean areas. Spread of architectural ideas by diffusion may still describe the mechanism behind the observed spatial distribution, but the specific model for diffusion clearly needs reexamination.

Because diffusion is so well documented and so common, and because evidence of more specific mechanisms such as trade, migration, invasion, and invention is sometimes difficult to demonstrate, culture historical interpretations have relied heavily on diffusion as a model. All too often, however, the concept is used uncritically, without considering the specific circumstances under which ideas might have been transmitted. Thus, any observed similarity between cultures may be attributed to diffusion. An extreme example of abuse of this concept is found in the diffusionist school of anthropology in the early 20th century, especially the branch of it that traced all civilizations of the world to dynastic Egypt (the so-called Heliocentric theory). Proponents of this model, such as Sir Grafton Elliot Smith, argued that the observed distribution of such widespread traits of civilization as divine kingship and pyramid construction resulted from diffusion from a single source culture: Egypt. Even when applied in less extreme ways, however, use of the concept of diffusion often raises questions about why the cultures involved should have been in communication in the first place and, if they were, why certain traits were accepted rather than rejected.

A more recent, comprehensive diffusionist model was presented by James A. Ford to describe the course of cultural change and the spread of ideas in pre-Columbian America. On the basis of finds at the Ecuadorian site of Valdivia, Betty J. Meggers, Clifford Evans, and Emilio Estrada had argued that a series of early-third-millennium innovations—including the oldest American occurrence of pottery—were derived by trans-Pacific

Prehistoric diffusion: Cases in Mesoamerica and Europe

Abuse of diffusion: Smith and the Heliocentric theory

Extreme diffusionism: Proposed Old World–New World links

contacts from the contemporary Japanese culture called Jomon. Ford accepted the Valdivia-Jomon thesis and went further, tracing the spread of selected cultural traits throughout the Americas from 3000 B.C. onward. The ultimate origins of a number of cultural traits, such as ring-shaped village plans in **Formative**-period coastal settlements, were often assigned to Asiatic sources, as were some of the human populations involved. Parts of Ford's scheme may have validity, but much does not. The Jomon question, for example, has been effectively refuted by the discovery of earlier local prototypes for the Valdivia pottery. Unfortunately, the Ford model has become embroiled in a recurring philosophical standoff between those who advocate independent invention as an overriding mechanism of cultural change and those who favor diffusion. Despite the polemics, each case must be examined individually; neither internal invention nor external contacts are likely alone to account for all instances of cultural change.

Although diffusion is often an elusive mechanism, easy to invoke and difficult to substantiate, contact and communication through **trade** can frequently be concretely demonstrated. Because trade involves the exchange of material objects, the less perishable of these may be recovered by archaeologists as artifacts and ecofacts. In Chapter 15 we discussed the nature and detection of exchange systems in some detail; thus only a brief review will be given here.

Artifacts and ecofacts may be initially identified as imported goods either because they are infrequently occurring items, distinct from the bulk of items found in a site, or because they are made of raw materials known to be unavailable locally. Various technical analyses have been developed to identify sources of raw materials, including such widely traded stone materials as obsidian, jade, and steatite. In a number of cases, archaeologists have been able to plot both the distribution of sources of a particular material and the observed distribution of products from those sources; they then use this information to reconstruct ancient trade routes. The important implication of trade distributions for cultural change is that archaeologists can use them to demonstrate contact between groups: When an obsidian trade route is reconstructed, for example, a minimal inference is that the obsidian was introduced to groups who could then add obsidian tools to their cultural inventory. But, along with the obsidian, traders probably carried other goods, many of which could not survive in the archaeological record, and certainly information about ways of life in their home community. Traders also certainly acquired other goods and information, which they then introduced at home. The obsidian in this case is concrete evidence of the means of transmitting a much broader array of materials and ideas.

Another mechanism of cultural change is actual movement of populations, both in **migrations** and in **invasions** and **conquests.** Culture historical interpretations often cite these movements to account for evidence of widespread and rapid change. Numerous authors have discussed detection of population movements in the archaeological record; Emil W.

Evidence for prehistoric migration: Haury at Point of Pines, Arizona

Haury presents the requirements succinctly in his postulation of a migration from northern Arizona into the Point of Pines region of east central Arizona at the end of the 13th century. Haury sets forth four conditions that must be met to argue that a migration has occurred:

1. A number of new cultural traits must suddenly appear, too many to be feasibly accounted for by diffusion, invention, or trade, and none having earlier local prototypes.
2. Some of the forms or styles of local materials should be modified or used in a different way by the newcomers.
3. A source for the immigrant population must be identified—a homeland where the intrusive cultural elements do have prototypes.
4. The artifacts used as indices of population movement must exist in the same form at the same time level in both the homeland and the newly adopted home.

At Point of Pines, Haury notes that new architectural styles, both sacred and secular, as well as very specific ceramic attributes appear suddenly in one particular sector of the site. At the same time level, some distinctively "foreign" design elements are found on locally made pottery vessels, also found in this one sector. These two conclusions supply the first two kinds of evidence needed to postulate a migration. Looking, then, for a source for these cultural traits, he finds the same elements in association at sites in northern Arizona, on an equivalent time level, and notes that independent evidence is available for a population decline in the proposed homeland at the appropriate time. His actual reconstructions are even more specific: He presents additional evidence to suggest that the size of the migrating group was about 50 or 60 families, and he posits that the community into which they moved did not take kindly to the intrusion, ultimately setting fire to the newcomers' homes and driving them out again.

The concept of peaceful migration as one means of introducing new culture traits into an area can be contrasted with its more typically violent counterparts, invasion and conquest. These, too, involve population movements, but with presumably more drastic effects on the way of life in the invaded society. Elements cited as evidence of invasion or conquest include massive burning or other destruction of buildings in a settlement, usually accompanied by large-scale loss of human life. An example of ancient invasion has been reconstructed from the excavations directed by Robert Dyson at the fortified city of Hasanlu, Iran. Evidence throughout levels of the site dating from the ninth century B.C. testified to a sudden and violent end. The most dramatic finds were in the walled palace compound in the heart of the city, where the ruins of burned buildings and remains of people caught in the falling debris were exposed (Fig. 17.4). A child had died on a street between two burning buildings, and an old man had been buried under the collapse of the palace walls. Several young men

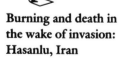

Burning and death in the wake of invasion: Hasanlu, Iran

FIGURE 17.4   Evidence of culture change through conquest can take dramatic forms. This photograph shows human skeletal remains sprawled among the remains of burned buildings in the walled palace compound of Hasanlu, Iran, the result of the ninth-century B.C. destruction of the city. (Courtesy of Robert H. Dyson, Jr., and The University Museum, University of Pennsylvania.)

had apparently been on the second floor of the burning palace when the floor gave way, hurling them to their deaths. They may have been seeking plunder or trying to save valuables, for a beautiful gold bowl was found with their remains, beneath the burned building. After this ancient event, no one had tried to recover the victims' bodies, and Hasanlu was abandoned for a time, although it was eventually rebuilt and reoccupied.

The change brought about by conquest or invasion may, of course, be simple annihilation of the existing population, sometimes with no replacement by the intruders. In many cases, however, part of the original population survives and stays on, often under new political domination. The invaders may bring in new cultural elements, but historically documented

Archaeological evidence of conquest: The 16th-century Spanish

invasions show up rather inconsistently in the archaeological record. A case in point is the Spanish Conquest of the Americas in the 16th century. Both European and native chronicles of the period attest to the extent and severity of the changes wrought by the Spanish. Even so, archaeologists working in a number of the affected areas, including Mexico, Guatemala, and Peru, have sometimes had difficulty actually identifying the dramatic onset of a Spanish presence. At some sites, distinctive features such as Catholic churches do appear, but pottery inventories often remain unchanged for long periods after the conquest. Numerous small communities, at varying distances from the civic and religious centers, must have undergone the change to Spanish rule without altering their tools, food, houses, or other material aspects of life. With reference to Haury's criteria, then, archaeologists can positively identify some prehistoric population movements, but the example just given argues rather strongly that not all such movements—violent or peaceful—can be detected in the archaeological record.

Environmental Change

Underlying culture historical interpretation is also a general descriptive model that concerns the relationship between culture and the natural **environment**. Although this model has been very useful in identifying and describing some important effects of environmental variables on culture and cultural change, the most common form of the model identifies the environmental sources of cultural change generally rather than specifically. In the next section we will discuss specific explanatory models that take the natural environment into account explicitly.

Environmental impact: Martin at Tularosa Cave, New Mexico

The usual culture historical model of culture and environment interaction holds that each has the potential to modify the other. This relationship is diagrammed in Figure 17.5. According to this model, environmental change may stimulate cultural change, or vice versa. For example, at Tularosa Cave, in the Mogollon area of western New Mexico, evidence indicates that maize and other cultivated plants generally increased in importance in the human diet over time. An exception, however, occurs between about A.D. 500 and A.D. 700; during this time maize consumption declined to almost nothing. This correlates with the period in which the total number of sites, as well as the area in square feet per house, reaches its lowest point. Paul S. Martin and his colleagues believe that a sustained series of short droughts may have been at least partially responsible for this dietary change, by making agriculture difficult at best and leading to a renewed reliance on wild foods.

Environmental impact: Sunset Crater, Arizona

A more dramatic example of the cultural impact of an environmental change also comes from the southwestern United States—the effects of the eruption of Sunset Crater, near Flagstaff, Arizona, sometime in the middle of the 11th century A.D. The initial effect of the eruption was to destroy or drive away all residents in the approximately 800 square miles

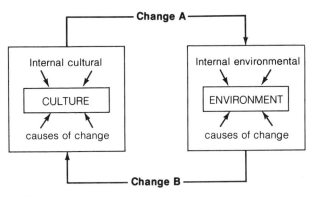

FIGURE 17.5 The culture historical approach stresses a simple interaction between culture and environment, based on the capability of each to modify the other (compare with Fig. 17.9, p. 558).

Key:
A: Environmental change caused by cultural factors
B: Culture change caused by environmental factors

blanketed by the black volcanic ash. A century later, however, the area was resettled by a diverse population who apparently took advantage of the rich mulching action of the volcanic soil. By A.D. 1300, however, the environment had changed again: Wind had converted the ash cover to shifting dunes, exposing the original hard clay soil. The settlers once again moved on.

In previous chapters we have given examples showing how culture changes environment. A change in technology may redefine the environment by increasing or decreasing the range of exploitable resources. Agricultural overuse may exhaust local soils; the clearing of trees on hillsides may foster erosion, landslides, and ultimately—by increasing the load deposited in a streambed by runoff—flooding. Alteration of the natural environment by cultural activities is not an exclusively modern phenomenon; the changes today may be more extensive than before, but they are part of a long, global tradition of cultural impact on the state of the natural world.

CULTURAL PROCESSUAL FRAMEWORKS

Just as some models are used more frequently in culture historical reconstruction, others are primarily associated with cultural processual explanation. We shall discuss three groups of models, all of them based on fundamental concepts introduced in Chapter 3. The first—systems models—derives from the **functional concept of culture,** especially as it has been refined by application of **general systems theory.** The ecological concept of culture provides archaeologists with the second set of models, those based on ecology; and the multilinear evolutionary concept furnishes the third group of models, founded on modern cultural evolutionary theory.

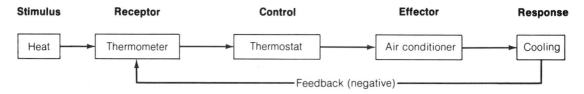

FIGURE 17.6 Diagram of a homeostatic temperature control system, illustrating the operation of a closed system.

Closed systems:
Thermostats

Systems Models

Descriptive studies of culture, such as those dealing with social organization of family units, kin groups, or whole communities, often focus on individual parts of the organization. But the dynamic qualities of any organization—how and why it survives and changes through time—can be understood only through examination of both its components and their relationships. Systems models recognize that an organization represents more than a simple sum of its parts; in fact, they emphasize the study of the relations between these parts.

The systems models used in cultural processual interpretation are based on general systems theory as set forth in the work of Ludwig von Bertalanffy and others. This theory defines a **system** as a set of parts and the relationships among the parts. *General systems theory* also holds that any organization, from amoebae to cultures to computers, may be studied as a system, to examine how its components are related and how changes in some components or in their relations produce changes in the overall system. The term *environment,* in a systems approach, refers to all factors that are external to the systems being studied and that may cause change in the system or be affected by the system.

Systems theorists distinguish two kinds of systems, open and closed. **Closed systems** receive no matter, energy, or information from the environment; all sources of change are internal. **Open systems** exchange matter, energy, and information with their environment; change can come either from within the system or from outside. Living organisms and sociocultural systems are both examples of open systems. To understand how systems operate, we will examine systems models that are often applied to cultural processual interpretation.

We will begin with a simple closed systems model. An example is a self-regulated or *homeostatic* temperature control system, such as those found within many modern buildings (Fig. 17.6). The components in the system are the air in the room or building, the thermometer, the thermostat, and the heater or the air conditioner. In this case, a change in the air temperature acts as a stimulus, which is detected by a thermometer and transmitted to the thermostat. When the temperature rises above a predetermined level, the thermostat triggers the air conditioner. The cooling response acts as **feedback** by stimulating the same interdependent components to shut down the air conditioner once the temperature has gone

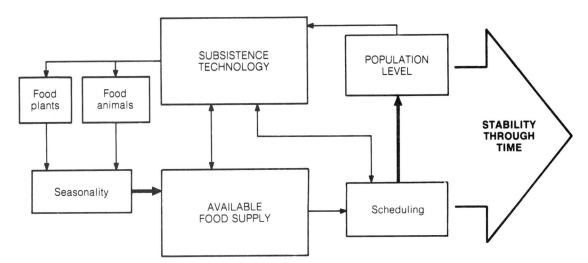

FIGURE 17.7 Simplified diagram of a system characterized by deviation-counteracting mechanisms (→) that lead to population and cultural stability through time; based on data from prehistoric Mesoamerica (ca. 8000–5000 B.C.). The larger arrow at the right indicates the trajectory of the system as a whole.

below the critical level. (Of course, the outside temperature ultimately influences that of the interior; to be truly closed, such a system would have to be completely insulated from exterior conditions.)

This closed system illustrates how certain systems operate to maintain a stable condition, or *steady state*. When a specific change in one part of the system threatens the steady state, this stimulates a response from other parts. When the steady state has been restored, a feedback loop shuts down the response. Feedback of this kind is **negative** in the sense that it dampens or cuts off the system's response and thus maintains a condition of *dynamic equilibrium,* in which the system's components are active but the overall system is stable and unchanging. Equilibrating systems such as the above example are characterized as regulatory or **deviation-counteracting systems** (Fig. 17.7). Although they are useful for illustrating the operation of systems, such models are applicable only to unchanging and stable aspects of human societies. Since archaeologists are at least as frequently concerned with processes of cultural change, we must also consider dynamic systems models that can account for cumulative systemic change.

The most commonly applied model for this deals with **deviation-amplifying systems.** Some changes stimulate further changes through **positive feedback** (Fig. 17.8). An interesting application of these concepts to an archaeological situation is Kent Flannery's systems model for the development of food production in Mesoamerica. In setting forth the model, Flannery first describes the food procurement system used by peoples of highland Mexico between about 8000 and 5000 B.C. The components of this system were the people themselves, their technology—including knowledge and equipment—for obtaining food, and the plants

Open systems: Flannery's food production models

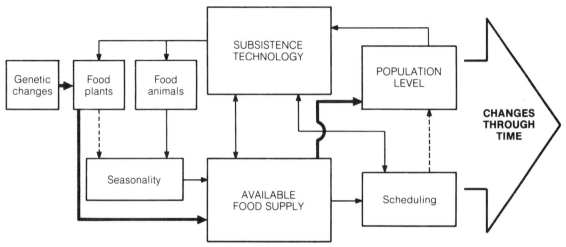

FIGURE 17.8 Simplified diagram of a system characterized by deviation-amplifying mechanisms that both weaken the deviation-counteracting mechanisms in Figure 17.7 and lead to population growth and cultural change, stimulated by genetic changes; based on data from prehistoric Mesoamerica (after 5000 B.C.).

and animals actually used for food. People in the highland valleys lived in small groups, periodically coming together into larger "macrobands" but never settling down in stationary villages. The subsistence technology available to them included knowledge of edible plants and animals that could be procured by gathering and hunting techniques; it also included the use of projectile points, baskets, storage pits, fiber shredders, and various other implements and facilities for collecting and processing the food. Among the food items actively used were cactus, avocado, white-tailed deer, and rabbits. Wild grasses related to maize were sometimes eaten but did not form a very important part of the diet.

This food procurement system was regulated and maintained by two deviation-counteracting processes, which Flannery calls "seasonality" and "scheduling." Seasonality refers to the characteristics of the food resources —some were available during only one season. To gather enough food, the people had to go where it was available; periodic abundance of particular resources allowed people to come together into temporary macrobands, but the seasons of lean resources placed sharply defined limits on both total valley population and effective social group size. Scheduling, the other deviation-counteracting process that Flannery posits, refers to the people's organizational response to seasonality: Seasonal population movement and diet diversity prevented exhaustion of resources by over-exploitation, but it also kept population levels low (see Fig. 17.7).

This stable system persisted for several thousand years. But eventually a series of genetic changes in some of the wild grasses of the genus *Zea* stimulated a deviation-amplifying feedback system. Improved traits of the maize, such as larger cob size, induced people to reproduce the "improved" grass by sowing. As a result of this behavior, scheduling patterns were gradually altered. For instance, planting and harvesting requirements increased the time spent in spring and autumn camps, precisely where larger population gatherings had been feasible. The larger, more stable population group then invested more time and labor in improving the quality and quantity of crop yield; this positive feedback continued to induce change in the subsistence system. For example, irrigation technology was developed to extend agriculture and settlement into more arid zones. As Flannery says (1968:79), the "positive feedback following these initial genetic changes caused one minor [sub]system to grow out of all proportion to the others, and eventually to change the whole ecosystem of the Southern Mexican Highlands" (see Fig. 17.8).

Although some cultural systems may maintain a state of dynamic equilibrium for long periods of time, all cultures do change. Not all change involves growth, however. Sometimes deviation-amplifying processes result in cultural loss or decline, and ultimately in dissolution of the system. The Ik of East Africa, described by ethnographer Colin Turnbull, provide a modern example of such decline. Disruption of traditional Ik behavior patterns by such factors as forced migration from preferred lands has led to apathy, intragroup hostility, a devaluation of human life, and population decline. The result in this case is as dramatically bleak as Flannery's is dramatically positive. Cultural systems are affected simultaneously by both growth and decline of subsystems within them, and they tend to fluctuate between periods of stability or gradual change and periods of rapid and profound transformations of the entire cultural system.

Dissolution of a system: The Ik of East Africa

Cultural Ecological Models

The second basic type of model used in cultural processual interpretation is provided by the perspective of **cultural ecology.** In its modern form, cultural ecology provides much more sophisticated models of the interaction between culture and environment than did the culture historical model, discussed earlier in this chapter. The cultural ecological models are more sophisticated because they are both systemic and comprehensive. The overall approach of cultural ecology incorporates the tenets of general systems theory, and models based on it partition the environment of a culture into three separate, complementary facets to offer a comprehensive view of it. Whereas the culture historical approach often treats "environment" as a single entity, cultural ecology considers a culture as interacting with an environmental system composed of three complex subsystems: the **physical environment** (habitat), the **biological environment** (biome), and the **cultural environment** (other human groups) (Fig. 17.9).

This basic ecological system seems superficially simple, but in fact it is very complex. We can appreciate this by considering that each subsystem is composed of further subordinate systems, which in turn comprise smaller component systems, and so on. For example, the cultural subsystem combines three component systems—technological, social, and

FIGURE 17.9 The cultural ecological system, illustrating the relationships between a given culture (subject human society) and its environment, composed of physical, cultural, and biological subsystems (compare with Fig. 17.5, p. 553).

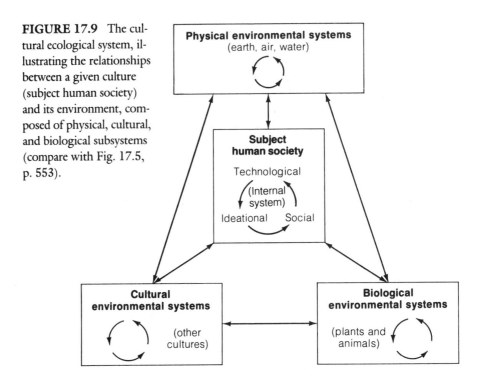

ideational; and the social component of that subsystem can be broken down further into such constituents as political, kinship, and economic subsystems.

For any given society, the sum of specific interactions contained within an overall cultural ecological system describes the nature of the society's **cultural adaptation.** Each society adapts to its environment primarily through its technological system but secondarily through its social and ideological systems. The technological system interacts directly with all three components of the environment—physical, biological, and cultural—by providing, for instance, the tools and techniques for securing shelter, food, and defense from attack. The social system adapts by integrating and organizing society. The relation, described earlier, between band organization, seasonality, and scheduling in preagricultural highland Mexican societies is an example of social system adaptation to the biological environment. And the ideological system adapts by reinforcing the organization and integration of society—providing motivation for, explanation of, and confidence in the appropriateness of the technological and social adaptations.

Of course, the full set of interactions within such a complex system is difficult to study all at once; as a result archaeologists often begin by isolating one or more of the subordinate systems directly involved in cultural

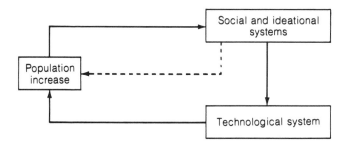

FIGURE 17.10   Diagram of the relationship between technological, social, and ideational systems and population increase within a culture.

adaptation. The technological system is the obvious focus of studies seeking to understand the adaptive process. Fortunately for the prehistoric archaeologist, not only is the technological system a principal agent of cultural adaptation, but also the remains of ancient technology are usually the fullest part of the archaeological record. These technological data may be used to reconstruct a particular aspect of the technological system, such as subsistence. Archaeologists then integrate their detailed models of different subsystems to create complex models of overall cultural adaptation (Fig. 17.10).

Because of the mass of information involved in such models, computers are often used for information storage. Computers also enable the archaeologist to perform experimental manipulation of the models: After a hypothetical change is introduced in one component of the stable hypothetical system, **computer simulation studies** determine what deviation-amplifying or deviation-counteracting reactions would be induced by the original change. For example, Ezra Zubrow used computer simulations to examine relationships among human population size and structure, biological resources of the environment, and settlement location in the prehistoric Southwest; he found that changing the characteristics of any of these system components produced different projected courses of growth and decline.

We should reiterate that, although many changes originate within the technological subsystem of culture, change may arise anywhere in the overall cultural ecological system. Technological development is important in **cultural evolution,** but it is not the only source of change.

In an analogy to biological adaptation, many archaeologists measure the effectiveness of cultural adaptation by the rate of population growth and resultant population size. In this sense, population growth and size are measurable responses to the overall cultural ecological system (see Fig. 17.10). Thus, with regard to population increase, some societies exhibit the characteristics of deviation-amplifying systems possessing one or more positive feedback mechanisms. For example, changes in the technological system may provide more abundant food production and storage capabilities, resulting in an increase in population. Changes in the social

Computer simulation: Zubrow's projections of Southwest cultural development

or ideational systems will follow, to accommodate the population growth; these in turn may allow more efficient food distribution or expansion through conquest or colonization to open new areas for food production; these changes result in further population growth; this may place new stress on the technology, which must respond with further changes to increase the food supply; and so forth. The result is an interrelated change-increase cycle, perhaps best illustrated by the phenomenon of recent world population growth.

However, some societies maintain their populations in dynamic equilibrium by negative feedback mechanisms. Such mechanisms include culturally acceptable population control methods (birth control, infanticide, warfare), migration, and social fission (breakup of communities into smaller or more dispersed units). Environmental mechanisms, including periodic famine or endemic disease, also contribute to deviation-counteracting systems.

The consideration of the dynamic consequences of cultural ecological models brings us to the final basic perspective on cultural processual interpretation—multilinear cultural evolution.

Multilinear Cultural Evolution Models

The systemic view of culture and the adaptation concept of cultural ecology are combined in the contemporary theory of **multilinear cultural evolution.** This theory sees the evolution of culture as the cumulative changes in a system resulting from the continuous process of cultural adaptation over extensive periods of time.

Unlike the 19th-century theory of **unilinear cultural evolution,** modern cultural evolutionary theory does not postulate any single inevitable course of change to be followed by all societies. Multilinear evolutionary theorists do, however, hold that certain recognizable regularities occur in the trajectory of cultural change and differentiation through time. Building on the work of Leslie White and others, Marshall Sahlins and Elman R. Service distinguished between *specific* cultural evolution, which describes the unique course followed by a particular cultural system, and *general* cultural evolution, in which a series of broad developmental stages may be discerned. We noted, in Chapter 3, a similar recognition in the recent evolutionary theory of Allen W. Johnson and Timothy Earle. As all these writers agree, the levels have been defined and labeled in various ways. Although most analysts agree that the continuum of complexity can and should be divided into such categories, no one categorization has achieved universal acceptance. One that is commonly used distinguishes *bands, tribes, chiefdoms,* and *states,* defined primarily by the related criteria of population size, social organizational complexity, and subsistence practices (Fig. 17.11). None of the categories is absolute or unvarying; intermediate or transitional versions can be found.

Bands are small, egalitarian societies that usually meet their subsistence

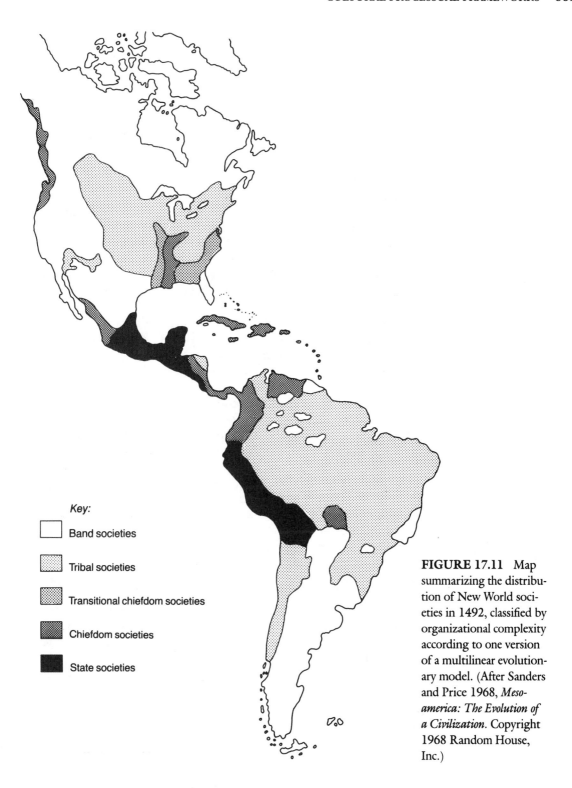

Key:

☐ Band societies

▫ Tribal societies

▨ Transitional chiefdom societies

▨ Chiefdom societies

■ State societies

FIGURE 17.11 Map summarizing the distribution of New World societies in 1492, classified by organizational complexity according to one version of a multilinear evolutionary model. (After Sanders and Price 1968, *Mesoamerica: The Evolution of a Civilization*. Copyright 1968 Random House, Inc.)

needs by hunting and gathering. Although they recognize a home territory, they do not live in settled communities but follow a seasonal migration pattern that corresponds to available food and water resources. Organizationally, a band consists of a single kin group; one example is a group composed of related adult males, wives who have been brought in from other bands, and dependent children. There is no formal political organization, no economic specialization, and no social ranking other than that based on sex and age. Population size generally ranges from 25 to 100. Richard MacNeish, on whose work Kent Flannery's highland Mexican agriculture model is based, has defined "macrobands" formed by the coalescence of several regular bands ("microbands") during seasons of relative abundance of food resources. These macrobands may consist of as many as 500 individuals, but they usually represent only temporary social gatherings. Such gatherings are known from the ethnological literature; they may be represented archaeologically by short-lived occupation sites that are uncharacteristically large for their area. Examples are found at Ipiutak, Alaska, as well as the posited sites in MacNeish's survey in the Tehuacán Valley of Mexico.

Band organizations: Tehuacán, Mexico

Tribes are usually egalitarian societies, but they are often larger in population size than bands, and they possess more varied subsistence strategies, which allow permanent village settlement. Specific subsistence modes usually include some form of food production—agriculture or horticulture—but may also involve some hunting and gathering. Tribal systems have a variety of crosscutting social institutions, beyond basic kinship ties, that integrate the members of the society; these include secret societies, age-grade groupings, and occupational groups, such as warrior or religious organizations. Permanent positions of leadership and authority do not exist, although some individuals may assume temporary leadership roles during times of stress, such as leaders of war parties. Tribal systems support populations ranging from about 500 to several thousand individuals. Under unusual conditions, however, "composite tribes" with populations of more than 10,000 may be formed: An example is the congregation of tribes of the North American Great Plains when they were faced with serious military threat from Euro-American forces in the 19th century. The tribe level of organization can usually be recognized archaeologically by village settlements that show evidence of food production subsistence practices but not of marked social status differentiation. Examples can be found the world over, from Pan P'o in central China to Basketmaker and early Pueblo sites in the southwestern United States.

Tribal organizations: Great Plains, central China, southwestern United States

Chiefdoms mark the appearance within age and sex groups of social rankings in which differential social status is conferred at birth. Kin groups such as lineages are often ranked, and the highest social status resides in a single hereditary position (the chief), who is normally the highest-ranked person within the highest-ranked lineage. The office and status of the chief are vital to the integration of the society. Although the chief exercises authority primarily by economic power, often acting as the arbitrator in distribution of surplus wealth, his right to wield this authority is usually reinforced by religious sanctions as well as by the prestige vested in the office of chief. Chiefdoms are characterized by the existence of full-time economic and political specialists, as well as such economic institutions as markets and long-distance trade networks. Population size varies from less than 1000 to more than 10,000. Some well-developed chiefdoms, such as groups along the northwestern coast of North America, are known to have supported populations approaching 100,000 by means of food *collecting* subsistence systems—in this case, intensive seacoast fishing and plant gathering. But such examples are exceptional; most chiefdoms rely on food production systems such as irrigation-based agriculture. Archaeological evidence of chiefdom systems is indicated by the material remains of the category's defining attributes—specified population size, marked social hierarchy, economic specialization, and so on. Examples include Pueblo Bonito, in Chaco Canyon, New Mexico, and—as argued by Christopher Peebles and Susan Kus—the site of Moundville, in Alabama.

State systems retain many characteristics of chiefdoms, at least in the initial period of their development. In many respects state systems merely elaborate and codify chiefdom-level institutions such as status ranking, occupational specialization, and market and trading institutions. State systems differ from chiefdoms in two crucial respects, however. First, authority is based on true political power, sanctioned by the explicit threat of legitimized force in case of deviant behavior. The means for carrying out the threat are usually manifested in permanent military, police, and judicial institutions. Second, states are too large and complex for the integrative functions of kin ties to be effective: Social integration in states is facilitated and expressed by concepts of nationality and citizenship, usually defined with reference to territorial boundaries. Thus membership in a state society is based less on genealogy and descent than on place of birth. A distinction is often made between urban and nonurban states, depending on relative size and density of major population centers. However, urbanism has proved a difficult concept to define ethnographically and sociologically, let alone for prehistoric situations; as a result, many archaeologists have come to disregard this distinction, focusing instead on attributes of organizational complexity. State systems are usually supported by intensive forms of agriculture, with agricultural technologies that include irrigation and fertilization. Populations range from about 10,000 to the millions of modern nation states. State systems have emerged at various times in different parts of the world. In Mesopotamia, state organization was established in the fourth millennium B.C.; in Mesoamerica, the site of Teotihuacan represents the locus of power of a state system that arose in the last few centuries B.C.

Taken together, the foregoing set of evolutionary levels encompasses the range of ancient social complexity. As we noted earlier, this range can be subdivided in alternative ways. Any version, however, is only a tool, and as Johnson and Earle have reminded us, it is far more important to

Chiefdom organizations: Northwest coast, Pueblo Bonito, and Moundville

State organizations: Mesopotamia and Mesoamerica

outline the mechanisms responsible for change between the levels than to simply describe the levels themselves. Recall that in their view, for example, it is population growth within an existing economic system that drives change and evolution.

POSTPROCESSUAL FRAMEWORKS

As we said at the outset of this chapter, postprocessual frameworks for interpretation are still under development. Some parts of the approach are already clear, however. Postprocessualists use a cognitive culture concept (see Chapter 3), in which culture consists of the set of meanings individuals actively construct and modify in living and making sense of their lives. Following this concept, postprocessualists emphasize the active role of individual decision makers as the molding force in cultural form, stability, and change. Not surprisingly, interpretations often stress synchronic and dynamic reconstructions of how culture is structured. In so doing, postprocessualists remind us that the specific decisions, symbols, and cultures of the past existed within their own distinct cultural contexts and should not be expected or assumed to mirror our own ideas and meanings. Rather, postprocessual archaeologists attempt to reconstruct meaning in its own specific cultural context as the key to understanding the archaeological record.

In Chapter 15, for example, we discussed the common assumption that certain artifact associations in the archaeological record represent gender distinctions. The meaning of gender-related or other kinds of patterning is often subject to alternative interpretation, depending on the kinds of models being applied to the data. To illustrate this, imagine finding clusters of cooking utensils near hearths and woodworking tools in a corner of a houseyard. A functional cultural model (often used in processual interpretation) would usually explain this pattern as defining female and male activity areas (Chapters 4 and 15), based on projecting our cultural expectations (an etic perspective) onto the archaeological record. Now assume that we have independent documentary evidence that this association between gender and activities was in fact accurate for this society, lending support for the functional (processual) explanation. But at the same time, this new evidence would facilitate the application of a cognitive cultural model. As a result, the meaning of the same data patterning might be understood as reinforcing past concepts of femaleness and maleness within this society. In other words, the definitions of these activity areas allow two different, but noncontradictory, interpretations (occupational roles and gender concepts). Both may well be correct, and in combination give a more complete account of the observed patterning in the archaeological record.

When dealing with culture change, postprocessual interpretive frameworks are dominated by internal change models. These differ in crucial ways from previous versions, however, especially ones associated with a culture historical approach. Postprocessual interpretations often deal with some of the concepts we have already seen, such as diffusion and exchange. But they recast the people of the past from faceless and passive participants into active agents. Postprocessualists also draw on processualists' call for attention to variability (as opposed to adherence to standardized norms), but treat such variability at the level of individual decision makers and symbol users, rather than focusing, as do processualists, on collective adaptations and variability between whole societies. In these and other ways, postprocessual syntheses are both a departure from and a new integration of frameworks of culture historians and processualists.

Decision-making Models

Strictly speaking, postprocessualists would probably argue against development of synchronic models, since they portray culture as dynamic, constantly in flux, being molded and reshaped on a daily basis. Nevertheless, we can speak of interpretive frameworks involving very short-term fluctuation, and therefore essentially synchronic portrayals, as well as interpretations involving longer time spans and culture change. Both of these are addressed by postprocessualists through decision-making models, where observed changes in forms and styles of the archaeological record are considered as the accumulation of conscious decisions by individuals within a particular cultural context and worldview. Again, the postprocessual emphasis is on active agents and meaning-laden behavior. Interpretation proceeds through identifying the nature of the settings in which decisions were made, the actors involved, and the meanings of the actions to those who made them. This attempt to integrate small-scale and large-scale phenomena has parallels in recent theories of biological evolution and other fields (see below, Microchange: The Multivariate Concept). Two specific instances will highlight how use of an active decision-making model differs—sometimes subtly, sometimes markedly—from culture historical and cultural processual approaches.

By the time Europeans arrived in eastern North America, many Native American groups were horticulturalists, and maize was the most important food crop grown. As we saw in earlier chapters, however, maize was originally domesticated in highland Mexico. Not only was maize an imported crop, but it also reached the Eastern Woodlands fairly late in prehistory, appearing about A.D. 150–200 among societies that had by then practiced cultivation of local plants for well over 1500 years. Culture historians would speak of the introduction of maize as a clear case of diffusion, the spread of recognition of the value of this productive crop among receptive new societies. Processualists would write instead of systems, ecology, and evolution. Bruce Smith, for example, has outlined the original development of Eastern Woodland horticulture in the **Archaic** period (4500–1500 B.C.), depicting this development as an evolutionary process,

Decision making in the Eastern Woodlands: Watson and Kennedy on ancient horticulture

in which people tended and very gradually modified available food plants within the local ecological system. As Patty Jo Watson and Mary C. Kennedy summarize Smith's account: "The plants virtually domesticate themselves." Watson and Kennedy don't directly dispute Smith's account, but they show how considering the role of individual decision makers offers expanded insights. They first argue that because maize was not native to the Eastern Woodlands, it required active care and tending, a deliberate decision to include and encourage this crop, rather than simply a passive or an accidental acceptance of a new cultigen. They further suggest that since the natural ecology of local domesticates remains poorly understood, it may be that even these had been removed from their original habitats by human cultivators. If so, such a finding would similarly imply quite purposeful behavior on the part of ancient individuals, almost certainly women. Watson and Kennedy do not claim their view has been demonstrated, but it both provides alternative perspectives on Eastern Woodland prehistory and specifies avenues (such as further study of native plant ecologies) for further research.

Watson and Kennedy stress the role of purposeful behavior by individuals, but their use of such a decision-making model does not in itself make them postprocessualists. As we said at the outset of this chapter, elements of the three approaches we distinguish are often combined in the work of individual archaeologists. Postprocessual use of a decision-making model is more fully illustrated by explicit attention to inferring ancient meaning.

Decision making and meaning: Hodder and the domestication of Europe

In *The Domestication of Europe,* Ian Hodder offers a postprocessual interpretation of the archaeological record of Neolithic Europe. In an evolutionary sense, he focuses on the same developmental transition as do Watson and Kennedy—the transition to sedentary, food-producing societies. Also like them, he emphasizes the role of individual decision makers in effecting changes in ancient life. In other ways, however, his approach is quite distinct and represents a more thoroughly postprocessual orientation. A brief summary of Hodder's thesis will illustrate clear contrast and complementarity with culture historical and processual frameworks in dealing with culture change.

Specifically, Hodder seeks to understand the form of the Neolithic European archaeological record and the ancient emic meanings it embodies. Instead of focusing on changes in plant or animal exploitation and their specific implications, he looks at the range of artifacts, ecofacts, and features pertaining to the Neolithic in Europe, to identify widespread and long-term structures in the forms of those data. For example, in central Europe, Hodder identifies consistent use of linear styles, in house form (Fig. 17.12), pottery decoration, and, later, the shape of tombs. In these linear styles, space (whether in buildings or on vessel surfaces) is broken into distinct units or fields. Moreover, Hodder notes parallel changes over time in ceramic design motifs and in division of space within houses. In brief, increasing emphasis was given to boundaries between spaces and

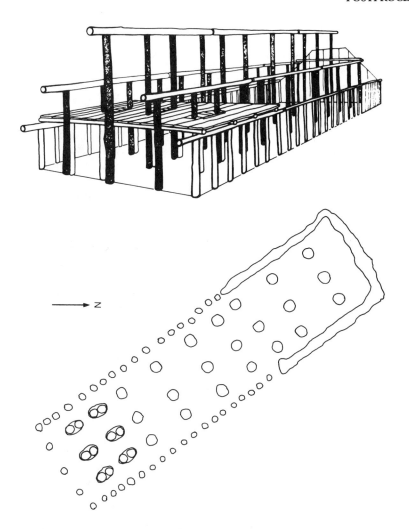

FIGURE 17.12 This reconstruction of the frame of a European Neolithic house (top) is based on evidence from the ground plan (bottom) revealed by excavation. (After Lüning, in Hodder 1990.)

overall complexity of design. In architecture this was especially evident in the elaboration of house entrances, which (not coincidentally?) tend to be where finds of decorated pottery concentrate. Hodder interprets these parallels as reflecting an emic meaning system that structured central European Neolithic society. In this system, boundaries and divisions became more important through time. The reason they did, Hodder believes, is that people used them to distinguish the "domesticated" human domain from the "wild" surrounding world. By dramatizing house entrances, for example, and arranging the rooms within the building in a linear sequence, the occupants increasingly chose to stress control over access by strangers, human or otherwise. The specific sequence of observable changes in house or ceramic style is, however, more gradual than abrupt because although the individual builders and potters were actively reinterpreting symbols, they did so within the context of an established expressive system, in which their houses and vessels had to still be meaningful.

Elsewhere in Europe, the particular patterns differed, but the meaning, to Hodder, is broadly the same. In southeastern Europe, for example, ovens and adjacent areas of houses (as opposed to entrances) were emphasized, and even the forms of ovens and houses were similar, as illustrated in miniature representations. Oven areas were associated with female figurines as well as with pottery and other equipment for grain storage and preparation. Despite the distinctions of form between southeast and central Europe, Hodder sees the meanings of the structured forms as parallel, each actively stressing establishment of a tamed, controlled, and sheltering house—a domesticated space—contrasting with the wild and dangerous world beyond the house. Ultimately, he interprets the European Neolithic as a time of such "domestication" of cultural forms generally, through the accumulation of individual, symbol-laden decisions in the creation and use of these cultural forms. Archaeologists have traditionally focused attention on the technological and economic side of the picture, on the Neolithic as the time of domestication of plants and animals. To Hodder, on the other hand, this was but one, relatively small reflection of what was going on.

The differences between this interpretive framework and those of culture history and processualism are marked. For example, both this framework and that of culture history focus on style. For culture historical archaeologists, however, studying stylistic change is undertaken for creating **time–space grids;** for postprocessualists, examining style allows inferring both the symbolic meaning behind the style and the manipulation of that meaning by its users. For processualists, on the other hand, we have seen that interpretive synthesis emphasizes functional and adaptive aspects of culture, usually by examining the most accessible parts of culture—subsistence, technology, and (more indirectly) social organization—and seeks broad, cross-cultural regularities. Illustrations include characterization of the multilinear stages outlined earlier and factors emphasized in specific theoretical views, such as Johnson and Earle's (see above). Postprocessualists, however, look to the structure and symbolic meaning behind cultural forms and, to do so, stay within the context of individual cultural traditions or sets of related traditions.

Different as these frameworks clearly are, we repeat that they are not mutually incompatible. They are different ways of looking at the data, and they ask different questions of the archaeological record. Hodder himself makes this point quite explicitly in several places in his book, and when he speaks of the role of economics in change, his remarks are sometimes compatible with views of Johnson and Earle. But the emphasis is quite different, as we have seen. Where processualists seek to explain, postprocessualists seek to understand, a sometimes subtle distinction explored first in Chapter 3.

The foregoing comments do not imply that all frameworks are always equally successful. Each provides working interpretations, however (Hodder describes his own as an "uncertain foray"), and each should be subjected to the kind of systematic examination we described in Chapter 3 as characterizing scientific pursuit.

CAUSES OF PREHISTORIC CULTURAL CHANGE

By using any one of the interpretive models discussed above, or a combination of several, archaeologists attempt to understand the basic causes of prehistoric culture change. But how does the archaeologist reveal those causes? Two basic schools of thought have emerged to address this question, each with many variations. The first emphasizes the general approach associated with processual archaeology and concerns the identification of what are held to be the **prime movers** of cultural change. That is, the prime-mover concept attempts to document the process of change in a universal context, revealing those primary causes that operate in all human societies. The second school, the multivariate concept, is more particularistic, attempting to isolate and understand individual causes to explain particular instances of cultural change. Although originating with processual archaeology, in its emphasis on the more fine-grained events of the past, the multivariate concept provides a bridge to postprocessual archaeology. In contrast to seeing change as being due to universal prime movers, the multivariate concept holds that cultural change can be understood only by investigating each individual instance of change. In the original processual version, the multivariate concept is rooted in the basic cultural adaptive process. In postprocessual versions, the multivariate concept is rooted in individual cultural contexts. But in both versions, the causes of change are seen as particularistic rather than universal.

Macrochange: The Prime-Mover Concept

The first perspective emphasizes identification of a few specific, primary factors that underlie the process of cultural change and, ultimately, cultural evolution. It is based on the premise that the regularities and patterns in evolutionary change result from regularities of cause. Accordingly, without necessarily denying the validity of research focused on individual subsystems and microchange, this approach emphasizes the testing of broader hypotheses that seek the fundamental, far-reaching causes of all cultural change.

The prime-mover approach is derived directly from the pioneering theories of Childe and Adams, discussed in Chapter 3. The idea of a prime mover has come to mean an emphasis on a crucial factor that sparks evolutionary change, but all archaeologists realize that cultural evolution is the product of complex interactions among many factors. Current workers

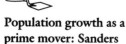

Population growth as a prime mover: Sanders and Price in Mesoamerica

in the field attempt to identify in detail the working of various prime movers in cultural change. Population growth is often proposed as a fundamental cause of cultural change. This prime mover has been applied in various regions to explain the course of cultural evolution. For example, William Sanders and Barbara Price based their thesis for the evolution of pre-Columbian Mesoamerican culture on population growth and its effects on two secondary factors, competition and cooperation. As noted earlier, Johnson and Earle argued the prime-mover role of population with reference to a worldwide set of examples. Other causal factors have been proposed to explain specific evolutionary developments, such as the rise of complex state societies. Prime movers proposed for this development include environmental circumscription and warfare (suggested by scholars such as Robert Carneiro and David Webster) and economic exchange systems (advanced by Malcolm Webb).

Microchange: The Multivariate Concept

The second perspective holds that no single factor or small group of "prime movers" causes cultural change. Rather, change is "multivariate"; each instance is unique, resulting from a specific combination of factors embedded in specific events. The strategy used is to direct research toward individual cases of culture change to delineate the specific factors involved in each instance. This strategy originated within processual archaeology as an alternative to the prime-mover concept, specifically as a consequence of cultural ecological research. In this version, the multivariate concept focuses on subsystems that are most directly involved in adaptation. To identify the causes of change, research of this kind may test hypotheses concerned, for example, with a variety of alternative subsistence modes or with the acquisition and distribution of critical natural resources.

The multivariate concept holds that cultural evolution, the overall product of change, is the product of a multitude of adaptive adjustments—each resulting in a microchange—that are a constant feature of all cultural systems. Specific multivariate models, such as that proposed by Kent Flannery for the transformation from hunting and gathering subsistence to food production, build on this premise and assume that substantial cumulative cultural changes occur over a sufficient period of time.

In processual terms, the multivariate perspective sees cultural evolution operating through an interlocking, hierarchical systems model of culture, whose basic structure is common to all human societies but whose details vary from culture to culture. The variations and unique features of certain systems produce the different patterns of cultural evolution in each society. These systemic variations account for the relative stability of some societies, characterized by deviation-counteracting relationships, whereas change occurs rapidly in others, characterized by deviation-amplifying relationships.

Thus the structure and operation of the multivariate concept of cultural evolution is based on the tenets of cultural ecological and systems models. This approach requires that the archaeologist identify the components, and understand the relationships, of those specific subsystems crucial to the cultural adaptive process. This is not an easy task, especially given the inherent limitations of archaeological data. The archaeologist must formulate and test a series of sophisticated hypotheses, using data that are often difficult to collect. Yet, when successful—as in the analysis of the transformation to food production in Mesoamerica described earlier in this chapter—such research may reveal multivariate causes to explain fundamental cultural change.

Multivariate causality must also allow for factors beyond ecological or systemic adaptations. Although, as we have seen, cultural evolution is often viewed in such materialist terms, the development of postprocessual archaeology has highlighted the need to consider nonmaterial or ideological factors that are often crucial in cultural process (see Chapter 16). Furthermore, postprocessual research focuses on the specific events in the past—including the activities of individuals and small groups that may direct or at least influence the developmental course of a society. Our concepts of specific culture change and long-term cultural evolution, therefore, must provide for the behavior of single individuals or small segments of society on all levels, ideological as well as technological or economic, as difficult as this may be to demonstrate archaeologically. Insofar as possible, these events should also be understood in their own terms—an emic as well as an etic perspective. And we must keep in mind that the activities of individual members and groups within society are often spawned by selfish motives, with results that are sometimes beneficial, sometimes disastrous. These points are summarized by Geoffrey Conrad and Arthur Demarest (1984:198): "World archaeology is littered with the remains of extinct civilizations driven to the point of systemic collapse by . . . maladaptive behavior—behavior that can only be explained by reference to the dominance of individual, small group, or class interests during critical periods of cultural evolution."

In this context, then, the multivariate concept of culture change becomes a link to the postprocessual approach. For in seeking the meaning of the past in emic terms, postprocessual archaeology views change in the same nondeterministic and unique terms as the multivariate concept. Of course, the postprocessual version of the multivariate concept sees the factors responsible for change in a different context from that usually associated with processualism. Thus a postprocessual version of the multivariate concept would attempt to identify the factors involved in change within specific events, but not only those involved with ecosystems and their adaptive adjustments.

Rather, for postprocessualists, all past events represent past decisions, as defined within a particular cultural context. Taken together, the sum of these decisions is the record of cultural evolution, within and ultimately across cultural contexts. It is noteworthy that, as Steven Mithen and others point out, a parallel view, of individual decisions as the building blocks of evolution, has emerged in recent theories of evolutionary biology.

SUMMARY

Culture historical interpretation is built on the temporal and spatial synthesis of archaeological data. It emphasizes a chronicling of events, a demonstration of shifting cultural connections between sites, and an outline of relative change and stability of cultural forms within sites. The descriptive models used as the basis for interpretation are usually broad, general analogs founded in a normative concept of culture. Interpretation by means of these models attempts to account for the similarities and differences observed in the synthesized data. Differences between sites may be ascribed either to inevitable cultural variation or to processes of internal cultural change. Similarities, on the other hand, are interpreted as the result of mechanisms that lead to transfer of ideas between communities.

Most archaeologists recognize that observed cultural similarities, such as equivalent form or style attributes in the artifacts from two different sites, do not *in themselves* constitute sufficient evidence to distinguish among various mechanisms of prehistoric communication and contact—that is, to determine whether diffusion, trade, or migration accounts for the observed correspondences. Only detailed analysis can resolve this question; constituent analysis, for instance, may establish whether the raw materials of various artifacts have the same source.

The problem of interpreting observed similarities is compounded by documented examples of independent but parallel invention—a phenomenon that also leads to cultural similarity. For instance, the mathematical concept of zero is thought to have been invented at least twice—once in India at least as early as the sixth century A.D., and apparently even earlier by the ancient Maya of Mesoamerica. The domestication of food plants is usually considered an independent but parallel cultural development in the Old and New Worlds. Thus, observed similarities in the data at two different sites may sometimes result from independent invention.

Deciding between internal and external sources for cultural change—and specifically settling the question of diffusion as opposed to independent invention in interpreting observed cross-cultural similarities—has absorbed a great deal of intellectual energy. The question can sometimes be resolved by new evidence. Discovery of local bronze tool prototypes would be evidence in favor of the postulated independent development of metallurgy in Southeast Asia. Models may originally arise as a result of a compilation of archaeological data in an unknown area. But to resolve the issues raised often requires further, problem-oriented research designed to test specific hypotheses.

We have seen that culture historical interpretation is the result of a rational process of inquiry that focuses on the gathering and synthesis of data representing temporal and spatial variation. The resulting time–space grids are tested, refined, and expanded by subsequent research, providing a necessary foundation for the new and different questions asked by the other approaches to the past. But the culture historical approach may also generate initial hypotheses about what happened in the past that can be tested by the more explicitly scientific procedures associated with the processual approach.

This second approach uses hypothesis testing to identify and explain cultural process—how cultures operate at any one point in time and why they change (or remain stable) through time. Certain explanatory models are most often associated with the cultural processual approach. Systems models see a culture as a set of interconnected components that change (or remain stable) as a result of the relationships between their parts. Cultural ecological models, based on the specialized study of cultural ecology, combine a systems model concept with a comprehensive view of the dynamic interaction between culture and environment. Multilinear cultural evolutionary models are based in part on systems and cultural ecological concepts but stress a broader, long-term perspective in tracing the developmental course of each human society. Regularities observed in the evolutionary careers of cultures have led to the definition of "stages" of societies (such as bands, tribes, chiefdoms, and states), but unlike earlier cultural evolutionary concepts, multilinear models stress the individual and nonpredictable trajectory of each society through time. Overall, it appears that cultural evolution fluctuates between times of gradual change or relative stability and times of rapid and profound transformation.

The causes of cultural evolution are often defined at two levels (which are actually part of the same continuum): prime movers, the one or more critical factors that broadly spark change; and microchanges, the multitude of individual adaptive adjustments that, in the aggregate, result in change. These causes have usually been viewed from a technological or material bias, given the prehistoric archaeological reliance on physical remains from the past. But archaeologists must also consider nonmaterial factors, such as ideology, which often play a critical role in the developmental course of human society.

The postprocessual approach offers a finer-grained framework for interpretation, emphasizing the active role of individuals as decision makers and the meaning-laden context in which decisions are made. The "meaning" cited here is emic, viewed from the perspective of the culture under study, not by imposition of the archaeologist's cultural viewpoint. Discovering the emic perspective for past situations is a serious challenge for postprocessual archaeologists, and frameworks for doing so are still under development. Although postprocessual interpretations are often based on synchronic models (or short-term fluctuations), they can have implications for evolutionary change. The postprocessual view of long-term change, then, is the cumulative sum of these decision-events over time.

Finally, although over the past few decades archaeologists have debated the relative merits of the culture historical, cultural processual, and post-processual approaches, we take the position that all three are essential to the development of the most complete and accurate understanding of the past. The combination of aspects of all available approaches offers the most comprehensive research strategy for the archaeologist confronting the complexities of the past.

GUIDE TO FURTHER READING

Culture Historical Frameworks

Adams 1968; S. R. Binford 1968; Bischof and Viteri 1972; Dyson 1960; Ford 1969; Haury 1958; Lathrap, Marcos, and Zeidler 1977; Martin et al. 1952; Meggers, Evans, and Estrada 1965; Mooney 1965; Rouse 1986; Rowe 1966; Smith 1928; Tschopik 1950

Cultural Processual Frameworks

Systems Models: Bertalanffy 1968; Clarke 1968; Doran 1970; Flannery 1968; Hill 1977; Plog 1975; Rappaport 1968; Turnbull 1972

Cultural Ecological Models: Flannery 1965, 1969, 1986; Netting 1977; Sanders and Price 1968; Steward 1955, 1977; Thomas 1973; Zubrow 1975

Multilinear Cultural Evolution Models: Adams 1966; Braun and Plog 1982; Conrad and Demarest 1984; Dunnell 1980; Feinman and Neitzel 1984; Flannery 1972a, 1986; Fried 1967; Johnson and Earle 1987; MacNeish 1964a; Peebles and Kus 1977; Preucel 1991; Sahlins and Service 1960; Sanders and Price 1968; Service 1962; Steward 1955, 1977

Postprocessual Frameworks

Gero and Conkey 1991; Gibbon 1989; Hodder 1982c, 1985, 1989, 1990, 1991a, 1991b; Leone and Potter 1988; Mithen 1989; Pinsky and Wylie 1990; Preucel 1991; Smith 1987; Watson and Kennedy 1991

Causes of Prehistoric Cultural Change

Adams 1966; L. R. Binford 1968b; Carneiro 1970; Childe 1954; Cohen 1977; Conrad and Demarest 1984; Flannery 1968, 1969, 1972a, 1986; Hodder 1985, 1990, 1991a, 1991b; Johnson and Earle 1987; Jones and Kautz 1981; Kelley and Hanen 1988; Reed 1977; Sanders, Parsons, and Santley 1979; Sanders and Price 1968; Service 1975; Stark 1986; Thomas 1986a; Trigger 1989; Webb 1973; Webster 1977; Wenke 1981; Wright 1986

OF POTS AND PILLAGE

Steven A. LeBlanc

LeBlanc was formerly Curator of Archaeology at the Southwest Museum. He is also the Director of the Mimbres Foundation, which has conducted six field seasons of research in southwestern New Mexico. In 1980, LeBlanc and several others founded the Archaeological Conservancy to help protect archaeological sites.

In the summer of 1975 I was directing fieldwork on the Mattocks Ruin in New Mexico. As my crew members excavated with shovels, trowels, and whisk brooms, we could hear the dull rumble of a looter's bulldozer about 3 miles away, completely obliterating a similar ruin to recover a few pots. Even worse, such destruction was legal, and there was no established means to do anything about it. We could only continue to dig and to hear the bulldozer. It was not a pleasant experience.

Graduate training in the 1960s and early 1970s did not result in a strong concern for the preservation of archaeological sites. As students, we were primarily concerned with the concepts of processual archaeology and the scientific method. Site preservation was relegated to the "lesson" that all looters were bad and that amateur archaeologists were just that—amateurs who usually caused more harm than good.

The consensus of the times was that the best way to deal with these problems was to avoid them. Dig the most pristine sites available; avoid the locals as much as possible. This was, and to some extent is, the prevalent approach to archaeology and society. It is quite possible to be a senior archaeologist whose excavations all have been undertaken on government land, thus avoiding local landowners. It is possible for an archaeologist to have never held an open house or produced a newspaper or popular report informing the community about either the purpose or the results of his or her work. Such archaeologists, nevertheless, will complain about pothunting and the lack of public awareness about the importance of archaeology and the need to protect sites. Until very recently, the training of most archaeologists ignored these concerns.

With this typical archaeological background, I began a long-term research project in the Mimbres area in southwestern New Mex-ico. It was well known that the Mimbres area, due to the beauty of its painted bowls, was one of the most severely looted areas in North America. To preserve what we could of the Mimbres cultural tradition, a few nonarchaeologists from Los Angeles and I instituted the Mimbres Foundation. It began with a five-year program of excavation and site survey. Crews composed of about 20 students excavated for several months each summer. We recognized that the looting problem was severe, but we were ill equipped to deal with it.

During the first season of digging, several things quickly became obvious. Even at sites that looked like battlefields as a result of the looters' holes (see Fig 18.2), important scientific information could still be obtained. Recovering it, however, was not easy. It turned out to be frustrating work, with lots of wasted effort. Many a dig crew member would excavate a room down to its floor only to discover an old, rusted Prince Albert tobacco can, revealing that all the carefully excavated deposits had been churned up by looters. Nevertheless, we determined that

(continued)

(continued)

with perseverance and an ever-increasing knowledge of how to excavate looted sites, it was possible to recover considerable information.

Local residents, amateur archaeologists, and ordinary folks knew a great deal about the locations of sites and their basic contents, and they willingly shared this information with us. Moreover, they were interested in archaeology, and often their interest was limited only by their inability to learn more about the local archaeology. After we realized this, we initiated an annual open house. We curated exhibits of recovered artifacts, opened excavated areas to tours, and presented demonstrations. Several hundred people visited the excavations and parked their cars, pickups, and horses everywhere, and the Future Farmers of America sold soft drinks—an experience both for us and for the local community! We also printed and distributed a brief annual report that summarized the season's excavations.

While we were teaching local people the difference between scientific archaeology and looting, professional looters were hard at work in the Mimbres area. The market value of Mimbres bowls had long encouraged such site destruction. In the late 1960s, a cost-effective method—the use of bulldozers—sped up the looters'

work of finding pots. Looters either leased sites or simply trespassed and quickly looted out as many bowls as possible. Even though this method left many bowls smashed beyond repair and crushed skeletons and artifacts of all kinds in the bulldozers' tracks, the commercial looters were not deterred.

Our strategy was to dig faster—to try to recover what we could before every site in the valley was destroyed. As luck would have it, the house we rented as a dig headquarters had a site adjacent to it that had great potential. When we leased the house, the owner included a purchase-option clause. Initially, we had not thought of invoking it, but we began to realize that although we could never out-dig bulldozers, we could own a site and protect it forever. If we could own this site, why not others?

I subsequently went on the fund-raising trail and obtained the funds to purchase this site and four others. I estimated the cost of the sites to be less than 2 percent of the money it would have taken to properly excavate and report the results.

The acquisition of these sites became known to a few archaeologists in the Southwest. One came to me about a very important site in the northern part of New Mexico, a site that was an outlying community of Chaco Canyon. This site was in the process of

being purchased by looters. With virtually no funds but lots of confidence, I approached the landowners and attempted to purchase the site. The looters quickly sued me. Because I had no resources and no experience in legal issues, the looters got the site and subsequently decimated it. Saving sites was going to be harder than I had imagined.

It was then that I decided a real organization rather than a lone, underfunded amateur was needed. We had been lucky in the Mimbres, but luck wasn't enough.

The board of directors of the Mimbres Foundation decided that a separate organization was needed, so the Archaeological Conservancy was incorporated with initial grants from the Ford Foundation and the Rockefeller Brothers Funds. The Conservancy now has a permanent staff, more than 4,000 members, and has protected sites in many states that span the prehistory and history of the United States.

Some interesting lessons about archaeology as a profession can be found in this story. Archaeologists have always had to do much more than archaeology. Today, additional skills or experience seem to be needed—such as the ability to deal with lawyers, officers of philanthropic foundations, government bureaucrats, politicians, and county courthouse records. Although such skills don't seem necessary when starting out in graduate school, they are becoming increasingly important.

There is also another side to the problem of looting and public education. There is no body of literature or knowledge on how to excavate heavily damaged sites. Sessions to share what knowledge does exist are not held at the annual archaeological meetings. We had to learn by trial and error when we dug in the Mimbres, and we made a lot of mistakes.

In addition, some professionals do not yet recognize or acknowledge the importance of site preservation. Looting is rightly condemned, but in the eyes of many, efforts to stop looting are not part of a professional archaeologist's job. There is no Hippocratic oath for archaeologists; there is no obligation to try to protect this heritage. With a few exceptions, such as Bob McGimsey, archaeologists are not acknowl-

edged for making significant efforts to protect sites. Certainly, society at large deserves to have the heritage of humankind preserved. But before archaeologists can play a leading role in halting the toll taken by looters, the professional duty and obligation to protect the past must be actively carried out by all archaeologists.

CHAPTER EIGHTEEN

CHALLENGES TO ARCHAEOLOGY

We in the modern world have turned more stones, listened to more buried
voices, than any culture before us. There should be a kind of pity that comes with
time, when one grows truly more conscious and looks behind as well as forward,
for nothing is more brutally savage than the man who is not aware he is a
shadow.

   Loren C. Eiseley, The Night Country, *1971*

A great challenge faces contemporary archaeologists: the threat posed by
the accelerating destruction of the remains of past societies. As we noted
at the beginning of this book, the processes of transformation—whether
natural forces or the impact of later societies—affect all forms of archaeological data. However, in recent decades the toll of archaeological destruction has reached immense proportions; many archaeologists fear that
unless immediate action is taken, critical information will be lost forever
(Fig. 18.1).

   During the past few years archaeologists have increasingly attempted to
stimulate public awareness of and concern about the threatened status of
archaeological remains throughout the world. This awakening is especially
apparent in the United States, where public awareness and governmental
protective action concerning archaeology have traditionally lagged behind
those of other nations. There are encouraging signs that public ignorance
and apathy are changing. An important book by Charles McGimsey, a
leading advocate of public and governmental support for archaeology in
the United States, reviewed the situation a generation ago and made recommendations for future programs on both state and federal governmental levels. McGimsey summarized the basic issues as follows:

> The next fifty years—some would say twenty-five—are going to be the most
> critical in the history of American archaeology. What is recovered, what is pre-
> served, and how these goals are accomplished during this period will largely
> determine *for all time* the knowledge available to subsequent generations of
> Americans concerning their heritage from the past. . . . The next generation
> cannot study or preserve what already has been destroyed. (McGimsey 1972:3)

MAJOR SOURCES OF CHALLENGE

The destruction of archaeological evidence has two sources: the **looter**
who ransacks the remnants of ancient societies for artifacts or "art" that
can be sold to **collectors;** and the constant destructive effects of expanding
societies all over the world. Everyday activities such as farming and construction, though not intended to obliterate archaeological information,
nevertheless take their toll. We will consider these threats in turn in the
remainder of this chapter.

FIGURE 18.1 The accelerating destruction of past cultural remains represents the most critical threat to archaeology today; here, archaeologists attempt to salvage evidence from a site being destroyed by highway construction. (Courtesy of Hester Davis and the Florida Bureau of Archives and History.)

Looting and Antiquities Collecting

The tragic destruction of archaeological sites by vandals and plunderers has accelerated dramatically over the past few decades. This is especially true for sites in the United States and Latin America, where the problem is clearly out of control, as we described at the outset of this book with reference to recent incidents at Slack Farm in Kentucky and Sipán in Peru. Words and even pictures cannot convey the full impact of the physical destruction of a plundered site, transformed into what looks like a wartime scene (Fig. 18.2). But what appears to be the result of aerial bombing is in fact the aftermath of gangs of looters using the tools of their illicit trade—shovels, pickaxes, dynamite, and even bulldozers—in frenzied attempts to find a few buried "treasures" that will fetch a high price on the art market. The amount of information that is lost each year to this destruction is astronomical. And the violence is not restricted to archaeological sites—looters are often armed and in some instances have used their weapons to drive away anyone who attempted to stop them. In several documented cases, people have been shot and even killed after surprising these criminals at work.

In discussing archaeological looting in the first part of this book, we concluded that the cause of the problem is economic. As long as collectors consider certain kinds of archaeological remains to be "art," the economics of supply and demand will lead to the plundering of sites to find artifacts

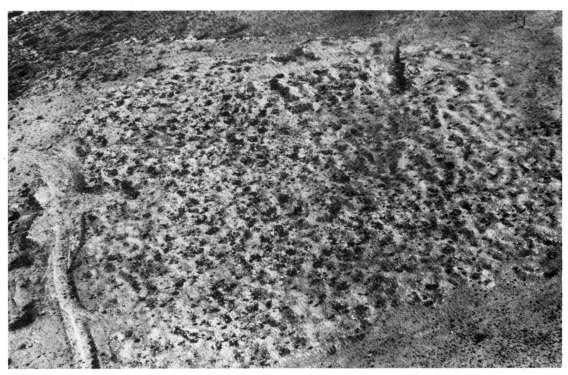

FIGURE 18.2 This aerial photograph shows the utter destruction caused by looters, who have transformed the archaeological site of Oldtown Village, New Mexico, into a cratered wasteland. Scenes like this are becoming all too common in many areas of the world, as collectors increase their demand for "authentic" archaeological specimens. (Photo courtesy of Steven LeBlanc.)

that have commercial value (Fig. 18.3). In this process, of course, information on the archaeological association and context of the objects is lost, and associated artifacts that lack commercial value are often destroyed.

Most archaeologists recognize that the looting of sites can never be stopped completely. Under most circumstances, about all that can be done is to reduce the toll until it reaches insignificant proportions, as it has in China because of aroused national concern and government vigilance. New laws that restrict the international traffic in archaeological materials are needed, and present laws should be better enforced. International cooperation and standardization of import-export regulations would help, but customs laws alone cannot solve the problem.

The only effective way to reduce archaeological looting is to discourage the collector. If collectors no longer sought "art" from archaeological contexts, there would be no market for archaeological items and thus no incentive for the plundering of sites. Paintings, sculptures, or other works *produced for* the art market or art patrons are not included here. But the line must be drawn at any item that derives from an archaeological context, whether it is a Maya vase from a tomb or a Greek sculpture dragged from the bottom of the sea. The distinction is based on context; archaeological

(a)

(b)

FIGURE 18.3 Valuable archaeological evidence is often destroyed because it is sought by collectors and commands a high price on the "art" market. (a) Stela 1 from Jimbal, Guatemala, photographed shortly after its discovery in 1965. (b) Less than ten years later, looters had sawed off the top panel to steal the sculptured figures; in the process, they destroyed the head of the Maya ruler and the top of the hieroglyphic inscription. (Photo (a) courtesy of the Tikal Project, The University Museum, University of Pennsylvania; photo (b) courtesy of Joya Hairs.)

remains ripped from their archaeological context have already lost their scientific value. Archaeologists must therefore direct their efforts to preventing further destruction of sites (Fig. 18.4).

When we speak of collectors, we are referring to a diverse group that includes both individuals and institutions. Only a few decades ago, most museums acquired at least some of the objects in their archaeological collections by purchase and thus encouraged (directly or indirectly) the looting of sites. Fortunately, that situation has changed: Most museums have signed or agreed to abide by a series of international agreements prohibiting commercial dealings in archaeological materials that lack documented "pedigrees" concerning the circumstances of their discovery. Unfortunately, some museums, including many art museums, have refused to abide by these agreements and continue to buy and sell archaeological "art."

The private market demand for prized archaeological specimens has swelled to such a degree that collectors are increasingly turning to museum collections to satisfy their appetite for antiquities. Burglaries at archaeological museums are becoming more commonplace; the most tragic proof of this occurred at Christmas 1985 when a series of world-famous pre-Columbian artifacts were stolen from their exhibit cases at the Museum of Anthropology in Mexico City. These objects are so well known that they can never be traded on the open market. Rather, it appears thefts of this

FIGURE 18.4 Not all looting is motivated by the inflated prices typical of the commercial art market. Here we see the destruction of a prehistoric archaeological site by weekend artifact collectors. (Courtesy of Hester Davis and the Society for California Archaeologists.)

kind are often carried out to satisfy a small number of wealthy collectors who pay millions of dollars for antiquities that will have to remain hidden away indefinitely. In the Mexican case, fortunately, most of the stolen items were eventually recovered; otherwise, the people of that nation would have lost a priceless portion of their national heritage.

In another example, red-painted pottery from the northeast Thailand site of Ban Chiang began to attract some foreign buyers by the late 1960s. As the site, and northeast Thailand generally, aroused more archaeological interest in the 1970s, becoming known as a precocious rival to ancient Mesopotamia as a center for the development of farming villages and bronze metallurgy, the demand for Ban Chiang pottery by private collectors stepped up dramatically. By the mid-1970s, archaeologists working in northeast Thailand to gather further evidence had trouble locating sites that had not been damaged or leveled by looting. And the insatiable demand for artifacts that caused so much destruction of archaeological sites also spawned a thriving business in the local production of high-quality fakes. By the early 1980s, sales of Ban Chiang pots, some authentic and some modern fakes, were bringing $3000 or more apiece on the illicit "art" market.

Thus it is the individual antiquities collector who remains the greatest threat to the world's archaeological resources, whether collectors are part of the vast majority who buy and sell artifacts looted from archaeological sites, or part of the most wealthy and mysterious clique who sponsor audacious burglaries from archaeological museums. In both cases, they are acquiring stolen property. About the best that can be said for museums that continue to purchase looted artifacts is that these remains almost

Museums as latest targets to supply collectors: Burglary at the Mexican Museum of Anthropology

Demand and supply: Ban Chiang pottery, looted and fake

always become public knowledge eventually, although the archaeological information is forever lost. But purchases of archaeological materials by private individuals usually take place in secrecy and remain unknown to archaeologists. We do not mean to imply that all collectors are evil. Many may not even be aware that their collecting spawns the destruction of knowledge. They need to be made aware of the destruction they are sponsoring, for as long as a market exists, looting will continue.

It is discouraging to note that some professional archaeologists retain close ties both to private collectors and to commercial dealers in antiquities. These archaeologists perform services such as authentication (distinguishing legitimate archaeological specimens from fakes) and evaluation (assessment of market value), often for a fee. They often defend their dealings on the ground that the archaeologists then have the opportunity to observe and even record (photographs are sometimes permitted) objects that would otherwise remain closeted in a private collection and thus unknown. Yet the harsh fact is that any archaeologist who provides such services, whether to evaluate, authenticate, or merely record a looted object, is engaged in an activity that *encourages* the further destruction of archaeological sites. Obviously, any archaeological specimen that has been authenticated or evaluated by an archaeologist commands a greater price. But the mere fact that an object has been of interest to a professional archaeologist—especially if it was of sufficient interest to be photographed—will also increase that object's market value. The excuse of recording information otherwise lost is a delusion; the true archaeological information is already lost, destroyed when the object was robbed of its archaeological context. No person and no photograph can restore that loss of information. Professional archaeologists should be committed to discouraging the destruction wrought by looting of sites, and therefore they must avoid any activity that fosters the plundering of the past, including interaction with dealers and encouragement of collectors. Severing such interactions might contribute to lowering commercial values for antiquities and thus begin to diminish the attractions of looting.

But the question remains how collectors can be discouraged from seeking and purchasing looted archaeological materials. Various solutions have been offered. One promising line of legal action, already implemented by some governments, is to change inheritance laws so that an individual cannot bequeath archaeological collections to his or her heirs. Instead of being part of an inheritance, those items defined by law as archaeological materials pass to the state. One motive for maintaining private collections of antiquities is that most antiquities, like legitimate art, increase in value over time and thus represent an investment. Legislation excluding such a collection from the individual's estate makes it a much less desirable investment and thus removes one powerful incentive for collecting archaeological objects. Many collectors may think twice about purchasing "art" that will ultimately be taken by the government. Although it is promising, however, this kind of legal action is now only partially effective, since some collectors avoid the law by moving their collections to other countries. Thus, uniform international laws are needed.

The United States, like many countries, has problems in protecting its archaeological resources, including Native American and historical sites. A recent focus of legislative attention has been the protection of historic shipwrecks. Traditionally under the jurisdiction of federal maritime salvage laws, shipwrecks of all ages have been available for exploitation by divers and commercial salvage companies. Recent wrecks are often beneficially salvaged, but the lack of discrimination between these and older remains has allowed many shipwrecks with unique archaeological and historical value to be destroyed by treasure seekers, sometimes innocently removing isolated "souvenirs," at other times dismantling entire sunken ships.

Unfortunately, in recent years several important wrecks have been "salvaged" to the point of utter destruction, including remains of pirate ships and Spanish treasure galleons. In several recent cases in Florida, for example, current federal admiralty law has taken precedence over state laws designed to protect underwater archaeological resources, and the broader implication of the Florida rulings is that, without new federal legislation, no state can assert confident and effective protective authority over historical shipwrecks. Some specific results of these rulings have been vividly described by Wilburn Cockrell, Underwater Archaeologist for the State of Florida. For example, the 1733 wreck of the *San Jose,* originally slated to become the world's first underwater shipwreck park, is now completely looted, almost all of its contents destroyed or scattered, so that what remains is "simply a hole in the ocean floor, with even the ballast stones removed for a fireplace." This tragic case contrasts with the fate of the 1554 wreck of the *San Esteban,* excavated off the coast of Texas in 1973 under the sponsorship of the Texas State Antiquities Committee. The results of this effort include recovery of important new data on little-known 16th-century ship architecture and construction methods, conservation of the remains of the ship and its contents, and publication of the results in book, movie, and exhibition formats aimed at diverse audiences.

We hope that the destruction of underwater sites such as the *San Jose* is a thing of the past. In 1988 Congress passed the Federal Abandoned Shipwreck Act, which ends most exploitation and destruction by removing sunken ships of archaeological interest from marine salvage jurisdiction. Now historic shipwrecks are protected by laws in most states without fear that these provisions will be overridden by salvage interests.

The antiquities problem is as complex as it is urgent. In formulating antiquities legislation, considerations of politics and patronage often weigh more heavily than the security of archaeological materials. Archaeologists and interested persons alike must therefore fight to protect the past, or we shall lose it forever.

Problems in protecting cultural resources: Ancient shipwrecks

Destruction in the Name of Progress

Vandalism and looting are serious problems, but well-intentioned activity can also be harmful. Although done in the name of progress, activities such as opening new lands to agriculture, constructing new roads and buildings, and creating flood-control projects inevitably destroy countless remains of past human activity (see Fig. 18.1). Almost any action that affects the earth's surface is a threat to the archaeological record, and preserving all archaeological remains is clearly impossible. But much has already been destroyed, and the pace of destruction continues to accelerate in step with world population growth, so that only a small proportion of the archaeological record remains intact. In some areas of the world, entire regions have already been lost, entire ancient cities destroyed.

McGimsey's estimate that we have very little time before the remains of the past are lost forever is true not only for the United States but also for the entire world. If the destructive forces are not controlled within a generation, so little may be left that further archaeological field research would be futile. The loss will be felt not only by the archaeologists (who will no longer be able to conduct field research) but also by all of humanity. Under the best of circumstances we can never answer all our questions about past cultural development, but as the physical remains continue to be obliterated, our ability to ask any new questions at all is drastically curtailed.

Obviously, we cannot simply stop population and construction growth, so a considerable number of sites are going to be destroyed. But an increasing number of archaeologists are adopting a conservationist attitude toward cultural remains. This attitude involves a heightened emphasis on planning and a restructuring of the relative roles of excavation and reconnaissance/survey in archaeological research. In the case of sites threatened with imminent destruction, the archaeologist's response has traditionally been to excavate quickly and recover as many data as possible—sometimes literally one step ahead of construction crews. Now, with the invaluable assistance of an increasing array of supportive legislation, archaeologists are more often able to take the time to assess the situation, to reconnoiter the area concerned, and then—if appropriate—to conduct excavations.

Since the excavation process itself destroys an archaeological site, it should be confined whenever possible to situations in which adequate planning, time, and money are available to ensure that maximum useful knowledge about the past is recovered. Archaeologists are thus becoming more actively concerned with ensuring that archaeological data are preserved in the ground, secure for future generations and future archaeologists. Of course, this philosophy applies to unthreatened sites as well as immediately endangered ones. As we discussed in Chapter 4, archaeologists have a responsibility to the future, when greater resources and more sophisticated techniques may allow a more complete recovery of data. Therefore, unthreatened sites should never be completely excavated; a portion should always be left undisturbed for future archaeologists to investigate.

FACING THE CHALLENGES TO ARCHAEOLOGY

We now turn to some of the responses being made by archaeologists to the problems and issues facing the discipline today. Specifically, these issues include safeguarding and conserving archaeological sites throughout the world, ensuring respect for the descendants of many of the ancient societies investigated by the archaeologists, and meeting the responsibilities archaeologists have to the past, including the dissemination of archaeological information to both the profession and the general public.

Contract Archaeology

Archaeologists have always attempted to respond to the threat of destruction. Traditionally, as we have said, this response was to excavate whatever could be recovered before a site was destroyed. This kind of response is usually known as **salvage archaeology.** Often, such salvage work was completely unforeseen and therefore unplanned. Almost every archaeologist has received an unexpected summons from a visitor or a telephone call that archaeological materials have just been discovered by a farmer plowing his field, a houseowner digging a well, or some similar situation. The recent acceleration of looting activity throughout the world has greatly increased the incidence of salvage operations springing from reported discoveries made originally by illicit excavators. In some cases, the discovery may be dramatic enough for the threat to be stopped, at least temporarily. Such a "stay of execution" may allow the archaeologist to plan an adequate salvage excavation, but seldom can the financial resources be gathered to support more than a few days or weeks of work. And even less frequently is any provision made for later analysis or publication of data gathered under such conditions.

In contrast to this unexpected, emergency salvage work, archaeologists in many countries have conducted numerous planned projects by arrangement with land-clearing and construction enterprises. This kind of salvage project is often referred to as **contract archaeology,** since it is carried out under a legal contract between an archaeologist (or an archaeological institution) and the agency undertaking the construction project, often a governmental or private institution. Unfortunately, contract archaeology has not enjoyed a uniformly good reputation among professional archaeologists. This stems from the fact that in the past many—though not all—contract projects were poorly funded, and almost all were rushed to meet deadlines imposed by the contracting agencies. These problems are

Contract archaeology: Problems with Depression-era projects

Recent contract archaeology: Rescue of Abu Simbel

well illustrated by the government-sponsored program of contract archaeology conducted in the United States during the Great Depression of the 1930s. Entire regions were being transformed by dam-building programs, and archaeological contract work was used to salvage threatened historic and prehistoric sites. But neither time nor money was ever adequate, and these shortages were often compounded by the use of untrained labor, sometimes without adequate supervision. The Depression-era salvage projects had a secondary role—giving work to great numbers of unemployed people—in addition to investigating threatened archaeological sites. Unfortunately, the employment aspect often took on a greater importance than the archaeological investigations. In general, the archaeological work was subordinate to the priorities of the contracting agency, the flood-control engineer, or the dam builder, with predictably disastrous results as far as archaeology was concerned. When good research was done, as it was in some cases, it was due to the extraordinary efforts of individual archaeologists in the face of these obstacles.

The lessons learned from Depression-era contract archaeology were not in vain. More recent work, both in the United States and in other countries, has benefited from this experience. In Egypt, the Aswan Dam salvage project conducted in the 1960s was well funded. Organized by UNESCO, the effort to save the site of Abu Simbel (Fig. 18.5) from the floodwaters cost an estimated $40 million, of which the government of Egypt supplied more than half. The salvage program also included work in the less spectacular aspects of archaeology, such as locating prehistoric occupation sites. Although this work was less heavily funded, its inclusion was important in itself.

The overall quality of contract archaeology has vastly improved in recent years, because of both changing attitudes on the part of archaeologists and changing policies on the part of sponsoring agencies. One of the most significant changes, from both points of view, is that archaeological research is given greater priority, usually more balanced with the demands of the sponsoring agency and less subject to its pressures. The incidence of contract archaeology is generally increasing in the climate of growing worldwide concern over the fate of humankind's heritage. Most governments now require that archaeologists (or archaeological institutions) enter into legal agreements or contracts before permission is granted to conduct archaeological research within their boundaries. Thus the term *contract archaeology* is no longer appropriate only to salvage situations but increasingly also refers to many kinds of archaeological projects, whether concerned with threatened or unthreatened sites. As part of the contract, archaeologists undertaking nonsalvage archaeology, motivated entirely by their own theoretical interests, may find that their project will be supervised, and perhaps even modified, by agencies that represent the national interests of the country in which the site is located. Although legal requirements vary, many nations rightfully require that excavations be planned to

FIGURE 18.5 The spectacular remains of the temple of Abu Simbel were saved from the rising waters behind the Aswan Dam by being cut apart, moved, and reassembled on higher ground at a cost of over $40 million. (Courtesy of David O'Connor.)

minimize destruction of sites, that visible features be restored or consolidated after excavation, that discovered artifacts remain the property of the host nation, and that copies of all research records and published reports be turned over to appropriate governmental agencies, such as national museums. In some cases, contracts may require that final research reports be published in the appropriate governmental publication of the host country.

The growth of contract archaeology in the context of protecting our heritage raises the possibility that nonsalvage investigations ("pure research") may be controlled or even dictated by government agencies granting contracts. The lesson here is the same as that learned in earlier examples of salvage-oriented contract archaeology. If nonarchaeological priorities are placed before archaeological needs, the result will be predictable: bad archaeology. The obvious solution is a balance of priorities. Archaeologists must expect and demand that their research be conducted according to the principles of freedom of inquiry and conducted to ensure maximum data conservation. Because the archaeological record is so vulnerable, and because each site represents a unique portion of that record, every nation has the right to ensure that archaeological research within its boundaries is of the highest quality, that sites are safeguarded during and after excavation, and that the results of research are made readily available to both the scholarly community and the general public.

FIGURE 18.6 Archaeological remains are recognized national symbols for many countries and provide huge revenues from tourists. One of the most famous examples is Teotihuacan, Mexico.

Cultural and economic benefits: Teotihuacan, the Great Pyramids, and Williamsburg, Virginia

Cultural Resource Management

After many years of neglect and destruction, many nations have enacted firm protective legislation, based on the premise that the remains of the past, both historic and prehistoric, are a nonrenewable national resource, analogous to such natural resources as petroleum or mineral deposits. Unfortunately, some nations have been slow to enact or enforce such legal conservation measures, but the worldwide trend is clearly in this direction. The motives for such conservation efforts are humanistic and scientific, but they also have a very practical basis. Knowledge of the past fosters self-esteem and national unity. It also fosters economic development: Tourism, founded at least in part on a well-documented and spectacular past, is a multimillion-dollar business in some nations. Sites such as Teotihuacan in Mexico, the Great Pyramids in Egypt, and Williamsburg in the United States not only serve as symbols of the national heritage but also attract millions of tourists every year (Fig. 18.6).

In the United States, a series of federal laws dating back to 1906 has been enacted to conserve archaeological sites (Table 18.1). Until recently, however, other countries, including many in Europe and several in Latin America, were far ahead of the United States in providing legal protection for their archaeological resources. Fortunately, recent legislative measures have helped the United States to catch up, and perhaps even to provide leadership in this area.

The most important of the new laws in the United States have been enacted by the federal government; these are sometimes reinforced by state and local laws designed to supplement the federal provisions.

The precedent for federal protection of archaeological and historical

Table 18.1   Major U.S. Federal Legislation for the Protection of Archaeological Resources

Antiquities Act of 1906	Protects sites on federal lands
Historic Sites Act of 1935	Provides authority for designating National Historic Landmarks and for archaeological survey before destruction by development programs
National Historic Preservation Act of 1966 (amended 1976 and 1980)	Strengthens protection of sites via National Register; integrates state and local agencies into national program for site preservation
National Environmental Policy Act of 1969	Requires all federal agencies to specify impact of development programs on cultural resources
Archaeological Resources Protection Act of 1979	Provides criminal and civil penalties for looting or damaging sites on public and Native American lands
Convention of Cultural Property of 1982	Authorizes U.S participation in 1970 UNESCO convention to prevent illegal international trade in cultural property
Cultural Property Act of 1983	Provides sanctions against U.S. import or export of illicit antiquities
Federal Abandoned Shipwreck Act of 1988	Removes sunken ships of archaeological interest from marine salvage jurisdiction; provides for protection under state jurisdiction
Federal Reburial and Repatriation Act of 1990	Specifies return of Native American remains and cultural property to Native American groups by U.S. museums

sites was set by the Antiquities Act of 1906, which was aimed at preserving ancient remains on federal lands. The Historic Sites Act of 1935 provided the Secretary of the Interior with the authority to protect archaeological and historical monuments throughout the United States (including authority to designate National Historic Landmarks), and established the important precedent for any federal agency sponsoring a construction project to allocate funds (up to 1 percent of the total cost)

Protection of cultural resources: United States legislation

for archaeological survey before beginning construction. This procedure was further strengthened by the National Environmental Policy Act of 1969, which required all federal agencies to prepare an Environmental Impact Statement to specify the effects federal projects would have on the environment (including cultural resources). The National Historic Preservation Act, originally enacted in 1966 but strengthened by amendments in 1976 and 1980, is the most important and powerful legal basis for the protection of the cultural resources of the United States. It and other laws established a National Register to identify and preserve the nation's archaeological and historic sites, an Advisory Council on Historic Preservation, the Historic Preservation Fund, and procedures that various federal agencies are to use in fulfilling their responsibilities for protecting cultural resources. Under these provisions the roles of state and local agencies are integrated into the national program; for example, a State Historic Preservation Officer (SHPO) is designated to be responsible for preserving cultural resources in each state and nominating state sites to the National Register. Beyond this, criminal and civil penalties for looting and otherwise damaging sites on public or Native American lands were enacted by the Archaeological Resources Protection Act of 1979.

United States participation in international efforts to stem the worldwide trade in looted archaeological materials has been somewhat hesitant, but substantial progress was made by passage in Congress of the 1982 Convention of Cultural Property, which authorized United States participation in the 1970 UNESCO Convention on the Means of Prohibiting and Preventing the Illicit Import, Export, and Transfer of Ownership of Cultural Property. This effort was further strengthened by the Cultural Property Act of 1983, which provided for strong sanctions against the import of illicit antiquities into the United States.

Within the United States, nearly a century of legislation designed to protect cultural resources has slowed but certainly not stopped the loss of the national heritage. As a result, all federal and state agencies are required to study and assess the effect of their programs on the total environment, including archaeological sites (and provide the crucial funding for these studies), before the programs take effect. This means that any federal construction program, or any similar program requiring a federal permit, must evaluate the impact of its project on archaeological evidence and must take action either to avoid or to mitigate any effects harmful to the archaeological record. As a result, a variety of governmental agencies, including some longtime sponsors of "salvage archaeology" (such as the National Park Service, the Department of Defense—Army Corps of Engineers, the Federal Highway Administration, and the Department of Housing and Urban Development), are now involved in a new kind of comprehensive cultural resource management that grants a high priority to archaeology. In addition, most state governments, through their State Historic Preservation Offices (SHPOs), have the means to protect sites on state lands. And some 850 municipalities possess the authority to conserve archaeological remains under historical landmark ordinances and by using their zoning powers. As a result, archaeologists are now being contracted on an unprecedented scale, not only to locate sites and gather data, but also to develop the methods and policies that will conserve the archaeological resources of the United States for future generations.

As mentioned in Chapter 1, **cultural resource management** was the fastest-growing area within American professional archaeology in the 1970s and 1980s. The federal government is now spending tens of millions of dollars each year on archaeology; funding has increased each year and will have to continue to expand if progress is to be made in protecting the cultural resources of the United States. The rapid expansion of government-funded research has not been without growing pains, chiefly from several related factors. First, the increase in both funds and demand for archaeologists to conduct studies has not always been anticipated, so that considerable confusion has arisen at times in dealing with the unfamiliar complexities of the federal laws, regulations, and bureaucratic procedures, and there has been a shortage of qualified archaeologists interested in undertaking a flood of new contracts. Second, archaeologists have had to seriously reexamine the ethics and professional standards appropriate for this kind of contract work, to avoid the well-known mistakes of past salvage archaeology. Third, the priorities and policies needed to guide archaeologists in their attempts to conserve archaeological resources have also been subject to debate.

The most encouraging development in this complex situation is the increasingly positive attitude of archaeologists toward contract archaeology and cultural resource management as areas in which creative research can be carried out. Traditional salvage archaeology programs earned the reputation of being conducted far too often without adequate planning and with little attention to analysis and interpretation of the data collected. There was a common attitude that as long as sites were dug, the data would be used and useful somewhere, sometime. A growing number of archaeologists today, however, are engaged in efforts to coordinate with State Historic Preservation Officers in formulating broad regional research goals and priorities. Though flexible, such goals and priorities can increase the applicability of data collected under contract to questions of current culture historical, processual, postprocessual, and general theoretical interest (see Chapter 1). They also provide guidelines for judging whether particular sites merit excavation or preservation. We cannot preserve or excavate all sites, and some sites have more to tell us than others. Clearly, then, increased attention should be paid to improving the means by which sites are evaluated for scientific importance and by which decisions are made between protection, immediate investigation, and sometimes necessary sacrifice. The question is not whether the past should be protected but how best to protect it in the context of a growing and changing world.

Cultural Resource Management: On the eve of destruction

Conservation Archaeology

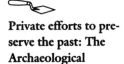

Private efforts to preserve the past: The Archaeological Conservancy

Not all archaeological sites are on public land; many sites, especially in the eastern United States, are situated on private property. To preserve such sites, often threatened by looting or destruction by development or neglect, Mark Michel and Steven LeBlanc conceived of a private organization modeled after the successful Nature Conservancy. The **Archaeological Conservancy** was incorporated in 1979. Headquartered in Santa Fe, New Mexico, it seeks to identify archaeological sites worthy of protection, to acquire these sites through purchase or donation, and to educate the public about the destruction of, and the need to preserve, our cultural heritage.

Although it is a private organization, the Archaeological Conservancy works closely with local, state, and federal government agencies to meet its objectives. State Historic Preservation Offices help identify sites worthy of protection, which are usually secured by direct negotiation with the landowner. Sometimes the site is donated to the Archaeological Conservancy, and the property owner receives considerable tax advantages, or the land is purchased with money from the Conservancy's rotating Preservation Fund or fund-raising efforts. For instance, an emergency loan from the National Trust for Historic Preservation and contributions from individuals, foundations, and corporations allowed the Conservancy to acquire and preserve the two largest Mesa Verde culture sites (ca. A.D. 900–1300), Mud Springs and Yellowjacket Pueblos, in Colorado. Once a site is secured, the Archaeological Conservancy ensures its short-term protection, but eventually each site is donated or sold to a public agency able to undertake its long-term conservation. The Fort Craig Site in New Mexico, for example, has been donated to the Bureau of Land Management, and two other sites—Savage Cave in Kentucky and Powers Fort in Missouri—have been given to local universities as centers for both environmental and archaeological research. As its resources grow, the Archaeological Conservancy promises to be a potent factor in the protection of the past (Fig. 18.7).

THE RESPONSIBILITIES OF ARCHAEOLOGY

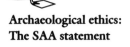

Archaeological ethics: The SAA statement

The archaeological profession has assumed responsibility for the cultural resources we have inherited from our past. This responsibility includes a variety of obligations, guided by ethical considerations, that are summarized in a statement of archaeological ethics adopted a number of years ago by the Society for American Archaeology:

> Collections made by competent archaeologists must be available for examination by qualified scholars; relevant supporting data must also be accessible for study whether the collection is in a museum or other institution or in private hands.

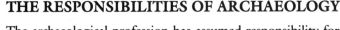

im...
ruins acq...
vation by the ...
cal Conservancy in ...
This ruin is located on
Oak Creek in the Verde
Valley of central Arizona
and dates to A.D. 1200–
1450. At one time there
were about 40 Sinagua culture ruins in the area, but
most have been destroyed
by looters and by development. The Sinagua are
thought to be ancestors of
the modern Hopi. (Photo
courtesy of the Archaeo-
logical Conservancy.)

It is the scholarly obligation of the archaeologist to report his findings in a recognized scientific medium. In the event that significance of the collection does not warrant publication, a manuscript report should be prepared and be available.

Inasmuch as the buying and selling of artifacts usually results in the loss of context and cultural associations, the practice is censured.

An archaeological site presents problems which must be handled by the excavator according to a plan. Therefore, members of the Society for American Archaeology do not undertake excavations on any site being studied by someone without the prior knowledge and consent of that person.

Willful destruction, distortion, or concealment of the data of archaeology is censured, and provides grounds for expulsion from the Society for American Archaeology, at the discretion of the Executive Committee. (Champe et al. 1961)

Preservation of the Archaeological Record

Today's archaeologists have a duty to protect and preserve the archaeological record for future generations. But this responsibility is far too great for professional archaeologists alone to bear; if the material remains of our human past are to survive the growing threats posed by the modern world, archaeologists must be joined by allies in both governmental and private sectors worldwide. The first step in accomplishing this goal is educational; archaeologists must foster a public awareness of the very real threats that

The archaeologist's obligation: Preservation of cultural resources

are destroying the cultural heritage of all peoples. Public awareness can then be translated into effective actions designed to ensure both the protection of cultural resources and the enforcement of sanctions against those individuals or groups who are deliberately destroying the archaeological record.

Working with Concerned Ethnic Groups

Archaeologists and ethnic awareness: The reburial issue

Archaeologists are not alone in their concern about protecting cultural resources. A growing number of ethnic minorities and societies are mobilizing efforts to ensure that their traditions and heritage are preserved. There is a measure of irony in this situation, since in several instances archaeologists and anthropologists have been the primary target of efforts to protect ethnic cultural resources. Native American groups, resentful over the callous disregard shown by a *very few* archaeologists in excavating and removing burials and artifacts, have succeeded in some parts of the United States (California and Iowa, for instance) in having laws enacted that restrict or even prohibit the excavation of Native American sites. Some ethnic groups are seeking return or reburial of excavated burials and artifacts. A similar situation exists in Australia, where new legislation requires that some Aborigine skeletal collections in universities and museums be returned to native control. Federal law recently enacted in the United States also provides for repatriation of Native American materials (discussed below).

These are examples of a new challenge facing archaeologists: an anti-archaeological trend, motivated by the desire to compensate ethnic groups for very real offenses committed in the past, as well as to protect cultural traditions. Although archaeologists were not actively involved in the worst of these past offenses—such as the genocidal treatment of Aborigine groups in Australia and some Native American tribes in the United States—at the very least some archaeologists have excavated sites without considering the feelings or belief systems of the living descendants of the people who once occupied those sites.

As a result of these past wrongs and the current actions of various ethnic groups, archaeological research in some instances is threatened with restriction or even prohibition. Although this may be a severe lesson, it may be one worth learning, provided *all* archaeologists in the future recognize, respect, and heed the traditions of the ethnic groups they are studying. Obviously, if an archaeological site is known or suspected to be linked to a living ethnic group, the permission and cooperation of that community should be obtained before excavation proceeds. Cooperation can only lead to very real benefits for both archaeologists and the ethnic group involved, by adding new information about the cultural and biological heritage of the living descendants. For example, knowledge about ancient disease patterns can contribute to today's health care programs (see Chapters 11 and 15). Unfortunately, because of the sensitivity of the issue in dealing with human remains, confrontation has sometimes superseded cooperation in relations between archaeologists and ethnic groups. This is particularly regrettable since the benefits to be gained for both are sometimes lost in the fray.

Both archaeologists and concerned ethnic groups recognize that the greatest agent of destruction of cultural resources is the looter, motivated by monetary greed rather than knowledge of or respect for the past. Archaeologists and ethnic groups must join forces to protect cultural resources from looting, while cooperating in research designed to increase our knowledge about the past for both science and the living descendants of an ancient society. Under such cooperative agreements, the professional expertise of archaeologists should be respected in conduct of the research process. On the other hand, archaeologists must respect the concerns of living descendants. Furthermore, in those cases where archaeological remains can be demonstrated to have cultural or biological affinities with living peoples, archaeologists have an obligation to ensure that those materials are returned to their rightful owners.

As long as the scientific information resulting from the archaeological recovery of such remains is safeguarded, and the final disposition of human remains is made in accordance with the law, archaeologists have an obligation to ensure that the treatment of these finds is consistent with the feelings and beliefs of the ethnic group involved. If, for instance, the living descendants do not object to public displays of excavated artifacts, an informative exhibit in a local museum might be appropriate. In other cases, descendants might prefer reburial of the remains after the scientific data had been obtained.

After some two years of gathering information and considering the full spectrum of opinions about this issue, the Society for American Archaeology adopted the following statement concerning the treatment of human remains:

SAA guidelines for treatment of human remains

> Archaeologists are committed to understanding and communicating the richness of the cultural heritage of humanity, and they acknowledge and respect the diversity of beliefs about, and interests in, the past and its material remains.
>
> It is the ethical responsibility of archaeologists "to advocate and to aid in the conservation of archaeological data," as specified in the Bylaws of the Society for American Archaeology. Mortuary evidence is an integral part of the archaeological record of past culture and behavior in that it informs directly upon social structure and organization and, less directly, upon aspects of religion and ideology. Human remains, as an integral part of the mortuary record, provide unique information about demography, diet, disease, and genetic relationships among human groups. Research in archaeology, bioarchaeology, biological anthropology, and medicine depends upon responsible scholars having collections of human remains available for replicative research and research that addresses new questions or employs new analytical techniques.

There is great diversity in cultural and religious values concerning the treatment of human remains. Individuals and cultural groups have legitimate concerns derived from cultural and religious beliefs about the treatment and disposition of remains of their ancestors or members that may conflict with legitimate scientific interests in those remains. The concerns of different cultures, as presented by their designated representatives and leaders, must be recognized and respected.

The Society for American Archaeology recognizes both scientific and traditional interests in human remains. Human skeletal materials must at all times be treated with dignity and respect. Commercial exploitation of ancient human remains is abhorrent. Whatever their ultimate disposition, all human remains should receive appropriate scientific study, should be responsibly and carefully conserved, and should be accessible only for legitimate scientific or educational purposes.

The Society for American Archaeology opposes universal or indiscriminate reburial of human remains, either from ongoing excavations or from extant collections. Conflicting claims concerning the proper treatment and disposition of particular human remains must be resolved on a case-by-case basis through consideration of the scientific importance of the material, the cultural and religious values of the interested individuals or groups, and the strength of their relationship to the remains in question.

The scientific importance of particular human remains should be determined by their potential to aid in present and future research, and thus depends on professional judgments concerning the degree of their physical and contextual integrity. The weight accorded any claim made by an individual or group concerning particular human remains should depend upon the strength of their demonstrated biological or cultural affinity with the remains in question. If remains can be identified as those of a known individual from whom specific biological descendants can be traced, the disposition of those remains, including possible reburial, should be determined by the closest living relatives.

The Society for American Archaeology encourages close and effective communication between scholars engaged in the study of human remains and the communities that may have biological or cultural affinities to those remains. Because vandalism and looting threaten the record of the human past, including human remains, the protection of this record necessitates cooperation between archaeologists and others who share that goal.

Because controversies involving the treatment of human remains cannot properly be resolved nation-wide in a uniform way, the Society opposes any Federal legislation that seeks to impose a uniform standard for determining the disposition of all human remains.

Recognizing the diversity of potential legal interests in the material record of the human past, archaeologists have a professional responsibility to seek to ensure that laws governing that record are consistent with the objectives, principles, and formal statements of the Society for American Archaeology.

In 1990 the U.S. Congress enacted a new federal law governing reburial of Native American remains and return of certain cultural property (artifacts) to Native American groups (see Table 18.1). The provisions of the new law are complex, and the details of its implementation have still to be worked out, but it is encouraging that museums and other institutions holding Native American skeletal and cultural material are committed to returning these remains to the bona fide tribal owners.

Professional Continuity

Archaeologists, as members of a professional discipline, have a responsibility for the continuity and improvement of their profession. This obligation is met with research designed to improve archaeological methods and theory and with recruitment and training of new generations of archaeologists. Interest in archaeology often begins as early as the primary and secondary grades, and archaeologists should ensure that up-to-date and accurate information about archaeology is available in the classroom and in textbooks. As discussed in Chapter 1, formal archaeological training usually takes place at the college or university level, in the classroom, laboratory, and field, for both undergraduate and graduate students, and advanced degrees (masters and doctorates) are the rule. But many people's interest in archaeology is first sparked by exposure from nonacademic sources, such as television programs, motion pictures, popular books, and magazines. Unfortunately, the picture painted of archaeology by the mass media is not always accurate, so at least part of the educational effort undertaken by archaeologists has to be directed toward correcting popular misconceptions.

The archaeologist's obligation: Training of new professionals

Publication

The ultimate responsibility of all archaeologists, like all scientists, is to ensure that their research is accurate and unbiased and that their results are available to all who would benefit from such knowledge, including both the professional and the public audiences. This obligation lies at the very heart of professional archaeological responsibility, for the dissemination of valid archaeological information is crucial to the mobilization of public awareness about both the value of understanding our past and the tragedy of loss of our heritage because of the destruction of cultural resources.

The archaeologist's obligation: To acquire and pass on knowledge

Archaeological information is usually made available by a variety of means, ranging from public lectures and museum exhibits to the **publication** of technical articles and books. In some cases, communication to the general public is the most neglected aspect. Archaeologists recognize the obligation to make the results of their research available to their professional colleagues, usually in scholarly journals and detailed site reports, but apparently not all accept the need to provide such information to a wider or more general audience. For example, some archaeologists seem to believe that it is "unprofessional" to write for popular publications. This attitude is especially prevalent in academic circles. At many colleges and universities achievement is measured in numbers of scholarly publications, but "popular" writings are discouraged since they are usually ignored when evaluating an individual's professional standing. Yet archaeologists have an obligation to communicate their results as widely as possible, especially when an increasing amount of archaeological research is supported by public funds. Because archaeologists are uniquely able to address the full range of the human past, they have an obligation to educate as many people as possible about the richness of our human heritage. The communication of archaeological information to the general public not only is an ethical responsibility but also aids in the recruitment of future archaeologists and counteracts the destruction of cultural resources that threatens to rob us all of our heritage.

SUMMARY

In this chapter we have considered the challenge posed by the irreversible destruction of archaeological data. This threat stems from two sources. The first is intentional destruction by looters, fostered by the market for archaeological "art," which provides an economic incentive for plundering archaeological sites. The second is unintentional—the disruption of archaeological sites by everyday activities of our expanding world. Both problems point out the seriously endangered status of archaeological remains throughout the world.

Archaeology today faces an unprecedented crisis from this rapidly increasing destruction of archaeological sites—loss of the cultural resources of humankind. Although there is no easy solution to this threat, success has been achieved by measures that range from legislation enacted at all levels of government, in the United States and in many other countries, to private preservation efforts such as the Archaeological Conservancy. A related trend, and one that archaeologists should welcome and work with rather than against, is the efforts of a growing number of ethnic groups worldwide to protect their cultural heritage. Overall, archaeologists have a professional responsibility not only to protect the record of the past but also, through training and publication, to ensure that the knowledge they acquire is preserved and passed on to future generations.

GUIDE TO FURTHER READING

Major Sources of Challenge

Arden 1989; Bassett 1986; Bator 1983; Cleere 1984, 1989; Coggins 1972; Fagan 1975, 1988; Giesecke 1985; R. A. Gould 1980b; Harrington 1991; Herscher 1989; Knudson 1989; McGimsey 1972; McKinley and Henderson 1985; Meisch 1985; Meyer 1977; Miller 1980; Muscarella 1984; Robertson 1972; Sheets 1973; Shelton 1986; Skowronek 1985; R. H. Smith 1974; Vitelli 1983; White 1982; Wiseman 1984; Young 1989

Facing the Challenges to Archaeology

Burnham 1974; Cleere 1984, 1989; Davis 1972, 1989; Ford 1983; D. D. Fowler 1982; M. L. Fowler 1974; Friedman 1985; Glassow 1977; Gumerman 1984; Gyrisco 1983; King 1971, 1983; King, Hickman, and Berg 1977; Layton 1989a, 1989b; LeBlanc 1983; Lipe 1974, 1984; MacDonald 1976; McGimsey 1972; McGimsey and Davis 1977; Michel 1981; Powell et al. 1983; Quimby 1979; Raab and Klinger 1977; Rahtz 1974; Schiffer and Gumerman 1977; Schiffer and House 1977; R. H. Smith 1974; Speser, Reinberg, and Porsche 1986; Speser et al. 1986; Wendorf 1973

The Responsibilities of Archaeology

Adkins and Adkins 1989; Anderson 1985; Champe et al. 1961; Cheek and Keel 1984; Dillon 1985; Green 1984; Hammil and Zimmerman 1983; Higgenbotham 1983; Karata 1989; McBryde 1985; Moberg 1985; Quick 1986; Renfrew 1983a; Rosen 1980; R. H. Smith 1974; Society for American Archaeology 1986; Talmadge 1982; Trigger 1980, 1990; Wiseman 1985

EXCAVATING BURIALS IN THE 1990S

Lynne Goldstein

Lynne Goldstein is an Associate Professor of Anthropology at the University of Wisconsin—Milwaukee. She focuses much of her attention on a regional archaeology program in southeastern Wisconsin, but is also noted for her expertise in the excavation and analysis of mortuary sites. She has been active locally and nationally in the development of burial and repatriation legislation, and serves as a member of the Smithsonian Institution Repatriation Advisory Committee. Goldstein presents her recent work at the historic Russian cemetery at Fort Ross as an example of how mortuary excavations can be successfully conducted under present burial and reburial laws.

There have been few issues in archaeology as emotionally charged and far-reaching as the issues of reburial and repatriation of human remains.

To archaeologists and physical anthropologists, human remains represent one of the few instances in which we actually encounter and can identify individual behavior and treatment. Mortuary sites probably yield more information per cubic inch than any other kind of archaeological site—data con-

cerning style, artifact associations, clothing, diet, disease, population statistics, and social organization are routinely recovered, and new and improved techniques are continually being developed. For example, physical anthropologists are perfecting the ability to extract DNA from bones; this means that in the future we may be able to actually determine to whom a particular burial is related. If bones are reburied, however, such studies will no longer be possible. It is not generally known that restudy of burials is common. For example, over the last 20 years at the Smithsonian Institution, an average of about 500 requests each year have been made to reexamine previously excavated human remains housed at the museum. The less one can restudy and reexamine previously excavated materials, the less one can conclude about the past.

In contrast, many Native Americans do not want remains excavated or kept. From their perspective, the issue can be cast as a human rights concern—these individuals, known elders or not, are ancestors and should be treated according to modern American In-

dian wishes. Native Americans argue that because the dead never gave their permission to be studied, they should be handed over or repatriated to people who are at least their spiritual relatives. Excavation and analysis should require the explicit permission of modern Native Americans.

Today, there is a federal law that requires the repatriation of certain human remains, funerary objects, and sacred objects from museums and other institutions that receive federal funds. At the state level, most states have written laws within the last fifteen years that apply to the excavation and analysis of human burials. If an archaeologist wishes to excavate a mortuary site, for *any* reason, he or she is usually required to get permission and permits from a variety of tribal people and state offices.

The net result is that most archaeologists in the United States excavate burials only if necessary—that is, in contract archaeology situations when burials are threatened by construction or development that falls under the jurisdiction of a particular law. It is rare for archaeologists to conduct burial excavations in other circumstances. Such excavations can be done, however, and the realities of undertaking such a project can provide some useful lessons.

Fort Ross State Historic Park is located on the Pacific coast in Sonoma County, California, and is operated by the California Department of Parks and Recreation (hereafter referred to as DPR). Fort Ross itself represents a Russian outpost occupied from 1812 to 1841. The development of Fort Ross was associated with expansion of the Pacific maritime fur trade. The Russian colonies in North America (in Alaska, in northern California, and very briefly in Hawaii) were established to gain access to productive sea otter territories, and Fort Ross was the southernmost colony.

In 1989, Sannie Osborn, one of my Ph.D. students and a native Californian, proposed that for her dissertation research she study mortuary practices in a frontier setting—specifically, Fort Ross. What happens to prescribed customs of funerary behavior when members of a society are removed from the familiar surroundings of family, friends, and church, and relocated to a frontier outpost such as the Russian colony at Fort Ross? An extensive review of archival records might locate the names, ages, sex, and causes of death of, and other information about, the individuals who are interred at the cemetery. Although

the general location of the cemetery was known, no one was certain about its precise location, its extent, or who was buried there. Osborn's dissertation would focus on the archival materials, but it would be important to locate and excavate the cemetery to see how well it matched the written record.

Our first step was to discover who could grant permission and what permits were needed. Since the park is in California—noted for its tough burial excavation laws—we knew that there would be many hurdles, particularly since the cemetery was on state land and was not threatened by development or construction.

I have argued that archaeologists should take the initiative and talk directly to the concerned group or groups to explain what they have learned, what they hoped to learn, and why that information was important. Similarly, I have suggested that archaeologists should also find out what those from whom they seek permission want to learn. In our case, we took an unusual step and tried to outline for each group specific benefits *they* would realize from our work.

We began the permission process in January 1989, and eventually received all necessary permissions in April 1990, about 15 months later. (We've had to renew all permissions in 1991 and 1992.) Getting permissions was an educational process, and I will never forget my first meeting. I

arrived at the Regional Offices of the DPR, expecting a small group of park and church officials who were immediately concerned with the project. I had been told that only those who had to "sign off" on the project would be present. I opened the door to discover a group of about 15 people, each of whom had to approve what we were doing, and all of whom were suspicious of the project for different reasons. Although that was a bit disconcerting, it was more depressing to discover that no Native Alaskans or Native Californians were there that day! Before I outline what had to be done, I will note that our work was made considerably easier with the assistance of an ally or two in the bureaucracy. In particular, E. Breck Parkman, DPR's regional archaeologist, believed in the project and helped guide our way.

DPR has different offices and levels of hierarchy that had to approve our plans. Obviously, the rangers at Fort Ross had to be willing to work with us, as did their bosses at the District and Regional levels. Although the Regional Director is the person who signs our permit, individuals in at least two state-level offices also had to approve. One office is the repository for artifacts, and the other is responsible for park interpretation. Add to the mix several archaeologists and physical anthropologists throughout the
(*continued*)

(continued)

hierarchy who had worked at Fort Ross at one time or another. Because of their experience, they rightly thought they should have input on our project. For all these cases, we prepared a written proposal of what we planned to do and why; then I also presented our plans and answered questions at a series of meetings. The strategy we adopted was: "If in doubt, ask for approval."

Although everyone in DPR ultimately agreed to support the project, that support was contingent upon permission from the Russian Orthodox church, Alaska Natives, and relevant California Indian groups. The Russian Orthodox church has two major branches in the United States, and the permission and support of *both* were mandatory. Because the two branches of the church are not close, we anticipated some difficulties. Surprisingly, those permissions were among the easiest to obtain. Each church branch considers the cemetery consecrated ground, and each has an annual ceremony at the site. Both branches of the church think that DPR has not properly cared for the cemetery and that the deceased employees of the Russian-American Company have not received proper recognition and respect.

The next group whose permission was required were Alaska Natives. The archival record is clear

that a number of these individuals were brought to Fort Ross, and we anticipated that the cemetery would contain many Alaska Native graves. Theoretically, every possible group of Alaska Natives could make a case for a relationship. Fortunately, this problem was circumvented because of previous work done at Fort Ross. On the basis of earlier research and negotiations, it was agreed that the Kodiak Area Native Association (KANA) could represent the Alaska Natives. To get their permission, someone had to make a presentation to the Association—it had already been discovered that they did not respond well to written correspondence. Since two projects at Fort Ross (ours and a separate project by archaeologists from the University of California at Berkeley wanted KANA's permission, we each helped pay Breck Parkman's airfare to Alaska for a meeting. We outlined a series of benefits to the tribe, and permission was granted: KANA would go along with the wishes of the church but asked to be kept regularly informed.

Of the California native populations who dealt directly with the Russians, the Kashaya Pomo had the closest interactions. They had villages close to the Fort, and many tribal members worked for the Russians. Today, the Kashaya Pomo are a small group of fewer than 90 individuals. Getting their permission proved somewhat

problematic because it was not clear who was tribal chair. Since it is always wrong to enter local politics of any sort as an outsider, our approach to the Kashaya was to ask permission from all four of the possible contenders for the tribal chair position, as well as talking with some of the Kashaya who were employed by DPR. The Kashaya were not necessarily in favor of the excavations, but at the same time, they did not think that any Pomo would be in the cemetery—it is their (and our) view that any Pomo who died would have been returned to their home village. After some discussion, the Pomo gave us limited permission: If we can determine that a grave is Pomo, we must immediately rebury the individual and notify the Pomo. Since this initial agreement, a number of Kashaya have visited our excavations, and one happens to be our main equipment operator—he drives the bulldozer that has uncovered all the graves!

There was some question as to whether other California native groups should be notified, but this potentially new maze was simplified by Parkman, who has a working relationship with these groups. He talked with them, explained the project, and invited each to come and visit. Similarly, although the excavation of Native American burials requires the permission of the California Native American Heritage Commission, the fact that all relevant local tribes had agreed to the project made this step simple.

We have kept an open-door policy on the project—anyone interested is welcome to visit at any time. We thought that the 15-month effort spent getting permission was worth the energy because we were confident that we would have few unforseen problems or surprises. You can't plan for everything, however. On our first day at the site, we were mapping and trying to tie the cemetery to a permanent United States Geological Survey benchmark down the road. We had a two-person crew doing the work, when a California Department of Transportation supervisor suddenly appeared and announced that he might have to close us down—he claimed we needed an "encroachment permit" to do any work on the right-of-way. No one had warned us of this (in fact, we later learned that no one in the park system had heard of such a permit). After some discussion, the official calmed down, particularly after I apologized, then I asked if hitch-hiking was illegal on this stretch of road. He assured me it was not, so I told him he had misunderstood—my crew was simply hitch-hiking because their equipment was too heavy.

In spite of the unforeseen and the sometimes absurd, the project has been an unqualified success; aside from finding more than we ever imagined, we have been blessed by priests and archbishops, and visited by hundreds. The venture has required huge amounts of energy and patience, but as an additional benefit, this effort will provide a model for undertaking cemetery excavations in a climate of cooperation among disparate interests.

GLOSSARY

Terms in italics are defined elsewhere in the glossary.

Absolute age determination: Determination of age on a specific time-scale, as in years before present (B.P.) or according to a fixed calendrical system (compare with *relative age determination*). (Chapter 9)

Acculturation: Changes induced within two cultures as a consequence of contact between them, one culture usually being dominant in such a relationship. (Chapter 17)

Achieved status: An individual's social standing gained by his or her accomplishments (compare with *ascribed status*). (Chapter 15)

Acquisition: The first stage of *behavioral processes,* in which raw materials are procured (see *manufacture, use,* and *deposition*). (Chapter 4)

Acquisition (of data): See *data acquisition.*

Activity area: A place where one or more specific ancient activities were located, usually corresponding to one or more *features* and associated *artifacts* and *ecofacts* (see *data cluster*). (Chapters 4 and 15)

Actualistic studies: Detailed observations of actual use of materials like those found in the *archaeological record* (*artifacts, ecofacts,* and *features*) to produce reliable *general analogies* for archaeological *interpretation.* (Chapter 13)

Adaptation: See *cultural adaptation.*

Aerial photographic map: A map of a *region* or a *site* made through use of *aerial photography,* providing good control over distance and direction measurements but, unless made by professional cartographic equipment, little control over elevation. (Chapter 6)

Aerial photography: A technique of photographic recording, used principally in *aerial reconnaissance,* to record environmental conditions and surface and buried *sites;* may be vertical (camera at a right angle to the ground surface) or oblique (camera at less than a right angle to the ground). (Chapter 6)

Aerial reconnaissance: *Remote sensing* techniques, carried out from an aerial platform (balloon, airplane, satellite, etc.); includes direct observation, as well as recording by photographic, thermographic, and radar images. (Chapter 6)

Aerial thermography: A method of *aerial reconnaissance* that detects differential retention and radiation of heat from ground surfaces and thus aids in the identification of buried sites. (Chapter 6)

Alidade: A surveyor's instrument used in conjunction with a *plane table* to produce *topographic* or *planimetric* maps. (Chapter 6)

Alloy: A mixture of two or more metals, such as bronze (copper and tin) or tumbaga (gold and copper), used to make *metal artifacts.* (Chapter 10)

Alluvium: Soil deposited by running water. (Chapter 9)

American Anthropological Association (AAA): A professional organization for anthropologists, among whom archaeologists constitute a distinct membership division; the AAA publishes *American Anthropologist* and the *Anthropology Newsletter,* and its Archeology Division publishes a monograph series entitled *Archeological Papers of the American Anthropological Association.* (Chapter 1)

American Society of Conservation Archaeologists (ASCA): A professional organization especially for archaeologists committed to the conservation of *cultural resources.* (Chapter 1)

Analogy: A process of reasoning in which similarity between two entities in some characteristics is taken to imply similarity of other characteristics as well; the basis of most archaeological *interpretation* (see *general* and *specific analogy*). (Chapter 13)

Analysis: A stage in archaeological *research design* in which data are isolated, described, and structured, usually by means of typological *classification,* along with chronological, functional, technological, and constituent determinations. (Chapters 5, 9–12)

Annealing: Application of heat in the manufacture of *metal artifacts.* (Chapter 10)

Anthropology: The comprehensive study of the human species from biological, social, and cultural perspectives using both *synchronic* and *diachronic* views; in North America, it includes the subdisciplines of physical anthropology and cultural anthropology, the latter including *prehistoric archaeology.* (Chapter 1)

Antiquarian: A person with nonprofessional interests in the past, usually someone who studies the past for its artistic or cultural value (compare with *archaeologist* and *looter*). (Chapter 2)

Arbitrary levels: *Excavation* units defined metrically, for example, in the excavation of 5-, 10-, or 20-cm levels (compare with *natural levels*). (Chapter 7)

Arbitrary sample unit: A subdivision of the *data universe* with no cultural relevance, such as a *sample unit* defined by a *site grid* (Compare with *nonarbitrary sample unit*). (Chapter 4)

Archaeoastronomy: Inference of ancient astronomical knowledge through study of alignments and other aspects of the *archaeological record;* it combines perspectives of *archaeology* and astronomy. (Chapters 12 and 16)

Archaeological Conservancy: A private, nonprofit organization dedicated to saving archaeological *sites* from destruction, primarily by purchasing threatened sites and ensuring their protection until they can be turned over to responsible agencies such as parks (see *conservation archaeology* and *cultural resource management*). (Chapter 18)

Archaeological culture: The maximum grouping of all *assemblages* assumed to represent the sum of human activities carried out within an ancient *culture*. (Chapter 8)

Archaeological Institute of America (AIA): A professional organization whose membership is predominantly specialists in Old World archaeology; it publishes the scholarly *American Journal of Archaeology* and the more popular magazine, *Archaeology*. (Chapter 1)

Archaeological method: The means used by archaeologists to find, recover, preserve, describe, and analyze the remains of past human activity (see also *research design*). (Chapter 1)

Archaeological record: The physical remains produced by past human activities, which are sought, recovered, studied, and interpreted by *archaeologists* to reconstruct the past (see *cultural resources*). (Chapter 1)

Archaeological theory: Information used to assess the meaning of the remains of past human activity and to guide its *interpretation* to reconstruct the past (see *constructs, middle-range theory,* and *general theory*). (Chapter 1)

Archaeologist: A professional scholar who studies the human past through its physical remains (compare with *antiquarian* and *looter*). (Chapters 1 and 2)

Archaeology: The study of the social and cultural past through material remains with the aim of ordering and describing the events of the past and explaining the meaning of those events. (Introduction, Chapters 1 and 2)

Archaeomagnetic age determination: Measurement of magnetic alignments within undisturbed *features,* such as hearths or kilns, for comparison with known schedules of past magnetic alignments within a region, to yield an absolute age. (Chapter 9)

Archaic: A New World chronological *period* characterized by permanent settlements and the transition from a hunting and gathering to an agricultural *economy*. (Chapters 15, 16, and 17)

Area excavation: A type of *clearing excavation* composed of large squares used to reveal the horizontal extent of data while preserving a stratigraphic record in the balks left between excavations (compare with *stripping excavations*). (Chapter 7)

Artifact: A discrete and portable object whose characteristics result wholly or in part from human activity; artifacts are individually assignable to *ceramic, lithic, metal, organic,* or other categories (see also *industry*). (Chapters 4 and 10)

Ascribed status: An individual's social standing inherited from his or her parents or other relatives (compare with *achieved status*). (Chapter 15)

Aspartic acid racemization: A process of cumulative change in the form of amino acids, beginning at the death of an organism; it is now being tested for use as a technique for *absolute age determination* of bone tissue. (Chapter 9)

Assemblage: A gross grouping of all *subassemblages* assumed to represent the sum of human activities carried out within an ancient community (see *archaeological culture*). (Chapter 8)

Association: Occurrence of an item of archaeological data adjacent to another and in or on the same *matrix*. (Chapter 4)

Attribute: The minimal characteristic used as a criterion for grouping *artifacts* into classes; includes *stylistic, form,* and *technological attributes* (also see *classification*). (Chapters 8 and 10)

Augering: A *subsurface detection* technique using a drill run by either human or machine power to determine the depth and characteristics of archaeological or natural deposits. (Chapter 6)

Band: A small, egalitarian society subsisting by hunting and gathering, with no status distinctions other than those based on age and sex; often used to define the simplest *multilinear cultural evolutionary* stage. (Chapter 17)

Battleship-shaped curve: A lens-shaped graph representing changes in *artifact* type frequencies through time, from origin to expanding popularity, decline, and finally disappearance. (Chapter 9)

Behavioral processes: Human activities, including *acquisition, manufacture, use,* and *deposition* behavior, that produce tangible archaeological remains (compare with *transformational processes*). (Chapter 4)

Biblical archaeology: A particular field of *historical archaeology* specializing in the investigation of the time period and places recorded by the bible. (Chapter 1)

Biological environment: Those elements of the habitat consisting of living organisms; a component of the total *environment* as seen by *cultural ecology* (see *cultural* and *physical environment*). (Chapters 3 and 17)

Blade: A long, thin, and parallel-sided *flake* usually made from a cylindrical *core* (see *lithic artifacts*). (Chapter 10)

Bone age determination: Use of any of a variety of *relative age determination* techniques applicable to bone material, including measurements of the depletion of nitrogen and the accumulation of fluorine and uranium. (Chapter 9)

Bowsing: A *subsurface detection* technique performed by striking the ground to locate buried features. (Chapter 6)

B.P.: Before present; used in age determinations; in calculating radiocarbon dates, "present" means 1950 (a fixed reference date). (Chapter 9)

Bulb of percussion: A small protrusion on the inside surface of a *flake* produced by the force that detached the flake from the *core* (see *negative bulb of percussion*). (Chapter 10)

Cache: A deliberate interment of one or more *artifacts,* often associated with *constructed features* and usually representing ancient safeguarding or ritual activities. (Chapters 7 and 12)

Calendrical age determination: A dating technique usable when objects are inscribed with calendrical dates or are associated with calendrical inscriptions; an *absolute age determination* technique, provided a correlation with a modern calendar exists. (Chapter 9)

Carrying capacity: The size and density of ancient populations that a given site or region could have supported under a specified subsistence *technology*. (Chapter 14)

Central place theory: The theory that human settlements will space themselves evenly across a landscape, depending on the availability of resources and communication routes, and that these settlements will become differentiated, forming a hierarchy of controlling centers called "central places" (see *locational analysis*). (Chapter 15)

Ceramic artifacts: *Artifacts* of fired clay, belonging to *pottery,* figurine, or other ceramic *industries*. (Chapter 10)

Ceramic sociology: Reconstruction of past *social systems* from distributions of *stylistic attributes* of *pottery* in time and space. (Chapter 15)

Chiefdom: A large and complex society with differential social status, full-time occupational specializations, and developed economic and political institutions headed by a hereditary authority, the chief; often used to define a *multilinear cultural evolutionary* stage. (Chapter 17)

Chipped-stone artifacts: A class of *lithic artifacts* produced by fracturing to drive *flakes* from a *core* (see *direct percussion, indirect percussion,* and *pressure flaking*). (Chapter 10)

Chronometric: See *absolute age determination.*

Classic: A New World chronological *period* marked by the appearance of initial urban *states* and limited to the Mesoamerican and Andean *culture areas*. (Chapter 3)

Classical archaeology: A particular field of *historical archaeology* specializing in the investigation of the classical civilizations of the Mediterranean region (Greece, Rome, and their antecedents and contemporaries). (Chapter 1)

Classification: The ordering of phenomena into groups (classes), based on the sharing of *attributes* (see *paradigmatic classification* and *taxonomic classification*). (Chapters 2, 8, 9, and 10)

Clearing excavations: Excavations designed primarily to reveal the horizontal and, by inference, functional dimensions of archaeological *sites,* the extent, distribution, and patterning of buried archaeological data (see *area* and *stripping excavations*). (Chapter 7)

Closed system: A *system* that receives no information, matter, or energy from its *environment;* all its sources of change are internal (compare with *open system*). (Chapter 17)

Cognitive archaeology: The study of past *ideological systems* from material remains. (Chapter 16)

Cognitive concept of culture: A *model* of *culture* as the set of meanings (categories and relationships) people construct for making sense of their lives; used in archaeological *interpretation* for both *synchronic* and *diachronic* descriptions of cultural meaning. (Chapter 3)

Coiled: Basketry made with a vertical stitch or weft (see *plaited* and *twined*). (Chapter 10)

Cold hammering: A technique for making *metal artifacts* in which the metal is shaped by percussion without heating (see *annealing*). (Chapter 10)

Collectors: Those individuals who accumulate *artifacts* and other archaeological remains, as opposed to collecting true works of art, for personal purposes (satisfaction, financial gain, etc.) and are thus destructive to *archaeology;* although collectors were important to the origins of archaeology, their demands today are met mostly by *looters* and thus are a major cause of the destruction of the world's *cultural resources.* (Chapters 2 and 18)

Colonial archaeology: In North America, a particular field of *historical archaeology* specializing in the investigation of the era of European colonization in the New World (generally, the 16th through the 18th centuries). (Chapter 1)

Compass map: A map of a *region* or a *site* made by using a compass to control geographical direction and, usually, pacing or tape measures to control distances, without control over elevation (compare with *sketch* and *instrument maps*). (Chapter 6)

Complex: An arbitrary chronological unit defined for data categories, such as artifact *industries,* and used in the *culture historical approach* (see *period, time–space grid*). (Chapter 3)

Composite data cluster: *Data clusters* that are internally heterogeneous and patterned in regard to activities other than those based on age or sex differences, such as activities reflecting status, occupational specializations, or wealth distinctions. (Chapter 4)

Computer simulation studies: Reconstructions of the past based on computerized *models* that describe ancient conditions and variables and then use computers to generate a sequence of events, to compare the results against the known *archaeological record,* thus refining and testing *hypotheses* about the past. (Chapters 15 and 17)

Conjoining studies: The refitting of *artifact* and *ecofact* fragments to determine the integrity of an archaeological deposit; such studies allow definition of *cumulative features,* such as *lithic artifact* and *debitage* scatters; they sometimes allow reconstruction of ancient *manufacture* and *use* behavior. (Chapter 12)

Conjunctive approach: A pioneering approach to archaeological *interpretation* advocated by Walter Taylor (1948) involving the reconstruction of ancient behavior by defining functional sets of archaeological data. (Chapter 3)

Conquest: Aggressive movement of human groups from one area to another, resulting in the subjugation of the indigenous society. (Chapter 17)

Conservation archaeology: A branch of *archaeology* seeking to preserve the *archaeological record* from destruction, by protective legislation, education, and efforts such as the *Archaeological Conservancy* (see also *cultural resource management*). (Chapter 18)

Constituent analysis: Techniques used to reveal the composition of *artifacts* and other archaeological materials; it is especially useful in determining raw material sources for the reconstruction of ancient *exchange systems* (see *secondary classification*). (Chapter 15)

Constructed feature: A *feature* deliberately built to provide a setting for one or more activities, such as a house, storeroom, or burial chamber (compare with *cumulative feature*). (Chapter 12)

Constructs: The most basic level of *archaeological theory,* referring to concepts through which time, space, *form,* and *function* are perceived and interpreted (see also *middle-range theory* and *general theory*). (Chapter 1)

Context: Characteristics of archaeological data that result from combined *behavioral* and *transformational processes,* evaluated by means of recorded *association, matrix,* and *provenience* (see *primary context* and *secondary context*). (Chapter 4)

Contract archaeology: Archaeological research conducted under legal agreement with a governmental or private agency; in the United States it is usually carried out under authority of legislation designed to protect the nation's *cultural resources* (see *cultural resource management*). (Chapter 18)

Coprolites: Preserved ancient feces that contain food residues used to reconstruct ancient diet and subsistence activities. (Chapter 11)

Core: A *lithic artifact* from which *flakes* are removed; it is used as a tool or a blank from which other tools are made. (Chapter 10)

Coring: A *subsurface detection* technique using a hollow metal tube driven into the ground to lift a column of earth for stratigraphic study. (Chapter 6)

Council on Underwater Archaeology (CUA): A professional organization especially for archaeologists specializing in nautical archaeology; affiliated with the *Society for Historical Archaeology.* (Chapter 1)

Cross-dating: See *sequence comparison.*

Cultural adaptation: The sum of the adjustments of a human society to its *environment* (see *cultural ecology*). (Chapter 17)

Cultural anthropology: One of the two major subdivisions of *anthropology*, the study of humankind from a cultural perspective (compare with *physical anthropology*); in the United States, *prehistoric archaeology* is usually considered a subdivision of cultural anthropology. (Chapter 1)

Cultural drift: Gradual cultural change due to the imperfect transmission of information between generations; it is analogous to genetic drift in biology. (Chapter 17)

Cultural ecology: The study of the dynamic interaction between human society and its *environment*, viewing *culture* as the primary adaptive mechanism in the relationship. (Chapters 3, 14, and 17)

Cultural environment: Those elements of the habitat created or modified by human cultures; a component of the total *environment* as seen by *cultural ecology* (see *biological* and *physical environment*). (Chapters 3 and 17)

Cultural evolution: The theory that human societies change via a process analogous to the evolution of biological species (see *evolution, unilinear cultural evolution,* and *multilinear cultural evolution*). (Chapters 2, 3, and 17)

Cultural invention: The origin of new cultural forms within a society, by either accident or design. (Chapter 17)

Cultural process: The cumulative effect of the mechanisms and interactions within a *culture* that produce stability and/or change. The delineation of cultural process is one of the goals of archaeological research, to explain how and why cultures change through time (see *form* and *function*). (Chapters 1, 3, and 17)

Cultural processual approach: An established approach to archaeological *interpretation* aimed at delineating the interactions and changes in cultural *systems* by the application of both descriptive and explanatory *models* based on *functional*, ecological, or *multilinear cultural evolutionary* concepts of culture. (Chapters 3 and 17)

Cultural resource management (CRM): The conservation and selective investigation of prehistoric and historic remains; specifically, the development of ways and means, including legislation, to safeguard the past (see *conservation archaeology, contract archaeology*). (Chapters 1 and 18)

Cultural resources: The remains that compose our nonrenewable heritage from the past, including both the *archaeological* and the *historical records*. (Chapter 1)

Cultural revival: Reacceptance of forms or ideas that had fallen into disuse. (Chapter 17)

Cultural selection: The process that leads to differential retention of cultural traits that increase a society's potential for successful *cultural adaptation*, while eliminating maladaptive traits (compare with *natural selection*). (Chapter 17)

Culture: The concept that both underlies and unites the discipline of *anthropology* and, in its various definitions, acts as a central *model* by which archaeological data are interpreted; a definition suited to *archaeology* sees culture as the cumulative resource of human society that provides the means for nongenetic adaptation to the environment by regulating behavior in three areas—*technology, social systems,* and *ideological systems*. (Chapters 1, 2, 3, and 14)

Culture area: A spatial unit defined by *ethnographically* observed cultural similarities within a given geographical area; used archaeologically to define spatial limits to *archaeological cultures* (see also *time–space grids*). (Chapter 3)

Culture historical approach: An established approach to archaeological *interpretation* based on temporal and spatial syntheses of data and the application of general descriptive *models* usually derived from a *normative concept of culture*. (Chapters 3 and 17)

Cumulative feature: A *feature* without evidence of deliberate construction, resulting instead from accretion, for example, in a *midden,* or subtraction, for example, in a *quarry* (compare with *constructed feature*). (Chapter 12)

Data acquisition: A stage in archaeological *research design* in which data are gathered, normally by three basic procedures—*reconnaissance, surface survey,* and *excavation*. (Chapters 5–7)

Data cluster: Archaeological data found in *association* and in *primary context* and used to define areas and kinds of ancient activity; such information may be divided into *composite, differentiated,* and *simple data clusters*. (Chapter 4)

Data pool: The archaeological evidence available within a given *data universe*, conditioned by both *behavioral* and *transformational processes*. (Chapter 4)

Data processing: A stage in archaeological *research design* usually involving, in the case of *artifacts*, cleaning, conserving, labeling, inventorying, and cataloging. (Chapters 5 and 8)

Data universe: A defined area of archaeological investigation, often a *region* or a *site*, bounded in both time and geographical space. (Chapter 4)

Debitage: The debris resulting from the *manufacture*

of *chipped-stone artifacts,* that provides evidence for the reconstruction of ancient manufacturing behavior (see *technological attributes*). (Chapter 10)

Dendrochronology: The study of tree ring patterns, which are linked to develop a continuous chronological sequence. (Chapter 9)

Depletion gilding: A New World metallurgical technique in which tumbaga (copper and gold *alloy*) *metal artifacts* were treated with chemicals that removed much of the copper from the surface, leaving a finish that appears to be pure gold. (Chapter 10)

Deposition: The last stage of *behavioral processes,* in which *artifacts* are discarded (see *acquisition, manufacture,* and *use*). (Chapter 4)

Deviation-amplifying system: A *system* that continues to change as a result of *positive feedback* (compare with *deviation-counteracting system*). (Chapter 17)

Deviation-counteracting system: A *system* that reaches equilibrium as a result of *negative feedback* (compare with *deviation-amplifying system*). (Chapter 17)

Diachronic: Pertaining to phenomena as they occur or change over a period of time; a chronological perspective (compare with *synchronic*). (Chapters 1, 2, 14, and 17)

Differentiated data cluster: Clustered data that are heterogeneous and patterned in regard to two or more activities reflective of age or sex differences; for example, a house floor with cooking utensils and hunting weapons in *primary context*. (Chapter 4)

Diffusion: Transmission of ideas from one *culture* to another. (Chapter 17)

Direct age determination: Determination of the age of archaeological data by analysis of an *artifact, ecofact,* or *feature* (compare with *indirect age determination*). (Chapter 9)

Direct historical approach: A method of chronological ordering based on comparison of historically documented or contemporary *artifacts* with those recovered from archaeological contexts. (Chapters 2, 3, 13, and 17)

Direct percussion: A technique used for the *manufacture* of *chipped-stone artifacts* in which *flakes* are produced by striking a *core* with a hammerstone or striking the core against a fixed stone or anvil (compare with *indirect percussion* and *pressure flaking*). (Chapter 10)

Disposal: See *deposition.*

Distance decay: The phenomenon of measurable decline with distance from a source; used to describe the decreasing frequency of trade goods at destinations increasingly distant from their source. (Chapter 15)

Domestication: Adaptations made by animal and plant species to the *cultural environment* as a result of human interference in reproductive or other behavior; it is often detectable as specific physical changes in *faunal* or *floral ecofacts.* (Chapter 11)

Ecofact: Nonartifactual evidence from the past that has cultural relevance; the category includes both *inorganic* and *organic ecofacts (faunal* and *floral ecofacts* and human remains). (Chapters 4 and 11)

Economy: The provisioning of human society (food, water, and shelter). (Chapters 14 and 15)

Egyptology: A branch of *archaeology* specializing in the investigation of ancient Egyptian civilization. (Chapter 1)

Electron spin resonance (ESR): An age determination technique for shell or bone, similar to *thermoluminescence* for determining the age of *pottery;* in ESR, the sample is placed in a strong magnetic field to measure the number of electrons and thereby the age of the specimen. (Chapter 9)

Elevation drawing: A two-dimensional rendering of a *feature,* viewed from the side, showing details of surface composition. (Chapter 7)

Emic: Referring to the perspective of the *culture* being studied; an internal, culture-specific point of view. (Chapters 3 and 8)

Environment: The conditions that surround and affect the *evolution* of *culture* and human society, subdivided into *biological, cultural,* and *physical environments* (see *cultural ecology* and *microenvironments*). (Chapters 3, 14, and 17)

Ethnoarchaeology: *Ethnographic* studies designed to aid archaeological *interpretation,* such as descriptions of *behavioral processes;* especially the ways material items enter the *archaeological record* after *disposal* (see *analogy*). (Chapter 13)

Ethnocentrism: Observational bias in which other societies are evaluated by standards relevant to the observer's *culture.* (Chapters 1 and 2)

Ethnography: The description of contemporary *cultures;* part of the subdiscipline of *cultural anthropology* (see *anthropology*). (Chapters 1 and 13)

Ethnology: The comparative study of contemporary *cultures;* part of the subdiscipline of *cultural anthropology* (see *anthropology*). (Chapter 1)

Etic: Referring to the perspective of the observer; a

view external to the *culture* being studied. (Chapters 3 and 8)

Evolution: The process of growth or change of one form into another, usually involving increasing complexity; it may be gradual or rapid; in biology, the theory that all forms of life derive from a process of change via *natural selection* (see *cultural evolution*). (Chapter 2)

Excavation: A method of *data acquisition* in which *matrix* is removed to discover and retrieve archaeological data from beneath the ground, revealing the three-dimensional structure of the data and matrix, both vertically (see *penetrating excavations*) and horizontally (see *clearing excavations*). (Chapters 5 and 7)

Exchange systems: Systems for *trade* or transfer of goods, services, and ideas between individuals and societies (see *reciprocal* and *redistributive exchange*). (Chapter 15)

Experimental archaeology: Studies designed to aid archaeological *interpretation* by attempting to duplicate aspects of *behavioral processes* experimentally under carefully controlled conditions (see *analogy*). (Chapter 13)

Experimental hypothesis: A specific *hypothesis,* deduced from a generalization or general law, which can then be directly tested against data (see *hypothesis testing*). (Chapter 3)

Explanation: The end product of scientific research; in *archaeology* this refers to determining what happened in the past, and when, where, how, and why it happened (see *interpretation*). (Chapters 13 and 17)

Faunal association: A *relative age determination* technique based on archaeological *associations* with remains of extinct species. (Chapter 9)

Faunal ecofacts: *Ecofacts* derived from animals, including bones, teeth, antlers, and so forth; they are usually subdivided into human remains and nonhuman ecofacts. (Chapter 11)

Feature: A nonportable *artifact,* not recoverable from its *matrix* without destroying its integrity (see *cumulative feature* and *constructed feature*). (Chapters 4 and 12)

Feedback: A response to a stimulus that acts within a *system* (see *positive feedback* and *negative feedback*). (Chapter 17)

Field notes: A written account of archaeological research, usually kept by each investigator, recording all stages of *research design,* but especially the conduct of *data acquisition* (see also *photography, scaled drawings,* and *standardized forms*). (Chapter 7)

Fission track age determination: A technique similar to *thermoluminescence,* based on the measure of scars of radioactivity (fission tracks) accumulated since a substance such as glass or obsidian was last heated above a critical temperature. (Chapter 9)

Flake: A *lithic artifact* detached from a *core,* either as *debitage* or as a tool. (Chapter 10)

Floral ecofacts: *Ecofacts* derived from plants; they are subdivided into microspecimens (pollen, *opal phytoliths*) and macrospecimens (seeds, plant fragments, impressions). (Chapter 11)

Flotation: Placing excavated *matrix* in water to separate and recover small *ecofacts* and *artifacts*. (Chapter 7)

Form: The physical characteristics—arrangement, composition, size, and shape—of any component of a *culture* or cultural *system;* in archaeological research, the first objective is to describe and analyze the physical *attributes* (form) of data to determine distributions in time and space (see *function* and *cultural process*). (Chapters 1 and 2)

Form attributes: *Attributes* based on the physical characteristics of an *artifact,* including overall shape, the shape of parts, and measurable dimensions; leads to form *classifications*. (Chapters 8, 10, and 15)

Form types: *Artifact* classes based on *form attributes*. (Chapters 8 and 10)

Formative (Preclassic): A New World chronological *period* characterized by initial complex societies (*chiefdoms*) and long-distance *trade* networks. (Chapters 3 and 17)

Formulation: The first stage in archaeological *research design,* involving definition of the research problem and goals, background investigations, and feasibility studies. (Chapter 5)

Fossiles directeurs: "Type fossils" or particular classes of *lithic artifacts* associated with specific time *periods* and *archaeological cultures* of the European *Paleolithic*. (Chapter 10)

Frequency seriation: A *relative age determination* technique in which *artifacts* or other archaeological data are chronologically ordered by ranking their relative frequencies to conform with *battleship-shaped curves* (see *seriation*). (Chapter 9)

Function: The purpose or use of a component of a *culture* or of a cultural *system;* the second goal of archaeological research is analysis of data and their relationships to determine function and thus reconstruct ancient behavior (see *form* and *cultural process*). (Chapters 1 and 2)

Functional concept of culture: A *model* of *culture* that is keyed to the *functions* of its various components united into a single network or structure; used in archaeological *interpretation* for *synchronic* descriptions of ancient behavior. (Chapters 3 and 17)

General analogy: An *analogy* used in archaeological *interpretation* based on broad and generalized comparisons that are documented across many cultural *traditions* (see *actualistic studies*). (Chapter 13)

General systems theory: The premise that any organization may be studied as a *system* to discover how its parts are related and how changes in either parts or their relationships produce changes in the overall system. (Chapters 3 and 17)

General theory: The broadest level of *archaeological theory*, referring to frameworks that describe and attempt to explain *cultural processes* that operated in the past (see also *constructs* and *middle-range theory*). (Chapter 1)

Geochronology: Age determination by *association* with geological formations. (Chapter 9)

Geographic Information Systems (GIS): Computerized technology for storage, analysis, and display of geographically referenced information. (Chapters 6, 14, and 15)

Geography: The descriptive study of the earth's surface and of its exploitation by life forms. (Chapter 15)

Geology: The study of the development of the earth, especially as preserved in its crust formations. (Chapters 1 and 2)

Geomorphology: That part of *geography* concerned with the form and development of the landscape. (Chapter 11)

Glaze: Specialized *slip* applied to *pottery*, which produces an impermeable and glassy surface when fired at high temperatures (see *vitrification*). (Chapter 10)

Global positioning system (GPS): An instrument used in determining the location of archaeological *sites* by triangulation from orbiting satellites. (Chapter 6)

Glume: A *floral ecofact;* the casing holding the wheat kernel; it can be an important focus of change during *domestication* (see *rachis*). (Chapter 11)

Grid: See *site grid.*

Ground-penetrating radar: An instrument used in *subsurface detection* that records differential reflection of radar pulses from buried *strata* and *features*. (Chapter 6)

Ground reconnaissance: The traditional method for the discovery of archaeological *sites* by visual inspection from ground level. (Chapter 6)

Ground-stone artifacts: A class of *lithic artifacts* produced by abrading and pecking hard stones to form tools with durable edges and surfaces (see *metates* and *querns*). (Chapter 10)

Ground survey: A *surface survey* technique using direct observation to gather archaeological data present on the ground surface; specifically, *mapping* and *surface collection*. (Chapter 6)

Ground truth: Determination of the causes of patterns revealed by *remote sensing*, such as by examining, on the ground, features identified by *aerial photography*. (Chapter 6)

Half-life: The period required for one-half of a radioactive isotope to decay and form a stable element; this decay rate, expressed as a statistical constant, provides the measurement scale for *radiometric age determination*. (Chapter 9)

Hieroglyphs: Literally "sacred carvings"; originally applied to the pictographic script of ancient Egypt, now commonly used to describe any pictographic writing system. (Chapters 2 and 16)

Historical archaeology: That area of *archaeology* concerned with literate societies, in contrast to *prehistoric archaeology*, although the distinction is not always clearcut (see *protohistory*); for obvious reasons historical archaeology is often allied to the discipline of *history*. (Chapter 1)

Historical record: The written texts produced by past human societies that are sought, recovered, studied, and interpreted by historians to reconstruct the past (see *cultural resources*). (Chapter 1)

History: The study of the past through written records, which are compared, judged for veracity, placed in chronological sequence, and interpreted in light of preceding, contemporary, and subsequent events. (Chapter 1)

Horizon: The cross-cultural regularities at one point in time; the spatial baseline of the New World *culture historical approach* synthesis proposed by Willey and Phillips (1958) (compare with *tradition*). (Chapter 3)

Horizontal stratigraphy: Chronological sequences based on successive horizontal displacements, such as sequential beach terraces, analogous to *stratigraphy*. (Chapter 9)

Household archaeology: A branch of *settlement archaeology* specializing in the study of the activities and facilities associated with ancient houses. (Chapter 15)

Hypothesis: A proposition, often derived from a broader generalization or law, that postulates relationships between two or more variables, based on specified assumptions. (Chapter 1)

Hypothesis testing: The process of examining how well various *hypotheses* explain the actual data, to eliminate those that are invalid and to identify those that best fit the observed phenomena; a successful hypothesis is not proved but found to be the best approximation of truth given the current state of knowledge. (Chapter 3)

Hypothesis-testing criteria: The standards for accepting or rejecting hypotheses; in archaeology the primary standard is compatibility with available data; other criteria include predictability, parsimony, completeness, and symmetry. (Chapter 3)

Ideofacts: Archaeological data resulting from past human ideological activities (see *ideological systems*). (Chapter 3)

Ideological systems: One of three components of *culture;* the knowledge or beliefs used by human societies to understand and cope with their existence (see also *technology* and *social systems*). (Chapters 2, 14, and 16)

Implementation: The second stage in archaeological *research design;* it involves obtaining permits, raising funds, and making logistical arrangements. (Chapter 5)

Index species: An animal species with a relatively restricted distribution in time and space, making it the basis for dating by *faunal association* when its remains are present in the *archaeological record*. (Chapter 9)

Indirect age determination: Determination of the age of archaeological data by *association* with a *matrix* or an object of known age (compare with *direct age determination*). (Chapter 9)

Indirect percussion: A technique used to *manufacture chipped-stone artifacts,* in which *flakes* are produced by striking a punch, usually made of wood or bone, placed against a *core* (compare with *direct percussion* and *pressure flaking*). (Chapter 10)

Industry: A gross *artifact* category defined by shared material and *technology,* such as a chipped-stone industry or a *pottery* industry. (Chapters 8 and 10)

Inevitable variation: The premise that all *cultures* vary and change through time without specific cause; a general and unsatisfactory descriptive *model* sometimes implied in the *culture historical approach*. (Chapter 17)

Infrared photography: A technique of *aerial photography* for detection and recording on film of infrared radiation reflected from the sun (compare with *aerial thermography*). (Chapter 6)

Inorganic ecofacts: *Ecofacts* derived from nonbiological remains, including soils, minerals, and the like (compare with *organic ecofacts*). (Chapter 11)

Instrument map: An archaeological map made by use of surveyor's instruments, providing the most accurate control over distance, direction, and elevation (compare with *compass* and *sketch maps*). (Chapter 6)

Interpretation: A stage in archaeological *research design* involving the *synthesis* of the results of data *analysis* and the *explanation* of their meaning, allowing a reconstruction of the past. (Chapters 4, 5, 9, 13–17)

Invasion: See *conquest.*

Isolated data: Unassociated archaeological remains (compare with *data clusters*). (Chapter 4)

Isometric drawing: A three-dimensional rendering, usually of a *feature* or a *site,* used to record and reconstruct the results of archaeological research. In contrast to *perspective drawings,* isometric drawings maintain a constant scale in all three dimensions (see *scaled drawings*). (Chapter 7)

Kiva: A semisubterranean *constructed feature* used for ritual purposes by both ancient and present-day Native Americans in the Southwestern United States. (Chapters 12 and 16)

Knapper: A producer of *chipped-stone artifacts*. (Chapter 10)

Landsat: The Earth Resources Technology Satellites that produce small-scale images of vast areas of the earth's surface; used to study regional patterns of use of land and other resources (see *aerial reconnaissance* and *pixel*). (Chapter 6)

Landscape archaeology: An approach within *archaeology* that emphasizes examination of the complete landscape, focusing on dispersed *features* and on areas between and surrounding traditional *sites* as well as on the sites themselves. (Chapter 7)

Law of superposition: The principle that the sequence of observable *strata,* from bottom to top, reflects the order of deposition, from earliest to latest (see *stratigraphy*). (Chapter 7)

Leather hard: A stage in the *manufacture* of *ceramic artifacts* between forming and firing when the clay is sufficiently dry to lose plasticity but still can be polished to compact its surface. (Chapter 10)

Lerici periscope: A *subsurface detection* probe fitted with a periscope or camera and light source, used to examine subterranean chambers (most often Etruscan tombs). (Chapter 6)

Levallois technique: A specialized method of manufacturing *chipped-stone artifacts,* in which a *core* is prepared to predetermine the shape of a single large *flake* that is subsequently removed. (Chapter 10)

Lithic artifacts: *Artifacts* made from stone, including chipped-stone and ground-stone *industries.* (Chapter 10)

Locational analysis: Techniques from *geography* used to study locations of human settlement and to infer the determinants of these locations (see *central place theory*). (Chapter 15)

Looter: An individual who plunders archaeological *sites* to find *artifacts* of commercial value, at the same time destroying the evidence that archaeologists rely upon to understand the past (compare with *antiquarian* and *archaeologist*). (Chapters 1, 2, and 18)

Lost wax process: A technique in the manufacture of *metal artifacts* in which a wax model is encased in a clay mold, and molten metal is poured into the mold, melting and replacing the wax. (Chapter 10)

Lot: See *provenience lot.*

Magnetometer: A device used in *subsurface detection* that measures minor variations in the earth's magnetic field, often revealing archaeological *features* as magnetic anomalies. (Chapter 6)

Manufacture: The second stage of *behavorial processes,* in which raw materials are modified to produce *artifacts* (see *acquisition, use,* and *deposition*). (Chapter 4)

Mapping: The scaled recording of the horizontal position of exposed *features* and, in some cases, *artifacts* and *ecofacts,* using standardized symbols; one of two basic *ground survey* methods used in *surface survey* of archaeological *sites,* the other being *surface collection* (see *planimetric* and *topographic maps*). (Chapter 6)

Matrix: The physical medium that surrounds, holds, or supports archaeological data. (Chapter 4)

Medieval archaeology: In Europe, a particular field of *historical archaeology* specializing in the investigation of the era between the Dark Ages and the Renaissance (generally the 11th through the 14th centuries A.D.). (Chapter 1)

Mesolithic: An Old World chronological *period* referring to the transition between the *Paleolithic* and the *Neolithic.* (Chapter 11)

Metal artifacts: *Artifacts* made from metal, including copper, bronze, and iron *industries.* (Chapter 10)

Metate: A common New World term for ground-stone basins used to process grains. (Chapter 10)

Microenvironments: Minimal subdivisions of the en-

vironment allowing alternative opportunities for exploitation (see *cultural ecology*). (Chapter 14)

Midden: An accumulation of debris, resulting from human *disposal* behavior, removed from areas of *manufacturing* and *use;* it may be the result of one-time refuse disposal or long-term disposal resulting in *stratification.* (Chapters 4 and 12)

Middle-range theory: The frameworks that link the *archaeological record* and the original activities that produced that record, allowing *archaeologists* to make inferences about past human behavior (see also *constructs* and *general theory*). (Chapter 1)

Migration: Movement of human populations from one area to another, usually resulting in cultural contact. (Chapter 17)

Minimum number of individuals (MNI): The minimum number of individuals represented in a given faunal or human bone collection; determined from the number in the largest category of skeletal elements recovered. (Chapter 11)

Mode: An *attribute* with special significance because it distinguishes one *type* from another. (Chapters 8 and 10)

Model: A theoretical scheme constructed to understand a specific set of data or phenomena; descriptive models deal with the form and structure of phenomena, while explanatory models seek underlying causes for phenomena; models may also be *diachronic* or *synchronic.* (Chapters 2 and 17)

Multilinear cultural evolution: A theory of *cultural evolution* that sees each society pursuing an individual evolutionary career, often defined by four general levels of complexity (see *band, tribe, chiefdom,* and *state*), rather than seeing all societies as pursuing a single course (compare with *unilinear cultural evolution*). (Chapters 3 and 17)

Multiple working hypotheses: The simultaneous testing of alternative *hypotheses* to minimize bias and maximize the chances of finding the best available choice (see *hypothesis testing*). (Chapters 3 and 17)

Natural levels: *Excavation* units corresponding to levels defined by *stratigraphy,* as opposed to *arbitrary levels.* (Chapter 7)

Natural secondary context: A *secondary context* resulting from natural *transformational processes* such as erosion or animal and plant activity (compare with *use-related secondary context*). (Chapter 4)

Natural selection: The mechanism that leads to differential survival and reproduction of those individuals suited to a given *environment* in contrast to others less well adapted (compare with *cultural selection*). (Chapter 2)

Negative bulb of percussion: A small depression on a *core* below the *striking platform,* produced by the force that detached a *flake* (see *bulb of percussion*). (Chapter 10)

Negative feedback: A response to changing conditions that acts to dampen or stop a *system's* reaction (see *deviation-counteracting system*). (Chapter 17)

Neolithic: An Old World chronological *period* characterized by the development of agriculture and the use of ground-stone tool *industries*. (Chapter 10)

Network analysis: Analysis of routes of communication among points such as human settlements. (Chapter 15)

Nonarbitrary sample unit: A subdivision of the *data universe* with cultural relevance, such as *sample units* defined by *data clusters* in remains of rooms or houses (compare with *arbitrary sample unit*). (Chapter 4)

Nonprobabilistic sampling: *Acquisition* of sample data based on informal criteria or personal judgment; it does not allow evaluation of how representative the sample is with respect to the data *population* (compare with *probabilistic sampling*). (Chapters 4, 6, and 7)

Normative concept of culture: A *model of culture* keyed to the abstracted set of rules (norms) that regulate and perpetuate human behavior; it is used in archaeological *interpretation* of both *synchronic* and *diachronic* descriptions of cultural *forms*. (Chapters 3 and 17)

Obsidian hydration: Absorption of water on exposed surfaces of obsidian; if the local hydration rate is known and constant, this phenomenon can be used as an *absolute age determination* technique through measurement of the thickness of the hydration layer. (Chapter 9)

Opal phytoliths: Microscopic silica bodies that form in living plants, providing a durable *floral ecofact* that allows the identification of plant remains in archaeological deposits. (Chapter 11)

Open system: A *system* that receives information, matter, or energy from its *environment* and that changes due to sources either internal or external to the system (compare with *closed system*). (Chapter 17)

Organic artifacts: *Artifacts* made of organic materials, including wood, bone, horn, fiber, ivory, or hide *industries*. (Chapter 10)

Organic ecofacts: *Ecofacts* derived from living remains (see *floral* and *faunal ecofacts*). (Chapter 11)

Osteodontokeratic: Literally "bone-tooth-horn"; refers to the controversial tool "*technology*" of some early hominids. (Chapter 10)

Paleodemography: The study of ancient human populations. (Chapter 11)

Paleolithic: An Old World chronological *period* characterized by the earliest known *lithic artifacts,* those of chipped stone, and by a hunting and gathering *economy*. (Chapter 10)

Palynology: The study of pollen (see *floral ecofacts*). (Chapter 11)

Paradigm: A conceptual framework for a scientific discipline; a strategy for integrating a research method, theory, and goals. (Chapter 3)

Paradigmatic classification: *Classification* based on an equal weighting of *attributes,* so that each class is defined by a cluster of unique attributes and is not dependent on the order in which the attributes were defined (compare with *taxonomic classification*). (Chapter 8)

Pedology: The study of soils. (Chapter 11)

Penetrating excavations: *Excavations* designed primarily to reveal the vertical and temporal dimensions within archaeological deposits—the depth, sequence, and composition of buried data (see *sondage, test pit, trench,* and *tunnel*). (Chapter 7)

Period: A broad and general chronological unit defined for a *site* or a *region,* based on combined data, such as defined *complexes* (see also *time–space grid*). (Chapter 3)

Perspective drawing: A three-dimensional rendering, usually of a *feature* or a *site,* used to record and reconstruct the results of archaeological research. In contrast to *isometric drawings,* perspective drawings do not maintain a constant scale in all three dimensions, so that size appears to diminish with distance from the viewer (see *scaled drawings*). (Chapter 7)

Phase: See *complex*.

Photography: The recording of archaeological data on photographic film, especially during *data acquisition, processing,* and *analysis* (see also *field notes, scaled drawings,* and *standardized forms*). (Chapters 7 and 8)

Physical anthropology: One of the two major subdivisions of *anthropology,* the study of humankind from a biological perspective (compare with *cultural anthropology*). (Chapters 1 and 11)

Physical environment: Those nonbiotic elements of the habitat created or modified by natural forces; a component of the total *environment* as seen by *cultural ecology* (see *biological* and *cultural environment*). (Chapter 17)

Phytoliths: See *opal phytoliths*.

Pixel: A picture element, the minimum unit recorded electronically by the *Landsat* satellites. (Chapter 6)

Plaited: Basketry made with both a horizontal and a vertical stitch or weft (see *coiled* and *twined*). (Chapter 10)

Plan drawing: A two-dimensional rendering at a constant scale, depicting the horizontal dimensions of archaeological data. (Chapter 7)

Plane table: A portable drawing surface used in conjunction with an *alidade* to produce *planimetric* or *topographic maps*. (Chapter 6)

Planimetric maps: Archaeological maps that depict *sites* or *features* using nontopographic symbols (compare with *topographic maps*). (Chapter 6)

Pleistocene: A geological period characterized by successive glacial advances and retreats, ending about 11,500 years ago. (Chapter 9)

Population: The aggregate of all *sample units* within a *data universe*. (Chapter 4)

Positive feedback: A response to changing conditions that acts to stimulate further reactions within a *system* (see *deviation-amplifying system*). (Chapter 17)

Positivism: A philosophical position holding that all natural and social phenomena can be understood by determining their origins or causes (see also *evolution* and *progress*). (Chapter 2)

Postclassic: A New World chronological *period* characterized by secular and militaristic emphases within societies in both Mesoamerica and the Andean area. (Chapter 3)

Postprocessual approach: A recent approach to archaeological *interpretation* that is based on a *cognitive concept of culture* and emphasizes both the active role of individuals as decision makers and the meaning-laden contexts in which decisions are made. (Chapter 17)

Potassium–argon age determination: A *radiometric age determination* technique based on the *half-life* of the radioactive isotope of potassium (^{40}K) that decays to form argon (^{40}Ar). (Chapter 9)

Pottery: A class of *ceramic artifacts* in which clay is formed into containers (by hand, in molds, or using a potter's wheel), often decorated, and fired. (Chapter 10)

Preclassic: See *Formative*.

Prehistoric archaeology: The area of *archaeology* concerned with preliterate or nonliterate societies, in contrast to *historical archaeology;* in North America prehistoric archaeology is considered a part of the discipline of *anthropology*. (Chapter 1)

Prehistory: Those eras in various parts of the world before the invention of writing. (Chapter 1)

Pressure flaking: A technique for manufacturing *chipped-stone artifacts,* in which *flakes* or *blades* are produced by applying pressure against a *core* with a punch usually made of wood or bone (compare with *direct percussion* and *indirect percussion*). (Chapter 10)

Primary classification: A *classification* based on directly observable *attributes,* often carried out by *archaeologists* in the field (see *secondary classification*). (Chapter 8)

Primary context: The condition where *provenience, association,* and *matrix* have not been disturbed since the original *deposition* of archaeological data (compare with *secondary context*). (Chapter 4)

Prime movers: Crucial factors that stimulate cultural change; they are emphasized in some *models* of *multilinear cultural evolution*. (Chapters 3 and 17)

Probabilistic sampling: *Sample data acquisition* based on formal statistical criteria in selecting *sample units* to be investigated; it allows evaluation of how representative the sample is with respect to the data *population* (compare with *nonprobabilistic sampling*). (Chapters 4, 6, and 7)

Process: See *cultural processes*.

Processing: See *data processing*.

Profile drawing: A two-dimensional rendering similar to a *section drawing* except that features are depicted in outline without showing their internal composition. (Chapter 7)

Progress: A philosophical position holding that change in natural or social phenomena implies increase in complexity or sophistication (see also *evolution* and *positivism*). (Chapter 2)

Protohistory: A transition period between the prehistoric and the historical eras (see *prehistoric* and *historical archaeology*). (Chapter 1)

Provenience (provenance): The three-dimensional location of archaeological data within or on the *matrix* at the time of discovery. (Chapter 4)

Provenience lot: A defined spatial area, in either two dimensions (for surface data) or three dimensions (for excavated data), used as a minimal unit for *provenience* determination and recording. (Chapters 6 and 7)

Pseudoarchaeology: Use of real or imagined archaeological evidence to justify nonscientific accounts about the past. (Chapter 1)

Publication: The final stage of archaeological *research design*, providing reports of the data and interpretations resulting from archaeological research. (Chapters 5 and 18)

Quadrat: An *arbitrary sample unit* defined as a square of specified size. (Chapters 4 and 6)

Quarry: A *cumulative feature* resulting from the mining of mineral resources. (Chapter 10)

Quenching: A technique used in the *manufacture of metal artifacts,* in which the strength of carbonized iron (steel) is increased by heating it and then rapidly cooling it by plunging the metal into water (see also *tempering*). (Chapter 10)

Quern: A common Old World term for ground-stone basins used to process grains. (Chapter 10)

Rachis: A *floral ecofact;* the stem connecting the wheat kernel to the shaft; it can be an important focus of change during *domestication* (see *glume*). (Chapter 11)

Radiocarbon age determination: A *radiometric age determination* technique based on measuring the decay of the radioactive isotope of carbon (^{14}C) to stable nitrogen (^{14}N). (Chapter 9)

Radiometric age determination: A variety of *absolute age determination* techniques based on the transformation of unstable radioactive isotopes into stable elements (see *potassium–argon* and *radiocarbon age determination*). (Chapter 9)

Random sampling: See *simple random sampling*.

Reciprocal exchange: Simple and direct *trade* between two parties, involving the exchange of goods, services, or monetary units (compare with *redistributive exchange*). (Chapter 15)

Reconnaissance: A method of *data acquisition* in which archaeological remains are systematically identified, including both discovery and plotting of their location; it is often conducted along with *surface survey.* (Chapters 5 and 6)

Redistributive exchange: Complex and indirect *trade* involving a third party or institution that collects goods, services, or monetary units and reallocates at least a portion to others (compare with *reciprocal exchange*). (Chapter 15)

Region: A geographically defined area containing a series of interrelated human communities sharing a single cultural–ecological *system.* (Chapter 4)

Regional maps: Maps designed to depict the distribution of archaeological *sites* within *regions.* (Chapter 6)

Relative age determination: Determining chronological sequence without reference to a fixed time scale (compare with *absolute age determination*). (Chapter 9)

Remote sensing: *Reconnaissance* and *surface survey* methods involving aerial or subsurface detection of archaeological data. (Chapter 6)

Research design: A systematic plan to coordinate archaeological research to ensure the efficient use of resources and to guide the research according to the *scientific method* (see *formulation, implementation, data acquisition, data processing, analysis, interpretation,* and *publication*). (Chapter 5)

Residence rule: The description of the household location of newly married couples within a given society, usually distinguishing between actual and ideal patterns of behavior. (Chapter 3)

Resistivity detector: An instrument used in *subsurface detection* that measures differences in the conductivity of electrical current, and thus may identify archaeological *features.* (Chapter 6)

Retouch: A technique of *chipped-stone artifact manufacture* in which *pressure flaking* is used to detach small steep flakes to modify the edges of *flake* tools. (Chapter 10)

Salvage archaeology: Collection of archaeological data from a *site* or a *region* in the face of the impending destruction of past remains (see *cultural resource management*). (Chapter 18)

Sample: A set of units selected from a *population.* (Chapter 4)

Sample data acquisition: Investigation of only a portion of the *sample units* in a *population,* by either *probabilistic* or *nonprobabilistic sampling* (compare with *total data acquisition*). (Chapters 4, 6–8, 10–12)

Sample size: The total number of *sample units* drawn from a *sampling frame.* (Chapter 4)

Sample unit: The basic unit of archaeological investigation; a subdivision of the *data universe,* defined by either arbitrary or nonarbitrary criteria (see *arbitrary* and *nonarbitrary sample units*). (Chapter 4)

Sampling fraction: The total number of *sample units* drawn from a *sampling frame,* expressed as a percentage of the *population* size. (Chapter 4)

Sampling frame: A list of *sample units* from which a *sample* is drawn. (Chapter 4)

Scaled drawings: Standardized renderings in pencil

used to record archaeological data, especially during *data acquisition;* they include *elevation, isometric, perspective, plan, profile,* and *section drawings* (see also *field notes, photography,* and *standardized forms*). (Chapters 7 and 8)

Science: The systematic pursuit of knowledge about natural phenomena (in contrast to the nonnatural or supernatural) by a continually self-correcting method of testing and refining the conclusions resulting from observation (see *scientific method*). (Chapter 1)

Scientific method: The operational means of *science,* by which natural phenomena are observed, conclusions are drawn, and *hypotheses* are tested. (Chapter 1)

Screening: Passing excavated *matrix* through a metal mesh to improve the recovery rate of *artifacts* and larger *ecofacts.* (Chapter 7)

Secondary classification: A *classification* based on inferred or analytic *attributes,* often carried out by technicians in specialized laboratories (see *primary classification*). (Chapter 8)

Secondary context: The condition where *provenience, association,* and *matrix* have been wholly or partially altered by *transformational processes* after original *deposition* of archaeological data (compare with *primary context*). (Chapters 4 and 7)

Section drawing: A two-dimensional rendering, at a constant scale, depicting archaeological data and *matrix* as seen in the wall of an *excavation.* (Chapter 7)

Sequence comparison: A *relative age determination* technique based on similarities between newly classified *artifacts* or *features* and established chronological sequences of similar materials. (Chapter 9)

Sequence dating: A *relative age determination* technique based on a *stylistic seriation* of Egyptian predynastic tomb pottery. (Chapter 9)

Seriation: Techniques used to order materials in a *relative age determination* sequence, in such a way that adjacent items in the series are more similar to each other than to items further apart in the series (see *frequency* and *stylistic seriation*). (Chapter 9)

Settlement archaeology: The study of the spatial distribution of ancient activities, from remains of single *activity areas* to those of entire *regions.* (Chapter 15)

Settlement pattern: The distribution of *features* and *sites* across the landscape. (Chapter 15)

Shovel testing: A *subsurface detection* technique using either posthole diggers or shovels to determine rapidly the density and distribution of archaeological remains. (Chapter 6)

Side-looking airborne radar (SLAR): An instrument used in *aerial reconnaissance* that can detect large archaeological *sites* using an oblique radar image; especially useful because it can penetrate cloud cover and, to a degree, vegetation. (Chapter 6)

Simple data cluster: Clustered data that are internally homogeneous with regard to a single function, such as those from an obsidian tool workshop. (Chapter 4)

Simple random sampling: A *probabilistic sampling* technique in which each *sample unit* has a statistically equal chance for selection. (Chapter 4)

Site: A spatial clustering of archaeological data, comprising *artifacts, ecofacts,* and *features* in any combination. (Chapter 4)

Site-catchment analysis: Definition of the available resources within a given distance of a *site;* it determines an area within which distance is assumed to be insignificant in differential access to these resources. (Chapter 14)

Site grid: A set of regularly spaced intersecting north–south and east–west lines, usually marked by stakes, providing the basic reference system for recording horizontal *provenience* (coordinates) within a *site.* (Chapter 6)

Site map: A map designed to depict the details of a *site,* usually by recording all observable surface *features.* (Chapter 6)

Site plan: A map designed to depict a specific detail within a *site,* usually a single *feature* or a group of features. (Chapter 6)

Sketch map: An impressionistic rendering of a *region, site,* or *feature* made without instruments so that there is no control over geographical direction or elevation; distances may be estimated by pacing (compare with *compass* and *instrument maps*). (Chapter 6)

Slip: A solution of clay and water applied to *pottery* to provide color and a smooth and uniform surface (see also *glaze*). (Chapter 10)

Smelting: Application of heat to ores to extract metals prior to the *manufacture* of *metal artifacts.* (Chapter 10)

Social systems: One of the three basic components of *culture;* the means by which human societies organize themselves and their interactions with other societies (see also *technology* and *ideological systems*). (Chapters 2, 14, and 15)

Society for American Archaeology (SAA): A professional organization especially for archaeologists specializing in New World archaeology; it publishes the scholarly journals *American Antiquity, Latin American*

Antiquity, and the *Bulletin of the Society for American Archaeology.* (Chapter 1)

Society for Historical Archaeology (SHA): A professional organization especially for archaeologists specializing in *historical archaeology;* it publishes the scholarly journal *Historical Archaeology* and a quarterly newsletter. (Chapter 1)

Society of Professional Archeologists (SOPA): A professional organization especially for archaeologists specializing in *contract archaeology* and *cultural resource management;* it publishes an annual directory of members and a monthly newsletter. (Chapter 1)

Sociofacts: Archaeological data resulting from past human social activities (see *social systems*). (Chapter 3)

Sondage: A sounding pit—an initial *test pit* placed so as to preview what lies beneath the ground. (Chapter 7)

Specific analogy: An *analogy* used in archaeological *interpretation* based on specific comparisons that are documented within a single cultural *tradition.* (Chapter 13)

Spiral fracture: A particular type of fracture observed in bones—breakage curving along and around the shaft; it is seen by some specialists as diagnostic of human use of bones for tools. (Chapter 10)

Spot: An *arbitrary sample unit* defined by geographical coordinates. (Chapters 4 and 6)

Stable carbon isotope analysis: A technique used in the analysis of human remains based on the measurement of ratio between ^{13}C and ^{12}C isotopes in ancient human bone collagen to determine past diets (plant foods). (Chapter 11)

Standardized forms: Preformatted information sheets completed in the field for recording archaeological data, especially during *data acquisition, data processing,* and *analysis* (see also *field notes, photography,* and *scaled drawings*). (Chapters 7 and 8)

State: A society retaining many *chiefdom* characteristics in elaborated form, but also including true political power sanctioned by legitimate force, and social integration through concepts of nationality and citizenship usually defined by territorial boundaries; often used to define the most complex *multilinear cultural evolutionary* stage. (Chapter 17)

Strata: The definable layers of archaeological *matrix* or *features* revealed by *excavation* (see *stratification*). (Chapter 7)

Strata (sampling): Divisions of a *population* based on

observed similarities (see *stratified sampling*). (Chapter 4)

Stratification: Multiple *strata* whose order of deposition reflects the *law of superposition* (see *stratigraphy*). (Chapter 7)

Stratified sampling: A *probabilistic sampling* technique in which *sample units* are drawn from two or more sampling *strata.* (Chapter 4)

Stratigraphy: The archaeological evaluation of the significance of *stratification* to determine the temporal sequence of data within stratified deposits by using both the *law of superposition* and *context* evaluations; also a specific *relative age determination* technique. (Chapters 7 and 9)

Striking platform: The surface area of a *chipped-stone artifact* where force is applied to detach a *flake* from a *core.* (Chapter 10)

Stripping excavations: *Clearing excavations* in which large areas of overburden are removed to reveal horizontal distributions of data without leaving balks (compare with *area excavations*). (Chapter 7)

Stylistic attributes: *Attributes* defined by the surface characteristics of *artifacts*—color, texture, decoration, and so forth—leading to stylistic *classifications.* (Chapters 8, 10, and 15)

Stylistic seriation: A *relative age determination* technique in which artifacts or other data are ordered chronologically according to stylistic similarities (see *seriation*). (Chapter 9)

Stylistic types: *Artifact* classes based on *stylistic attributes.* (Chapters 8, 10, and 15)

Subassemblage: A grouping of *artifact* classes, based on *form* and *functional* criteria, that is assumed to represent a single occupational group within an ancient community (see *assemblage* and *archaeological culture*). (Chapter 8)

Subsurface detection: *Remote sensing* techniques carried out from ground level, including *bowsing, augering,* and *coring,* by use of the *Lerici periscope, magnetometer, resistivity detector,* and similar means. (Chapter 6)

Surface collection: The systematic gathering of exposed *artifacts* or *ecofacts;* one of two basic *ground survey* methods used in *surface survey* of archaeological *sites,* the other being *mapping.* (Chapter 6)

Surface survey: A method of *data acquisition* in which data are gathered and evaluated from the surface of archaeological *sites,* usually by *mapping* of *features* and *surface collection* of *artifacts* and *ecofacts* (Chapters 5 and 6)

Synchronic: Pertaining to phenomena at one point in time; a concurrent perspective (compare with *diachronic*). (Chapters 2, 14, and 17)

Synthesis: The reassembling of analyzed data as the prelude to *interpretation*. (Chapters 13–17)

System: An organization that functions through the interdependence of its parts (see *general systems theory*). (Chapters 3 and 17)

Systematic sampling: A *probabilistic sampling* technique in which the first *sample unit* is selected at random and all other units are selected by a predetermined interval from the first. (Chapter 4)

Taphonomy: Study of the *transformational processes* of *faunal* and *floral ecofacts* after the death of the original organisms. (Chapter 11)

Taxonomic classification: A *classification* based on an unequal weighting of *attributes* that are imposed in a hierarchical order so that the attributes defining each class are dependent on the order in which the attributes were considered (compare with *paradigmatic classification*). (Chapter 8)

Technofacts: Archaeological data resulting from past technological activities (see *technology*). (Chapter 3)

Technological attributes: *Attributes* consisting of raw material characteristics (constituents) and those resulting from manufacturing methods; these attributes lead to technological *classifications*. (Chapters 8 and 10)

Technological types: *Artifact* classes based on *technological attributes*. (Chapters 8 and 10)

Technology: One of the three basic components of *culture;* the means used by human societies to interact directly with and adapt to the *environment* (see *ideological* and *social systems*). (Chapters 3 and 14)

Tell or tepe: Literally "hill"; a term used in southwest Asia to refer to a mounded archaeological *site*. (Chapter 6)

Temper: A nonplastic substance (such as sand) added to clay prior to *pottery manufacture* to reduce shrinkage and breakage during drying and firing. (Chapter 10)

Tempering: A technique used in the *manufacture of metal artifacts,* in which carbonized iron is reheated after *quenching* to reduce brittleness. (Chapter 10)

Terminus ante quem (TAQ): Referring to the date before which an *artifact* or a *feature* must have been deposited (see *terminus post quem*). (Chapter 9)

Terminus post quem (TPQ): Referring to the date after which an *artifact* or a *feature* must have been deposited (see *terminus ante quem*). (Chapter 9)

Test pit: A *penetrating excavation* used to probe the depth of archaeological *sites* within a very restricted area. (Chapter 7)

Thermography: See *aerial thermography.*

Thermoluminescence (TL): An age determination technique in which the amount of light energy released in a *pottery* sample during heating gives a measure of the time elapsed since the material was last heated to a critical temperature. (Chapter 9)

Thiessen polygons: Areas described by drawing perpendiculars midway between points, such as *sites* on a *regional map,* and connecting these lines to form polygons around each point; they are used in *locational analysis.* (Chapter 15)

Thin-section: A prepared slice of stone or ceramic (about 0.03 mm thick) used by specialists to identify constituents and recognize *quarry* sources. (Chapter 10)

Three-age sequence: A traditional *diachronic model* describing the sequence of technological *periods* in the Old World, each period characterized by predominant use of stone, bronze, or iron tools. (Chapter 2)

Time–space grid: A *synthesis* of temporal and spatial distributions of data used in the *culture historical approach* based on *period* sequences within *culture areas.* (Chapters 3 and 17)

Topographic maps: Maps that depict topographic (landform) data in combination with representations of archaeological *sites* (compare with *planimetric maps*). (Chapter 6)

Total data acquisition: Investigation of all *sample units* in a *population* (compare with *sample data acquisition*). (Chapters 4, 6–8, 10–12)

Trade: Transmission of material objects from one society to another; a descriptive cultural *model* used in the *culture historical approach* (see *exchange systems*). (Chapters 15 and 17)

Tradition: Cultural continuity through time; the temporal basis of the New World *culture historical approach* synthesis proposed by Willey and Phillips (1958) (compare with *horizon*). (Chapters 3 and 17)

Transect: An *arbitrary sample unit* defined as a linear corridor of uniform specified width. (Chapters 4 and 6)

Transformational processes: Conditions and events that affect archaeological data from the time of *deposition* to the time of recovery (compare with *behavioral processes;* see also *taphonomy*). (Chapter 4)

Transit: A surveyor's instrument used to produce *topographic* or *planimetric maps.* (Chapter 6)

Transposed primary context: A *primary context* resulting from depositional activities leading to *midden* formation (compare with *use-related primary context*). (Chapter 4)

Trench: A long and narrow *penetrating excavation* used to reveal the vertical dimension of archaeological data and to explore the horizontal dimension along one axis. (Chapter 7)

Tribe: An egalitarian society possessing a subsistence base stable enough to support permanent settlement and social institutions such as age–grade groupings that supplement the kinship ties that integrate society; often used to define a *multilinear cultural evolutionary* stage. (Chapter 17)

Tunnel: A *penetrating excavation* that, instead of cutting through *strata* vertically, follows buried *strata* or *features* along one horizontal dimension. (Chapter 7)

Twined: Basketry made with a horizontal stitch or weft (see *coiled* and *plaited*). (Chapter 10)

Type: A class of data defined by a consistent clustering of *attributes* (see *classification*). (Chapter 8)

Type-variety-mode analysis: A standardized *taxonomic classification* of pottery based on *stylistic attributes* that defines a hierarchy of classes: *modes* and varieties (minimal units); *types,* groups, *complexes,* and spheres (maximal units). (Chapter 10)

Unilinear cultural evolution: A 19th-century version of *cultural evolution* holding that all human societies change according to a single fixed evolutionary course, passing through the same stages (described as "savagery," "barbarism," and "civilization" by L. H. Morgan). (Chapters 2, 13, and 17)

Use: The third stage of *behavioral processes,* in which *artifacts* are utilized (see *acquisition, manufacture,* and *deposition*). (Chapter 4)

Use-related primary context: A *primary context* resulting from abandonment of materials during either manufacturing or use activities (compare with *transposed primary context*). (Chapter 4)

Use-related secondary context: A *secondary context* resulting from disturbance by human activity after original *deposition* of materials (compare with *natural secondary context*). (Chapter 4)

Varves: Fine layers of *alluvium* deposited in glacial lakes by retreating ice sheets; they are used for age determination, based on annual cycles of deposition. (Chapter 9)

Vitrification: Melting and fusion of glassy minerals within clay during high-temperature firing of *pottery* (above 1000°C), resulting in loss of porosity. (Chapter 10)

BIBLIOGRAPHY

Adams, J. L. 1988. Use-wear analysis on manos and hide processing stones. *Journal of Field Archaeology* 15: 307–315.

Adams, R. E. W. 1974. A trial estimation of palace populations at Uaxactún. In *Mesoamerican Archaeology: New Approaches,* ed. N. Hammond, pp. 285–296. Austin: University of Texas Press.

———. 1975. Stratigraphy. In *Field Methods in Archaeology,* 6th ed., ed. T. R. Hester, R. F. Heizer, and J. A. Graham, pp. 147–162. Palo Alto, Calif.: Mayfield.

———, ed. 1977. *The Origins of Maya Civilization.* School of American Research Advanced Seminar Series. Albuquerque: University of New Mexico Press.

Adams, R. E. W., W. E. Brown, Jr., and T. P. Culbert. 1981. Radar mapping, archaeology, and ancient Maya land use. *Science* 213: 1457–1463.

Adams, R. M. 1965. *Land behind Baghdad: A History of Settlement on the Diyala Plains.* Chicago: University of Chicago Press.

———. 1966. *The Evolution of Urban Society.* Chicago: Aldine-Atherton.

———. 1974. Anthropological perspectives on ancient trade. *Current Anthropology* 15: 239–258.

Adams, R. M., and H. Nissen. 1972. *The Uruk Countryside.* Chicago: University of Chicago Press.

Adams, W. Y. 1968. Invasion, diffusion, evolution? *Antiquity* 42: 194–215.

———. 1988. Archaeological classification: Theory versus practice. *Antiquity* 62: 40–56.

Addington, L. R. 1985. *Lithic Illustration.* Chicago: University of Chicago Press.

Adkins, L., and R. Adkins. 1989. *Archaeological Illustration.* Cambridge: Cambridge University Press.

Adovasio, J. M. 1977. *Basketry Technology: A Guide to Identification and Analysis.* Manuals on Archaeology. Chicago: Aldine.

Agurcia Fasquelle, R. 1986. Snakes, jaguars, and outlaws: Some comments on Central American archaeology. In *Research and Reflections in Archaeology and History. Essays in Honor of Doris Stone,* ed. E. W. Andrews V, pp. 1–9. New Orleans: Middle American Research Institute, Tulane University.

Aitken, M. J. 1960. Magnetic dating. *Archaeometry* 3: 41–44.

———. 1985. *Thermoluminescence Dating.* Orlando: Academic Press.

———. 1990. *Science-Based Dating in Archaeology.* London: Longman.

Aldenderfer, M. S. 1983. Review of *Essays on Archaeological Typology,* edited by R. Whallon and J. A. Brown. *American Antiquity* 48: 652–654.

———. 1991. The analytical engine: Computer simulation and archaeological research. In *Archaeological Method and Theory,* vol. 3, ed. M. B. Schiffer, pp. 195–247. Tucson: University of Arizona Press.

Alexander, D. 1983. The limitations of traditional surveying techniques in a forested environment. *Journal of Field Archaeology* 10: 133–144.

Alexander, J. 1970. *The Directing of Archaeological Excavations.* London: John Baker.

Allen, K. M. S., S. W. Green, and E. B. W. Zubrow, eds. 1990. *Interpreting Space: GIS and Archaeology.* London: Taylor & Francis.

Allen, R. O., ed. 1989. *Archaeological Chemistry IV.* Advances in Chemistry Series No. 220. Washington, D.C.: American Chemical Society.

Allen, W. L., and J. B. Richardson III. 1971. The reconstruction of kinship from archaeological data: The concepts, the methods, and the feasibility. *American Antiquity* 36: 41–53.

Altman, N., J. P. Dwyer, M. R. Beckes, and R. D. Hake. 1982. ASP: A simplified computer sampling package for the field archaeologist. *Journal of Field Archaeology* 9: 136–140.

Alva, W. 1988a. Discovering the New World's richest unlooted tomb. *National Geographic Magazine* 174 (4): 510–514.

———. 1988b. Into the tomb of a Moche lord. *National Geographic Magazine* 174 (4): 516–549.

———. 1990. New tomb of royal splendor. *National Geographic Magazine* 177 (6): 2–15.

Ammerman, A. J. 1981. Surveys and archaeological research. *Annual Review of Anthropology* 10: 63–88.

———. 1985. Plow-zone experiments in Calabria, Italy. *Journal of Field Archaeology* 8: 151–165.

Ammerman, A. J., and M. W. Feldman. 1978. Replicated collection of site surfaces. *American Antiquity* 43: 734–740.

Anderson, B. A. 1978. Excavations at Laguna Cuzcachapa and Laguna Seca. In *The Prehistory of Chalchuapa, El Salvador,* vol. 1, pt. 3, ed. R. J. Sharer, pp. 43–60. Philadelphia: University of Pennsylvania Press.

Anderson, D. D. 1985. Reburial: Is it reasonable? *Archaeology* 38 (5): 48–51.

Anderson, K. M. 1969. Ethnographic analogy and archaeological interpretation. *Science* 163: 133–138.

Andresen, J. M., B. F. Byrd, M. D. Elson, R. H. McGuire, R. G. Mendoza, E. Staski, and J. P. White. 1981. The deer hunters: Star Carr reconsidered. *World Archaeology* 13: 31–46.

Angel, J. L. 1969. The bases of paleodemography. *American Journal of Physical Anthropology* 30: 427–438.

Arden, H. 1989. Who owns our past? *National Geographic Magazine* 175 (3): 376–392.

Arnold, D. 1985. *Ceramic Theory and Cultural Process.* Cambridge: Cambridge University Press.

Arnold, J. R., and W. F. Libby. 1949. Age determinations by radiocarbon content: Checks with samples of known age. *Science* 110: 678–680.

Aronoff, S. 1989. *Geographic Information Systems: A Management Perspective.* Ottawa: WDL Publications.

Ascher, M., and R. Ascher. 1963. Chronological ordering by computer. *American Anthropologist* 65: 1045–1052.

Ascher, R. M. 1961a. Analogy in archaeological interpretation. *Southwestern Journal of Anthropology* 17: 317–325.

———. 1961b. Experimental archaeology. *American Anthropologist* 63: 793–816.

———. 1968. Time's arrow and the archaeology of a contemporary community. In *Settlement Archaeology,* ed. K. C. Chang, pp. 43–52. Palo Alto, Calif.: National Press.

Ashmore, W. 1980. Discovering Early Classic Quiriguá. *Expedition* 23 (1): 35–44.

———, ed. 1981. *Lowland Maya Settlement Patterns.* School of American Research Advanced Seminar Series. Albuquerque: University of New Mexico Press.

———. 1991. Site-planning principles and concepts of directionality among the ancient Maya. *Latin American Antiquity* 2: 199–226.

Aveni, A. F. 1980. *Skywatchers of Ancient Mexico.* Austin: University of Texas Press.

———. 1981. Archaeoastronomy. *Advances in Archaeological Method and Theory,* vol. 4, ed. M. B. Schiffer, pp. 1–77. New York: Academic Press.

———, ed. 1982. *Archaeoastronomy in the New World.* Cambridge: Cambridge University Press.

———, ed. 1989. *World Archaeoastronomy.* Cambridge: Cambridge University Press.

———, ed. 1990. *The Lines of Nazca.* Memoirs, vol. 183. Philadelphia: American Philosophical Society.

Bada, J. L., and P. M. Helfman. 1975. Amino acid racemization dating of fossil bones. *World Archaeology* 7: 160–173.

Bahn, P. G., and J. Vertut. 1988. *Images of the Ice Age.* New York: Facts on File.

Baillie, M. G. L. 1982. *Tree-Ring Dating and Archaeology.* Chicago: University of Chicago Press.

Baity, E. C. 1973. Archaeoastronomy and ethnoastronomy so far. *Current Anthropology* 14: 389–449.

Baker, C. M. 1978. The size effect: An explanation of variability in surface artifact assemblage content. *American Antiquity* 43: 288–293.

Baker, J., and D. R. Brothwell. 1980. *Animal Diseases in Archaeology.* New York: Academic Press.

Bamforth, D. B., and A. C. Spaulding. 1982. Human behavior, explanation, archaeology, history, and science. *Journal of Anthropological Archaeology* 1: 170–195.

Bannister, B. 1962. The interpretation of tree-ring dates. *American Antiquity* 27: 508–514.

———. 1970. Dendrochronology. In *Science in Archaeology,* 2nd ed., ed. D. Brothwell and E. S. Higgs, pp. 191–205. New York: Praeger.

Bannister, B., and T. L. Smiley. 1955. Dendrochronology. In *Geochronology,* ed. T. L. Smiley, pp. 177–195. Physical Science Bulletin no. 2. Tucson: University of Arizona.

Bapty, I., and T. Yates, eds. 1990. *Archaeology after Structuralism: Post-Structuralism and the Practice of Archaeology.* London: Routledge.

Barker, G. 1985. *Prehistoric Farming in Europe.* Cambridge: Cambridge University Press.

Barker, P. 1977. *Techniques of Archaeological Investigation.* New York: Universe Books.

———. 1988. *The Techniques of Archaeological Excavation.* London: Batsford.

Barnatt, J., and P. Hering. 1986. Stone circles and megalithic geometry: An experiment to test alternative design practices. *Journal of Archaeological Science* 13: 431–449.

Bartel, B. 1982. A historical review of ethnological and archaeological analyses of mortuary practice. *Journal of Anthropological Archaeology* 1: 32–58.

Bass, G. F. 1966. *Archaeology under Water.* London: Thames & Hudson.

Bass, G. F., and P. Throckmorton. 1961. Excavating a Bronze Age shipwreck. *Archaeology* 14: 78–87.

Bass, W. M. 1986. *Human Osteology: A Laboratory and Field Manual of the Human Skeleton*. Columbia: Missouri Archaeological Society.

Bassett, C. A. 1986. The culture thieves. *Science 86* 7 (6): 22–29.

Bator, P. M. 1983. *The International Trade in Art*. Chicago: University of Chicago Press.

Baudez, C. F., ed. 1983. *Introducción a la Arqueología de Copán, Honduras*. 3 vols. Tegucigalpa: SECTUR.

Bawden, G. 1982. Community organization reflected by the household. *Journal of Field Archaeology* 9: 165–181.

Bayard, D. T. 1972. Early Thai bronze: Analysis and new dates. *Science* 176: 1411–1412.

Beadle, G. W. 1980. The ancestry of corn. *Scientific American* 242 (1): 112–119.

Beaudry, M. C., ed. 1989. *Documentary Archaeology in the New World*. Cambridge: Cambridge University Press.

Beck, C., and G. T. Jones. 1989. Bias and archaeological classification. *American Antiquity* 54: 244–262.

Beck, C. W., ed. 1974. *Archaeological Chemistry*. Advances in Chemistry Series No. 138. Washington, D.C.: American Chemical Society.

Behrensmeyer, A. K. 1984. Taphonomy and the fossil record. *American Scientist* 72: 558–566.

Behrensmeyer, A. K., and A. P. Hill. 1980. *Fossils in the Making: Vertebrate Taphonomy and Paleoecology*. Chicago: University of Chicago Press.

Bellhouse, D. R. 1980. Sampling studies in archaeology. *Archaeometry* 22: 123–132.

Bement, L. C. 1985. Spray foam: A new bone encasement technique. *Journal of Field Archaeology* 12: 371–372.

Benner, S. M., and R. S. Brodkey. 1984. Underground detection using differential heat analysis. *Archaeometry* 26: 21–36.

Bennett, C. L., R. P. Beukens, M. R. Clover, H. E. Gove, R. B. Liebert, A. E. Litherland, K. H. Purser, and W. E. Sondheim. 1977. Radiocarbon dating using electrostatic accelerators: Negative ions provide the key. *Science* 198: 508–510.

Bennett, M. A. 1974. *Basic Ceramic Analyses*. Contributions in Anthropology 6. Portales: Eastern New Mexico University.

Benson, E. P., ed. 1975. *Death and the Afterlife in Pre-Columbian America*. Washington, D.C.: Dumbarton Oaks.

———, ed. 1979. *Pre-Columbian Metallurgy of South America*. Washington, D.C.: Dumbarton Oaks.

———, ed. 1980. *Mesoamerican Sites and World-Views*. Washington, D.C.: Dumbarton Oaks.

Bertalanffy, L. von. 1968. *General System Theory: Foundations, Development, Applications*. New York: Braziller.

Betancourt, J. L., T. R. Van Devender, and P. S. Martin, eds. 1990. *Packrat Middens: The Last 40,000 Years of Biotic Change*. Tucson: University of Arizona Press.

Bettinger, R. L. 1980. Explanatory/predictive models of hunter-gatherer adaptation. In *Advances in Archaeological Method and Theory*, vol. 3, ed. M. B. Schiffer, pp. 189–255. New York: Academic Press.

Biddle, M., ed. 1977. Architecture and archaeology. *World Archaeology* 9 (whole no. 2).

Binford, L. R. 1961. A new method of calculating dates from kaolin pipe stem samples. *Southeastern Archaeological Conference Newsletter* 9 (1): 19–21.

———. 1962. Archaeology as anthropology. *American Antiquity* 28: 217–225.

———. 1964. A consideration of archaeological research design. *American Antiquity* 29: 425–441.

———. 1967. Smudge pits and hide smoking: The use of analogy in archaeological reasoning. *American Antiquity* 32: 1–12.

———. 1968a. Archeological perspectives. In *New Perspectives in Archeology*, ed. S. R. Binford and L. R. Binford, pp. 5–32. Chicago: Aldine.

———. 1968b. Post-Pleistocene adaptations. In *New Perspectives in Archeology*, ed. S. R. Binford and L. R. Binford, pp. 313–341. Chicago: Aldine.

———. 1971. Mortuary practices: Their study and their potential. In *Approaches to the Social Dimensions of Mortuary Practices*, ed. J. A. Brown, pp. 6–29. Memoir no. 25. Washington, D.C.: Society for American Archaeology.

———. 1972a. *An Archaeological Perspective*. New York: Seminar Press.

———. 1972b. Archaeological reasoning and smudge pits—revisited. In *An Archaeological Perspective*, by L. R. Binford, pp. 52–58. New York: Seminar Press.

———. 1973. Interassemblage variability—the Mousterian and the "functional" argument. In *The Explanation of Culture Change: Models in Prehistory*, ed. C. Renfrew, pp. 227–254. Pittsburgh: University of Pittsburgh Press.

———, ed. 1977. *For Theory Building in Archaeology*. New York: Academic Press.

————. 1978. *Nunamiut Ethnoarchaeology*. New York: Academic Press.

————. 1981a. Behavioral archaeology and the "Pompeii premise." *Journal of Anthropological Research* 37: 195–208.

————. 1981b. *Bones: Ancient Men and Modern Myths*. New York: Academic Press.

————. 1982. The archaeology of place. *Journal of Anthropological Archaeology* 1: 5–31.

————. 1983. *Working at Archaeology*. New York: Academic Press.

————. 1985. Human ancestors: Changing views of their behavior. *Journal of Anthropological Archaeology* 4: 292–327.

————. 1987. Data, relativism and archaeological science. *Man* 22: 391–404.

————. 1989. *Debating Archaeology*. San Diego: Academic Press.

Binford, L. R., and S. R. Binford. 1966. A preliminary analysis of functional variability in the Mousterian of Levallois facies. In Recent studies in paleoanthropology, ed. J. D. Clark and F. C. Howell, special issue of *American Anthropologist* 68 (2, pt. 2): 238–295.

Binford, L. R., S. R. Binford, R. Whallon, and M. A. Hardin. 1970. *Archaeology at Hatchery West*. Memoir no. 24. Washington, D.C.: Society for American Archaeology.

Binford, S. R. 1968. Ethnographic data and understanding the Pleistocene. In *Man the Hunter,* ed. R. B. Lee and I. DeVore, pp. 274–275. Chicago: Aldine.

Binford, S. R., and L. R. Binford, eds. 1968. *New Perspectives in Archeology*. Chicago, Aldine.

Bintleff, J. L., and C. F. Gaffney, eds. 1986. *Archaeology at the Interface: Studies in Archaeology's Relationships with History, Geography, Biology and Physical Science*. British Archaeological Reports International Series 300. Oxford: BAR.

Bird, J. B. 1968. More about earth-shaking equipment. *American Antiquity* 33: 507–509.

Bird, J. B., and J. A. Ford. 1956. A new earth-shaking machine. *American Antiquity* 21: 399–401.

Bischof, H., and J. Viteri Gamboa. 1972. Pre-Valdivia occupation on the southwest coast of Ecuador. *American Antiquity* 37: 548–551.

Biscott, J. L., and R. J. Rosenbauer. 1981. Uranium series dating of human skeletal remains from the Del Mar and Sunnyvale sites, California. *Science* 213: 1003–1006.

Bishop, R. L., R. L. Rands, and G. R. Holley. 1982. Ceramic compositional analysis in archaeological perspective. In *Advances in Archaeological Method and Theory,* vol. 5, ed. M. B. Schiffer, pp. 275–330. New York: Academic Press.

Blanton, R. E. 1976. Anthropological studies of cities. *Annual Review of Anthropology* 5: 249–264.

Bleed, P. 1983. Management techniques and archaeological fieldwork. *Journal of Field Archaeology* 10: 494–498.

Blumenschine, R. J. 1986. *Early Hominid Scavenging Opportunities: Implications of Carcass Availability in the Serengeti and Ngorongoro Ecosystems*. British Archaeological Reports International Series 283. Oxford: BAR.

Blumenschine, R. J., and M. M. Selvaggio. 1988. Percussion marks on bone surfaces as a new diagnostic of hominid behaviour. *Nature* 333: 763–765.

Boas, F. 1948. *Race, Language and Culture*. New York: Macmillan.

Bodner, C. C., and R. M. Rowlett. 1980. Separation of bone, charcoal, and seeds by chemical flotation. *American Antiquity* 45: 110–116.

Bonnichsen, R., and M. H. Sorg, eds. 1989. *Bone Modification*. Orono, Maine: Center for the Study of the First Americans, University of Maine.

Boone, E. H., and G. R. Willey, eds. 1988. *The Southeast Classic Maya Zone*. Washington, D.C.: Dumbarton Oaks.

Bordaz, J. 1970. *Tools of the Old and New Stone Age*. Garden City, N.Y.: Natural History Press.

Bordes, F. 1968. *The Old Stone Age*. New York: McGraw-Hill.

————. 1969. Reflections on typology and techniques in the Palaeolithic. *Arctic Anthropology* 6: 1–29.

Bordes, F., and D. de Sonneville-Bordes. 1970. The significance of variability in Palaeolithic assemblages. *World Archaeology* 2: 61–73.

Bourdieu, P. 1977. *Outline of a Theory of Practice*. Cambridge: Cambridge University Press.

Bowman, S. 1990. *Radiocarbon Dating*. Berkeley and Los Angeles: University of California Press.

Brain, C. K. 1981. *Hunters or the Hunted? An Introduction to African Cave Taphonomy*. Chicago: University of Chicago Press.

Brainerd, G. W. 1951. The place of chronological ordering in archaeological analysis. *American Antiquity* 16: 301–313.

Braun, D. P., and S. Plog. 1982. Evolution of "tribal" social networks: Theory and prehistoric North American evidence. *American Antiquity* 47: 504–525.

Bray, W., ed. 1973. Trade. *World Archaeology* 5 (whole no. 2).

———, ed. 1976. Climatic change. *World Archaeology* 8 (whole no. 2).

Bray, W., and N. Seeley, eds. 1989. Archaeometallurgy. *World Archaeology* 20 (whole no. 3).

Breiner, S., and M. D. Coe. 1972. Magnetic exploration of the Olmec civilization. *American Scientist* 60: 566–575.

Brew, J. O. 1946. The use and abuse of taxonomy. In *The Archaeology of Alkali Ridge, Southern Utah,* by J. O. Brew, pp. 44–66. Papers of the Peabody Museum, 21. Cambridge: Harvard University.

———, ed. 1968. *One Hundred Years of Anthropology.* Cambridge: Harvard University Press.

Brodrick, A. H. 1949. *Lascaux, A Commentary.* London: Benn.

Bronitsky, G., ed. 1989. *Pottery Technology: Ideas and Approaches.* Boulder, Colo.: Westview Press.

Brothwell, D. R. 1971. Paleodemography. In *Biological Aspects of Demography,* ed. W. Brass, pp. 111–130. London: Taylor & Francis.

———. 1981. *Digging up Bones,* 3rd ed. Ithaca, N.Y.: Cornell University Press.

Brothwell, D. R., and A. T. Sandison, eds. 1967. *Diseases in Antiquity.* Springfield, Ill.: Thomas.

Browman, D. L. 1981. Isotopic discrimination and correction factors in radiocarbon dating. In *Advances in Archaeological Method and Theory,* vol. 4, ed. M. B. Schiffer, pp. 241–295. New York: Academic Press.

Brown, J. A., ed. 1971. *Approaches to the Social Dimensions of Mortuary Practices.* Memoir no. 25. Washington, D.C.: Society for American Archaeology.

———. 1975. Spiro art and its mortuary contexts. In *Death and the Afterlife in Pre-Columbian America,* ed. E. P. Benson, pp. 1–32. Washington, D.C.: Dumbarton Oaks.

———. 1981. The search for rank in prehistoric burials. In *The Archaeology of Death,* ed. R. Chapman, I. Kinnes, and K. Randsborg, pp. 25–37. Cambridge: Cambridge University Press.

Brown, J. A., and S. Struever. 1973. The organization of archaeological research: An Illinois example. In *Research and Theory in Current Archaeology,* ed. C. L. Redman, pp. 261–280. New York: Wiley-Interscience.

Brunhouse, R. L. 1973. *In Search of the Maya: The First Archaeologists.* Albuquerque: University of New Mexico Press.

Bryant, V. M., Jr., and R. G. Holloway. 1983. The role of palynology in archaeology. In *Advances in Archaeological Method and Theory,* vol. 6, ed. M. B. Schiffer, pp. 191–224. New York: Academic Press.

Buikstra, J. E. 1976. *Hopewell in the Lower Illinois Valley: A Regional Study of Human Biological Variability.* Evanston, Ill.: Center for American Archaeology Press.

———. 1981a. Mortality practices, paleodemography, and paleopathology: A case study from the Koster site (Illinois). In *The Archaeology of Death,* ed. R. Chapman, I. Kinnes, and K. Randsborg, pp. 123–132. Cambridge: Cambridge University Press.

———, ed. 1981b. *Prehistoric Tuberculosis in the Americas.* Evanston, Ill.: Center for American Archaeology Press.

Buikstra, J. E., and D. C. Cook. 1980. Paleopathology: An American account. *Annual Review of Anthropology* 9: 433–470.

Buikstra, J. E., and L. W. Konigsberg. 1985. Paleodemography: Critiques and controversies. *American Anthropologist* 87: 316–333.

Bunn, H. T. 1981. Archaeological evidence for meat-eating by Plio-Pleistocene hominids from Koobi Fora and Olduvai Gorge. *Nature* 29: 574–577.

———. 1983. Evidence on the diet and subsistence patterns of Plio-Pleistocene hominids at Koobi Fora, Kenya, and Olduvai Gorge, Tanzania. In *Animals and Archaeology: 1. Hunters and Their Prey,* ed. J. Clutton-Brock and C. Grigson, pp. 21–30. British Archaeological Reports International Series 163. Oxford: BAR.

Bunn, H. T., J. W. K. Harris, G. Isaac, Z. Kaufulu, E. Kroll, K. Schick, N. Toth, and A. K. Behrensmeyer. 1980. FxJj50: An early Pleistocene site in northern Kenya. *World Archaeology* 12: 109–136.

Burnham, B., comp. 1974. *The Protection of Cultural Property: Handbook of National Legislations.* Paris: International Council of Museums, Tunisia.

Burnham, B. C., and J. Kingsbury, eds. 1979. *Space, Hierarchy and Society: Interdisciplinary Studies in Social Area Analysis.* British Archaeological Reports International Series 59. Oxford: BAR.

Butler, W. B. 1987. Significance and other frustrations in the CRM process. *American Antiquity* 52: 820–829.

Butzer, K. W. 1964. *Environment and Archaeology: An Introduction to Pleistocene Geography.* Chicago: Aldine.

———. 1982. *Archaeology as Human Ecology: Method and Theory for a Contextual Approach.* New York: Cambridge University Press.

Byrd, B. 1980. A standardized system for recording survey-project information. *Journal of Field Archaeology* 8: 381–383.

Cahan, D., and L. H. Keeley. 1980. Not less than two, not more than three. *World Archaeology* 12: 166–180.

Cahan, D., L. H. Keeley, and F. L. Van Noten. 1979. Stone tools, toolkits and human behaviour in prehistory. *Current Anthropology* 20: 661–683.

Callen, E. O. 1970. Diet as revealed by coprolites. In *Science in Archaeology*, 2nd ed., ed. D. Brothwell and E. S. Higgs, pp. 235–243. New York: Praeger.

Callender, D. W., Jr. 1976. Reliving the past: Experimental archaeology in Pennsylvania. *Archaeology* 29: 173–177.

Camden, W. [1789, orig. pub. 1586] 1977. *Britannia*. Trans. R. Gough. London: J. Nichol. Reprint, annotated and edited by G. J. Copley. London: Hutchinson.

Cann, J. R., and C. Renfrew. 1964. The characterization of obsidian and its application to the Mediterranean region. *Proceedings of the Prehistoric Society* 30: 111–133.

Carneiro, R. L. 1970. A theory of the origin of the state. *Science* 169: 733–738.

Carr, C. 1982. *Handbook on Soil Resistivity Surveying*. Evanston, Ill.: Center for American Archaeology Press.

———. 1984. The nature of organization of intrasite archaeological records and spatial analytic approaches to their investigation. In *Advances in Archaeological Method and Theory*, vol. 7, ed. M. B. Schiffer, pp. 103–222. Orlando: Academic Press.

———, ed. 1985. *For Concordance in Archaeological Analysis: Bridging Data Structure, Quantitative Technique and Theory*. Kansas City: Westport Publishers, Inc. Reprint. Prospect Heights, Ill.: Waveland Press, Inc., 1989.

Carr, D. R., and J. L. Kulp. 1957. Potassium–argon method of geochronometry. *Bulletin of the Geological Society of America* 68: 763–784.

Carr, R. F., and J. E. Hazard. 1961. *Map of the Ruins of Tikal, El Petén, Guatemala*. Tikal Reports no. 11. Philadelphia: University Museum.

Carter, G. F., ed. 1978. *Archaeological Chemistry II*. Advances in Chemistry Series No. 171. Washington, D.C.: American Chemical Society.

Carter, H. [1922] 1972. *The Tomb of Tutankhamen*. Reprint. New York: Excalibur Books.

Casteel, R. W. 1970. Core and column sampling. *American Antiquity* 35: 465–466.

———. 1976. *Fish Remains in Archaeology and Paleo-Environmental Studies*. New York: Academic Press.

Cavallo, J. A. 1984. Fish, fires, and foresight: Middle Woodland economic adaptations in the Abbott Farm National Landmark. *North American Archaeologist* 5: 111–138.

Chamberlain, T. C. 1897. The method of multiple working hypotheses. *Journal of Geology* 39: 155–165.

Champe, J. L., D. S. Byers, C. Evans, A. K. Guthe, H. W. Hamilton, E. B. Jelks, C. W. Meighan, S. Olafson, G. I. Quimby, W. Smith, and F. Wendorf. 1961. Four statements for archaeology. *American Antiquity* 27: 137–138.

Champion, S. 1980. *A Dictionary of Terms and Techniques in Archaeology*. Oxford: Phaidon Press.

Chang, C., and H. A. Koster. 1986. Beyond bones: Toward an archaeology of pastoralism. In *Advances in Archaeological Method and Theory*, vol. 9, ed. M. B. Schiffer, pp. 97–148. Orlando: Academic Press.

Chang, K. C. 1958. Study of the Neolithic social groupings: Examples from the New World. *American Anthropologist* 60: 298–334.

———. 1967. Major aspects of the interrelationship of archaeology and ethnology. *Current Anthropology* 8: 227–243.

———, ed. 1968. *Settlement Archaeology*. Palo Alto, Calif.: National Press Books.

———. 1972. *Settlement Patterns in Archaeology*. Modules in Anthropology, no. 24. Reading, Mass.: Addison-Wesley.

———. 1983. *Art, Myth and Ritual: The Path to Political Authority in Ancient China*. Cambridge: Harvard University Press.

Chaplin, R. E. 1971. *The Study of Animal Bones from Archaeological Sites*. New York: Seminar Press.

Chapman, C. H. 1985. The amateur archaeological society: A Missouri example. *American Antiquity* 50: 241–248.

Chapman, R., and K. Randsborg. 1981. Approaches to the archaeology of death. In *The Archaeology of Death*, ed. R. Chapman, I. Kinnes, and K. Randsborg, pp. 1–24. Cambridge: Cambridge University Press.

Chapman, R., I. Kinnes, and K. Randsborg, eds. 1981. *The Archaeology of Death*. Cambridge: Cambridge University Press.

Charleton, T. H. 1981. Archaeology, ethnohistory, and ethnology: Interpretive interfaces. In *Advances in Archaeological Method and Theory*, vol. 4, ed. M. B. Schiffer, pp. 129–176. New York: Academic Press.

Chartkoff, J. L. 1978. Transect interval sampling in forests. *American Antiquity* 43: 46–53.

Chase, A. F., and P. M. Rice, eds. 1985. *The Lowland Maya Postclassic*. Austin: University of Texas Press.

Chenhall, R. G. 1975. *Museum Cataloging in the Computer Age*. Nashville: American Association for State and Local History.

Cherry, J. F. 1983. Frogs around the pond: Perspectives on current archaeological survey projects in the Mediterranean region. In *Archaeological Survey in the Mediterranean Area,* ed. D. R. Keller and D. W. Rupp, pp. 375–416. British Archaeological Reports International Series 155. Oxford: BAR.

———. 1984. Common sense in Mediterranean survey? *Journal of Field Archaeology* 11: 117–120.

Childe, V. G. 1954. *What Happened in History.* Rev. ed. Harmondsworth, England: Penguin.

Chippindale, C. 1986. Stonehenge astronomy: Anatomy of a modern myth. *Archaeology* 39 (1): 48–52.

Chippindale, C., P. Devereux, P. Fowler, R. Jones, and T. Sebastian. 1990. *Who Owns Stonehenge?* London: B. T. Batsford, Ltd.

Christaller, W. 1933. *Die zentralen Orte in Suddeutschland.* Jena, Germany: Fischer.

Christenson, A. L., ed. 1989. *Tracing Archaeology's Past: The Historiography of Archaeology.* Carbondale: Southern Illinois University Press.

Claasen, C. P. 1991a. Gender, shellfishing, and the Shell Mound Archaic. In *Engendering Archaeology: Women and Prehistory*, ed. J. M. Gero and M. W. Conkey, pp. 276–300. Oxford: Basil Blackwell.

———. 1991b. Normative thinking and shell-bearing sites. In *Archaeological Method and Theory*, vol. 3, ed. M. B. Schiffer, pp. 249–298. Tucson: University of Arizona Press.

Clark, G. A. 1982. Quantifying archaeological research. In *Advances in Archaeological Method and Theory,* vol. 5, ed. M. B. Schiffer, pp. 217–273. New York: Academic Press.

Clark, G. A., and C. R. Stafford. 1982. Quantification in American archaeology: A historical perspective. *World Archaeology* 14: 98–119.

Clark, J. G. D. 1952. *Prehistoric Europe: The Economic Basis.* London: Methuen.

———. [1954] 1971. *Excavations at Star Carr.* Reprint. Cambridge: Cambridge University Press.

———. 1972. *Star Carr: A Case Study in Bioarchaeology.* Modules in Anthropology, no. 10. Reading, Mass.: Addison-Wesley.

Clarke, D. L. 1968. *Analytical Archaeology.* London: Methuen.

———. 1972a. Models and paradigms in contemporary archaeology. In *Models in Archaeology,* ed. D. L. Clarke, pp. 1–60. London: Methuen.

———. 1972b. A provisional model of an Iron Age society. In *Models in Archaeology,* ed. D. L. Clarke, pp. 801–869. London: Methuen.

———. 1973. Archaeology: The loss of innocence. *Antiquity* 47: 6–18.

———, ed. 1977. *Spatial Archaeology.* New York: Academic Press.

———. 1978. Introduction and polemic. In *Analytical Archaeology,* 2nd ed., by D. L. Clarke, pp. 1–41. London: Methuen.

Clay, R. B. 1976. Typological classification, attribute analysis, and lithic variability. *Journal of Field Archaeology* 3: 303–311.

Cleere, H., ed. 1984. *Approaches to the Archaeological Heritage: A Comparative Study of World Cultural Resource Management Systems.* Cambridge: Cambridge University Press.

———, ed. 1989. *Archaeological Heritage Management in the Modern World.* London: Unwin Hyman.

Cleghorn, P. L. 1986. Organizational structure at the Mauna Kea adze quarry complex, Hawaii. *Journal of Archaeological Science* 13: 375–387.

Clutton-Brock, J., and C. Grigson, eds. 1983. *Animals and Archaeology: 1. Hunters and Their Prey.* British Archaeological Reports International Series 163. Oxford: BAR.

———, eds. 1984. *Animals and Archaeology: 3. Early Herders and Their Flocks.* British Archaeological Reports International Series 203. Oxford: BAR.

Coe, M. D., and K. V. Flannery. 1964. Microenvironments and Mesoamerican prehistory. *Science* 143: 650–654.

———. 1967. *Early Cultures and Human Ecology in South Coastal Guatemala.* Smithsonian Contributions to Anthropology, vol. 3. Washington, D.C.: Smithsonian Institution.

Coe, W. R. 1967. *Tikal, A Handbook of the Ancient Maya Ruins.* Philadelphia: University Museum, University of Pennsylvania.

Coggins, C. C. 1972. Archaeology and the art market. *Science* 175: 263–266.

Coggins, C. C., and O. G. Shane III, eds. 1984. *Cenote of Sacrifice.* Austin: University of Texas Press.

Cohen, M. N. 1977. *The Food Crisis in Prehistory.* New Haven: Yale University Press.

Cohen, M. N., and G. J. Armelagos, eds. 1984. *Paleopathology at the Origins of Civilization.* Orlando: Academic Press.

Cole, J. R. 1980. Cult archaeology and unscientific method and theory. In *Advances in Archaeological Method and Theory,* vol. 3, ed. M. B. Schiffer, pp. 1–33. New York: Academic Press.

Coles, B., and J. M. Coles. 1986. *Sweet Track to Glastonbury: The Somerset Levels in Prehistory.* New York and London: Thames & Hudson.

———. 1989. *People of the Wetlands: Bogs, Bodies and Lake-Dwellers.* New York: Thames & Hudson.

Coles, J. M. 1973. *Archaeology by Experiment.* New York: Scribner's.

———. 1984. *The Archaeology of Wetlands.* Edinburgh: Edinburgh University Press.

———. 1989. The world's oldest road. *Scientific American* 261 (5): 100–106.

Collingwood, R. G. 1946. *The Idea of History.* Oxford: Oxford University Press.

Conkey, M. W. 1984. To find ourselves: Art and social geography of prehistoric hunter gatherers. In *Past and Present in Hunter-Gatherer Studies,* ed. C. Schrire, pp. 253–276. Orlando: Academic Press.

———. 1985. Ritual communication, social elaboration, and the variable trajectories of Paleolithic material culture. In *Prehistoric Hunter-Gatherers: The Emergence of Cultural Complexity,* ed. T. D. Price and J. A. Brown, pp. 299–323. Orlando: Academic Press.

———. 1987. New approaches in the search for meaning? A review of research in "Paleolithic art." *Journal of Field Archaeology* 14: 413–430.

———. 1991. Contexts of action, contexts for power: Material culture and gender in the Magdalenian. In *Engendering Archaeology: Women and Prehistory,* ed. J. M. Gero and M. W. Conkey, pp. 57–92. Oxford: Basil Blackwell.

Conkey, M. W., and C. Hastorf, eds. 1990. *The Uses of Style in Archaeology.* Cambridge: Cambridge University Press.

Conkey, M. W., and J. Spector. 1984. Archaeology and the study of gender. In *Advances in Archaeological Method and Theory,* vol. 7, ed. M. B. Schiffer, pp. 1–38. Orlando: Academic Press.

Conrad, G. W., and A. A. Demarest. 1984. *Religion and Empire: The Dynamics of Aztec and Inca Expansionism.* Cambridge: Cambridge University Press.

Cook, B. F. 1991. The archaeologist and the art market: Policies and practice. *Antiquity* 65: 533–537.

Cook, D. C. 1981. Mortality, age-structure and status in the interpretation of stress indicators in prehistoric skeletons: A dental example from the lower Illinois valley. In *The Archaeology of Death,* ed. R. Chapman, I. Kinnes, and K. Randsborg, pp. 133–144. Cambridge: Cambridge University Press.

Cook, S. F. 1972. *Prehistoric Demography.* Modules in Anthropology, no. 16. Reading, Mass.: Addison-Wesley.

Cooper, M. A., and J. D. Richards, eds. 1985. *Current Issues in Archaeological Computing.* British Archaeological Reports International Series 271. Oxford: BAR.

Cordell, L. S. 1979. Prehistory: Eastern Anasazi. In *Handbook of North American Indians,* vol. 9, ed. W. C. Sturtevant and A. Ortiz, pp. 131–151. Washington, D.C.: Smithsonian Institution.

———. 1984a. *Prehistory of the Southwest.* Orlando: Academic Press.

———. 1984b. Southwestern archaeology. *Annual Review of Anthropology* 13: 301–332.

Cordell, L. S., and F. Plog. 1979. Escaping the confines of normative thought: A reevaluation of Puebloan prehistory. *American Antiquity* 44: 405–429.

Cornwall, I. W. 1970. Soil, stratification and environment. In *Science in Archaeology,* 2nd ed., ed. D. R. Brothwell and E. S. Higgs, pp. 120–134. New York: Praeger.

Costin, C. L. 1991. Craft specialization: Issues in defining, documenting, and explaining the organization of production. In *Archaeological Method and Theory,* vol. 3, ed. M. B. Schiffer, pp. 1–56. Tucson: University of Arizona Press.

Cotterell, B., and J. Kamminga. 1987. The formation of flakes. *American Antiquity* 52: 675–708.

Cottrell, A. 1981. *The First Emperor of China, the Greatest Archaeological Find of Our Time.* New York: Holt, Rinehart & Winston.

Courbin, P. 1988. *What Is Archaeology? An Essay on the Nature of Archaeological Research.* Trans. P. Bahn. Chicago: University of Chicago Press.

Courty, M. A., P. Goldberg, and R. Macphail. 1989. *Soils and Micromorphology in Archaeology.* Cambridge: Cambridge University Press.

Cowgill, G. L. 1964. The selection of samples from large sherd collections. *American Antiquity* 29: 467–473.

———. 1968. Archaeological applications of factor, cluster and proximity analysis. *American Antiquity* 33: 367–375.

———. 1974. Quantitative studies of urbanization at Teotihuacan. In *Mesoamerican Archaeology: New Approaches,* ed. N. Hammond, pp. 363–397. Austin: University of Texas Press.

———. 1977. The trouble with significance tests and what we can do about it. *American Antiquity* 42: 350–368.

———. 1986. Archaeological applications of mathematical and formal methods. In *American Archaeology Past and Future: A Celebration of the Society for American Archaeology 1935–1985,* ed. D. J. Meltzer, D. D. Fowler, and J. A. Sabloff, pp. 369–393. Washington, D.C.: Smithsonian Institution Press.

Cowgill, G. L., J. H. Altschul, and R. S. Sload. 1984. Spatial analysis of Teotihuacan: A Mesoamerican metropolis. In *Intrasite Spatial Analysis in Archaeology,* ed. H. J. Hietala, pp. 154–195. Cambridge: Cambridge University Press.

Crabtree, D. E. 1972. *An Introduction to Flintworking: Part I. An Introduction to the Technology of Stone Tools.* Occasional Paper no. 28. Pocatello: Idaho State University.

Crabtree, P. J. 1990. Zooarchaeology and complex society: Some uses of faunal analysis for the study of trade, social status, and ethnicity. In *Archaeological Method and Theory*, vol. 2, ed. M. B. Schiffer, pp. 155–205. Tucson: University of Arizona Press.

Cronyn, J. M. 1990. *The Elements of Archaeological Conservation.* London: Routledge.

Crumley, C. 1979. Three locational models: An epistemological assessment for anthropology and archaeology. In *Advances in Archaeological Method and Theory,* vol. 2, ed. M. B. Schiffer, pp. 141–173. New York: Academic Press.

Crumley, C. L., and W. H. Marquardt, eds. 1987. *Regional Dynamics: Burgundian Landscapes in Historical Perspective.* San Diego: Academic Press.

———. 1990. Landscape: A unifying concept in regional analysis. In *Interpreting Space: GIS and Archaeology*, ed. K. M. S. Allen, S. W. Green, and E. B. W. Zubrow, pp. 73–79. Bristol, Pa.: Taylor & Francis, Inc.

Culbert, T. P., ed. 1973. *The Classic Maya Collapse.* School of American Research Advanced Seminar Series. Albuquerque: University of New Mexico Press.

———, ed. 1991. *Classic Maya Political History: Hieroglyphic and Archaeological Evidence.* Cambridge: Cambridge University Press.

Culbert, T. P., and D. S. Rice, eds. 1990. *Precolumbian Population History in the Maya Lowlands.* Albuquerque: University of New Mexico Press.

Cunliffe, B., ed. 1978. Landscape archaeology. *World Archaeology* 9 (whole no. 3).

———. 1984. Ceramics. *World Archaeology* 15 (whole no. 3).

Curtis, G. H. 1975. Improvements in potassium–argon dating: 1962–1975. *World Archaeology* 7: 198–209.

Cushing, F. H. 1890. Preliminary notes on the origin, working hypotheses and preliminary researches of the Hemenway Expedition. *Seventh International Congress of Americanists,* Berlin, pp. 151–194.

Custer, J. F., T. Eveleigh, V. Klemas, and I. Wells. 1986. Application of LANDSAT data and synoptic remote sensing to predictive models for prehistoric archaeological sites: An example from the Delaware coastal plain. *American Antiquity* 51: 572–588.

Dales, G. F. 1966. The decline of the Harappans. *Scientific American* 214 (5): 92–100.

Daniel, G. 1943. *The Three Ages: An Essay on Archaeological Method.* Cambridge: Cambridge University Press.

———. 1962. *The Idea of Prehistory.* Baltimore: Penguin.

———. 1967. *The Origins and Growth of Archaeology.* Baltimore: Penguin.

———. 1971a. Editorial. *Antiquity* 45: 246–249.

———. 1971b. From Worsaae to Childe: The models of prehistory. *Proceedings of the Prehistoric Society* 38: 140–153.

———. 1976a. *A Hundred and Fifty Years of Archaeology.* Cambridge: Harvard University Press.

———. 1976b. Stone, bronze and iron. In *To Illustrate the Monuments: Essays on Archaeology Presented to Stuart Piggott,* ed. J. V. S. Megaw, pp. 35–42. London: Thames & Hudson.

———. 1981a. *A Short History of Archaeology.* London: Thames & Hudson.

———, ed. 1981b. *Towards a History of Archaeology.* New York: Thames & Hudson.

Daniel, G., and C. Chippindale, eds. 1989. *The Pastmasters: Eleven Modern Pioneers of Archaeology.* London: Thames & Hudson.

Daniels, S. G. H. 1972. Research design models. In *Models in Archaeology,* ed. D. L. Clarke, pp. 201–229. London: Methuen.

Dart, R. A. 1949. The predatory implemental technique of the australopithecines. *American Journal of Physical Anthropology* 7: 1–16.

———. 1957. *The Osteodontokeratic Culture of Australopithecus prometheus.* Memoir no. 10. Pretoria, South Africa: Transvaal Museum.

Darwin, C. R. 1859. *On the Origin of Species.* London: J. Murray.

David, N. 1971. The Fulani compound and the archaeologist. *World Archaeology* 3: 111–131.

Davies, M. 1987. The archaeology of standing structures. *Australian Journal of Historical Archaeology* 5: 54–64.

Davis, D. D. 1985. Hereditary emblems: Material culture in the context of social change. *Journal of Anthropological Archaeology* 4: 149–176.

Davis, E. L. 1975. The "exposed archaeology" of China Lake, California. *American Antiquity* 40: 39–53.

Davis, H. A. 1972. The crisis in American archaeology. *Science* 175: 267–272.

———. 1982. Professionalism in archaeology. *American Antiquity* 47: 158–162.

Davis, S. J. M. 1987. *The Archaeology of Animals.* New Haven: Yale University Press.

Davis, W. 1986. The origins of image making. *Current Anthropology* 27: 193–215.

Deagan, K. 1982. Avenues of inquiry in historical archaeology. In *Advances in Archaeological Method and Theory*, vol. 5, ed. M. B. Schiffer, pp. 151–177. New York: Academic Press.

Deal, M. 1985. Household pottery disposal in the Maya highlands: An ethnoarchaeological interpretation. *Journal of Anthropological Archaeology* 4: 243–291.

Dean, J. S. 1978. Independent dating in archaeological analysis. In *Advances in Archaeological Method and Theory*, vol. 1, ed. M. B. Schiffer, pp. 223–255. New York: Academic Press.

De Atley, S. P., and F. J. Findlow, eds. 1984. *Exploring the Limits: Frontiers and Boundaries in Prehistory*. British Archaeological Reports International Series 223. Oxford: BAR.

Deetz, J. 1965. *The Dynamics of Stylistic Change in Arikara Ceramics*. Illinois Studies in Anthropology, no. 4. Urbana: University of Illinois Press.

———. 1967. *Invitation to Archaeology*. Garden City, N.Y.: Natural History Press.

———. 1968. The inference of residence and descent rules from archaeological data. In *New Perspectives in Archaeology*, ed. S. R. Binford and L. R. Binford, pp. 41–48. Chicago: Aldine.

———. 1977. *In Small Things Forgotten: The Archaeology of Early American Life*. Garden City, N.Y.: Doubleday/ Anchor.

———. 1988a. History and archaeological theory: Walter Taylor revisited. *American Antiquity* 53: 13–22.

———. 1988b. American historical archaeology: Methods and results. *Science* 239: 362–367.

Deetz, J., and E. Dethlefsen. 1965. The Doppler effect and archaeology: A consideration of the spatial aspects of seriation. *Southwestern Journal of Anthropology* 21: 196–206.

———. 1967. Death's head, cherub, urn and willow. *Natural History* 76 (3): 28–37.

Deevey, E. S., Jr. 1960. The human population. *Scientific American* 203 (3): 195–205.

DeNiro, M. J. 1987. Stable isotopy and archaeology. *American Scientist* 75: 182–191.

Dethlefsen, E., and J. Deetz. 1966. Death's heads, cherubs, and willow trees: Experimental archaeology in colonial cemeteries. *American Antiquity* 31: 502–510.

Diamant, S. 1979. Archaeological sieving at Franchthi cave. *Journal of Field Archaeology* 6: 203–219.

Diaz del Castillo, B. [1632] 1956. *The Discovery and Conquest of Mexico, 1517–1521*. Trans. A. P. Maudslay. Reprint. New York: Grove Press.

Dickson, D. B. 1980. Ancient agriculture and population at Tikal, Guatemala: An application of linear programming to the simulation of an archaeological problem. *American Antiquity* 45: 697–712.

———. 1981. Further simulation of ancient agriculture and population at Tikal, Guatemala. *American Antiquity* 46: 922–926.

———. 1990. *The Dawn of Belief: An Archaeological Reconstruction of Religion in the Upper Paleolithic of Southwestern Europe*. Tucson: University of Arizona Press.

Dillon, B., ed. 1985. *Student's Guide to Archaeological Illustrating*. Rev. ed. Archaeological Research Tools 1. Los Angeles: UCLA Institute of Archaeology.

———. 1989. *Practical Archaeology: Field and Laboratory Techniques and Archaeological Logistics*. Rev. ed. Archaeological Research Tools 2. Los Angeles: UCLA Institute of Archaeology.

Dimbleby, G. W. 1967. *Plants and Archaeology*. London: John Baker.

———. 1985. *The Palynology of Archaeological Sites*. Orlando: Academic Press.

Dinsmoor, W. B., Jr. 1977. The archaeological field staff: The architect. *Journal of Field Archaeology* 4: 309–328.

Donley, L. W. 1982. House power: Swahili space and symbolic markers. In *Symbolic and Structural Archaeology*, ed. I. Hodder, pp. 63–73. Cambridge: Cambridge University Press.

Donnan, C. B. 1964. An early house from Chilca, Peru. *American Antiquity* 30: 137–144.

Doran, J. 1970. Systems theory, computer simulations and archaeology. *World Archaeology* 1: 289–298.

Doran, J. E., and F. R. Hodson. 1975. *Mathematics and Computers in Archaeology*. Cambridge: Harvard University Press.

Dorrell, P. G. 1989. *Photography in Archaeology and Conservation*. Cambridge: Cambridge University Press.

Douglas, M. 1972. Symbolic orders in the use of domestic space. In *Man, Settlement and Urbanism*, ed. P. J. Ucko, R. Tringham, and G. W. Dimbleby, pp. 513–521. London: Duckworth.

Doumas, C. 1974. The Minoan eruption of the Santorini volcano. *Antiquity* 48: 110–115.

Dowman, E. A. 1970. *Conservation in Field Archaeology*. London: Methuen.

Drennan, R. D. 1976. Religion and social evolution in Formative Mesoamerica. In *The Early Mesoamerican Village*, ed. K. V. Flannery, pp. 345–368. New York: Academic Press.

Drucker, P. 1972. *Stratigraphy in Archaeology: An Intro-*

duction. Modules in Anthropology, no. 30. Reading, Mass.: Addison-Wesley.

Dumond, D. E. 1977. Science in archaeology: The saints go marching in. *American Antiquity* 42: 33–49.

Dunnell, R. C. 1971. *Systematics in Prehistory*. New York: Free Press.

——. 1980. Evolutionary theory and archaeology. In *Advances in Archaeological Method and Theory*, vol. 3, ed. M. B. Schiffer, pp. 35–99. New York: Academic Press.

——. 1982. Science, social science, and common sense: The agonizing dilemma of modern archaeology. *Journal of Anthropological Research* 38: 1–25.

——. 1986a. Five decades of American archaeology. In *American Archaeology Past and Future: A Celebration of the Society for American Archaeology 1935–1985*, ed. D. J. Meltzer, D. D. Fowler, and J. A. Sabloff, pp. 23–49. Washington, D.C.: Smithsonian Institution Press.

——. 1986b. Methodological issues in Americanist artifact classification. In *Advances in Archaeological Method and Theory*, vol. 9, ed. M. B. Schiffer, pp. 149–207. Orlando: Academic Press.

Dunnell, R. C., and W. S. Dancey. 1983. The siteless survey: A regional scale data collection strategy. In *Advances in Archaeological Method and Theory*, vol. 6, ed. M. B. Schiffer, pp. 267–288. New York: Academic Press.

Dyson, R. H., Jr. 1960. Hasanlu and early Iran. *Archaeology* 13 (2): 118–129.

Earle, T. K., and J. E. Ericson, eds. 1977. *Exchange Systems in Prehistory*. New York: Academic Press.

Earle, T. K., and R. W. Preucel. 1987. Processual archaeology and the radical critique. *Current Anthropology* 28: 501–538.

Ebert, J. I. 1984. Remote sensing applications in archaeology. In *Advances in Archaeological Method and Theory*, vol. 7, ed. M. B. Schiffer, pp. 293–362. Orlando: Academic Press.

Eddy, J. A. 1974. Astronomical alignment of the Big Horn Medicine Wheel. *Science* 184: 1035–1043.

Edgerton, H. E. 1976. Underwater archaeological search with sonar. *Historical Archaeology* 10: 46–53.

Edwards, S. W. 1978. Nonutilitarian activities in the lower Paleolithic: A look at the two kinds of evidence. *Current Anthropology* 19: 135–137.

Ehrich, R. W., ed. 1990. *Chronologies in Old World Archaeology*. 3rd ed. Chicago: University of Chicago Press.

Eidt, R. C. 1977. Detection and examination of anthrosols by phosphate analysis. *Science* 197: 1327–1333.

——. 1985. Theoretical and practical considerations in the analysis of anthrosols. In *Archaeological Geology*, ed. G. Rapp, Jr., and J. A. Gifford, pp. 155–190. New Haven: Yale University Press.

Eighmy, J. L., and R. S. Sternberg, eds. 1990. *Archaeomagnetic Dating*. Tucson: University of Arizona Press.

Eiseley, L. 1958. *Darwin's Century: Evolution and the Men Who Discovered It*. Garden City, N.Y.: Doubleday/Anchor.

Elachi, C. 1982. Radar images of the earth from space. *Scientific American* 247 (6): 54–61.

El-Baz, F., B. Moores, and C. E. Petrone. 1989. Remote sensing at an archaeological site in Egypt. *American Scientist* 77: 60–66.

Ellis, F. H. 1975. A thousand years of the Pueblo sun-moon-star calendar. In *Archaeoastronomy in Pre-Columbian America*, ed. A. F. Aveni, pp. 59–87. Austin: University of Texas Press.

Ericson, J. E., and T. K. Earle, eds. 1982. *Contexts for Prehistoric Exchange*. New York: Academic Press.

Ericson, J. E., and B. A. Purdy, eds. 1984. *Prehistoric Quarries and Lithic Production*. Cambridge: Cambridge University Press.

Ester, M. 1981. A column-wise approach to seriation. *American Antiquity* 46: 496–512.

Estes, J. E., J. R. Jensen, and L. R. Tinney. 1977. The use of historical photography for mapping archaeological sites. *Journal of Field Archaeology* 4: 441–447.

Evernden, J. F., and G. H. Curtis. 1965. The potassium–argon dating of Late Cenozoic rocks in East Africa and Italy. *Current Anthropology* 6: 343–385.

Fagan, B. M. 1975. *The Rape of the Nile*. New York: Scribner's.

——. 1978. *Quest for the Past: Great Discoveries in Archaeology*. Reading, Mass.: Addison-Wesley.

——. 1985. *The Adventure of Archaeology*. Washington, D.C.: National Geographic Society.

——. 1988. Black day at Slack Farm. *Archaeology* 41 (8): 15–16, 73.

Falk, L., ed. 1991. *Historical Archaeology in Global Perspective*. Washington, D.C.: Smithsonian Institution Press.

Farnsworth, P., J. E. Brady, M. J. DeNiro, and R. S. MacNeish. 1985. A re-evaluation of the isotopic and archaeological reconstructions of diet in the Tehuacán Valley. *American Antiquity* 50: 102–116.

Fash, W. L. 1988. A new look at Maya statecraft at Copán, Honduras. *Antiquity* 62: 157–169.

——. 1991. *Scribes, Warriors and Kings: The City of Copán and the Ancient Maya*. New York: Thames & Hudson.

Fash, W. L., and B. W. Fash. 1990. Scribes, warriors, and kings. *Archaeology* 45 (3): 26–35.

Fash, W. L., and R. J. Sharer. 1991. Sociopolitical developments and methodological issues at Copán, Honduras: A conjunctive perspective. *Latin American Antiquity* 2: 166–187.

Feder, K. L. 1990. *Frauds, Myths, and Mysteries: Science and Pseudoscience in Archaeology.* Mountain View, Calif.: Mayfield Publishing Company.

Fehon, J. R., and S. C. Scholtz. 1978. A conceptual framework for the study of artifact loss. *American Antiquity* 43: 271–273.

Feinman, G., and J. Neitzel. 1984. Too many types: An overview of prestate societies in the Americas. In *Advances in Archaeological Method and Theory,* vol. 7, ed. M. B. Schiffer, pp. 39–102. Orlando: Academic Press.

Fell, B. 1976. *America B.C.* New York: Pocket Books.

Findlow, F. J., and J. E. Ericson, eds. 1980. *Catchment Analysis: Essays on Prehistoric Resource Space.* Anthropology UCLA, vol. 10, nos. 1 and 2. Los Angeles: University of California.

Finley, M. I. 1971. Archaeology and history. *Daedalus* 100: 168–186.

Finney, B. R. 1977. Voyaging canoes and the settlement of Polynesia. *Science* 196: 1277–1285.

Fish, S. K., and S. A. Kowalewski, eds. 1990. *The Archaeology of Regions: A Case for Full-Coverage Survey.* Washington, D.C.: Smithsonian Institution Press.

Fish, S. K., P. R. Fish, and J. H. Madsen. 1990. Analyzing regional agriculture: A Hohokam example. In *The Archaeology of Regions: A Case for Full-coverage Survey,* ed. S. K. Fish and S. A. Kowalewski, pp. 189–218. Washington, D.C.: Smithsonian Institution Press.

Fitting, J. E., ed. 1973. *The Development of North American Archaeology: Essays in the History of Regional Traditions.* Garden City, N.Y.: Doubleday/Anchor.

Fladmark, K. R. 1982. Microdebitage analysis: Initial considerations. *Journal of Archaeological Science* 9: 205–220.

Flannery, K. V. 1965. The ecology of early food production in Mesopotamia. *Science* 147: 1247–1256.

———. 1967. Culture history vs. cultural process: A debate in American archaeology. *Scientific American* 217 (2): 119–122.

———. 1968. Archaeological systems theory and early Mesoamerica. In *Anthropological Archeology in the Americas,* ed. B. J. Meggers, pp. 67–87. Washington, D.C.: Anthropological Society of Washington.

———. 1969. Origins and ecological effects of early domestication in Iran and the Near East. In *The Domesti-*

cation and Exploitation of Plants and Animals, ed. P. J. Ucko and G. W. Dimbleby, pp. 73–100. Chicago: Aldine-Atherton.

———. 1972a. The cultural evolution of civilizations. *Annual Review of Ecology and Systematics* 2: 399–426.

———. 1972b. The origins of the village as a settlement type in Mesoamerica and the Near East: A comparative study. In *Man, Settlement and Urbanism,* ed. P. J. Ucko, R. Tringham, and G. W. Dimbleby, pp. 23–53. London: Duckworth.

———. 1973. Archeology with a capital S. In *Research and Theory in Current Archeology,* ed. C. L. Redman, pp. 47–53. New York: Wiley-Interscience.

———. 1976a. Contextual analysis of ritual paraphernalia from Formative Oaxaca. In *The Early Mesoamerican Village,* ed. K. V. Flannery, pp. 333–345. New York: Academic Press.

———, ed. 1976b. *The Early Mesoamerican Village.* New York: Academic Press.

———. 1976c. Excavating deep communities by transect samples. In *The Early Mesoamerican Village,* ed. K. V. Flannery, pp. 68–72. New York: Academic Press.

———. 1976d. Sampling by intensive surface collecting. In *The Early Mesoamerican Village,* ed. K. V. Flannery, pp. 51–62. New York: Academic Press.

———, ed. 1982a. *Maya Subsistence: Studies in Memory of Dennis E. Puleston.* New York: Academic Press.

———. 1982b. The Golden Marshalltown: A parable for the archeology of the 1980s. *American Anthropologist* 84: 265–278.

———. 1986. A visit to the master. In *Guilá Naquitz, Archaic Foraging and Early Agriculture in Oaxaca, Mexico,* ed. K. V. Flannery, pp. 511–519. Orlando: Academic Press.

Flannery, K. V., and J. Marcus. 1976a. Evolution of the public building in Formative Oaxaca. In *Cultural Change and Continuity: Essays in Honor of James Bennett Griffin,* ed. C. E. Cleland, pp. 205–221. New York: Academic Press.

———. 1976b. Formative Oaxaca and the Zapotec cosmos. *American Scientist* 64: 374–383.

Fleming, S. J. 1979. *Thermoluminescence Techniques in Archaeology.* Oxford: Clarendon Press.

Flenley, J. R., and S. M. King. 1984. Late Quaternary pollen records from Easter Island. *Nature* 307: 47–50.

Flenniken, J. J. 1984. The past, present, and future of flint-knapping: An anthropological perspective. *Annual Review of Anthropology* 13: 187–203.

Flint, R. N. 1971. *Glacial and Quaternary Geology.* New York: Wiley.

Folan, W. J., J. Gunn, J. D. Eaton, and R. W. Patch. 1983. Paleoclimatological patterning in southern Mesoamerica. *Journal of Field Archaeology* 10: 453–468.

Foley, R. 1981. Off-site archaeology: An alternative approach for the short-sited. In *Pattern of the Past*, ed. I. Hodder, G. Isaac, and N. Hammond, pp. 157–183. Cambridge: Cambridge University Press.

Forbes, R. J. 1963. *Studies in Ancient Technology*, vol. 7. Leiden, Netherlands: Brill.

Ford, J. A. 1954. The type concept revisited. *American Anthropologist* 56: 42–53.

———. 1962. *A Quantitative Method for Deriving Cultural Chronology*. Pan American Union, Technical Manual 1. Washington, D.C.: Organization of American States.

———. 1969. *A Comparison of Formative Cultures in the Americas*. Smithsonian Contributions to Anthropology, vol. 11. Washington, D.C.: Smithsonian Institution.

Ford, R. I. 1977. The state of the art in archaeology. In *Perspectives on Anthropology, 1976,* ed. A. F. C. Wallace, J. L. Angel, R. Fox, S. McLendon, R. Sady, and R. J. Sharer, pp. 101–115. Special Publication 10. Washington, D.C.: American Anthropological Association.

———. 1979. Paleoethnobotany in American archaeology. In *Advances in Archaeological Method and Theory,* vol. 2, ed. M. B. Schiffer, pp. 285–336. New York: Academic Press.

———. 1983. The Archaeological Conservancy, Inc.: The goal is site preservation. *American Archaeology* 3: 221–224.

Fowler, D. D. 1982. Cultural resources management. In *Advances in Archaeological Method and Theory,* vol. 5, ed. M. B. Schiffer, pp. 1–50. New York: Academic Press.

———. 1987. Uses of the past: Archaeology in the service of the state. *American Antiquity* 52: 229–248.

Fowler, M. L. 1974. *Cahokia: Ancient Capital of the Midwest*. Modules in Anthropology, no. 48. Reading, Mass.: Addison-Wesley.

Fowler, P. J. 1988/89. The experimental earthworks 1958–88. *Annual Report of the Council for British Archaeology* 39: 83–98.

Fox, C. 1922. *The Archaeology of the Cambridge Region*. Cambridge: Cambridge University Press.

Freidel, D. A. 1979. Culture areas and interaction spheres: Contrasting approaches to the emergence of civilization in the Maya lowlands. *American Antiquity* 44: 36–54.

———. 1981. Civilization as a state of mind: The cultural evolution of the lowland Maya. In *The Transition to Statehood in the New World*, ed. G. D. Jones and R. R. Kautz, pp. 188–227. Cambridge: Cambridge University Press.

Frere, J. 1800. Account of flint weapons discovered at Hoxne in Suffolk. *Archaeologia* 13: 204–205.

Fried, M. H. 1967. *The Evolution of Political Society*. New York: Random House.

Friedman, I., and R. L. Smith. 1960. A new dating method using obsidian: Part I. The development of the method. *American Antiquity* 25: 476–493.

Friedman, I., and F. W. Trembour. 1978. Obsidian: The dating stone. *American Scientist* 66: 44–51.

———. 1983. Obsidian hydration dating update. *American Antiquity* 48: 544–547.

Friedman, J. L., ed. 1985. A history of the Archaeological Resources Protection Act: Law and regulations. *American Archaeology* 5: 82–119.

Frink, D. S. 1984. Artifact behavior within the plow zone. *Journal of Field Archaeology* 11: 356–363.

Fritz, J. M. 1978. Paleopsychology today: Ideational systems and human adaptation in prehistory. In *Social Archaeology: Beyond Subsistence and Dating*, ed. C. L. Redman, M. J. Berman, E. V. Curtin, W. T. Langhorne, Jr., N. M. Versaggi, and J. C. Wanser, pp. 37–59. New York: Academic Press.

———. 1986. Vijayanagara: Authority and meaning of a South Indian imperial capital. *American Anthropologist* 88: 44–55.

Fritz, J. M., G. Michell, and M. S. N. Rao. 1986. Vijayanagara: The city of victory. *Archaeology* 39 (2): 22–29.

Fry, R. E. 1972. Manually operated post-hole diggers as sampling instruments. *American Antiquity* 37: 259–262.

———, ed. 1980. *Models and Methods in Regional Exchange*. SAA Paper, no. 1. Washington, D.C.: Society for American Archaeology.

Gallatin, A. 1836. A synopsis of the Indian tribes within the United States east of the Rocky Mountains, in the British and Russian possessions in North America. *Archaeologia Americana* 2: 1–422.

Gardin, J.-C. 1980. *Archaeological Constructs: An Aspect of Theoretical Archaeology*. Cambridge: Cambridge University Press.

Gasparini, G., and L. Margolies. 1980. *Inca Architecture*. Trans. P. J. Lyon. Bloomington: Indiana University Press.

Gathercole, P., and D. Lowenthal, eds. 1989. *The Politics of the Past*. London: Unwin Hyman.

Gero, J. M. 1991. Genderlithics: Women's roles in stone tool production. In *Engendering Archaeology: Women and Prehistory*, ed. J. M. Gero and M. W. Conkey, pp. 163–193. Oxford: Basil Blackwell.

Gero, J. M., and M. W. Conkey, eds. 1991. *Engendering Archaeology: Women and Prehistory.* Oxford: Basil Blackwell.

Gibbon, G. 1984. *Anthropological Archaeology.* New York: Columbia University Press.

———. 1989. *Explanation in Archaeology.* Oxford: Basil Blackwell.

Gibbons, A. 1991. A "new look" for archeology. *Science* 252: 918–920.

Gibson, A., and A. Woods. 1990. *Prehistoric Pottery for the Archaeologist.* Leicester: Leicester University Press.

Giddings, J. L. 1964. *The Archeology of Cape Denbigh.* Providence, R.I.: Brown University Press.

———. 1966. Cross-dating the archaeology of northwestern Alaska. *Science* 153: 127–135.

———. 1967. *Ancient Men of the Arctic.* New York: Knopf.

Giesecke, A. G. 1985. Shipwrecks, states and the courts. *Archaeology* 38 (5): 80.

Gifford, D. P. 1981. Taphonomy and paleoecology: A critical review of archaeology's sister disciplines. In *Advances in Archaeological Method and Theory,* vol. 4, ed. M. B. Schiffer, pp. 365–438. New York: Academic Press.

Gifford, J. C. 1960. The type-variety method of ceramic classification as an indicator of cultural phenomena. *American Antiquity* 25: 341–347.

———. 1976. *Prehistoric Pottery Analysis and the Ceramics of Barton Ramie in the Belize Valley.* Memoirs of the Peabody Museum, 18. Cambridge: Harvard University.

Gilbert, B. M. 1973. *Mammalian Osteoarchaeology.* Missouri Archaeological Society Special Publications. Columbia: Missouri Archaeological Society.

Gilbert, R. I., Jr., and J. H. Mielke, eds. 1985. *The Analysis of Prehistoric Diets.* Orlando: Academic Press.

Gladfelter, B. G. 1981. Developments and directions in geoarchaeology. In *Advances in Archaeological Method and Theory,* vol. 4, ed. M. B. Schiffer, pp. 343–364. New York: Academic Press.

Glassie, H. 1975. *Folk Housing in Middle Virginia: A Structural Analysis of Historic Artifacts.* Knoxville: University of Tennessee Press.

Glassow, M. A. 1977. Issues in evaluating the significance of archaeological resources. *American Antiquity* 42: 413–420.

———. 1978. The concept of carrying capacity in the study of culture process. In *Advances in Archaeological Method and Theory,* vol. 1, ed. M. B. Schiffer, pp. 31–48. New York: Academic Press.

Glob, P. V. 1969. *The Bog People: Iron Age Man Preserved.* Trans. R. Bruce-Mitford. Ithaca, N.Y.: Cornell University Press.

Glover, I., and D. Griffiths, eds. 1989. Ceramic technology. *World Archaeology* 21 (whole no. 1).

Goodman, A. H., R. B. Thomas, A. C. Swedlund, and G. J. Armelagos. 1988. Biocultural perspectives on stress in prehistoric, historical and contemporary population research. *Yearbook of Physical Anthropology* 31: 169–202.

Goodwin, A. J. H. 1960. Chemical alteration (patination) of stone. In *The Application of Quantitative Methods in Archaeology,* ed. R. F. Heizer and S. F. Cook, pp. 300–312. Viking Fund Publications in Anthropology, no. 28. New York: Wenner-Gren Foundation for Anthropological Research.

Goodyear, A. C., L. M. Raab, and T. C. Klinger. 1978. The status of archaeological research design in cultural resource management. *American Antiquity* 43: 159–173.

Gorenstein, S. 1977. History of American archaeology. In *Perspectives on Anthropology, 1976,* ed. A. F. C. Wallace, J. L. Angel, R. Fox, S. McLendon, R. Sady, and R. J. Sharer, pp. 86–100. Special Publication 10. Washington, D.C.: American Anthropological Association.

Gould, R. A. 1969. Subsistence behavior among the Western Desert Aborigines of Australia. *Oceania* 39: 251–274.

———, ed. 1978. *Explorations in Ethnoarchaeology.* Albuquerque: University of New Mexico Press.

———. 1980a. *Living Archaeology.* Cambridge: Cambridge University Press.

———, ed. 1980b. *Shipwreck Anthropology.* School of American Research Advanced Seminar Series. Albuquerque: University of New Mexico Press.

Gould, R. A., and M. B. Schiffer, eds. 1981. *Modern Material Culture: The Archaeology of Us.* New York: Academic Press.

Gould, R. A., and P. J. Watson. 1982. A dialogue on the meaning and use of analogy in ethnoarchaeological reasoning. *Journal of Anthropological Archaeology* 1: 355–381.

Gould, S. J. 1980. *The Panda's Thumb.* New York: Norton.

———. 1982. Darwinism and the expansion of evolutionary theory. *Science* 216: 380–387.

———. 1983. *Hen's Teeth and Horse's Toes.* New York: Norton.

———. 1985. *The Flamingo's Smile.* New York: Norton.

————. 1986. Evolution and the triumph of homology, or why history matters. *American Scientist* 74: 60–69.

Gowlett, J. A. J. 1987. The archaeology of radiocarbon accelerator dating. *Journal of World Prehistory* 1: 127–170.

Graham, I., ed. 1985a. Ethnoarchaeology. *World Archaeology* 17 (whole no. 2).

————, ed. 1985b. Water-craft and water transport. *World Archaeology* 16 (whole no. 3).

Graham, I., P. Galloway, and I. Scollar. 1976. Model studies in computer seriation. *Journal of Archaeological Science* 3: 1–30.

Grant, M. 1990. *The Visible Past: Greek and Roman History from Archaeology 1960–1990.* New York: Charles Scribner's Sons.

Grayson, D. K. 1979. On the quantification of vertebrate archaeofaunas. In *Advances in Archaeological Method and Theory,* vol. 2, ed. M. B. Schiffer, pp. 199–237. New York: Academic Press.

————. 1983. *The Establishment of Human Antiquity.* New York: Academic Press.

————. 1984. *Quantitative Zooarchaeology: Topics in the Analysis of Archaeological Faunas.* New York: Academic Press.

Green, E. L., ed. 1984. *Ethics and Values in Archaeology.* New York: Free Press.

Green, J. 1990. *Maritime Archaeology: A Technical Handbook.* London: Academic Press.

Green, S. W. 1980. Toward a general model of agricultural systems. In *Advances in Archaeological Method and Theory,* vol. 3, ed. M. B. Schiffer, pp. 311–355. New York: Academic Press.

Green, S. W., and S. M. Perlman, eds. 1985. *The Archaeology of Frontiers and Boundaries.* Orlando: Academic Press.

Greenfield, J. 1989. *The Return of Cultural Treasures.* Cambridge: Cambridge University Press.

Griffin, J. B. 1959. The pursuit of archaeology in the United States. *American Anthropologist* 61: 379–388.

Grigson, C., and J. Clutton-Brock, eds. 1983. *Animals and Archaeology: 2. Shell Middens, Fishes, and Birds.* British Archaeological Reports International Series 183. Oxford: BAR.

Grinsell, L., P. Rahtz, and D. P. Williams. 1974. *The Preparation of Archaeological Reports.* 2nd ed. London: Baker.

Gumerman, G. J. 1984. *A View from Black Mesa: The Changing Face of Archaeology.* Tucson: University of Arizona Press.

Gumerman, G. J., and T. R. Lyons. 1971. Archaeological methodology and remote sensing. *Science* 172: 126–132.

Gumerman, G. J., and D. A. Phillips, Jr. 1978. Archaeology beyond anthropology. *American Antiquity* 43: 184–191.

Gurfinkel, D. M., and U. M. Franklin. 1988. A study of the feasibility of detecting blood residue on artifacts. *Journal of Archaeological Science* 15: 83–98.

Gyrisco, G. M. 1983. Tools suggested and coalitions to preserve archaeological resources. *American Archaeology* 3: 224–227.

Hadingham, E. 1984. *Early Man and the Cosmos.* New York: Walker.

Hall, R. L. 1977. An anthropocentric perspective for eastern United States prehistory. *American Antiquity* 42: 499–518.

————. 1989. The material symbols of the Winnebago Sky and Earth moieties. In *The Meaning of Things: Material Culture and Symbolic Expression,* ed. I. Hodder, pp. 178–184. London: Unwin Hyman.

Hamilton, D. L., and R. Woodward. 1984. A sunken 17th-century city: Port Royal, Jamaica. *Archaeology* 37 (1): 38–45.

Hammil, J., and L. J. Zimmerman, eds. 1983. *Reburial of Human Skeletal Remains: Perspectives from Lakota Holy Men and Elders.* Indianapolis: American Indians Against Desecration.

Hammond, N. 1972. Obsidian trade routes in the Mayan area. *Science* 178: 1092–1093.

————. 1974. The distribution of Late Classic Maya major ceremonial centres in the Central Area. In *Mesoamerican Archaeology: New Approaches,* ed. N. Hammond, pp. 313–334. Austin: University of Texas Press.

————. 1982. *Ancient Maya Civilization.* New Brunswick, N.J.: Rutgers University Press.

Hanson, J. A., and M. B. Schiffer. 1975. The Joint Site—a preliminary report. In *Chapters in the Prehistory of Eastern Arizona,* vol. 4, pp. 47–91. Fieldiana: Anthropology 65. Chicago: Field Museum of Natural History.

Harbottle, G. 1982. Chemical characterization in archaeology. In *Contexts for Prehistoric Exchange,* ed. J. E. Ericson and T. K. Earle, pp. 13–51. New York: Academic Press.

Hardesty, D. L. 1980. The use of general ecological principles in archaeology. In *Advances in Archaeological Method and Theory,* vol. 3, ed. M. B. Schiffer, pp. 157–187. New York: Academic Press.

Harlan, J. R. 1967. A wild wheat harvest in Turkey. *Antiquity* 20: 197–201.

Harp, E., Jr., ed. 1975. *Photography in Archaeological Research*. School of American Research Advanced Seminar Series. Albuquerque: University of New Mexico Press.

Harré, R., and P. F. Secord. 1972. *The Explanation of Social Behavior*. Oxford: Basil Blackwell.

Harrington, J. C. 1954. Dating stem fragments of seventeenth and eighteenth century clay tobacco pipes. *Bulletin of the Archaeological Society of Virginia* 9 (1): 9–13.

Harrington, S. P. M. 1991. The looting of Arkansas. *Archaeology* 44 (3): 22–30.

Harris, D. M., and G. Hillman, eds. 1989. *Foraging and Farming*. London: Unwin Hyman.

Harris, E. C. 1975. The stratigraphic sequence: A question of time. *World Archaeology* 7: 109–121.

———. 1989. *Principles of Archaeological Stratigraphy*. 2nd ed. London: Academic Press.

Harris, M. 1968. *The Rise of Anthropological Theory: A History of Theories of Culture*. New York: Crowell.

Harrison, P. D., and B. L. Turner II, eds. 1978. *Pre-Hispanic Maya Agriculture*. Albuquerque: University of New Mexico Press.

Hart, D., ed. 1983. *Disease in Ancient Man*. Agincourt, Ontario: Irwin.

Hassan, F. A. 1978. Demographic archaeology. In *Advances in Archaeological Method and Theory*, vol. 1, ed. M. B. Schiffer, pp. 49–103. New York: Academic Press.

Hastings, C. M., and M. E. Moseley. 1975. The adobes of Huaca del Sol and Huaca de la Luna. *American Antiquity* 40: 196–203.

Hastorf, C. A., and V. S. Popper, eds. 1988. *Current Paleoethnobotany: Analytical Methods and Cultural Interpretations of Archaeological Plant Remains*. Chicago: University of Chicago Press.

Hatch, J. W., and P. E. Miller. 1985. Procurement, tool production and sourcing research at the Vera Cruz jasper quarry in Pennsylvania. *Journal of Field Archaeology* 12: 219–230.

Haury, E. W. 1945. Arizona's ancient irrigation builders. *Natural History* 54: 300–310, 335.

———. 1958. Evidence at Point of Pines for a prehistoric migration from northern Arizona. In *Migrations in New World Culture History*, ed. R. H. Thompson, pp. 1–6. Social Science Bulletin, no. 27. Tucson: University of Arizona.

Haven, S. F. 1856. *Archaeology of the United States*. Smithsonian Contributions to Knowledge 8 (article 2). Washington, D.C.: Smithsonian Institution.

Haviland, W. A. 1967. Stature at Tikal, Guatemala: Implications for ancient demography and social organization. *American Antiquity* 32: 316–325.

———. 1981. Dower houses and minor centers at Tikal, Guatemala: An investigation into the identification of valid units in settlement hierarchies. In *Lowland Maya Settlement Patterns*, ed. W. Ashmore, pp. 89–117. School of American Research Advanced Seminar Series. Albuquerque: University of New Mexico Press.

———. 1982. Where the rich folks lived: Deranging factors in the statistical analysis of Tikal settlement. *American Antiquity* 47: 427–429.

———. 1985. Population and social dynamics: The dynasties and social structure of Tikal. *Expedition* 27 (3): 34–41.

Hawkins, G. S. 1965. *Stonehenge Decoded*. New York: Doubleday.

Hawley, F. M. 1937. Reverse stratigraphy. *American Antiquity* 2: 297–299.

Hayden, B., ed. 1979. *Lithic Use-Wear Analysis*. New York: Academic Press.

Hayden, B., and A. Cannon. 1983. Where the garbage goes: Refuse disposal in the Maya highlands. *Journal of Anthropological Archaeology* 2: 117–163.

Hayes, A. C., D. M. Brugge, and W. J. Judge. 1981. *Archaeological Surveys of Chaco Canyon, New Mexico*. Washington, D.C.: Government Printing Office.

Haynes, G. 1983. Frequencies of spiral and green-bone fractures on ungulate limb bones in modern surface assemblages. *American Antiquity* 48: 102–114.

Hecker, H. M. 1982. Domestication revisited: Its implications for faunal analysis. *Journal of Field Archaeology* 9: 217–236.

Hedges, J. W. 1984. *Tomb of the Eagles: Death and Life in a Stone Age Tribe*. New York: New Amsterdam.

Hedges, R. E. M., and J. A. J. Gowlett. 1986. Radiocarbon dating by accelerator mass spectrometry. *Scientific American* 254 (1): 100–107.

Heggie, D. C. 1981. *Megalithic Science*. London: Thames & Hudson.

———, ed. 1982. *Archaeoastronomy in the Old World*. Cambridge: University of Cambridge Press.

Heider, K. G. 1967. Archaeological assumptions and ethnographical facts: A cautionary tale from New Guinea. *Southwestern Journal of Anthropology* 23: 52–64.

Heizer, R. F. 1962. *Man's Discovery of His Past: Literary Landmarks in Archaeology.* Englewood Cliffs, N.J.: Prentice-Hall.

Hempel, C. G. 1966. *Philosophy of Natural Science.* Englewood Cliffs, N.J.: Prentice-Hall.

Hempel, C. G., and P. Oppenheim. 1948. Studies in the logic of explanation. *Philosophy of Science* 15: 135–175.

Henderson, J., ed. 1989. *Scientific Analysis in Archaeology and Its Interpretation.* Archaeological Research Tools 5/Monograph 19. Los Angeles and Oxford: UCLA Institute of Archaeology/Oxford University.

Henry, D. O., and G. H. Odell, eds. 1989. *Alternative Approaches to Lithic Analysis.* Archeological Papers of the American Anthropological Association, No. 1. Washington, D.C.: American Anthropological Association.

Herscher, E. 1989. A future in ruins. *Archaeology* 42 (1): 67–70.

Hess, B., and P. Wapnish. 1985. *Animal Bone Archaeology: From Objectives to Analysis.* Manuals on Archaeology. Washington, D.C.: Taraxacum.

Hester, T. A., and R. F. Heizer. 1973. *Bibliography of Archaeology: I. Experiments, Lithic Technology, and Petrography.* Modules in Anthropology, no. 29. Reading, Mass.: Addison-Wesley.

Hester, T. A., R. F. Heizer, and J. A. Graham, eds. 1975. *Field Methods in Archaeology,* 6th ed. Palo Alto, Calif.: Mayfield.

Heyerdahl, T. 1950. *The Kon-Tiki Expedition: By Raft across the South Seas.* London: Allen & Unwin.

———, ed. 1961/1965. *Reports of the Norwegian Archaeological Expedition to Easter Island and the East Pacific.* 2 vols. London: Allen & Unwin.

Hietala, H. J., ed. 1984. *Intrasite Spatial Analysis in Archaeology.* Cambridge: Cambridge University Press.

Higgenbotham, C. D. 1983. Native Americans versus archaeologists: The legal issues. *American Indian Law Review* 10: 91–115.

Higgs, E. S., ed. 1972. *Papers in Economic Prehistory.* Cambridge: Cambridge University Press.

———, ed. 1975. *Paleoeconomy.* Cambridge: Cambridge University Press.

Higham, C. F. W. 1984. Prehistoric rice cultivation in Southeast Asia. *Scientific American* 250 (4): 138–146.

Hill, A. P. 1979. Butchery and natural disarticulation: An investigatory technique. *American Antiquity* 44: 739–744.

Hill, J. N. 1966. A prehistoric community in eastern Arizona. *Southwestern Journal of Anthropology* 22: 9–30.

———. 1967. The problem of sampling. In *Chapters in the Prehistory of Eastern Arizona,* vol. 3, pp. 145–157. Fieldiana: Anthropology 57. Chicago: Field Museum of Natural History.

———. 1970. *Broken K Pueblo: Prehistoric Social Organization in the American Southwest.* Anthropological Paper no. 18. Tucson: University of Arizona Press.

———, ed. 1977. *Explanation of Prehistoric Change.* School of American Research Advanced Seminar Series. Albuquerque: University of New Mexico Press.

Hill, J. N., and R. K. Evans. 1972. A model for classification and typology. In *Models in Archaeology,* ed. D. L. Clarke, pp. 231–273. London: Methuen.

Hill, J. N., and J. Gunn, eds. 1977. *The Individual in Prehistory.* New York: Academic Press.

Hillson, S. 1986. *Teeth.* Cambridge: Cambridge University Press.

Hirth, K. G. 1978. Problems in data recovery and management in settlement archaeology. *Journal of Field Archaeology* 5: 125–131.

———, ed. 1984. *Trade and Exchange in Early Mesoamerica.* Albuquerque: University of New Mexico Press.

Hodder, I., ed. 1978a. *Simulation Studies in Archaeology.* Cambridge: Cambridge University Press.

———, ed. 1978b. *The Spatial Organisation of Culture.* Pittsburgh: University of Pittsburgh Press.

———, ed. 1982a. *Symbolic and Structural Archaeology.* Cambridge: Cambridge University Press.

———. 1982b. *Symbols in Action: Ethnoarchaeological Studies of Material Culture.* Cambridge: Cambridge University Press.

———. 1982c. *The Present Past: An Introduction to Anthropology for Archaeologists.* New York: Pica Press.

———. 1985. Postprocessual archaeology. In *Advances in Archaeological Method and Theory,* vol. 8, ed. M. B. Schiffer, pp. 1–26. Orlando: Academic Press.

———. 1987. The meaning of discard: Ash and domestic space in Baringo. In *Method and Theory for Activity Area Research: An Ethnoarchaeological Approach,* ed. S. Kent, pp. 424–488. New York: Columbia University Press.

———, ed. 1989. *The Meaning of Things: Material Culture and Symbolic Expression.* London: Unwin Hyman.

———. 1990. *The Domestication of Europe: Structure and Contingency in Neolithic Societies.* Oxford: Basil Blackwell.

———. 1991a. *Reading the Past: Current Approaches to Interpretation in Archaeology.* 2nd ed. Cambridge: Cambridge University Press.

———. 1991b. Interpretive archaeology and its role. *American Antiquity* 56: 7–18.

Hodder, I. R., and M. Hassall. 1971. The non-random spacing of Romano-British walled towns. *Man* 6: 391–407.

Hodder, I. R., and C. Orton. 1976. *Spatial Analysis in Archaeology*. Cambridge: Cambridge University Press.

Hodges, H. 1964. *Artifacts: An Introduction to Early Materials and Technology*. London: Baker.

Hodson, F. R. 1970. Cluster analysis and archaeology: Some new developments and applications. *World Archaeology* 1: 299–320.

Hole, B. 1980. Sampling in archaeology: A critique. *Annual Review of Anthropology* 9: 217–234.

Hole, F., and M. Shaw. 1967. *Computer Analysis of Chronological Seriation*. Rice University Studies 53. Houston: Rice University.

Hole, F., K. V. Flannery, and J. A. Neely. 1969. *Prehistoric Human Ecology of the Deh Luran Plain: An Early Village Sequence from Khuzistan, Iran*. Memoirs of the Museum of Anthropology, no. 1. Ann Arbor: University of Michigan.

Holmes, W. H. 1900. The obsidian mines of Hidalgo. *American Anthropologist* 2: 405–416.

Hope-Simpson, R. 1984. The analysis of data from surface surveys. *Journal of Field Archaeology* 11: 115–117.

Hope-Taylor, B. 1966. Archaeological draughtsmanship: Principles and practice: Part II. Ends and means. *Antiquity* 40: 107–113.

———. 1967. Archaeological draughtsmanship: Principles and practice: Part III. Lines of communication. *Antiquity* 41: 181–189.

Horne, P. D. 1985. A review of the evidence of human endoparasitism in the pre-Columbian New World through the study of coprolites. *Journal of Archaeological Science* 12: 299–310.

Houston, S. D. 1989. *Maya Glyphs*. Berkeley and Los Angeles: University of California Press.

Hurley, W. M. 1979. *Prehistoric Cordage, Identification of Impressions on Pottery*. Manuals on Archaeology. Washington, D.C.: Taraxacum.

Huss-Ashmore, R., A. H. Goodman, and G. J. Armelagos. 1982. Nutritional inference from paleopathology. In *Advances in Archaeological Method and Theory,* vol. 5, ed. M. B. Schiffer, pp. 395–474. New York: Academic Press.

Hyslop, J. 1984. *The Inca Road System*. Orlando: Academic Press.

Isaac, G. L. 1967. Towards the interpretation of occupation debris: Some experiments and observations. *Kroeber Anthropological Society Papers* 37: 371–375.

———. 1971. Whither archaeology? *Antiquity* 45: 123–129.

———. 1983. Bones in contention: Competing explanations for the juxtaposition of early Pleistocene artifacts and faunal remains. In *Animals and Archaeology: 1. Hunters and Their Prey*, ed. J. Clutton-Brock and C. Grigson, pp. 3–19. British Archaeological Reports International Series 163. Oxford: BAR.

———. 1984. The archaeology of human origins: Studies of the Lower Pleistocene in East Africa 1971–1981. In *Advances in World Archaeology,* ed. F. Wendorf and A. E. Close, pp. 1–87. Orlando: Academic Press.

Isbell, W. H. 1978. The prehistoric ground drawings of Peru. *Scientific American* 239 (4): 140–153.

Jackson, T. L. 1991. Pounding acorn: Women's production as social and economic focus. In *Engendering Archaeology: Women and Prehistory*, ed. J. M. Gero and M. W. Conkey, pp. 301–325. Oxford: Basil Blackwell.

Jakes, K. A., and A. Angel. 1989. Determination of elemental distribution in ancient fibers. In *Archaeological Chemistry IV*, ed. R. O. Allen, pp. 451–464. Advances in Chemistry Series No. 220. Washington D.C.: American Chemical Society.

Jarman, M. R., C. Vita-Finzi, and E. S. Higgs. 1972. Site catchment analysis in archaeology. In *Man, Settlement and Urbanism,* ed. P. J. Ucko, R. Tringham, and G. W. Dimbleby, pp. 61–66. London: Duckworth.

Jelinek, A. J. 1976. Form, function, and style in lithic analysis. In *Cultural Change and Continuity: Essays in Honor of James Bennett Griffin*, ed. C. E. Cleland, pp. 19–34. New York: Academic Press.

Jennings, J. D. 1957. *Danger Cave*. Memoir no. 14. Salt Lake City: University of Utah Press and Society for American Archaeology.

Jewell, P. A. 1963. *The Experimental Earthwork on Overton Down, Wiltshire, 1960*. London: British Association for the Advancement of Science.

Jewell, P. A., and G. W. Dimbleby. 1968. The experimental earthwork on Overton Down, Wiltshire, England: The first four years. *Proceedings of the Prehistoric Society* 32: 313–342.

Jochim, M. A. 1979. Breaking down the system: Recent ecological approaches in archaeology. In *Advances in Archaeological Method and Theory,* vol. 2, ed. M. B. Schiffer, pp. 77–117. New York: Academic Press.

Johnson, A. W., and T. Earle. 1987. *The Evolution of Hu-*

man Societies: From Foraging Group to Agrarian State. Stanford: Stanford University Press.

Johnson, E. 1985. Current developments in bone technology. In *Advances in Archaeological Method and Theory,* vol. 8, ed. M. B. Schiffer, pp. 157–235. Orlando: Academic Press.

Johnson, G. A. 1972. A test of the utility of central place theory in archaeology. In *Man, Settlement and Urbanism,* ed. P. J. Ucko, R. Tringham, and G. W. Dimbleby, pp. 769–786. London: Duckworth.

———. 1973. *Local Exchange and Early State Development in Southwestern Iran.* Anthropological Papers, no. 51. Ann Arbor: University of Michigan.

———. 1977. Aspects of regional analysis in archaeology. *Annual Review of Anthropology* 6: 479–508.

Johnson, J. K., T. L. Sever, S. L. H. Madry, and H. T. Hoff. 1988. Remote sensing and GIS analysis in large scale survey design in north Mississippi. *Southeastern Archaeology* 7 (2): 124–131.

Johnson, L. L. 1978. A history of flint-knapping experimentation, 1838–1976. *Current Anthropology* 19: 337–372.

Johnstone, P. 1980. *The Sea-Craft of Prehistory.* Cambridge: Harvard University Press.

Jones, C. 1977. Inauguration dates of three Late Classic rulers of Tikal, Guatemala. *American Antiquity* 42: 28–60.

Jones, G. D., and R. R. Kautz, eds. 1981. *The Transition to Statehood in the New World.* Cambridge: Cambridge University Press.

Jones, P. 1980. Experimental butchery with modern stone tools and its relevance for Paleolithic archaeology. *World Archaeology* 12: 153–165.

Joukowsky, M. 1980. *A Complete Manual of Field Archaeology.* Englewood Cliffs, N.J.: Prentice-Hall.

Jovanovic, B. 1980. The origins of copper mining in Europe. *Scientific American* 242 (5): 152–167.

Karata, H. M., ed. 1989. *Non-Topographic Photogrammetry.* 2nd ed. Falls Church, Va.: American Society for Photogrammetry and Remote Sensing.

Kardiner, A., and E. Preble. 1961. *They Studied Man.* New York: World/New American Library.

Keatinge, R. W., and K. C. Day. 1974. Chan Chan: A study of Precolumbian urbanism and the management of land and water resources in Peru. *Archaeology* 27: 228–235.

Keeley, L. H. 1974. Technique and methodology in microwear studies: A critical review. *World Archaeology* 5: 323–336.

———. 1977. The functions of Paleolithic stone tools. *Scientific American* 237 (5): 108–126.

———. 1980. *Experimental Determination of Stone Tool Uses: A Microwear Analysis.* Chicago: University of Chicago Press.

Keeley, L. H., and N. Toth. 1981. Microwear polishes on early stone tools from Koobi Fora, Kenya. *Nature* 293: 464–465.

Keesing, R. M. 1974. Theories of culture. *Annual Review of Anthropology* 3: 71–97.

Kehoe, A. B., and T. F. Kehoe. 1973. Cognitive models for archaeological interpretation. *American Antiquity* 38: 150–154.

Kelley, J. H., and M. P. Hanen. 1988. *Archaeology and the Methodology of Science.* Albuquerque: University of New Mexico Press.

Kelley, M. A., P. Dale, and J. G. B. Haigh. 1984. A microcomputer system for data logging in geophysical surveying. *Archaeometry* 26: 183–191.

Kennedy, D., ed. 1989. *Into the Sun: Essays in Air Photography in Archaeology in Honour of Derrick Riley.* Sheffield: J. R. Collis Publications, University of Sheffield.

Kennedy, D., and D. Riley. 1990. *Rome's Desert Frontier from the Air.* Austin: University of Texas Press.

Kent, K. P. 1983. *Prehistoric Textiles of the Southwest.* School of American Research. Albuquerque: University of New Mexico Press.

Kent, S. 1984. *Analyzing Activity Areas: An Ethnoarchaeological Study of the Use of Space.* Albuquerque: University of New Mexico Press.

———, ed. 1987. *Method and Theory for Activity Area Research—An Ethnoarchaeological Approach.* New York: Columbia University Press.

———, ed. 1990. *Domestic Architecture and the Use of Space.* Cambridge: Cambridge University Press.

Kenworthy, M. A., E. M. King, M. E. Ruwell, and T. Van Houten. 1985. *Preserving Field Records: Archival Techniques for Archaeologists and Anthropologists.* Philadelphia: University Museum, University of Pennsylvania.

Kenyon, J. L., and B. Bevan. 1977. Ground penetrating radar and its application to a historical archaeological site. *Historical Archaeology* 11: 48–55.

Kenyon, K. M. 1961. *Beginning in Archaeology.* Rev. ed. London: Phoenix House.

Kidder, A. V. [1924] 1962. *An Introduction to the Study of Southwestern Archaeology.* Reprint with introduction, Southwestern archaeology today, by I. Rouse. New Haven: Yale University Press.

————. 1932. *The Artifacts of Pecos.* Papers of the Southwestern Expedition, no. 6. Andover, Mass.: Phillips Academy.

————. 1947. *The Artifacts of Uaxactún, Guatemala.* Publication 576. Washington, D.C.: Carnegie Institution.

————. 1961. Archaeological investigations at Kaminaljuyú, Guatemala. *Proceedings of the American Philosophical Society* 105: 559–570.

Kidder, A. V., and S. J. Guernsey. 1919. *Archaeological Explorations in Northeastern Arizona.* Bureau of American Ethnology, Bulletin 65. Washington, D.C.: Smithsonian Institution.

Kidder, A. V., J. D. Jennings, and E. M. Shook. 1946. *Excavations at Kaminaljuyú, Guatemala.* Publication 561. Washington, D.C.: Carnegie Institution.

King, M. E. 1978. Analytical methods and prehistoric textiles. *American Antiquity* 43: 89–96.

King, T. F. 1971. A conflict of values in American archaeology. *American Antiquity* 36: 255–262.

————. 1978a. *The Archaeological Survey: Methods and Uses.* Washington, D.C.: U.S. Department of the Interior, Heritage Conservation and Recreation Service.

————. 1978b. Don't that beat the band? Nonegalitarian political organization in prehistoric central California. In *Social Archeology: Beyond Subsistence and Dating,* ed. C. L. Redman, M. J. Berman, E. V. Curtin, W. T. Langhorne, Jr., N. M. Versaggi, and J. C. Wanser, pp. 225–248. New York: Academic Press.

————. 1983. Professional responsibility in public archaeology. *Annual Review of Anthropology* 12: 143–164.

King, T. F., P. P. Hickman, and G. Berg. 1977. *Anthropology in Historic Preservation: Caring for Culture's Clutter.* New York: Academic Press.

Kingery, W. D., ed. 1985. *Ceramics and Civilization: I. From Ancient Technology to Modern Science.* Columbus, Ohio: American Ceramic Society.

————, ed. 1986. *Ceramics and Civilization: II. Technology and Style.* Columbus, Ohio: American Ceramic Society.

Kintigh, K. W. 1988. The effectiveness of subsurface testing: A simulation approach. *American Antiquity* 53: 686–707.

Kintigh, K. W., and A. J. Ammerman. 1982. Heuristic approaches to spatial analysis in archaeology. *American Antiquity* 47: 31–63.

Kirch, P. V. 1980. The archaeological study of adaptation: Theoretical and methodological issues. In *Advances in Archaeological Method and Theory,* vol. 3, ed. M. B. Schiffer, pp. 101–156. New York: Academic Press.

————. 1984. *The Evolution of the Polynesian Chiefdoms.* Cambridge: Cambridge University Press.

Klein, J., J. C. Lerman, P. E. Damon, and E. K. Ralph. 1982. Calibration of radiocarbon dates: Tables based on the consensus data of the workshop on calibrating the radiocarbon time scale. *Radiocarbon* 24: 103–150.

Klein, R. G. 1973. *Ice-Age Hunters of the Ukraine.* Chicago: University of Chicago Press.

Klein, R. G., and K. Cruz-Uribe. 1984. *The Analysis of Animal Bones from Archaeological Sites.* Chicago: University of Chicago Press.

Klejn, L. S. 1977. A panorama of theoretical archaeology. *Current Anthropology* 18: 1–42.

————. 1982. *Archaeological Typology.* Trans. P. Dole. British Archaeological Reports International Series 153. Oxford: BAR.

Klindt-Jensen, O. 1975. *A History of Scandinavian Archaeology.* London: Thames & Hudson.

Knudson, R. 1989. North America's threatened heritage. *Archaeology* 42 (1): 71–73, 106.

Koch, A., and W. Peden, eds. 1944. *The Life and Selected Writings of Thomas Jefferson.* New York: Modern Library.

Koch, C. 1989. *Taphonomy: A Bibliographic Guide to the Literature.* Orono, Maine: Center for the Study of the First Americans, University of Maine.

Kopper, J. S., and G. Rossello-Bordoy. 1974. Megalithic quarrying techniques and limestone technology in eastern Spain. *Journal of Field Archaeology* 1: 161–170.

Kosso, P. 1991. Method in archaeology: Middle-range theory as hermeneutics. *American Antiquity* 56: 621–627.

Kraft, J. C., S. E. Aschenbrenner, and G. Rapp, Jr. 1977. Paleogeographic reconstructions of coastal Aegean archaeological sites. *Science* 195: 941–947.

Krakker, J. J., M. J. Shott, and P. D. Welch. 1983. Design and evaluation of shovel-test sampling in regional archaeological survey. *Journal of Field Archaeology* 10: 469–480.

Kramer, C., and M. Stark. 1988. The status of women in archaeology. *Anthropology Newsletter (American Anthropological Association)* 29 (9): 1, 11–12.

Krieger, A. D. 1944. The typological concept. *American Antiquity* 9: 271–288.

————. 1946. *Culture Complexes and Chronology in Northern Texas with Extension of Puebloan Datings to the Mississippi Valley.* Publication 4640. Austin: University of Texas.

————. 1960. Archaeological typology in theory and practice. In *Selected Papers of the Fifth International Congress of Anthropological and Ethnological Sciences,* ed. A. F. C. Wallace, pp. 141–151. Philadelphia: University of Pennsylvania Press.

Kroeber, A. L. 1939. *Cultural and Natural Areas of Native North America.* Berkeley and Los Angeles: University of California Press.

Kroll, E. M., and G. Isaac. 1984. Configurations of artifacts and bones at early Pleistocene sites in East Africa. In *Intrasite Spatial Analysis in Archaeology,* ed. H. J. Hietala, pp. 4–31. Cambridge: Cambridge University Press.

Kroll, E. M., and T. D. Price, eds. 1991. *The Interpretation of Archaeological Spatial Patterning.* New York: Plenum.

Kuhn, T. S. 1970. *The Structure of Scientific Revolutions.* 2nd ed. Chicago: University of Chicago Press.

Kvamme, K. L. 1989. Geographic Information Systems in regional archaeological research and data management. In *Archaeological Method and Theory*, vol. 1, ed. M. B. Schiffer, pp. 139–203. Tucson: University of Arizona Press.

Lamberg-Karlovsky, C. C., ed. 1988. *Archaeological Thought in America.* Cambridge: Cambridge University Press.

Lambert, J. B., ed. 1984. *Archaeological Chemistry III.* Advances in Chemistry Series No. 205. Washington, D.C.: American Chemical Society.

Lange, F. W., and C. R. Rydberg. 1972. Abandonment and post-abandonment behavior at a rural Central American house-site. *American Antiquity* 37: 419–432.

Lathrap, D. W., J. G. Marcos, and J. Zeidler. 1977. Real Alto: An ancient ceremonial center. *Archaeology* 30: 2–13.

Lawrence, R. A. 1979. Experimental evidence for the significance of attributes used in edge-damage analysis. In *Lithic Use-Wear Analysis,* ed. B. Hayden, pp. 113–121. New York: Academic Press.

Layton, R., ed. 1989a. *Conflict in the Archaeology of Living Traditions.* London: Unwin Hyman.

———, ed. 1989b. *Who Needs the Past? Indigenous Values and Archaeology.* London: Unwin Hyman.

Leach, E. R. 1983. The gatekeepers of heaven: Anthropological aspects of grandiose architecture. *Journal of Anthropological Research* 39: 243–264.

LeBlanc, S. A. 1975. Micro-seriation: A method for fine chronologic differentiation. *American Antiquity* 40: 22–28.

———. 1976. Archaeological recording systems. *Journal of Field Archaeology* 3: 159–168.

———. 1983. *The Mimbres People: Ancient Pueblo Painters of the American Southwest.* New York: Thames & Hudson.

Lechtman, H. 1976. A metallurgical site survey in the Peruvian Andes. *Journal of Field Archaeology* 3: 1–42.

———. 1984a. Andean value systems and the development of prehistoric metallurgy. *Technology and Culture* 25: 1–36.

———. 1984b. Pre-Columbian surface metallurgy. *Scientific American* 250 (6): 56–63.

Lee, R. B. 1968. What hunters do for a living, or, how to make out on scarce resources. In *Man the Hunter,* ed. R. B. Lee and I. DeVore, pp. 30–48. Chicago: Aldine.

Lee, R. B., and I. DeVore, eds. 1968. *Man the Hunter.* Chicago: Aldine.

———, eds. 1976. *Kalahari Hunter-Gatherers.* Cambridge: Harvard University Press.

Lennstrom, H. A., and C. A. Hastorf. 1992. Testing old wives' tales in palaeoethnobotany: A comparison of bulk and scatter sampling schemes from Pancán, Peru. *Journal of Archaeological Science* 19: 205–229.

Leone, M. P. 1972. Issues in anthropological archaeology. In *Contemporary Archaeology,* ed. M. P. Leone, pp. 14–27. Carbondale: Southern Illinois University Press.

———. 1977. The new Mormon temple in Washington, D.C. In *Historical Archaeology and the Importance of Material Things,* ed. L. Ferguson, pp. 43–61. Lansing, Mich.: Society for Historical Archaeology.

———. 1982. Some opinions about recovering mind. *American Antiquity* 47: 742–760.

———. 1986. Symbolic, structural, and critical archaeology. In *American Archaeology Past and Future: A Celebration of the Society for American Archaeology 1935–1985,* ed. D. J. Meltzer, D. D. Fowler, and J. A. Sabloff, pp. 415–438. Washington, D.C.: Smithsonian Institution Press.

Leone, M. P., and P. B. Potter, eds. 1988. *The Recovery of Meaning.* Washington, D.C.: Smithsonian Institution Press.

Leroi-Gourhan, A. 1975. The flowers found with Shanidar IV, a Neanderthal burial in Iraq. *Science* 190: 562–564.

———. 1982. *The Dawn of European Art.* Cambridge: Cambridge University Press.

Levin, A. M. 1986. Excavation photography: A day on a dig. *Archaeology* 39 (1): 34–39.

Levi-Strauss, C. 1963. *Structural Anthropology.* Trans. C. Jacobson and B. G. Schoepf. Garden City, N.Y.: Doubleday/Anchor.

Lewarch, D. E., and M. J. O'Brien. 1981. The expanding role of surface assemblages in archaeological research. In *Advances in Archaeological Method and Theory,* vol. 4, ed. M. B. Schiffer, pp. 297–342. New York: Academic Press.

Lewin, R. 1984. Extinction threatens Australian anthropology. *Science* 225: 393–394.

Lewis-Williams, J. D. 1986. Cognitive and optical illusions in San rock art research. *Current Anthropology* 27: 171–178.

Libby, W. F. 1955. *Radiocarbon Dating*. 2nd ed. Chicago: University of Chicago Press.

Lightfoot, K. 1986. Regional surveys in the Eastern United States: The strengths and weaknesses of implementing subsurface testing programs. *American Antiquity* 51: 484–504.

———. 1989. A defense of shovel-test-sampling: A reply to Shott. *American Antiquity* 54: 413–416.

Limp, W. F. 1974. Water separation and flotation processes. *Journal of Field Archaeology* 1: 337–342.

Lipe, W. D. 1974. A conservation model for American archaeology. *The Kiva* 39: 213–245.

———. 1984. Value and meaning in cultural resources. In *Approaches to the Archaeological Heritage: A Comparative Study of World Cultural Resource Management Systems,* ed. H. Cleere, pp. 1–11. Cambridge: Cambridge University Press.

Little, B. J., ed. 1991. *Text-Aided Archaeology*. Boca Raton: CRC Press.

Lloyd, S. 1955. *Foundations in the Dust: A Story of Mesopotamian Exploration*. Baltimore: Penguin.

———. 1963. *Mounds of the Near East*. Edinburgh: Edinburgh University Press.

———. 1976. Illustrating monuments: Drawn reconstructions of architecture. In *To Illustrate the Monuments: Essays on Archaeology Presented to Stuart Piggott,* ed. J. V. S. Megaw, pp. 27–34. London: Thames & Hudson.

Lock, G., and J. Wilcock. 1987. *Computer Archaeology*. Aylesbury: Shire Publications, Ltd.

Longacre, W. A. 1970a. *Archaeology as Anthropology: A Case Study*. Anthropological Paper no. 17. Tucson: University of Arizona Press.

———. 1970b. Current thinking in American archaeology. In *Current Directions in Anthropology,* ed. A. Fischer, pp. 126–138. Bulletin 3 (no. 3, pt. 2). Washington, D.C.: American Anthropological Association.

———. 1981. Kalinga pottery: An ethnoarchaeological study. In *Pattern of the Past: Studies in Honour of David Clarke,* ed. I. Hodder, G. Isaac, and N. Hammond, pp. 49–66. Cambridge: Cambridge University Press.

Longacre, W. A., and J. E. Ayres. 1968. Archeological lessons from an Apache wickiup. In *New Perspectives in Archeology,* ed. S. R. Binford and L. R. Binford, pp. 151–159. Chicago: Aldine.

Longworth, I., ed. 1971. Archaeology and ethnography. *World Archaeology* 3 (whole no. 2).

———, ed. 1984. Mines and quarries. *World Archaeology* 16 (whole no. 2).

Longyear, J. M., III. 1952. *Copán Ceramics: A Study of Southeastern Maya Pottery*. Publication 597. Washington, D.C.: Carnegie Institution of Washington.

Lovejoy, A. O. [1936] 1960. *The Great Chain of Being: A Study of the History of an Idea*. Cambridge: Harvard University Press. Reprint. New York: Harper.

Lovis, W. A., Jr. 1976. Quarter sections and forests: An example of probability sampling in the northeastern woodlands. *American Antiquity* 41: 364–372.

Loy, T. H. 1983. Prehistoric blood residues: Detection on tool surfaces and identification of species of origin. *Science* 220: 1269–1271.

Lubbock, J. (Lord Avebury). 1865. *Prehistoric Times*. London: Williams & Norgate.

Luckenbach, A. H., C. G. Holland, and R. O. Allen. 1975. Soapstone artifacts: Tracing prehistoric trade patterns in Virginia. *Science* 187: 57–58.

Lyell, C. 1830–1833. *Principles of Geology*. London: Murray.

Lyman, R. L. 1982. Archaeofaunas and subsistence studies. In *Advances in Archaeological Method and Theory,* vol. 5, ed. M. B. Schiffer, pp. 331–393. New York: Academic Press.

Lynch, B. D., and T. F. Lynch, 1968. The beginnings of a scientific approach to prehistoric archaeology in 17th and 18th century Britain. *Southwestern Journal of Anthropology* 24: 33–65.

Lynch, B. M. 1980. Site artifact density and the effectiveness of shovel probes. *Current Anthropology* 21: 516–517.

McBryde, I., ed. 1985. *Who Owns the Past?* Melbourne: Oxford University Press.

McCauley, J. F., G. G. Schaber, C. S. Breed, M. J. Grolier, C. V. Haynes, B. Issaw, C. Elachi, and R. Blom. 1982. Subsurface valleys and geoarchaeology of the eastern Sahara revealed by shuttle radar. *Science* 218: 1004–1020.

McConnell, D. 1962. Dating of fossil bone by the fluorine method. *Science* 136: 241–244.

MacDonald, W. K., ed. 1976. *Digging for Gold: Papers on Archaeology for Profit*. Ann Arbor: University of Michigan, Museum of Anthropology.

McGhee, R. 1977. Ivory for the sea woman: The symbolic attributes of a prehistoric technology. *Canadian Journal of Archaeology* 1: 141–149.

McGimsey, C. R., III. 1972. *Public Archeology*. New York: Seminar Press.

McGimsey, C. R., III, and H. A. Davis, eds. 1977. *The Management of Archaeological Resources: The Airlie House Report*. Washington, D.C.: Society for American Archaeology.

McGuire, R. H., and R. Paynter, eds. 1991. *The Archaeology of Inequality*. Oxford: Basil Blackwell.

McIntosh, R. J. 1974. Archaeology and mud wall decay in a West African village. *World Archaeology* 6: 154–171.

———. 1977. The excavation of mud structures: An experiment from West Africa. *World Archaeology* 9: 185–199.

McKern, W. C. 1939. The Midwestern Taxonomic Method as an aid to archaeological study. *American Antiquity* 4: 301–313.

McKinley, J. R., and G. J. Henderson. 1985. The protection of historic shipwrecks: A New Zealand case study. *Archaeology* 38 (6): 48–51.

McKusick, M. 1982. Psychic archaeology: Theory, method and mythology. *Journal of Field Archaeology* 9: 99–118.

———. 1984. Psychic archaeology from Atlantis to Oz. *Archaeology* 37 (6): 48–52.

McManamon, F. P. 1984. Discovering Sites Unseen. In *Advances in Archaeological Method and Theory*, vol. 7, ed. M. B. Schiffer, pp. 223–292. Orlando: Academic Press.

McNally, S., and V. Walsh. 1984. The Akhmim data base: A multi-stage system for computer-assisted analysis of artifacts. *Journal of Field Archaeology* 11: 47–59.

MacNeish, R. S. 1964a. Ancient Mesoamerican civilization. *Science* 143: 531–537.

———. 1964b. The origins of New World civilization. *Scientific American* 211 (5): 29–37.

———. 1967. An interdisciplinary approach to an archaeological problem. In *The Prehistory of the Tehuacán Valley*, vol. 1, ed. D. S. Byers, pp. 14–24. Austin: University of Texas Press.

———. 1974. Reflections on my search for the beginnings of agriculture in Mexico. In *Archaeological Researches in Retrospect*, ed. G. R. Willey, pp. 207–234. Cambridge, Mass.: Winthrop.

MacNeish, R. S., M. L. Fowler, A. G. Cook, F. A. Peterson, A. Nelken-Terner, and J. A. Neely. 1972. *Excavations and Reconnaissance: The Prehistory of the Tehuacán Valley*, vol. 5. Austin: University of Texas Press.

MacNeish, R. S., T. C. Patterson, and D. L. Browman. 1975. *The Central Peruvian Prehistoric Interaction Sphere*. Andover, Mass.: Phillips Academy.

McWeeney, L. 1984. Wood identification and archaeology in the Northeast. *North American Archaeologist* 5: 183–195.

Maddin, R., ed. 1988. *The Beginning of the Use of Metals and Alloys*. Cambridge: MIT Press.

Maddin, R., J. D. Muhly, and T. S. Wheeler. 1977. How the Iron Age began. *Scientific American* 237 (4): 122–131.

Madeira, P. C. 1931. An aerial expedition to Central America. *Philadelphia Museum Journal* 22 (whole no. 2).

Madry, S. L. H., and C. L. Crumley. 1990. An application of remote sensing and GIS in a regional archaeological settlement pattern analysis: The Arroux River valley, Burgundy, France. In *Interpreting Space: GIS and Archaeology*, ed. K. M. S. Allen, S. W. Green, and E. B. W. Zubrow, pp. 364–380. Bristol, Pa.: Taylor & Francis, Inc.

Malinowski, B. 1944. *A Scientific Theory of Culture*. Chapel Hill: University of North Carolina Press.

Marquardt, W. H. 1978. Advances in archaeological seriation. In *Advances in Archaeological Method and Theory*, vol. 1, ed. M. B. Schiffer, pp. 257–314. New York: Academic Press.

Marquardt, W. H., A. Montet-White, and S. C. Scholtz. 1982. Resolving the crisis in archaeological collections curation. *American Antiquity* 47: 409–418.

Marshack, A. 1972a. *The Roots of Civilization*. New York: McGraw-Hill.

———. 1972b. Upper Paleolithic notation and symbol. *Science* 178: 817–827.

Martin, P. S. 1971. The revolution in archaeology. *American Antiquity* 36: 1–8.

Martin, P. S., J. B. Rinaldo, E. Bluhm, H. C. Cutler, and R. Grange, Jr. 1952. *Mogollon Cultural Continuity and Change: The Stratigraphic Analysis of Tularosa and Cordova Caves*. Fieldiana: Anthropology, vol. 40. Chicago: Field Museum of Natural History.

Martin, W. A., J. E. Bruseth, and R. J. Huggins. 1991. Assessing feature function and spatial patterning of artifacts with geophysical remote-sensing data. *American Antiquity* 56: 701–720.

Martlew, R., ed. 1984. *Information Systems in Archaeology*. Gloucester: Alan Sutton.

Mason, J. 1984. An unorthodox magnetic survey of a large forested historic site. *Historical Archaeology* 18: 54–63.

Matheny, R. T. 1976. Maya lowland hydraulic systems. *Science* 193: 639–646.

Matos Moctezuma, E. 1989. *The Aztecs*. Trans. A. Ellis. New York: Rizzoli.

Matson, F. R., ed. 1965. *Ceramics and Man*. Chicago: Aldine.

Mayr, E. 1972. The nature of the Darwinian revolution. *Science* 176: 981–989.

Mazar, B. 1985. *Biblical Archaeology Today*. Biblical Archaeological Society.

Mazess, R. B., and D. W. Zimmerman. 1966. Pottery dating from thermoluminescence. *Science* 152: 347–348.

Meeks, N. D., G. de G. Sieveking, M. S. Tite, and J. Cook. 1982. Gloss and use-wear traces on flint sickles and similar phenomena. *Journal of Archaeological Science* 9: 317–340.

Meggers, B. J., C. Evans, and E. Estrada. 1965. *Early Formative Period of Coastal Ecuador: The Valdivia and Machalilla Phases*. Smithsonian Contributions to Anthropology, vol. 1. Washington, D.C.: Smithsonian Institution.

Meighan, C. W. 1959. A new method for the seriation of archaeological collections. *American Antiquity* 25: 203–211.

Meisch, L. A. 1985. Machu Picchu: Conserving an Inca treasure. *Archaeology* 38 (6): 18–25.

Meltzer, D. J. 1979. Paradigms and the nature of change in American archaeology. *American Antiquity* 44: 644–657.

———. 1983. The antiquity of man and the development of archaeology. In *Advances in Archaeological Method and Theory*, vol. 6, ed. M. B. Schiffer, pp. 1–51. New York: Academic Press.

Meltzer, D. J., D. D. Fowler, and J. A. Sabloff, eds. 1986. *American Archaeology Past and Future: A Celebration of the Society for American Archaeology 1935–1985*. Washington, D.C.: Smithsonian Institution Press.

Mendelssohn, K. 1971. A scientist looks at the pyramids. *American Scientist* 59: 210–220.

Meyer, K. E. 1977. *The Plundered Past*. New York: Atheneum.

Michael, H. N. 1985. Correcting radiocarbon dates with tree ring dates at MASCA. *University Museum Newsletter* (University of Pennsylvania) 23 (3): 1–2.

Michel, M. 1981. Preserving America's prehistoric heritage. *Archaeology* 34 (2): 61–63.

Michels, J. W., and I. S. T. Tsong. 1980. Obsidian hydration dating: A coming of age. In *Advances in Archaeological Method and Theory*, vol. 3, ed. M. B. Schiffer, pp. 405–444. New York: Academic Press.

Miller, D. 1980. Archaeology and development. *Current Anthropology* 21: 709–826.

Miller, D., and C. Tilley, eds. 1984. *Ideology, Power and Prehistory*. Cambridge: Cambridge University Press.

Millon, R. 1973. *The Teotihuacan Map: Urbanization at Teotihuacan, Mexico*, vol. 1. Austin: University of Texas Press.

———. 1974. The study of urbanism at Teotihuacan, Mexico. In *Mesoamerican Archaeology: New Approaches*, ed. N. Hammond, pp. 335–362. Austin: University of Texas Press.

———. 1981. Teotihuacan: City, state, and civilization. In *Supplement to the Handbook of Middle American Indians*, vol. 1, ed. J. A. Sabloff, pp. 198–243. Austin: University of Texas Press.

Minchinton, W. 1983. World industrial archaeology: A survey. *World Archaeology* 15: 125–136.

Mithen, S. 1989. Evolutionary theory and post-processual archaeology. *Antiquity* 63: 483–494.

Moberg, C.-A. 1985. Archaeology in the television age. *Archaeology* 38 (4): 80.

Moeller, R. W. 1982. *Practicing Environmental Archaeology*. Washington, Conn.: American Indian Archaeological Institute.

Mohrman, H. 1985. Memoir of an avocational archaeologist. *American Antiquity* 50: 237–240.

Money, J. 1973. The destruction of Acrotiri. *Antiquity* 47: 50–53.

Monks, G. G. 1981. Seasonality studies. In *Advances in Archaeological Method and Theory*, vol. 4, ed. M. B. Schiffer, pp. 177–240. New York: Academic Press.

Mooney, J. [1896] 1965. *The Ghost-Dance Religion and the Sioux Outbreak of 1890*. Reprint abridged, with an introduction by A. F. C. Wallace. Chicago: University of Chicago Press/Phoenix.

Morgan, L. H. 1877. *Ancient Society*. New York: Holt.

Mori, J. L. 1970. Procedures for establishing a faunal collection to aid in archaeological analysis. *American Antiquity* 35: 387–389.

Morley, S. G. 1920. *The Inscriptions at Copán*. Publication 219. Washington, D.C.: Carnegie Institution of Washington.

Moseley, M. E. 1975. Prehistoric principles of labor organization in the Moche valley, Peru. *American Antiquity* 40: 190–196.

———. 1983. Patterns of settlement and preservation in the Virú and Moche valleys. In *Prehistoric Settlement Patterns: Essays in Honor of Gordon R. Willey*, ed. E. Z. Vogt and R. M. Leventhal, pp. 423–442. Albuquerque and Cambridge: University of New Mexico Press, and Harvard University, Peabody Museum of Archaeology and Ethnology.

Moseley, M. E., and C. J. Mackey. 1974. *Twenty-four Architectural Plans of Chan Chan, Peru: Structure and Form at the Capital of Chimor.* Cambridge: Harvard University, Peabody Museum Press.

Moss, E. H. 1983. Some comments on edge damage as a factor in functional analysis of stone artifacts. *Journal of Archaeological Science* 10: 231–242.

Movius, H. L., Jr. 1966. The hearths of the Upper Perigordian and Aurignacian horizons at the Abri Pataud, Les Eyzies (Dordogne), and their possible significance. In Recent Studies in Paleoanthropology, ed. J. D. Clark and F. C. Howell, special issue of *American Anthropologist* 68 (2, pt. 2): 296–325.

———. 1974. The Abri Pataud program of the French Upper Paleolithic in retrospect. In *Archaeological Researches in Retrospect,* ed. G. R. Willey, pp. 87–116. Cambridge, Mass.: Winthrop.

———. 1977. *Excavation of the Abri Pataud, Les Eyzies (Dordogne): Stratigraphy.* Bulletin 31. Cambridge, Mass.: American School of Prehistoric Research.

Mueller, J. W. 1974. *The Uses of Sampling in Archaeological Survey.* Memoir no. 28. Washington, D.C.: Society for American Archaeology.

———, ed. 1975. *Sampling in Archaeology.* Tucson: University of Arizona Press.

———. 1978. A reply to Plog and Thomas. *American Antiquity* 43: 286–287.

Muller, R. A. 1977. Radioisotope dating with a cyclotron. *Science* 196: 489–494.

Müller-Beck, H. 1961. Prehistoric Swiss lake dwellers. *Scientific American* 205 (6): 138–147.

Munsen, P. J. 1969. Comments on Binford's "Smudge pits and hide smoking: The use of analogy in archaeological reasoning." *American Antiquity* 34: 83–85.

Muscarella, O. W. 1984. On publishing unexcavated artifacts. *Journal of Field Archaeology* 11: 61–66.

Myers, J. W., and E. E. Myers. 1985. An aerial atlas of ancient Crete. *Archaeology* 38 (5): 18–25.

Nance, J. D. 1979. Regional subsampling and statistical inference in forested habitats. *American Antiquity* 44: 172–176.

———. 1981. Statistical fact and archaeological faith: Two models in small site sampling. *Journal of Field Archaeology* 8: 151–165.

———. 1983. Regional sampling in archaeological survey: The statistical perspective. In *Advances in Archaeological Method and Theory,* vol. 6, ed. M. B. Schiffer, pp. 289–356. New York: Academic Press.

Nance, J. D., and B. F. Ball. 1986. No surprises? The reliability and validity of test pit sampling. *American Antiquity* 51: 457–483.

———. 1989. A shot in the dark: Shott's comments on Nance and Ball. *American Antiquity* 54: 405–412.

Napton, L. K. 1975. Site mapping and layout. In *Field Methods in Archaeology,* 6th ed., ed. T. R. Hester, R. F. Heizer, and J. A. Graham, pp. 37–63. Palo Alto, Calif.: Mayfield.

Naroll, R. 1962. Floor area and settlement population. *American Antiquity* 27: 587–588.

Nelson, B., ed. 1985. *Decoding Prehistoric Ceramics.* Carbondale: Southern Illinois University Press.

Nelson, D. E., R. G. Korteling, and W. R. Stott. 1977. Carbon-14: Direct detection at natural concentrations. *Science* 198: 507–508.

Nelson, M. C. 1991. The study of technological organization. In *Archaeological Method and Theory,* vol. 3, ed. M. B. Schiffer, pp. 57–100. Tucson: University of Arizona Press.

Nelson, S. M., and A. B. Kehoe, eds. 1990. *Powers of Observation: Alternative Views in Archeology.* Archeological Papers of the American Anthropological Association, No. 2. Washington D.C.: American Anthropological Association.

Netting, R. M. 1977. *Cultural Ecology.* Menlo Park, Calif.: Cummings.

———. 1982. Some home truths on household size and wealth. In Archaeology of the household: Building a prehistory of domestic life, ed. R. R. Wilk and W. L. Rathje, special issue of *American Behavioral Scientist* 25: 641–662.

Newcomer, M. H., and L. H. Keeley. 1979. Testing a method of microwear analysis with experimental flint tools. In *Lithic Use-Wear Analysis,* ed. B. Hayden, pp. 195–205. New York: Academic Press.

Niles, S. A. 1987. *Callachaca: Style and Status in an Inca Community.* Iowa City: University of Iowa Press.

Noël Hume, I. 1969. *Historical Archaeology.* New York: Knopf.

———. 1979. *Martin's Hundred: The Discovery of a Lost Colonial Virginia Settlement.* New York: Knopf.

Numbers, R. L. 1982. Creationism in 20th-century America. *Science* 218: 538–544.

Oakley, K. P. 1948. Fluorine and the relative dating of bones. *Advancement of Science* 4: 336–337.

———. 1956. *Man the Tool-Maker.* 3rd ed. London: British Museum.

———. 1970. Analytical methods of dating bones. In *Science in Archaeology,* 2nd ed., ed. D. Brothwell and E. S. Higgs, pp. 35–45. New York: Praeger.

Odell, G. H., and F. Cowan. 1987. Estimating tillage effects on artifact distributions. *American Antiquity* 52: 456–484.

Olin, J. S., ed. 1982. *Future Directions in Archaeometry: A Round Table*. Washington, D.C.: Smithsonian Institution Press.

Olsen, S. J. 1964. *Mammal Remains from Archaeological Sites*. Papers of the Peabody Museum 56. Cambridge: Harvard University.

———. 1971. *Zooarchaeology: Animal Bones in Archaeology and Their Interpretation*. Modules in Anthropology, no. 2. Reading, Mass.: Addison-Wesley.

———. 1979. Archaeologically, what constitutes an early domestic animal? In *Advances in Archaeological Method and Theory*, vol. 2, ed. M. B. Schiffer, pp. 175–197. New York: Academic Press.

———. 1985. *Origins of the Domestic Dog: The Fossil Record*. Tucson: University of Arizona Press.

Organ, R. M. 1968. *Design for Scientific Conservation of Antiquities*. Washington, D.C.: Smithsonian Institution Press.

Orme, B., ed. 1982. *Problems in Case Studies in Archaeological Dating*. Atlantic Highlands, N.J.: Humanities Press.

Ortner, D. J., and W. G. J. Putschar. 1987. *Identification of Pathological Conditions in Human Skeletal Remains*. Rev. ed. Washington, D.C.: Smithsonian Institution Press.

Orton, C. 1980. *Mathematics in Archaeology*. Cambridge: Cambridge University Press.

O'Shea, J. M. 1984. *Mortuary Variability: An Archaeological Investigation*. Orlando: Academic Press.

Paddayya, K. 1990. *The New Archaeology and Aftermath: A View from Outside the Anglo-American World*. Pune, India: Ravish Publishers.

Palmer, R. 1977. A computer method for transcribing information graphically from oblique aerial photographs to maps. *Journal of Archaeological Science* 4: 283–290.

Parrington, M. 1983. Remote Sensing. *Annual Review of Anthropology* 12: 105–124.

Parsons, E. C. 1939. *Pueblo Indian Religion*. 2 vols. Chicago: University of Chicago Press.

Parsons, J. R. 1972. Archaeological settlement patterns. *Annual Review of Anthropology* 1: 127–150.

———. 1974. The development of a prehistoric complex society: A regional perspective from the Valley of Mexico. *Journal of Field Archaeology* 1: 81–108.

Patrik, L. S. 1985. Is there an archaeological record? In *Advances in Archaeological Method and Theory*, vol. 8, ed. M. B. Schiffer, pp. 27–62. Orlando: Academic Press.

Patterson, T. C. 1963. Contemporaneity and cross-dating in archaeological interpretation. *American Antiquity* 28: 129–137.

———. 1986. The last sixty years: Toward a social history of Americanist archaeology in the United States. *American Anthropologist* 88: 7–26.

Pearce, S. M. 1990. *Archaeological Curatorship*. Washington, D.C.: Smithsonian Institution Press.

Pearsall, D. M. 1989. *Paleoethnobotany: A Handbook of Procedures*. San Diego: Academic Press.

Peebles, C. S., and S. M. Kus. 1977. Some archaeological correlates of ranked societies. *American Antiquity* 42: 421–448.

Perkins, D., Jr., and P. Daly. 1968. A hunters' village in Neolithic Turkey. *Scientific American* 219 (5): 96–106.

Petersen, W. 1975. A demographer's view of prehistoric demography. *Current Anthropology* 16: 227–245.

Petrie, W. M. F. 1901. *Diospolis Parva*. Memoir no. 20. London: Egyptian Exploration Fund.

Pickersgill, B. 1972. Cultivated plants as evidence for cultural contacts. *American Antiquity* 37: 97–104.

Piggott, S. 1959. The discipline of archaeology. In *Approach to Archaeology*, by S. Piggott. Cambridge: Harvard University Press.

———. 1965. Archaeological draughtsmanship: Principles and practice: Part I. Principles and retrospect. *Antiquity* 39: 165–176.

———. 1985. *William Stukeley, an Eighteenth-Century Antiquary*. London: Thames & Hudson.

Pinsky, V., and A. Wylie, eds. 1990. *Critical Traditions in Contemporary Archaeology*. Cambridge: Cambridge University Press.

Piperno, D. R. 1988. *Phytolith Analysis: An Archaeological and Geological Perspective*. San Diego: Academic Press.

Platt, C., ed. 1976. Archaeology and history. *World Archaeology* 7 (whole no. 3).

Plog, F. T. 1974. *The Study of Prehistoric Change*. New York: Academic Press.

———. 1975. Systems theory in archaeological research. *Annual Review of Anthropology* 4: 207–224.

Plog, S. 1976. Relative efficiencies of sampling techniques for archaeological surveys. In *The Early Mesoamerican Village*, ed. K. V. Flannery, pp. 136–158. New York: Academic Press.

———. 1978a. Sampling in archaeological surveys: A critique. *American Antiquity* 43: 280–285.

———. 1978b. Social interaction and stylistic similarity: A reanalysis. In *Advances in Archaeological Method and*

Theory, vol. 1, ed. M. B. Schiffer, pp. 143–182. New York: Academic Press.

———. 1980. *Stylistic Variation in Prehistoric Ceramics.* Cambridge: Cambridge University Press.

———. 1983. Analysis of style in artifacts. *Annual Review of Anthropology* 12: 125–142.

Plog, S., F. Plog, and W. Wait. 1978. Decision making in modern surveys. In *Advances in Archaeological Method and Theory,* vol. 1, ed. M. B. Schiffer, pp. 383–421. New York: Academic Press.

Polanyi, K., C. M. Arensburg, and H. W. Pearson, eds. 1957. *Trade and Market in the Early Empires.* Glencoe, Ill.: Free Press.

Pollock, S. 1983. Style and information: An analysis of Susiana ceramics. *Journal of Anthropological Archaeology* 2: 354–390.

Poole, L., and G. J. Poole. 1966. *One Passion, Two Loves: The Story of Heinrich and Sophia Schliemann, Discoverers of Troy.* New York: Crowell.

Potts, R. 1984. Home bases and early hominids. *American Scientist* 72: 338–347.

———. 1986. Temporal span of bone accumulations at Olduvai Gorge and implications for early hominid foraging behavior. *Paleobiology* 12: 25–31.

Potts, R., and P. Shipman. 1981. Cutmarks made by stone tools on bones from Olduvai Gorge, Tanzania. *Nature* 291: 577–580.

Powell, S., P. P. Andrews, D. L. Nichols, and F. E. Smiley. 1983. Fifteen years on the rock: Archaeological research, administration, and compliance on Black Mesa, Arizona. *American Antiquity* 48: 228–252.

Preucel, R. W., ed. 1991. *Processual and Postprocessual Archaeologies: Multiple Ways of Knowing the Past.* Center for Archaeological Investigations, Occasional Papers 16. Carbondale: Southern Illinois University.

Price, T. D., ed. 1989. *The Chemistry of Prehistoric Human Bone.* Cambridge: Cambridge University Press.

Price, T. D., M. J. Schoeninger, and G. J. Armelagos. 1985. Bone chemistry and past behavior: An overview. *Journal of Human Evolution* 14: 419–447.

Protzen, J.-P. 1986. Inca stonemasonry. *Scientific American* 254 (2): 94–105.

Pugh, J. C. 1975. *Surveying for Field Scientists.* Pittsburgh: University of Pittsburgh Press.

Pulak, C., and D. A. Frey. 1985. The search for a Bronze Age shipwreck. *Archaeology* 38 (4): 18–24.

Puleston, D. E. 1971. An experimental approach to the function of Classic Maya chultuns. *American Antiquity* 36: 322–335.

———. 1974. Intersite areas in the vicinity of Tikal and Uaxactún. In *Mesoamerican Archaeology: New Approaches,* ed. N. Hammond, pp. 303–311. Austin: University of Texas Press.

———. 1979. An epistemological pathology and the collapse, or why the Maya kept the Short Count. In *Maya Archaeology and Ethnohistory,* ed. N. Hammond and G. R. Willey, pp. 63–71. Austin: University of Texas Press.

Purdy, B. A., ed. 1990. *Wet Site Archaeology.* Boca Raton: CRC Press.

Quick, P. M. 1986. *Proceedings: Conference on Reburial Issues.* Washington, D.C.: Society for American Archaeology.

Quimby, G. I. 1979. A brief history of WPA archaeology. In *The Uses of Anthropology,* ed. W. Goldschmidt, pp. 110–123. Washington, D.C.: American Anthropological Association.

Raab, L. M., and A. C. Goodyear. 1984. Middle-range theory in archaeology: A critical review of origins and applications. *American Antiquity* 49: 255–268.

Raab, L. M., and T. C. Klinger. 1977. A critical appraisal of "significance" in contract archaeology. *American Antiquity* 42: 629–634.

Ragir, S. 1975. A review of techniques for archaeological sampling. In *Field Methods in Archaeology,* 6th ed., ed. T. R. Hester, R. F. Heizer, and J. A. Graham, pp. 283–310. Palo Alto, Calif.: Mayfield.

Rahtz, P. A. 1974. *RESCUE Archaeology.* Harmondsworth, England: Penguin.

Ralph, E. K., and H. N. Michael. 1974. Twenty-five years of radiocarbon dating. *American Scientist* 62: 553–560.

Ralph, E. K., H. N. Michael, and M. C. Han. 1973. Radiocarbon dates and reality. *MASCA Newsletter* 9 (whole no. 1).

Rands, R. L., and R. L. Bishop. 1980. Resource procurement zones and patterns of ceramic exchange in the Palenque region, Mexico. In *Models and Methods in Regional Exchange,* ed. R. E. Fry, pp. 19–46. SAA Paper no. 1. Washington, D.C.: Society for American Archaeology.

Rapoport, Amos. 1982. *The Meaning of the Built Environment: A Nonverbal Communication Approach.* Beverly Hills: Sage.

Rapoport, Anatol. 1968. Foreword. In *Modern Systems Research for the Behavioral Scientist,* ed. W. Buckley, pp. xiii–xxii. Chicago: Aldine.

Rapp, G., Jr. 1975. The archaeological field staff: The geologist. *Journal of Field Archaeology* 2: 229–237.

Rapp, G., Jr., and J. A. Gifford, eds. 1985. *Archaeological Geology*. New Haven: Yale University Press.

Rappaport, R. A. 1971a. Ritual, sanctity, and cybernetics. *American Anthropologist* 73: 59–76.

———. 1971b. The sacred in human evolution. *Annual Review of Ecology and Systematics* 2: 23–44.

Rathje, W. L. 1978. The ancient astronaut myth. *Archaeology* 31: 4–7.

Read, D. W. 1986. Sampling procedures for regional surveys: A problem of representativeness and effectiveness. *Journal of Field Archaeology* 13: 479–491.

Read-Martin, C. E., and D. W. Read. 1975. Australopithecine scavenging and human evolution: An approach from faunal analysis. *Current Anthropology* 16: 359–368.

Redman, C. L. 1973. Multistage fieldwork and analytical techniques. *American Antiquity* 38: 61–79.

———. 1974. *Archaeological Sampling Strategies*. Modules in Anthropology, no. 55. Reading, Mass.: Addison-Wesley.

———. 1982. Archaeological survey and the study of Mesopotamian urban systems. *Journal of Field Archaeology* 9: 375–382.

———. 1987. Surface collection, sampling, and research design: A retrospective. *American Antiquity* 52: 249–265.

Redman, C. L., and P. J. Watson. 1970. Systemic, intensive surface collection. *American Antiquity* 35: 279–291.

Redman, C. L., M. J. Berman, E. V. Curtin, W. T. Langhorne, Jr., N. M. Versaggi, and J. C. Wanser, eds. 1978. *Social Archeology: Beyond Subsistence and Dating*. New York: Academic Press.

Reed, C. A., ed. 1977. *Origins of Agriculture*. The Hague: Mouton.

Reed, N. A., J. W. Bennett, and J. W. Porter. 1968. Solid core drilling of Monks Mound: Technique and findings. *American Antiquity* 33: 137–148.

Renfrew, C. 1969. Trade and culture process in European prehistory. *Current Anthropology* 10: 151–169.

———. 1971. Carbon 14 and the prehistory of Europe. *Scientific American* 225 (4): 63–72.

———. 1973a. *Before Civilization: The Radiocarbon Revolution and Prehistoric Europe*. New York: Knopf.

———. 1973b. Monuments, mobilization and social organization in Neolithic Wessex. In *The Explanation of Culture Change: Models in Prehistory*, ed. C. Renfrew, pp. 539–558. Pittsburgh: University of Pittsburgh Press.

———. 1975. Trade as action at a distance: Questions of integration and communication. In *Ancient Civilization and Trade*, ed. J. A. Sabloff and C. C. Lamberg-Karlovsky, pp. 3–59. School of American Research Advanced Seminar Series. Albuquerque: University of New Mexico Press.

———. 1980. The great tradition versus the great divide: Archaeology as anthropology? *American Journal of Archaeology* 84: 287–298.

———. 1983a. Divided we stand: Aspects of archaeology and information. *American Antiquity* 48: 3–16.

———. 1983b. The social archaeology of megalithic monuments. *Scientific American* 249 (5): 152–163.

———. 1984. Social archaeology, societal change and generalisation. In *Approaches to Social Archaeology*, by C. Renfrew, pp. 3–21. Cambridge: Harvard University Press.

Renfrew, C., M. J. Rowlands, and B. A. Segraves, eds. 1982. *Theory and Explanation in Archaeology: The Southampton Conference*. New York: Academic Press.

Renfrew, J. M. 1973. *Palaeoethnobotany*. New York: Columbia University Press.

Rice, D. S. 1976. Middle Preclassic Maya settlement in the central Maya lowlands. *Journal of Field Archaeology* 3: 425–445.

Rice, P. M. 1977. Whiteware pottery production in the Valley of Guatemala: Specialization and resource utilization. *Journal of Field Archaeology* 4: 221–233.

———. 1987. *Pottery Analysis: A Sourcebook*. Chicago: University of Chicago Press.

Richards, J. D., and N. S. Ryan. 1985. *Data Processing in Archaeology*. Cambridge: Cambridge University Press.

Rick, J. W. 1976. Downslope movement and archaeological intrasite spatial analysis. *American Antiquity* 41: 133–144.

Roberts, F. H. H. [1929] 1979. *Shabik'eschee Village: A Late Basket Maker Site in the Chaco Canyon, New Mexico*. Bureau of American Ethnology, Bulletin 92. Washington, D.C.: Smithsonian Institution. Reprints in Anthropology, vol. 17. Lincoln, Neb.: J&L Reprint Co.

Robertshaw, P. T., and D. P. Collett. 1983. The identification of pastoral peoples in the archaeological record: An example from East Africa. *World Archaeology* 15: 67–78.

Robertson, M. G. 1972. Monument thievery in Mesoamerica. *American Antiquity* 37: 147–155.

Robinson, W. S. 1951. A method for chronologically ordering archaeological deposits. *American Antiquity* 16: 293–301.

Roe, D., ed. 1971. Subsistence. *World Archaeology* 2 (whole no. 3).

———, ed. 1985. Studying stones: *World Archaeology* 17 (whole no. 1).

Rogers, J., and T. Waldron. 1989. Infections in paleopathology: The basis of classification according to most probable cause. *Journal of Archaeological Science* 16: 611–625.

Roosevelt, A. C. 1980. *Parmana: Prehistoric Maize and Manioc Subsistence along the Amazon and Orinoco.* New York: Academic Press.

———. 1989. Lost civilizations of the lower Amazon. *Natural History* 98 (2): 74–83.

———. 1991. *Mound-builders of the Amazon: Geophysical Archaeology in the Marajoara Chiefdom.* San Diego: Academic Press.

Roper, D. C. 1976. Lateral displacement of artifacts due to plowing. *American Antiquity* 41: 372–375.

———. 1979. The method and theory of site catchment analysis: A review. In *Advances in Archaeological Method and Theory,* vol. 2, ed. M. B. Schiffer, pp. 119–140. New York: Academic Press.

Rothenberg, B., ed. 1990. *The Ancient Metallurgy of Copper.* London: Institute for Archaeo-Metallurgical Studies.

Rothschild, N. A. 1979. Mortuary behavior and social organization at Indian Knoll and Dickson Mounds. *American Antiquity* 44: 658–675.

Rouse, I. 1953. The strategy of culture history. In *Anthropology Today,* ed. A. L. Kroeber, pp. 57–76. Chicago: University of Chicago Press.

———. 1960. The classification of artifacts in archaeology. *American Antiquity* 25: 313–323.

———. 1986. *Migrations in Prehistory.* New Haven: Yale University Press.

Rovner, I. 1983. Plant opal phytolith analysis: Major advances in archaeobotanical research. In *Advances in Archaeological Method and Theory,* vol. 6, ed. M. B. Schiffer, pp. 225–266. New York: Academic Press.

Rowe, J. H. 1954. Max Uhle, 1856–1944: A memoir of the father of Peruvian archaeology. *University of California Publications in Archaeology and Ethnology* 46: 1–134.

———. 1961a. Archaeology as a career. *Archaeology* 14: 45–55.

———. 1961b. Stratigraphy and seriation. *American Antiquity* 26: 324–330.

———. 1965. The Renaissance foundations of anthropology. *American Anthropologist* 67: 1–20.

———. 1966. Diffusionism and archaeology. *American Antiquity* 31: 334–338.

Rowell, R. M., and J. Barbour, eds. 1990. *Archaeological Wood.* Advances in Chemistry Series No. 225. Washington, D.C.: American Chemical Society.

Rowlands, M. J. 1971. The archaeological interpretation of prehistoric metalworking. *World Archaeology* 3: 210–224.

Rowlett, R. M. 1970. A random number generator for field use. *American Antiquity* 35: 491.

———. 1982. 1000 years of American archaeology. *American Antiquity* 47: 652–654.

Ryder, M. L. 1983. *Sheep and Man.* London: Duckworth.

———. 1984. Wools from textiles in the *Mary Rose,* a sixteenth-century English warship. *Journal of Archaeological Science* 11: 337–343.

Rye, O. S. 1981. *Pottery Technology: Principles and Reconstruction.* Washington, D.C.: Taraxacum Inc.

Sabloff, J. A. 1990. *The New Archaeology and the Ancient Maya.* Scientific American Library 30. New York: Freeman.

Sabloff, J. A., and E. W. Andrews V, eds. 1986. *Late Lowland Maya Civilization.* School of American Research Advanced Seminar Series. Albuquerque: University of New Mexico Press.

Sabloff, J. A., and C. C. Lamberg-Karlovsky, eds. 1975. *Ancient Civilization and Trade.* School of American Research Advanced Seminar Series. Albuquerque: University of New Mexico Press.

———. 1982. Introduction. In *Archaeology: Myth and Reality: Readings from Scientific American,* ed. J. A. Sabloff, pp. 1–26. San Francisco: Freeman.

Sabloff, J. A., and W. L. Rathje. 1973. Ancient Maya commercial systems: A research design for the island of Cozumel, Mexico. *World Archaeology* 5: 221–231.

Sabloff, J. A., and R. E. Smith. 1969. The importance of both analytic and taxonomic classification in the type-variety system. *American Antiquity* 34: 278–285.

Sackett, J. R. 1966. Quantitative analysis of Upper Paleolithic stone tools. In Recent Studies in Paleoanthropology, ed. J. D. Clark and F. C. Howell, special issue of *American Anthropologist* 68 (2, pt. 2): 356–394.

———. 1977. The meaning of style in archaeology: A general model. *American Antiquity* 42: 369–380.

———. 1982. Approaches to style in lithic technology. *Journal of Anthropological Archaeology* 1: 59–112.

Sahlins, M. D., and E. R. Service, eds. 1960. *Evolution and Culture.* Ann Arbor: University of Michigan Press.

Salmon, M. 1982. *Philosophy and Archaeology.* New York: Academic Press.

Salwen, B. 1962. Sea levels and archaeology in the Long Island Sound area. *American Antiquity* 28: 46–55.

Sanders, W. T., ed. 1986. *Excavaciones en el Area Urbana de Copán*, vol. I. Tegucigalpa: Secretaria de la Cultura y Turismo, Instituto Hondureño de Antropología e Historia.

———, ed. 1990. *Excavaciones en el Area Urbana de Copán*, vol. II. Tegucigalpa: Secretaria de la Cultura y Turismo, Instituto Hondureño de Antropología e Historia.

Sanders, W. T., J. R. Parsons, and R. S. Santley. 1979. *The Basin of Mexico*. New York: Academic Press.

Sanders, W. T., and B. J. Price. 1968. *Mesoamerica: The Evolution of a Civilization*. New York: Random House.

Saraydar, S., and I. Shimada. 1973. Experimental archaeology: A new outlook. *American Antiquity* 38: 344–350.

Satterthwaite, L., Jr., and E. K. Ralph. 1960. New radiocarbon dates and the Maya correlation problem. *American Antiquity* 26: 165–184.

Saxe, A. A. 1971. Social dimensions of mortuary practices in a Mesolithic population from Wadi Halfa, Sudan. In *Approaches to the Social Dimensions of Mortuary Practices*, ed. J. A. Brown, pp. 39–57. Memoir no. 25. Washington, D.C.: Society for American Archaeology.

Sayre, E.V., P. B. Vandiver, J. Druzik, and C. Stevenson, eds. 1988. *Materials Issues in Art and Archaeology I*. MRS Symposium Proceedings Volume 123. Pittsburgh: Materials Research Society.

Scarre, C. 1984. Archaeology and sea-level in west-central France. *World Archaeology* 16: 98–107.

Schaafsma, P. 1980. *Indian Rock Art of the Southwest*. Albuquerque: University of New Mexico Press.

Schacht, R. M. 1981. Estimating past population trends. *Annual Review of Anthropology* 10: 119–140.

Schele, L., and D. A. Freidel. 1990. *A Forest of Kings: The Untold Story of the Ancient Maya*. New York: William Morrow.

Schele, L., and M. E. Miller. 1986. *The Blood of Kings: Dynasty and Ritual in Maya Art*. Fort Worth: Kimbell Art Museum.

Schiffer, M. B. 1972. Archaeological context and systemic context. *American Antiquity* 37: 156–165.

———. 1976. *Behavioral Archeology*. New York: Academic Press.

———. 1978. Taking the pulse of method and theory in American archaeology. *American Antiquity* 43: 153–158.

———. 1985. Is there a "Pompeii premise" in archaeology? *Journal of Anthropological Research* 41: 18–41.

———. 1987. *Formation Processes of the Archaeological Record*. Albuquerque: University of New Mexico Press.

———. 1988. The structure of archaeological theory. *American Antiquity* 53: 461–485.

Schiffer, M. B., and G. J. Gumerman, eds. 1977. *Conservation Archaeology: A Guide for Cultural Resource Management Studies*. New York: Academic Press.

Schiffer, M. B., and J. H. House. 1977. Cultural resource management and archaeological research: The Cache Project. *Current Anthropology* 18: 43–68.

Schiffer, M. B., A. P. Sullivan, and T. C. Klinger. 1978. The design of archaeological surveys. *World Archaeology* 10: 1–28.

Schliemann, H. [1881] 1968. *Ilios, the City and Country of the Trojans*. Reissue. New York: Benjamin Blom.

Schmandt-Besserat, D. 1978. The earliest precursors of writing. *Scientific American* 238 (6): 50–59.

———. 1992. *Before Writing*. 2 vols. Austin: University of Texas Press.

Schmidt, P. R., assisted by D. H. Avery. 1983. More evidence for an advanced prehistoric iron technology in Africa. *Journal of Field Archaeology* 10: 421–434.

Schorr, T. S. 1974. Aerial ethnography in regional studies: A reconnaissance of adaptive change in the Cauca Valley of Colombia. In *Aerial Photography in Anthropological Field Research*, ed. E. Z. Vogt, pp. 40–53. Cambridge: Harvard University Press.

Schortman, E. M. 1986. Maya/non-Maya interaction along the Late Classic southeast Maya periphery: The view from the lower Motagua valley. In *The Southeast Maya Periphery*, ed. P. A. Urban and E. M. Schortman, pp. 114–137. Austin: University of Texas Press.

———. 1989. Interregional interaction in prehistory: The need for a new perspective. *American Antiquity* 54: 52–65.

Schrire, C., ed. 1984. *Past and Present in Hunter-Gatherer Studies*. Orlando: Academic Press.

Schrire, C., J. Deetz, D. Lubinsky, and C. Poggenpoel. 1990. The chronology of Oudepost I, Cape, as inferred from an analysis of clay pipes. *Journal of Archaeological Science* 17: 269–300.

Schuyler, R. L. 1971. The history of American archaeology: An examination of procedure. *American Antiquity* 36: 383–409.

———. 1976. Images of America: The contribution of historical archaeology to the national identity. *Southwestern Lore* 42 (4): 27–39.

———, ed. 1978. *Historical Archaeology: A Guide to Substantive and Theoretical Contributions*. Farmingdale, N.Y.: Baywood.

Schwarcz, H. P., W. M. Buhay, R. Grün, H. Valladas, E. Tchernov, O. Bar-Yosef, and B. Vandermeersch. 1989. ESR dating of the Neanderthal site, Kebara Cave, Israel. *Journal of Archaeological Science* 16: 653–659.

Scollar, I., A. Tabbagh, A. Hesse, and I. Herzog. 1990. *Image Processing in Archaeology.* Cambridge: Cambridge University Press.

Sealy, J. C., and N. van der Merwe. 1986. Isotope assessment and the seasonal-mobility hypothesis in the southwestern cape of South Africa. *Current Anthropology* 27: 135–150.

Sears, W. H. 1961. The study of social and religious systems in North American archaeology. *Current Anthropology* 2: 223–246.

Sease, C. 1987. *Conservation for the Field Archaeologist.* Archaeological Research Tools 4. Los Angeles: UCLA Institute of Archaeology.

Semenov, S. A. 1964. *Prehistoric Technology.* New York: Barnes & Noble.

Service, E. R. 1962. *Primitive Social Organization: An Evolutionary Perspective.* New York: Random House.

———. 1975. *Origins of the State and Civilization: The Process of Cultural Evolution.* New York: Norton.

Sever, T., and J. Wiseman. 1985. *Remote Sensing and Archaeology: Potential for the Future.* National Space Technology Laboratories, Miss.: National Aeronautics and Space Administration, Earth Resources Laboratory.

Shackleton, J., T. H. van Andel, and C. N. Runnels. 1984. Coastal paleogeography of the central and western Mediterranean during the last 125,000 years and its archaeological implications. *Journal of Field Archaeology* 11: 307–314.

Shackley, M. L. 1975. *Archaeological Sediments.* New York: Wiley/Halsted.

———. 1981. *Environmental Archaeology.* London: Allen & Unwin.

———. 1985. *Using Environmental Archaeology.* London: Batsford.

Shafer, H. J., and R. G. Holloway. 1979. Organic residue analysis in determining stone tool function. In *Lithic Use-Wear Analysis,* ed. B. Hayden, pp. 385–399. New York: Academic Press.

Shanks, M., and C. Tilley. 1987. *Re-Constructing Archaeology.* Cambridge: Cambridge University Press.

Shapiro, G. 1984. A soil resistivity survey of 15th-century Puerto Real, Haiti. *Journal of Field Archaeology* 11: 101–110.

Sharer, R. J. 1978. The surface surveys. In *The Prehistory of Chalchuapa, El Salvador,* vol. 1, pt. 2, ed. R. J. Sharer,

pp. 15–26. Philadelphia: University of Pennsylvania Press.

———. 1990. *Quiriguá: A Classic Maya Center and Its Sculpture.* Durham, N.C.: Carolina Academic Press.

Sheets, P. D. 1971. An ancient natural disaster. *Expedition* 14 (1): 24–31.

———. 1973. The pillage of prehistory. *American Antiquity* 38: 317–320.

———. 1975. Behavioral analysis and the structure of a prehistoric industry. *Current Anthropology* 16: 369–391.

Shelton, D. 1986. Law and looting. *Archaeology* 39 (4): 80.

Shennan, S. J., ed. 1988. *Quantifying Archaeology.* San Diego: Academic Press.

———. 1989. *Archaeological Approaches to Cultural Identity.* London: Unwin Hyman.

Shepard, A. O. 1971. *Ceramics for the Archaeologist.* Publication 609. Washington, D.C.: Carnegie Institution.

Shimada, I. 1978. Economy of a prehistoric urban context: Commodity and labor flow at Moche V Pampa Grande, Peru. *American Antiquity* 43: 569–592.

———. 1981. The Batan Grande-La Leche archaeological project: The first two seasons. *Journal of Field Archaeology* 8: 405–446.

Shimada, I., S. Epstein, and A. K. Craig. 1982. Batan Grande: A prehistoric metallurgical center in Peru. *Science* 216: 952–959.

Shimada, I., and J. F. Merkel. 1991. Copper-alloy metallurgy in ancient Peru. *Scientific American* 265 (1): 80–86.

Shipman, P. 1981. *Life History of a Fossil: An Introduction to Taphonomy and Paleoecology.* Cambridge: Harvard University Press.

———. 1986. Scavenging or hunting in early hominids: Theoretical framework and tests. *American Anthropologist* 88: 27–43.

Shipman, P., and J. Rose. 1983. Early hominid hunting, butchering, and carcass-producing behaviors: Approaches to the fossil record. *Journal of Anthropological Archaeology* 2: 57–98.

Shipman, P., A. Walker, and D. Bichell. 1985. *The Human Skeleton.* Cambridge: Harvard University Press.

Shook, E. M., and W. R. Coe. 1961. *Tikal: Numeration, Terminology and Objectives.* Tikal Reports, no. 5. Philadelphia: University Museum, University of Pennsylvania.

Shook, E. M., and A. V. Kidder. 1952. Mound E-III-3, Kaminaljuyú, Guatemala, *Contributions to American*

Anthropology and History 11 (53): 33–127. Publication 596. Washington, D.C.: Carnegie Institution.

Shott, M. 1985. Shovel-test sampling as a site discovery technique: A case study from Michigan. *Journal of Field Archaeology* 12: 457–468.

———. 1989a. Shovel-test sampling in archaeological survey: Comments on Nance and Ball, and Lightfoot. *American Antiquity* 54: 396–404.

———. 1989b. On tool-class use lives and the formation of archaeological assemblages. *American Antiquity* 54: 9–30.

Sieveking, A. 1979. *The Cave Artists*. London: Thames & Hudson.

Sillen, A., J. C. Sealy, and N. J. van der Merwe. 1989. Chemistry and paleodietary research: No more easy answers. *American Antiquity* 54: 504–512.

Sjoberg, A. 1976. Phosphate analysis of anthropic soils. *Journal of Field Archaeology* 3: 447–454.

Skowronek, R. K. 1985. Sport divers and archaeology: The case of the Legare Anchorage ship site. *Archaeology* 38 (3): 22–27.

Smith, A. L. 1973. *Uaxactún: A Pioneering Excavation in Guatemala*. Modules in Anthropology, no. 40. Reading, Mass.: Addison-Wesley.

Smith, B. D. 1974. Middle Mississippi exploitation of animal populations: A predictive model. *American Antiquity* 39: 274–291.

———. 1983. Selectivity determinations: A continuum from conservative to confident. In *Animals and Archaeology: 1. Hunters and Their Prey,* ed. J. Clutton-Brock and C. Grigson, pp. 205–304. British Archaeological Reports International Series 163. Oxford: BAR.

———. 1987. The independent domestication of the indigenous seed-bearing plants in Eastern North America. In *Emergent Horticultural Economies of the Eastern Woodlands,* ed. W. Keegan, pp. 3–47. Center for Archaeological Investigations, Occasional Paper No. 7. Carbondale: Southern Illinois University.

Smith, C. S. 1973. Bronze technology in the East: A metallurgical study of early Thai bronzes, with some speculation on the cultural transmission of technology. In *Changing Perspectives in the History of Science,* ed. M. Teich and R. Young, pp. 21–32. London: Heinemann.

Smith, G. E. 1928. *In the Beginning: The Origin of Civilization*. New York: Morrow.

Smith, G. S., and J. E. Ehrenhard, eds. 1991. *Protecting the Past*. Boca Raton: CRC Press.

Smith, N. 1978. Roman hydraulic technology. *Scientific American* 238 (5): 154–161.

Smith, P., and L. K. Horwitz. 1984. Radiographic evidence for changing patterns of animal exploitation in the Southern Levant. *Journal of Archaeological Science* 11: 467–475.

Smith, P. E. L. 1976. *Food Production and Its Consequences*. Menlo Park, Calif.: Cummings.

Smith, R. E., G. R. Willey, and J. C. Gifford. 1960. The type-variety concept as a basis for the analysis of Maya pottery. *American Antiquity* 25: 330–340.

Smith, R. H. 1974. Ethics in field archaeology. *Journal of Field Archaeology* 1: 375–383.

Society for American Archaeology. 1986. Statement concerning the treatment of human remains. *Bulletin of the Society for American Archaeology* 4 (3): 7–8.

Society of Professional Archeologists. 1978. Qualifications for recognition as a professional archeologist. *SOPADOPA: Newsletter of the Society of Professional Archeologists* 2 (whole no. 3).

Solecki, R. S. 1975. Shanidar IV, a Neanderthal flower burial in northern Iraq. *Science* 190: 880–881.

South, S. A. 1977. *Method and Theory in Historical Archeology*. New York: Academic Press.

Spaulding, A. C. 1953. Statistical techniques for the discovery of artifact types. *American Antiquity* 18: 305–313.

———. 1960. The dimensions of archaeology. In *Essays in the Science of Culture in Honor of Leslie A. White,* ed. G. E. Dole and R. L. Carneiro, pp. 437–456. New York: Crowell.

———. 1968. Explanation in archeology. In *New Perspectives in Archeology,* ed. S. R. Binford and L. R. Binford, pp. 33–39. Chicago: Aldine.

———. 1977. On growth and form in archaeology. *Journal of Anthropological Research* 33: 1–15.

Spector, J. D. 1991. What this awl means: Toward a feminist archaeology. In *Engendering Archaeology: Women and Prehistory,* ed. J. M. Gero and M. W. Conkey, pp. 388–406. Oxford: Basil Blackwell.

Spector, J. D., and M. K. Whelan. 1989. Incorporating gender into archaeology courses. In *Gender and Anthropology: Critical Reviews for Research and Teaching,* ed. S. Morgen, pp. 65–94. Washington, D.C.: American Anthropological Association.

Spencer, H. 1876. *Principles of Sociology*. New York: Appleton.

Speser, P., K. Reinburg, and A. Porsche. 1986. *The Procurement of Archaeology*. Archaeology and the Federal Government Publication Series. Washington, D.C.: Foresight Science and Technology.

Speser, P., K. Reinburg, A. Porsche, S. Arter, and P. Bienenfeld. 1986. *The Politics of Archaeology.* Archaeology and the Federal Government Publication Series. Washington, D.C.: Foresight Science and Technology.

Squier, E. G., and E. H. Davis. 1848. *Ancient Monuments of the Mississippi Valley.* Smithsonian Contributions to Knowledge 1. Washington, D.C.: Smithsonian Institution.

Stahle, D. W., and D. Wolfman. 1985. The potential for archaeological tree-ring dating in eastern North America. In *Advances in Archaeological Method and Theory,* vol. 8, ed. M. B. Schiffer, pp. 279–302. Orlando: Academic Press.

Stallings, W. S., Jr. 1949. *Dating Prehistoric Ruins by Tree-Rings.* Rev. ed. Tucson: University of Arizona Laboratory of Tree-Ring Research.

Stanford, D., R. Bonnichsen, and R. E. Morlan. 1981. The Ginsberg experiment: Modern and prehistoric evidence of a bone-flaking technology. *Science* 212: 438–440.

Stanislawski, M. B. 1973. Review of *Archeology as Anthropology: A Case Study,* by W. A. Longacre. *American Antiquity* 38: 117–121.

Stark, B. L. 1986. Origins of food production in the New World. In *American Archaeology Past and Future: A Celebration of the Society for American Archaeology 1935–1985,* ed. D. J. Meltzer, D. D. Fowler, and J. A. Sabloff, pp. 277–321. Washington, D.C.: Smithsonian Institution Press.

Staski, E. 1982. Advances in urban archaeology. In *Advances in Archaeological Method and Theory,* vol. 5, ed. M. B. Schiffer, pp. 97–149. New York: Academic Press.

Steen-McIntyre, V. 1985. Tephrochronology and its application to archaeology. In *Archaeological Geology,* ed. G. Rapp, Jr., and J. A. Gifford, pp. 265–302. New Haven: Yale University Press.

Stein, J. K. 1983. Earthworm activity: A source of potential disturbance of archaeological sediments. *American Antiquity* 48: 277–289.

———. 1987. Deposits for archaeologists. In *Advances in Archaeological Method and Theory*, vol. 11, ed. M. B. Schiffer, pp. 337–395. New York: Academic Press.

Stein, J. K., and W. R. Farrand, eds. 1985. *Archaeological Sediments in Context.* Orono, Maine: Center for the Study of Early Man.

Stephen, D. V. M., and D. B. Craig. 1984. Recovering the past bit by bit with microcomputers. *Archaeology* 37 (4): 20–26.

Stephens, J. L. [1841] 1969. *Incidents of Travel in Central America, Chiapas, and Yucatan.* 2 vols. New York: Harper. Reprint. New York: Dover.

———. [1843] 1963. *Incidents of Travel in Yucatan.* 2 vols. New York: Harper. Reprint. New York: Dover.

Steponaitis, V. P., and J. P. Brain. 1976. A portable differential proton magnetometer. *Journal of Field Archaeology* 3: 455–463.

Sterud, E. L. 1978. Changing aims of Americanist archaeology: A citations analysis of *American Antiquity*—1946–1975. *American Antiquity* 43: 294–302.

Sterud, E. L., and P. P. Pratt. 1975. Archaeological intrasite recording with photography. *Journal of Field Archaeology* 2: 151–167.

Steward, J. H. 1938. *Basin-Plateau Aboriginal Sociopolitical Groups.* Bureau of American Ethnology, Bulletin 120. Washington, D.C.: Smithsonian Institution.

———. 1942. The direct historical approach to archaeology. *American Antiquity* 7: 337–343.

———. 1955. *Theory of Culture Change.* Urbana: University of Illinois Press.

Steward, J. H., and F. M. Setzler. 1938. Function and configuration in archaeology. *American Antiquity* 1: 4–10.

Stiles, D. 1977. Ethnoarchaeology: A discussion of methods and applications. *Man* 12: 87–103.

Stoltman, J. B. 1989. A quantitative approach to the petrographic analysis of ceramic thin-sections. *American Antiquity* 54: 147–160.

Stone, P., and R. MacKenzie, eds. 1989. *The Excluded Past: Archaeology in Education.* London: Unwin Hyman.

Story, R. 1976. *The Space-Gods Revealed.* New York: Harper & Row.

Stover, L. E., and H. Harrison. 1970. *Apeman, Spaceman: Anthropological Science Fiction.* New York: Berkley.

Struever, S. 1968. Flotation techniques for the recovery of small-scale archaeological remains. *American Antiquity* 33: 353–362.

———. 1971. Comments on archaeological data requirements and research design. *American Antiquity* 36: 9–19.

Struever, S., and J. Carlson. 1977. Koster site: The new archaeology in action. *Archaeology* 30: 93–101.

Stuart, G. E. 1976. *Your Career in Archaeology.* Washington, D.C.: Society for American Archaeology.

Stuiver, M. 1982. A high-precision calibration of the A.D. radiocarbon time scale. *Radiocarbon* 24: 1–26.

Sullivan, G. 1980. *Discover Archaeology: An Introduction to the Tools and Techniques of Archaeological Fieldwork.* New York: Penguin.

Swanson, E., ed. 1975. *Lithic Technology: Making and Using Stone Tools.* Chicago: Aldine.

Swart, P., and B. D. Till. 1984. Bronze carriages from the tomb of China's first emperor. *Archaeology* 37 (6): 18–25.

Tainter, J. A. 1978. Mortuary practices and the study of prehistoric social systems. In *Advances in Archaeological Method and Theory,* vol. 1, ed. M. B. Schiffer, pp. 105–141. New York: Academic Press.

Talmadge, V. A. 1982. The violation of sepulture: Is it legal to excavate human burials? *Archaeology* 35 (6): 44–49.

Tarling, D. H. 1985. Archaeomagnetism. In *Archaeological Geology,* ed. G. Rapp, Jr., and J. A. Gifford, pp. 237–263. New Haven: Yale University Press.

Taylor, R. E. 1987. *Radiocarbon Dating.* San Diego: Academic Press.

Taylor, R. E., and I. Longworth, eds. 1975. Dating: New methods and new results. *World Archaeology* 7 (whole no. 2).

Taylor, R. E., and C. W. Meighan, eds. 1978. *Chronologies in New World Archaeology.* New York: Academic Press.

Taylor, R. E., P. J. Slota, Jr., W. Henning, W. Kutschera, and M. Paul. 1989. Radiocalcium dating: Potential applications in archaeology and paleoanthropology. In *Archaeological Chemistry IV*, ed. R. O. Allen, pp. 321–335. Advances in Chemistry Series No. 220. Washington, D.C.: American Chemical Society.

Taylor, W. W. [1948] 1964 and 1967. *A Study of Archeology.* American Anthropological Association, Memoir 69. Reprint. Carbondale: Southern Illinois University Press.

———. 1972. Old wine and new skins: A contemporary parable. In *Contemporary Archaeology,* ed. M. P. Leone, pp. 28–33. Carbondale: Southern Illinois University Press.

Thom, A. 1971. *Megalithic Lunar Observatories.* Oxford: Clarendon Press.

Thomas, C. 1894. *Report of the Mound Explorations of the Bureau of Ethnology.* Washington, D.C.: Smithsonian Institution.

Thomas, D. H. 1969. Regional sampling in archaeology: A pilot Great Basin research design. *UCLA Archaeological Survey Annual Report* 11: 87–100.

———. 1973. An empirical test for Steward's model of Great Basin settlement patterns. *American Antiquity* 38: 155–176.

———. 1975. Non-site sampling: Up the creek without a site? In *Sampling in Archaeology,* ed. James Mueller, pp. 61–81. Tucson: University of Arizona Press.

———. 1978. The awful truth about statistics in archaeology. *American Antiquity* 43: 231–244.

———. 1983. *The Archaeology of Monitor Valley: I. Epistemology.* Anthropological Papers vol. 58, no. 1. New York: American Museum of Natural History.

———. 1986a. Contemporary hunter-gatherer archaeology in America. In *American Archaeology Past and Future: A Celebration of the Society for American Archaeology 1935–1985,* ed. D. J. Meltzer, D. D. Fowler, and J. A. Sabloff, pp. 237–276. Washington, D.C.: Smithsonian Institution Press.

———. 1986b. *Refiguring Anthropology: First Principles of Probability and Statistics.* Prospect Heights, Ill.: Waveland Press.

Thompson, D. E., and J. V. Murra. 1966. The Inca bridges in the Huánuco area. *American Antiquity* 31: 632–639.

Thompson, F. C. 1970. Microscopic studies of ancient metals. In *Science in Archaeology,* ed. D. Brothwell and E. S. Higgs, pp. 555–563. New York: Praeger.

Thompson, J. E. S. 1963. *Maya Archaeologist.* Norman: University of Oklahoma Press.

Tilley, C. 1990. *Reading Material Culture.* Oxford: Basil Blackwell.

Tolstoy, P. 1958. Surface survey of the northern Valley of Mexico: The Classic and Postclassic periods. *Transactions of the American Philosophical Society* 48 (whole no. 5).

Tolstoy, P., and S. K. Fish. 1975. Surface and subsurface evidence for community size at Coapexco, Mexico. *Journal of Field Archaeology* 2: 97–104.

Topping, A. 1978. China's incredible find. *National Geographic* 153: 440–459.

Torrence, R., ed. 1989. *Time, Energy and Stone Tools.* Cambridge: Cambridge University Press.

Toth, N. 1985. The Oldowan reassessed: A close look at early stone artifacts. *Journal of Archaeological Science* 12: 101–120.

Toth, N., and K. D. Schick. 1986. The first million years: The archaeology of protohuman culture. In *Advances in Archaeological Method and Theory,* vol. 9, ed. M. B. Schiffer, pp. 1–96. Orlando: Academic Press.

Toulmin, S., and J. Goodfield. 1965. *The Discovery of Time.* New York: Harper & Row.

Trigger, B. G. 1968a. *Beyond History: The Methods of Prehistory.* New York: Holt, Rinehart & Winston.

———. 1968b. The determinants of settlement patterns. In *Settlement Archaeology,* ed. K. C. Chang, pp. 53–78. Palo Alto, Calif.: National Press.

———. 1970. Aims in prehistoric archaeology. *Antiquity* 44: 26–37.

———. 1980. *Gordon Childe: Revolutions in Archaeology*. London: Thames & Hudson.

———. 1984. Archaeology at the crossroads: What's new? *Annual Review of Anthropology* 13: 275–300.

———. 1989. *A History of Archaeological Thought*. Cambridge: Cambridge University Press.

Trigger, B. G., and I. Glover, eds. 1981. Regional traditions of archaeological research: I. *World Archaeology* 13 (whole no. 2).

———, eds. 1982. Regional traditions of archaeological research: II. *World Archaeology* 13 (whole no. 3).

Trigger, B. G., and I. Longworth, eds. 1974. Political systems. *World Archaeology* 6 (whole no. 1).

Tringham, R. 1983. V. Gordon Childe 25 years after: His relevance for the archaeology of the eighties. *Journal of Field Archaeology* 1: 171–196.

Trinkaus, K. M., ed. 1986. *Polities and Partitions: Human Boundaries and the Growth of Complex Societies*. Tempe, Ariz.: Anthropological Research Papers.

Tschopik, H., Jr. 1950. An Andean ceramic tradition in historical perspective. *American Antiquity* 15: 196–218.

Tuan, Y. 1977. *Space and Place: The Perspective of Experience*. Minneapolis: University of Minnesota Press.

Tuggle, H. D., A. H. Townsend, and T. J. Riley. 1972. Laws, systems and research designs. *American Antiquity* 37: 3–12.

Turnbaugh, W. A., C. L. Vandebrock, and J. S. Jones. 1983. The professionalism of amateurs in archaeology. *Archaeology* 36 (6): 24–29.

Turnbull, C. 1972. *The Mountain People*. New York: Simon & Schuster.

Turner, B. L., and P. D. Harrison. 1983. *Pulltrouser Swamp*. Austin: University of Texas Press.

Tylor, E. B. 1871. *Primitive Culture*. London: Murray.

Ubelaker, D. H. 1989. *Human Skeletal Remains: Excavation, Analysis, Interpretation*. 2nd ed. Washington, D.C.: Taraxacum.

Ucko, P. J. 1968. *Anthropomorphic Figurines of Predynastic Egypt and Neolithic Crete, with Comparative Material from the Prehistoric Near East and Mainland Greece*. Royal Anthropological Institute Occasional Paper 24. London: Szmidla.

———. 1969. Ethnography and archaeological interpretation of funerary remains. *World Archaeology* 1: 262–280.

Ucko, P. J., and G. W. Dimbleby, eds. 1969. *The Domestication and Exploitation of Plants and Animals*. London: Duckworth.

Ucko, P. J., and A. Rosenfeld. 1967. *Palaeolithic Cave Art*. New York: McGraw-Hill.

Ucko, P. J., R. Tringham, and G. W. Dimbleby, eds. 1972. *Man, Settlement and Urbanism*. London: Duckworth.

UNESCO. 1968. *The Conservation of Cultural Property*. N.p.: UNESCO Press.

Urban, P. A., and E. M. Schortman, eds. 1986. *The Southeast Maya Periphery*. Austin: University of Texas Press.

van der Merwe, N. J. 1982. Carbon isotopes, photosynthesis, and archaeology. *American Scientist* 70: 596–606.

van der Merwe, N. J., and D. H. Avery. 1982. Pathways to steel. *American Scientist* 70: 146–155.

van der Veen, M., and N. Fieller. 1982. Sampling seeds. *Journal of Archaeological Science* 9: 287–298.

Vandiver, P. B., J. Druzik, and G. S. Wheeler, eds. 1991. *Materials Issues in Art and Archaeology II*. MRS Symposium Proceedings Volume 185. Pittsburgh: Materials Research Society.

Van Noten, F., D. Cahan, and L. Keeley. 1980. A Paleolithic campsite in Belgium. *Scientific American* 242 (4): 48–55.

Veit, U. 1989. Ethnic concepts in German prehistory: A case study on the relationship between cultural identity and archaeological objectivity. In *Archaeological Approaches to Cultural Identity*, ed. Stephen Shennan, pp. 35–56. London: Unwin Hyman.

Villa, P. 1982. Conjoinable pieces and site formation processes. *American Antiquity* 27: 276–290.

Villa, P., and J. Courtin. 1983. The interpretation of stratified sites: A view from underground. *Journal of Archaeological Science* 10: 267–282.

Vita-Finzi, C., and E. S. Higgs. 1970. Prehistoric economy in the Mount Carmel area of Palestine. *Proceedings of the Prehistoric Society* 36: 1–37.

Vitelli, K. D. 1983. To remove the double standard: Historic shipwreck legislation. *Journal of Field Archaeology* 10: 105–106.

Vogt, E. Z., ed. 1974. *Aerial Photography in Anthropological Field Research*. Cambridge: Harvard University Press.

von Däniken, E. 1969. *Chariots of the Gods?* New York: Bantam.

———. 1970. *Gods from Outer Space*. New York: Bantam.

von den Driesch, A. 1976. *A Guide to the Measurement of Animal Bones from Archaeological Sites*. Bulletin 1. Cambridge: Harvard University, Peabody Museum of Archaeology and Ethnology.

Wagner, G. E. 1982. Testing flotation recovery rates. *American Antiquity* 47: 127–132.

Ward, R. H., and K. M. Weiss. 1976. *The Demographic*

Evolution of Human Populations. London: Academic Press.

Waselkov, G. A. 1987. Shellfish gathering and shell midden archaeology. In *Advances in Archaeological Method and Theory,* vol. 10, ed. M. B. Schiffer, pp. 93–210. San Diego: Academic Press.

Watanabe, N., and M. Suzuki. 1969. Fission-track dating of archaeological glass materials from Japan. *Nature* 222: 1057–1058.

Watson, P. J. 1973. The future of archeology in anthropology: Cultural history and social science. In *Research and Theory in Current Archeology,* ed. C. L. Redman, pp. 113–124. New York: Wiley-Interscience.

———. 1977. Design analysis of painted pottery. *American Antiquity* 42: 381–393.

———. 1986. Archaeological interpretation, 1985. In *American Archaeology Past and Future: A Celebration of the Society for American Archaeology 1935–1985,* ed. D. J. Meltzer, D. D. Fowler, and J. A. Sabloff, pp. 439–457. Washington, D.C.: Smithsonian Institution Press.

Watson, P. J., and M. C. Kennedy. 1991. The development of horticulture in the Eastern Woodlands of North America: Women's role. In *Engendering Archaeology: Women and Prehistory,* ed. J. M. Gero and M. W. Conkey, pp. 255–275. Oxford: Basil Blackwell.

Watson, P. J., S. A. LeBlanc, and C. L. Redman. 1971. *Explanation in Archeology: An Explicitly Scientific Approach.* New York: Columbia University Press.

———. 1984. *Archaeological Explanation: The Scientific Method in Archaeology.* New York: Columbia University Press.

Watson, R. A. 1990. Ozymandias, king of kings: Postprocessual radical archaeology as critique. *American Antiquity* 55: 673–689.

———. 1991. What the New Archaeology has accomplished. *Current Anthropology* 32: 275–291.

Wauchope, R. 1938. *Modern Maya Houses.* Publication 502. Washington, D.C.: Carnegie Institution.

———. 1962. *Lost Tribes and Sunken Continents.* Chicago: University of Chicago Press.

———. 1965. *They Found the Buried Cities.* Chicago: University of Chicago Press.

Webb, M. 1973. The Petén Maya decline viewed in the perspective of state formation. In *The Classic Maya Collapse,* ed. T. P. Culbert, pp. 367–404. School of American Research Advanced Seminar Series. Albuquerque: University of New Mexico Press.

Webster, D. L. 1977. Warfare and the evolution of Maya civilization. In *The Origins of Maya Civilization,* ed.

R. E. W. Adams, pp. 335–372. School of American Research Advanced Seminar Series. Albuquerque: University of New Mexico Press.

———. 1981. Egregious energetics. *American Antiquity* 46: 919–922.

———, ed. 1989. *The House of the Bacabs, Copán, Honduras.* Studies in Pre-Columbian Art and Archaeology No. 29. Washington, D.C.: Dumbarton Oaks.

Webster, D., and E. M. Abrams. 1983. An elite compound at Copán, Honduras. *Journal of Field Archaeology* 10: 285–296.

Webster, D. L., and A. Freter. 1990a. Settlement history and the Classic collapse at Copán: A redefined chronological perspective. *Latin American Antiquity* 1: 66–85.

———. 1990b. The demography of Late Classic Copán. In *Precolumbian Population History in the Maya Lowlands,* ed. T. P. Culbert and D. S. Rice, pp. 37–61. Albuquerque: University of New Mexico Press.

Webster, D. L., and N. Gonlin. 1988. Households of the humblest Maya. *Journal of Field Archaeology* 15: 169–190.

Weiner, J. S. 1955. *The Piltdown Forgery.* London: Oxford University Press.

Weiss, K. M. 1976. Demographic theory and anthropological inference. *Annual Review of Anthropology* 5: 351–381.

Wendorf, F. 1973. "Rescue" archaeology along the Nile. In *In Search of Man: Readings in Archaeology,* ed. E. L. Green, pp. 39–42. Boston: Little, Brown.

Wenke, R. J. 1981. Explaining the evolution of cultural complexity: A review. In *Advances in Archaeological Method and Theory,* vol. 4, ed. M. B. Schiffer, pp. 79–127. New York: Academic Press.

Wertime, T. A. 1973. The beginnings of metallurgy: A new look. *Science* 182: 875–887.

———. 1983. The furnace vs. the goat: The pyrotechnologic industries and Mediterranean deforestation in antiquity. *Journal of Field Archaeology* 10: 445–452.

Wertime, T., and J. Muhly, eds. 1980. *The Coming of the Age of Iron.* New Haven: Yale University Press.

Wertime, T., and S. Wertime, eds. 1982. *Early Pyrotechnology.* Washington, D.C.: Smithsonian Institution Press.

Weymouth, J. M. 1986. Geophysical methods of archaeological site surveying. In *Advances in Archaeological Method and Theory,* vol. 9, ed. M. B. Schiffer, pp. 311–395. Orlando: Academic Press.

Whallon, R., Jr. 1968. Investigations of late prehistoric social organization in New York State. In *New Perspectives in Archeology,* ed. S. R. Binford and L. R. Binford, pp. 223–244. Chicago: Aldine.

———. 1972. A new approach to pottery typology. *American Antiquity* 37: 13–33.

———. 1973. Spatial analysis of occupation floors: I. Application of dimensional analysis of variance. *American Antiquity* 38: 266–278.

———. 1974. Spatial analysis of occupation floors: II. The application of nearest neighbor analysis. *American Antiquity* 39: 16–34.

———. 1984. Unconstrained clustering for the analysis of spatial distributions in archaeology. In *Intrasite Spatial Analysis in Archaeology,* ed. H. J. Hietala, pp. 242–277. Cambridge: Cambridge University Press.

Whallon, R., and J. A. Brown, eds. 1982. *Essays on Archaeological Typology.* Evanston, Ill.: Center for American Archaeology Press.

Wheat, J. B. 1967. A Paleo-Indian bison kill. *Scientific American* 216 (1): 44–52.

———. 1972. *The Olsen-Chubbuck Site: A Paleo-Indian Bison Kill.* Memoir no. 26. Washington, D.C.: Society for American Archaeology.

Wheeler, A., and A. K. G. Jones. 1989. *Fishes.* Cambridge: Cambridge University Press.

Wheeler, M. 1943. *Maiden Castle, Dorset.* London: Society of Antiquaries of London.

———. 1954. *Archaeology from the Earth.* Harmondsworth, England: Penguin.

———. 1955. *Still Digging.* London: Joseph.

White, J. C. 1982. *Ban Chiang: Discovery of a Lost Bronze Age.* Philadelphia: University Museum, University of Pennsylvania.

White, J. R., and P. N. Kardulias. 1985. The dynamics of razing: Lessons from the Barnhisel House. *Historical Archaeology* 19: 65–75.

White, L. A. 1949. *The Science of Culture.* New York: Grove Press.

White, P. 1974. *The Past Is Human.* New York: Taplinger.

White, T. D. 1990. *Human Osteology.* San Diego: Academic Press.

Whiting, J. W. M., and B. Ayres. 1968. Inferences from the shape of dwellings. In *Settlement Archaeology,* ed. K. C. Chang, pp. 117–133. Palo Alto, Calif.: National Press.

Wiessner, P. 1974. A functional estimator of population from floor area. *American Antiquity* 39: 343–350.

———. 1983. Style and social information in Kalahari San projectile points. *American Antiquity* 48: 253–276.

———. 1984. Reconsidering the behavioral basis for style: A case study among the Kalahari San. *Journal of Anthropological Archaeology* 3: 190–234.

Wilk, R. R., and W. Ashmore, eds. 1988. *Household and Community in the Mesoamerican Past.* Albuquerque: University of New Mexico Press.

Wilk, R. R., and W. L. Rathje, eds. 1982. Archaeology of the household: Building a prehistory of domestic life. *American Behavioral Scientist* 25 (whole no. 6).

Willey, G. R. 1953. *Prehistoric Settlement Patterns in the Virú Valley, Peru.* Bureau of American Ethnology, Bulletin 155. Washington, D.C.: Smithsonian Institution.

———, ed. 1956. *Prehistoric Settlement Patterns in the New World.* Viking Fund Publications in Anthropology, no. 23. New York: Wenner-Gren Foundation for Anthropological Research.

———. 1962. The early great styles and the rise of the pre-Columbian civilizations. *American Anthropologist* 64: 1–14.

———. 1966. *An Introduction to American Archaeology.* Vol. 1: *North and Middle America.* Englewood Cliffs, N.J.: Prentice-Hall.

———. 1971. *An Introduction to American Archaeology.* Vol. 2: *South America.* Englewood Cliffs, N.J.: Prentice-Hall.

———, ed. 1974. *Archaeological Researches in Retrospect.* Cambridge, Mass.: Winthrop.

———. 1976. Mesoamerican civilization and the idea of transcendence. *Antiquity* 50: 205–215.

———. 1982. Maya archaeology. *Science* 215: 260–267.

———. 1983. Settlement patterns and archaeology: Some comments. In *Prehistoric Settlement Patterns: Essays in Honor of Gordon R. Willey,* ed. E. Z. Vogt and R. M. Leventhal, pp. 445–462. Albuquerque and Cambridge: University of New Mexico Press, and Harvard University.

Willey, G. R., W. R. Coe, and R. J. Sharer. 1976. Un proyecto para el desarrollo de investigación y preservación arqueológica en Copán (Honduras) y vecindad. *Yaxkin* 1 (2): 10–29.

Willey, G. R., and R. M. Leventhal. 1979. A preliminary report on prehistoric Maya settlements in the Copán valley. In *Maya Archaeology and Ethnohistory,* ed. N. Hammond and G. R. Willey, pp. 75–102. Austin: University of Texas Press.

Willey, G. R., R. M. Leventhal, and W. L. Fash, Jr. 1978. Maya settlement in the Copán valley. *Archaeology* 31 (4): 32–43.

Willey, G. R., and P. Phillips. 1958. *Method and Theory in*

American Archaeology. Chicago: University of Chicago Press.

Willey, G. R., and J. A. Sabloff. 1980. *A History of American Archaeology.* 2nd ed. San Francisco: Freeman.

Williams, L., D. H. Thomas, and R. L. Bettinger. 1973. Notions to numbers: Great Basin settlements as polythetic sets. In *Research and Theory in Current Archaeology*, ed. C. L. Redman, pp. 215–237. New York: Wiley-Interscience.

———. 1985. Notions to numbers: Great Basin settlements as polythetic sets. In *For Concordance in Archaeological Analysis: Bridging Data Structure, Quantitative Technique and Theory*, ed. C. Carr, pp. 274–296. Kansas City: Westport Publisher, Inc. Reprint. Prospect Heights, Ill.: Waveland Press, Inc., 1989.

Williams, S. 1991. *Fantastic Archaeology: The Wild Side of North American Prehistory.* Philadelphia: University of Pennsylvania Press.

Williamson, R. A. 1979. Field report: Hovenweep National Monument. *Archaeoastronomy* 2 (3): 11–12.

———, ed. 1981. *Archaeoastronomy in the Americas.* Los Altos, Calif., and College Park, Md.: Ballena Press and the Center for Archaeoastronomy.

Williamson, R. A., H. J. Fisher, and D. O'Flynn. 1977. Anasazi solar observations. In *Native American Astronomy*, ed. A. F. Aveni, pp. 203–217. Austin: University of Texas Press.

Wilmsen, E. N. 1970. *Lithic Analysis and Cultural Inference: A Paleo-Indian Case.* Anthropological Paper no. 16. Tucson: University of Arizona Press.

———. 1974. *Lindenmeier: A Pleistocene Hunting Society.* New York: Harper & Row.

Wilshusen, R. H., and G. D. Stone. 1990. An ethnoarchaeological perspective on soils. *World Archaeology* 22: 104–114.

Wilson, B., C. Grigson, and S. Payne, eds. 1982. *Ageing and Sexing Animal Bones from Archaeological Sites.* British Archaeological Reports, British Series 109. Oxford: BAR.

Wing, E. S., and A. R. Brown. 1980. *Paleonutrition: Method and Theory in Prehistoric Foodways.* New York: Academic Press.

Winter, M. C. 1976. Excavating a shallow community by random sampling quadrats. In *The Early Mesoamerican Village*, ed. K. V. Flannery, pp. 62–67. New York: Academic Press.

Winterhalder, B., and E. A. Smith. 1981. *Hunter-Gatherer Foraging Strategies: Ethnographic and Archaeological Analyses.* Chicago: University of Chicago Press.

Winters, H. D. 1968. Value systems and trade cycles of the Late Archaic in the Midwest. In *New Perspectives in Archeology,* ed. S. R. Binford and L. R. Binford, pp. 175–221. Chicago: Aldine.

Wiseman, J. 1980. Archaeology as archaeology. *Journal of Field Archaeology* 7: 149–151.

———. 1984. Scholarship and provenience in the study of artifacts. *Journal of Field Archaeology* 11: 67–77.

———. 1985. Odds and ends: Multimedia documentation in archaeology. *Journal of Field Archaeology* 12: 389.

Wittry, W. L. 1977. The American woodhenge. In *Explorations in Cahokia Archaeology,* ed. M. L. Fowler, pp. 43–48. Illinois Archaeology Survey Bulletin 7. Urbana: University of Illinois.

Wobst, H. M. 1977. Stylistic behavior and information exchange. In *For the Director: Essays in Honor of James B. Griffin,* ed. C. E. Cleland, pp. 317–342. Anthropological Paper no. 61. Ann Arbor: University of Michigan, Museum of Anthropology.

———. 1983. We can't see the forest for the trees: Sampling and the shapes of archaeological distributions. In *Archaeological Hammers and Theories,* ed. J. A. Moore and A. S. Keene, pp. 37–85. New York: Academic Press.

Wolf, E. R. 1982. *Europe and the People without History.* Berkeley and Los Angeles: University of California Press.

Wolfman, D. 1984. Geomagnetic dating methods in archaeology. In *Advances in Archaeological Method and Theory,* vol. 7, ed. M. B. Schiffer, pp. 363–458. Orlando: Academic Press.

Wood, M. 1985. *In Search of the Trojan War.* New York: Facts on File Publications.

Wood, W. R., and D. L. Johnson. 1978. A survey of disturbance processes in archaeological site formation. In *Advances in Archaeological Method and Theory,* vol. 1, ed. M. B. Schiffer, pp. 315–381. New York: Academic Press.

Woodbury, R. B. 1973. *Alfred V. Kidder.* New York: Columbia University Press.

Woolley, C. L. 1934. *Ur Excavations. Vol. II: The Royal Cemetery.* Oxford and Philadelphia: British Museum, and University Museum, University of Pennsylvania.

Wright, H. T. 1986. The evolution of civilizations. In *American Archaeology Past and Future: A Celebration of the Society for American Archaeology 1935–1985,* ed. D. J. Meltzer, D. D. Fowler, and J. A. Sabloff, pp. 323–365. Washington, D.C.: Smithsonian Institution Press.

Wright, R. V. S., ed. 1977. *Stone Tools as Cultural Markers.* Canberra: Australian Institute of Aboriginal Studies.

Wylie, A. 1985. The reaction against analogy. In *Advances in Archaeological Method and Theory,* vol. 8, ed. M. B. Schiffer, pp. 63–111. Orlando: Academic Press.

Yellen, J. E. 1977. *Archaeological Approaches to the Present: Models for Reconstructing the Past.* New York: Academic Press.

Young, D., and R. Bonnichsen. 1984. *Understanding Stone Tools.* Peopling of the Americas Series No. 1. Orono: University of Maine.

Young, P., ed. 1989. Archaeology in the 21st century. *Archaeology* 42 (whole no. 1).

Young, T. C. 1988. Since Herodotus, has history been a valid concept? *American Antiquity* 53: 7–12.

Zeilik, M. 1984. Archaeoastronomy at Chaco Canyon: The historic-prehistoric connection. In *New Light on Chaco Canyon,* ed. D. G. Noble, pp. 65–72. Santa Fe: School of American Research Press.

Zeuner, F. E. 1958. *Dating the Past: An Introduction to Geochronology.* London: Methuen.

Zimmerman, D. W. 1971. Uranium distributions in archaeological ceramics. *Science* 174: 818–819.

Zubrow, E. 1975. *Prehistoric Carrying Capacity: A Model.* Menlo Park, Calif.: Cummings.

———, ed. 1976. *Demographic Anthropology: Quantitative Approaches.* School of American Research Advanced Seminar Series. Albuquerque: University of New Mexico Press.

INDEX

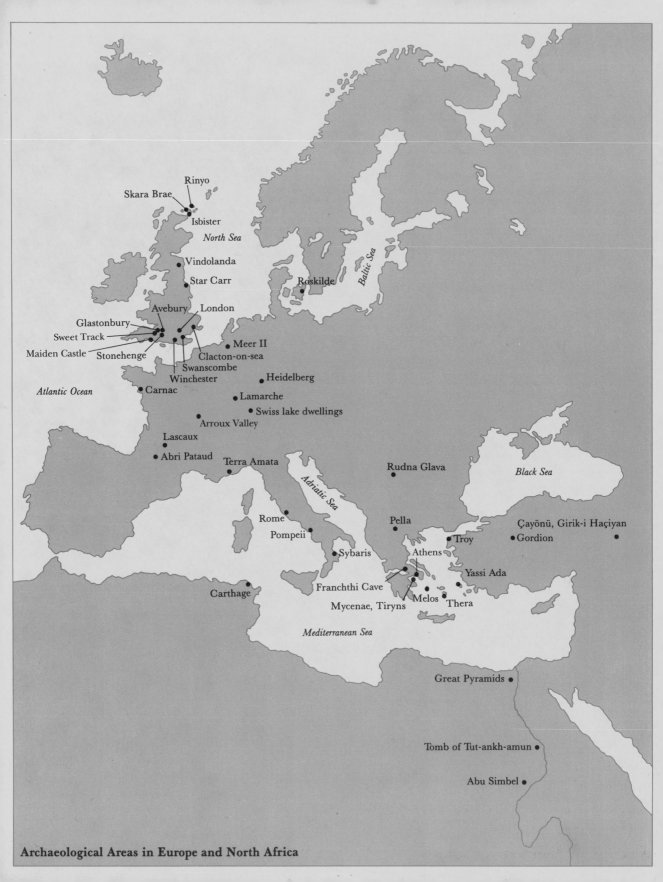

Rinyo

Skara Brae

Isbister

North Sea

Vindolanda

Star Carr

Roskilde

Baltic Sea

Avebury · London

Glastonbury

Sweet Track

Maiden Castle · Stonehenge

Meer II

Clacton-on-sea

Swanscombe

Winchester

Heidelberg

Carnac

Lamarche

Swiss lake dwellings

Arroux Valley

Lascaux

Abri Pataud

Terra Amata

Adriatic Sea

Rudna Glava

Black Sea

Rome

Pella

Çayönü, Girik-i Haçiyan

Pompeii

Troy

Gordion

Sybaris

Athens

Carthage

Franchthi Cave

Yassi Ada

Mycenae, Tiryns

Melos

Thera

Mediterranean Sea

Great Pyramids

Tomb of Tut-ankh-amun

Abu Simbel

Atlantic Ocean

Archaeological Areas in Europe and North Africa